uo Youzhengye
azhan Yanjiu Baogao

政业
研究报告

策法规司◎编著

美国商标审查指南

美国专利商标局　译

中国工商总局商标局　校

商务印书馆

2008年·北京

图书在版编目(CIP)数据

美国商标审查指南/美国专利商标局译;中国工商总局商标局校.—北京:商务印书馆,2008

ISBN 978-7-100-05767-7

I. 美… II. ①美…②中… III. 商标法—美国
IV. D971.23

中国版本图书馆 CIP 数据核字(2008)第 017597 号

MĚIGUÓ SHĀNGBIĀO SHĚNCHÁ ZHǏNÁN

美国商标审查指南

美国专利商标局 译

中国工商总局商标局 校

商 务 印 书 馆 出 版
(北京王府井大街36号 邮政编码 100710)
商 务 印 书 馆 发 行
北 京 瑞 古 冠 中 印 刷 厂 印 刷
ISBN 978-7-100-05767-7

2008 年 9 月第 1 版 开本 700×1000 1/16
2008 年 9 月北京第 1 次印刷 印张 53¼ 插页 2

定价: 108.00 元

美国商务部部长兼专利商标局局长 Dudas 先生
向中国国家工商总局商标局局长安青虎先生递
交美国《商标审查指南》译稿光盘

序　言

中华人民共和国国家工商行政管理总局商标局局长

安青虎

经过中国国家工商行政管理总局商标局(CTMO)和美国专利商标局(USPTO)的共同努力,美国专利商标局《商标审查指南》(*Trademark Manual of Examining Procedure*)第四版第1200章(申请的实质审查)及第1300章(不同类型商标的审查)同读者见面了。

1972年发表《中美上海联合公报》后,中美两国的直接贸易开始恢复并逐渐上升。自2001年12月中国加入世界贸易组织以来,中美两国经贸合作持续快速发展。据统计,2006年中美贸易额达2627亿美元,同比增长24.1%,截至2007年6月底,美国在华设立外商投资企业2.4万余户。美国成为中国第一大出口市场和第二大贸易伙伴。中国成为美国第三大出口市场和第二大贸易伙伴。

与此同时,在与贸易有关的重要知识产权之一的商标领域,中美的交流与合作积极发展。1979年12月中国恢复商标注册后,美国来华商标申请量逐年上升。1980年,美国企业在华商标注册申请仅为数百件,2000年,美国企业在华商标注册申请突破1万件,2006年,美国企业在华商标注册申请突破2万件。截至2007年6月底,美国在华累计商标注册申请量为16.1万件,累计商标注册量为10.5万件,占130多个外国和地区在华注册商标总量的21%,是在中国申请和注册商标最多的国家。

2004年3月,美国专利商标局局长杜达智先生首次访问中国商标局,双方均表达了希望在商标方面加强合作的愿望。同年6月,杜达智先生再次率团来访,双方在会谈中就具体合作项目进行了磋商。由于当时商标局正在修订《商标审查准则》,因此,我提出希望美国专利商标局能提供其《商标审查指南》的中文本,以为借鉴。杜达智先生爽快地答应了。之后不久,杜达智先生托美国驻华使馆高级知识产权专员柯恒先生捎话给我,说由于其《商标审查指南》内容繁杂,全部翻译难度较大,且费时会很长,怕来不及供中国商标局修改《商标审查准则》时参考,故拟先将其认为是对中国修改《商标审查准则》具有价值、最具参考作用的部分译出。我表示同意和理解。

2005 年 1 月,杜达智先生访问中国,将《商标审查指南》有关章节(第 1200 章和第 1300 章)中文译稿亲手交给我。我和我的同事看后认为,该稿翻译质量具有相当水准,无须大改。于是,我又向杜达智先生提出,以两局的名义用中英文在中国出版《商标审查指南》这部分内容,以供中国更多的业内人士分享。杜达智先生欣然同意。同年 11 月,杜达智先生将《商标审查指南》稿件的电子版及其为该书所写的序稿面交给我。2007 年 6 月,杜达智先生托柯恒先生捎来该序的中英文修改稿,之后又寄来该序的签名稿。对于杜达智先生积极热情的合作、富有成效的工作和认真负责的精神,我十分赞赏。

美国是普通法国家。在商标审查工作中,美国专利商标局依据美国商标法和联邦法规的规定确立了一整套应用法律的具体原则,并结合多年的商标审查实践积累起大量对后来的相似案件具有很强指导作用的判例以及适用于各审查环节的应用程序。《商标审查指南》是美国专利商标局审查员所遵守的审查指南和程序,对美国商标申请人、代理人进行商标工作也具有参考意义。内容包括审查员手册及信息和解释,大致描述了审查员在审查过程中所需遵守或需授权遵守的程序。

该《商标审查指南》于 1974 年 1 月制定,之后于 1993 年、2002 年、2005 年作了三次修修订,以适应美国联邦法院系统的新判决对美国专利商标局的影响。目前执行的第四版共 19 章,1005 页,具体章节标题为:基本情况、申请日期、申请书件的提交和受理、申请书件处理和费用、所有权变更、代理人或代表人、申请的审查程序、申请要求、商业使用、国际协议下的申请、意图使用与相关文件、申请的实质审查、不同种类商标的审查、商品和服务的分类与确认、审查后程序、注册和注册后程序、提交局长的事项、申请和注册的公众查询、马德里协议。

本书尽管只是其中两章,但内容涉及商标申请中的实质审查部分,内容丰富,案例众多,其中的很多案例都是经过指南的编写者精心挑选出来的,具有较高的参考价值。中国商标局在修订《商标审查准则》、商标评审委员会在制定《商标审理标准》的过程中,均参考和借鉴了这两章的部分内容。2005 年 12 月,中国商标局和商标评审委员会共同发布了《商标审查及审理标准》,并在中国商标局的官方网站"中国商标网"(www.ctmo.gov.cn)上全文刊载。

本书的成功出版，是中美两国商标领域合作交流的一项重要成果。本书不仅对中国的商标审查人员具有参考价值，而且对中国知识产权领域的立法人员、法官、学者、代理人、企业家等均具有借鉴意义。我衷心希望，中美两国的有关机构能继续保持并不断深化和加强双方在商标领域的合作，为保护知识产权，促进中美经济和贸易的不断发展作出更多的贡献。

安青虎

2007 年 8 月

Foreword

By Mr. An Qinghu, Director General of Trademark Office
State Administration for Industry and Commerce
The People's Republic of China

With the joint efforts by the Trademark Office of the State Administration for Industry and Commerce of the People's Republic of China (CTMO) and the United States Patent and Trademark Office (USPTO), Chapter 1200 (Substantive Examination of Applications) and Chapter 1300 (Examination of Different Types of Marks) of the *Trademark Manual of Examination Procedure* (TMEP) of the USPTO is now available to readers.

Since the *Shanghai Sino-US Joint Communique* was publicized in 1972, the direct trade between China and US has resumed and risen gradually. The bilateral economic and trade cooperation has witnessed continuous and even rapid increase since China entered into the World Trade Organization (WTO) in December 2001. According to statistics, the trade volume reported a 24.1% year on year increase to 262.7 billion USD in 2006. By the end of June 2007, there had been 24,000 US-invested enterprises in China. The United States of America has become China's largest export destination and the second largest trade partner. And China is the US's third largest export destination and the second largest trade partner.

Meanwhile, the two countries have also developed exchanges and cooperation in the trademark field, which is one of the important intellectual property rights related to trade. Since China resumed trademark registration in December 1979, there has been a steady growth of trademark applications from the United States. In 1980, only a few hundreds of applications for trademark registration from the

United States were received. While in 2000, the figure was more than 10,000 and in 2006, in exceeded 20,000. By the end of June 2007, there had been accumulatively 161,000 applications for trademark registration from the United States, with 105,000 trademark registration in total, accounting for 21% of the total registered trademarks by 130 foreign countries and regions. Among the foreign countries, the United States ranks first in terms of trademark applications and registrations in China.

In March 2004, Mr. Jon W. Dudas, Under Secretary of Commerce for Intellectual Property and Director of the USPTO paid his first visit to CTMO when the two Offices expressed wishes to strengthen the cooperation in the trademark field. In June when Mr. Dudas headed a delegation to visit the CTMO again, both sides discussed cooperative programs in details. Since at that time CTMO was revising its *Trademark Examination Guidelines*, I asked if USPTO could provide its TMEP in Chinese version for out reference. And I got a positive answer. Soon after that, Mr. Mark Cohen, the Intellectual Property Attache of the U.S. Embassy in Beijing passed on a message of Mr. Dudas to me, that due to the complexity of the TMEP, the USPTO would probably be unable to have it translated in time. He suggested that the most useful parts be translated first. I agreed and expressed my understanding.

In January 2005, Mr. Dudas visited China and in person gave me the Chinese version of related Chapters (Chapter 1200 and Chapter 1300) of the TMEP. My colleagues and I thought the translated version was of such high quality that there would be no need for further amendment. Then I proposed that the chapters be published both in Chinese and English in the name of the two Offices so that more practitioners can share the content. Mr. Dudas agreed. In November the same year, Mr. Dudas sent me the electronic version as well as his preface for publication. In June 2007, Mr. Dudas asked Mr. Cohen to send me the revised preface both in Chinese and English, and soon the signed preface. I appreciate the active cooperation, fruitful work and responsible attitude of Mr. Dudas very much.

The United States uses a system of common law. In its trademark examination, USPTO has established a whole set of concrete principles of applying laws in accordance with the provisions of the US Lanham Act and relevant federal acts. In addition, combined with years of practices there have been case laws that can be applied to similar cases as well as some procedures that are applicable to various processes. The TMEP is the guidance for USPTO examiners, and also offers references for trademark applicants and agents. It contains the examiners' manual, information and explanation, which describe the procedures that examiners should abide by or should be authorized to abide by during examination.

The TMEP was formulated in January 1974 and was revised three times in 1993, 2002 and 2005 respectively in order to be adapted to the new judgment of the federal court. The current fourth edition of the manual is composed of 19 chapters and 1005 pages in total. The captions of each chapter are as follows: General Information; Application Filing Date; Filing and Receipt of Documents; Processing Documents and Fees; Change of Ownership; Attorney and Representative; Procedure for Examining Applications; Application Requirements; Use in Commerce; Applications under International Agreements; Intent-to-Use Applications and Related Documents; Substantive Examination of Applications; Examination of Different Types of Marks; Classification and Identification of Goods and Services; Post-Examination Procedures; Registration and Post-Registration Procedures; Matters Submitted to the Director; Public Inquires about Applications and Registrations; Madrid Protocol.

Although the publication only includes two chapters, it contains the substantive examination of trademark applications. Many of the cases are cautiously selected by compliers to provide references. Both CTMO and Trademark Review and Adjudication Board (TRAB) referred to and borrowed parts of the two chapters when they revised and drafted their trademark examination guidelines respectively. In December 2005, CTMO and TRAB jointly publicized the *Trademark Examination and Guidelines* on CTMO's official website www.ctmo.gov.cn.

The successful publication is a significant fruit of cooperative exchanges in Sino-US trademark realm. The publication provides reference not only to the Chinese trademark examiners, but also to law-makers, judges, scholars, agents as well as applicants who are intending to apply for trademark registration in the US. I sincerely hope that the relevant bodies of the two countries can maintain and further reinforce their trademark cooperation, and make more contributions to IPR protection as well as economic and trade development of the two countries.

August 2007

序　言

美国商务部主管知识产权副部长兼专利商标局局长

杜　达　智

首先感谢您对美国专利商标局商标审查指南的关注。

能与中国的同事分享我们的审查指南是一个非常难得的机会。中国商标局是一个令人印象如此深刻的商标主管机关。中国商标局的同事都是工作勤奋且具有相当学术水平的专家，领导层则目光远大，无私奉献。应中国商标局安青虎局长的要求，美国专利商标局非常高兴能提供《美国商标审查指南》第四版第1200章（申请的实质审查）和第1300章（不同类型商标的审查）的中译本，内容主要涉及美国专利商标局在商标实质审查中的实践经验。至于完整的最新修订版的审查指南，请参照网页http://tess2.uspto.gov/tmdb/tmep/。

本审查指南具有多重意义：1.为商标审查员规定了统一标准。2.由于标准统一，我们可以利用本审查指南协助评估审查员的工作质量。3.由于任何人均可以登陆美国专利商标局网站免费查阅本审查指南，申请人和商标从业者据此可以正确预测商标审查结果。4.由于申请人或其代理人能够看到本审查指南，他们可以据此质疑任何不正确的审查实践，也可以更好地理解商标局提出某些具体要求或作出驳回决定的理由。5.世界各国商标局的同事可以据此对美国专利商标局的审查实践进行评价。

我们赞赏中国商标局在进行第三次商标法修改过程中向国内外商标所有人及包括美国专利商标局在内的其他各国商标主管机关征求意见的做法。在安青虎局长的领导下，中国商标局在改善权利人在华保护商标权和商标执法方面作出了巨大的努力。中国商标局的网站http://www.ctmo.gov.cn，不仅提供中国有关商标保护的综合公共信息，同时也提供中国商标审查及审理标准和商标注册信息网上查询系统的链接。

我们将继续与中国商标局共同努力，进一步推动这些合作，尤其是支持中国商标局应用最新技术优化审查流程，减少案件积压的努力。同时，中国商标局和美国专利商标局已经同意共同采取措施，例如编写和交换信息小册子，以帮助中小型企业更好地了解如何在对方国家保护自己的商标。这个由安青虎局长提议的项目，主要是考虑到中国培育更多国际知名商标的需要，鼓励中国企业使用美国专利商标局商标在线查询系统，并且在美国申请注册他们的商标。同时，也帮助美国企业了解在中国注册和保护商标的法律及程序。

我谨代表美国专利商标局全体雇员，期待着与中国商标局在上述各方面以及其他重要领域进行更多的合作，以促进双方的知识产权保护工作。

Jon W. Dudas
杜达智

United States Patent and Trademark Office Trademark Manual of Examining Procedure, 4th Edition (TMEP) Chapters 1200 (Substantive Examination of Applications) and 1300 (Examination of Different Types of Marks)

Foreword from the Under Secretary for Intellectual Property and Director of the United States Patent and Trademark Office Jon W. Dudas:

Welcome and thank you for your interest in this guide to examination of trademarks by the United States Patent and Trademark Office (USPTO).

The ability to share our TMEP with colleagues in China is an incredible opportunity. The China Trademark Office (CTMO) is quite an impressive organization. Our colleagues at the CTMO are hard-working professionals with scholarly ability, and the CTMO leadership is visionary and dedicated. In response to the request of CTMO's Director General An Qinghu, the USPTO is pleased to provide a translation of Chapters 1200 (Substantive Examination of Applications) and 1300 (Examination of Different Types of Marks) of the 4th Edition of USPTO's *Trademark Manual of Examining Procedure* (TMEP). These two chapters contain the most pertinent information about the USPTO's examination practice as to substantive trademark law issues. The complete TMEP featuring all of the latest updates is available online at http://tess2.uspto.gov/tmdb/tmep/.

The TMEP serves several purposes. First, it provides uniform guidance to our trademark examining attorneys. Second, because of the uniform guidance, we use the TMEP to help us assess the quality of work performed by our examiners. Third, applicants and practitioners know what to expect, because the TMEP is available, free of charge, to everyone at USPTO's website. Fourth, because applicants and their representatives can read the TMEP, they are able to challenge any incorrect practices — or better understand why a particular requirement or rejection is made. Finally, the TMEP gives our colleagues in trademark offices around the world the opportunity to review our examination practices at the USPTO.

We applaud the CTMO's leadership in soliciting input from foreign and domestic brand owners and from other trademark offices, including the USPTO, in undertaking the third revision to China's Trademark Law. Under Director General An, the CTMO has instituted significant changes to improve right holders' ability to protect and enforce their trademarks in China. The CTMO's website, http://www.ctmo.gov.cn, serves as a comprehensive public resource of information about protecting trademarks in China, with links to the trademark examination guidelines and to the online trademark search database.

We continue to work with the CTMO to further these advances and, in particular, to support the CTMO in realizing its vision to streamline operations and improve pendency by implementing the latest technological advancements. Together, the CTMO and the USPTO have agreed to take steps, including the development and exchange of informational brochures, to help smaller businesses better understand how to protect their marks in our respective countries. This project, initiated by Director General An, is designed in large part to encourage Chinese companies to consult the USPTO online trademark search database and apply to register their marks as China develops more international brands. At the same time, it would help U.S. enterprises understand the laws and procedures relating to trademark registration and protection in China.

On behalf of all the Trademark Office employees at the USPTO, we look forward to working with the CTMO on these and other important efforts to advance intellectual property rights protection for all.

Jon W. Dudas

Contents

Chapter 1200
Substantive Examination of Applications

目　　录

第1200章　申请的实质审查

Chapter 1300

Examination of Different Types of Marks

第 1300 章　不同类型的商标审查

美国商标审查指南

Chapter 1200
Substantive Examination of Applications

1201 Ownership of Mark

Under Section 1(a)(1) of the Trademark Act, 15 U.S.C. §1051(a)(1), an application based on use in commerce must be filed by the owner of the mark. A §1(a) application must include a verified statement that the applicant believes it is the owner of the mark sought to be registered. 15 U.S.C. §1051(a)(3)(A); 37 C.F.R. §2.33(b)(1). An application that is not filed by the owner is void. *See* TMEP §1201.02(b).

An application under §1(b) or §44 of the Act, 15 U.S.C. §1051(b) or §1126, must be filed by a party who is entitled to use the mark in commerce, and must include a verified statement that the applicant is entitled to use the mark in commerce and that the applicant has a bona fide intention to use the mark in commerce as of the application filing date. 15 U.S.C. §§1051(b)(3), 1126(d)(2) and 1126(e); 37 C.F.R. §2.33(b)(2). When the person designated as the applicant was not the person with a bona fide intention to use the mark in commerce, the application is void. *See* TMEP §1201.02(b). However, the examining attorney will not inquire into the bona fides, or good faith, of an applicant's asserted intent to use a mark in commerce during *ex parte* examination unless there is evidence in the record clearly indicating that the applicant does not have a bona fide intention to use the mark in commerce. *See* TMEP §1101.

In a §1(b) application, before the mark can be registered, the applicant must file an amendment to allege use under 15 U.S.C. §1051(c) (*see* TMEP §§1104 *et seq.*) or a statement of use under 15 U.S.C. §1051(d) (*see* TMEP §§1109 *et seq.*) that states that the applicant is using the mark in commerce on or in connection

第 1200 章

申请的实质审查

1201　商标的所有权

根据《商标法》15 U.S.C.§1051(a)(1),Section 1(a)(1)的规定,基于商业使用提出的申请必须由商标的所有人提出。根据 §1(a)提出的申请必须包含一份经鉴定的声明,证明申请人确信自己是申请注册商标的所有人。见 15 U.S.C.§1051(a)(3)(A);37 C.F.R.§2.33(b)(1)。只有所有人提出的申请方为有效。*参见* TMEP §1201.02(b)。

根据该法 §1(b)或 §44、15 U.S.C.§1051(b)或 §1126 的规定提出的申请,必须由有权在商业活动中使用该商标的当事人提出,且必须包含一份经鉴定的声明,证明申请人有权在商业活动中使用该商标,并且在提交申请之日,确有在商业活动中使用该商标的真实意图。见 15 U.S.C.§§1051(b)(3),1126(d)(2)和 1126(e);37 C.F.R.§2.33(b)(2)。若指定的申请人并非真实地意图在商业中使用该商标者,申请无效。*参见* TMEP §1201.02(b)。不过,在单方面审查期间,审查员对于申请人所称的在商业上使用商标的意图是否真实或诚信并不进行调查,除非在记录中有证据明确显示该申请人并无在商业中使用该商标的真实意图。*参见* TMEP §1101。

对于根据 §1(b)提出的申请,申请人必须根据 15 U.S.C.§1051(c)(*参见* TMEP §§1104 及以下)的规定提交一份宣称使用修正书,或者根据 15 U.S.C.§1051(d)(*参见* TMEP §§1109 及以下)的规定提交一份使用声明书,说明申请人在商业上使用

with the goods or services and that the applicant is the owner of the mark. 15 U.S.C. §§1051(b)(3)(A) and (B); 37 C.F.R. §§2.76(b)(1), and 2.88(b)(1).

In a §44 application, the applicant must be the owner of the foreign application or registration on which the United States application is based as of the filing date of the United States application. *See* TMEP §1005. In an application based solely on §44, the applicant does not have to allege use prior to registration. TMEP §1009.

1201.01 Claim of Ownership May Be Based on Use By Related Companies

In an application under §1 of the Trademark Act, an applicant may base its claim of ownership of a trademark or a service mark on:

(1) its own exclusive use of the mark;

(2) use of the mark solely by a related company whose use inures to the applicant's benefit (*see* TMEP §§1201.03 *et seq.*); or

(3) use of the mark both by the applicant and by a related company whose use inures to the applicant's benefit (*see* TMEP §1201.05).

Where the mark is used by a related company, the owner is the party who controls the nature and quality of the goods sold or services rendered under the mark. The owner is the only proper party to apply for registration of a mark. 15 U.S.C. §1051. *See* TMEP §§1201.03 *et seq.* for additional information about use by related companies.

The examining attorney should accept the applicant's statement regarding ownership of the mark unless it is clearly contradicted by information in the record. The Office does not inquire about the relationship between the applicant and other parties named on the specimens or elsewhere in the record, except when the reference to another party clearly contradicts the applicant's verified statement that it is the owner of the mark or entitled to use the mark. Moreover, where the

该商标或在商品或服务上使用该商标，而且申请人是该商标的所有人，商标才可以注册。见 15 U.S.C.§§1051(b)(3)(A)和(B)；37 C.F.R.§§2.76(b)(1)和 2.88(b)(1)。

对于根据 §44 提出的申请，申请者若以在外国的申请或注册作为在美国申请注册的基础，那么，申请人在美国提出申请时必须是该外国申请或注册的所有人。*参见* TMEP §1005。对于只依据 §44 提出的申请，申请人无须在注册之前宣称使用商标。见 TMEP §1009。

1201.01 可以根据相关公司的使用声明自己的所有权

对于根据《商标法》§1 的规定提出的申请，申请人可以根据以下宣称其拥有某商标或服务商标的所有权：

(1) 该商标由申请人自己独家使用；

(2) 该商标由某相关公司单独使用，相关公司的使用给申请人带来利益(*参见* TMEP §§1201.03 以下)；或者

(3) 该商标由申请人和相关公司共同使用，相关公司的使用给申请人带来利益(*参见* TMEP §1201.05)。

在相关公司使用该商标的情况下，所有人对使用该商标销售的商品或提供的服务的性质及质量进行控制。所有人是申请注册商标的唯一适格当事人。见 15 U.S.C.§1051。有关相关公司使用的其他情况，*参见* TMEP §§1201.03 及以下。

审查员应当接受申请人关于商标所有权的声明，除非记录的信息明显地与之有悖。本局对于申请人与样本或记录提及的他方之间的关系不作调查，除非提及他方时明显悖于申请人关于其为该商标所有人或有权使用该商标的经鉴定的声明。此

application states that use of the mark is by related companies, the examining attorney should not require any explanation of how the applicant controls such use.

The above provisions also apply to service marks, collective marks and certification marks, except that, by definition, collective marks and certification marks are not used by the owner of the mark, but are used by others under the control of the owner. 15 U.S.C. §§1053 and 1054. *See* TMEP §§1303.01, 1304.03 and 1306.01(a).

See TMEP §1201.04 for information about when an examining attorney should issue an inquiry or refusal with respect to ownership.

1201.02 Identifying the Applicant in the Application

1201.02(a) Identifying the Applicant Properly

The applicant may be any person or entity capable of suing and being sued in a court of law. *See* TMEP §§803 *et seq*. for the appropriate format for identifying the applicant and setting forth the relevant legal entity. *See* TMEP §1201.03(a) regarding the form for indicating that the mark is used solely by a related company.

1201.02(b) Application Void if Wrong Party Identified as the Applicant

An application must be filed by the party who is the owner of (or is entitled to use) the mark as of the application filing date. *See* TMEP §1201.

An application based on use in commerce under 15 U.S.C. §1051(a) must be filed by the party who owns the mark on the application filing date. If the applicant does not own the mark on the application filing date, the application is *void*. 37 C.F.R. §2.71(d). *Huang v. Tzu Wei Chen Food Co. Ltd.*, 849 F.2d 1458, 7 USPQ2d 1335 (Fed. Cir. 1988).

If the record indicates that the applicant is not the owner of the mark, the examining attorney should refuse registration on that ground.

外，在申请中说明商标由相关公司使用的情况下，审查员对于申请人如何控制此类使用不应要求作任何解释。

以上规定同样适用于服务商标、集体商标及证明商标，除非根据定义，集体商标和证明商标并非由商标的所有人使用，而是由他人在所有人的控制之下使用。见 15 U.S.C.§§1053 和 1054。*参见* TMEP §§1303.01、1304.03 和 1306.01(a)。

有关审查员何时应当就所有权问题发出查询函或驳回，*参见* TMEP §1201.04。

1201.02　确定申请的申请人

1201.02(a)　正确确定申请人

任何拥有诉讼能力的个人或实体均可成为申请人。有关确定申请人和写明相关法人实体的适当格式，*参见* TMEP §§803 及以下。有关标明商标系由相关公司单独使用的表格，*参见* TMEP §1201.03(a)。

1201.02(b)　申请人错误时申请无效

提出申请的人在提出申请时必须是商标的所有人（或使用权人）。*参见* TMEP §1201。

依据 15 U.S.C.§1051(a)的规定根据商业使用而提出的申请，申请人在提交申请时必须是拥有商标所有权之人。如果在提交申请时申请人并非商标的所有人，则申请无效。见 37 C.F.R.§2.71(d)。相关判例：*Huang v. Tzu Wei Chen Food Co. Ltd.*，849 F.2d 1458，7 USPQ2d 1335 (Fed. Cir. 1988)。

如果记录表明申请人并非商标的所有人，则审查员应当以此为理由拒绝予以注册。

The statutory basis for this refusal is §1 of the Trademark Act, 15 U.S.C. §1051, and, where related-company issues are relevant, §§5 and 45, 15 U.S.C. §§1055 and 1127. The examining attorney should not have the filing date cancelled or refund the application filing fee.

In an application under §1(b) or §44 of the Trademark Act, 15 U.S.C. §1051(b) or §1126, the applicant must be entitled to use the mark in commerce on the application filing date, and the application must include a verified statement that the applicant has a bona fide intention to use the mark in commerce. 15 U.S.C. §§1051(b)(3)(A), 1051(b)(3)(B), 1126(d)(2) and 1126(e). When the person designated as the applicant was not the person with a bona fide intention to use the mark in commerce at the time the application was filed, the application is void. *American Forests v. Sanders*, 54 USPQ2d 1860 (TTAB 1999), *aff'd*, 232 F. 3d 907 (Fed. Cir. 2000) (intent-to-use application filed by an individual held void, where the entity that had a bona fide intention to use the mark in commerce on the application filing date was a partnership composed of the individual applicant and her husband). However, the examining attorney will not inquire into the bona fides, or good faith, of an applicant's asserted intention to use a mark in commerce during *ex parte* examination, unless there is evidence in the record clearly indicating that the applicant does not have a bona fide intention to use the mark in commerce. *See* TMEP §1101.

When an application is filed in the name of the wrong party, this defect cannot be cured by amendment or assignment. 37 C.F.R. §2.71(d); TMEP §803.06. However, if the application was filed by the owner, but there was a mistake in the manner in which the applicant's name is set forth in the application, this may be corrected. *See* TMEP §1201.02(c) for examples of correctable and non-correctable errors.

1201.02(c) Correcting Errors in How the Applicant Is Identified [R-1]

If the party applying to register the mark is in fact the owner of the mark, but there is a mistake in the manner in which the name of the applicant is set out in

此类拒绝的法律依据是《商标法》§1,15 U.S.C.§1051,在涉及相关公司问题时,拒绝的法律依据是 §§5 和 45, 15 U.S.C.§§1055 和 1127。审查员不应注销申请日期,也不应退还申请费。

对于根据《商标法》§1(b)或 §44、15 U.S.C.§1051(b)或 §1126 提出的申请,申请人在提出申请之时必须有权在商业上使用该商标,而且申请必须包含一份经鉴定的声明,说明申请人真实地意图在商业上使用该商标。15 U.S.C.§§1051(b)(3)(A), 1051(b)(3)(B), 1126(d)(2)和 1126(e)。如果指定的申请人并非真实地意图在商业中商标使用者,则申请无效。相关判例:*American Forests v. Sanders*, 54 USPQ2d 1860 (TTAB 1999), *aff'd*, 232 F.3d 907 (Fed. Cir. 2000)(由于在提出申请之日,真实地意图在商业上使用商标的实体是个体申请人与其丈夫组成的合伙企业,因此该申请人提交的意图使用申请被认定为无效)。不过,在单方面审查中,审查员对于申请人所称的在商业上使用商标的意图是否真实或诚信并不进行调查,除非记录中有证据明确显示申请人没有将商标用于商业活动的真实意图。*参见* TMEP §1101。

如果申请是以不适格当事人的名义提出,此种缺陷不能通过修正书或转让书更正。37 C.F.R.§2.71(d); TMEP §803.06。不过,如果申请确由所有人提出,只是在申请书中把申请人的名称写错,则可以予以更正。有关可更正和不可更正错误的例子,*参见* TMEP §1201.02(c)。

1201.02(c) 纠正确定申请人方面的错误 [R-1]

如果申请注册商标的申请人确系商标的所有人,只是在申请书中把申请人的名

the application, the mistake may be corrected by amendment. *U.S. Pioneer Electronics Corp. v. Evans Marketing, Inc.*, 183 USPQ 613 (Comm'r Pats. 1974). However, the application may *not* be amended to designate another entity as the applicant. 37 C.F.R. §2.71(d); TMEP §803.06. An application filed in the name of the wrong party is void and cannot be corrected by amendment. *In re Tong Yang Cement Corp.*, 19 USPQ2d 1689 (TTAB 1991).

The following are examples of correctable errors in identifying the applicant:

(1) If the applicant identifies itself by a name under which it does business, which is not its name as a legal entity, then amendment to state the applicant's correct legal name is permitted.

(2) If the applicant mistakenly names an operating division that is not a legal entity as the owner, then the applicant's name may be amended. *See* TMEP §1201.02(d).

(3) Clerical errors such as the mistaken addition or omission of "The" or "Inc." in the applicant's name may be corrected by amendment.

(4) If the record is ambiguous as to who owns the mark, *e.g.*, an individual and a corporation are each identified as the owner in different places in the application, the application may be amended to indicate the proper applicant.

(5) If the owner of a mark legally changed its name before filing an application, but mistakenly lists its former name on the application, the error may be corrected because the correct party filed, but merely identified itself incorrectly. *In re Techsonic Industries, Inc.*, 216 USPQ 619 (TTAB 1982).

(6) If the applicant has been identified as "A and B, doing business as The AB Company, a partnership," and the true owner is a partnership organized under the name The AB Company and composed of A and B,

称写错，那么这种错误可以通过修正书加以更正。相关判例：*U.S. Pioneer Electronics Corp. v. Evans Marketing, Inc.*, 183 USPQ 613（Comm'r Pats.1974）。但是，不得以指定另一实体为申请人的方式对申请进行修正。见 37 C.F.R. §2.71(d)；TMEP §803.06。以不适格当事人名义提出的申请无效，且不能通过修正书进行更正。相关判例：*Tong Yang Cement Corp.*, 19 USPQ2d 1689（TTAB 1991）。

以下是确定申请人方面的可更正错误的例子：

(1) 如果申请人从事商业活动所使用的名称与其作为法人实体的名称不一样，则准许通过修正书的方式，说明申请人的正确法人名称。

(2) 如果申请人错误地把某个并非法人实体的职能部门的名称写成所有人，则申请人的名称是可以更正的。*参见* TMEP §1201.02(d)。

(3) 申请人名称存在笔误，例如不慎增加或删减了"The"或"Inc."（有限公司），则可以通过修正书进行更正。

(4) 如果记录上对商标的所有人记载不明，比如，在申请书中的不同地方分别把某个人或某公司作为所有人，则可以通过修正申请书，指明正确的申请人。

(5) 如果在提出申请之前，商标所有人合法地变更了名称，而在申请书中不慎地写入了变更前的名称，则此错误可以加以更正，因为申请确系由正确的申请人提出，只是写错自己的名称而已。相关判例：*Techsonic Industries, Inc.*, 216 USPQ 619（TTAB 1982）。

(6) 如果把申请人写成"甲和乙，二者合伙组成丙公司从事商业活动"，而真正的所有人是甲和乙的合伙企业丙公司，

the applicant's name should be amended to "The AB Company, a partnership composed of A and B."

To correct an obvious mistake of this nature, a verification or declaration is not normally necessary.

The following are examples of non-correctable errors in identifying the applicant:

(1) If the president of a corporation is identified as the owner of the mark when in fact the corporation owns the mark, the application is void as filed because the applicant is not the owner of the mark.

(2) If an application is filed in the name of entity A, when the mark was assigned to entity B before the application filing date, the application is void as filed because the applicant was not the owner of the mark at the time of filing. *Huang v. Tzu Wei Chen Food Co. Ltd.*, 849 F.2d 1458, 7 USPQ2d 1335 (Fed. Cir. 1988) (application filed by an individual two days after ownership of the mark was transferred to a newly formed corporation held void).

(3) If the application is filed in the name of a joint venturer when the mark is owned by the joint venture, the application cannot be amended. *In re Tong Yang Cement Corp., supra*.

(4) If an application is filed in the name of corporation A and a sister corporation (corporation B) owns the mark, the application is void as filed because the applicant is not the owner of the mark.

1201.02(d) Operating Divisions

An operating division that is not a legal entity that can sue and be sued does not have standing to own a mark or to file an application to register a mark. The application must be filed in the name of the company of which the division is a part. *In re Cambridge Digital Systems*, 1 USPQ2d 1659, 1660 n.1 (TTAB 1986). An operating division's use is

则申请人的名称应当修正为“丙公司，系甲和乙组成的合伙企业”。

修正此类明显的错误，一般无需确认书或声明书。

以下是确定申请人方面的不可更正的错误的例子：

(1) 如果公司总裁被写成是商标的所有人，而实际上公司是商标的所有人，则申请无效，因为申请人并非商标的所有人。

(2) 如果申请以实体甲的名义提出，而在提出申请之前该商标已经转让给实体乙了，则申请无效，因为在申请提出之时，申请人并非商标的所有人。相关判例：*Huang v. Tzu Wei Chen Food Co. Ltd.*, 849 F.2d 1458, 7 USPQ2d 1335 (Fed. Cir. 1988)（某人在将商标所有权转让给一个新成立公司两天之后提出的申请被认定无效）。

(3) 如果申请是以某合资企业的合资人的名义提出，而商标的所有人是合资企业，则申请不可修正。相关判例：*Tong Yang Cement Corp.*，见上述。

(4) 如果申请以公司甲同其姊妹公司（公司乙）的名义提出，则该申请无效，因为申请人并非商标的所有人。

1201.02(d) 职能部门

职能部门不具有诉讼资格，不是法人实体，故不享有拥有商标所有权及提出商标注册申请的资格。申请必须以该部门所属公司的名义提出。相关判例：*Cambridge Digital Systems*, 1 USPQ2d 1659, 1660 n.1 (TTAB 1986)。职能部门使用被视作申

considered to be use by the applicant and not use by a related company; therefore, reference to related-company use is permissible but not necessary.

1201.02(e) Changes in Ownership After Application Is Filed

See TMEP Chapter 500 regarding changes of ownership and changes of name subsequent to filing an application for registration, and recordation in the Office's Assignment Services Division of assignment documents, certificates of merger, certificates of change of name, security agreements, etc.

Recording a document with the Assignment Services Division does not change the owner of record in the TRAM (Trademark Reporting and Monitoring) System. The new owner must also notify the examining attorney that ownership has changed, to ensure that the registration issues in the name of the new owner. 37 C.F.R. §3.85. *See* TMEP §502.01 regarding the procedure for requesting that a certificate of registration be issued in the name of an assignee or in an applicant's new name.

1201.03 Use by Related Companies

Section 5 of the Trademark Act, 15 U.S.C. §1055, states, in part, as follows:

> Where a registered mark or a mark sought to be registered is or may be used legitimately by related companies, such use shall inure to the benefit of the registrant or applicant for registration, and such use shall not affect the validity of such mark or of its registration, provided such mark is not used in such manner as to deceive the public.

Section 45 of the Act, 15 U.S.C. §1127, defines "related company" as follows:

> The term "related company" means any person whose use of a mark is controlled by the owner of the mark with respect to the nature and quality of the goods or services on or in connection with which the mark is used.

请人使用而非相关公司使用；因此，可提及相关公司使用，但并非必须这样做。

1201.02(e)　提出申请后所有权的变更

有关注册申请提交后变更所有权及名称的情况，以及到本局转让事务部登记转让文件、合并证明、名称变更证明、担保协议等情况，*参见* TMEP Chapter 500。

在转让事务部登记文件并不改变 TRAM（商标报告及监督）系统中记录的所有人。新所有人也必须向审查员通知所有权变更事项，以确保以新所有人的名称进行注册。见 37 C.F.R.§3.85。有关请求颁发以受让人的名称或申请人的新名称登记的注册证明书的手续，*参见* TMEP §502.01。

1201.03　相关公司的使用

《商标法》第 5 节 15 U.S.C.§1055 作如下规定（节选）：

> 如果已经注册或正在申请注册的商标已经或可能由相关公司合法地使用，那么此类使用应使注册人或申请注册人获利，并且此类使用不应影响商标或其注册的有效性，但商标不得以欺骗公众的方式使用。

《商标法》第 45 节 15 U.S.C.§1127 对“相关公司”作以下定义：

> “相关公司”这一术语是指在商标所有人控制使用商标的商品或服务的性质和质量的情况下使用商标的任何人。

Thus, §5 of the Act permits applicants for registration to rely on use of the mark by related companies. Either a natural person or a juristic person may be a related company. 15 U.S.C. §1127.

The essence of related-company use is the control exercised over the nature and quality of the goods or services on or in connection with which the mark is used. When a mark is used by a related company, use of the mark inures to the benefit of the party who controls the nature and quality of the goods or services. This party is the owner of the mark and, therefore, is the only party that may apply to register the mark. *Smith International, Inc. v. Olin Corp.*, 209 USPQ 1033, 1044 (TTAB 1981).

Reliance on related-company use requires, *inter alia*, that the related company use the mark in connection with the same goods or services recited in the application. *In re Admark, Inc.*, 214 USPQ 302 (TTAB 1982) (related-company use not at issue where the applicant sought registration of a mark for advertising agency services and the purported related company used the mark for retail store services).

A related company is different from a successor in interest who is in privity with the predecessor in interest for purposes of determining the right to register. *Wells Cargo, Inc. v. Wells Cargo, Inc.*, 197 USPQ 569 (TTAB 1977), *aff'd*, 606 F.2d 961, 203 USPQ 564 (C.C.P.A. 1979).

See TMEP §1201.03(c) regarding wholly owned related companies, §1201.03(d) regarding corporations with common stockholders, directors or officers, §1201.03(e) regarding sister corporations, and §1201.03(f) regarding license and franchise situations.

1201.03(a) Use Solely by Related Company Must be Disclosed

If the mark is not being used by the applicant but is being used by one or more related companies whose use inures to the benefit of the applicant under §5 of the Act, then these facts must be disclosed in the application. 37 C.F.R. §2.38(b). *See Pease Woodwork Co., Inc. v. Ready Hung Door Co., Inc.*, 103 USPQ 240

因此,《商标法》§5 准许根据相关公司的使用提出注册申请。自然人和法人均可成为相关公司。见 15 U.S.C.§1127。

相关公司使用的本质是,使用商标的商品或服务的性质和质量受到控制。当相关公司使用商标时,商标的使用给控制使用商标的商品或服务的性质和质量的一方带来利益。这一方是商标的所有人,因而也是申请注册商标的唯一适格申请人。相关判例:*Smith International, Inc. v. Olin Corp.*, 209 USPQ 1033, 1044 (TTAB 1981)。

以相关公司使用为基础的申请要求(除其他要求外)相关公司将商标用于申请书所述的相同商品或服务上。相关判例:*Admark, Inc.*, 214 USPQ 302 (TTAB 1982)(相关公司使用并不存在,因为申请人申请注册的商标是用于广告代理服务,但据说相关公司将商标用于零售商店服务)。

相关公司不同于利益继承者,在决定注册权利上,后者与被继承者有着同样的利益。相关判例:*Wells Cargo, Inc. v. Wells Cargo, Inc.*, 197 USPQ 569 (TTAB 1977), *aff'd*, 606 F.2d 961, 203 USPQ 564 (C.C.P.A.1979)。

有关独资相关公司的情况,*参见* TMEP §1201.03(c);有关具有共同股东、董事或管理者的公司的情况,*参见* §1201.03(d);有关姊妹公司的情况,*参见* §1201.03(e);有关许可和特许经营的情况,*参见* §1201.03(f)。

1201.03(a)　相关公司的单独使用必须披露

如果申请人并没有使用商标,而是由一个及一个以上的相关公司根据《商标法》§5 进行使用,而且相关公司的使用给申请人带来利益,那么这些事实情况必须在申请书中披露。见 37 C.F.R.§2.38(b)。*参见 Pease Woodwork Co., Inc. v. Ready Hung Door Co., Inc.*, 103 USPQ 240 (Comm'r Pats.1954); *Industrial Abrasives*,

(Comm'r Pats. 1954); *Industrial Abrasives, Inc. v. Strong*, 101 USPQ 420 (Comm'r Pats. 1954). Use that inures to the applicant's benefit is a proper and sufficient support for an application and satisfies the requirement of 37 C.F.R. §2.33(b)(1) that a §1(a) application specify that the *applicant* has adopted and is using the mark.

The party who controls the nature and quality of the goods or services on or in connection with which the mark is used should be set forth as the applicant. In an application under §1(a) of the Trademark Act, the applicant should state in the body of the application that the applicant has adopted and is using the mark *through its related company* (or equivalent explanatory wording). In a §1(b) application, the statement that the applicant is using the mark through a related company should be included in the amendment to allege use under 15 U.S.C. §1051(c) (*see* TMEP §§1104 *et seq.*) or statement of use under 15 U.S.C. §1051 (d) (*see* TMEP §§1109 *et seq.*).

The applicant is not required to give the name of the related-company user unless it is necessary to explain information in the record that clearly contradicts the applicant's verified claim of ownership of the mark.

The applicant may claim the benefit of use by a related company in an amendment to the application. *Greyhound Corp. v. Armour Life Insurance Co.*, 214 USPQ 473, 475 (TTAB 1982).

If the applicant and a related company both use the mark, and it is the applicant's own use of the mark that is relied on in the application, then the applicant does not have to include a reference to use by a related company in the application. *See* TMEP §1201.05.

1201.03(b) No Explanation of Applicant's Control Over Use of Mark by Related Companies Required

Where the application states that use of the mark is by a related company or com-

Inc. v. Strong, 101 USPQ 420 (Comm'r Pats. 1954)。给申请人带来利益的使用可以适当并充分地支持一项申请，并且满足了 37 C.F.R.§2.33(b)(1)的要求，即根据§1(a)提出的申请必须说明*申请人*已经采用并正在使用该商标。

对使用商标的商品或服务的性质和质量进行控制的一方应当被列为申请人。对于根据《商标法》§1(a)提出的申请，申请人应在申请书正文中说明，申请人已经采用并正在*通过其相关公司*（或类似的解释性措辞）使用该商标。对于根据 §1(b)提出的申请，申请人正在通过相关公司使用商标的声明应包含在根据 15 U.S.C.§1051(c)规定提交的宣称使用修正书(*参见* TMEP §§1104 及以下)或根据 15 U.S.C.§1051(d)规定提交的使用声明书(*参见* TMEP §§1109 及以下)之中。

除非因为记录中存在明显有悖于申请人拥有该商标的主张的信息，而有必要对这些信息进行解释时，申请人不必提供相关公司使用者的名称。

申请人可以用申请书的修正书的方式，主张由相关公司的使用而获得的利益。相关判例：*Greyhound Corp. v. Armour Life Insurance Co.*, 214 USPQ 473, 475 (TTAB 1982)。

如果申请人与相关公司同时使用该商标，而申请人是根据自己使用商标提出申请，那么申请人就不必在申请书中加入有关相关公司使用的证明。*参见* TMEP §1201.05。

1201.03(b)　申请人无须对控制相关公司使用商标的情况进行解释

对于申请书中指出商标由一个或多个相关公司使用，本局并不要求申请人解释如何控制商标的使用。

panies, the Office does not require an explanation of how the applicant controls the use of the mark.

Similarly, the Office does not inquire about the relationship between the applicant and other parties named on the specimens or elsewhere in the record, except when the reference to another party clearly contradicts the applicant's verified statement that it is the owner of the mark or entitled to use the mark. *See* TMEP §1201.04.

1201.03(c) Wholly Owned Related Companies

Related-company use includes situations where a wholly owned related company of the applicant uses the mark or the applicant is wholly owned by a related company that uses the mark.

Frequently, related companies comprise parent and wholly owned subsidiary corporations. Either a parent corporation or a subsidiary corporation may be the proper applicant, depending on the facts concerning ownership of the mark. The Office will consider the filing of the application in the name of either the parent or the subsidiary to be the expression of the intention of the parties as to ownership in accord with the arrangements between them.

Either an individual or a juristic entity may own a mark that is used by a wholly owned related company. *See In re Hand*, 231 USPQ 487 (TTAB 1986).

1201.03(d) Common Stockholders, Directors or Officers

Corporations are not "related companies" within the meaning of §5 of the Trademark Act, 15 U.S.C. §1055, merely because they have the same stockholders, directors or officers, or because they occupy the same premises. *In re Raven Marine, Inc.*, 217 USPQ 68, 69 (TTAB 1983) (statement that both the applicant corporation and the corporate user of the mark have the same principal stockholder

同样地，本局对于申请人与样本或记录提及的他方之间的关系不作调查，除非提及他方时明显悖于申请人关于其为该商标所有人或有权使用该商标的经鉴定的声明。*参见* TMEP §1201.04。

1201.03(c)　独资相关公司

相关公司使用也包括申请人独资的相关公司使用商标以及申请人为使用商标的相关公司所独有这两种情况。

通常，相关公司包括母公司和独资子公司。根据商标所有权的具体情况，母公司和子公司均可成为适格的申请人。本局将认为以母公司或子公司的名义提出的申请表明了母子双方按照母子公司之间的协议确定所有人的意图。

无论是自然人还是法人，均可拥有由独资相关公司使用的商标。*参见*相关判例：*Hand*，231 USPQ 487（TTAB 1986）。

1201.03(d)　共同股东、董事或管理者

如果两家公司只属于具有共同的股东、董事或管理者，或者占有同一个房产的情况，则不属于《商标法》§5 15 U.S.C.§1055 所规定的“相关公司”。相关判例：*Raven Marine*，*Inc*.，217 USPQ 68，69（TTAB 1983）（声明商标的法人申请人和商标的法人使用者具有相同的主要股东和管理者，不足以表明使用者为相关公司）。

and officer held insufficient to show that the user is a related company).

If an individual applicant is not the sole owner of the corporation that is using the mark, the question of whether the corporation is a "related company" depends on whether the applicant maintains control over the nature and quality of the goods or services such that use of the mark inures to the applicant's benefit. A formal written licensing agreement between the parties is not necessary, nor is its existence sufficient to establish ownership rights. The critical question is whether the applicant sufficiently controls the nature and quality of the goods or services with which the mark is used. *See Pneutek, Inc. v. Scherr*, 211 USPQ 824 (TTAB 1981) (detailed written agreement and substantial evidence in the record indicating that the applicant, an individual, exercised control over the nature and quality of the goods sold under the mark by the user corporation held sufficient to show that the corporation was a related company).

Similarly, where an individual applicant is not the sole owner of the corporation that is using the mark, the fact that the individual applicant is a stockholder, director of officer in the corporation is insufficient by itself to establish that the corporation is a related company. The question depends on whether the applicant maintains control over the nature and quality of the goods or services.

See TMEP §1201.03(c) regarding use by wholly owned related companies.

1201.03(e) Sister Corporations

The fact that two sister corporations are controlled by a single parent corporation does not mean that they are related companies. Where two corporations are wholly owned subsidiaries of a common parent, use by one sister corporation is not considered to inure to the benefit of the other unless the applicant sister corporation exercises appropriate control over the nature and quality of the goods or services on or in connection with which the mark is used. *In re Pharmacia Inc.*, 2 USPQ2d 1883 (TTAB 1987); *Greyhound Corp. v. Armour Life Insurance Co.*, 214 USPQ 473 (TTAB 1982).

如果自然人申请人并非使用商标的公司的唯一所有人，那么该公司是否为“相关公司”的问题就取决于申请人对使用商标并为其带来利益的商品或服务的性质和质量是否具有控制权。双方之间的正式书面许可协议并非必要，但即使存在此书面许可协议，也不足以证明所有权。问题的关键在于申请人对使用商标的商品或服务的性质和质量是否具有充分的控制权。*参见* *Pneutek, Inc. v. Scherr*, 211 USPQ 824 (TTAB 1981)（详细的书面协议以及记录中的实质性证据表明，个人申请人对公司使用者使用商标出售的商品的性质和质量行使了控制，因而我们认定这一事实充分显示了该公司为相关公司）。

类似地，如果个人申请人并非使用商标的公司的唯一所有人，而只是其股东、董事或管理者，则不能认定该公司为相关公司。问题取决于申请人是否对商品或服务的性质和质量进行控制。

有关独资相关公司使用的情况，*参见* TMEP §1201.03(c)。

1201.03(e)　姊妹公司

两家姊妹公司由同一家母公司控制，并不表示它们是相关公司。两家公司为同一家母公司所独有的子公司时，其中一家姊妹公司的使用并不视作给另一家姊妹公司带来了利益，除非作为申请人的姊妹公司对于使用商标的商品或服务的性质和质量行使了相应的控制。相关判例：*Pharmacia Inc.*, 2 USPQ2d 1883 (TTAB 1987)；*Greyhound Corp. v. Armour Life Insurance Co.*, 214 USPQ 473 (TTAB 1982)。

See TMEP §1201.03(c) regarding use by wholly owned related companies.

1201.03(f) License and Franchise Situations

The Office accepts applications by parties who claim to be owners of marks through use by controlled licensees, pursuant to a contract or agreement. *Pneutek, Inc. v. Scherr*, 211 USPQ 824, 833 (TTAB 1981).

A controlled licensing agreement may be recognized whether oral or written in form. *In re Raven Marine, Inc.*, 217 USPQ 68, 69 (TTAB 1983).

If the application indicates that use of the mark is pursuant to a license or franchise agreement, and the record contains nothing that contradicts the assertion of ownership by the applicant (*i.e.*, the licensor or franchisor), the examining attorney will not inquire about the relationship between the applicant and the related company (*i.e.*, the licensee or franchisee).

Ownership rights in a trademark or service mark may be acquired and maintained through the use of the mark by a controlled licensee even when the only use of the mark has been made, and is being made, by the licensee. *Turner v. HMH Publishing Co., Inc.*, 380 F.2d 224, 154 USPQ 330, 334 (5th Cir. 1967), *cert. denied*, 389 U.S. 1006, 156 USPQ 720 (1967); *Central Fidelity Banks, Inc. v. First Bankers Corp. of Florida*, 225 USPQ 438, 440 (TTAB 1984) (use of the mark by petitioner's affiliated banks considered to inure to the benefit of petitioner bank holding company, even though the bank holding company could not legally render banking services and thus could not use the mark).

Joint applicants enjoy rights of ownership to the same extent as any other "person" who has a proprietary interest in a mark. Therefore, joint applicants may license others to use a mark and, by exercising sufficient control and supervision of the nature and quality of the goods or services to which the mark is applied, the

有关独资相关公司使用的情况，参见 TMEP §1201.03(c)。

1201.03(f) 许可和特许的情况

当事人通过依据合同或协议控制被许可人使用商标的方式主张其为商标所有人时，可以向本局提出申请。见 *Pneutek, Inc. v. Scherr*, 211 USPQ 824, 833 (TTAB 1981)。

被控制的许可协议可以是书面形式，也可以是口头形式。相关判例：*Raven Marine, Inc.*, 217 USPQ 68, 69 (TTAB 1983)。

如果提交的申请书表明，商标的使用是依照许可或特许协议进行的，而且记录的情况与申请人(即许可人或特许人)对所有权的主张并不相悖，则审查员对于申请人和相关公司(即被许可人或被特许人)之间的关系不进行调查。

可以通过控制被许可人对商标的使用，获得并保持对商标或服务商标的所有权，即使被许可人对商标的使用是唯一的商标使用。见 *Turner v. HMH Publishing Co., Inc.*, 380 F.2d 224, 154 USPQ 330, 334 (5th Cir. 1967), *cert. denied*, 389 U.S.1006, 156 USPQ 720 (1967); *Central Fidelity Banks, Inc. v. First Bankers Corp. of Florida*, 225 USPQ 438, 440 (TTAB 1984)(申请人的附属银行对商标的使用被认为给申请人的银行控股公司带来了利益，尽管该银行控股公司不能合法地提供银行服务因而不能使用商标)。

共同申请人享有与享有商标所有权利益的任何其他“人”相同的所有权权利。因此，共同申请人可以许可他人使用商标，而且，通过对使用商标的商品或服务的性质

joint applicants/licensors may claim the benefits of the use by the related company/licensee. *In re Diamond Walnut Growers, Inc. and Sunsweet Growers Inc.*, 204 USPQ 507, 510 (TTAB 1979).

Stores that are operating under franchise agreements from another party are considered "related companies" of that party, and use of the mark by the franchisee/store inures to the benefit of the franchisor. *Mr. Rooter Corp. v. Morris*, 188 USPQ 392, 394 (E.D. La. 1975); *Southland Corp. v. Schubert*, 297 F. Supp. 477, 160 USPQ 375, 381 (C.D. Cal. 1968).

In all franchise and license situations, the key to ownership is the nature and extent of the control by the applicant of the goods or services to which the mark is applied. A trademark owner who fails to exercise necessary controls over licensees or franchisees may be found to have abandoned its rights in the mark. *See Hurricane Fence Co. v. A-1 Hurricane Fence Co. Inc.*, 468 F. Supp. 975, 208 USPQ 314, 325-27 (S.D. Ala. 1979).

In general, where the application states that a mark is used by a licensee or franchisee, the Office does not require an explanation of how the applicant controls the use. *See* TMEP §1201.03(b).

1201.04 Inquiry Regarding Parties Named on Specimens or Elsewhere in Record

The Office does not inquire about the relationship between the applicant and other parties named on the specimens or elsewhere in the record, except when the reference to another party clearly contradicts the applicant's verified statement that it is the owner of the mark or entitled to use the mark.

The examining attorney should inquire about another party if the record specifically states that another party is the owner of the mark, or if the record specifically identifies the applicant in a manner that contradicts the claim of ownership, for example, as a licensee. In these circumstances, registration should be refused

和质量实施充分的控制及监督，共同申请人/许可人可以对相关公司/被许可人使用该商标所产生的利益提出权利要求。相关判例：*Diamond Walnut Growers, Inc. and Sunsweet Growers Inc.*, 204 USPQ 507, 510 (TTAB 1979)。

依照另一方的特许协议进行经营的商店被视作是该另一方的“相关公司”，被特许人/商店对商标的使用给特许人带来了利益。见 *Mr. Rooter Corp. v. Morris*, 188 USPQ 392, 394 (E. D. La. 1975); *Southland Corp. v. Schubert*, 297 F. Supp. 477, 160 USPQ 375, 381 (C. D. Cal. 1968)。

在一切特许和许可的情形中，所有权问题的关键在于申请人对使用商标的商品或服务所实施的控制的性质和范围。未对被许可人或被特许人实施必要控制的商标所有人可以被视作放弃其对该商标的权利。*参见 Hurricane Fence Co. v. A-1 Hurricane Fence Co. Inc.*, 468 F. Supp. 975, 208 USPQ 314, 325-27 (S. D. Ala. 1979)。

一般情况下，如果申请中称商标是由被许可人或被特许人使用，则本局并不要求申请人解释如何控制商标的使用。*参见* TMEP §1201.03(b)。

1201.04　对样本或记录他处提及的当事人的调查

本局对于申请人与样本或记录他处提及的他方之间的关系不作调查，除非提及他方时明显有悖于申请人关于其为商标所有人或有权使用商标的经鉴定的声明。

如果记录特别指出他方为该商标的所有人，或者记录中特别指明的申请人身份与对所有权的主张有悖，比如指明申请人为被许可人，则审查员应当对该他方进行调查。在这种情况下，应当根据《商标法》§1的规定拒绝注册，因为申请人并非商标的

under §1 of the Trademark Act, on the ground that the applicant is not the owner of the mark. Similarly, when the record indicates that the applicant is a United States distributor, importer or other distributing agent for a foreign manufacturer, the examining attorney should require the applicant to establish its ownership rights in the United States in accordance with TMEP §1201.06(a).

Where the specimen of use indicates that the goods are manufactured in a country other than the applicant's home country, the examining attorney normally should not inquire whether the mark is used by a foreign manufacturer. *See* TMEP §1201.06(b). Also, where the application states that use of the mark is by related companies, an explanation of how the applicant controls use of the mark by the related companies is not required. *See* TMEP §1201.03(b).

1201.05 Acceptable Claim of Ownership Based on Applicant's Own Use

An applicant's claim of ownership of a mark may be based on the applicant's own use of the mark, even though there is also use by a related company. The applicant is the owner by virtue of the applicant's own use, and the application does not have to refer to use by a related company.

An applicant may claim ownership of a mark when the mark is applied on the applicant's instruction. For example, if the applicant contracts with another party to have goods produced for the applicant and instructs the party to place the mark on the goods, that is the equivalent of the applicant itself placing the mark on its own goods and reference to related-company use is not necessary.

1201.06 Special Situations Pertaining to Ownership

1201.06(a) Applicant Is Merely Distributor or Importer

A distributor, importer or other distributing agent of the goods of a manufacturer

所有人。类似地,如果记录显示申请人是某外国生产商在美国的分销商、进口商或其他销售代理,则审查员应当要求申请人根据 TMEP §1201.06(a)的规定,证明其在美国的所有人权利。

如果使用样本显示商品不是在申请人本国生产,审查员一般不应调查该商标是否由某外国生产商使用。*参见* TMEP §1201.06(b)。同样地,如果申请中称商标是由相关公司使用,则不要求申请人解释如何控制相关公司对商标的使用。*参见* TMEP §1201.03(b)。

1201.05　根据申请人自己使用提出的可接受的所有权主张

申请人可以根据自己的使用提出对商标的所有权,即使同时也存在相关公司使用的情况。由于自己使用,申请人即为所有人,而无需在申请中提供相关公司使用的情况。

当商标是根据申请人的指示进行使用时,申请人可以提出对商标的所有权。例如,如果申请人与他方订立合同,由对方为其生产产品,并根据申请人的指示将商标置于商品之上,这种情况等同于申请人自己将商标用在商品上,故无需提供相关公司使用的情况。

1201.06　有关所有权的特殊情形

1201.06(a)　申请人只是经销商或进口商

制造商或生产商商品的经销商、进口商或其他经销代理人对于制造商或生产商

or producer does not acquire a right of ownership in the manufacturer's or producer's mark merely because it moves the goods in trade. *In re Bee Pollen from England Ltd*., 219 USPQ 163 (TTAB 1983); *Audioson Vertriebs - GmbH v. Kirksaeter Audiosonics, Inc*., 196 USPQ 453 (TTAB 1977); *Jean D'Albret v. Henkel-Khasana G.m.b.H*., 185 USPQ 317 (TTAB 1975); *In re Lettmann*, 183 USPQ 369 (TTAB 1974); *Bakker v. Steel Nurse of America Inc*., 176 USPQ 447 (TTAB 1972). A party that merely distributes goods bearing the mark of a manufacturer or producer is neither the owner nor a related-company user of the mark.

If the applicant merely distributes or imports goods for the owner of the mark, registration must be refused under §1 of the Trademark Act, *except* in the following situations:

(1) If a parent and wholly owned subsidiary relationship exists between the distributor and the manufacturer, then the applicant's statement that such a relationship exists disposes of an ownership issue. *See* TMEP §1201.03(c).

(2) If an applicant is the United States importer or distribution agent for a foreign manufacturer, then the applicant can register the foreign manufacturer's mark in the United States, if the applicant submits one of the following:

(a) written consent from the owner of the mark to registration in the applicant's name, or

(b) written agreement or acknowledgment between the parties that the importer or distributor is the owner of the mark in the United States, or

(c) an assignment (or true copy) to the applicant of the owner's rights in the mark as to the United States together with the business and good will appurtenant thereto.

的商标不享有所有权，因为其只是在贸易中移转商品。相关判例：*Bee Pollen from England Ltd.*，219 USPQ 163（TTAB 1983）；*Audioson Vertriebs-GmbH v. Kirksaeter Audiosonics, Inc.*，196 USPQ 453（TTAB 1977）；*Jean D'Albret v. Henkel-Khasana G.m.b.H.*，185 USPQ 317（TTAB 1975）；*Lettmann*，183 USPQ 369（TTAB 1974）；*Bakker v. Steel Nurse of America Inc.*，176 USPQ 447（TTAB 1972）。仅仅经销带有制造商或生产商商标的商品的当事人既不是商标的所有人，也不是商标的相关公司使用者。

如果申请人只是为商标的所有人经销或进口商品，则应当根据《商标法》§1 的规定拒绝其注册申请，*除非*存在下列情形：

（1） 如果在经销商和制造商之间存在母公司和独资子公司的关系，则只要申请人声明存在此种关系，即可解决所有权问题。*参见* TMEP §1201.03(c)。

（2） 如果申请人是外国制造商在美国的进口商或代理经销商，只要申请人提交下列文件之一，即可在美国注册该外国制造商的商标：

（a） 商标所有人同意以申请人的名义进行注册的书面文件，或

（b） 双方的书面协议或确认书，同意以进口商或经销商为该商标在美国的所有人，或

（c） 所有人将该商标在美国的权利，随同附随的业务及商誉一并让与申请人的转让书（或正式副本）。

See In re Pharmacia Inc., 2 USPQ2d 1883 (TTAB 1987); *In re Geo. J. Ball, Inc*., 153 USPQ 426 (TTAB 1967).

1201.06(b) Goods Manufactured in a Country Other than Where Applicant Is Located

Where a specimen of use indicates that the goods are manufactured in a country other than the applicant's home country, the examining attorney normally should not inquire whether the mark is used by a foreign manufacturer. If, however, information in the record clearly contradicts the applicant's verified claim of ownership (*e.g*., a statement in the record that the mark is owned by the foreign manufacturer and that the applicant is only an importer or distributor), then registration must be refused under §1, 15 U.S.C. §1051, unless registration in the United States by the applicant is supported by the applicant's submission of one of the documents listed in TMEP §1201.06(a).

1201.07 Related Companies and Likelihood of Confusion

1201.07(a) "Single Source"—"Unity of Control"

Section 2(d) of the Trademark Act, 15 U.S.C. §1052(d), requires that the examining attorney refuse registration when an applicant's mark, as applied to the specified goods or services, so resembles a registered mark as to be likely to cause confusion. In general, registration of confusingly similar marks to separate legal entities is barred by §2(d). *See, e.g., In re Citibank, N.A*., 225 USPQ 612 (TTAB 1985); *In re Champion International Corp*., 220 USPQ 478 (TTAB 1982); *In re Air Products, Inc*., 124 USPQ 81 (TTAB 1960). However, the Court of Appeals for the Federal Circuit has held that, where the applicant is related in ownership to a company that owns a registered mark that would otherwise give rise to a likelihood of confusion, the examining attorney must consider whether, in view of all the circumstances, use of the mark by the applicant is likely to con-

相关判例：*Pharmacia Inc.*, 2 USPQ2d 1883 (TTAB 1987)；*Geo. J. Ball, Inc.*, 153 USPQ 426 (TTAB 1967)。

1201.06(b)　在申请人所在地以外国家制造的商品

如果样本表明，商品是在申请人本国以外的国家生产的，则审查员一般不对该商标是否由某外国制造商使用进行调查。但是，如果记录中的信息明显有悖于申请人的所有权主张(例如，记录中声明该商标是由某外国制造商所有，而申请人只是其进口商或经销商)，那么就必须根据 §1，15 U.S.C.§1051 的规定拒绝其注册申请，除非申请人提交 TMEP §1201.06(a)中规定的文件之一，方可在美国注册。

1201.07　相关公司及混淆的可能性

1201.07(a)　"单一来源"——"统一控制"

《商标法》Section 2(d)，15 U.S.C.§1052(d)规定，如果申请人的商标在特定商品或服务上使用时，与已注册的商标很相似并可能导致混淆，则审查员应当拒绝注册。一般说来，§2(d)禁止了不同的法人实体分别注册混淆性的类似商标。*参见*相关判例：*Citibank, N.A.*, 225 USPQ 612 (TTAB 1985)；*Champion International Corp.*, 220 USPQ 478 (TTAB 1982)； *Air Products, Inc.*, 124 USPQ 81 (TTAB 1960)。不过，联邦巡回上诉法院认为，当申请人在所有权问题上遇到了可能与其他公司拥有的已注册商标相混淆的情况时，审查员必须考虑，是否在一切情况下，申请

fuse the public about the source of the applicant's goods because of the resemblance of the applicant's mark to the mark of the other company. The Court stated that:

> The question is whether, despite the similarity of the marks and the goods on which they are used, the public is likely to be confused about the source of the hair straightening products carrying the trademark "WELLASTRATE." In other words, is the public likely to believe that the source of the product is Wella U.S. rather than the German company or the Wella organization.

In re Wella A. G., 787 F.2d 1549, 1552, 229 USPQ 274, 276 (Fed. Cir. 1986). The Court remanded the case to the Board for consideration of the likelihood of confusion issue.

In ruling on that issue, the Board concluded that there was no likelihood of confusion, stating as follows:

> [A] determination must be made as to whether there exists a likelihood of confusion as to *source*, that is, whether purchasers would believe that particular goods or services emanate from a single source, when in fact those goods or services emanate from more than a single source. Clearly, the Court views the concept of "source" as encompassing more than "legal entity." Thus, in this case, we are required to determine whether Wella A. G. and Wella U.S. are the same source or different sources ...
>
> The existence of a related company relationship between Wella U.S. and Wella A. G. is not, in itself, a basis for finding that any "WELLA" product emanating from either of the two companies emanates from the same source. Besides the existence of a legal relationship, there must also be a unity of control over the use of the trademarks. "Control" and "source" are inextricably linked. If, notwithstanding the legal relationship between entities, each entity exclusively controls the nature and

人对商标的使用都可能由于与其他公司的商标相类似而造成公众混淆申请人商品的来源。法院指出：

> 问题的关键是，撇开商标的相似性以及使用商标的商品，公众是否可能混淆带有“WELLASTRATE”商标的用于拉直头发的产品的来源。换句话说，公众是否可能认为该产品的来源是 Wella U.S.公司，而非德国公司或 Wella 组织。

相关判例：*Wella A.G.*，787 F.2d 1549，1552，229 USPQ 274，276（Fed. Cir. 1986）。法院将该案发回委员会，以审查混淆的可能性问题。

对于此问题，委员会判定不存在混淆的可能性，陈述如下：

> 在此必须判断是否可能构成了对于来源的混淆，也就是说，购买者是否认为特定的商品或服务的来源只有一个，而实际上那些商品或服务的来源不止一个。很明显，法院认为“来源”的概念比“法人实体”的概念范围更广。因此，在本案中，要求我们判断 Wella A.G. 和 Wella U.S. 是同一来源还是不同的来源。

> 尽管 Wella U.S. 和 Wella A.G. 之间存在相关公司关系，但这种关系本身不足以产生任何“WELLA”产品——无论由这两家公司中哪一家生产——都来自于同一来源这一结论。除了存在法律关系之外，还必须存在对商标使用的统一控制。“控制”和“来源”不可分割地联系在一起。如果，尽管两个实体之间存在法律关系，但每个实体分别单独地对使用各种“WELLA”

> quality of the goods to which it applies one or more of the various "WELLA" trademarks, the two entities are in fact separate sources. Wella A.G. has made of record a declaration of the executive vice president of Wella U.S., which declaration states that Wella A.G. owns substantially all the outstanding stock of Wella U.S. and "thus controls the activities and operations of Wella U.S., including the selection, adoption and use of the trademarks." While the declaration contains no details of how this control is exercised, the declaration is sufficient, absent contradictory evidence in the record, to establish that control over the use of all the "WELLA" trademarks in the United States resides in a single source.

In re Wella A.G., 5 USPQ2d 1359, 1361 (TTAB 1987) (emphasis in original), *rev'd on other grounds*, 858 F.2d 725, 8 USPQ2d 1365 (Fed. Cir. 1988).

Therefore, in some limited circumstances, the close relationship between related companies will obviate any likelihood of confusion in the public mind because the related companies constitute a single source. *See* TMEP §§1201.07(b) *et seq*. for further information.

1201.07(b) Appropriate Action with Respect to Assertion of Unity of Control

First, it is important to note that analysis under *Wella* is not triggered until an applicant affirmatively asserts that a §2(d) refusal is inappropriate because the applicant and the registrant, though separate legal entities, constitute a single source, or the applicant raises an equivalent argument. Examining attorneys should issue §2(d) refusals in any case where an analysis of the marks and the goods or services of the respective parties indicates a bar to registration under §2(d). The examining attorney should not attempt to analyze the relationship between an applicant and registrant until an applicant, in some form, relies on the nature of the relationship to obviate a refusal under §2(d).

商标中的一种或多种的产品的性质和质量进行控制，那么这两个实体实际上是不同的来源。Wella A.G.在记录中提供了 Wella U.S.执行副总裁的声明，称 Wella A.G.实际上拥有 Wella U.S.所有的已发行股票，并“因此控制了 Wella U.S.的活动和经营，包括对商标的选择、采用和使用”。尽管该声明并没有详细说明如何行使此种控制，但由于在记录中不存在相反的证据，因此该声明足以证明：在美国对“WELLA”商标使用的控制来自单一的来源。

相关判例：*Wella A.G.*, 5 USPQ2d 1359, 1361 (TTAB 1987)(重点在于来源)，以其他理由推翻了原判，858 F.2d 725, 8 USPQ2d 1365 (Fed. Cir. 1988)。

因此，在有限的情况下，相关公司之间的亲密关系可以排除给公众造成混淆的可能，因为相关公司构成了一种单一来源。*参见* TMEP §§1201.07(b)及以下，了解更多信息。

1201.07(b)　确定统一控制的适当行动

首先，很重要的一点是，直到申请人明确主张根据 §2(d)而拒绝注册是不适当的——因为尽管申请人和注册人为单独的两个法人实体，但二者构成了单一来源——或者提出同类抗辩的情况下，才引发 *Wella* 案中的分析。一旦对商标和各方当事人的商品或服务的分析表明，存在 §2(d)所规定的禁止注册事由，那么审查员就应当拒绝注册。只有在申请人在某种程度上依据其与注册人之间的关系性质，以排除 §2(d)规定的拒绝注册事由时，审查员才应对申请人和注册人之间的关系进行分析。

Once an applicant has made this assertion, the question is whether the specific relationship is such that the two entities constitute a "single source," so that there is no likelihood of confusion. The following guidelines may assist the examining attorney in resolving questions of likelihood of confusion when the marks are owned by related companies and the applicant asserts unity of control. (Of course, in many of these situations, the applicant may choose to attempt to overcome the §2(d) refusal by submitting a consent agreement or other conventional evidence to establish no likelihood of confusion. *See In re Sumitomo Electric Industries, Ltd.*, 184 USPQ 365 (TTAB 1974). Another way to overcome a §2(d) refusal is to assign all relevant registrations to the same party.)

1201.07(b)(i) When Either Applicant or Registrant Owns All of the Other Entity

If the applicant or the applicant's attorney represents that *either* the applicant or the registrant owns *all* of the other entity, and there is no contradictory evidence, then the examining attorney should conclude that there is unity of control, a single source and no likelihood of confusion. This would apply to an individual who owns all of the stock of a corporation, and to a corporation and a wholly owned subsidiary. In this circumstance, additional representations or declarations should generally *not* be required, absent contradictory evidence.

1201.07(b)(ii) When Either Applicant or Registrant Owns Substantially All of the Other Entity

In *Wella*, the applicant provided a declaration stating that the applicant owned *substantially all* of the stock of the registrant and that the applicant thus controlled the activities of the registrant, including the selection, adoption and use of trademarks. The Board concluded that this declaration alone, absent contradictory evidence, established unity of control, a single source and no likelihood of confusion. Therefore, if *either* the applicant or the registrant owns substantially all of

一旦申请人做出这种声明，那么问题就在于具体的关系是否属于二实体构成"单一来源"的情况，从而排除了混淆的可能性。在商标由相关公司拥有，而申请人主张存在统一管理的情况下，下列指导方针可以帮助审查员解决混淆可能性的问题。（当然，在许多此类情况下，申请人可能选择提交一份双方同意的协议或者其他证明不存在混淆可能性的协议证据以克服 §2(d)规定的拒绝注册事由。*参见* 相关判例：*Sumitomo Electric Industries, Ltd.*, 184 USPQ 365 (TTAB 1974)。另一种克服 §2(d)规定的拒绝注册事由的方法是，将所有相关注册全部转让给同一方。）

1201.07(b)(i)　当申请人或注册人对于对方实体拥有完全所有权时

如果申请人或其代理人声明，申请人或注册人完全拥有对方实体，同时不存在相反的证据，则审查员应判定存在统一管理、单一来源，并不存在混淆的可能性。这种情况适用于拥有公司所有股份的个人，也适用于拥有独资子公司的公司。在这种情况下，如无相反证据，通常无需另外提供说明或声明。

1201.07(b)(ii)　当申请人或注册人实质上完全拥有对方实体时

在 *Wella* 一案中，申请人提供了一份声明，称申请人实质上拥有注册人的所有股份，因此申请人控制了注册人的活动，包括对于商标的选择、采用和使用。委员会判定，由于没有相反证据，单独根据这份声明即可证明存在统一控制、单一来源，并不存在混淆的可能性。因此，如果申请人或者注册人实质上完全拥有对方，并且宣称控

the other entity and asserts control over the activities of the other entity, including its trademarks, and there is no contradictory evidence, the examining attorney should conclude that unity of control is present, that the entities constitute a single source, and that there is no likelihood of confusion under §2(d). In such a case the applicant should generally provide these assertions in the form of an affidavit or declaration under 37 C.F.R. §2.20.

1201.07(b)(iii) When the Record Does Not Support a Presumption of Unity of Control

If neither the applicant nor the registrant owns all or substantially all of the other entity, the applicant bears a more substantial burden to establish that unity of control is present. For instance, if both the applicant and the registrant are wholly owned by a third common parent, the applicant would have to provide detailed evidence to establish how one sister corporation controlled the trademark activities of the other to establish unity of control to support the contention that the sister corporations constitute a single source. *See In re Pharmacia Inc.*, 2 USPQ2d 1883 (TTAB 1987); *Greyhound Corp. v. Armour Life Ins. Co.*, 214 USPQ 473 (TTAB 1982). Likewise, where an applicant and registrant have certain stockholders, directors or officers in common, the applicant must demonstrate with detailed evidence or explanation how those relationships establish unity of control. *See Pneutek, Inc. v. Scherr*, 211 USPQ 824 (TTAB 1981). The applicant's evidence or explanation should generally be supported by an affidavit or a declaration under 37 C.F.R. §2.20.

1201.07(b)(iv) When the Record Contradicts an Assertion of Unity of Control

In contrast to those circumstances where the relationship between the parties may support a presumption of unity of control or at least afford an applicant the opportunity to demonstrate unity of control, some relationships, by their very na-

制对方实体的行为，且并无相反证据，则审查员就应判定存在统一控制，故二者构成了单一来源，而不存在 §2(d)规定的混淆可能。在这种情况下，申请人通常应以宣誓书或 37 C.F.R.§2.20 所规定的声明书的形式作出此类宣称。

1201.07(b)(iii) 当记录不支持统一控制的假定时

如果申请人和注册人都没有完全拥有或实质上完全拥有对方实体，那么申请人证明存在统一控制的负担大大增加。例如，如果申请人和注册人均为第三方的共同母公司所完全拥有，则申请人必须提供详细证据以证明姊妹公司之一控制了对方的商标活动，从而证明存在统一控制，以表明姊妹公司共同构成了单一来源。参见相关判例：*Pharmacia Inc.*，2 USPQ2d 1883（TTAB 1987）；*Greyhound Corp. v. Armour Life Ins. Co.*，214 USPQ 473（TTAB 1982）。类似地，如果申请人和注册人具有一些共同的股东、董事或管理者，申请人必须通过详细的证据或解释表明这些关系如何构成了统一控制。参见 *Pneutek，Inc. v. Scherr*，211 USPQ 824（TTAB 1981）。申请人通常应以宣誓书或 37 C.F.R.§2.20 所规定的声明书的形式提出证据或解释。

1201.07(b)(iv) 当记录有悖于声称统一控制时

与双方之间的关系可以支持统一控制假定或者至少使申请人有机会证明存在统一控制的那些情况不同的是，某些关系由于其特殊性，有悖于任何存在统一控制的声

ture, contradict any claim that unity of control is present. For instance, if the relationship between the parties is that of licensor and licensee, unity of control will ordinarily not be present. The licensing relationship suggests ownership in one party and control by that one party over only the use of a specific mark or marks, but not over the operations or activities of the licensee generally. Thus, there is no unity of control and no basis for concluding that the two parties form a single source. Precisely because unity of control is absent, a licensing agreement is necessary. The licensing agreement enables the licensor/owner to control specific activities to protect its interests as the sole source or sponsor of the goods or services provided under the mark. Therefore, in these situations, it is most unlikely that an applicant could establish unity of control to overcome a §2(d) refusal.

1202 Use of Subject Matter as Trademark

In an application under §1 of the Act, the examining attorney must determine whether the subject matter for which registration is sought is used as a trademark by reviewing all evidence (*e.g.*, the specimens of use and any promotional material) of record in the application. *See In re Safariland Hunting Corp.*, 24 USPQ2d 1380 (TTAB 1992) (examining attorney should look primarily to specimens to determine whether a designation would be perceived as a source indicator, but may also consider other evidence, if there is other evidence of record).

The Trademark Trial and Appeal Board has noted that "not everything that a party adopts and uses with the intent that it function as a trademark necessarily achieves this goal or is legally capable of doing so and not everything that is recognized or associated with a party is necessarily a registrable trademark." As the Court of Customs and Patent Appeals observed in *In re Standard Oil Co.*, 275 F. 2d 945, 947, 125 USPQ 227, 229 (C.C.P.A. 1960):

> The Trademark Act is not an act to register words but to register trademarks. Before there can be registrability, there must be a trademark (or a service mark) and, unless words have been so used, they cannot qualify

称。例如,如果双方的关系是许可人和被许可人的关系,统一控制通常不存在。许可关系表明,一方享有所有权,而另一方则只对特定商标的使用进行控制,而不对被许可人的经营或活动进行总体的控制。如此一来,就不存在统一控制的情况,于是也就无法推定双方构成了单一来源。正是由于不存在统一控制,所以就需要一份许可协议。许可协议使许可人/所有人能够控制特定的活动,以保护其作为使用商标的商品或服务的唯一来源或资助者的利益。因此,在此类情况下,申请人几乎不可能通过证明统一控制而克服 §2(d)规定的拒绝注册事由。

1202 作为商标使用的标的物

对于根据《商标法》§1 提出的申请,审查员必须审查申请书中的所有记录证据(例如,使用样本以及一切宣传促销材料),以判断申请注册的标的物是否作为商标使用。参见 相关判例:*Safariland Hunting Corp*., 24 USPQ2d 1380 (TTAB 1992)(审查员应主要审查样本以判定某种商标是否可以被认为是识别来源的商标,但如果存在其他记录证据,也可以考虑其他证据)。

商标审判和上诉委员会指出:"并非当事人以作为商标使用为目的而采用和使用的任何物体都必然达到这一目的,或者必然在法律上能够起到商标的作用,而且,并非任何识别当事人或与当事人相关联的物体都是可注册的商标。"正如关税及专利上诉法院在 *Standard Oil Co*., 275 F.2d 945, 947, 125 USPQ 227, 229 (C.C.P.A. 1960)一案中所说的:

> 《商标法》这部法律是用来注册商标,而非注册词语。在存在可注册性之前,必须先存在商标(或者服务商标),而且,除非词语用于此途,否则不能

for registration. Words are not registrable *merely* because they do not happen to be descriptive of the goods or services with which they are associated.

Sections 1 and 2 of the Trademark Act, 15 U.S.C.§§1051 and 1052, require that the subject matter presented for registration be a "trademark."Section 45 of the Act, 15 U.S.C.§1127, defines that term as follows:

> The term "trademark" includes any word, name, symbol, or device, or any combination thereof—
>
> (1) used by a person, or
>
> (2) which a person has a bona fide intention to use in commerce and applies to register on the principal register established by this Act,
>
> to identify and distinguish his or her goods, including a unique product, from those manufactured or sold by others and to indicate the source of the goods, even if that source is unknown.

Thus, §§1, 2 and 45 of the Trademark Act, 15 U.S.C.§§1051, 1052, and 1127, provide the statutory basis for refusal to register on the Principal Register subject matter that, due to its inherent nature or the manner in which it is used, does not function as a mark to identify and distinguish the applicant's goods. The statutory basis for refusal of registration on the Supplemental Register of matter that does not function as a trademark because it does not fit within the statutory definition of a trademark is §§23 and 45, 15 U.S.C.§§1091 and 1127.

When the examining attorney refuses registration on the ground that the subject matter is not used as a trademark, the examining attorney should explain the specific reason for the conclusion that the subject matter is not used as a trademark. *See* TMEP §§1202.01 through 1202.15 for a discussion of situations in which it may be appropriate, depending on the circumstances, for the examining attorney to refuse registration on the ground that the asserted trademark does not function

注册。词语本身不具有可注册性，*仅仅*因为它们并非刚好是用来描述与它们相关联的商品或服务的。

《商标法》第1和2节，15 U.S.C.§§1051和1052规定，申请注册的标的物必须是“商标”。《商标法》第45节，15 U.S.C.§1127，对商标一词作了如下定义：

> “商标”一词包括任何文字、名称、符号或图案，或以上元素的任何组合，它——
>
> (1) 为某人所使用，或者
>
> (2) 某人真实地计划将其用于商业用途，并向注册机构申请，在依据本法设立的联邦商标登记簿上注册，
>
> 用以识别某人的产品(包括独特的产品)，与他人制造或销售的产品区分开来，并表明商品的来源——即使来源未知。

因此，《商标法》§§1，2和45，15 U.S.C.§§1051，1052和1127以法律形式规定了，标的物若由于其固有性质或其使用方式，不能作为商标使用以识别和区分申请人的商品的，应拒绝其在联邦商标登记簿上注册。标的物因为不符合法律对商标的定义而不能作为商标使用的，应拒绝其在联邦商标补充登记簿上注册，拒绝的法律依据是《商标法》§§23和45，15 U.S.C.§§1091和1127。

如果审查员以注册的标的物不能作为商标使用为由而拒绝注册，则应当对得出标的物不能作为商标使用的结论的具体理由作出解释。有关审查员在何种情况下可以根据具体的情况以申请注册的商标不能作为商标使用为由拒绝注册的讨论，*参见*

as a trademark, *e.g.*, TMEP §§1202.01 (trade names), 1202.02(a) *et seq.* (functionality), 1202.03 (ornamentation), 1202.04 (informational matter), 1202.05 (color marks), 1202.06 (goods in trade), 1202.07 (columns or sections of publications), 1202.08 (title of single creative work), 1202.09 (names of artists and authors), 1202.10 (model or grade designations), 1202.11 (background designs and shapes), 1202.12 (varietal and cultivar names).

The presence of the letters "SM" or "TM" cannot transform an otherwise unregistrable designation into a mark. *In re Remington Products Inc.*, 3 USPQ2d 1714 (TTAB 1987); *In re Anchor Hocking Corp.*, 223 USPQ 85 (TTAB 1984); *In re Minnetonka, Inc.*, 212 USPQ 772 (TTAB 1981).

See TMEP §§1301.02 *et seq.* regarding use of subject matter as a service mark; TMEP §§1302 through 1304 regarding use of subject matter as a collective mark; and TMEP §1306 regarding use of subject matter as a certification mark.

1202.01 Refusal of Matter Used Solely as a Trade Name

The name of a business or company is a trade name. The Trademark Act distinguishes trade names from trademarks by definition. While a trademark is used to identify and distinguish the trademark owner's goods from those manufactured or sold by others and to indicate the source of the goods, "trade name" and "commercial name" are defined in §45 of the Act, 15 U.S.C. §1127, as follows:

> The terms "trade name" and "commercial name" mean any name used by a person to identify his or her business or vocation.

The Trademark Act does not provide for registration of trade names. *See In re Letica Corp.*, 226 USPQ 276, 277 (TTAB 1985) ("[T]here was a clear intention by the Congress to draw a line between indicia which perform only trade name functions and indicia which perform or also perform the function of trademarks or service marks.").

TMEP §§1202.01 至 1202.15,*例如*:TMEP §§1202.01(商号)、1202.02(a)及以下(功能性)、1202.03(装饰)、1202.04(信息性物质)、1202.05(颜色商标)、1202.06(贸易中的商品)、1202.07(出版物专栏或章节)、1202.08(单个创造性作品的标题)、1202.09(艺术家和作者的名字)、1202.10(型号或等级名称)、1202.11(背景图案和形状)、1202.12(品种或变种名称)。

存在字母"SM"或"TM"不能将一个不可注册的图案转变为商标。相关判例:*Remington Products Inc.*, 3 USPQ2d 1714 (TTAB 1987);*Anchor Hocking Corp.*, 223 USPQ 85 (TTAB 1984);*Minnetonka, Inc.*, 212 USPQ 772 (TTAB 1981)。

有关标的物作为服务商标使用的情况,*参见* TMEP §§1301.02 及以下;有关标的物作为集体商标使用的情况,*参见* TMEP §§1302 至 1304;有关标的物作为证明商标使用的情况,*参见* TMEP §1306。

1202.01 仅作为商号使用的标的物不得注册

企业或公司的名称是商号。《商标法》通过定义对商号和商标进行了区分。商标是用来识别商标所有者的商品,与他人制造或销售的商品区分开来,并指出商品的来源,而《商标法》§45, 15 U.S.C.§1127 对"商号"和"商业名称"的定义如下:

> "商号"和"商业名称"是指个人用于识别其业务或行业的任何名称。

《商标法》对商号的注册没有规定。*参见* 相关判例:*Letica Corp.*, 226 USPQ 276, 277 (TTAB 1985)("很显然,国会意图在仅仅作为商号使用的标记和作为或同时作为商标或服务商标使用的标记之间划出一条界线")。

If the examining attorney determines that matter for which registration is requested is merely a trade name, registration must be refused both on the Principal Register and on the Supplemental Register. The statutory basis for refusal of trademark registration on the ground that the matter is used merely as a trade name is found in §§1, 2 and 45 of the Trademark Act, 15 U.S.C. §§1051, 1052 and 1127, and, in the case of matter sought to be registered for services, §§1, 3, and 45, 15 U.S.C. §§1051, 1053 and 1127.

A designation may function as both a trade name and a trademark or service mark. *See In re Walker Process Equipment Inc.*, 233 F.2d 329, 332, 110 USPQ 41, 43 (C.C.P.A. 1956), *aff'g* 102 USPQ 443 (Comm'r Pats. 1954).

A determination of whether matter serves solely as a trade name rather than as a mark requires consideration of the way the mark is used, as evidenced by the specimens. Therefore, no refusal on that ground will be issued in an intent-to-use application until the applicant has submitted specimens of use in conjunction with either an amendment to allege use under 15 U.S.C. §1051(c) or a statement of use under 15 U.S.C. §1051(d).

If subject matter presented for registration in an application is a trade name or part of a trade name, the examining attorney must determine whether it is also used as a trademark or service mark by examining the specimens and other evidence of record in the application file. *See In re Diamond Hill Farms*, 32 USPQ2d 1383 (TTAB 1994) (DIAMOND HILL FARMS, as used on containers for goods, found to be a tradename that identifies applicant as a business entity rather than a mark that identifies applicant's goods and distinguishes them from those of others).

Whether matter that is a trade name or a portion thereof also performs the function of a trademark depends on the manner of its use and the probable impact of the use on customers. *See In re Unclaimed Salvage & Freight Co., Inc.*, 192 USPQ 165, 168 (TTAB 1976) ("It is our opinion that the foregoing material reflects use by applicant of the notation 'UNCLAIMED SALVAGE & FREIGHT CO.' mere-

如果审查员认定申请注册的标的物只是一个商号，必须拒绝其在联邦商标登记簿和补充登记簿上注册。以仅用作商号使用为由拒绝商标注册的法律依据是《商标法》§§1，2 和 45，15 U.S.C.§§1051，1052 和 1127，在申请服务商标的情况，拒绝的法律依据是 §§1，3 和 45，15 U.S.C.§§1051，1053 和 1127。

一种符号可以同时作为商号和商标或服务商标使用。*参见* 相关判例：*Walker Process Equipment Inc.*, 233 F.2d 329, 332, 110 USPQ 41, 43 (C.C.P.A.1956), *aff'g* 102 USPQ 443 (Comm'r Pats.1954)。

对于某标的物是一种商标还是商号，要根据样本提供的证据，考虑该商标使用的方式，然后作出判断。因此，对于一项意图使用的申请，直到申请人提交使用样本以及 15 U.S.C.§1051(c)所规定的宣称使用修正书或者 15 U.S.C.§1051(d)所规定的使用声明书，否则不能以这种理由拒绝注册。

如果申请注册的标的物是一个商号或是商号的一部分，则审查员必须对样本和申请文件中的其他记录证据进行审查，判断该标的物是否同时也作为商标或服务商标使用。*参见* 相关判例：*Diamond Hill Farms*, 32 USPQ2d 1383 (TTAB 1994)（在商品容器上使用的"DIAMOND HILL FARMS"被认定是一个识别申请人作为商业实体的商号，而不是识别其商品并区别于他人商品的商标）。

某个作为商号或商号的一部分的标的物是否同时也作为商标使用，取决于其使用的方式以及其使用可能对消费者产生的影响。*参见* 相关判例：*Unclaimed Salvage & Freight Co., Inc.*, 192 USPQ 165, 168 (TTAB 1976)（"我们的观点是，上述材料反映出申请人仅仅将'UNCLAIMED SALVAGE & FREIGHT CO.'标记作为一种

ly as a commercial, business, or trade name serving to identify applicant as a viable business entity; and that this is or would be the general and likely impact of such use upon the average person encountering this material under normal circumstances and conditions surrounding the distribution thereof."); *In re Lytle Engineering & Mfg. Co.*, 125 USPQ 308 (TTAB 1960) ("'LYTLE' is applied to the container for applicant's goods in a style of lettering distinctly different from the other portion of the trade name and is of such nature and prominence that it creates a separate and independent impression.").

The presence of an entity designator in a name sought to be registered and the proximity of an address are both factors to be considered in determining whether a proposed mark is merely a trade name. *In re Univar Corp.*, 20 USPQ2d 1865, 1869 (TTAB 1991) ("[T]he mark 'UNIVAR' independently projects a separate commercial impression, due to its presentation in a distinctively bolder, larger and different type of lettering and, in some instances, its additional use in a contrasting color, and thus does more than merely convey information about a corporate relationship.") *See also Book Craft, Inc. v. BookCrafters USA, Inc.*, 222 USPQ 724,727 (TTAB 1984)("That the invoices ... plainly show ... service mark use is apparent from the fact that, not only do the words 'BookCrafters, Inc.' appear in larger letters and a different style of print than the address, but they are accompanied by a design feature (the circularly enclosed ends of two books).").

1202.02 Registration of Trade Dress

When an applicant applies to register a product's design, product packaging, color, or other trade dress for goods or services, the examining attorney must consider two issues: (1) functionality; and (2) distinctiveness. *See TrafFix Devices, Inc. v. Marketing Displays, Inc.*, 532 U. S. 23, 58 USPQ2d 1001, 1004-1005 (2001); *Two Pesos, Inc. v. Taco Cabana, Inc.*, 505 U.S. 763, 775, 23 USPQ2d 1081, 1086 (1992) (only nonfunctional distinctive trade dress is protected). *See* TMEP §§1202.02(a) *et seq.* regarding functionality, TMEP §§1202.02(b) and

商号或商业、贸易名称使用，指出申请人为可行的商业实体；而且这就是标记的使用在通常情况和条件下会对或可能对一般人产生的一般和可能的印象”)；*Lytle Engineering & Mfg. Co.*，125 USPQ 308（TTAB 1960)(“‘LYTLE’以一种显然有别于商号其他部分的书写方式用在申请人商品的容器上，而且其性质和显著性给人一种单独和独立的印象”)。

在判断申请的商标是否仅仅是一个商号时，要考虑商标的名称中是否存在实体名称以及地址与商标是否邻近这两个因素。相关判例：*Univar Corp.*，20 USPQ2d 1865，1869（TTAB 1991)(“‘UNIVAR’商标给人一种独立的商业印象，因为它以显然加粗、加大及不同书写方式进行显示，并且有时还以对比色彩进行显示，因此它所传递的信息不仅仅是法人关系”)。*另参见 Book Craft，Inc. v. BookCrafters USA，Inc.*，222 USPQ 724，727（TTAB 1984)(“发票……明显地表明……存在明显的服务商标使用，因为‘BookCrafters，Inc.’这几个字不仅字体放大，而且字体风格也不同于地址，而且还带有图案的特点(两个 book 的圆形封闭端部)”)。

1202.02 产品外观的注册

如果申请人申请注册某产品的设计、产品包装、色彩，或者商品及服务的其他外观，则审查员必须考虑两点：(1)功能性；以及(2)特色性。*参见 TrafFix Devices，Inc. v. Marketing Displays，Inc.*，532 U.S. 23，58 USPQ2d 1001，1004 - 1005 (2001)；*Two Pesos，Inc. v. Taco Cabana，Inc.*，505 U.S. 763，775，23 USPQ2d 1081，1086 (1992)(只有非功能性的有特色的外观方可受到保护)。关于功能性，*参见* TMEP §§1202.02(a)及以下；关于特色性，*参见* TMEP §§1202.02(b)和 1212 及

1212 *et seq*. regarding distinctiveness, and TMEP §1202.02(c) regarding separate treatment of the two issues procedurally. With respect to the functionality and distinctiveness issues in the specific context of color as a mark, *see* TMEP §§1202.05 and 1202.05(f).

1202.02(a) Functionality

1202.02(a)(i) Statutory Basis for Functionality Refusal

Before October 30, 1998, there was no specific statutory reference to functionality as a ground for refusal, and functionality refusals were thus issued as failure-to-function refusals under Sections 1, 2 and 45 of the Trademark Act, 15 U.S.C. §§1051, 1052 and 1127.

Effective October 30, 1998, the Technical Corrections to Trademark Act of 1946, Pub.L.No.105-330, §201, 112 Stat.3064, 3069, amended the Trademark Act to expressly prohibit registration on either the Principal or Supplemental Register of matter that is functional:

- Section 2(e)(5) of the Trademark Act, 15 U.S.C. §1052(e)(5), prohibits registration on the Principal Register of "matter that, as a whole, is functional."
- Section 2(f) of the Act, 15 U.S.C. §1052(f), provides that matter that, as a whole, is functional may not be registered even on a showing that it has become distinctive.
- Section 23(c) of the Act, 15 U.S.C. §1091(c), provides that a mark that, as a whole, is functional may not be registered on the Supplemental Register.
- Section 14(3) of the Act, 15 U.S.C. §1064(3), lists functionality as a ground that can be raised in a cancellation proceeding more than five years after the date of registration.

以下;关于在程序上分别处理这两个问题的情况,*参见* TMEP §1202.02(c)。关于色彩作为商标的特殊情况下的功能性和特色性问题,*参见* TMEP §§1202.05 和 1202.05(f)。

1202.02(a) 功能性

1202.02(a)(i) 以功能性为由拒绝注册的法律依据

1998 年 10 月 30 日之前,并没有以功能性为拒绝注册理由的具体法律依据,因此,因功能性而拒绝注册的理由是以《商标法》第 1、2 和 45 节,15 U.S.C. §§1051、1052 和 1127 规定的不能作为商标使用这一理由拒绝注册的。

1998 年 10 月 30 日生效的《1946 年商标法技术修正》,Pub. L. No. 105 - 330, §201, 112 Stat.3064, 3069,对《商标法》作了修订,明确禁止具有功能性的标的物在联邦商标登记簿或补充登记簿上注册:

- 《商标法》第 2(e)(5)节,15 U.S.C.§1052(e)(5)规定,禁止"整体上具备功能性的标的物"在联邦商标登记簿上注册。
- 《商标法》第 2(f)节,15 U.S.C.§1052(f)规定,整体上具备功能性的标的物,即使显示出特色性,也不得注册。
- 《商标法》第 23(c)节,15 U.S.C.§1091(c)规定,整体上具备功能性的标的物不得在联邦商标补充登记簿上注册。
- 《商标法》第 14(3)节 15 U.S.C.§1064(3)列出在注册五年之后仍可启动撤消程序以功能性为由撤消注册的情况。

- Section 33(b)(8) of the Act, 15 U.S.C. §1115(b)(8), lists functionality as a statutory defense to infringement in a suit involving an incontestable registration.

These amendments codified case law and the longstanding Office practice of refusing registration of matter that is functional.

1202.02(a)(ii) Purpose of Functionality Doctrine

The functionality doctrine, which prohibits registration of functional product features, is intended to encourage legitimate competition by maintaining the proper balance between trademark law and patent law. As the Supreme Court explained, in *Qualitex Co. v. Jacobson Products Co., Inc.*, 514 U.S. 159, 164, 34 USPQ2d 1161, 1163 (1995):

> The functionality doctrine prevents trademark law, which seeks to promote competition by protecting a firm's reputation, from instead inhibiting legitimate competition by allowing a producer to control a useful product feature. It is the province of patent law, not trademark law, to encourage invention by granting inventors a monopoly over new product designs or functions for a limited time, 35 U.S.C. §§154, 173, after which competitors are free to use the innovation. If a product's functional features could be used as trademarks, however, a monopoly over such features could be obtained without regard to whether they qualify as patents and could be extended forever (because trademarks may be renewed in perpetuity).

In other words, the functionality doctrine ensures that protection for utilitarian product features be properly sought through a limited-duration utility patent, and not through the potentially unlimited protection of a trademark registration. Upon expiration of a utility patent, the invention covered by the patent enters the pub-

• 《商标法》第 33(b)(8)节 15 U.S.C.§1115(b)(8)列出在涉及无可争辩注册的侵权诉讼案中,以功能性为法定抗辩事由的情况。

这些修正使得以功能性为理由拒绝标的物注册的判例法和长久以来商标局的实际做法有了成文法律作为依据。

1202.02(a)(ii) 功能性原则的目的

功能性原则禁止注册具有功能性的产品外观,其目的在于通过保持商标法和专利法之间的适当平衡,鼓励合法竞争。正如最高法院在 *Qualitex Co. v. Jacobson Products Co., Inc.*, 514 U.S. 159, 164, 34 USPQ2d 1161, 1163 (1995)一案中所解释的:

> 商标法的目的是通过保护企业声誉促进竞争,功能性原则可以防止商标法通过允许生产商控制某有用产品特色而抑制合法的竞争。授予发明人在有限的时间(35 U.S.C.§§154, 173)内对新的产品设计或功能的垄断权,而在时限过后,竞争者则可以自由使用该项发明,通过这种方式鼓励发明是属于专利法的管辖范畴,而不属于商标法的管辖范畴。但是,如果产品的具有功能性的特点能够用作商标,那么无论这些特点是否可以获得专利,都可以对其进行垄断,而且期限可以无限延长(因为商标可以无限期地延续)。

换句话说,功能性原则确保通过有时间期限的实用新型专利对实用性的产品特点进行恰当的保护,而不是通过可能无限延长的商标注册来加以保护。实用新型专

lic domain, and the functional features disclosed in the patent may then be copied by others—thus encouraging advances in product design and manufacture. In *TrafFix Devices, Inc. v. Marketing Displays, Inc.*, 532 U. S. 23, 34-35, 58 USPQ2d 1001, 1007 (2001), the Supreme Court reiterated this rationale, also noting that the functionality doctrine is not affected by evidence of acquired distinctiveness:

> The Lanham Act does not exist to reward manufacturers for their innovation in creating a particular device; that is the purpose of the patent law and its period of exclusivity. The Lanham Act, furthermore, does not protect trade dress in a functional design simply because an investment has been made to encourage the public to associate a particular functional feature with a single manufacturer or seller.

Thus, even where the evidence establishes that consumers have come to associate a functional product feature with a single source, trademark protection will not be granted in light of the public policy reasons just stated. *Id*.

1202.02(a)(iii) Definitions

1202.02(a)(iii)(A) Functionality [R-1]

Functional matter cannot be protected as trade dress or a trademark. 15 U.S.C. §§1052(e)(5) and (f), 1091(c), 1064(3), and 1115(b). A feature is functional as a matter of law if it is "essential to the use or purpose of the product or if it affects the cost or quality of the product." *TrafFix Devices, Inc. v. Marketing Displays, Inc.*, 532 U.S. 23, 58 USPQ2d 1001, 1006 (2001); *Qualitex Co. v. Jacobson Products Co., Inc.*, 514 U. S. 159, 165, 34 USPQ2d 1161, 1163-64 (1995); *Inwood Laboratories, Inc. v. Ives Laboratories, Inc.*, 456 U. S. 844, 850, 214 USPQ 1, 4 n.10 (1982).

While some courts had developed a definition of functionality that focused solely

利到期后，专利所保护的发明就进入公共领域，专利中揭示的功能性特点就可以为他人所复制——从而鼓励产品设计和制造的进步。在 *TrafFix Devices*, *Inc*. *v*. *Marketing Displays*, *Inc*., 532 U.S. 23, 34 - 35, 58 USPQ2d 1001, 1007 (2001) 一案中，最高法院重申这一原则，同时指出，具有特色性的证据不能影响功能性原则。

> 《兰哈姆法》存在的目的并非对制造商创造某特定装置的创新行为进行奖励；那是专利法及其专有权保护期的目的。此外，《兰哈姆法》也不保护功能性设计中的产品外观，因为已为鼓励公众将特定功能性特点与单个制造商或销售商相联系而进行了投资。

因此，即使有证据证明消费者已经将某种功能性的产品特点与单一来源相联系，出于前述的公共政策原因，也不得授予其商标保护。*同前*。

1202.02(a)(iii)　定义

1202.02(a)(iii)(A)　功能性 [R-1]

具有功能性的标的物不能作为产品外观或商标进行保护。15 U.S.C. §§1052 (e)(5)和(f)、1091(c)、1064(3)和 1115(b)。在法律上，如果某特点“对于产品的使用或目的而言必不可少，或者影响到产品的成本或质量”，那么它就具有功能性。见 *TrafFix Devices*, *Inc*. *v*. *Marketing Displays*, *Inc*., 532 U.S. 23, 58 USPQ2d 1001, 1006 (2001); *Qualitex Co*. *v*. *Jacobson Products Co*., *Inc*., 514 U.S. 159, 165, 34 USPQ2d 1161, 1163 - 64 (1995); *Inwood Laboratories*, *Inc*. *v*. *Ives Laboratories*, *Inc*., 456 U.S. 844, 850, 214 USPQ 1, 4 n.10 (1982)。

一些法院曾经建立了一种仅仅关注“竞争性需要”的功能性定义——只要竞争者

on "competitive need" — thus finding a particular product feature functional only if competitors needed to copy that design in order to compete effectively —the Supreme Court held that this "was incorrect as a comprehensive definition" of functionality. *TrafFix*, 532 U.S. at 33, 58 USPQ2d at 1006. The Court emphasized that where a product feature meets the traditional functionality definition — that is, it is essential to the use or purpose of the product or affects the cost or quality of the product — then the feature is functional. *Id*. However, an inquiry into competitive need for the product design or feature at issue may be appropriate in cases where the mark sought to be registered is a color or other matter that does not easily fit within the "utilitarian" definition of functionality. *Id*. at 1006-07 (stating that inquiring into the issue of "significant non-reputation-related disadvantage" (*i. e*., competitive need) would be appropriate in cases of "aesthetic functionality," such as *Qualitex*). *See* TMEP §§1202.02(a)(iii)(C) and 1202.05 regarding the issues of "aesthetic functionality" and color as a mark.

The determination that a proposed mark is functional constitutes, for public policy reasons, an absolute bar to registration on either the Principal Register or the Supplemental Register — regardless of evidence showing that the proposed mark has acquired distinctiveness. *TrafFix*, 532 U.S. at 29, 58 USPQ2d at 1006. *See also Valu Engineering, Inc. v. Rexnord Corp*., 278 F.3d 1268, 61 USPQ2d 1422 (Fed. Cir. 2002); *In re Controls Corp. of America*, 46 USPQ2d 1308, 1311 (TTAB 1998).

See TMEP §§1202.02(a)(v) *et seq*. regarding evidentiary considerations pertaining to functionality refusals.

1202.02(a)(iii)(B) "*De Jure*" and "*De Facto*" Functionality [R-1]

Prior to this revision of the TMEP, the Office used the terms "*de facto*" and "*de jure*" in assessing whether "subject matter" (usually a product feature or the configuration of the goods) presented for registration was functional. This distinction originated with the Court of Customs and Patent Appeals' *Morton-Norwich* deci-

为了获得更有力的竞争力而需要复制该设计，那么这种特定的产品外观就是功能性的——最高法院认为这“并不是一种（关于功能性的）全面的定义”。见 *TrafFix*，532 U.S. 33，58 USPQ2d 1006。法院强调如果某种产品特征符合传统的功能性定义——即对于产品的使用或目的而言必不可少，或者影响到产品的成本或质量——那么该外观就是功能性的。*同前*。不过，如果申请注册的商标是一种色彩，或者是其他不完全符合“实用”功能性定义的标的物，那么对产品设计或特征的竞争性需求就要加以调查。*同前* 1006 - 07（阐述了在涉及“美学功能性”的案件中，如 *Qualitex* 案，对于“重大的、与声誉无关的缺点”（即竞争性需求）问题的调查）。有关“美学功能性”以及色彩用作商标的问题，*参见* TMEP §§1202.02(a)(iii)(C)和 1202.05。

出于公共政策的理由，一旦申请注册的商标被判定具有功能性，就绝对不能在联邦商标登记簿或补充登记簿上注册——不论是否有证据表明该商标已经具备了特色性。见 *TrafFix*，532 U.S. at 29，58 USPQ2d at 1006. *另见 Valu Engineering*，*Inc. v. Rexnord Corp.*，278 F. 3d 1268，61 USPQ2d 1422（Fed. Cir. 2002）；*Controls Corp. of America*，46 USPQ2d 1308，1311（TTAB 1998）。

有关以功能性为由拒绝注册的证据方面的考虑事项，*参见* TMEP §§1202.02(a)(v)及以下。

1202.02(a)(iii)(B)　“法律上”和“事实上”的功能性［R - 1］

此次 TMEP 修订之前，商标局在评定申请注册的“标的物”（通常是一种产品特征或商品配置）是否具有功能性时使用“事实上”和“法律上”两个术语。这种区分始创于关税及专利上诉法院对 *Morton-Norwich* 案的判决，对此联邦巡回法院在 *Valu En-*

sion, which was discussed by the Federal Circuit in *Valu Engineering, Inc. v. Rexnord Corp.*, 278 F.3d 1268, 61 USPQ2d 1422, 1425 (Fed. Cir. 2002):

> Our decisions distinguish *de facto* functional features, which may be entitled to trademark protection, from *de jure* functional features, which are not. 'In essence, *de facto* functional means that the design of a product has a function, *i.e.*, a bottle of any design holds fluid.' *In re R.M. Smith, Inc.*, 734 F.2d 1482, 1484, 222 USPQ 1, 3 (Fed. Cir. 1984). *De facto* functionality does not necessarily defeat registrability. *Morton-Norwich*, 671 F.2d [1332,] at 1337, 213 USPQ [9] at 13 [(C.C.P.A. 1982)] (A design that is *de facto* functional, *i.e.*, 'functional' in the lay sense ... may be legally recognized as an indication of source.). *De jure* functionality means that the product has a particular shape 'because it works better in this shape.' *Smith*, 734 F.2d at 1484, 222 USPQ at 3.

However, in the three recent Supreme Court decisions which discuss functionality—*Qualitex Co. v. Jacobson Products Co., Inc.*, 514 U.S. 159, 34 USPQ2d 1161 (1995), *Wal-Mart Stores, Inc. v. Samara Brothers, Inc.*, 529 U.S. 205, 54 USPQ2d 1065 (2000), and *TrafFix Devices, Inc. v. Marketing Displays, Inc.*, 532 U.S. 23, 58 USPQ2d 1001 (2001) — the Court has not used the "*de facto/de jure*" distinction. Nor were these terms used when the Trademark Act was amended to expressly prohibit registration of matter that is "functional." Technical Corrections to Trademark Act of 1946, Pub. L. No. 105-330, §201, 112 Stat. 3064, 3069 (1998). Accordingly, in general, examining attorneys will no longer make this distinction in Office actions which refuse registration based on functionality.

De facto functionality is not a ground for refusal. *In re Ennco Display Systems Inc.*, 56 USPQ2d 1279, 1282 (TTAB 2000); *In re Parkway Machine Corp.*, 52 USPQ2d 1628, 1631 n.4 (TTAB 1999).

1202.02(a)(iii)(C) Aesthetic Functionality

The concept of "aesthetic functionality" (as opposed to "utilitarian functionality")

gineering，*Inc*. *v*. *Rexnord Corp*.，278 F.3d 1268，61 USPQ2d 1422，1425（Fed. Cir. 2002）一案中也进行了讨论：

> 我们的判决对事实上的和法律上的功能性特征进行了区分，前者可以获得商标保护，而后者则不能。"本质上，事实上的功能性意味着产品的设计具有某种功能，*比如*，任何结构设计的瓶子都可以容纳液体。"见 *R. M. Smith*，*Inc*.，734 F.2d 1482，1484，222 USPQ 1，3（Fed. Cir. 1984）。事实上的功能性并非一定使可注册性无效。见 *Morton-Norwich*，671 F.2d [1332,] 1337，213 USPQ [9] 13 [(C. C. P. A. 1982)]（"事实上的功能性——即一般意义上的'功能性'——的设计可以合法地被识别为来源标识"）。法律上的功能性是指，产品具备某种特定的外形，"因为这种形状更有利于其工作"。*Smith*，734 F.2d 1484，222 USPQ 3。

但是，最高法院在最近三个有关功能性的案件判决中——*Qualitex Co*. *v*. *Jacobson Products Co*.，*Inc*.，514 U. S. 159，34 USPQ2d 1161（1995），*Wal-Mart Stores*，*Inc*. *v*. *Samara Brothers*，*Inc*.，529 U.S. 205，54 USPQ2d 1065（2000），以及 *TrafFix Devices*，*Inc*. *v*. *Marketing Displays*，*Inc*.，532 U. S. 23，58 USPQ2d 1001（2001）——都没有使用"事实上/法律上"这一区分。在修订《商标法》以明确禁止注册"具有功能性的"标的物时，也没有使用这两个术语。见《1946 年商标法技术修正》Pub. L. No. 105－330，§201，112 Stat. 3064，3069（1998）。相应地，在通常情况下，在以功能性为由拒绝注册的商标局决定中，审查员也就不再作这种区分了。

事实上的功能性不能作为拒绝注册的理由。相关判例：*Ennco Display Systems Inc*.，56 USPQ2d 1279，1282（TTAB 2000）；*Parkway Machine Corp*.，52 USPQ2d 1628，1631 n.4（TTAB 1999）。

1202. 02(a)(iii)(C)　美学功能性

多年以来，"美学功能性"概念（相对于"实用功能性"）的精确含义一直是一个含

has for many years been the subject of much confusion as to its precise meaning, as well as whether it is even a viable legal principle. While the Court of Customs and Patent Appeals (the predecessor to the Court of Appeals for the Federal Circuit) appeared to reject the doctrine of aesthetic functionality in *In re DC Comics, Inc.*, 689 F.2d 1042, 215 USPQ 394 (C.C.P.A. 1982), the Supreme Court more recently referred to aesthetic functionality as a valid legal concept in *TrafFix Devices, Inc. v. Marketing Displays, Inc.*, 532 U.S. 23, 58 USPQ2d 1001 (2001). In discussing the proper definition of "functionality," the Court distinguished its previous decision in *Qualitex Co. v. Jacobson Products Co., Inc.*, 514 U.S. 159, 34 USPQ2d 1161 (1995), specifically contrasting the fact that, unlike the issue currently before the Court, in *Qualitex* "aesthetic functionality was the central question, there having been no indication that the green-gold color of the laundry press pad had any bearing on the use or purpose of the product or its cost or quality." *TrafFix*, 532 U.S. at 33, 58 USPQ2d at 1006-07. Although the references to aesthetic functionality in the *TrafFix* decision are *dicta*, the Court's use of this terminology appears to indicate that the concept of aesthetic functionality — at least when used properly — is a viable legal principle.

The confusion regarding this concept stems from widespread misuse of the term "aesthetic functionality" in cases involving ornamentation issues, with some courts having mistakenly expanded the category of "functional" marks to include matter that is solely ornamental, essentially on the theory that such matter serves an "aesthetic function" or "ornamentation function." It is this incorrect use of the term "aesthetic functionality" in connection with ornamentation cases that was rejected by the Court of Customs and Patent Appeals. *See In re DC Comics, Inc.*, 689 F.2d 1042, 215 USPQ 394, 397, 399-401 (majority opinion and Rich, J., concurring) (C.C.P.A. 1982) (holding, in a case involving features of toy dolls, that the Board had improperly "intermingled the concepts of utilitarian functionality and what has been termed 'aesthetic functionality'"; and rejecting the concept of aesthetic functionality where it is used as a substitute for "the more traditional source identification principles of trademark law," such as the ornamentation and

混不清的问题，甚至其是否属于可行的法律原则都还存在争议。虽然关税及专利上诉法院(前身是联邦巡回区上诉法院)在 *DC Comics*，*Inc*.，689 F.2d 1042，215 USPQ 394 (C.C.P.A.1982)一案中拒绝适用美学功能性原则，但是最高法院在较近期的 *TrafFix Devices*，*Inc*. *v*. *Marketing Displays*，*Inc*.，532 U.S.23，58 USPQ2d 1001 (2001)一案中却认为美学功能性是一项有效的法律概念。在讨论"功能性"适当定义的过程中，法院区别了以往在 *Qualitex Co*. *v*. *Jacobson Products Co*.，*Inc*.，514 U.S.159，34 USPQ2d 1161 (1995)一案中所作的判决，尤其是比较了 *Qualitex* 案中与当前问题不同的事实情况："美学功能性是 *Qualitex* 一案的中心问题，没有迹象表明，洗衣店烫衣垫的金绿色与产品的使用或用途或其成本或质量有任何的联系。"*TrafFix*，532 U.S.33，58 USPQ2d 1006－07。尽管 *TrafFix* 案的判决只是在附论中提到了美学功能性，但法庭对该术语的使用表明美学功能性的概念——至少在正确使用的情况下——是一项可行的法律原则。

对于此概念的混淆，来自于在涉及装饰问题的案件中对"美学功能性"一词的广泛误用，有些法院错误地扩大了"功能性"商标的范畴而将仅仅具有装饰性的标的物包括在内，本质上是基于此类标的物是具有"美学功能"还是具有"装饰功能"的理论。正是由于将"美学功能性"错误地与装饰案件相关地使用，使关税及专利上诉法院作出驳回的判决。*见 DC Comics*，*Inc*.，689 F.2d 1042，215 USPQ 394，397，399－401(多数人的意见且 Rich 法官同意)(C.C.P.A.1982)(认为，在一个涉及玩具娃娃特征的案件中，委员会错误地"混淆了'实用功能性'与'美学功能性'两个概念"；并且反对用美学功能性的概念替代"商标法更传统的来源识别原则"，例如装饰性和功

functionality doctrines).

Where the issue presented is whether the proposed mark is ornamental in nature, it is improper to refer to "aesthetic functionality," because the doctrine of "functionality" is inapplicable to such cases. The proper refusal is on the basis that the matter is ornamental and thus does not function as a mark under §§1, 2 and 45 of the Trademark Act, 15 U.S.C. §§1051, 1052 and 1127. *See* TMEP §§1202.03 *et seq*. regarding ornamentation.

The Supreme Court's use of the term "aesthetic functionality" in the *TrafFix* case appears limited to cases where the issue is one of actual functionality, but where the nature of the proposed mark makes it difficult to evaluate the functionality issue from a purely utilitarian standpoint. This is the case with color marks and product features that enhance the attractiveness of the product. The color or feature does not normally give the product a truly utilitarian advantage (in terms of making the product actually perform better), but may still be found to be functional because it provides other real and significant competitive advantages and thus should remain in the public domain.

For example, in *Qualitex*, *supra*, referred to as an "aesthetic functionality" case in *TrafFix*, *supra*, the Supreme Court considered whether a green-gold color used on the pads for dry cleaning presses was barred from trademark protection under the functionality doctrine. While the Court ultimately concluded that the color at issue was not functional, the Court evaluated the proposed mark not only in light of the traditional "utilitarian" definition of functionality (*i.e.*, whether the proposed mark is essential to the use or purpose of the product or affects the cost or quality of the product), but also in terms of whether there was a competitive need for the color in that industry, stating that the color would be considered functional if its exclusive use "would put competitors at a significant non-reputation-related disadvantage." *Qualitex*, 514 U.S. 165, 34 USPQ2d at 1163-65. *See also Brunswick Corp. v. British Seagull Ltd.*, 35 F.3d 1527, 32 USPQ2d 1120 (Fed. Cir. 1994) (affirming the Board's determination that the color black for outboard mo-

能性原则)。

问题的关键在于,申请注册的商标是否是装饰性的,在此并不应适用“美学功能性”,因为“功能性”原则不适用于此类案件。正确的拒绝注册理由是,标的物是装饰性的,因此根据《商标法》§§1, 2 和 45,15 U.S.C.§§1051, 1052 和 1127 的规定,不能作为商标。有关装饰的情况,*参见* TMEP §§1202.03 及以下。

最高法院在 *TrafFix* 案中对于“美学功能性”一词的使用表明其仅限于涉及实际功能性问题的案件,不过由于申请注册的商标本身的性质,有时很难从纯粹的实用观点出发衡量功能性的问题。这里存在通过色彩商标和产品特征增强产品吸引力的情况。尽管色彩或特征通常不会给产品带来一种真正的实用优点(也就是说,使产品实际上更好用),但是仍然可以认为是功能性的,因为其提供其他真实重要的竞争优势,因此应当留在公共领域。

例如,在上述 *Qualitex* 案中(在上述 *TrafFix* 案中称为“美学功能性”案件),最高法院认为,根据功能性原则,在干洗烫衣垫上使用的金绿色不能获得商标保护。虽然法庭最终判定该案中涉及的色彩不具有功能性,但是法庭不仅通过功能性传统的“实用”定义(即申请注册的商标对于该产品的使用或目的是否不可缺少,或者影响了产品的成本或质量)衡量申请注册的商标,同时还从该行业中是否存在使用该色彩的竞争需求的角度进行了衡量,并认为,如果该色彩的专属使用“使竞争者处于重大的非涉及声誉的不利地位”,那么该色彩就具有功能性。*Qualitex*, 514 U.S.165, 34 USPQ2d 1163-65。*另参见 Brunswick Corp. v. British Seagull Ltd.*, 35 F.3d 1527, 32 USPQ2d 1120 (Fed. Cir. 1994)(确认了委员会的决定,即外置马达的黑色具备功

tors was functional because while it had no utilitarian effect on the mechanical working of the engines, it nevertheless provided other identifiable competitive advantages — *i.e.*, ease of coordination with a variety of boat colors and reduction in the apparent size of the engines.

In *M-5 Steel Mfg., Inc. v. O'Hagin's Inc.*, 61 USPQ2d 1086 (TTAB 2001), the Board considered the proper use of the aesthetic functionality doctrine in connection with product designs for metal ventilating ducts and vents for tile or concrete roofs:

> This case seems to involve elements of both utilitarian and aesthetic functionality. Here, for example, there is evidence of utility in applicant's patent application, as well as statements touting the superiority of applicant's design in applicant's promotional literature, and statements that applicant's design results in reduced costs of installation. On the other hand, there is no question that applicant's roof designs which match the appearance of surrounding roof tiles are more pleasing in appearance because the venting tiles in each case are unobtrusive.

M-5 Steel, 61 USPQ2d at 1096. Citing extensively from the *TrafFix*, *Qualitex* and *Brunswick* cases, the Board concluded that the product designs were functional for a combination of utilitarian and aesthetic reasons:

> [W]e agree with opposer that applicant's product designs are functional in the sense that these configurations blend in or match the roof tiles with which they are used better than alternative products. As in *Brunswick*, these configurations do not make the roof vents work better because they are in these shapes. Rather, like the advantages of color compatibility and reduction in apparent engine size afforded by the color black, applicant's designs are compatible with the roof tiles with which they are used and supply applicant with a competitive advantage in each case. Because applicant's vents match the contours of the roof vents with which they are used, alternatives will not have this advantage.

能性,因为尽管其对于引擎的机械工作并没有实际的效果,但是却带来了可以确认的竞争优势——即可以与各种船只颜色搭配,并缩小了引擎的外观尺寸)。

在 *M-5 Steel Mfg., Inc. v. O'Hagin's Inc.*, 61 USPQ2d 1086 (TTAB 2001)一案中,涉及金属通风管道以及砖瓦水泥屋顶通风口的产品设计,对此委员会考虑了美学功能性原则的正确适用:

> 本案看来同时涉及实用功能性和美学功能性。例如,申请人的专利申请书中存在有关实用性的证据,同时也有关于申请人的设计在其促销材料中的优越性的陈述,还有关于其设计导致安装成本降低的陈述。而另一方面,毫无疑问,申请人的屋顶设计同四周的屋瓦相匹配,从而使得外表更美观,因为在各种情况下通风口的瓦片都是看不到的。

见 *M-5 Steel*, 61 USPQ2d 1096。委员会广泛引用了 *TrafFix*, *Qualitex* 及 *Brunswick* 诸案,综合考虑实用性和美学性的理由,最终判定该产品设计具备功能性:

> 我们同意反对者的意见,认为申请人的产品设计具有功能性,因为这些同屋瓦相配或匹配的结构设计使得该产品相比其他替代产品在使用上更加优越。同 *Brunswick* 案一样,这些结构设计并没有因为其形状而改善了屋顶通风孔的工作状况。进一步说,就像黑色所带来的色彩兼容性以及减小了引擎的外观尺寸所带来的优点那样,申请人的设计同屋瓦相兼容,从而使申请人拥有了一种竞争优势。由于申请人的通风孔同其所使用的屋瓦相

Applicant's patent application and other evidence of record, including applicant's promotional literature and applicant's own testimony, tout the designs' unobtrusive appearance, state that they are "functional in design," camouflage the existence of the vents and are aesthetically pleasing. Applicant also represents in its promotional material that its vents are cheaper to install. We conclude that applicant's product design are, as a whole, functional, and that registration by applicant would hinder competition by placing competitors at a substantial competitive disadvantage.

M-5 *Steel*, 61 USPQ2d at 1097.

Note that this type of functionality determination — while employed in connection with a normally "aesthetic" feature such as color — is a proper use of the functionality doctrine, necessitating a §2(e)(5) refusal where the evidence establishes that a color or other matter at issue provides identifiable competitive advantages and thus should remain in the public domain. This is the opposite of an ornamentation refusal, where the matter at issue serves no identifiable purpose other than that of pure decoration.

Generally speaking, examining attorneys should exercise caution in the use of the term "aesthetic functionality," in light of the confusion that historically has surrounded this issue. In most situations, reference to aesthetic functionality will be unnecessary, since a determination that the matter sought to be registered is purely ornamental in nature will result in an ornamentation refusal under §§1, 2 and 45, and a determination that the matter sought to be registered is functional will result in a functionality refusal under §2(e)(5). Use of the term "aesthetic functionality" may be appropriate in limited circumstances where the proposed mark presents issues similar to those involved in the *M*-5 *Steel* and *Brunswick* cases, *supra* — *i.e.*, where the issue is one of true functionality under §2(e)(5), but where the nature of the mark makes the functionality determination turn on evidence of particular competitive advantages that are not necessarily categorized as

配合，因此替代品无法获得这种优点。申请人的专利申请和其他记录证据，包括促销材料、申请人自己的陈述、对于该设计一体化外形的夸耀，都声称该设计具有隐蔽通风孔存在的“设计功能”并且更美观。申请人在其促销材料中还声称，其通风孔的安装费用低廉。由此，我们判定申请人的产品设计在整体上具有功能性，并且，如果同意申请人的注册申请，就会给竞争者造成一种实质性的竞争劣势，从而妨碍竞争。

见 *M－5 Steel*, 61 USPQ2d 1097。

需要注意的是，这类功能性判定——与通常是“美学”的特征（比如色彩）相关地使用时——正确地适用了功能性原则，在有证据表明申请的色彩或其他标的物可以提供可识别的竞争优势时，就应当将其保留在公共领域，因而按 §2(e)(5)的规定必须拒绝注册。这种情况与以装饰性为由拒绝注册的情况相反，对于后者，申请注册的标的物除了纯粹的装饰之外并不具有可识别的用途。

一般说来，考虑到长久以来在这一问题上的混淆，审查员应当谨慎使用“美学功能性”一词。在大多数情况下，并不需要提到美学功能性，因为如果判定申请注册的标的物属于纯粹的装饰性质，就可以根据 §§1, 2 和 45 以装饰性为由拒绝注册，而如果申请注册的标的物被判定具有功能性，则可以根据 §2(e)(5)以功能性为由拒绝注册。在有限的情况下，比如申请注册的商标类似于前述 *M－5 Steel* 和 *Brunswick* 各案中的情况——即确实存在 §2(e)(5)规定的功能性，但商标的性质又使得功能性判定激发了在性质上无法归入“实用”类型的某些特定的竞争优势。“美学功能性”一词

"utilitarian" in nature. Any such use of the term "aesthetic functionality" should be closely tied to a discussion of specific competitive advantages resulting from use of the proposed mark at issue, so that it is clear that the refusal is properly based on the functionality doctrine and not on an incorrect use of "aesthetic functionality" to mean ornamentation.

See TMEP §§1202.05 and 1202.05(f) for additional discussion and case references regarding the functionality issue in connection with color marks.

1202.02(a)(iv) Burden of Proof in Functionality Determinations [R-1]

The examining attorney must establish a *prima facie* case that the trade dress sought to be registered is functional. The burden then shifts to the applicant to present sufficient evidence to rebut the examining attorney's *prima facie* case of functionality. *In re R.M. Smith, Inc.*, 734 F.2d 1482, 222 USPQ 1, 3 (Fed. Cir. 1984); *In re Bio-Medicus Inc.*, 31 USPQ2d 1254, 1257 n.5 (TTAB 1993).

The functionality determination is a question of fact, and depends on the totality of the evidence presented in each particular case. *Valu Engineering, Inc. v. Rexnord Corp.*, 278 F.3d 1268, 61 USPQ2d 1422 (Fed. Cir. 2002); *In re Caterpillar Inc.*, 43 USPQ2d 1335, 1339 (TTAB 1997). While there is no set amount of evidence that an examining attorney must present to establish a *prima facie* case of functionality, it is clear that there must be evidentiary support for the refusal in the record. *See, e.g., In re Morton-Norwich Products, Inc.*, 671 F.2d 1332, 213 USPQ 9, 16-17 (C.C.P.A. 1982) (admonishing both the examining attorney and the Board for failing to support the functionality determination with even "one iota of evidence").

If the trade dress sought to be registered as a mark is the subject of a utility patent that discloses the feature's utilitarian advantages, then the applicant bears an especially "heavy burden of overcoming the strong evidentiary inference of functionality." *TrafFix Devices, Inc. v. Marketing Displays, Inc.*, 532 U.S. 23, 58 US-

的这种使用应当与使用申请注册商标而导致的具体竞争优势的讨论紧密相关，使拒绝的理由很显然：正确地根据功能性原则，并非根据不当地使用"美学功能性"来表示装饰。

有关色彩商标功能性问题的其他讨论和参考案例，*参见* TMEP §§1202.05 和 1202.05(f)。

1202.02(a)(iv) 功能性判定中的举证责任 [R-1]

审查员必须确立申请注册的商品外观具备功能性的初步证据。然后，举证责任就转移到申请人身上，申请人必须提出充分的证据来反驳审查员对功能性的初步证据。相关判例：*R.M.Smith, Inc.*, 734 F.2d 1482, 222 USPQ 1, 3 (Fed. Cir. 1984); *Bio-Medicus Inc.*, 31 USPQ2d 1254, 1257 n.5 (TTAB 1993)。

对于功能性判定属于事实问题，有赖于在每个具体案件中所提出的全部证据。参见 *Valu Engineering, Inc. v. Rexnord Corp.*, 278 F.3d 1268, 61 USPQ2d 1422 (Fed. Cir. 2002); *Caterpillar Inc.*, 43 USPQ2d 1335, 1339 (TTAB 1997)。如果审查员没有确定数量的证据初步证明存在功能性，很明显，记录中必定有证据支持拒绝注册的理由。*参见，例如 Morton-Norwich Products, Inc.*, 671 F.2d 1332, 213 USPQ 9, 16-17 (C.C.P.A. 1982)(告诫审查员和委员会，哪怕只要有"一丝一毫的证据"支持存在功能性的判定，即应当作出如此判定)。

如果申请注册为商标的商品外观是某实用新型专利的对象，该项专利揭示了该特征的实用性优点，那么申请人就负有一种特别"沉重的举证责任，以求推翻强有力的、得到证据支持的功能性推论"。见 *TrafFix Devices, Inc. v. Marketing Displays, Inc.*, 532 U.S. 23, 58 USPQ2d 1001, 1005 (2001)。*参见* TMEP §1202.02(a)(v)。

PQ2d 1001, 1005 (2001). *See* TMEP §1202.02(a)(v).

1202.02(a)(v) Evidence and Considerations Regarding Functionality Determinations [R-1]

Trade dress is functional if it is essential to the use or purpose of a product or if it affects the cost or quality of the product. *Inwood Laboratories, Inc. v. Ives Laboratories, Inc.*, 456 U.S. 844, 850, 214 USPQ 1, 4 n. 10 (1982).

In *TrafFix Devices, Inc. v. Marketing Displays, Inc.*, 532 U.S. 23, 58 USPQ2d 1001, 1005 (2001), the Supreme Court resolved a circuit split regarding the proper weight to be afforded a utility patent in the functionality determination, stating:

> A utility patent is strong evidence that the features claimed therein are functional. If trade dress protection is sought for those features the strong evidence of functionality based on the previous patent adds great weight to the statutory presumption that features are deemed functional until proved otherwise by the party seeking trade dress protection. Where the expired patent claimed the features in question, one who seeks to establish trade dress protection must carry the heavy burden of showing that the feature is not functional, for instance by showing that it is merely an ornamental, incidental, or arbitrary aspect of the device.

See also In re Bose Corp., 772 F.2d 866, 227 USPQ 1 (Fed. Cir. 1985); *In re Visual Communications Co., Inc.*, 51 USPQ2d 1141 (TTAB 1999); *In re Edward Ski Products, Inc.*, 49 USPQ2d 2001 (TTAB 1999); *In re Caterpillar Inc.*, 43 USPQ2d 1335 (TTAB 1997).

The Court in *TrafFix* went on to hold that where the evidence includes a utility patent that claims the product features at issue, it is unnecessary to consider evidence relating to the availability of alternative designs:

> There is no need, furthermore, to engage, as did the Court of Appeals,

1202.02(a)(v)　有关功能性判定的证据和考虑［R-1］

如果某种产品外观对于产品的使用或目的而言必不可少,或者影响到产品的成本或质量,那么它就是功能性的。*Inwood Laboratories, Inc. v. Ives Laboratories, Inc.*, 456 U.S.844, 850, 214 USPQ 1, 4 n.10 (1982)。

在 *TrafFix Devices, Inc. v. Marketing Displays, Inc.*, 532 U.S. 23, 58 USPQ2d 1001, 1005 (2001)一案中,最高法院解决了各巡回法院之间在功能性判定中实用新型专利所应占据的适当分量上存在的分歧,阐述如下:

> 实用新型专利是证明所主张的特征具有功能性的强有力的证据。如果为这些特征申请商品外观保护,那么根据先前的专利得出的强有力的功能性证据将大大增加了将该外观特征视为具有功能性的法律推定的分量,除非申请商品外观保护的当事人提出相反的证据,推翻了这一推定。如果有过期的专利主张保护所申请的外观特征,那么寻求商品外观保护的当事人必须负担沉重的举证责任,以表明该外观特征并不具有功能性,例如,表明它仅仅是装置的装饰性的、附带的或者任意的一面。

另参见:*Bose Corp.*, 772 F. 2d 866, 227 USPQ 1 (Fed. Cir. 1985); *Visual Communications Co., Inc.*, 51 USPQ2d 1141 (TTAB 1999); *Edward Ski Products, Inc.*, 49 USPQ2d 2001 (TTAB 1999); *Caterpillar Inc.*, 43 USPQ2d 1335 (TTAB 1997)。

法院在 *TrafFix* 案中继续坚持认为,如果证据中包括了主张所申请的产品特征的实用新型专利,那么就没有必要考虑有关使用可替代设计的证据:

> 此外,没有必要像上诉法院那样考虑其他的设计可能性,例如:使用三条或

in speculation about other design possibilities, such as using three or four springs which might serve the same purpose. Here, the functionality of the spring design means that competitors need not explore whether other spring juxtapositions might be used. The dual-spring design is not an arbitrary flourish in the configuration of MDI's product; it is the reason the device works. Other designs need not be attempted.

TrafFix, 532 U.S. at 23, 58 USPQ2d at 1007 (citation omitted).

Therefore, in those instances where the examining attorney is presented with facts similar to those in *TrafFix*—*i.e.*, where there is a utility patent establishing the utilitarian nature of the product design at issue — the examining attorney may properly issue a final functionality refusal based primarily on the utility patent.

In relevant cases, the examining attorney should ask the applicant to provide copies of any patent(s) or any pending or abandoned patent application(s). *See Valu Engineering, Inc. v. Rexnord Corp.*, 278 F.3d 1268, 61 USPQ2d 1422, 1429 (Fed. Cir. 2002) ("We agree with the Board that an abandoned patent application should be considered under the first Morton-Norwich factor, because an applied-for utility patent that never issued has evidentiary significance for the statements and claims made in the patent application concerning the utilitarian advantages, just as an issued patent has evidentiary significance.").

It is important to read the patent to determine whether the patent actually claims the features presented in the proposed mark. If it does not, or if the features are referenced in the patent, but only as arbitrary or incidental features, then the probative value of the patent as evidence of functionality is substantially diminished or negated entirely. *TrafFix*, 532 U.S. at 34, 58 USPQ2d at 1007 (where a manufacturer seeks to protect arbitrary, incidental or ornamental aspects or features of a product found in the patent claims, such as arbitrary curves in the legs or an ornamental pattern painted on the springs, functionality will not be established if the manufacturer can prove that those aspects do not serve a purpose within the terms of utility patent); *see also Black & Decker Inc. v. Hoover Service*

> 四条弹簧也可能达到同样的效果。在此，弹簧设计的功能性在于，竞争者不必再探索是否可以使用其他弹簧设置法。双弹簧设计在 MDI 产品的结构中并不是无端地流行；而是因为这种设计是装置工作的原因。因而无需尝试其他设计。

TrafFix, 532 U.S. at 23, 58 USPQ2d at 1007(引文略)。

因此，在这些例子中，审查员遇到了同 *TrafFix* 案中类似的情况——即存在一项实用新型专利证明受审查产品设计的实用性质——审查员就可以主要以该实用新型专利为由，正确地作出以功能性为由拒绝注册的最终决定。

在相关案件中，审查员应要求申请人提供专利文件或者过期失效的专利文件的副本。*参见 Valu Engineering, Inc. v. Rexnord Corp.*, 278 F.3d 1268, 61 USPQ2d 1422, 1429 (Fed. Cir. 2002)("我们同意委员会的意见，在涉及第一项 Morton-Norwich 因素的情况下，应当考虑失效的专利申请，因为一项未被核准的实用新型专利申请对于有关实用性优点的专利申请书中的陈述和主张具有证据性的意义，就如同被核准的专利一样具有证据性的意义")。

应当审查该专利以判断该专利是否实际上对申请注册的商标中的外观特征提出了主张。如果并没有提出主张，或者虽然提到了该外观特征，但只是作为一种任意或附带的特征，则该专利作为功能性证据的证明力就实质上消失或完全被否定了。见 *TrafFix*, 532 U.S 34, 58 USPQ2d 1007(制造商寻求对专利主张中产品的任意、附带或装饰性的方面或外观进行保护，诸如木支架上的任意刻文、弹簧上印刷的装饰性图案等，但是如果该制造商能够证明这些方面不属于实用新型专利中的用途，那么就不能确立存在功能性)；*另参见 Black & Decker Inc. v. Hoover Service Ctr.*, 886 F.

Ctr., 886 F.2d 1285, 12 USPQ2d 1250 (Fed. Cir. 1989); *In re Zippo Mfg. Co*., 50 USPQ2d 1852 (TTAB 1999); *In re Weber-Stephen Products Co*., 3 USPQ2d 1659 (TTAB 1987).

It is not necessary that the utility patent be owned by the applicant; a third-party utility patent is also relevant to the functionality determination if the patent claims the features in the product design sought to be registered. *See In re Virshup*, 42 USPQ2d 1403 (TTAB 1997); *In re American National Can Co*., 41 USPQ2d 1841 (TTAB 1997); *In re Cabot Corp*., 15 USPQ2d 1224 (TTAB 1990). Therefore, the examining attorney may also search the Office's patent records to see if there are utility patents owned by third parties that disclose the functional advantages of the product design that the applicant seeks to register.

Statements regarding utilitarian advantages of the design made in the course of the prosecution of the patent application can be very strong evidence of functionality. *TrafFix*, 532 U.S. at 32, 58 USPQ2d at 1006 ("These statements [regarding specific functional advantages of the product design] made in the patent applications and in the course of procuring the patents demonstrate the functionality of the design. MDI does not assert that any of these representations are mistaken or inaccurate, and this is further strong evidence of the functionality of the dual-spring design.").

Where a utility patent claims more than what is sought to be registered, this fact does not establish the nonfunctionality of the product design if the patent shows that the part claimed as a trademark is an essential or integral part of the invention and has utilitarian advantages. *Cf*. *TrafFix*, 532 U.S. at 31, 58 USPQ2d at 1006.

The fact that the proposed mark is *not* the subject of a utility patent does not establish that the product feature is nonfunctional. *TrafFix*, 532 U.S. at 31, 58 USPQ2d at 1006; *In re Gibson Guitar Corp*., 61 USPQ2d 1948, 1950 n.3, (TTAB 2001). If the patent does not disclose utilitarian advantages of the design features at issue, or if no utility patent/application is of record, the evidence normally in-

2d 1285，12 USPQ2d 1250（Fed. Cir. 1989）；*Zippo Mfg. Co.*，50 USPQ2d 1852（TTAB 1999）；*Weber-Stephen Products Co.*，3 USPQ2d 1659（TTAB 1987）。

实用新型专利不必为申请人所有；只要专利主张了申请注册的产品设计特征，第三方的实用新型专利也可以用于对功能性的判定。*参见 Virshup*，42 USPQ2d 1403（TTAB 1997）；*American National Can Co.*，41 USPQ2d 1841（TTAB 1997）；*Cabot Corp.*，15 USPQ2d 1224（TTAB 1990）。因此，审查员也可以搜索本局的专利记录，检查是否有第三方的实用新型专利揭示了申请注册的产品设计的功能性优点。

在专利申请执行过程中所作的有关设计的实用性优点的陈述可以成为证明功能性的强有力证据。*参见 TrafFix*，532 U.S.32，58 USPQ2d 1006（"这些在专利申请书以及在获得专利过程中[有关该产品设计的具体功能性优点方面]的陈述证明了设计的功能性。MDI 并没有主张任何这些陈述是错误或不准确的，而这就成为双弹簧设计具有功能性的进一步重要证据"）。

在实用新型专利的主张范围大于申请注册范围的情况下，如果该专利表明作为商标的这部分是该发明不可缺少或固有的部分，且具有实用性优点，那么范围超出就并不能证明该产品设计不具有功能性。*比较*：*TrafFix*，532 U.S.31，58 USPQ2d 1006。

如果申请注册的商标并*非*实用新型专利的对象，这一事实并不能证明产品特征不具有功能性。见 *TrafFix*，532 U.S.31，58 USPQ2d 1006；*Gibson Guitar Corp.*，61 USPQ2d 1948，1950 n.3，（TTAB 2001）。如果专利并没有揭示相关设计特征的实用性优点，或者记录中不存在实用新型专利/申请，则证据通常设计考虑一个或

volves consideration of one or more of the other factors commonly known as the "*Morton-Norwich* factors":

(1) the existence of a utility patent that discloses the utilitarian advantages of the design sought to be registered;

(2) advertising by the applicant that touts the utilitarian advantages of the design;

(3) facts pertaining to the availability of alternative designs; and

(4) facts pertaining to whether the design results from a comparatively simple or inexpensive method of manufacture.

In re Morton-Norwich Products, Inc., 671 F.2d 1332, 213 USPQ 9, 15-16 (C.C.P.A.1982).

Moreover, even in the absence of a utility patent or utility patent application, it is not necessary to consider all these factors in every case. The Supreme Court held that "[w]here the design is functional under the *Inwood* formulation there is no need to proceed further to consider if there is a competitive necessity for the feature." *TrafFix Devices, Inc. v. Marketing Displays, Inc.*, 532 U. S. 23, 58 USPQ2d 1001, 1006 (2001). *See also Gibson Guitar Corp., supra* (where there was no utility patent, and no evidence that applicant's guitar configuration resulted from a simpler or cheaper method of manufacture, these factors did not weigh in Board's decision).

Relevant technical information is usually more readily available to an applicant. *In re Witco Corp.*, 14 USPQ2d 1557, 1560 (TTAB 1990). Therefore, the applicant will often be the source of most of the evidence relied upon by the examining attorney in establishing a *prima facie* case of functionality in an *ex parte* case. *In re Teledyne Industries Inc.*, 696 F.2d 968, 971, 217 USPQ 9, 11 (Fed.Cir.1982). When there is reason to believe the proposed mark may be functional, in the first Office action the examining attorney should require the applicant to provide in-

一个以上的其他因素，这些因素称为“*Morton-Norwich* 因素”：

(1) 存在一项实用新型专利，其揭示了申请注册的设计的实用性优点；

(2) 申请人所做的广告，宣传该设计的实用性优点；

(3) 有关是否有可替代设计的事实；以及

(4) 有关该设计是否来源于某项相对简单或便宜的制造方法的事实。

见 *Morton-Norwich Products, Inc.*, 671 F.2d 1332, 213 USPQ 9, 15 - 16 (C.C.P.A.1982)。

此外，甚至在缺乏实用新型专利或实用新型专利申请的情况下，也不是在每一个案件中都必须考虑所有这些因素。最高法院认为：“如果根据 *Inwood* 公式该设计被认定为具有功能性，就不必再进一步考虑是否存在对该设计特征的竞争需要。”见 *TrafFix Devices, Inc. v. Marketing Displays, Inc.*, 532 U.S. 23, 58 USPQ2d 1001, 1006 (2001)。*另参见 Gibson Guitar Corp.,如前*（没有实用新型专利，也没有证据证明申请人的吉他设计来源于一种更简单或更便宜的制造方法，但在委员会的裁决中也没有考虑这些因素）。

通常申请人可以更容易地获得相关的技术信息。相关判例：*Witco Corp.*, 14 USPQ2d 1557, 1560 (TTAB 1990)。因此，在单方面案件中，通常审查员初步证明具有功能性所依据的证据大多是申请人提供的资料。相关判例：*Teledyne Industries Inc.*, 696 F.2d 968, 971, 217 USPQ 9, 11 (Fed. Cir. 1982)。如果有理由相信，申请注册的商标可能存在功能性，审查员要做的第一件事是，要求申请人提供必要的资

formation necessary to permit an informed determination concerning the registrability of the proposed mark. *See* 37 C.F.R. §2.61(b); *In re Babies Beat Inc.*, 13 USPQ2d 1729, 1731 (TTAB 1990) (registration properly refused where applicant failed to comply with examining attorney's request for copies of patent applications and other patent information). In addition to requesting whether the proposed mark is or has been the subject of a utility patent or a pending or abandoned patent application, the examining attorney should require an applicant to provide advertising or promotional materials. The examining attorney should also inquire whether the feature makes the product easier or cheaper to manufacture and whether alternative designs are available.

It is important that the inquiry focus on the utility of the feature or combination of features that is claimed as protectible trade dress, and not on the usefulness of the article overall. *Morton-Norwich*, 671 F.2d at 1338, 213 USPQ at 13. Generally, dissecting the design into its individual features and analyzing the utility of each separate feature does not establish that the overall design is functional. 15 U.S.C. §1052(e)(5); *Teledyne Industries Inc.*, 696 F.2d at 971, 217 USPQ at 11. However, it is sometimes helpful to analyze the design from the standpoint of its various features. *In re R.M. Smith, Inc.*, 734 F.2d 1482, 1484, 222 USPQ 1, 2 (Fed. Cir. 1984) (affirming the functionality determination, where the Board had initially considered the six individual features of the design, and then had concluded that the design as a whole was functional); *In re Controls Corp. of America*, 46 USPQ2d 1308, 1312 (TTAB 1998) (finding the entire configuration at issue functional because it consisted of several individual features, each of which was functional in nature). *See also Elmer v. ICC Fabricating Inc.*, 67 F.3d 1571, 1579-80, 36 USPQ2d 1417, 1422-23 (Fed. Cir. 1995) (rejecting the argument that the combination of individually functional features in the configuration resulted in an overall nonfunctional product design).

Where the evidence shows that the overall design is functional, the inclusion of a few arbitrary or otherwise nonfunctional features in the design will not change the result. *See Textron, Inc. v. U.S. International Trade Commission*, 753 F.2d

料，以便能够就所申请的商标的可注册性作出有根据的决定。*参见* 37 C.F.R.§2.61(b)；*Babies Beat Inc*., 13 USPQ2d 1729，1731 (TTAB 1990)（如果申请人未能提供符合审查员要求的专利申请书复印件以及其他专利资料，可以正当地驳回申请）。除了要求提供申请注册的商标是否为某一项实用新型专利的对象，或者曾经是某一项已经过期或失效的专利申请的对象方面的资料之外，审查员还应要求申请人提供广告或促销宣传材料。审查员还应调查该特征是否使产品更易于制造或降低了制造成本，以及是否存在替代性的设计。

对于主张为可保护的商品外观，调查的重点应放在特征或特征组合的实用性上，而非放在其整体有用性上。见 *Morton-Norwich*，671 F.2d 1338，213 USPQ 13。一般说来，将设计分解成单独的特征，并对每个单独的特征的实用性进行分析，不能证明整体设计具有功能性。见 15 U.S.C.§1052(e)(5)；*Teledyne Industries Inc*.，696 F.2d 971，217 USPQ 11。不过，这样做有时有助于从其各种特征出发对设计进行分析。相关判例：*R. M. Smith，Inc*.，734 F.2d 1482，1484，222 USPQ 1，2 (Fed. Cir. 1984)（维持了认定具有功能性的裁决，在该裁决中，委员会首先考虑了相关设计的六个单独特征，然后得出结论认为该设计在整体上具有功能性）；*Controls Corp. of America*，46 USPQ2d 1308，1312 (TTAB 1998)（判定相关设计在整体上具有功能性，因为该设计由若干单独的特征构成，而每项特征均具备了功能性）。*另参见 Elmer v. ICC Fabricating Inc*.，67 F.3d 1571，1579－80，36 USPQ2d 1417，1422－23 (Fed. Cir. 1995)（当事人抗辩说，设计的各个单独特征均具备功能性，但组合在一起后，作为整体的产品设计不具有功能性，此种抗辩遭到了驳回）。

证据显示了整体设计具有功能性，尽管该设计包含了一些任意的或者不具功能性的特征，但这并不能改变其结果。*参见 Textron，Inc. v. U.S. International Trade Commission*，753 F.2d 1019，224 USPQ 625，628－29 (Fed. Cir. 1985)；*Vico*

1019, 224 *USPQ* 625, 628-29 (*Fed. Cir.* 1985); *In re Vico Products Mfg. Co., Inc.*, 229 USPQ 364, 368 (TTAB 1985).

A design patent is a factor that weighs against a finding of functionality because design patents by definition protect only ornamental and nonfunctional features. However, ownership of a design patent does not in and of itself establish that a product feature is nonfunctional, and can be outweighed by other evidence supporting the functionality determination. *R. M. Smith, Inc.*, 734 F. 2d at 1485, 222 USPQ at 3; *American National Can Co.*, 41 USPQ2d at 1843; *Caterpillar Inc.*, 43 USPQ2d at 1339; *Witco Corp.*, 14 USPQ2d at 1559.

1202.02(a)(v)(A) Advertising, Promotional or Explanatory Material in Functionality Determinations [R-1]

The examining attorney should examine the specimens of record, and should also ask an applicant to provide any available advertising, promotional or explanatory material concerning the goods/services, particularly any material specifically related to the features embodied in the proposed mark. The examining attorney should also check to see if the applicant has a website on which the product is advertised or described.

The applicant's own advertising touting the utilitarian aspects of its design is often strong evidence supporting a functionality refusal. *See, e.g., In re Gibson Guitar Corp.*, 61 USPQ2d 1948 (TTAB 2001); *M-5 Steel Mfg., Inc. v. O'Hagin's Inc.*, 61 USPQ2d 1086 (TTAB 2001); *In re Visual Communications Co., Inc.*, 51 USPQ2d 1141 (TTAB 1999); *In re Edward Ski Products, Inc.*, 49 USPQ2d 2001 (TTAB 1999); *In re Caterpillar Inc.*, 43 USPQ2d 1335 (TTAB 1997); *In re Bio-Medicus Inc.*, 31 USPQ2d 1254 (TTAB 1993); *In re Witco Corp.*, 14 USPQ2d 1557 (TTAB 1989).

An applicant will often assert that statements in its promotional materials touting the utilitarian advantages of the product feature are mere "puffery" and thus enti-

Products Mfg. Co., Inc., 229 USPQ 364, 368 (TTAB 1985)。

设计专利是反驳功能性裁决的一个因素,因为根据定义,设计专利只保护装饰性和不具功能性的特征。不过,拥有一项设计专利本身并不能证明产品特征不具功能性,并且可以被其他支持功能性裁判的证据所压倒。相关判例:*R. M. Smith, Inc.*, 734 F.2d 1485, 222 USPQ 3; *American National Can Co.*, 41 USPQ2d 1843; *Caterpillar Inc.*, 43 USPQ2d 1339; *Witco Corp.*, 14 USPQ2d 1559。

1202.02(a)(v)(A) 功能性判决中的广告、促销或说明性材料[R-1]

审查员应审查记录样本,并应同时要求申请人提供任何现有的有关该商品/服务的广告、促销或说明性材料,尤其是任何特别有关于申请注册的商标所体现的特征的材料。审查员还应查看申请人是否有对其产品进行广告宣传或介绍的网站。

申请人自己宣传其设计具有实用性的广告通常是以功能性为由作出拒绝注册决定的强有力证据。参见判例: *Gibson Guitar Corp.*, 61 USPQ2d 1948 (TTAB 2001); *M-5 Steel Mfg., Inc. v. O'Hagin's Inc.*, 61 USPQ2d 1086 (TTAB 2001); *Visual Communications Co., Inc.*, 51 USPQ2d 1141 (TTAB 1999); *Edward Ski Products, Inc.*, 49 USPQ2d 2001 (TTAB 1999); *Caterpillar Inc.*, 43 USPQ2d 1335 (TTAB 1997); *Bio-Medicus Inc.*, 31 USPQ2d 1254 (TTAB 1993); *Witco Corp.*, 14 USPQ2d 1557 (TTAB 1989)。

申请人通常会声称,在其促销材料中宣传产品特征的实用性优点,只是在"吹嘘",

tled to little weight in the functionality analysis. However, where the advertising statements clearly emphasize specific utilitarian features of the design claimed as a mark, the Board will reject such assertions of "puffing." *See*, *e.g.*, *In re Gibson Guitar Corp.*, *supra*; *Goodyear Tire and Rubber Co. v. Interco Tire Corp.*, 49 USPQ2d 1705, 1716-17 (TTAB 1998); *In re BioMedicus Inc.*, 31 USPQ2d 1254, 1260 (TTAB 1993); *In re Witco Corp.*, 14 USPQ2d 1557, 1559-61 (TTAB 1989).

In *Gibson Guitar*, the Board found the design of a guitar body to be functional, noting that applicant's literature clearly indicated that the shape of applicant's guitar produced a better musical sound. Applicant's advertisements stated that "This unique body shape creates a sound which is much more balanced and less 'muddy' than other ordinary dreadnought acoustics." 61 USPQ2d at 1951.

The examining attorney may also check trade publications and computer databases to determine whether others have written about the applicant's design and its functional features or characteristics. In *Gibson Guitar*, the record included an advertisement obtained from the website of a competitor whose guitar appeared to be identical in shape to applicant's configuration, touting the acoustical advantages of the shape of the guitar.

1202.02(a)(v)(B) Availability of Alternative Designs in Functionality Determinations [R-1]

An applicant attempting to rebut a *prima facie* case of functionality will often submit evidence of alternative designs to demonstrate that there is no "competitive need" in the industry for the applicant's particular product design. *See* TMEP §1202.02(a)(iii)(A).

However, in *TrafFix Devices, Inc. v. Marketing Displays, Inc.*, 532 U.S. 23, 58 USPQ2d 1001 (2001), the Supreme Court clearly indicated that if the record shows that a design is essential to the use or purpose of a product, or if it affects the cost or quality of the product, it is unnecessary to consider whether there is a

对于功能性分析应该没有什么分量。不过，如果广告的陈述明显地强调了申请注册的设计的具体实用性特征，则委员将驳回是在作“吹嘘”的主张。*参见* 判例：*Gibson Guitar Corp.*，*supra*；*Goodyear Tire and Rubber Co. v. Interco Tire Corp.*，49 USPQ2d 1705，1716－17（TTAB 1998）；*Bio-Medicus Inc.*，31 USPQ2d 1254，1260（TTAB 1993）；*Witco Corp.*，14 USPQ2d 1557，1559－61（TTAB 1989）。

在 *Gibson Guitar* 案中，委员会判定一项吉他琴体的设计具有功能性，认为申请人的文本资料明显表示，申请人吉他的形状能够产生更好的乐音。申请人在广告中称：“这种独一无二的形状能够创造出比其他普通的声响更加平衡且更少‘浑浊’的声音。”61 USPQ2d 1951。

审查员还可以查验商业出版物和计算机数据库，以判断是否有其他人曾论及申请人的设计及其功能性特征或特性。在 *Gibson Guitar* 案中，记录中包含了一份从某竞争者网站上获得的广告，他的吉他同申请人设计的形状相同，并且宣传该吉他形状带来的音色优点。

1202.02(a)(v)(B) 功能性判决中关于是否存在替代设计的问题［R－1］

为了反驳功能性的初步证明，申请人通常会提交可替代设计的证据，以此证明其特定的产品设计在本行业中不存在“竞争需要”。*参见* TMEP §1202.02(a)(iii)(A)。

但是，在 *TrafFix Devices, Inc. v. Marketing Displays, Inc.*，532 U.S. 23，58 USPQ2d 1001 (2001)一案中，最高法院明确表示，如果记录表明某项设计对于产品的用途或目的必不可少，或者影响到产品的成本或质量，就不必考虑是否存在对该产

competitive need for the product feature. The Court explained:

> [W]e have said "in general terms, a product feature is functional, and cannot serve as a trademark, if it is essential to the use or purpose of the article or if it affects the cost or quality of the article." Expanding upon the meaning of this phrase, we have observed that a functional feature is one the "exclusive use of [which] would put competitors at a significant non-reputation-related disadvantage." The Court of Appeals in the instant case seemed to interpret this language to mean that a necessary test for functionality is "whether the particular product configuration is a competitive necessity." ... This was incorrect as a comprehensive definition. As explained in *Qualitex*, *supra*, and *Inwood*, *supra*, a feature is also functional when it is essential to the use or purpose of the device or when it affects the cost or quality of the device ... *Where the design is functional under the Inwood formulation there is no need to proceed further to consider if there is a competitive necessity for the feature.*
>
> * * *
>
> *There is no need, furthermore, to engage, as did the Court of Appeals, in speculation about other design possibilities*, such as using three or four springs which might serve the same purpose. Here, the functionality of the spring design means that *competitors need not explore whether other spring juxtapositions might be used*. The dual-spring design is not an arbitrary flourish in the configuration of MDI's product; it is the reason the device works. *Other designs need not be attempted* (emphasis added).

TrafFix, 58 USPQ2d at 1006-1007 (citations and additional internal quotations omitted).

Thus, where the evidence clearly establishes the utilitarian nature of the trade dress at issue in view of a utility patent and/or advertising statements and facts showing a positive effect on the cost or quality of manufacture, it is unnecessary

品特征的竞争需要。法庭解释道：

> 我们曾经说过："一般说来，如果某项产品特征是其用途或目的必不可少的，或者影响到该物品的成本或质量，就具备了功能性，因而不能作为商标。"为了进一步阐明这段话的含义，我们也曾论述，一种功能性的特征是指"[该特征]的专属使用将使竞争者处于一种显著的、与声誉无关的劣势"。上诉法院在所举的案件中似乎将上述论述解释为，功能性的一个必要测试是"该特定产品设计是否具有竞争必要性"。……作为一个全面的定义，这是不正确的。在*Qualitex*案和*Inwood*案中已经解释过了，如果某个特征对于装置的用途或目的必不可少，或者影响到装置的成本或质量，那么它也就具备了功能性。*如果根据Inwood公式该设计被认定为具有功能性，就不必再进一步考虑该特征对于竞争是否必要。*
>
> * * *
>
> *此外，没有必要像上诉法院那样考虑其他的设计可能性，如：使用三条或四条弹簧也可能达到同样的效果。*在此，弹簧设计的功能性在于，*竞争者不必再探索是否可以使用其他弹簧设置法。*双弹簧设计在MDI产品的结构中并不是无端地流行；而是因为这种设计是装置工作的原因。*因而无需尝试其他设计*（给予了强调）。

TrafFix, 58 USPQ2d 1006－1007（引文和附加内部引用均略去）。

因此，如果由于某项实用新型专利和/或广告陈述，以及事实表明对产品制造的成本或质量产生了积极影响，从而有明确的证据证明所申请的商品外观具有实用性，

to consider whether alternative designs are available. *See Valu Engineering, Inc. v. Rexnord Corp.*, 278 F.3d 1268, 61 USPQ2d 1422, 1427 (Fed.Cir.2002) discussing the Supreme Court's decision in *TrafFix* ("once a product feature is found functional based on other considerations there is no need to consider the availability of alternative designs, because the feature cannot be given trade dress protection merely because there are alternative designs available.").

Evidence of the availability of alternative designs may be helpful where the record is otherwise unclear regarding the utilitarian functionality of the design at issue. *Id*. Accordingly, examining attorneys may continue to request information about alternative designs in the initial Office action, *i.e.*, inquire whether alternative designs are available for the feature embodied in the proposed mark, and whether the alternatives are more costly to produce. *See* TMEP 1212.02(a)(v).

In *In re Gibson Guitar Corp.*, 61 USPQ2d 1948 (TTAB 2001), the Board found that the applicant had not shown that there were alternative guitar shapes that could produce the same sound as applicant's configuration. The Board noted that the record contained an advertisement obtained from the website of a competitor whose guitar appeared to be identical in shape to applicant's configuration, stating that the shape of the guitar produces a better sound.

In order to be probative, the alternative design evidence must pertain to the same category of goods as the applicant's goods. *See, e.g., In re Zippo Mfg. Co.*, 50 USPQ2d 1852, 1854 (TTAB 1999); *In re EBSCO Industries Inc.*, 41 USPQ2d 1917, 1919 (TTAB 1997).

1202.02(a)(v)(C) Ease or Economy of Manufacture in Functionality Determinations

As noted in TMEP §1202.02(a)(iii)(A), a product feature is "functional" if it is essential to the use or purpose of the product *or if it affects the cost or quality of the product*. *Inwood Laboratories, Inc. v. Ives Laboratories, Inc.*, 456 U.S.844,

那么就不必再考虑是否存在可用的替代设计。参见 *Valu Engineering, Inc. v. Rexnord Corp.*, 278 F.3d 1268, 61 USPQ2d 1422, 1427 (Fed. Cir. 2002),讨论了最高法院在 *TrafFix* 案中所作的裁决("一旦某产品特征根据其他考虑被判定具有功能性,就没有必要再考虑替代设计的可行性,因为仅凭替代设计的可行性已不能授予该特征商品外观保护了")。

如果对于所申请设计的实用功能性的记录不明确,在这种情况下替代设计可行性的证据可能有所帮助。*同前*。如此,审查员就可以继续在初步审查中要求提供有关替代设计的资料,亦即,调查申请注册的商标所体现的特征是否存在替代设计,以及该替代设计是否会导致更大的生产成本。参见 TMEP 1212.02(a)(v)。

在 *Gibson Guitar Corp.*, 61 USPQ2d 1948 (TTAB 2001)一案中,委员会判定申请人未能表明存在其他吉他形状可以产生与申请人设计所能达到的相同声音效果。委员会称,记录包含了一份从某竞争者网站上获得的广告,其吉他与申请人设计的形状相同,并称该吉他形状能够产生更好的声音。

为了能够进行检验,替代设计的证据必须与申请人的商品属于同一类商品。参见相关判例:*Zippo Mfg. Co.*, 50 USPQ2d 1852, 1854 (TTAB 1999); *EBSCO Industries Inc.*, 41 USPQ2d 1917, 1919 (TTAB 1997)。

1202.02(a)(v)(C) 功能性裁判中有关制造方便性或经济性的问题

正如在 TMEP §1202.02(a)(iii)(A)一案中所述,如果某产品特征对于产品的用途或目的必不可少,*或者影响到产品的成本或质量*,那么它就是功能性的。见 *Inwood Laboratories, Inc. v. Ives Laboratories, Inc.*, 456 U.S. 844, 850, 214 USPQ

850, 214 USPQ 1, 4 n.10 (1982). Therefore, a showing that a design results from a comparatively simple or inexpensive method of manufacture will support a finding that the design is functional.

In most cases, there is little or no evidence pertaining to this factor. However, the examining attorney should still ask the applicant for information as to whether the subject design makes the product simpler or less costly to manufacture, since evidence on this issue weighs strongly in favor of a finding of functionality. *See*, *e.g.*, *TrafFix Devices*, *Inc. v. Marketing Displays*, *Inc.*, 532 U. S. 23, 58 USPQ2d 1001 (2001); *In re Virshup*, 42 USPQ2d 1403 (TTAB 1997). Statements pertaining to the cost or ease of manufacture may sometimes also be found in informational or advertising materials submitted by the applicant. *See M*-5 *Steel Mfg.*, *Inc. v. O'Hagin's Inc.*, 61 USPQ2d 1086, 1097 (TTAB 2001) (statements in promotional material that applicant's design results in reduced costs of installation found to be evidence of functionality of applicant's configurations of metal ventilating ducts and vents for tile or concrete roofs).

While evidence showing that the product feature results from a comparatively simple or inexpensive method of manufacture supports a finding that the design is functional, the opposite is not necessarily the case — *i.e.*, assertions by the applicant that its design is more expensive or more difficult to make will not establish that the configuration is not functional.

1202.02(b) Distinctiveness of Trade Dress [R-1]

In *Wal-Mart Stores*, *Inc. v Samara Brothers*, *Inc.*, 529 U. S. 205, 215, 54 USPQ2d 1065, 1069 (2000) the Supreme Court distinguished between two types of trade dress-product design and product packaging. If the trade dress falls within the category of "product design," it can never be inherently distinctive. *Id.* 529 U. S. at 212, 54 USPQ2d at 1068 ("It seems to us that design, like color, is not inherently distinctive."). Moreover, the Court held that in close cases in which it is difficult to determine whether the trade dress at issue is product packaging or

1，4 n.10 (1982)。因此，如果能够表明某设计来源于一种相对简单或者便宜的制造方法，就能够判定该设计具有功能性。

在大多数案件中，很少或没有关于此因素的证据。不过，审查员仍然应当向申请人要求提供有关该设计是否使产品制造更简便或者降低成本的资料，因为这方面的证据在判定功能性的过程中有重要作用。*参见*相关判例：*TrafFix Devices, Inc. v. Marketing Displays, Inc.*, 532 U.S. 23, 58 USPQ2d 1001 (2001)；*Virshup*, 42 USPQ2d 1403 (TTAB 1997)。在申请人提交的广告材料中有时也可以发现有关制造成本或简易性的陈述。*参见 M-5 Steel Mfg., Inc. v. O'Hagin's Inc.*, 61 USPQ2d 1086, 1097 (TTAB 2001)（促销材料中称，申请人的设计能够降低安装成本，结果被认定为申请人金属通风管道以及砖瓦水泥屋顶通风口设计具有功能性的证据）。

如果证据表明某产品特征来源于一种相对简单或者便宜的制造方法，则可以支持该设计具有功能性的判定，但是相反的情况则未必能得出相反的结论——亦即，申请人主张其设计的成本更高或更困难并不能证明该设计不具有功能性。

1202.02(b) 产品外观的独特性 [R-1]

在 *Wal-Mart Stores, Inc. v Samara Brothers, Inc.*, 529 U.S. 205, 215, 54 USPQ2d 1065, 1069 (2000) 一案中，最高法院对两类商品外观——商品设计和商品包装作了区别。如果商品外观属于"产品设计"范畴，就不具备固有的独特性。*同前*。529 U.S. 212, 54 USPQ2d 1068（"在我们看来，该设计与色彩一样，并不具有固有的独特性"）。此外，法庭还认为，在难以判断涉案商品外观究竟是产品包装还是产品设

product design, "courts should err on the side of caution and classify ambiguous trade dress as product design, thereby requiring secondary meaning." *Id*. at 215, 54 USPQ2d at 1070. (*Note*: If the trade dress is functional, it cannot be registered despite acquired distinctiveness. *TrafFix Devices, Inc. v. Marketing Displays, Inc*., 532 U.S. 23, 58 USPQ2d 1001, 1007 (2001).)

The statutory basis for refusal of registration on the Principal Register on the ground that the trade dress is nondistinctive is 15 U.S.C. §§1051, 1052, and 1127.

1202.02(b)(i) Distinctiveness and Product Design Trade Dress

In addition to determining whether a proposed mark is functional, the examining attorney must refuse to register, on the Principal Register, any mark that consists of a product design, unless the applicant establishes that the mark has acquired distinctiveness under §2(f). *Wal-Mart Stores, Inc. v. Samara Brothers, Inc*., 529 U.S. 205, 210, 54 USPQ2d 1065, 1068 (2000). Features of a product's design can never be inherently distinctive and are registrable only upon a showing of secondary meaning. *Id*. at 213-14, 54 USPQ2d at 1069. The Supreme Court noted that product design almost invariably serves purposes other than source identification, and that consumers are aware that even the most unusual product design (such as a cocktail shaker shaped like a penguin) is intended not to identify the source, but to render the product itself more useful or appealing. *Id*.

The examining attorney must issue this refusal in *all* applications seeking registration of a product design unless the application is filed under the provisions of §2(f) and includes sufficient evidence to show that the mark has secondary meaning. The ground for refusal is that the proposed mark consists of a nondistinctive product design, and thus does not function as a mark under §§1, 2 and 45 of the Trademark Act, 15 U.S.C. §§1051, 1052 and 1127. If the product design is not functional, the mark may be registered on the Supplemental Register, or, if the applicant shows that the product design has acquired distinctiveness, on the Principal Register under §2(f). *See* TMEP §1202.02(a) regarding functionality,

计的情况下，“法庭应宁可谨慎一些，将模糊不清的商品外观定性为产品设计，并因此要求第二含义”。同前 215，54 USPQ2d 1070。（注：如果商品外观具有功能性，那么即使具备了独特性也不能注册。见 *TrafFix Devices，Inc. v. Marketing Displays，Inc.*，532 U.S.23，58 USPQ2d 1001，1007（2001）。）

因商品外观不具有独特性而拒绝在联邦商标登记簿上注册的法律依据是 15 U.S.C.§§1051，1052 和 1127。

1202.02(b)(i)　独特性和产品设计的商品外观

除了判定申请注册的商标是否具有功能性外，对于含有产品设计的任何商标，审查员都必须拒绝在联邦商标登记簿上注册，除非申请人证明该商标具有 §2(f)所规定的独特性。见 *Wal-Mart Stores，Inc. v. Samara Brothers，Inc.*，529 U.S.205，210，54 USPQ2d 1065，1068（2000）。不能仅仅根据产品设计特征显示出的第二含义而认定该特征具有固有的独特性和可注册性。*同前* 213 – 14，54 USPQ2d 1069。最高法院解释道，产品设计几乎总是有除了识别来源以外的其他用途，消费者知道即使是最不同寻常的产品设计（比如企鹅形状的鸡尾酒调酒器）也不是用来识别商品来源，而是使产品本身更好用或更有吸引力。*同前*。

对于*所有*要求注册产品设计的申请，审查员均应以此驳回，除非申请是根据 §2(f)的规定提出，并且有充分证据表明商标具有第二含义。拒绝注册的理由是，申请注册的商标包含了不具独特性的产品设计，所以根据《商标法》§§1，2 和 45，15 U.S.C.§§1051、1052 和 1127 的规定，不能作为商标使用。如果产品设计并不具有功能性，那么商标可以在联邦商标补充登记簿上注册，或者，如果申请人证明产品设计具有独特性，那么可以根据§2(f)的规定，在联邦商标登记簿上注册。有关功能性的情

TMEP §§815 and 816 *et seq*. regarding the Supplemental Register, and TMEP §§1212 *et seq*. regarding acquired distinctiveness.

For applications based on §1(b) of the Trademark Act, 15 U.S.C. §1051(b), the examining attorney must issue the refusal even if the applicant has not filed an amendment to allege use or statement of use. *See* TMEP §1202.02(e) regarding examination of intent-to-use applications.

1202.02(b)(ii) Distinctiveness and Product Packaging Trade Dress for Goods or Services

Where a proposed mark consists of product packaging trade dress for goods or services, the examining attorney must determine whether the proposed mark is inherently distinctive. If it is not inherently distinctive, the examining attorney must refuse registration on the Principal Register on the ground that the proposed mark is nondistinctive trade dress under §§1, 2 and 45 of the Trademark Act, 15 U.S.C. §§1051, 1052 and 1127, for trademark applications; or §§1, 3 and 45 of the Act, 15 U.S.C. §§1051, 1053 and 1127, for service mark applications.

In *Wal-Mart Stores, Inc., v. Samara Brothers, Inc.*, 529 U.S. 205, 54 USPQ2d 1065 (2000), the Supreme Court discussed the distinction between the trade dress at issue in *Two Pesos, Inc. v. Taco Cabana, Inc.*, 505 U.S. 763, 23 USPQ2d 1081 (1992), and the product design trade dress (designs for children's clothing) under consideration in *Wal-Mart*:

> *Two Pesos* unquestionably establishes the legal principle that trade dress can be inherently distinctive, but it does not establish that *product design* trade dress can be. *Two Pesos* is inapposite to our holding here because the trade dress at issue, the decor of a restaurant, seems to us not to constitute product *design*. It was either product packaging — which, as we have discussed, normally is taken by the consumer to indicate origin — or else some *tertium quid* that is akin to product packaging.

况，*参见* TMEP §1202.02(a)；关于联邦商标补充登记簿的信息，*参见* TMEP §§815 和 816 及以下；关于获得性独特性的情况，*参见* TMEP §§1212 及以下。

对于根据《商标法》§1(b)，15 U.S.C.§1051(b)提出的申请，即使申请人尚未提出宣称使用修正书或使用声明书，审查员也必须拒绝注册。有关意图使用申请的审查的信息，*参见* TMEP §1202.02(e)。

1202.02(b)(ii)　独特性和商品或服务的产品包装性商品外观

如果申请注册的商标包含了商品或服务的产品包装性商品外观，审查员就必须判断申请注册的商标是否具备固有的独特性。如果不存在固有的独特性，审查员就必须以申请注册的商标属于不具独特性的商品外观为由拒绝在联邦商标登记簿上注册，法律依据对于商标注册申请是《商标法》§§1，2 和 45，15 U.S.C.§§1051、1052 和 1127；对于服务商标注册申请是《商标法》§§1，3 和 45，15 U.S.C.§§1051、1053 和 1127。

在 *Wal-Mart Stores, Inc., v. Samara Brothers, Inc.*, 529 U.S.205, 54 USPQ2d 1065 (2000)一案中，最高法院讨论了 *Two Pesos, Inc. v. Taco Cabana, Inc.*, 505 U.S.763, 23 USPQ2d 1081 (1992)案中涉及的商品外观与 *Wal-Mart* 案中考虑的产品设计性商品外观（童装的设计）之间的区别：

> *Two Pesos* 案无可争辩地确立了一项法律原则，即：商品外观可以具有固有的独特性，但它并未确立*产品设计性*商品外观也是如此。不过在此 *Two Pesos* 案对于我们的裁定并不适合，因为在我们看来，涉案的商品外观——某餐馆的装饰——并没有构成产品*设计*。这种装饰要么是产品包装——对此我们已经讨论过，消费者通常把它看作表明来源——要么是某些类似于产品包装的“第三物”。

Wal-Mart, 529 U.S. at 215, 54 USPQ2d at 1069.

Thus, unlike product design trade dress, trade dress constituting product packaging may be inherently distinctive for goods or services and registrable on the Principal Register without a showing of acquired distinctiveness. However, the examining attorney should be mindful of the Supreme Court's admonishment that where there are close cases, trade dress should be classified as product design for which secondary meaning is always required. *Id*., 529 U.S. at 215, 54 USPQ2d at 1070.

"[A] mark is inherently distinctive if [its] intrinsic nature serves to identify a particular source." *Id*. at 210, 54 USPQ2d at 1068 (citing *Two Pesos*, *Inc*. *v*. *Taco Cabana*, *Inc*., 505 U.S. 763, 768, 23 USPQ2d 1081 (1992)). The test for determining inherent distinctiveness set forth in *Seabrook Foods*, *Inc*. *v*. *Bar-Well Foods*, *Ltd*., 568 F.2d 1342, 1344, 196 USPQ 289, 291 (C.C.P.A. 1977), although not applicable to product design trade dress, is still viable in the examination of product packaging trade dress. The examining attorney should consider the following "*Seabrook*" factors. Whether the proposed mark is:

(1) a "common" basic shape or design;

(2) unique or unusual in the field in which it is used;

(3) a mere refinement of a commonly-adopted and well-known form of ornamentation for a particular class of goods viewed by the public as a dress or ornamentation for the goods;

(4) capable of creating a commercial impression distinct from the accompanying words.

Id. *See also Yankee Candle Co*. *v*. *Bridgewater Candle Co*., *LLC*, 259 F.3d 25, 59 USPQ2d 1720 (1st Cir. 2001) (trade dress for common elements of candle labels was nondistinctive product packaging for which insufficient evidence of acquired distinctiveness was shown; also insufficient evidence of acquired distinctiveness

Wal-Mart, 529 U.S. 215, 54 USPQ2d 1069。

因此,与产品设计性商品外观不同的是,包含产品包装的商品或服务的商品外观无需显示出获得性独特性便可以具有固有的独特性,并可以在联邦商标登记簿上注册。不过,审查员应当注意最高法院的警告,在具有相近案例的情况下,商品外观应当被定性为产品设计,从而必定要求第二含义。*同前*。529 U.S. 215, 54 USPQ2d 1070。

"如果'商标的固有属性是用来识别某特定来源',那么它就具有固有的独特性。"*同前*。210, 54 USPQ2d 1068(引用 *Two Pesos, Inc. v. Taco Cabana, Inc.*, 505 U.S. 763, 768, 23 USPQ2d 1081 (1992))。在 *Seabrook Foods, Inc. v. Bar-Well Foods, Ltd.*, 568 F.2d 1342, 1344, 196 USPQ 289, 291 (C.C.P.A. 1977)一案中确定了判断固有独特性的评判标准,尽管不适用于产品设计性商品外观,但在判断产品包装性商品外观的过程中仍然可行。审查员应当考虑下列"*Seabrook*"因素。申请注册的商标是否:

(1) 为"共有的"基本形状或设计;

(2) 在其使用领域内具有独特性或不同寻常;

(3) 仅仅是对某常用、知名的、用于特定等级商品的装饰进行了改进,而且会被公众看做是商品的外观或装饰;

(4) 能够产生一种有别于伴随词语的商业印象。

另参见:*Yankee Candle Co. v. Bridgewater Candle Co., LLC*, 259 F.3d 25, 59 USPQ2d 1720 (1st Cir. 2001)(蜡烛标签共同部分的商品外观是非独特性产品包装,因为没有充分证据表明存在获得性独特性,也没有充分证据表明由标签、蜡烛架、演

for trade dress comprised of label elements, candle holders, display systems, and candle containers); *Tone Brothers, Inc. v. Sysco Corp.*, 28 F.3d 1192, 1205, 31 USPQ2d 1321, 1331 (Fed. Cir. 1994) (citing *Seabrook*); *In re Hudson News Co.*, 39 USPQ2d 1915, 1923 (TTAB 1996), *aff'd per curiam*, 114 F.3d 1207 (Fed. Cir. 1997) ("[f]or the 'blue motif' of a retail store to be registrable on the Principal Register without resort to Section 2(f), the trade dress would have to be immediately recognizable as a distinctive way of identifying the source of the store services."); *In re File*, 48 USPQ2d 1363, 1367 (TTAB 1998) (novel tubular lights used in connection with bowling alley services would be perceived by customers as "simply a refinement of the commonplace decorative or ornamental lighting ... and would not be inherently regarded as a source indicator."); *In re J. Kinderman & Sons Inc.*, 46 USPQ2d 1253, 1255 (TTAB 1998) ("... while the designs applicant seeks to register [the packaging for electric lights for Christmas trees] may be unique in the sense that we have no evidence that anyone else is using designs which are identical to them, they are nonetheless not inherently distinctive.").

Unlike §1(b) applications for product design trade dress, §1(b) applications for product packaging trade dress generally will not be refused registration on the ground of nondistinctiveness until the applicant has filed an amendment to allege use or a statement of use. *See* TMEP §1202.02(e).

Regardless of the bases for filing, if a proposed mark is inherently distinctive, it may be registered on the Principal Register. *See In re Creative Beauty Innovations, Inc.*, 56 USPQ2d 1203 (TTAB 2000) (bottle configuration found inherently distinctive); *In re Fre-Mar Industries, Inc.*, 158 USPQ 364, 367 (TTAB 1968) ("[A]lthough the particular shape is a commonplace one for flashlights, it is nevertheless so unique and arbitrary as a container in the tire repair field that it may be inherently distinctive and, therefore, by reason of its shape alone, serve to identify applicant's goods and distinguish them from like goods of others."); *In re International Playtex Corp.*, 153 USPQ 377 (TTAB 1967) (container configuration having the appearance of an ice cream cone found inherently distinctive as a

示系统以及蜡烛容器构成的商品外观具有获得性独特性）；*Tone Brothers, Inc. v. Sysco Corp.*, 28 F.3d 1192, 1205, 31 USPQ2d 1321, 1331 (Fed. Cir. 1994)（引用了 *Seabrook* 案）；*Hudson News Co.*, 39 USPQ2d 1915, 1923 (TTAB 1996), *aff'd per curiam*, 114 F.3d 1207 (Fed. Cir. 1997)（"要使某零售商店的'蓝色图案'无需适用 Section 2(f)而在联邦商标登记簿上注册，它必须能够立即被识别为是一种识别商店服务来源的独特方式"）；*File*, 48 USPQ2d 1363, 1367 (TTAB 1998)（在消费者看来，在提供保龄球道服务的过程中所使用的新颖的管状灯"只是通常的灯光装饰的一种改进，……因此不能认为是一种固有的识别来源的方式"）；*J. Kinderman & Sons Inc.*, 46 USPQ2d 1253, 1255 (TTAB 1998)（"……尽管我们并没有证据可以证明其他人使用了同样的设计，因而从这种意义上说，申请人申请注册的［圣诞树电灯包装］可能是独一无二的，但它们并不具有固有的独特性"）。

与根据 §1(b)规定而提出的产品设计性商品外观申请不同的是，根据 §1(b)规定提出的产品包装性商品外观申请通常不会由于不具有独特性而遭到拒绝，除非申请人提交了宣称使用修正书或使用声明书。*参见* TMEP §1202.02(e)。

无论提出申请的依据为何，只要商标具有固有的独特性，就可以在联邦商标登记簿上注册。*参见 Creative Beauty Innovations, Inc.*, 56 USPQ2d 1203 (TTAB 2000)（一种瓶子的设计被判定具有固有的独特性）；*Fre-Mar Industries, Inc.*, 158 USPQ 364, 367 (TTAB 1968)（"尽管该特定形状对于手电筒而言是平常的，但是作为轮胎修理厂的容器则是独特的，可以认为具有固有的独特性，因此，仅从其形状的理由出发，也可以识别申请人的商品，并将其同他人的商品区分开来"）；*International Playtex Corp.*, 153 USPQ 377 (TTAB 1967)（判定外形像冰淇淋筒的容器设计作

trademark for baby pants).

If a proposed mark is *not* inherently distinctive, the mark may be registered on either the Principal Register under §2(f) or on the Supplemental Register. Secondary meaning is acquired when the public views its primary significance as identifying the source of the product rather than the product itself. *Wal-Mart*, 529 U.S. at 211, 54 USPQ2d at 1068. In the following cases, the applicant's evidence was found to be sufficient to support a claim of acquired distinctiveness: *In re World's Finest Chocolate, Inc.*, 474 F.2d 1012, 177 USPQ 205 (C.C.P.A. 1973) (package design found to identify applicant's candy bars and distinguish them from those of others); *Ex parte Haig & Haig Ltd.*, 118 USPQ 229, 230 (Comm'r Pats. 1958) ("The decree recited that because of the original, distinctive and peculiar appearance of the 'Pinched Decanter' the brand of whiskey in such bottles had come to be known and recognized by the public, by dealers and by consumers; and that the whiskey contained in such bottles had come to be identified with the 'Pinched Decanter' in the minds of the public generally.").

In *In re Usher, S.A.*, 219 USPQ 920, 921 (TTAB 1983), the evidence of secondary meaning was insufficient. (The configuration of a package for mint candies was not functional but the package design was not shown to possess secondary meaning.)

See TMEP §§1212 *et seq*. regarding acquired distinctiveness and TMEP §§815 and 816 *et seq*. regarding the Supplemental Register.

1202.02(c) Distinctiveness and Functionality are Separate Issues

As stated in TMEP §1202.02, in an application for trade dress, distinctiveness and functionality are two separate issues, both of which must be considered by the examining attorney.

In many cases, registration is refused on both grounds. In any case where a product design or product packaging is refused because it is functional, registration

为童裤的商标使用,具有固有的独特性)。

如果所申请的商标不具有固有的独特性,那么商标可以依据 §2(f)的规定在联邦商标登记簿上注册或者在联邦商标补充登记簿上注册。如果公众认为它的主要意义在于识别产品的来源,而非产品本身,那么它就获得了第二含义。见 *Wal-Mart*,529 U.S.211, 54 USPQ2d 1068。在下列案件中,判定申请人提供的证据足以支持具有获得性独特性的主张:*World's Finest Chocolate, Inc.*, 474 F.2d 1012, 177 USPQ 205 (C.C.P.A.1973)(包装设计被认为能够识别申请人的糖果并将其同他人的产品区分开来);*Haig & Haig Ltd.*, 118 USPQ 229, 230 (Comm'r Pats.1958)("所引用的判决表明,由于'收缩玻璃瓶'独创、独特和罕见的外观,使用此类瓶子灌装的威士忌品牌已经为公众、商家和消费者所熟知和承认;而公众也已经普遍地以'收缩玻璃瓶'来识别装在这种瓶子里的威士忌")。

在 *Usher, S.A.*, 219 USPQ 920, 921 (TTAB 1983)一案中,第二含义的证据不够充分。(薄荷糖的包装设计被判定不具有功能性,但没有显示包装设计具有第二含义。)

有关获得性独特性的情况,*参见* TMEP §§1212 及以下;有关联邦商标补充登记簿的信息,*参见* TMEP §§815 和 816 及以下。

1202.02(c) 独特性和功能性是两个独立的问题

正如在 TMEP §1202.02 中所述,在一项商品外观申请中,独特性和功能性是两个独立的问题,审查员对两者都必须考虑。

在许多案件中,有以两个理由拒绝注册的情况。如果一项产品设计或产品包装

should also be refused on the ground that the proposed mark is nondistinctive.

In appropriate cases, the issues of functionality and acquired distinctiveness should be argued in the alternative. For example, if the examining attorney has determined that a mark is functional and the applicant has made a claim of acquired distinctiveness, the examining attorney must determine whether the showing of acquired distinctiveness would be sufficient to warrant registration if the examining attorney's decision on the functionality issue is reversed. Of course, if the mark is ultimately determined to be functional, evidence of acquired distinctiveness is irrelevant and registration will be refused. *TrafFix Devices, Inc. v. Marketing Displays, Inc.*, 532 U.S.23, 58 USPQ2d 1001, 1007 (2001).

1202.02(d) Drawing and Description of Mark in Trade Dress Applications

In an application to register a mark with three-dimensional features, the applicant must submit a drawing that depicts the mark in a single rendition. 37 C.F.R. §2.52(a)(2)(iii). If the mark comprises the design of only a portion of a product or container, broken lines should be used in the drawing to indicate that portion of the product or container that is not claimed as part of the mark. 37 C.F.R. §2.52(a)(2)(ii). *See In re Water Gremlin Co.*, 635 F.2d 841, 208 USPQ 89 (C.C.P.A.1980); *In re Famous Foods, Inc.*, 217 USPQ 177 (TTAB 1983). The matter that is shown in broken (dotted) lines does not have to be disclaimed, because it does not form part of the mark. If the drawing does not meet the requirements of 37 C.F.R. §2.52, the examining attorney should require the applicant to submit a substitute drawing.

If an acceptable statement describing the mark is not in the record, the examining attorney *must* require the applicant to submit a description to clarify what the applicant seeks to register. The description of the mark should include a statement that the matter shown in broken lines is not part of the mark. *See* 37 C.F.R. §§2.37, 2.52(a)(2)(iii) and 2.52(a)(2)(vi); TMEP §§808 *et seq*. The descrip-

由于具有功能性而遭到驳回，那么在任何情况下，也应以不具有独特性为理由驳回商标的申请。

在某些案件中，应当分别论证功能性和独特性问题。例如，如果审查员判定某商标具有功能性，而申请人已经提出了具有独特性的主张，在这种情况下，如果所作出的具有功能性的裁决被推翻，那么审查员必须判断所显示的独特性是否足以批准注册。当然，如果商标最终被判定具有功能性，那么有关具有独特性的证据就无关紧要，申请也将遭到驳回。见 *TrafFix Devices, Inc. v. Marketing Displays, Inc.*, 532 U.S.23, 58 USPQ2d 1001, 1007 (2001)。

1202.02(d)　商品外观注册申请的商标附图和说明

如果申请注册的商标带有立体特征，申请人必须提交以单个呈现图描绘商标的附图。37 C.F.R.§2.52(a)(2)(iii)。如果商标由产品或容器的某一部分设计组成，则应在图中以虚线显示不构成商标的产品或容器的部分。37 C.F.R.§2.52(a)(2)(ii)。*参见 Water Gremlin Co.*, 635 F.2d 841, 208 USPQ 89 (C.C.P.A.1980)；*Famous Foods, Inc.*, 217 USPQ 177 (TTAB 1983)。不必放弃对以虚线(点线)表示的部分的主张，因为该部分并不构成商标的一部分。如果附图不符合 37 C.F.R.§2.52 的规定要求，审查员应要求申请人提供另外的附图。

如果记录中没有包含符合要求的、对商标进行描述的陈述，审查员*必须*要求申请人提交对商标的描述以说明其申请注册的对象。商标的描述应当包含一份表明以虚线表示的部分不属于商标组成部分的声明书。*参见* 37 C.F.R.§§2.37, 2.52(a)(2)(iii) 和 2.52(a)(2)(vi)；TMEP §§808 及以下。商标描述将印刷在《官方公报》和注

tion is printed in the *Official Gazette* and on the registration certificate. Examples of acceptable language are, "The mark consists of the design of the blade portion of a flyswatter," and "The mark consists of the design of a perfume or cologne bottle and cap therefor, both having a 'V' shape as viewed from above." The description must adequately describe the mark, with unnecessary matter kept to a minimum. If applicable, the description must clearly indicate the portion of the product or container that the mark comprises. An example of acceptable language for this purpose is, "The mark consists of a red button positioned on the lower front area of a shirt. The dotted outline of the shirt is not part of the mark but is merely intended to show the position of the mark." As in this example, the description should make it clear what the dotted lines represent. The examining attorney should indicate in the file that the description statement should be printed. *See* TMEP §1202.05(d)(i) and (d)(ii) regarding drawings in applications for color marks consisting solely of one or more colors.

1202.02(e) Trade Dress in Intent-to-Use Applications

Distinctiveness and Product Design

A product design trademark can never be inherently distinctive and is registrable only upon a showing of secondary meaning. *Wal-Mart Stores, Inc. v. Samara Brothers, Inc.*, 529 U.S. 205, 212, 54 USPQ2d 1065, 1069 (2000); TMEP §1202.02(b)(i). Therefore, if the mark is comprised of a product design, the examining attorney will refuse registration on the Principal Register on the ground that the proposed mark consists of a nondistinctive product design under 15 U. S. C. §§1051, 1052 and 1127. The examining attorney will make this refusal even in an intent-to-use application under 15 U.S.C. §1051(b) for which no statement of use or amendment to allege use has been filed.

Distinctiveness and Product Packaging

If the mark comprises product packaging trade dress for goods or services, the ex-

册证书上。可接受的描述用语如:“商标由苍蝇拍叶片部分的设计构成”以及“商标由一个古龙水瓶及其盖子的设计组成,俯视时二者均有‘V’字形状”。商标描述必须对商标进行充分的描述,并尽可能减少不必要的内容。如果适当,商标描述必须清楚地表明构成商标的产品或容器的部分。关于这一点可接受的描述用语如:“商标由位于衬衫正面下方的一颗红色纽扣组成。虚线所显示的衬衫轮廓不是商标的组成部分,而只是用来表明商标所处的位置。”正如本例所示,商标描述必须明确说明虚线所代表的内容。审查员应在文件中注明,应当印刷商标的描述声明。

有关包含一种或一种以上颜色的彩色商标申请书的附图的情况,*参见* TMEP §1202.05(d)(i)和(d)(ii)。

1202.02(e) 意图使用申请的商品外观

独特性和产品设计

不能仅仅依据产品设计商标显示出第二含义就判定它具有固有的独特性以及可以注册。见 *Wal-Mart Stores, Inc. v. Samara Brothers, Inc.*, 529 U.S. 205, 212, 54 USPQ2d 1065, 1069 (2000);TMEP §1202.02(b)(i)。因此,如果商标由一项产品设计构成,审查员将根据 15 U.S.C.§§1051,1052 和 1127 的规定,以申请注册的商标含有不具独特性的产品设计为由拒绝其在联邦商标登记簿上注册。甚至在一项根据 15 U.S.C.§1051(b)提出的意图使用申请中,尚未提交使用声明书或宣称使用修正书,审查员也将以此为由拒绝注册。

独特性和产品包装

如果商标由商品或服务的产品包装性商品外观组成,审查员必须判断商标是否

amining attorney must determine whether the mark is inherently distinctive. *Wal-Mart Stores, Inc., v. Samara Brothers, Inc.*, 529 U.S. 205, 54 USPQ2d 1065 (2000); *Two Pesos, Inc. v. Taco Cabana, Inc.*, 505 U.S. 763, 23 USPQ2d 1081 (1992). This requires consideration of the context in which the mark is used and the impression it would make on purchasers. Generally, no refusal based on lack of inherent distinctiveness will be issued in an intent-to-use application until the applicant has submitted specimens with an amendment to allege use or a statement of use. However, if appropriate, the examining attorney has discretion to issue this refusal before specimens are submitted.

Functionality

To determine whether a proposed mark is functional, the examining attorney must consider how the asserted mark is used. Generally, in a §1(b) application the examining attorney will not issue a refusal on the ground that the mark is functional until the applicant has filed either an amendment to allege use under §1(c), or a statement of use under §1(d), 15 U.S.C. §§1051(c) or (d).

Advisory Statement

In a §1(b) application for which no specimens have been submitted, if the examining attorney anticipates that a refusal based on functionality or nondistinctive trade dress will be made, the potential refusal should be brought to the applicant's attention in the first action issued by the Office. This is done strictly as a courtesy. If information regarding this possible ground for refusal is not provided to the applicant before the allegation of use is filed, the Office is not precluded from refusing registration on this basis.

1202.03 Refusal on Basis of Ornamentation

Subject matter that is merely a decorative feature does not identify and distinguish the applicant's goods and, thus, does not function as a trademark. A decorative feature may include words, designs, slogans or other trade dress. This matter

具备固有的独特性。见 *Wal-Mart Stores, Inc., v. Samara Brothers, Inc.*, 529 U.S. 205, 54 USPQ2d 1065 (2000); *Two Pesos, Inc. v. Taco Cabana, Inc.*, 505 U.S. 763, 23 USPQ2d 1081 (1992)。在此要求考虑该商标使用的背景，以及可能给购买者的印象。通常，对于一项意图使用申请，不会以缺乏固有的独特性为由拒绝注册，除非申请人提交了样本和宣称使用修正书或使用声明书。不过，审查员在样本提交之前有权酌情自行以此为由驳回申请。

功能性

为了判断申请注册的商标是否具有功能性，审查员必须考虑商标的使用方式。通常，对于一项根据 §1(b)提出的申请，审查员不会以商标具有功能性为由拒绝注册，除非申请人已提交了 §1(c)所规定的宣称使用修正书或 §1(d)、15 U.S.C. §§1051(c)或(d)所规定的使用声明书。

告诫性声明

如果在一项根据 §1(b)提出的申请中，申请人没有提交样本，若审查员认为可能以功能性或无独特性商品外观为由拒绝注册，则商标局应在第一行动提请申请人注意。此种告诫纯粹是出于礼貌。如果在宣称使用提交之前，未向申请人告知关于该可能的驳回注册理由的信息，商标局仍然可以以该理由作出拒绝注册的决定。

1202.03　以装饰性为由拒绝注册

仅仅是装饰性特征的标的物不能识别和区分申请人的商品，因此，不能作为商标使用。装饰性特征可以包括文字、图案、标语或其他商品外观。对于这种物质应当拒

should be refused registration because it is merely ornamentation and, therefore, does not function as a trademark as required by §§1, 2 and 45 of the Trademark Act, 15 U.S.C. §§1051, 1052 and 1127.

Generally, the ornamentation refusal applies only to trademarks, not to service marks. *See* TMEP §§1301.02 *et seq*. regarding matter that does not function as a service mark.

Matter that serves primarily as a source indicator, either inherently or as a result of acquired distinctiveness, and that is only incidentally ornamental or decorative, can be registered as a trademark. *In re Soccer Sport Supply Co., Inc.*, 507 F.2d 1400, 184 USPQ 345 (C.C.P.A. 1975); *In re Paramount Pictures Corp.*, 213 USPQ 1111 (TTAB 1982).

With regard to registrability, ornamental matter may be categorized along a continuum ranging from ornamental matter that is registrable on the Principal Register, to purely ornamental matter that is incapable of trademark significance and unregistrable under any circumstances, as follows:

(1) Ornamental matter that serves as an identifier of a "secondary source" is considered an arbitrary symbol and is registrable on the Principal Register. For example, ornamental matter on a T-shirt (*e.g.*, the designation "NEW YORK UNIVERSITY") can convey to the purchasing public the "secondary source" of the T-shirt (rather than the manufacturing source). Thus, even where the T-shirt is distributed by a party other than that identified by the designation, sponsorship or authorization by the identified party is indicated. *See* TMEP §1202.03(c).

(2) Ornamental matter that is neither inherently distinctive nor a secondary source indicator may be registered on the Principal Register under §2(f) if the applicant establishes that the subject matter has acquired distinctiveness as a mark in relation to the goods. *See* TMEP §1202.03(d).

(3) Ornamental matter that is neither inherently distinctive nor an indica-

绝注册,因为它仅仅是装饰性的,因此不能作为《商标法》§§1,2 和 45,15 U.S.C. §§1051,1052 和 1127 所规定的商标。

通常,以装饰性为由拒绝注册只适用于商标,而不适用于服务商标。有关不作为服务商标的标的物,*参见* TMEP §§1301.02 及以下。

主要用于标示来源的标的物,无论是固有地还是由于获得性独特性而具有此作用,并且只是附带地具有装饰性的,可以作为商标注册。相关判例:*Soccer Sport Supply Co., Inc.*, 507 F.2d 1400, 184 USPQ 345 (C.C.P.A.1975); *Paramount Pictures Corp.*, 213 USPQ 1111 (TTAB 1982)。

关于可注册性,装饰性物质具有很大的范围,包括从可以在联邦商标登记簿上注册的装饰性物质,直到那些不具有商标意义、在任何情况下都不能注册的纯粹装饰性物质,包括如下:

(1) 作为标示"第二来源"的装饰性物质被认为是任意性标记,可以在联邦商标登记簿上注册。例如,一件 T 恤衫上的装饰性物质(*例如*,"纽约大学"名称)能够向购买公众传达该 T 恤衫的"第二来源"(除了制造生产来源外)。因此,即使 T 恤衫是由该名称识别的当事人以外的人经销的,它仍然指出了是由被识别的当事人赞助或授权的。*参见* TMEP §1202.03(c)。

(2) 既不具有固有独特性,也没有标示出第二来源的装饰性物质也可以根据§2(f)的规定在联邦商标登记簿上注册,只要申请人能够证明该物质获得了可以作为与该商品相关的商标的独特性。*参见* TMEP §1202.03(d)。

(3) 既不具有固有独特性,也没有标示出第二来源,且未获得独特性,但是能够

tor of secondary source, and has not acquired distinctiveness, but is capable of attaining trademark significance, may be registered on the Supplemental Register.

(4) Some matter is determined to be purely ornamental and thus incapable of trademark significance and unregistrable on either the Principal Register or the Supplemental Register. *See* TMEP §1202.03(a).

The examining attorney should consider the following factors to determine whether ornamental matter can be registered: (1) the commercial impression of the proposed mark; (2) the relevant practices of the trade; (3) secondary source, if applicable; and (4) evidence of distinctiveness. These factors are discussed in the following sections.

1202.03(a) Commercial Impression

The examining attorney must determine whether the overall commercial impression of the proposed mark is that of a trademark. Matter that is purely ornamental or decorative does not function as a trademark and is unregistrable on either the Principal Register or the Supplemental Register.

The significance of the proposed mark is a factor to consider when determining whether ornamental matter serves a trademark function. Common expressions and symbols (*e.g.*, the peace symbol, "smiley face," or the phrase "Have a Nice Day") are normally not perceived as marks.

The examining attorney must also consider the size, location and dominance of the proposed mark, as applied to the goods, to determine whether ornamental matter serves a trademark function. *In re Dimitri's Inc.*, 9 USPQ2d 1666, 1667 (TTAB 1988); *In re Astro-Gods Inc.*, 223 USPQ 621, 623 (TTAB 1984). A small, neat and discrete word or design feature (*e.g.*, small design of animal over pocket or breast portion of shirt) may be likely to create the commercial impression of a trademark, whereas a larger rendition of the same matter emblazoned across the

获得商标意义的装饰性物质可以在联邦商标补充登记簿上注册。

(4) 某些物质被判定属于纯粹的装饰性,因此而无法具有商标意义,不能在联邦商标登记簿或补充登记簿上注册。参见 TMEP §1202.03(a)。

在判断装饰性物质是否可以注册时,审查员应考虑下列因素:(1)申请注册的商标的商业印象;(2)该行业的相关做法;(3)第二来源(如果适当);以及(4)独特性的证据。这些因素在以下各节讨论。

1202.03(a) 商业印象

审查员必须判断申请注册的商标是否在整体上具有商标的商业印象。纯粹属于装饰性的物质,不能作为商标,不能在联邦商标登记簿或补充登记簿上注册。

在判断装饰性物质是否具有商标功能时,申请注册的商标的意义是需要考虑的一个因素。公用的词语和符号(*例如*,和平符号、"笑脸"以及短语"祝你今天快乐!")通常不会被认为是商标。

审查员还必须考虑申请注册的商标用在商品上时的大小、位置和主导地位,以判断装饰性物质是否具有商标的功能。相关判例:*Dimitri's Inc*., 9 USPQ2d 1666, 1667 (TTAB 1988); *Astro-Gods Inc*., 223 USPQ 621, 623 (TTAB 1984)。简洁且离散的短语或图案特征(*例如*,衬衫口袋或胸口部位上的动物小图案)可能给人商

front of a garment (or a tote bag, or the like) may be likely to be perceived merely as a decorative or ornamental feature of the goods. However, a small, neat and discrete word or design feature will not necessarily be perceived as a mark in all cases.

1202.03(b) Practices of the Trade

In determining whether a proposed mark is inherently distinctive, factors to be considered include whether the subject matter is unique or unusual in a particular field or whether it is a mere refinement of a commonly-adopted and well-known form of ornamentation for a particular class of goods that would be viewed by the public as a dress or ornamentation for the goods. *See*, *e.g.*, *In re Soccer Sport Supply Co., Inc.*, 507 F.2d 1400, 184 USPQ 345 (C.C.P.A. 1975) (pentagon-shaped repetitive design applied to the entire surface of soccer balls); *In re General Tire & Rubber Co.*, 404 F.2d 1396, 160 USPQ 415 (C.C.P.A. 1969) (three narrow white concentric rings of approximately equal width applied to the outer surface of a dark sidewall tire); *In re Chung, Jeanne & Kim Co., Inc.*, 226 USPQ 938 (TTAB 1985) (stripe design applied to sides of sport shoes).

Even if a proposed mark is not inherently distinctive, it may be registered on the Principal Register if it has become distinctive of the applicant's goods in commerce. *See* TMEP §1202.03(d). The practices of the trade may be relevant in assessing the applicant's burden of proving that the proposed mark has become distinctive. Typically, more evidence is required if the proposed mark is a type of ornamental matter used so frequently in the relevant industry that consumers would be less apt to discern a source-indicating significance from its use. *See Anchor Hocking Glass Corp. v. Corning Glass Works*, 162 USPQ 288 (TTAB 1969) (cornflower design recognized as a trademark for coffee percolators and culinary vessels and utensils). *Cf. In re Villeroy & Boch S.A.R.L.*, 5 USPQ2d 1451, 1454 (TTAB 1987) (affirming refusal to register design of morning glories and leaves for tableware, the Board noting that the design "has not been shown to be other than another decorative pattern without trademark significance ...").

标的商业印象，而将同样的东西放大了放在衣服（或大手提袋之类）的前面作为装饰时，却可能被人看做是商品的装饰性特征。不过，并不是在所有情况下简洁且离散的短语或图案特征都会给人商标的印象。

1202.03(b) 行业做法

在判断申请注册的商标是否具有固有的独特性时，需要考虑的因素包括：该标的物在某特定领域是否具有独特性或不同寻常，还是仅仅是对某常用和知名的、用于特定等级商品的装饰进行了改进，而且会被公众看做是商品的外观或装饰。参见相关判例：*Soccer Sport Supply Co., Inc.*, 507 F.2d 1400, 184 USPQ 345 (C.C.P.A. 1975)（分布在整个足球表面上的重复的五边形图案）；*General Tire & Rubber Co.*, 404 F.2d 1396, 160 USPQ 415 (C.C.P.A. 1969)（分布在黑色侧壁轮胎外表面上的三个基本等宽的白色同心圆）；*Chung, Jeanne & Kim Co., Inc.*, 226 USPQ 938 (TTAB 1985)（运动鞋侧面的斑纹图案）。

甚至即使申请注册的商标并不具有固有的独特性，但只要它使申请人的商品在商业流通中具有独特性，也可以在联邦商标登记簿上注册。*参见* TMEP §1202.03(d)。行业做法可能关系到如何确定申请人在证明相关商标具备独特性过程中的举证责任。典型地，如果申请注册的商标在相关行业中常常作为一种装饰性物质使用，使得消费者较少倾向于将其使用同一种标示来源的意义相联系，那么就需要举出更多的证据。*参见* *Anchor Hocking Glass Corp. v. Corning Glass Works*, 162 USPQ 288 (TTAB 1969)（矢车菊图案被认为是一种咖啡过滤器以及厨房用具的商标）。比较 *In re Villeroy & Boch S.A.R.L.*, 5 USPQ2d 1451, 1454 (TTAB 1987)（维持对用于餐具的牵牛花及叶子图案的不予注册决定，委员会解释道，该图案“并没有表现出与不具有商标意义的另一种装饰图案有所不同……”）。

If the applicant cannot show that the proposed mark has acquired distinctiveness, the mark may be registered on the Supplemental Register if it is "capable of distinguishing the applicant's goods or services." 15 U.S.C. §1091. The practices of the trade may be relevant in determining a proposed mark is capable of distinguishing the goods or services. If the practices of the trade suggest that certain matter performs the function of a trademark by signifying to purchasers and prospective purchasers the goods of a particular entity and distinguishing the goods from those of others (*e.g.*, design on hip pockets of jeans or design on athletic shoes), the matter is assumed to be capable of distinguishing the applicant's goods and, therefore, may be registered on the Supplemental Register. *See In re Todd Co., Inc.*, 290 F.2d 597, 129 USPQ 408 (C.C.P.A. 1961) (repeating pattern of green lines, used to cover the entire back surface of safety paper products (*e.g.*, checks), held registrable on the Supplemental Register for safety paper products, where the record showed that it had long been the practice in the industry to use distinctive overall surface designs to indicate origin of the products).

1202.03(c) "Secondary Source"

To show that a proposed mark that is used on the goods in a decorative or ornamental manner also serves a source-indicating function, the applicant may submit evidence that the proposed mark would be recognized as a mark through its use with goods or services other than those identified in the application. To show secondary source, the applicant may show: (1) ownership of a U.S. registration on the Principal Register of the same mark for other goods or services based on use in commerce under §1 of the Trademark Act; (2) non-ornamental use of the mark in commerce on other goods or services; or (3) ownership of a pending use-based application for the same mark, used in a non-ornamental manner, for other goods or services. Ownership of an intent-to-use application for which no allegation of use has been filed is not sufficient to show secondary source. If the applicant establishes that the proposed mark serves as an identifier of a secondary source, the matter is registrable on the Principal Register.

如果申请人无法证明申请注册的商标已经具备独特性，只要其“能够区分申请人的商品或服务”，就可以在联邦商标登记簿上注册。15 U.S.C.§1091。行业做法可能关系到判断申请注册的商标是否能够区别商品或服务。如果行业做法表明，通过向购买者及潜在的购买者表示商品属于某特定实体，并且将其同他人的商品区别开来，从而使得某些物质具有了商标的功能(*例如*，牛仔裤后口袋或运动鞋上的图案)，那么该物质就被推定能够区分申请人的商品，因而就可以在联邦商标补充登记簿上注册。*参见 Todd Co., Inc.*,'290 F.2d 597, 129 USPQ 408 (C.C.P.A.1961)(用于覆盖保险纸产品(*例如*，支票)背面的连续绿线条图案，被认为可以因安全纸制品而在联邦商标补充登记簿注册，只要记录显示，长久以来在行业实践中一直使用具有独特性的整体表面图案来标示产品的来源)。

1202.03(c) “第二来源”

为了表明尽管提出申请的商标是以一种装饰性的方式用于商品，但同时也承担了标示来源的功能，申请人可以提交证据以证明通过用于商品或服务，提出申请的商标可以被辨认为不同于申请书中已经识别的商标。为了表明第二来源，申请人可以表明：(1)在联邦商标登记簿拥有一项相同的用于其他类别商品或服务的美国注册商标，系根据《商标法》§1 的规定，基于商业使用而获得；(2)该商标在商业中没有用于装饰其他商品或服务；或(3)拥有一项尚未裁决的相同商标的申请，系以非装饰性的方式用于其他类别的商品或服务。拥有一项尚未提交使用证明的意图使用申请不足以表明第二来源。如果申请人证明，申请注册的商标用于识别一种第二来源，那么该物品就可以在联邦商标登记簿上注册。

See In re Paramount Pictures Corp., 213 USPQ 1111 (TTAB 1982), in which MORK & MINDY was held registrable for decals, because applicant had a television series of that name and had previously registered MORK & MINDY for various goods and services. The Board found that the *primary* significance of the term MORK & MINDY to a prospective purchaser of decals was to indicate the television series and the principal characters of the television series. *Id*. at 1112. The Board held that the case was controlled by its decision in *In re Olin Corp.*, 181 USPQ 182 (TTAB 1973) (stylized "O" design registrable for T-shirts, where applicant had previously registered the "O" design for skis), in which that Board had stated:

> It is a matter of common knowledge that T-shirts are "ornamented" with various insignia ... or ... various sayings such as "Swallow Your Leader." In that sense what is sought to be registered could be construed to be ornamental. If such ornamentation is without any meaning other than as mere ornamentation it is apparent that the ornamentation could not and would not serve as an indicia of source. Thus, to use our own example, "Swallow Your Leader" probably would not be considered as an indication of source.
>
> The "ornamentation" of a T-shirt can be of a special nature which inherently tells the purchasing public the source of the T-shirt, not the source of manufacture but the secondary source ...

181 USPQ at 182.

In *Paramount*, applying the test set forth in *Olin*, the Board found that "the paired names 'MORK & MINDY,' while certainly part of the ornamentation of the decal, also indicate source or origin in the proprietor of the Mork & Mindy television series in the same sense as the stylized 'O' in Olin."213 USPQ at 1113. The Board noted that "while purchasers may be accustomed to seeing characters' names and images as part of the ornamentation of decals, T-shirts and the like, they are also accustomed to seeing characters' names and images used as trade-

参见 *Paramount Pictures Corp*., 213 USPQ 1111（TTAB 1982），在该案中，"MORK & MINDY"被认为可以注册为贴纸商标，因为申请人拥有一部以此为名的电视剧，并且先前已经在很多商品及服务领域注册了"MORK & MINDY"商标。委员会判定，MORK & MINDY 一词对于潜在的贴纸购买者的主要意义在于标示该电视剧以及该剧的主要角色。*同前* 1112。委员会认为，在 *Olin Corp*., 181 USPQ 182（TTAB 1973）案中（固定的"O"图案可以为 T 恤衫注册，因为申请人先前已经为雪橇注册了该"O"图案），通过其裁决对情况进行了控制，在该案中委员会论述道：

> 尽人皆知，T 恤衫"装饰"有各种标记……或者……各种诸如"别理我烦着呢"之类的话语。在这种意义上，申请注册的物质可以被解释为是装饰性的。如果此类装饰物质不具有任何装饰以外的含义，那么很明显，这种装饰就不具有来源标示的功能。因此，借用上文我们自己的例子，"别理我烦着呢"可能就不会被认为是一种来源标示。
>
> 而 T 恤衫的"装饰"可能具有某种特殊的性质，自然地告诉购买公众该 T 恤衫的来源，不是生产来源而是第二来源……。

181 USPQ 182。

在 *Paramount* 案中，委员会适用了 *Olin* 案中确定的评判标准，认定："尽管这两个名字'MORK & MINDY'无疑是贴纸装饰的一部分，但同时也标示了其来源于与电视剧 MORK & MINDY 相同的所有者，就像 Olin 案中固定格式的'O'一样。"213 USPQ 1113。委员会解释道："尽管购买者可能习惯于将角色的名字及图案视为贴纸、T 恤衫或诸如此类的装饰的一部分，但他们同样也习惯于将角色的名字及图案用

marks to indicate source ..." *Id*. at 1114.

See also In re Watkins Glen International, Inc., 227 USPQ 727 (TTAB 1985) (stylized checkered flag design registrable for patches and clothing items, where applicant had previously registered WATKINS GLEN and checkered flag design (with "WATKINS GLEN" disclaimed) for services); *In re Expo '74*, 189 USPQ 48 (TTAB 1975) (EXPO '74 registrable for handkerchiefs and T-shirts, where applicant, organizer of the 1974 World's Fair, had previously registered EXPO '74 for goods and services).

A series of ornamental uses of the subject matter on various items will not establish that the subject matter functions as an indicator of secondary source; use as a trademark for the other goods or services must be shown. *See In re Astro-Gods Inc*., 223 USPQ 621 (TTAB 1984) (refusal to register ASTRO GODS and design for T-shirts affirmed despite applicant's ornamental use of the proposed mark on other goods and appearance of applicant's trade name "Astro Gods Inc." on the T-shirt as part of a copyright notice).

1202.03(d) Evidence of Distinctiveness

As noted above, even if a proposed mark is not inherently distinctive, it may nevertheless be registered on the Principal Register under §2(f), 15 U.S.C. §1052(f), if it becomes distinctive of the applicant's goods in commerce. *See* TMEP §§1212 *et seq*. regarding acquired distinctiveness.

1202.03(e) Ornamentation with Respect to Intent-to-Use Applications

Generally, the issue of ornamentation is tied to the use of the mark as evidenced by the specimens. Therefore, no ornamentation refusal will be issued in an intent-to-use application until the applicant has submitted specimens of use with either an amendment to allege use under §1(c), or a statement of use under §1(d), 15 U.S.C.§§1051(c) or (d).

作商标以标示来源……”*同前*1114。

另参见 Watkins Glen International, Inc., 227 USPQ 727 (TTAB 1985)(固定的各色旗帜图案被认为可以为缀片及衣料注册,因为申请人先前曾为服务注册了“WATKINS GLEN”和各色旗帜图案(后放弃了“WATKINS GLEN”));*Expo '74*, 189 USPQ 48 (TTAB 1975)(“EXPO '74”被认为可以为手帕和T恤衫注册,因为申请人系1974年世界博览会的组织者,先前已经为商品和服务注册了“EXPO '74”商标)。

将有关标的物在各种物品上作一系列的装饰性使用不能证明该标的物就是一种第二来源的商标;必须表明作为商标用于其他商品或服务。*参见 Astro-Gods Inc.*, 223 USPQ 621 (TTAB 1984)(维持拒绝注册“ASTRO GODS”及T恤衫图案的决定,尽管申请人将申请注册的商标用于装饰其他商品,并且其商号“Astro Gods Inc.”也作为一种著作权标记用于T恤衫)。

1202.03(d)　独特性的证据

如上所述,即使申请注册的商标不具有固有的独特性,根据 §2(f), 15 U.S.C. §1052(f)的规定也可以在联邦商标登记簿注册,只要它能够通过申请人进入商业流通的商品而获得独特性。有关获得性独特性的情况,*参见* TMEP §§1212 及以下。

1202.03(e)　有关意图使用申请的装饰

通常,装饰性问题通过样本的证据而同商标的使用联系在一起。因此,对于一项意图使用的申请,在申请人提交使用样本以及§1(c)所规定的证明使用修正书,或是§1(d)所规定的使用声明书之前,不会以装饰性为由拒绝注册,15 U.S.C.§1051(c)及(d)。

1202.03(f) Ornamentation: Case References

The following cases show the various ways in which ornamental matter was found not to function as a mark.

1202.03(f)(i) Slogans or Words Used on the Goods

Slogans or phrases used on items such as T-shirts and sweatshirts, jewelry, and ceramic plates have been refused registration as ornamentation that purchasers will perceive as conveying a message rather than indicating source of the goods. *See Damn I'm Good Inc. v. Sakowitz, Inc.*, 514 F.Supp.1357, 212 USPQ 684 (S.D. N.Y. 1981) ("DAMN I'M GOOD," inscribed in large letters on bracelets and used on hang tags affixed to the goods, found to be without any source-indicating significance); *In re Pro-Line Corp.*, 28 USPQ2d 1141 (TTAB 1993) (BLACKER THE COLLEGE SWEETER THE KNOWLEDGE primarily ornamental slogan that is not likely to be perceived as source indicator); *In re Dimitri's Inc.*, 9 USPQ2d 1666 (TTAB 1988) ("SUMO," as used in connection with stylized representations of sumo wrestlers on applicant's T-shirts and baseball-style caps); *In re Astro-Gods Inc.*, 223 USPQ 621, 624 (TTAB 1984) ("[T]he designation 'ASTRO GODS' and design is not likely to be perceived as anything other than part of the thematic whole of the ornamentation of applicant's shirts."); *In re Original Red Plate Co.*, 223 USPQ 836 (TTAB 1984) ("YOU ARE SPECIAL TODAY" for ceramic plates found to be without any source-indicating significance).

See also TMEP §1202.04 regarding informational matter.

1202.03(f)(ii) Designs Used on the Goods

See In re Soccer Sport Supply Co., Inc., 507 F.2d 1400, 184 USPQ 345 (C.C.P.A.1975) (evidence of record insufficient to establish distinctiveness of pentagon-

1202.03(f)　装饰性:参考案例

以下案例说明了装饰性物质被判定不能作为商标的各种方式。

1202.03(f)(i)　用在商品上的标语或语词

用在物品上的标语或短语,诸如用于T恤衫、运动衫、珠宝以及陶瓷碗碟等等,被判定不得注册,因为在购买者看来,这些装饰只是传达了某种信息而非标示商品的来源。*参见 Damn I'm Good Inc. v. Sakowitz, Inc.*, 514 F. Supp. 1357, 212 USPQ 684 (S. D. N. Y. 1981)(以大写字母刻在手镯上,以及用于商品保养说明上的"DAMN I'M GOOD"被判定不具有标示来源的意义);*Pro-Line Corp.*, 28 USPQ2d 1141 (TTAB 1993)("BLACKER THE COLLEGE SWEETER THE KNOWLEDGE"主要是一种装饰性的标语,不太可能被认知为来源标示);*Dimitri's Inc.*, 9 USPQ2d 1666 (TTAB 1988)("SUMO"同固定的相扑手形象相联系,用于申请人的T恤衫和棒球帽);*Astro-Gods Inc.*, 223 USPQ 621, 624 (TTAB 1984)("'ASTRO GODS'字样及图案只是申请人衬衫装饰的一部分,并没有表达另外的含义");*Original Red Plate Co.*, 223 USPQ 836 (TTAB 1984)(陶瓷碗碟上的"YOU ARE SPECIAL TODAY"被判定不具有标示来源的意义)。

有关信息性物质的情况,*另参见* TMEP §1202.04。

1202.03(f)(ii)　商品上使用的外观设计

参见 Soccer Sport Supply Co., Inc., 507 F.2d 1400, 184 USPQ 345 (C.C.P.A. 1975)(记录证据不足以证明分布在整个足球表面上的重复的五边形图案的独特

shaped repetitive design applied to the entire surface of soccer balls); *In re General Tire & Rubber Co.*, 404 F.2d 1396, 160 USPQ 415 (C.C.P.A. 1969) (three narrow white concentric rings of approximately equal width applied to the outer surface of a dark sidewall tire considered just a refinement of a general ornamental concept rather than a trademark); *In re David Crystal, Inc.*, 296 F.2d 771, 132 USPQ 1 (C.C.P.A. 1961) (two parallel colored bands at the top of the sock, the upper band red and the lower band blue, for men's ribbed socks); *In re Sunburst Products, Inc.*, 51 USPQ2d 1843 (TTAB 1999) (combination of matching color of watch bezel and watch band and contrasting colors of watch case and watch bezel for sports watches found to be nothing more than a mere refinement of a common or basic color scheme for sports watches and therefore would not immediately be recognized or perceived as a source indicator); *In re Villeroy & Boch S.A.R.L.*, 5 USPQ2d 1451 (TTAB 1987) (floral pattern design of morning glories and leaves for tableware not distinctive and not shown to be other than decorative pattern without trademark significance).

1202.03(f)(iii) Trade Dress on the Containers for the Goods

See In re J. Kinderman & Sons Inc., 46 USPQ2d 1253 (TTAB 1998) (design of container for Christmas decorations that resembles a wrapped Christmas gift not inherently distinctive); *In re F.C.F. Inc.*, 30 USPQ2d 1825 (TTAB 1994) (rose design used on cosmetics packaging is essentially ornamental or decorative background and does not function as mark); *In re Petersen Mfg. Co.*, 2 USPQ2d 2032 (TTAB 1987) (design representing the rear panel of a container for hand tools held unregistrable as merely ornamental, notwithstanding §2(f) claim).

1202.03(g) Ornamentation Cases and Acquired Distinctiveness

In the following cases, subject matter sought to be registered was found to have acquired distinctiveness as a trademark: *In re Jockey International, Inc.*, 192 USPQ 579 (TTAB 1976) (inverted Y design used on underwear found to have ac-

性）；*General Tire & Rubber Co.*，404 F.2d 1396，160 USPQ 415（C.C.P.A.1969）（黑色侧壁轮胎外表面的三个基本等宽的白色同心圆被认为只是对一种普通装饰概念的改进，而不是商标）；*David Crystal，Inc.*，296 F.2d 771，132 USPQ 1（C.C.P.A.1961）（男式棱纹袜上端上红下蓝的两条色带）；*Sunburst Products，Inc.*，51 USPQ2d 1843（TTAB 1999）（运动手表上嵌沟和表带相配的颜色与表壳和嵌沟的对比的颜色组合被认为只是对于运动手表普通和基本色彩的改进，因而无法立即被认知或感知为一种来源标示）；*Villeroy & Boch S.A.R.L.*，5 USPQ2d 1451（TTAB 1987）（用于餐具的牵牛花及叶子的图案设计被认为不具有独特性，只是一种装饰图案，而不具有商标意义）。

1202.03(f)(iii)　　商品容器的外观

参见 J.Kinderman & Sons Inc.，46 USPQ2d 1253（TTAB 1998）（类似于小包装圣诞礼物的圣诞装饰品容器设计不具有固有的独特性）；*F.C.F.Inc.*，30 USPQ2d 1825（TTAB 1994）（化妆盒上的玫瑰图案本质上属于装饰性背景，而不具商标的功能）；*In re Petersen Mfg.Co.*，2 USPQ2d 2032（TTAB 1987）（尽管系根据§2(f)提出主张，但工具箱上的后面板图案被认为只是装饰性的，因而不得注册）。

1202.03(g)　　涉及装饰性的案例和获得性独特性

在下列案例中，申请注册的标的物被判定具有获得性显著性，因而可以作为商标注册：*Jockey International，Inc.*，192 USPQ 579（TTAB 1976）（用于内衣上倒转的"Y"图案被认为具有获得性显著性，因为证据表明，该图案广泛地用于包装，以及使

quired distinctiveness, where evidence showed extensive use on packaging and in advertising in a manner calculated to draw the attention of prospective purchasers to the design and for them to look at the design as a badge of origin); *Anchor Hocking Glass Corp. v. Corning Glass Works*, 162 USPQ 288 (TTAB 1969) (blue cornflower design for coffee percolators and culinary vessels and utensils found to have acquired distinctiveness, where evidence showed extensive and prominent use of the design in advertising, use of the design on pins and aprons worn by sales promotion representatives in the course of their duties, and surveys and statements of purchasers indicating that they recognized the design as indicating origin in applicant).

1202.04 Informational Matter

Slogans that are considered to be merely informational in nature or to be common laudatory phrases or statements that would ordinarily be used in business or in the particular trade or industry are not registrable. *In re Volvo Cars of North America Inc.*, 46 USPQ2d 1455 (TTAB 1998) (DRIVE SAFELY perceived as an everyday, commonplace safety admonition that does not function as mark); *In re Manco Inc.*, 24 USPQ2d 1938, 1942 (TTAB 1992) (THINK GREEN and design found unregistrable for weatherstripping and paper products, the Board stating, "[R]ather than being regarded as an indicator of source, the term 'THINK GREEN' would be regarded simply as a slogan of environmental awareness and/or ecological consciousness ..."); *In re Southbrook Entertainment Corp.*, 8 USPQ2d 1166 (TTAB 1988) (HI-YO-SILVER, for videotapes and cassettes, held to be a well known expression closely linked to a character, but did not function as a trademark for the goods); *In re Remington Products Inc.*, 3 USPQ2d 1714 (TTAB 1987) (PROUDLY MADE IN USA, for electric shavers, held incapable of functioning as a mark, notwithstanding use of letters "TM" in connection with prominent display of slogan on packages for the goods and claim of acquired distinctiveness); *In re Tilcon Warren, Inc.*, 221 USPQ 86 (TTAB 1984) (WATCH THAT CHILD held not to function as a mark for construction material notwithstanding

用吸引潜在购买者注意的广告宣传方式，使得购买者将该图案视为一种来源的商标)；*Anchor Hocking Glass Corp. v. Corning Glass Works*，162 USPQ 288 (TTAB 1969)(用于咖啡过滤器以及厨房用具的矢车菊图案被认为具有获得性独特性，因为证据显示，在广告中广泛、显著地使用该图案，以及在推销员的别针和围裙上使用该图案，以及购买者的调查和陈述表明他们认为该图案显示了申请人的来源)。

1202.04　　信息性物质

被认为仅具有信息性的标语，或者通常用于商业或特定行业中的普通赞美之词或陈述不得注册。*Volvo Cars of North America Inc.*，46 USPQ2d 1455 (TTAB 1998)(“安全驾驶”(DRIVE SAFELY)只是一种日常、普通的安全警示，不能作为商标)；*Manco Inc.*，24 USPQ2d 1938，1942 (TTAB 1992)(“绿色思考”(THINK GREEN)及图案被判定不得为挡风雨条和纸制品注册，委员会认为：“‘绿色思考’一词仅被认为是一种环境保护意识和/或生态意识的口号，而不是一种来源标示……”)；*Southbrook Entertainment Corp.*，8 USPQ2d 1166 (TTAB 1988)(用于录像带和磁带的“HI-YO-SILVER”被认为是同特征紧密联系的著名短语，但是不能作为商品的商标)；*Remington Products Inc.*，3 USPQ2d 1714 (TTAB 1987)(用于电动剃须刀的“PROUDLY MADE IN USA”被认为不能作为商标，尽管在商品包装上明显使用该标语时同“TM”字母相联系，并且主张具有获得性独特性)；*Tilcon Warren, Inc.*，221 USPQ 86 (TTAB 1984)(尽管已经长期使用，“WATCH THAT CHILD”仍然被认为不能用作建材商标，因为其仅仅用于运输该商品车辆的保险杠上)；*Schwauss*，

long use, where the only use was on the bumpers of construction vehicles in which the goods were transported); *In re Schwauss*, 217 USPQ 361 (TTAB 1983) (FRAGILE used on labels and bumper stickers does not function as a mark).

See TMEP §1301.02(a) regarding informational matter that does not function as a service mark, and TMEP §1202.03(f)(i) regarding slogans used on goods.

A slogan can function as a trademark if it is not merely descriptive or informational. *See e.g., Roux Laboratories, Inc. v. Clairol Inc.*, 427 F.2d 823, 166 USPQ 34 (C.C.P.A.1970) (affirming the Board's dismissal of an opposition to the registration of HAIR COLOR SO NATURAL ONLY HER HAIRDRESSER KNOWS FOR SURE for a hair coloring preparation); *In re The Hallicrafters Co.*, 153 USPQ 376 (TTAB 1967) (QUALITY THROUGH CRAFTSMANSHIP found registrable for radio equipment). *See* TMEP §1202.03(f)(i) regarding ornamental slogans used on goods.

1202.05 Color as a Mark

Color marks are marks that consist *solely* of one or more colors used on particular objects. For marks used in connection with goods, the color may be used on the entire surface of the goods, on a portion of the goods, or on all or part of the packaging for the goods. For example, a color trademark might consist of purple used on a salad bowl, or pink used on the handle of a shovel, or a blue background and a pink circle used on all or part of a product package. *See Qualitex Co. v. Jacobson Products Co., Inc.*, 514 U.S. 159, 34 USPQ2d 1161 (1995) (green-gold used on dry cleaning press pads held to be a protectible trademark, where the color had acquired secondary meaning); *In re Owens-Corning Fiberglas Corp.*, 774 F.2d 1116, 227 USPQ 417 (Fed. Cir. 1985) (the color pink as applied to fibrous glass residential insulation registrable where the evidence showed the color had acquired secondary meaning). Similarly, service marks may consist of color used on all or part of materials used in the advertising and rendering of the services.

217 USPQ 361 (TTAB 1983)(用于标签和保险杠上的"易碎"(FRAGILE)不具有商标功能)。

有关不能用作商标的信息性物质的情况,*参见* TMEP §1301.02(a);有关用在商品上的标语,*参见* TMEP §1202.03(f)(i)。

如果一种标语不仅仅是描述性或信息性的,那么就可以作为商标。*参见 Roux Laboratories, Inc. v. Clairol Inc.*, 427 F.2d 823, 166 USPQ 34 (C.C.P.A.1970)(维持委员会驳回一项针对"自然色泽,难辨真假"(HAIR COLOR SO NATURAL ONLY HER HAIRDRESSER KNOWS FOR SURE)染发剂注册的反对意见);*The Hallicrafters Co.*, 153 USPQ 376 (TTAB 1967)("精工制作"(QUALITY THROUGH CRAFTSMANSHIP)被判定可以为无线电设备注册)。有关用于商品的装饰性标语的情况,*参见* TMEP §1202.03(f)(i)。

1202.05 用作商标的色彩

色彩商标是用于特定物的由一种或一种以上色彩*单独*构成的商标。对于同商品联系使用的商标而言,该色彩可以用于商品全体表面,或者商品的某一部分,或者是商品包装的全部或部分。例如,一种色彩商标可以由用于色拉盆的紫色,或是铲柄的粉色,或者产品包装的蓝色底色或粉色圆圈构成。*参见 Qualitex Co. v. Jacobson Products Co., Inc.*, 514 U.S.159, 34 USPQ2d 1161 (1995)(干洗衬垫的金－绿间色被认为是可以受到保护的商标,因为该色彩具有第二含义);*Owens-Corning Fiberglas Corp.*, 774 F.2d 1116, 227 USPQ 417 (Fed. Cir. 1985)(用于家用绝缘玻璃纤维的粉色被判定可以注册,因为证据表明该色彩具有第二含义)。类似地,服务提供过程中以及广告中所使用材料的全部或部分色彩也可以构成服务商标。

The registrability of a color mark depends on the manner in which the proposed mark is used. *In re Owens-Corning*, 227 USPQ at 419, 774 F. 2d at 1120. A color(s) takes on the characteristics of the object or surface to which it is applied, and the commercial impression of a color will change accordingly. *See In re Thrifty, Inc.*, 274 F.3d 1349, 61 USPQ2d 1121, 1124 (Fed. Cir. 2001) ("a word mark retains its same appearance when used on different objects, but color is not immediately distinguishable as a service mark when used in similar circumstances").

Color marks are never inherently distinctive, and cannot be registered on the Principal Register without a showing of acquired distinctiveness under §2(f) of the Trademark Act, 15 U.S.C. §1052(f). *Wal-Mart Stores, Inc. v. Samara Brothers, Inc.*, 529 U. S. 205, 211-212, 54 USPQ2d 1065, 1068 (2000). *See* TMEP §1202.05(a) and cases cited therein.

Color, whether a single overall color or multiple colors applied in a specific and arbitrary fashion, is usually perceived as an ornamental feature of the goods or services. *In re Owens-Corning*, 227 USPQ at 422, 774 F.2d at 1124; *In re Hudson News Co.*, 39 USPQ2d 1915, 1923 (TTAB 1996), *aff'd per curiam*, 114 F. 3d 1207 (Fed. Cir. 1997) ("blue motif" used in retail stores would likely be perceived by prospective purchasers as "nothing more than interior decoration" that "could be found in any number of retail establishments. Undoubtedly such features are usually perceived as interior decoration or ornamentation"). However, color can function as a mark if it is used in the manner of a trademark/service mark and if it is perceived by the purchasing public to identify and distinguish the goods or services on or in connection with which it is used and to indicate their source. The United States Supreme Court has held that color alone may sometimes meet the basic legal requirements for a trademark. When it does, there is no rule that prevents color from serving as a mark. *Qualitex*, 514 U. S. at 161, 34 USPQ2d at 1162. If a color is not functional and is shown to have acquired distinctiveness on or in connection with the applicant's goods or services, it is registrable as a mark.

色彩商标的注册性取决于申请注册的商标以何种方式使用。见 *Owens-Corning*, 227 USPQ 419, 774 F.2d 1120。色彩表现了其所使用对象或表面的特性,而某种色彩的商业印象会相应地发生变化。*参见 Thrifty, Inc.*, 274 F.3d 1349, 61 USPQ2d 1121, 1124 (Fed. Cir. 2001)("一个词语商标用于不同的对象时仍然维持同样的表现,而当色彩作为服务商标用于类似的情况时则不能立即作出区分")。

色彩商标不具有固有的独特性,并且如果不显示《商标法》§2(f),15 U.S.C. §1052(f)所规定的获得性显著性,就不能在联邦商标登记簿上注册。见 *Wal-Mart Stores, Inc. v. Samara Brothers, Inc.*, 529 U.S. 205, 211, 54 USPQ2d 1065, 1068 (2000)。*参见* TMEP §1202.05(a)以及所引用的判例。

色彩,无论是单一的色彩还是多种色彩,如果以一种特定和任意的方式使用,通常被认为是商品或服务的一种装饰性外观特征。*Owens-Corning*, 227 USPQ 422, 774 F.2d 1124; *Hudson News Co.*, 39 USPQ2d 1915, 1923 (TTAB 1996), *aff'd per curiam*, 114 F.3d 1207 (Fed. Cir. 1997)(零售商店所使用的"蓝色图形"给潜在的购买者造成的感觉"只是内部装饰","可以在任何零售商协会成员那里看到,毫无疑问,此类外观特征通常会造成内部装饰的感觉")。不过,如果以商标/服务商标的方式使用色彩,而且,如果购买公众以此识别该商品和服务并标示其来源,该色彩就能够具备商标的功能。美国联邦最高法院也已经裁决,单独的色彩有时也可以符合商标的基本法律要求。如果是这样,则并不存在不准许色彩注册为商标的规定。*Qualitex*, 514 U.S. 161, 34 USPQ2d 1162。如果色彩不具有功能性,并且表明,已经在申请人的商品或服务上或通过与之相联系而具有获得性独特性,则可作为商标注册。

Functional color marks are not registrable. *See* TMEP §1202.05(b) and cases cited therein.

1202.05(a) Color Marks Never Inherently Distinctive

Color marks are never inherently distinctive. *Wal-Mart Stores, Inc. v. Samara Brothers, Inc.*, 529 U.S. 205, 211-212, 54 USPQ2d 1065, 1068 (2000) (citing *Qualitex Co. v. Jacobson Products Co., Inc.*, 514 U.S. 159, 162-163, 34 USPQ2d 1161, 1162-1163 (1995)); *In re Thrifty, Inc.*, 274 F.3d 1349, 61 USPQ2d 1121, 1124 (Fed. Cir. 2001). Therefore, the examining attorney must refuse to register a color mark on the Principal Register unless the applicant establishes that the mark has acquired distinctiveness under §2(f). The examining attorney must issue this refusal in *all* color mark applications where acquired distinctiveness has not been shown, regardless of the filing basis of the application. The ground for refusal is that the color is not inherently distinctive and thus does not function as a trademark under §§1, 2 and 45, or does not function as a service mark under §§1, 3 and 45.

If the proposed color mark is not functional, it may be registrable on the Principal Register if it is shown to have acquired distinctiveness under §2(f). If it is not distinctive, it is registrable only on the Supplemental Register. *See In re Hudson News Co.*, 39 USPQ2d 1915 (TTAB 1996), *aff'd per curiam*, 114 F.3d 1207 (Fed. Cir. 1997) ("blue motif" applied to retail store services not registrable on Principal Register without resort to Section 2(f)); *Edward Weck Inc. v. IM Inc.*, 17 USPQ2d 1142 (TTAB 1990) (the color green, as uniformly applied to medical instruments, not barred from registration on the basis of functionality; however, evidence failed to establish that the color had become distinctive of the goods); *In re Deere & Co.*, 7 USPQ2d 1401 (TTAB 1988) (the colors green and yellow, as applied to body and wheels of machines, respectively, not barred from registration on the basis of functionality; evidence held to establish that the colors had become distinctive of the goods).

功能性的色彩商标不得注册。参见 TMEP §1202.05(b)以及所引用的判例。

1202.05(a) 色彩商标绝不具有固有的独特性

色彩商标绝不具有固有的独特性。见 *Wal-Mart Stores, Inc. v. Samara Brothers, Inc.*, 529 U.S.205, 211-212, 54 USPQ2d 1065, 1068 (2000)(引用了 *Qualitex Co. v. Jacobson Products Co., Inc.*, 514 U.S. 159, 162-163, 34 USPQ2d 1161, 1162-1163 (1995)); *Thrifty, Inc.*, 274 F.3d 1349, 61 USPQ2d 1121, 1124 (Fed. Cir. 2001)。因此,除非申请人证明色彩商标具有 §2(f)规定的获得性显著性,否则审查员必须拒绝在联邦商标登记簿注册该商标。如果未显示出获得性显著性,不管基于何种理由提出申请,审查员都必须拒绝*一切*色彩商标的注册申请。拒绝的理由在于,色彩不具有固有的独特性,因此不具有 §§1, 2 和 45 所规定的商标功能,也不具有 §§1, 3 和 45 所规定的服务商标功能。

如果申请注册的色彩商标不具有功能性,那么一旦证明其具有 §2(f)规定的获得性独特性,就可以在联邦商标登记簿上注册。如果不具有独特性,就只能在联邦商标补充登记册上注册。参见 *Hudson News Co.*, 39 USPQ2d 1915 (TTAB 1996), *aff'd per curiam*, 114 F.3d 1207 (Fed. Cir. 1997)(零售商店服务所使用的"蓝色图案"如不适用 Section 2(f)就不能在联邦商标登记簿上注册); *Edward Weck Inc. v. IM Inc.*, 17 USPQ2d 1142 (TTAB 1990)(均匀涂在医疗器具上的绿色并非由于功能性,而是因为未能证明其成为商品所独有的特性而不能获得注册); *Deere & Co.*, 7 USPQ2d 1401 (TTAB 1988)(分别涂在机器机体和轮机的绿色和黄色,并未因为功能性而被拒绝注册;证据表明这些色彩成为商品所独有的特性)。

The burden of proving that a color mark has acquired distinctiveness is substantial. *See In re Owens-Corning Fiberglas Corp.*, 774 F.2d 1116, 227 USPQ 417 (Fed. Cir. 1985) (the color pink, as uniformly applied to fibrous glass residential insulation, shown to have acquired distinctiveness as a trademark for the goods); *In re Benetton Group S.p.A.*, 48 USPQ2d 1214 (TTAB 1998) (evidence insufficient to establish that green rectangular background design had acquired distinctiveness as applied to clothing and footwear); *In re American Home Products Corp.*, 226 USPQ 327 (TTAB 1985) (tri-colored, three-dimensional circular-shaped design found to have become distinctive of analgesic and muscle relaxant tablets); *In re Star Pharmaceuticals, Inc.*, 225 USPQ 209 (TTAB 1985) (evidence found insufficient to establish that two-colored drug capsules and multi-colored seeds or granules contained therein had become distinctive of methyltestosterone).

As noted above, the commercial impression of a color may change depending on the object to which it is applied. Therefore, evidence submitted to demonstrate acquired distinctiveness of a color may show consumer recognition with respect to certain objects, but not for other objects. *See In re Thrifty, Inc.*, 61 USPQ2d at 1124. *Cf. Qualitex*, 514 U.S. at 163, 34 USPQ2d at 1162-1163 ("The imaginary word 'Suntost,' or the words 'Suntost Marmalade,' on a jar of orange jam immediately would signal a brand or a product 'source'; the jam's orange color does not do so. But, over time, customers may come to treat a particular color on a product or its packaging (say, a color that in context seems unusual, such as pink on a firm's insulating material or red on the head of a large industrial bolt) as signifying a brand. And, if so, that color would have come to identify and distinguish the goods — *i.e.*, 'to indicate' their 'source ...'").

1202.05(b) Functional Color Marks Not Registrable

A color mark is not registrable on the Principal Register under §2(f), or the Supplemental Register, if the color is functional. *Brunswick Corp. v. British Seagull Ltd.*, 35 F. 3d 1527, 32 USPQ2d 1120 (Fed. Cir. 1994), *cert. denied*, 514 U.S.

证明色彩商标是否具有获得性独特性的工作量相当大。参见 *Owens-Corning Fiberglas Corp.*，774 F.2d 1116，227 USPQ 417（Fed. Cir. 1985）（均匀涂在家用绝缘玻璃纤维上的粉色被判定具有作为商品的商标的独特性）；*Benetton Group S.p.A.*，48 USPQ2d 1214（TTAB 1998）（没有充分证据证明，服装和鞋子上的绿色矩形背景设计具有获得性显著性）；*American Home Products Corp.*，226 USPQ 327（TTAB 1985）（止痛药和肌肉弛缓药的三色、立体圆形设计被判定具有独特性）；*Star Pharmaceuticals, Inc.*，225 USPQ 209（TTAB 1985）（没用充分证据证明，甲基睾丸素的二色胶囊以及内部装载的各色颗粒具有独特性）。

如上所述，根据所适用对象的不同，色彩的商业印象也可能变化。因此，所提交的证明一种色彩的获得性独特性的证据可能显示，消费者可能对某些对象存在这种认知，但对其他对象则不存在。*参见 Thrifty, Inc.*，61 USPQ2d 1124。*比较 Qualitex*，514 U.S.163，34 USPQ2d 162－1163（"橘子果酱罐上的虚构词汇'Suntost'或'Suntost Marmalade'能够立即反映出一种品牌或产品'来源'；而果酱的橙色则不能。但是，随着时间流逝，消费者可能会逐渐将某种特定的产品或包装的色彩（即在其环境中不同寻常的色彩，如某公司绝缘材料上的粉色，或大号工业螺栓顶部的红色）认作一种品牌。如果是这样，该色彩就可以识别和区分商品——亦即，'标示'其'来源……'"）。

1202.05(b) 功能性色彩商标不得注册

如果一种色彩具有功能性，那么根据§2(f)的规定，该色彩商标就不得在联邦商标登记簿及补充登记簿注册。见 *Brunswick Corp. v. British Seagull Ltd.*，35 F.3d 1527，32 USPQ2d 1120（Fed. Cir. 1994），*cert. denied*，514 U.S.1050 (1995)；

1050 (1995); *In re Owens-Corning Fiberglas Corp.*, 774 F.2d 1116, 227 USPQ 417 (Fed. Cir. 1985). A color may be functional if it yields a utilitarian or functional advantage, for example, yellow or orange for safety signs. *Brunswick Corp. v. British Seagull, supra* (holding the color black functional for outboard motors because while the color did not provide utilitarian advantages in terms of making the engines work better, it nevertheless provided recognizable competitive advantages in terms of being compatible with a wide variety of boat colors and making the engines appear smaller); *In re Ferris Corporation*, 59 USPQ2d 1587 (TTAB 2000) (color pink used on surgical wound dressings is functional because the actual color of the goods closely resembles Caucasian human skin); *In re Orange Communications, Inc.*, 41 USPQ2d 1036 (TTAB 1996) (colors yellow and orange held to be functional for public telephones and telephone booths, since they are more visible under all lighting conditions in the event of an emergency); *In re Howard S. Leight & Associates Inc.*, 39 USPQ2d 1058 (TTAB 1996) (color coral held to be functional for earplugs, because it is more visible during safety checks). A color may also be functional if it is more economical to manufacture or use. For example, a color may be a natural by-product of the manufacturing process for the goods. In such a case, appropriation of the color by a single party would place others at a competitive disadvantage by requiring them to alter the manufacturing process.

See also In re Pollak Steel Co., 314 F. 2d 566, 136 USPQ 651 (C. C. P. A. 1963) (reflective color on fence found to be functional); *R. L. Winston Rod Co. v. Sage Mfg. Co.*, 838 F. Supp. 1396, 29 USPQ2d 1779 (D. Mont. 1993) (color green used on graphite fishing rods found to be functional); *Russell Harrington Cutlery Inc. v. Zivi Hercules Inc.*, 25 USPQ2d 1965 (D. Mass. 1992) (color white used on cutlery handles found to be functional); *Kasco Corp. v. Southern Saw Service Inc.*, 27 USPQ2d 1501 (TTAB 1993) (color green used as wrapper for saw blades is functional when the color is one of the six colors used in a color-coding system to identify the type of blade).

The doctrine of "aesthetic functionality" may apply in some cases where the evi-

Owens-Corning Fiberglas Corp., 774 F.2d 1116, 227 USPQ 417 (Fed. Cir. 1985)。色彩可能具有功能性,只要该色彩产生了实用或功能性的优点,例如,黄色或橙色用作警示商标。*参见 Brunswick Corp. v. British Seagull*,*案卷号同前*(认为外置马达的黑色具备功能性,因为尽管其对于引擎的机械工作并没有实际的效果,但是却带来了可以确认的竞争优势——即同各种船只颜色更易于协调,并且减小了引擎的外观尺寸);*Ferris Corporation*, 59 USPQ2d 1587 (TTAB 2000)(外科用绷带的粉色具有功能性,因为该商品色彩同高加索人种的皮肤颜色非常相近);*Orange Communications, Inc*., 41 USPQ2d 1036 (TTAB 1996)(公用电话及电话亭的黄色和橙色被认为具有功能性,因为一旦紧急情况发生,这些颜色在任何灯光条件下都更加醒目);*Howard S. Leight & Associates Inc*., 39 USPQ2d 1058 (TTAB 1996)(耳塞的珊瑚色被认定具有功能性,因为它在安检时更醒目)。一种色彩如果对于制造和使用而言更经济,也可以被认为具有功能性。例如,某种色彩可能是商品制造过程的自然副产品。在这样的案件中,当事人通过将色彩用于改变生产制造过程,从而将他方置于一种竞争劣势的地位。

另参见 Pollak Steel Co., 314 F.2d 566, 136 USPQ 651 (C.C.P.A. 1963)(栅栏上的反射色彩被认为具有功能性);*R. L. Winston Rod Co. v. Sage Mfg. Co*., 838 F. Supp. 1396, 29 USPQ2d 1779 (D. Mont. 1993)(石墨钓竿的绿色被认为具有功能性);*Russell Harrington Cutlery Inc. v. Zivi Hercules Inc*., 25 USPQ2d 1965 (D. Mass. 1992)(餐具手柄的白色被认为具有功能性);*Kasco Corp. v. Southern Saw Service Inc*., 27 USPQ2d 1501 (TTAB 1993)(由于一种色彩识别系统使用了六种颜色以识别锯条的型号,锯条包装纸的绿色被认为具有功能性)。

如果有证据表明,涉案色彩带来了特定的竞争优势,即使不能必然归为纯粹

dence indicates that the color at issue provides specific competitive advantages that, while not necessarily categorized as purely "utilitarian" in nature, nevertheless dictate that the color remain in the public domain. *Brunswick Corp. v. British Seagull, supra*. *See also TrafFix Devices, Inc. v. Marketing Displays, Inc.*, 532 U.S. 23, 58 USPQ2d 1001, 1006 (2001) (in which the Supreme Court discussed aesthetic functionality, distinguishing *Qualitex*, *supra*, as a case where "aesthetic functionality was the central question ..."). *See* TMEP §1202.02(a)(iii)(C) regarding the "aesthetic functionality" doctrine.

1202.05(c) Color as a Separable Element [R-1]

As with all trademarks, a color mark may contain only those elements that make a separable commercial impression. *See* TMEP §807.14(b). Accordingly, an applicant may not seek to register the color of the wording or design apart from the words or designs themselves if the color does not create a separate commercial impression. For example, an applicant may not register the color of words that make up its mark apart from the words themselves, if the color does not create a separate commercial impression apart from the words. However, the applicant may register the color of the background material on which the words or design appear apart from the words or design. *See* TMEP §1202.11.

The commercial impression of a color may change depending on the object to which it is applied. *In re Thrifty, Inc.*, 274 F.3d 1349, 61 USPQ2d 1121, 1124 (Fed. Cir. 2001); *In re Hayes*, 62 USPQ2d 1443 (TTAB 2002). An application seeking registration of color in the abstract, without considering the manner or context in which the color is used, would be contrary to law and public policy because it would result in an unlimited number of marks being claimed in a single application. *Cf. In re International Flavors & Fragrances Inc.*, 183 F.3d 1361, 1368, 51 USPQ2d 1513, 1517-18 (Fed. Cir. 1999) (mark with changeable or "phantom" element unregistrable because it would "encompass too many combinations and permutations to make a thorough and effective search possible," and, therefore,

"实用性",也表明了该色彩仍应保持在公共领域中,在这种情况下,可以适用"美学功能性"原则。*Brunswick Corp. v. British Seagull*,*案卷号同前*。*另参见 TrafFix Devices, Inc. v. Marketing Displays, Inc.*, 532 U.S. 23, 58 USPQ2d 1001, 1006 (2001)(在该案中,最高法院讨论了美学功能性,同 *Qualitex* 案作了区分,认为在该案中"美学功能性是中心问题……")。有关"美学功能性"原则,*参见* TMEP §1202.02(a)(iii)(C)。

1202.05(c) 作为独立因素的色彩 [R-1]

与所有的商标一样,一项色彩商标也可能只包含那些造成一种独立商业印象的因素。*参见* TMEP §807.14(b)。据此,如果色彩没有创造出一种独立的商业印象,申请人就不能将语词或图案的色彩分割开来单独注册。例如,如果色彩没有创造出独立于语词的商业印象,申请人就不能将构成商标的语词的颜色同语词本身分割开来进行注册。不过,申请人可以将语词及图案附着于其上的背景材料的颜色同该语词及图案分割开来独立注册。*参见* TMEP §1202.11。

根据所适用对象的不同,色彩的商业印象也可能随之变化。见 *Thrifty, Inc.*, 274 F.3d 1349, 61 USPQ2d 1121, 1124 (Fed. Cir. 2001); *Hayes*, 62 USPQ2d 1443 (TTAB 2002)。不考虑色彩使用的方式及环境,申请注册一种抽象的色彩,是不符合法律和公共政策的,因为这会导致在一项申请中对无数种商标提出主张。*比较 International Flavors & Fragrances Inc.*, 183 F.3d 1361, 1368, 51 USPQ2d 1513, 1517-18 (Fed. Cir. 1999)(含有可变或"虚幻"元素的商标不得注册,因为这将"包含过多的排列组合,从而难以进行完整有效的查询",并且,因此而无法使公众充分注

would not provide adequate notice to the public); *In re Upper Deck Co*., 59 USPQ2d 1688 (TTAB 2001) (hologram used on trading cards in varying shapes, sizes, contents and positions constitutes more than one "device" as contemplated by §45 of the Trademark Act). Only one mark can be registered in a single application. TMEP §807.04.

1202.05(d) Drawings of Color Marks Required

All marks, other than sound and scent marks, require a drawing. TMEP §807. An application for a color mark that is filed without a drawing will be denied a filing date. 37 C. F. R. §2.21(a)(3). Similarly, an application for a color mark with a proposed drawing page that states "no drawing" or sets forth only a written description of the mark will be denied a filing date. The drawing provides notice of the nature of the mark sought to be registered. Only marks that are not capable of representation in a drawing, such as sound or scent marks, are excluded from the requirement for a drawing. Color marks are visual, and should be depicted in a black and white drawing, accompanied by a detailed written description of the color and how it is used. 37 C. F. R. §2.52(a)(2)(v); TMEP §§807.09(a) and (c).

1202.05(d)(i) Drawings of Color Marks in Trademark Applications

In most cases, the drawing will consist of a representation of the product or product package. The drawing of the mark must be a substantially exact representation of the mark as used or intended to be used on the goods. 37 C. F. R. §2.51. A depiction of the object on which the color is used is needed to meet this requirement.

The object depicted on the drawing should appear in broken lines. The broken lines inform the viewer where and how color is used on the product or package, while at the same time making it clear that the shape of the product, or the shape

意)；*Upper Deck Co*., 59 USPQ2d 1688 (TTAB 2001)(以各种不同的形状、大小、内容和位置用于系列卡片的全息图构成了一种以上《商标法》§45 所规定的"图案设计")。一项申请只能注册一个商标。TMEP §807.04。

1202.05(d)　色彩商标所需的附图

除了声音和气味商标，所有的商标都要求有附图。TMEP §807。色彩商标的申请书如无附图将被拒绝接受。37 C.F.R.§2.21(a)(3)。相似地，如果色彩商标申请书的附图页称"无图"，或者仅有该商标的书面说明，也将被拒绝接受。附图表明了申请注册商标的性质。只有无法以图来表示的商标，诸如声音及气味商标，可以不要求提交附图。色彩商标是可视的，应当以黑白图表示，同时附有关于该色彩如何使用的详细说明。37 C.F.R.§2.52(a)(2)(v)；TMEP §§807.09(a)和(c)。

1202.05(d)(i)　商标申请书中色彩商标的附图

在大多数情况下，附图包含产品或产品包装的图像。商标的图画必须对用于或意图用于商品的商标作出充分准确的表示。37 C.F.R.§2.51。还必须有对于使用该色彩的对象物的描述。

该物在图中以虚线表示。虚线须表示出色彩在产品或包装的何处如何使用，同

of the package, is not claimed as part of the mark. 37 C.F.R. §2.52(a)(2)(ii); TMEP §807.10. In the absence of a broken-line drawing, the Office will assume that the mark is a composite mark consisting of the product shape, or the packaging shape, in a particular color.

Color used on multiple goods

If the mark is used on multiple goods, the drawing required will depend on the nature of the goods. The drawing of the mark must be a substantially exact representation of the mark as used or intended to be used on the goods. 37 C.F.R. §2.51. A drawing consisting of a depiction of only one of the goods will be accepted if the goods, or the portions of the goods on which color appears, are similar in form and function so that a depiction of only one of the products is still a substantially exact representation of the mark as used on all of the products. For example, if the mark is the color purple used on refrigerators and freezers, a drawing of a freezer (in broken lines, with a description of the mark indicating the color purple is used on the mark) would be sufficient. Or, if the mark is the color pink used on the handles of rakes, shovels and hoes, a drawing of any of those items (in dotted lines with a description of the mark stating the handle is pink) would be sufficient. Or, if the mark consists of packaging for various food items that is always blue with a pink circle, a drawing of any one of the packages (in dotted lines with a description of the colors) would be sufficient.

If the mark is used on multiple goods that are dissimilar or unrelated, or if color is used in different ways on different goods, so that a depiction of one of the goods is not a substantially exact representation of the mark as used on all of the goods (for example, the color purple used on microscopes and vending machines), a separate application must be submitted for each item.

Color used on liquids or powders

Sometimes a color mark consists of color(s) used on liquids or powders. For example, the mark might consist of fuchsia body oil or red, white and blue granular

时必须解释未作为商标一部分加以主张的产品或包装的形状。37 C.F.R.§2.52(a)(2)(ii)；TMEP §807.10。如无虚线图，商标局将推定该商标系由特定颜色的产品形状或包装形状构成的组合商标。

用于多种商品的色彩

如果该商标用于多种商品，则附图将取决于这项商品的性质。商标的图画必须与用于或意图用于商品的商标完全一致。37 C.F.R.§2.51。如果使用该色彩的各商品或商品各部分在形式和功能上相似，因此一种商品的图画就可以对用于所有商品的商标作出充分准确的表示，那么也可以接受只由一种商品图画构成的附图。例如，如果该商标是用于各种冰箱及冰柜的紫色，那么一幅冰箱的图(以虚线表示，附有表明紫色如何用于该商标的说明)就足够了。或者，如果该商标是用于耙、铲及锄柄的粉色，那么只要有这些工具中任何一种的图画(虚线表示，附有柄部为粉色的说明)就可以了。或者，如果该商标由各种食品包装图案组成，均为带有粉色圆圈的蓝色，那么其中一种包装的图画(虚线表示，附有对色彩的说明)就足够了。

如果该商标用于各种不相似或不相关的商品，或在不同商品中色彩的使用方式不同，那么其中一种商品的图画就不足以充分准确地表示使用该商标的所有商品(例如，用于显微镜和自动贩售机的紫色)，于是就必须为各物件分别提交申请书。

液体或粉末的颜色

有时，一项色彩商标由涂在液体或粉末上的色彩构成。例如，商标可以由润肤油紫红色或红色、颗粒状洗衣粉的白和蓝色组成。在这种情况下，附图的性质取决于液

washing machine detergent. In these cases, the nature of the drawing will depend on the manner of use of the liquid or powder. If the liquid or powder is visible through the product package, then the drawing should consist of the shape of the product package in broken lines, with the description of the mark identifying the color of the liquid or powder.

1202.05(d)(ii) Drawings of Color Marks in Service Mark Applications

It is difficult to anticipate all of the issues that may arise, because there are a myriad of ways that color can be used in connection with services. However, the following general guidelines will be used to determine the sufficiency of drawings in these cases:

- The purpose of a drawing is to provide notice to the public of the nature of the mark. As with color used on goods, a color service mark does not consist of color in the abstract. Rather, the mark consists of color used in a particular manner, and the context in which the color is used is critical to provide notice of the nature of the mark sought to be registered. Therefore, as with color marks used on goods, a drawing, supplemented with a written description, is required.

- The drawing must display the manner in which the mark is used in connection with the services. As with any application, only one mark can be registered in a single application. TMEP §807.04. The mark depicted on the drawing must, as used on the specimens, make a separate and distinct commercial impression to be considered one mark. *See In re Thrifty, Inc.*, 274 F.3d 1349, 61 USPQ2d 1121 (Fed. Cir. 2001); *In re Chemical Dynamics Inc.*, 839 F.2d 1569, 5 USPQ2d 1828 (Fed. Cir. 1988). *See* TMEP §1202.05(a) regarding color as a separable element.

- If color is used in a variety of ways, but in a setting that makes a single commercial impression, such as a retail outlet with various color fea-

体或粉末的使用方式。如果通过产品包装可以看到这种液体或粉末，那么附图就应当包含着种产品包装的形状，以虚线表示，并附有对识别该液体或粉末颜色的商标的说明。

1202.05(d)(ii)　服务商标申请书中色彩商标的附图

很难预期所有可能发生的问题，因为色彩有无数种方式可以同服务联系起来使用。不过，在判断不同情况下附图是否充分时，可以适用下列一般指导原则：

- 附图的目的在于向公众告知该商标的性质。由于色彩是用于商品的，因此一种色彩服务商标不能包含抽象物的色彩。此外，构成商标的色彩进行实用的特定方式，及其使用的情景环境，对于提示该申请注册商标的性质非常重要。因而，除了用于商品的色彩商标以外，还必须提供附有书面说明的附图。

- 附图必须展示商标是以何种方式与服务相关地使用。无论何种申请，一项申请只能注册一个商标。TMEP §807.04。样本上使用的商标，其附图必须表明能够造成一种独立和独特的商业印象，如此才能被认为是一种商标。*参见* *Thrifty, Inc.*, 274 F.3d 1349, 61 USPQ2d 1121 (Fed. Cir. 2001)；*Chemical Dynamics Inc.*, 839 F.2d 1569, 5 USPQ2d 1828 (Fed. Cir. 1988)。作为独立因素的色彩的有关情况，*参见* TMEP §1202.05(a)。

- 如果色彩通过各种方式进行使用，但通过某种组合造成了一种独立的商业印象，比如使用各种颜色的零售商店，就必须提交该种组合的虚线图，

tures, a broken-line drawing of the setting must be submitted, with a detailed description of the color(s).

- If an applicant seeks to register a single color as a service mark used on a variety of items not viewed simultaneously by purchasers, *e.g.*, stationery, uniforms, pens, signs, shuttle buses, the store awning and the walls of the store, the drawing must display a solid-colored square with a dotted peripheral outline and include a detailed description of the mark. *Thrifty*, 274 F.3d at 1353, 61 USPQ2d at 1124. Applicant will receive a filing date for its application. However, as yet, the issues raised by the use of this type of drawing, *e.g.*, sufficient notice and phantom marks, have not yet been decided by the Office. *Cf. In re International Flavors & Fragrances Inc.*, 183 F.3d 1361, 1368, 51 USPQ2d 1513, 1517-18 (Fed. Cir. 1999). *See* TMEP §1202.05(c).

- The commercial impression of a color may change depending on the object on which it is applied. *See Thrifty*, 61 USPQ2d at 1124.

1202.05(d)(iii) Drawings for Marks Including Both Color and Words or Design

Sometimes a product or advertisement for a service will include both color and words or a design. For example, the surface of a toaster might be green, with the trademark "ABC" and design displayed on the toaster. In this situation, the applicant must decide whether to seek registration for the color green used on toasters, the letters "ABC" with or without the design, the design, or some combination of those elements. If applicant only seeks registration for the use of the color, no word or design elements should appear on the drawing.

1202.05(e) Written Explanation of a Color Mark [R-1]

The drawing of a color mark must be supplemented with a written description of

并附有关色彩的详细说明。

- 如果申请人申请将一种单一色彩注册为服务商标，而该色彩用于各种购买者不认为相似的物品，*例如*：文具、制服、钢笔、标牌、往返公交车、商店雨棚及墙壁等，则附图必须展示出有虚线轮廓的单色色块，包括详细的商标说明。*Thrifty*，274 F.3d 1353，61 USPQ2d 1124。申请人的申请书就可以被接受并注明申请日。不过，对于使用此类附图所产生的问题，*例如*，充分告知和虚构商标问题，至今商标局还没有作出规定。*比较 International Flavors & Fragrances Inc.*，183 F.3d 1361，1368，51 USPQ2d 1513，1517–18（Fed. Cir. 1999）。*参见* TMEP §1202.05(c)。

- 根据所适用对象的不同，色彩的商业印象也可能随之变化。*参见 Thrifty*，61 USPQ2d 1124。

1202.05(d)(iii) 同时包含色彩、语词或图案的商标的附图

有时产品或服务广告会同时包含色彩和语词或图案。例如，多士炉的表面可以是绿色的，同时带有“ABC”商标和图案。在这种情况下，申请人必须决定是为多士炉的绿色、附带或不附带图案的字母“ABC”、图案，还是这些元素中某一些的组合申请注册。如果申请人只对该色彩的使用申请注册，那么附图中就不应出现任何语词或图案。

1202.05(e) 色彩商标的书面解释［R-1］

色彩商标的附图必须附有该商标的书面说明，以解释该色彩以及用于商标何处。

the mark, explaining the color(s) and where they appear on the mark. 37 C. F. R. §§2.37 and 2.52(a)(2)(v); TMEP §807.09(c).

The description of the mark must be clear and specific, use ordinary language, and identify the mark as consisting of the particular color as applied to the goods or services. This description of the mark must appear both in the heading of the drawing, and in the written application. If the color is applied only to a portion of the goods, the description must indicate the specific portion. Similarly, if the mark includes gradations of color, the description should so indicate. If the applicant is claiming a shade of color, the shade must be described in ordinary language, for example, "maroon," "turquoise," "navy blue," "reddish orange." This is required even if the applicant also describes the color using a commercial coloring system.

The applicant may not amend the description of the mark if the amendment is a material alteration of the mark on the drawing filed with the original application. 37 C. F. R. §§2.52(a) and 2.72. *See In re Thrifty, Inc.*, 274 F.3d 1349, 61 USPQ2d 1121 (Fed. Cir. 2001); *cf. In re Hacot-Colombier*, 105 F.3d 616, 41 USPQ2d 1523 (Fed. Cir. 1997). *See* TMEP §807.14(a) regarding material alteration.

The description of a color mark must be limited to a single mark, because only one mark can be registered in a single application. *See In re International Flavors & Fragrances Inc.*, 83 F.3d 1361 51 USPQ2d 1513 (Fed. Cir. 1999); *In re Hayes*, 62 USPQ2d 1443 (TTAB 2002). *See* TMEP §1202.05(a) regarding color as a separable element. *Cf.* TMEP §807.04 (drawing must be limited to a single mark).

1202.05(f) Specimens for Color Marks

An application for a color mark must be supported by a specimen that shows use of the color mark depicted in the drawing. Therefore, an applicant who applies to register a color mark must submit a specimen showing use of color, either with a §1(a) application or with an allegation of use in a §1(b) application. If a black

见 37 C.F.R.§§2.37 和 2.52(a)(2)(v)；TMEP §807.09(c)。

对于商标的说明必须清楚详细，使用一般语言，以使用于商品或服务的特定色彩对其构成的商标进行识别。此种对商标的说明必须同时标明在附图的首部和书面申请中。如果色彩仅适用于商品的一部分，说明必须标示出该特定部分。类似地，如果商标包括了色彩的浓淡，说明中也必须相应地表明。如果申请人所主张的是一种色度，就必须以通常语言对其进行描述，例如："栗棕色"、"青绿色"、"藏青色"、"红橙色"等。即使申请人使用了一种商业色度系统对该色彩进行了描述，也必须如此。

如果修正是对于原始申请附图中商标的质料改变，那么对于该商标的说明可以不作修订。37 C.F.R.§§2.52(a)和 2.72。*参见 Thrifty, Inc.*, 274 F.3d 1349, 61 USPQ2d 1121 (Fed. Cir. 2001)；*比较 Hacot-Colombier*, 105 F.3d 616, 41 USPQ2d 1523 (Fed. Cir. 1997)。有关材料变化的信息，*参见* TMEP §807.14(a)。

对于色彩商标的说明限于一个商标，因为在一项申请只能注册一个商标。*参见 International Flavors & Fragrances Inc.*, 83 F.3d 1361 51 USPQ2d 1513 (Fed. Cir. 1999)；*Hayes*, 62 USPQ2d 1443 (TTAB 2002)。有关作为独立元素的色彩，*参见* TMEP §1202.05(a)。*比较* TMEP §807.04(附图必须限于一个商标)。

1202.05(f) 色彩商标的样本

一项色彩商标的申请必须有样本支持，样本必须显示附图所示的对色彩商标的使用。因而，申请注册色彩商标的申请人必须提交一份表明对色彩进行使用的样本，同时，在根据§1(a)提出的申请中须提交一份申请书，在根据§1(b)提出的申请中则

and white specimen is submitted, the examining attorney will require a substitute specimen. *See* TMEP §904.02(a).

See TMEP §§904.04 *et seq*. regarding trademark specimens and TMEP §§1301.04 *et seq*. regarding service mark specimens.

1202.05(g) Special Considerations for Service Mark Applications

No service mark registrations have issued for a single color *per se*. Although the applicant in *In re Thrifty, Inc*., 274 F.3d 1349, 61 USPQ2d 1121 (Fed. Cir. 2001) argued that it applied for the color blue *per se* as a service mark, the Court determined that the drawing controlled, such that the application was for the color blue applied to a building. Although the Court did not reach the issue of color *per se* as a service mark, the Court acknowledged the special evidentiary problem associated with showing acquired distinctiveness in this context. *Thrifty*, 274 F.3d at 1353, 61 USPQ2d at 1124 ("... [E]vidence submitted to demonstrate acquired distinctiveness of a color may show consumer recognition with respect to certain objects (*e.g.*, blue vehicle rental centers), but not for other objects (*e.g.*, blue rental cars)"). Accordingly, any claim to color *per se* needs to be specific as to use and include evidence of acquired distinctiveness for each claimed use.

1202.05(h) Applications for Color Marks Based on Intent-to-Use

As discussed in TMEP §1202.05, a color mark can never be inherently distinctive. *Wal-Mart Stores, Inc. v. Samara Brothers, Inc*., 529 U.S. 205, 211-212, 54 USPQ2d 1065, 1068 (2000) (citing *Qualitex Co. v. Jacobson Products Co., Inc*., 514 U.S. 159, 162-163, 34 USPQ2d 1161, 1162-1163 (1995)); TMEP §1202.05. Therefore, the examining attorney must refuse to register a color mark on the Principal Register unless the applicant establishes that the mark has acquired distinctiveness under §2(f). The ground for refusal is that the color is not inherently distinctive and thus does not function as a trademark under §§1, 2 and 45, or does

须提交一份使用证明书。如果提交的是黑白样本，审查员应要求提供一份备用样本。*参见* TMEP §904.02(a)。

有关商标样本的信息，*参见* TMEP §§904.04 及以下。有关服务商标样本，*参见* TMEP §§1301.04 及以下。

1202.05(g) 服务商标申请的特别考虑

一种单一色彩本身不能作为服务商标注册。尽管申请人在 *Thrifty*, *Inc*., 274 F.3d 1349, 61 USPQ2d 1121 (Fed. Cir. 2001)一案中抗辩称，申请将蓝色*本身*注册为一项服务商标，但法庭裁决，由于受到附图的约束，因此该项申请乃是针对用于某建筑物的蓝色提出的。尽管法庭并未涉及色彩*本身*作为服务商标的问题，但法庭承认在这种情况中存在关于显示出获得性显著性的特殊的证据问题。*Thrifty*, 274 F.3d 1353, 61 USPQ2d 1124("……提交用以证明某种色彩获得性显著性的证据可以表明，消费者将色彩同特定的对象(*例如*，蓝色的汽车租赁中心)，而不与其他对象(*例如*，蓝色的租赁汽车)相联系")。于是，任何对于色彩*本身*的主张，都需要根据其使用情况以及各种相应的获得性独特性证据进行特定化。

1202.05(h) 基于意图使用的色彩商标申请

正如 TMEP §1202.05 所讨论，色彩商标绝不可能具有固有的独特性。见 *Wal-Mart Stores*, *Inc*. *v*. *Samara Brothers*, *Inc*., 529 U.S. 205, 211－212, 54 USPQ2d 1065, 1068 (2000)(引用 *Qualitex Co*. *v*. *Jacobson Products Co*., *Inc*., 514 U.S. 159, 162－163, 34 USPQ2d 1161, 1162－1163 (1995))；TMEP §1202.05。因此，除非申请人证明色彩商标具有 §2(f)所规定的获得性显著性，否则审查员必须拒绝在联邦商标登记簿上注册该商标。拒绝的理由在于，色彩不具有固有的独特性，因此不具有 §§1, 2 和 45 所规定的商标的功能，也不具有 §§1, 3 和 45 所规定的服务商标的功能。

not function as a service mark under §§1, 3 and 45.

The issue of whether the proposed mark is functional requires consideration of the manner in which the mark is used. Generally, no refusal on these grounds will be issued in a §1(b) application until the applicant has submitted specimens of use with an amendment to allege use or statement of use. *See* TMEP §§1102.01, 1202.02(e) and 1202.03(e). In appropriate cases, the examining attorney will bring the potential refusal to the applicant's attention in the initial Office action. This is done strictly as a courtesy. If information regarding this possible ground for refusal is not provided to the applicant before the allegation of use is filed, the Office is not precluded from refusing registration on this basis.

1202.06 Goods in Trade

Section 45 of the Trademark Act, 15 U.S.C. §1127, defines a "trademark" as a "word, name, symbol, or device, or any combination thereof' that is used or intended to be used in commerce to *identify and distinguish his or her goods* (emphasis added)." Before rights in a term as a trademark can be established, the subject matter to which the term is applied must be "goods in trade." Incidental items that an applicant uses in conducting its business (such as letterhead, invoices and business forms), as opposed to items sold or transported in commerce for use by others, are not "goods in trade." *See In re Shareholders Data Corp.*, 495 F.2d 1360, 181 USPQ 722 (C.C.P.A. 1974) (reports not goods in trade, where applicant is not engaged in the sale of reports, but solely in furnishing financial reporting services, and reports are merely conduit through which services are rendered); *In re Compute-Her-Look, Inc.*, 176 USPQ 445 (TTAB 1972) (reports and printouts not goods in trade, where they are merely the means by which the results of a beauty analysis service is transmitted and have no viable existence separate and apart from the service); *Ex parte Bank of America National Trust and Savings Association*, 118 USPQ 165 (Comm'r Pats. 1958) (mark not registrable for passbooks, checks and other printed forms, where forms are used only as necessa-

要解决申请注册的商标是否具有功能性的问题，需要考虑该商标使用的方式。通常，在根据 §1(b)提出的申请中，不会以此为由拒绝注册，除非申请人提交了使用样本以及证明使用修正书或者使用声明书。*参见* TMEP §§1102.01，1202.02(e)和1202.03(e)。在适当情况下，在商标局初步程序中，审查员会提请申请人注意可能会作出拒绝注册的决定。此种告诫必须有礼貌地进行。如果在使用证明提交之前，未向申请人告知关于该可能的驳回注册理由的信息，商标局仍然可以以此为理由作出拒绝注册的决定。

1202.06　　贸易商品

《商标法》第 45 节，15 U.S.C.§1127，将“商标”定义为“用于或意图用于商业、以*识别或区分其商品*（斜体强调为后加）的文字、名称、符号或图案，或这些元素的组合”。在商标权利确立之前，商标所应用的标的物必须是“贸易商品”。申请者在商业活动中使用的附带物体（如信笺抬头、发票和商业表格等），与在商业中销售或运输、供他人使用的物体相对立，不属于“贸易商品”。*参见* 相关判例：*Shareholders Data Corp.*，495 F.2d 1360，181 USPQ 722 (C.C.P.A.1974)（报告不是贸易商品，因为申请者所从事的并非销售报告，而仅仅是提供金融报告服务，报告仅仅是传递此项服务的渠道）；*Compute-Her-Look*，*Inc.*，176 USPQ 445 (TTAB 1972)（报告及打印输出不是贸易商品，它们仅仅是传达美容分析服务结果的一种方式，与服务不可分离且不独立于服务而存在）；*Bank of America National Trust and Savings Association*，118 USPQ 165 (Comm’r Pats.1958)（存折、支票及其他印刷表格不能作为商标注册，这些表格只是提供银行服务的必要工具，而申请者并没有把印制或销售表格作为

ry tools in the performance of banking services, and the applicant is not engaged in printing or selling forms as commodities in trade).

1202.06(a) Goods Must Have Utility to Others

Affixing a mark to an item that is transported in commerce does not in and of itself establish that the mark is used on "goods." While a formal sale is not always necessary, items sold or transported in commerce are not "goods in trade" unless they have utility to others as the type of product named in the application.

> *Example*: Holiday greeting cards sent by a law firm to its clients are not "goods," where applicant is merely sending its own cards through the mail as a holiday greeting, and the cards are not suitable for use by the recipients as a greeting card.

See Gay Toys, Inc. v. McDonald's Corp., 585 F.2d 1067, 199 USPQ 722 (C.C.P.A. 1978) (plaster mockup of toy truck not goods in trade, where there is no evidence the mockup is actually used as a toy); *Paramount Pictures Corp. v. White*, 31 USPQ2d 1768 (TTAB 1994), *aff'd*, 108 F.3d 1392 (Fed. Cir. 1997) (mark not registrable for games, where purported games are advertising flyers used to promote applicant's services and have no real utilitarian function or purpose as games); *In re Douglas Aircraft Co., Inc.*, 123 USPQ 271 (TTAB 1959) (books, pamphlets and brochures that serve only to explain and advertise the goods in which applicant deals are not "goods"). *Cf. In re Snap-On Tools Corp.*, 159 USPQ 254 (TTAB 1968) (ball point pens used to promote applicant's tools are goods in trade, where they have a utilitarian function and purpose, and have been sold to applicant's franchised dealers and transported in commerce under mark); *In re United Merchants & Manufacturers, Inc.*, 154 USPQ 625 (TTAB 1967) (calendar used to promote applicant's plastic film constitutes goods in trade, where calendar has a utilitarian function and purpose in and of itself, and has been regularly distributed in commerce for several years).

贸易商品进行经营)。

1202.06(a) 商品必须对他人具备实用性

在商业运输中的物品上贴商标本身并不能确立商标在"商品"上使用。尽管并非一定要求具备正式的销售形式,但在商业中销售或运输的物品只有作为申请中所指产品对他人有用时,才是"贸易商品"。

> *例如*:某律师事务所向客户寄出的节日贺卡并非"商品",因为申请者只是通过邮政寄出了自己所拥有的卡片,以此问候客户,收到的人不宜再将贺卡作为问候卡片使用。

参见 Gay Toys, Inc. v. McDonald's Corp., 585 F.2d 1067, 199 USPQ 722 (C.C.P.A.1978)(玩具卡车的石膏模型不是贸易商品,因为没有证据表明石膏模型实际上作为玩具使用);*Paramount Pictures Corp. v. White*, 31 USPQ2d 1768 (TTAB 1994), *aff'd*, 108 F.3d 1392 (Fed. Cir. 1997)(这些游戏不能作为商标注册,因为游戏只是作为促销申请者服务的广告传单使用,并没有游戏的实际功效);*Douglas Aircraft Co., Inc.*, 123 USPQ 271 (TTAB 1959)(只是用于说明和宣传申请者商品的书籍、宣传册和目录册不属于"商品")。*比较*:*Snap-On Tools Corp.*, 159 USPQ 254 (TTAB 1968)(用来促销申请者工具的圆珠笔是贸易商品,因为其具有实用功能和目的,并且以此商标出售给了申请者的特许经营商并在商业中使用商标进行传输);*United Merchants & Manufacturers, Inc.*, 154 USPQ 625 (TTAB 1967)(用来促销申请者塑料薄膜的日历构成了贸易商品,因为日历本身具有实用功能和目的,并且已在商业中销售达数年之久)。

1202.06(b) Registration Must Be Refused if Trademark Not Used on Goods in Trade

If the specimens, identification of goods, or other evidence in the record indicate that the applicant uses the mark only on items incidental to conducting its own business, as opposed to items intended to be used by others, the examining attorney should refuse registration on the Principal Register under §§1, 2 and 45 of the Trademark Act; 15 U.S.C.§§1051, 1052 and 1127, on the ground that the mark is not used on "goods in trade."

If a mark is not used on "goods in trade," it is not registrable on the Principal Register under §2(f) of the Trademark Act, 15 U.S.C.§1052(f), or on the Supplemental Register.

If some, but not all of the items listed in the identification of goods are found not to be "goods in trade," it is not necessary to refuse registration of the entire application, but the examining attorney should require that these items be deleted from the identification of goods.

1202.06(c) "Goods in Trade" in Intent-to-Use Applications

In an intent-to-use application under §1(b) of the Trademark Act, the question of whether a mark is used on goods in trade usually does not arise until the applicant files an allegation of use under §1(c) or §1(d) of the Act, because this issue is based on the manner in which the mark is used. However, if the identification of goods in an intent-to-use application includes items that do not appear to be goods in trade, the potential refusal should be brought to the applicant's attention in the first action issued by the Office. This is done strictly as a courtesy. If information regarding this possible ground for refusal is not provided to the applicant before the allegation of use is filed, the Office is not precluded from refusing registration on this basis.

1202.06(b) 商标未在贸易商品上使用则必须拒绝予以注册

如果样本、商品识别符号或记录的其他证据表明,与在意图由他人使用的物品上使用商标不同,申请者仅在商业活动的附带物品上使用商标,审查员应根据《商标法》§§1, 2 和 45,15 U.S.C.§§1051, 1052 和 1127 的规定,以商标并非用于"贸易商品"为由拒绝该商标在联邦商标登记簿上注册。

如果商标不是用于"贸易商品",根据《商标法》§2(f),15 U.S.C.§1052(f),不得在联邦商标登记簿或补充登记簿上注册。

如果判定所识别的商品中有一部分不属于"贸易商品",则审查员不应拒绝整个申请,而应要求从识别的商品中删除这一部分物品。

1202.06(c) 意图使用申请中的"贸易商品"

在根据《商标法》§1(b)提出的申请中,除非申请者根据 §1(c)或 §1(d)提出了宣称使用声明,通常不会发生商标是否用于贸易商品的问题,因为问题的关键是商标的使用方式。不过,如果一项意图使用申请中识别的商品包含了不属于贸易商品的物品,商标局应在第一行动提请当事人注意其注册可能会被拒绝。此种告诫纯粹是出于礼貌。即使在宣称使用证明提交之前,未向申请者告知关于该可能的驳回注册理由的信息,商标局仍然可以以此为理由作出拒绝注册的决定。

1202.07 Marks That Identify Columns or Sections of Publications

1202.07(a) Marks That Identify Columns or Sections of Printed Publications

A column, section or supplement of a printed publication is normally not considered to be separate "goods" or "goods in trade" unless it is sold, syndicated, or offered for syndication separate and apart from the larger publication in which it appears. *In re Broadcasting Publications, Inc.*, 135 USPQ 374 (TTAB 1962); *Ex parte Meredith Publishing Co.*, 109 USPQ 426 (Comm'r Pats. 1956). This is true even of a removable or separable "pullout" section of a newspaper or other publication. In *Meredith*, the issue was analyzed as follows:

> The basic question is whether or not, under the circumstances of use, the section title is a name adopted and used by the publisher to identify his goods and distinguish them from those of others. The "goods" actually are magazines-not sections of magazines. When the magazine is purchased, the purchaser receives the sections whether he wants them or not, and it is doubtful that magazine readers *ordinarily* purchase a magazine merely to receive a section of it, or think of a magazine merely in terms of a section title. Sections of magazines are not in and of themselves articles of commerce other than as a part of an integrated whole; and we must therefore be concerned with whether a section title actually identifies and distinguishes, and if so, what it distinguishes. Under these circumstances it becomes necessary to ask: Was the mark adopted to identify a section of applicant's magazine and distinguish it from sections of other publishers' magazines, or was it adopted to distinguish one section of applicant's magazine from the other sections of its magazine? *Ordinarily*, it is the latter (emphasis in original).

109 USPQ 426.

1202.07　　识别出版物专栏或版面的商标

1202.07(a)　识别印刷出版物专栏或栏目的商标

印刷出版物的专栏、栏目或增刊通常被认为不是独立的"商品"或"贸易商品"，除非与其所在的出版物分离并独立销售或者进行辛迪加制作。相关判例：*Broadcasting Publications, Inc.*, 135 USPQ 374（TTAB 1962）；*Meredith Publishing Co.*, 109 USPQ 426（Comm'r Pats. 1956）。即使是报纸或其他出版物的可分离或独立的"插页"栏目也是如此。在 *Meredith* 一案中，对这一问题的分析如下：

> 基本问题在于，在使用条件下，栏目的标题是否是出版商使用和采用以识别其商品并与他人的商品区分开来的名称。"商品"实际上是杂志——而非杂志的栏目。购买者在购买杂志时，无论是否想要这些栏目都会收到这些栏目，而且杂志读者在购买杂志时是否*通常*只想收到其中的一个栏目或者在想到杂志时是否只想到某一栏目的标题，这是很值得怀疑的。杂志栏目本身并不是商业物体，而仅仅是整体的一部分；因此，我们必须考虑的是，某一个栏目标题实际上是否能够起识别和区分作用，如果能，所识别和区分的又是什么。在这些情况下，需要探究：商标是用来识别申请者杂志的某一栏目，并将其同其他出版商杂志的栏目区分开来，还是用以将申请者杂志中的某一栏目与同一杂志的其他栏目区分开来？在*通常情况下*，是属于后一种情况（斜体强调为后加）。
>
> 109 USPQ 426。

1202.07(a)(i) Syndicated Columns and Sections

Columns or sections that are separately sold, syndicated, or offered for syndication do constitute goods in trade. A mark that identifies a column or section that is separately syndicated or offered for syndication is registrable on the Principal Register without resort to §2(f) of the Trademark Act, 15 U.S.C.§1052(f), if registration is not barred by other sections of the Act.

1202.07(a)(ii) Non-Syndicated Columns and Sections

A column or section of a printed publication that is not separately sold, syndicated, or offered for syndication is not, in and of itself, considered to be separate goods in trade. Therefore, where the specimens, identification of goods, or other evidence in the record indicates that the mark identifies a column or section of a printed publication that is not separately sold, syndicated, or offered for syndication, the examining attorney should refuse registration on the Principal Register under §§1, 2 and 45 of the Trademark Act; 15 U.S.C.§§1051, 1052 and 1127, on the ground that the mark is not used on separate goods in trade.

Marks that identify non-syndicated columns or sections of printed publications are registrable on the Principal Register under §2(f) of the Trademark Act, 15 U.S.C.§1052(f), if the column or section is shown to have acquired separate recognition and distinctiveness. The applicant who seeks registration on the Principal Register bears the burden of establishing, through evidence of promotion, long use, advertising expenditures, and breadth of distribution or sales figures, that the public has come to recognize the proposed mark as an indicator of source.

The evidence of acquired distinctiveness must show that the column or section title is used and promoted to distinguish applicant's column or section from the columns or sections of other publishers' publications rather than merely to distinguish applicant's column or section from other columns or sections of applicant's publi-

1202.07(a)(i) 辛迪加的专栏和栏目

单独销售或者进行辛迪加运作的专栏或栏目的确构成了贸易商品。如果没有为《商标法》其他部分的规定所禁止，识别某一独立的辛迪加运作的专栏或栏目的商标可以不采用商标法 §2(f)，15 U.S.C.§1052(f)的规定，而在联邦商标登记簿上注册。

1202.07(a)(ii) 非辛迪加专栏和栏目

非单独销售或者进行辛迪加运作的印刷出版物专栏或栏目，本身不能被认为是独立的贸易商品。因此，如果样本、商品识别书以及档案中的其他证据表明，商标所识别的印刷出版物专栏或栏目并非单独销售或者进行辛迪加运作，则审查员应根据《商标法》§§1，2 和 45，15 U.S.C.§§1051，1052 和 1127 的规定，以商标并非用在单独的“贸易商品”之上为理由拒绝商标在联邦商标登记簿上注册。

如果某专栏或栏目显示出获得性单独的认知和独特性，那么识别印刷出版物的非辛迪加专栏或栏目的商标就可以根据《商标法》§2(f)，15 U.S.C.§1052(f)的规定，在联邦商标登记簿上注册。申请在联邦商标登记簿上注册的申请者，必须通过促销、长期使用、广告支出以及经营广度或销售数据来证明，公众已经将申请注册的商标认知为一种识别来源的商标。

获得性独特性的证据必须证明，专栏或栏目标题通过使用和促销，将申请者的专栏或栏目与其他出版商出版物的专栏或栏目区分开来，而不只是将该专栏或栏目与同

cation. *Metro Publishing v. San Jose Mercury News*, 987 F.2d 637, 25 USPQ2d 2049 (9th Cir. 1993); *In re Broadcasting Publications, Inc.*, 135 USPQ 374 (TTAB 1962).

The amount of evidence needed to establish distinctiveness must be evaluated by the examining attorney on a case-by-case basis, in light of the type of column or supplement. If the mark identifies a removable or pull-out section, a lesser degree of evidence might be required to establish distinctiveness. Of course, the amount of evidence needed to establish distinctiveness in any particular case will also vary depending on the strength or weakness of the mark. TMEP §1212.04(a).

Marks that identify non-syndicated columns or sections of printed publications, but have not yet acquired distinctiveness and therefore are not registrable under §2(f) of the Act, are registrable on the Supplemental Register, if registration is not barred by other sections of the Act. *Ex parte Meredith Publishing Co.*, 109 USPQ 426 (Comm'r Pats. 1956).

1202.07(a)(iii) Marks That Identify Columns and Sections of Printed Publications in Intent-to-Use Applications

Since a refusal to register a mark that identifies a column or section of a printed publication is based on whether the column or section is separately sold or syndicated, the issue ordinarily does not arise in an intent-to-use application under §1(b) of the Trademark Act, 15 U.S.C. §1051(b), until the applicant has filed either an amendment to allege use under §1(c), or a statement of use under §1(d), 15 U.S.C. §§1051(c) and (d). However, if the identification of goods indicates that the mark is intended to be used to identify a column or section of a printed publication that is not separately sold or syndicated, the potential refusal on the ground that the proposed mark is not used on separate goods in trade should be brought to the applicant's attention in the first Office Action. This is done strictly as a courtesy. If information regarding this possible ground for refusal is not provided to the applicant prior to the filing of the allegation of use, the Office is not precluded from refusing registration on this basis.

一出版物中的其他专栏或栏目区分开来。见 *Metro Publishing v. San Jose Mercury News*，987 F.2d 637，25 USPQ2d 2049（9th Cir. 1993）；*Broadcasting Publications, Inc.*，135 USPQ 374（TTAB 1962）。

审查员必须根据专栏或增刊的不同类型，根据每个个案的具体情况，确定证明具有独特性的证据的数量。如果商标所识别的是一种可分离的或插页的栏目，证明独特性所需的证据量就较少。当然，任何具体案件中证明独特性所需的证据量，应根据商标特性的强弱程度而有所不同。TMEP §1212.04(a)。

识别印刷出版物的非辛迪加专栏或栏目的商标，由于尚未具备独特性而不能根据《商标法》§2(f)的规定进行注册，但如果商标法的其他部分没有禁止其注册，则可以在联邦商标补充登记簿上注册。见 *Meredith Publishing Co.*，109 USPQ 426（Comm'r Pats. 1956）。

1202.07(a)(iii) 意图使用申请中识别印刷出版物专栏和栏目的商标

由于对一项识别印刷出版物的专栏或栏目的商标拒绝予以注册必须根据该专栏或栏目是否独立销售或进行辛迪加运作，因此对于根据《商标法》§1(b)，15 U.S.C. §1051(b)而提出的意图使用申请，通常不会发生争论，除非申请者已经根据 §1(c)提交了宣称使用修正书，或者根据 §1(d)，15 U.S.C. §§1051(c)及(d)提交了使用声明书。不过，如果识别商品的行为表明意图用于识别印刷出版物专栏或栏目的商标不是独立销售或进行辛迪加运作，则应当在第一行动提请当事人注意其注册可能会被拒绝。此种告诫纯粹是出于礼貌。即使在宣称使用声明书提交之前，未向申请者告知关于该可能的驳回注册理由的信息，商标局仍然可以以此为理由作出拒绝注册的决定。

1202.07(b) Marks That Identify Columns and Sections of On-Line Publications

An on-line publication is considered a service rather than a product. Therefore, refusal of registration on the ground that the proposed mark is not used on goods in trade is inappropriate. Unlike a printed column or section, an on-line column or section can be accessed directly and can exist independent of any single publication. *See Ludden v. Metro Weekly*, 8 F. Supp. 2d 7, 47 USPQ2d 1087, 1093 (D.D.C. 1998). Therefore, a mark that identifies an on-line column is registrable on the Principal Register without resort to §2(f) of the Trademark Act, 15 U.S.C. §1052(f), if registration is not barred by other sections of the Act.

1202.08 Title of a Single Creative Work [R-2]

The title of a single creative work is not registrable on the Principal Register or the Supplemental Register. Examples of "single creative works" include books, videotapes, films and theatrical performances. *Herbko International, Inc. v. Kappa Books, Inc.*, 308 F.3d 1156, 1162, 64 USPQ2d 1375, 1378 (Fed. Cir. 2002) ("the title of a single book cannot serve as a source identifier"); *In re Cooper*, 254 F.2d 611, 615-16, 117 USPQ 396, 400 (C.C.P.A. 1958), *cert. denied*, 358 U.S. 840, 119 USPQ 501 (1958) ("A book title ... identifies a specific literary work ... and is not associated in the public mind with the publisher, printer or bookseller ..."); *In re Posthuma*, 45 USPQ2d 2011 (TTAB 1998) (title of a live theater production held unregistrable); *In re Hal Leonard Publishing Corp.*, 15 USPQ2d 1574 (TTAB 1990) (INSTANT KEYBOARD, as used on music instruction books, found unregistrable as the title of a single work); *In re Appleby*, 159 USPQ 126 (TTAB 1968) (title of single phonograph record, as distinguished from series, does not function as mark).

The name of a series of books or other creative works may be registrable if it

1202.07(b) 识别在线出版物的专栏或栏目的商标

在线出版物被认为是一种服务，而不是一种产品。因此，以申请注册的商标并非用于贸易商品为理由拒绝注册是不适当的。与印刷专栏或栏目不同的是，在线专栏或栏目可以直接读取，并且能够独立于任何出版物而存在。参见 *Ludden v. Metro Weekly*, 8 F.Supp.2d 7, 47 USPQ2d 1087, 1093 (D.D.C.1998)。因此，如果没有为《商标法》其他部分的规定所禁止，识别某一在线专栏或栏目的商标可以根据商标法 §2(f),15 U.S.C.§1052(f)的规定，在联邦商标登记簿上注册。

1202.08 单件创造性作品的标题［R-2］

单件创造性作品的标题不能在联邦商标登记簿或补充登记簿上注册。“单件创造性作品”的例子包括书籍、录像带、影片及戏剧表演。相关判例：*Herbko International, Inc. v. Kappa Books, Inc.*, 308 F.3d 1156, 1162, 64 USPQ2d 1375, 1378 (Fed. Cir. 2002)(“一本书的标题不能作为一种识别来源的商标”)；*Cooper*, 254 F.2d 611, 615-16, 117 USPQ 396, 400 (C.C.P.A.1958), *cert. denied*, 358 U.S. 840, 119 USPQ 501 (1958)(“一本书的标题……仅识别一件具体的文学作品……而在公众心目中并没有将它与出版商、印刷商以及图书销售商联系起来……”)；*Posthuma*, 45 USPQ2d 2011 (TTAB 1998)(现场戏院表演的名称被认为不能注册)；*Hal Leonard Publishing Corp.*, 15 USPQ2d 1574 (TTAB 1990)(在音乐辅导书上使用的“INSTANT KEYBOARD”被判定是单件作品的标题，不能注册)；*Appleby*, 159 USPQ 126 (TTAB 1968)(一张唱片的标题，与同一系列的其他唱片相区别，并不具有商标功能)。

只要能够识别并区分商品的来源，一系列书籍或其他创造性作品的名称就可以

serves to identify and distinguish the source of the goods. *In re Scholastic Inc.*, 23 USPQ2d 1774, 1778 (TTAB 1992) (THE MAGIC SCHOOL BUS, prominently displayed on the cover of a series of books, has come to represent a source to purchasers and would be recognized as a trademark). However, a term used in the title of a series of books is not registrable if it merely identifies a character in the books. *In re Scholastic Inc.*, 223 USPQ 431 (TTAB 1984) (THE LITTLES, used in the title of each in a series of children's books, does not function as a mark where it merely identifies the main characters in the books). *Cf. In re Caserta*, 46 USPQ2d 1088 (TTAB 1998) (FURR-BALL FURCANIA, used as the principal character in a single children's book, was found not to function as a mark even though the character's name appeared on the cover and every page of the story); *In re Frederick Warne & Co. Inc.*, 218 USPQ 345 (TTAB 1983) (an illustration of a frog used on the cover of a single book served only to depict the main character in the book and did not function as a trademark).

See TMEP §1301.02(d) regarding the registrability of titles of radio and television programs as service marks, and TMEP §1202.09(a) regarding the registrability of the names of performing artists on sound recordings.

1202.09 Names of Artists and Authors

Generally, subject matter used solely as an author's name, even on multiple books, does not function as a trademark. *See In re Chicago Reader Inc.*, 12 USPQ2d 1079 (TTAB 1989) (CECIL ADAMS, as used on the specimens, merely identifies the author and is not used as a trademark). *Cf. In re Wood*, 217 USPQ 1345 (TTAB 1983) (artist's pseudonym YSABELLA, affixed to an original work of art, functioned as a trademark).

See TMEP §1202.09(a) regarding the registrability of the names of performing artists used on sound recordings.

See also TMEP §1301.02(b) regarding the registrability of the names of charac-

注册。见 *Scholastic Inc*., 23 USPQ2d 1774, 1778 (TTAB 1992)("THE MAGIC SCHOOL BUS"(魔法校车)醒目地显示在一系列书籍的封面上,对于购买者而言代表一种来源,因而可以作为商标注册)。不过,如果系列书籍标题中的某一个词仅仅识别了书中的一个角色,则不能注册。见 *Scholastic Inc*., 223 USPQ 431 (TTAB 1984)(在某一系列儿童图书的每一本书上使用的"THE LITTLES"不具有商标的功能,因为它只识别这些书中的一个主要人物而已)。*比较 Caserta*, 46 USPQ2d 1088 (TTAB 1998)("FURR - BALL FURCANIA",一本儿童书的主要人物名,被判定不具有商标的功能,尽管该人物的名字出现在封面以及故事的每一页上);*Frederick Warne & Co. Inc*., 218 USPQ 345 (TTAB 1983)(一本书封面上的青蛙图案只用来描绘该书的主要人物,而不具有商标的功能)。

有关广播电视节目标题是否可作为服务商标注册的情况,*参见* TMEP §1301.02(d);有关录音带上的表演艺术家的名字是否可注册的情况,*参见* TMEP §1202.09(a)。

1202.09　艺术家和作者的名字

通常,只作为作者名字使用的标的物,即使在多本书籍上使用,也不具有商标的功能。*参见 Chicago Reader Inc*., 12 USPQ2d 1079 (TTAB 1989)(样本上使用的"CECIL ADAMS",只是识别了作者而不是作为商标使用)。*比较 Wood*, 217 USPQ 1345 (TTAB 1983)(艺术家的笔名"YSABELLA",签署在原创艺术作品上,具有商标的功能)。

有关录音带表演艺术家的名字是否可注册的情况,*参见* TMEP §1202.09(a)。

另参见 TMEP§1301.02(b),查阅关于人物名及人名是否可作为服务标准注册

ters and personal names as service marks.

1202.09(a) Names of Performing Artists Used on Sound Recordings

Subject matter that, as used on sound recordings, *merely* serves to identify the artist or artists whose performance comprises the content of the recording is not registrable as a trademark for the recordings. *In re Spirer*, 225 USPQ 693 (TTAB 1985). As noted by the Court of Appeals for the Federal Circuit in *In re Polar Music International AB*, 714 F.2d 1567, 1572, 221 USPQ 315, 318 (Fed. Cir. 1983), "just showing the name of the recording group on a record will not by itself enable that name to be registered as a trademark. Where, however, the owner of the mark controls the quality of the goods, and where the name of that recording group has been used numerous times on different records and has therefore come to represent an assurance of quality to the public, the name may be registered as a trademark since it functions as one." Personal names of individuals or groups function as service marks for entertainment services only if they identify and distinguish the services recited and not merely the individual or group. *See* TMEP §1301.02(b).

The following guidelines must be followed to ensure consistent action on applications to register the names of performers for sound recordings in accordance with *In re Polar Music International AB* and *In re Spirer*.

First, the names of performers may only be registered as a trademark if the mark is used on a series of sound recordings. The identification of goods must specifically indicate that there is a series. If the application does not identify the goods in this fashion, the examining attorney must require an appropriate amendment.

Secondly, the applicant must provide evidence that the mark has been applied to at least two different recordings in the series. In an intent-to-use application, the applicant must provide evidence of use on at least two recordings at the time the applicant files either the amendment to allege use or the statement of use. It is advisable to provide advance notice of this requirement during initial examination,

的情况。

1202.09(a) 录音带上使用的表演艺术家的名字

在录音带上使用的标的物*仅仅*识别该录音带的表演艺术家(们)的名字,不能作为该录音带的商标进行注册。见 *Spirer*, 225 USPQ 693 (TTAB 1985)。在 *Polar Music International AB*, 714 F.2d 1567, 1572, 221 USPQ 315, 318 (Fed. Cir. 1983)一案中,联邦巡回上诉法院论道:"只在一张唱片上显示录音团体的名称,这一行为本身不能使该名称作为商标进行注册。但是,如果商标的所有人对商品的质量进行了控制,而且录音团体的名称多次用在不同的录音带,并因此对公众代表了质量保证,那么该名称就可以作为商标注册,因为它具备了商标的功能。"个人或团体的个人名称,只有在其识别并区分了相关服务而不只是该个人或团体时,才能构成娱乐服务的商标。*参见* TMEP §1301.02(b)。

根据 *Polar Music International AB* 案和*Spirer* 案,为了保证注册录音带表演者名字在程序上保持一致性,必须遵守以下指导原则。

首先,表演者的名字只有用于一系列录音带上方可作为商标注册。所识别的商品必须特别标明存在一系列的商品。如果申请中并未以这一方式识别商品,审查员必须要求提供适当的修正书。

其次,申请者必须提供证据,表明商标已经用于系列中至少两个不同的录音带上。在意图使用申请中,申请者必须在提交宣称使用修正书或使用声明书时,提供已经在至少两个录音带上使用的证据。如果适当,可以在初审期间提前通知此项要求。

where appropriate. If the applicant is unable to demonstrate use on a series, the mark may be registered on the Supplemental Register, provided it is otherwise proper. These procedures apply specifically to performers' names used on recordings and not to other types of marks used on other types of artistic material.

Finally, it is only necessary to inquire about the applicant's control over the nature and quality of the goods if information in the application record clearly contradicts the applicant's verified statement that it is the owner of the mark or entitled to use the mark.

Similarly, the name of a performer is not registrable as a service mark for entertainment services unless the record shows the name identifies a continuing series of presentations, performances or recordings. *See* TMEP §1301.02(d).

1202.10 Model or Grade Designations

Subject matter used solely as a model, style or grade designation within a product line does not function as a trademark. *In re Dana Corp*., 12 USPQ2d 1748 (TTAB 1989) (alphanumeric designations, such as "5-469X," held unregistrable for universal joint couplings; evidence insufficient to establish distinctiveness and recognition as a mark). *Cf*. *In re Clairol Inc*., 457 F.2d 509, 173 USPQ 355 (C.C.P.A.1972) (SWEDISH CRYSTAL found to be a registrable trademark, not merely a color designation, for a hair coloring preparation, the Court relying on the arbitrariness of the mark, its manner of use and the fact that it was always used in addition to a shade designation); *In re Petersen Mfg. Co., Inc*., 229 USPQ 466, 468 (TTAB 1986) (letter-number combinations found registrable for locking hand tools, the Board stating, "[T]here is no question that such model designations can, through use and promotion, be perceived as marks indicating origin in addition to functioning as model designations.")

1202.11 Background Designs and Shapes

"A background design which is always used in connection with word marks must

如果申请者未能证明商标用在一系列产品上，但在其他方面合乎要求，也可以在联邦商标补充登记簿上注册。这些程序特别适用于录音带表演者的名字，而不适用于其他形式的艺术品的其他类型的商标。

最后，只有当申请记录中存在明显有悖于申请者关于其为商标所有人或有权使用商标的经验证的声明时，才有必要调查申请者是否控制商品的性质和质量。

类似地，只有当档案显示表演者的名字识别了一种连续的演出、表演或录音制品系列时，表演者的名字才可以作为娱乐服务商标注册。参见 TMEP §1301.02(d)。

1202.10　型号或等级名称

只是作为型号、风格或等级名称而在产品线中使用的标的物，不具有商标功能。见 *Dana Corp.*，12 USPQ2d 1748 (TTAB 1989)(混合符号，如"5－469X"被认为不能注册为万向管接头的商标，因为没有充分证据表明具备了独特性并被识别为商标)。*Cf.* 比较 *Clairol Inc.*，457 F.2d 509，173 USPQ 355 (C.C.P.A.1972)(法庭基于该商标的任意性、使用方式以及一直与一种色调名称配合使用，从而判定"SWEDISH CRYSTAL"可以注册为染发剂商标，而不只是色彩名称)；*Petersen Mfg. Co.，Inc.*，229 USPQ 466，468 (TTAB 1986)(数字和字母组合被认为可以作为手工具锁的商标注册，委员会指出："毫无疑问，此类型号名称通过使用和宣传，可以给人识别来源的商标的印象，而不只是作为一种型号的名称。")。

1202.11　背景图案和形状

"总是与文字商标联合使用的背景图案，必须给购买者一种独立于该文字商标的

create a commercial impression on buyers separate and apart from the word marks for the design to be protectible as a separate mark. In deciding whether the design background of a word mark may be separately registered, the essential question is whether or not the background material is or is not inherently distinctive ... If the background portion is inherently distinctive, no proof of secondary meaning need be introduced; if not, such proof is essential (citations omitted)." *In re Chemical Dynamics, Inc.*, 839 F. 2d 1569, 1570-1571, 5 USPQ2d 1828, 1829 (Fed. Cir. 1988).

Common geometric shapes, when used as vehicles for the display of word marks, are not regarded as indicators of origin absent evidence of distinctiveness of the design alone. Additionally, the Supreme Court stated in *Wal-Mart Stores, Inc. v. Samara Brothers, Inc.*, 529 U. S. 205, 211-212, 54 USPQ2d 1065, 1068 (2000) that color can never be inherently distinctive.

In the following cases, the evidence of distinctiveness was insufficient: *In re Benetton Group S. p. A.*, 48 USPQ2d 1214 (TTAB 1998) (green rectangular background design not inherently distinctive; evidence of acquired distinctiveness found insufficient); *In re Anton/Bauer Inc.*, 7 USPQ2d 1380 (TTAB 1988) (parallelogram designs used as background for word marks found not inherently distinctive; evidence of record held insufficient to establish acquired distinctiveness pursuant to §2(f)); *In re Kerr-McGee Corp.*, 190 USPQ 204 (TTAB 1976) (affirming refusals to register escutcheon design used as a frame or border for words, under §2(f)).

In the following cases, the evidence of distinctiveness was sufficient: *In re Schenectady Varnish Co., Inc.*, 280 F. 2d 169, 126 USPQ 395 (C. C. P. A. 1960) (where use of applicant's design of a cloud and a lightning flash was always used as a background for the word "SCHENECTADY," evidence of record found sufficient to show acquired distinctiveness of the design alone as a trademark for synthetic resins); *In re Raytheon Co.*, 202 USPQ 317 (TTAB 1979) (light-colored oval within black rectangular carrier considered not inherently distinctive; evi-

商业印象,方能成为独立的商标。在判断文字商标的背景图案是否可以单独注册时,关键问题在于,该背景材料是否具有固有的独特性……如果背景部分具有固有的独特性,就不需要证明具有第二含义;否则,此项必须有这种证明(引语略)。"见 *Chemical Dynamics, Inc.*, 839 F.2d 1569, 1570 - 1571, 5 USPQ2d 1828, 1829 (Fed. Cir. 1988)。

作为显示文字商标的一种工具的普通几何图形被认为不是识别来源的商标,因为图案本身缺乏独特性证据。此外,最高法院在 *Wal-Mart Stores, Inc. v. Samara Brothers, Inc.*, 529 U.S. 205, 211 - 212, 54 USPQ2d 1065, 1068 (2000)一案中称,色彩绝不具有固有的独特性。

在下列案件中,独特性证据不足: *Benetton Group S. p. A.*, 48 USPQ2d 1214 (TTAB 1998)(绿色的矩形背景图案不具有固有的独特性;获得性独特性也证据不足); *Anton/Bauer Inc.*, 7 USPQ2d 1380 (TTAB 1988)(文字商标的平行四边形背景图案被判定不具有固有的独特性;档案证据也被认为不足以证明具有 §2(f)所规定的获得性独特性); *Kerr-McGee Corp.*, 190 USPQ 204 (TTAB 1976)(根据 §2(f)的规定,维持拒绝作为文字边框的盾形图案注册)。

在下列案件中,独特性的证据充分: *Schenectady Varnish Co., Inc.*, 280 F.2d 169, 126 USPQ 395 (C.C.P.A. 1960)(申请者一直使用乌云闪电的图案,作为"SCHENECTADY"一词的背景,档案证据被判定足以证明该图案独立地具有获得性独特性,可以作为人造树脂的商标注册); *Raytheon Co.*, 202 USPQ 317 (TTAB 1979)(黑色矩形框架内的浅色椭圆形被认为不具有固有的独特性;但档案证据被判

dence of record found sufficient to establish acquired distinctiveness).

An applicant may respond to a refusal to register by submitting evidence that the subject matter has acquired distinctiveness, under §2(f) of the Trademark Act, 15 U.S.C. §1052(f). The examining attorney should scrutinize any submission that asserts distinctiveness solely on the basis of a statement of substantially exclusive and continuous use for five years to determine whether it truly establishes that the subject matter is perceived as a trademark by the purchasing public. The examining attorney may continue to refuse registration if he or she believes that the applicant's assertion does not establish that the matter is perceived as a trademark. The applicant may submit additional evidence to establish distinctiveness. *See* TMEP §§1212 *et seq*.

1202.12 Varietal and Cultivar Names (Examination of Applications for Seeds and Plants)

Varietal or cultivar names are designations given to cultivated varieties or subspecies of live plants or agricultural seeds. They amount to the generic name of the plant or seed by which such variety is known to the public. These names can consist of a numeric or alphanumeric code or can be a "fancy" (arbitrary) name. The terms "varietal" and "cultivar" may have slight semantic differences but pose indistinguishable issues and are treated identically for trademark purposes.

Subspecies are types of a particular species of plant or seed that are members of a particular genus. For example, all maple trees are in the genus *Acer*. The sugar maple species is known as *Acer saccharum*, while the red maple species is called *Acer rubrum*. In turn, these species have been subdivided into various cultivated varieties that are developed commercially and given varietal or cultivar names that are known to the public.

If the examining attorney determines that wording sought to be registered as a mark for live plants or agricultural seeds comprises a varietal or cultivar name,

定足以证明其具有获得性独特性)。

申请者可以提交证明标的物具有《商标法》§2(f),15 U.S.C.§1052(f)所规定的获得性独特性的证据,作为对拒绝注册的回应。审查员应仔细审查一切基于五年实质专属和持续使用声明而提出的独特性主张,以判断是否确实能够证明该标的物被购买公众认知为一种商标。如果审查员认为申请者的主张未能确立该标的物确实被认知为商标,则仍然可以继续拒绝予以注册。申请者可以提交另外的证据,以证明具有独特性。参见 TMEP §§1212 及以下。

1202.12 植物品种或变种名称(种子和植物申请的审查)

植物品种或变种名称是活植物或农业种子的栽培品种或亚种的名称。它们成为植物或种子的一般名称,植物或种子的品种以此为公众所知晓。这些名称可以由数字或字母数字混合代码组成或者是一个"假想"(任意)的名称。"植物品种"和"植物变种"在语义上可能有些许不同,但问题不大,在商标问题上可以作同等处理。

亚种是植物或种子的某特定物种的种类,这些种类为某一特定属的成员。例如,所有的槭树都属于*枫木*属。糖槭被称为*糖枫木*,而红花槭则被称为*红枫木*。这些物种再细分为各种栽培品种,这些品种通过商业发展,获得各种为公众所知的植物品种和变种的名称。

如果审查员判定,申请作为活体植物或农业种子商标注册的文字中包含了品种

the examining attorney must refuse registration, or require a disclaimer, on the ground that the matter is the varietal name of the goods and does not function as a trademark under §§1, 2 and 45 of the Trademark Act, 15 U.S.C. §§1051, 1052 and 1127. *See Dixie Rose Nursery v. Coe*, 131 F.2d 446, 55 USPQ 315 (D.C. Cir. 1942), *cert. denied* 318 U.S. 782, 57 USPQ 568 (1943); *In re Hilltop Orchards & Nurseries, Inc.*, 206 USPQ 1034 (TTAB 1979); *In re Farmer Seed & Nursery Co.*, 137 USPQ 231 (TTAB 1963); *In re Cohn Bodger & Sons Co.*, 122 USPQ 345 (TTAB 1959). Likewise, if the mark identifies the prominent portion of a varietal name, it must be refused. *In re Delta and Pine Land Co.*, 26 USPQ2d 1157 (TTAB 1993) (Board affirmed refusal to register DELTAPINE, which was a portion of the varietal names Deltapine 50, Deltapine 20, Deltapine 105 and Deltapine 506).

A varietal or cultivar name is used in a plant patent to identify the variety. Thus, even if the name was originally arbitrary, it "describe[s] to the public a [plant] of a particular sort, not a [plant] from a particular [source]." *Dixie Rose*, 131 F.2d at 447, 55 USPQ at 316. It is against public policy for any one supplier to retain exclusivity in a patented variety of plant, or the name of a variety, once its patent expires. *Id*.

Market realities and lack of laws concerning the registration of varietal and cultivar names have created a number of problems in this area. Some varietal names are not attractive or easy to remember by the public. As a result, many arbitrary terms are used as varietal names. Problems arise when trademark registration is sought for varietal names, when arbitrary varietal names are thought of as being trademarks by the public, and when terms intended as trademarks by plant breeders become generic through public use. These problems make this a difficult area for the examining attorney in terms of gathering credible evidence and knowing when to make refusals.

Whenever an application is filed to register a mark containing wording for live plants or agricultural seeds, the examining attorney must inquire of the applicant

或变种名称，则审查员必须以标的物属于植物品种名称、不具有《商标法》§§1，2 和 45，15 U.S.C. §§1051，1052 和 1127 所规定的商标功能为理由拒绝予以注册，或者要求弃权。*参见*相关判例 *Dixie Rose Nursery v. Coe*，131 F.2d 446，55 USPQ 315（D.C. Cir. 1942），*cert. denied* 318 U.S. 782，57 USPQ 568（1943）；*Hilltop Orchards & Nurseries，Inc.*，206 USPQ 1034（TTAB 1979）；*Farmer Seed & Nursery Co.*，137 USPQ 231（TTAB 1963）；*Cohn Bodger & Sons Co.*，122 USPQ 345（TTAB 1959）。同样地，如果商标识别的是某一植物品种名称的主要部分，也必须拒绝予以注册。见 *Delta and Pine Land Co.*，26 USPQ2d 1157（TTAB 1993）(委员会维持了拒绝"DELTAPINE"注册的决定，因为这是植物品种名称 Deltapine 50、Deltapine 20、Deltapine 105 以及 Deltapine 506 的一部分)。

在植物专利中，植物品种或变种的名称用于识别物种。因此，即使名称最初是任意性的，它"向公众描述了某一特定种类的[植物]，而不是来自于某一特定[来源]的[植物]"*Dixie Rose*，131 F.2d at 447，55 USPQ at 316。任何供应商在专利到期之后，仍然独占某种专利物种或者品种的名称，是有悖于公共政策的。*同前*。

市场现实和缺乏植物品种和变种注册方面的法律，使这个领域产生了若干问题。一些植物品种的名称缺乏吸引力，或者难以为公众所记忆。结果，使用许多任意性名词用为植物品种的名称。当任意性植物品种名称被公众认作商标，并且植物生产者意图作为商标的名词经过公共使用而变成一般性名词时，品种名称作为商标注册，将出现问题。这些问题在收集可信证据以及判断在何种情况下必须拒绝注册时，给审查员造成了困难。

如果某项商标的注册申请包含了活体植物或农业种子名称，审查员必须对申请

whether the term has ever been used as a varietal name, and whether such name has been used in connection with a plant patent, a utility patent, or a certificate for plant variety protection. *See* 37 C. F. R. §2. 61(b). The examining attorney should also undertake an independent investigation of any evidence that would support a refusal to register, using sources of evidence that are appropriate for the particular goods specified in the application (*e. g.*, laboratories and repositories of the United States Department of Agriculture, plant patent information from the United States Patent and Trademark Office, a variety name search of plants certified under the Plant Variety Protection Act listed at www. ars-grn. gov/npgs/searchgrin. html).

1202. 13 Scent or Fragrance

The scent of a product may be registrable if it is used in a non-functional manner. *See In re Clarke*, 17 USPQ2d 1238 (TTAB 1990), in which the Trademark Trial and Appeal Board held that a scent functioned as a mark for "sewing thread and embroidery yarn."Scents that serve a utilitarian purpose, such as the scent of perfume, would be functional and not registrable. *See*, *generally*, TMEP §1202. 02 (a) regarding functionality. When a scent is not functional, it may be registered on the Principal Register under §2(f), or on the Supplemental Register. The amount of evidence required to establish that a scent or fragrance functions as a mark is substantial. *Cf. In re Owens-Corning Fiberglas Corp.*, 774 F. 2d 1116, 227 USPQ 417 (Fed. Cir. 1985).

The requirement for a drawing does not apply to scent marks. 37 C. F. R. §2. 52(a)(3). *See* TMEP §807. 11.

1202. 14 Holograms

A hologram used in varying forms does not function as a mark in the absence of evidence that consumers would perceive it as a trademark. *See In re Upper Deck*

者进行调查,调查该名词是否曾被用作植物品种名,以及该名称是否曾被用于某项植物专利、实用新型专利,或者一项植物品种保护证书。*参见* 37 C.F.R.§2.61(b)。审查员应当对一切可能支持拒绝注册决定的证据进行独立的调查,使用与申请书中特别指明的、与特定商品相适应的证据来源(例如,美国农业部实验室和资料库;美国专利和商标局的植物专利资料;搜索在www.arsgrin.gov/npgs/searchgrin.html上列举的、经《植物多样性保护法》认证的植物品种名称等等)。

1202.13 气味或香味

产品的气味,如果以一种非功能性的方式使用,是可以注册的。参见 *Clarke*, 17 USPQ2d 1238 (TTAB 1990),在本案中,商标评审及上诉委员会认为气味可以作为"缝纫线和刺绣纱线"的商标。具有实用目的的气味,诸如香水的气味,具有功能性,不能注册。有关功能性的信息,*参见* TMEP §1202.02(a)。如果气味不具有功能性,那么就可以根据 §2(f)的规定在联邦商标登记簿或补充登记簿上注册。证明一种气味或香味可以作为商标使用需要大量的证据。比较 *Owens-Corning Fiberglas Corp.*, 774 F.2d 1116, 227 USPQ 417 (Fed.Cir.1985)。

气味商标不要求附图。37 C.F.R.§2.52(a)(3)。*参见* TMEP §807.11。

1202.14 全息图

各种形状的全息图如果缺乏消费者将其看作商标的证据,则不具有商标的功能。

Co., 59 USPQ2d 1688 (TTAB 2001), where the Board held that a hologram used on trading cards in varying shapes, sizes, and positions did not function as a mark, because the record showed that other companies used holograms on trading cards and other products as anti-counterfeiting devices, and there was no evidence that the public would perceive applicant's hologram as an indicator of source. The Board noted that "the common use of holograms for non-trademark purposes means that consumers would be less likely to perceive applicant's uses of holograms as trademarks." 59 USPQ2d at 1693.

Therefore, in the absence of evidence of consumer recognition as a mark, the examining attorney should refuse registration on the ground that the hologram does not function as a mark, under §§1, 2 and 45 of the Trademark Act, 15 U.S.C. §§1051, 1052 and 1127.

Generally, if a hologram has two or more views, the examining attorney should also refuse registration under §§1 and 45 of the Trademark Act, 15 U.S.C. §§1051 and 1127, on the ground that the application seeks registration of more than one mark. *In re Upper Deck*, *supra*. *See* TMEP §807.03.

1202.15 Sound Marks

A sound mark identifies and distinguishes a product or service through audio rather than visual means. Examples of sound marks include: (1) a series of tones or musical notes, with or without words, and (2) a word or words accompanied by music. For a discussion of the criteria for registration of sound marks, *see In re General Electric Broadcasting Co., Inc.*, 199 USPQ 560 (TTAB 1978).

The requirement for a drawing does not apply to sound marks. 37 C.F.R. §2.52(a)(3). *See* TMEP §807.11.

Audio cassettes and compact disks may be accepted as specimens for sound marks. 37 C.F.R. §2.56(d)(3). To show that the sound mark actually identifies and distinguishes the services and indicates their source, the cassette should contain a suf-

参见 *Upper Deck Co*., 59 USPQ2d 1688（TTAB 2001），在本案中，委员会认为具有不同形状和大小、以各种放置位置用在游戏卡上的全息图不具有商标的功能，因为档案显示，其他公司也在游戏卡及其他产品上将全息图作为防伪标记使用，并没有证据表明公众会将申请者的全息图看做是识别来源的商标。委员会认为："全息图通常作为非商标用途使用，这意味着消费者不太可能将申请者使用的全息图看作是商标。" 59 USPQ2d at 1693。

因此，如果缺乏消费者将其认知为商标的证据，审查员应当根据《商标法》§§1，2 和 45，15 U.S.C.§§1051，1052 和 1127 的规定以全息图不具有商标功能为理由拒绝予以注册。

一般情况下，如果全息图有两个或两个以上的视图，审查员也应当根据《商标法》§§1 和 45，15 U.S.C.§§1051 和 1127 的规定，以申请注册不止一个商标为理由拒绝予以注册。见 *Upper Deck*，*案卷号同前*。*参见* TMEP §807.03。

1202.15 声音商标

声音商标通过听觉而不是视觉的方法识别并区分一种产品或服务。声音商标的例子包括：(1)一系列的音调或音符，有字或无字，以及(2)有音乐伴奏的一个或多个文字。要了解有关声音商标申请注册标准的讨论，请参见 *General Electric Broadcasting Co*., *Inc*., 199 USPQ 560（TTAB 1978）。

声音商标不要求附图。37 C.F.R.§2.52(a)(3)。*参见* TMEP §807.11。

音乐磁带和 CD 光盘可以作为声音商标的样本。37 C.F.R.§2.56(d)(3)。为了表明声音商标实质上识别并区分了服务，并标示了来源，磁带应当含有可以充分显

ficient portion of the audio content to indicate the nature of the services. If the mark comprises music or words set to music, the applicant may also submit the musical score as a specimen.

1203 Refusal on Basis of Immoral or Scandalous Matter; Deceptive Matter; Matter which May Disparage, Falsely Suggest a Connection, or Bring into Contempt or Disrepute

Extract from 15 U.S.C.§1052. No trademark by which the goods of the applicant may be distinguished from the goods of others shall be refused registration on the principal register on account of its nature unless it—

(a) Consists of or comprises immoral, deceptive, or scandalous matter; or matter which may disparage or falsely suggest a connection with persons, living or dead, institutions, beliefs, or national symbols, or bring them into contempt, or disrepute; or a geographical indication which, when used on or in connection with wines or spirits, identifies a place other than the origin of the goods and is first used on or in connection with wines or spirits by the applicant on or after one year after the date on which the WTO Agreement (as defined in section 2(9) of the Uruguay Round Agreements Act) enters into force with respect to the United States.

The provisions of 15 U.S.C. §1052(a) apply to both the Principal Register and the Supplemental Register.

1203.01 Immoral or Scandalous Matter

Section 2(a) of the Trademark Act, 15 U.S.C. §1052(a), is an absolute bar to the registration of immoral or scandalous matter on either the Principal Register or the Supplemental Register.

Although the words "immoral" and "scandalous" may have somewhat different

示服务性质的音乐内容。如果商标包含了音乐或者音乐配词，申请者也可以提交乐谱作为样本。

1203 以内容不道德或令人反感；内容具有欺骗性；内容可能贬损、虚假地暗示某种关系或导致不光彩或不名誉为理由拒绝注册

摘自 15 U.S.C.§1052。凡商标的性质是用来将申请者商品与他人商品区分开来的，都可以在联邦商标登记簿上注册，除非——

(a)其包含不道德、欺骗或令人反感的内容；或者可能贬损或虚假地暗示与某在世者或死者、机构、信仰或国家象征有关系或是导致不光彩或不名誉的内容；或者地理标记用在酒类商品上或与酒类商品相关的，属于在《世界贸易总协定》(根据《乌拉圭回合协议法》2(9)的规定)在美国生效一年之日起，才首次由申请者作这种使用，以识别酒类商品原产地以外的其他地点的情况。

15 U.S.C.§1052(a)的规定对联邦商标登记簿和补充登记簿都适用。

1203.01 不道德或令人反感的内容

《商标法》第2(a)节，15 U.S.C.§1052(a)规定，严禁不道德或令人反感的标的物在联邦商标登记簿或补充登记簿上注册。

尽管“不道德的”和“令人反感”两词的含义可能稍有不同，但判例法将不道德的

connotations, case law has included immoral matter in the same category as scandalous matter. *See In re McGinley*, 660 F.2d 481, 484 n.6, 211 USPQ 668, 672 n. 6 (C.C.P.A.1981), *aff'g* 206 USPQ 753 (TTAB 1979) ("Because of our holding, *infra*, that appellant's mark is 'scandalous,' it is unnecessary to consider whether appellant's mark is 'immoral.' We note the dearth of reported trademark decisions in which the term 'immoral' has been directly applied.")

The prohibition against the registration of marks that consist of or comprise immoral or scandalous matter was originally enacted as §5(a) of the Act of 1905, and was reenacted as part of §2(a) of the Act of 1946. There is little legislative history concerning the intent of Congress with regard to the provision; therefore, the term "scandalous" is interpreted by looking to "its ordinary and common meaning." *In re Riverbank Canning Co*., 95 F.2d 327, 328, 37 USPQ 268, 269 (C.C.P.A.1938). This may be established by referring to court decisions, decisions of the Trademark Trial and Appeal Board and dictionary definitions. *In re McGinley*, 660 F.2d at 485, 211 USPQ at 673.

In affirming a refusal to register a mark as scandalous under §2(a), the Court of Customs and Patent Appeals noted dictionary entries that defined "scandalous" as, *inter alia*, shocking to the sense of propriety, offensive to the conscience or moral feelings or calling out for condemnation. *In re McGinley*, 660 F.2d at 486, 211 USPQ at 673 (mark comprising a photograph of a nude, reclining man and woman, kissing and embracing, for a "newsletter devoted to social and interpersonal relationship topics" and for "social club services," held scandalous). The statutory language "scandalous" has also been considered to encompass matter that is "vulgar," defined as "lacking in taste, indelicate, morally crude." *In re Runsdorf*, 171 USPQ 443, 444 (TTAB 1971). *See also In re Tinseltown, Inc*., 212 USPQ 863, 864 (TTAB 1981) (BULLSHIT, which the Board termed "profane," held scandalous for "accessories of a personal nature, ... attaché cases, hand bags, purses, belts, and wallets").

The meaning imparted by a mark must be determined in the context of the current

内容与令人反感的内容归入同一类别。参见 *McGinley*，660 F.2d 481，484 n.6，211 USPQ 668，672 n.6（C.C.P.A.1981），*aff'g* 206 USPQ 753（TTAB 1979）（"由于我们认为，*见下文*：上诉人的商标'令人反感'，不必再考虑该商标是否是'不道德的'。我们注意到，缺乏直接适用'不道德'一词的相关商标案件判例。"）。

禁止包含不道德或令人反感的内容的商标注册的法律规定最初见于《1905 年商标法》§5(a)，后来在《1946 年商标法》§2(a)中作了规定。对于此项规定，并没有多少有关国会用意的立法历史档案；因此"令人反感"一词以其"通常和普遍的含义"来解释。见 *Riverbank Canning Co*.，95 F.2d 327，328，37 USPQ 268，269（C.C.P.A.1938）。其含义可以通过法庭的判决、商标评审及上诉委员会的裁决以及辞典的定义确立。见 *McGinley*，660 F.2d 485，211 USPQ 673。

在维持一项根据 §2(a)作出的、对含有令人反感的内容的商标拒绝予以注册的决定时，关税和专利上诉法院引用辞典条目将"令人反感"定义为：与社会习俗有激烈冲突、违背良心或道德感情或会受到谴责等的事物。见 *McGinley*，660 F.2d 486，211 USPQ 673（对于"致力于社会及人际关系主题"并且为"社会俱乐部服务"的目的而言，包含赤裸男女倚靠在一起接吻拥抱照片的商标被认为是令人反感的。法律语言上的"令人反感"还被认为包括了"庸俗的"内容，即"缺乏品位的、没有教养的、粗俗的"内容。见 *Runsdorf*，171 USPQ 443，444（TTAB 1971）。*另参见 Tinseltown*，*Inc*.，212 USPQ 863，864（TTAB 1981）（委员会认为，对于"个人性质的随身物品……公文包、手提包、钱包、皮带、皮夹"而言，具有亵渎含义的"BULLSHIT"（狗屎）一词是令人反感的。

商标所表达的含义必须根据当代人的态度进行判断。

attitudes of the day. *See In re Mavety Media Group Ltd.*, 33 F.3d 1367, 31 USPQ2d 1923 (Fed. Cir. 1994) (evidence found insufficient to establish that BLACK TAIL used on adult entertainment magazines comprises scandalous matter; court noted that there were both vulgar and non-vulgar definitions of "tail," and that the record was devoid of evidence demonstrating which of these definitions a substantial composite of the general public would choose in the context of the relevant marketplace); *In re Old Glory Condom Corp.*, 26 USPQ2d 1216 (TTAB 1993) (OLD GLORY CONDOM CORP and design comprising the representation of a condom decorated with stars and stripes in a manner to suggest the American flag held not to be scandalous); *In re Thomas Laboratories, Inc.*, 189 USPQ 50, 52 (TTAB 1975) ("[I]t is imperative that fullest consideration be given to the moral values and conduct which contemporary society has deemed to be appropriate and acceptable.")

The determination of whether a mark is scandalous must be made in the context of the relevant marketplace for the goods or services identified in the application, and must be ascertained from the standpoint of not necessarily a majority, but a "substantial composite of the general public." *In re McGinley*, 660 F.2d at 485, 211 USPQ at 673 ("[T]he Lanham Act does not require, under the rubric of 'scandalous,' any inquiry into the specific goods or services not shown in the application itself."); *In re Wilcher Corp.*, 40 USPQ2d 1929 (TTAB 1996) (mark for restaurant and bar services consisting of words DICK HEADS positioned directly underneath caricature of a human head composed primarily of graphic and readily recognizable representation of male genitalia held scandalous, as it would be considered offensive by a substantial portion of the public); *Greyhound Corp. v. Both Worlds Inc.*, 6 USPQ2d 1635, 1639 (TTAB 1988) (graphic design of a dog defecating, as applied to polo shirts and T-shirts, held scandalous, given the broad potential audience that may view applicant's mark in sales establishments and "virtually all public places"); *In re Hepperle*, 175 USPQ 512 (TTAB 1972) (while the words might be a reference to marijuana, ACAPULCO GOLD found not scandalous when used as a mark for suntan lotion).

参见 *Mavety Media Group Ltd*., 33 F.3d 1367, 31 USPQ2d 1923 (Fed. Cir. 1994)(没有充分证据证明成人娱乐杂志所使用的"BLACK TAIL"(黑尾)一词包含了令人反感的内容;法庭解释道,"tail"一词具有粗俗和不粗俗的两种含义,档案中没有充分证据表明在相应的市场环境中,一般大众的实质混合会选择哪一种含义); *Old Glory Condom Corp*., 26 USPQ2d 1216 (TTAB 1993)(避孕套饰有星条图案,以代表美国国旗,以及"OLD GLORY CONDOM CORP"字样,被认为并不是令人反感的); *Thomas Laboratories, Inc*., 189 USPQ 50, 52 (TTAB 1975)("必须在当代社会认为适当及可接受的前提下,对道德价值和行为规范进行最完整的考虑。")。

判断商标是否令人反感必须在申请的商标所识别的商品或服务的相关市场中进行,并且必须从"一般公众的实质混合"而不必是"大多数人"的观点来确定。相关判例: *McGinley*, 660 F.2d 485, 211 USPQ 673("《兰哈姆法》并没有要求以'令人反感'为理由对申请本书本身没有提及的具体商品或服务进行调查"); *Wilcher Corp*., 40 USPQ2d 1929 (TTAB 1996)(直接位于主要由可清晰辨认为男性生殖器图形和画像构成的人头漫画的下方的"DICK HEADS"(鸟头)二字,作为餐馆和酒吧服务的商标被认为是令人反感的,因为大部分的公众会认为这是无礼的。); *Greyhound Corp. v. Both Worlds Inc*., 6 USPQ2d 1635, 1639 (TTAB 1988)(用于运动衫和T恤衫上的一幅狗正在大便的图案被认为是令人反感的,因为委员会认为人们可能在销售场所以及"实际上一切公共场所"看到申请者的这个商标); *Hepperle*, 175 USPQ 512 (TTAB 1972)(由于"ACAPULCO GOLD"这两个字可能指大麻,因此在防晒露上使用的这两个字被判定是令人反感的)。

Therefore, to support a refusal on the ground that a proposed mark is immoral or scandalous, the examining attorney must provide evidence that a substantial portion of the general public would consider the mark to be scandalous in the context of contemporary attitudes and the relevant marketplace. *In re Mavety Media*, 33 F.3d at 1371-1372, 31 USPQ2d at 1925. This evidence could include dictionary definitions, newspaper articles and magazine articles.

It has been noted that the threshold is lower for what can be described as "scandalous" than for "obscene." Refusal to register immoral or scandalous matter has been found not to abridge First Amendment rights, because no conduct is proscribed and no tangible form of expression is suppressed. Also, the term "scandalous" has been held sufficiently precise to satisfy due process requirements under the Fifth Amendment. *In re McGinley*, 660 F.2d at 484-85, 211 USPQ at 672.

The prohibition in §2(a) of the Act against the registration of scandalous matter pertains only to *marks* that are scandalous. The authority of the Act does not extend to goods that may be scandalous. *See In re Madsen*, 180 USPQ 334, 335 (TTAB 1973) (WEEK-END SEX for magazines held not scandalous, the Board observing that whether the magazine contents may be pornographic was not an issue before the Board).

The examining attorney may look to the specimen(s) or other aspects of the record to determine how the mark will be seen in the marketplace. *See In re McGinley*, 660 F.2d at 482 n.3, 211 USPQ at 670 n.3 (containing excerpts from appellant's newsletters pertaining to their subject matter); *In re Hershey*, 6 USPQ2d 1470, 1472 (TTAB 1988) (BIG PECKER BRAND for T-shirts found not scandalous, the Board considering the labels that were submitted as specimens in determining the question of how the mark might be perceived. "[T]he inclusion of the bird design would make it less likely that purchasers would attribute any vulgar connotation to the word mark and we note that it is proper to look to the specimens of record to determine connotation or meaning of a mark.").

To ensure consistency in examination with respect to immoral or scandalous mat-

因此,为了支持一项以申请注册的商标不道德或令人反感为理由而作出的拒绝予以注册的决定,审查员必须提供证据,证明以现代人的态度以及在相关的市场中,一般公众中大部分人认为该商标是令人反感的。见 *Mavety Media*, 33 F.3d 1371–1372, 31 USPQ2d 1925。这种证据可以包括辞典定义以及报纸杂志的文章。

需要注意的是,可以被称为"令人反感的"事物的阈限比"淫秽事物"更低。对不道德及令人反感的内容拒绝予以注册并不违反宪法第一修正案,因为并没有禁止任何行为,也没有压制任何有形的语言表达。而且,"令人反感"一词被认为充分、精确地满足了宪法第一修正案所规定的正当程序要求。见 *McGinley*, 660 F.2d 484–85, 211 USPQ 672。

《商标法》§2(a)关于令人反感内容禁止注册的规定只适用于确属令人反感的*商标*。商标法的权利不可延伸至令人反感的商品。*参见 Madsen*, 180 USPQ 334, 335 (TTAB 1973)(杂志的"WEEK-END SEX"被认为是令人反感的,委员会认为,杂志的内容是否属于色情并不是本委员会所要考察的问题。)。

审查员可以参考样本或档案的其他部分,以判断在市场中该商标是如何被看待的。*参见 McGinley*, 660 F.2d 482 n.3, 211 USPQ 670 n.3(包括引自上诉人提交的、与标的物有关的时事通讯摘要);*Hershey*, 6 USPQ2d 1470, 1472 (TTAB 1988)(T 恤衫上的"BIG PECKER BRAND"(大啄木鸟头)被认为不是令人反感的,委员会在判断该商标可能造成何种认知的过程中,参考了提交作为样本的标签。"由于包含了小鸟图案,这使购买者不太可能认为该文字商标具有任何粗俗的含义,因而我们认为,参考档案样本以判断商标的含义或意义是适宜的。")。

为了在不道德或令人反感的内容的审查中保持一致性,如果无论出于何种理由

ter, when an examining attorney believes, for whatever reason, that a mark may be considered to comprise such matter, the examining attorney must consult with his or her supervisor.

1203.02 Deceptive Matter

Section 2(a) of the Trademark Act, 15 U.S.C. §1052(a), is an absolute bar to the registration of deceptive matter on either the Principal Register or the Supplemental Register. Neither a disclaimer of the deceptive matter nor a claim that it has acquired distinctiveness under §2(f) can obviate a refusal under §2(a) on the ground that the mark consists of or comprises deceptive matter. *See American Speech-Language-Hearing Association v. National Hearing Aid Society*, 224 USPQ 798, 808 (TTAB 1984); *In re Charles S. Loeb Pipes, Inc.*, 190 USPQ 238, 241 (TTAB 1975).

Deceptive marks may include marks that falsely describe the material content of a product (*see In re Intex Plastics Corp.*, 215 USPQ 1045 (TTAB 1982)) and marks that are geographically deceptive (*see Stabilisierungsfonds fur Wein v. Peter Meyer Winery GmbH*, 9 USPQ2d 1073 (TTAB 1988); *In re House of Windsor, Inc.*, 221 USPQ 53 (TTAB 1983), *recon. denied*, 223 USPQ 191 (TTAB 1984)). *See* TMEP §1210.05(a) regarding geographically deceptive marks.

The Court of Appeals for the Federal Circuit has articulated the following test for whether a mark consists of or comprises deceptive matter:

(1) Is the term misdescriptive of the character, quality, function, composition or use of the goods?

(2) If so, are prospective purchasers likely to believe that the misdescription actually describes the goods?

(3) If so, is the misdescription likely to affect the decision to purchase?

In re Budge Mfg. Co. Inc., 857 F. 2d 773, 775, 8 USPQ2d 1259, 1260 (Fed. Cir.

审查员相信某项商标可以被认为包含了此类内容，审查员必须同其上司协商。

1203.02 欺骗性内容

《商标法》第2(a)节，15 U.S.C. §1052(a)，严禁欺骗性的内容在联邦商标登记簿或补充登记簿上注册。无论是欺骗性内容免责声明书，还是主张具有 §2(f)所规定的获得性独特性的声明书，都不能阻止按 §2(a)的规定以商标含有欺骗性内容为理由作出拒绝予以注册的决定。参见 *American Speech-Language-Hearing Association v. National Hearing Aid Society*，224 USPQ 798，808 (TTAB 1984)；*Charles S. Loeb Pipes, Inc.*，190 USPQ 238，241 (TTAB 1975)。

欺骗性商标可以包括虚假地描述产品的材料内容的商标(参见 *Intex Plastics Corp.*，215 USPQ 1045 (TTAB 1982))以及具有地理欺骗性的商标(参见 *Stabilisierungsfonds fur Wein v. Peter Meyer Winery GmbH*，9 USPQ2d 1073 (TTAB 1988)；*House of Windsor, Inc.*，221 USPQ 53 (TTAB 1983)，*recon. denied*，223 USPQ 191 (TTAB 1984))。有关地理欺骗性商标的信息，参见 TMEP §1210.05(a)。

联邦巡回上诉法院在一项商标是否含有欺骗性内容上，明确了以下测试方法：

(1) 所用的文字是否对商品的特征、质量、功能、成分或用途进行误导性描述？

(2) 如果有，潜在购买者是否可能相信该误导性描述是对商品的真实描述？

(3) 如果是，该误导性描述是否可能影响购买决定？

见 *Budge Mfg. Co. Inc.*，857 F.2d 773，775，8 USPQ2d 1259，1260 (Fed. Cir. 1988)，*aff'g* 8 USPQ2d 1790 (TTAB 1987)。

1988), *aff'g* 8 USPQ2d 1790 (TTAB 1987).

The fact that only those knowledgeable in the relevant trade, and not average purchasers, would be deceived does not preclude a finding that a mark comprises deceptive matter. *In re House of Windsor, Inc.*, 223 USPQ 191, 192 (TTAB 1984).

1203.02(a) Distinction between Marks Comprising Deceptive Matter (§2(a)) and Deceptively Misdescriptive Marks (§2(e)(1)) or Geographically Deceptively Misdescriptive Marks (§2(e)(3))

If the first two inquiries set forth by the Federal Circuit in *In re Budge Mfg. Co. Inc.*, 857 F.2d 773, 775, 8 USPQ2d 1259, 1260 (Fed. Cir. 1988) (*i.e.*, whether a mark is misdescriptive of the goods or services and whether prospective purchasers are likely to believe the misdescription), are answered affirmatively, the mark is either deceptively misdescriptive of the goods/services under §2(e)(1), or primarily geographically deceptively misdescriptive of them under §2(e)(3). With regard to geographic marks, the second inquiry, whether purchasers are likely to believe the misrepresentation, may also be characterized as whether there is a goods/place association. *See* TMEP §§1210.04 *et seq*.

The third inquiry, whether the misdescription is likely to affect the decision to purchase, distinguishes marks that are deceptive under §2(a) from marks that are deceptively misdescriptive under §2(e)(1) or primarily geographically deceptively misdescriptive under §2(e)(3). Marks that are deceptive under §2(a) are unregistrable on either the Principal Register or the Supplemental Register.

Marks that are deceptively misdescriptive under §2(e)(1) are unregistrable on the Principal Register without a showing of acquired distinctiveness under §2(f), 15 U.S.C. §1052(f). Marks that are primarily geographically deceptively misdescriptive under §2(e)(3) are unregistrable on either the Principal Register or the Supplemental Register with the following exceptions. A mark that is primarily geo-

即使只有了解相关行业者，并非一般的购买者可能受到欺骗，这一事实并不能排除作出商标包含欺骗性内容的结论。见 *House of Windsor, Inc.*, 223 USPQ 191, 192 (TTAB 1984)。

1203.02(a) 包含欺骗性内容的商标（§2(a)）与欺骗性误导描述的商标（§2(e)(1)）或地理欺骗性误导描述的商标（§2(e)(3)）之间的区别

如果联邦巡回法院在 *Budge Mfg. Co. Inc.*, 857 F.2d 773, 775, 8 USPQ2d 1259, 1260 (Fed. Cir. 1988)案中所设定的前两项调查（即商标是否对商品或服务进行误导性描述，以及潜在的购买者是否可能相信这种误导性描述）得到了肯定的答案，那么该商标要么具有 §2(e)(1)所规定的对商品/服务进行欺骗性误导描述，要么主要是具有 §2(e)(3)所规定的对商品/服务进行地理欺骗性误导描述。对于地理商标，第二项调查即调查购买者是否可能相信该误导性描述，也可以表现为是否存在商品与地点之间的联系。参见 TMEP §§1210.04 及以下。

第三项调查，即该误导性描述是否可能对购买决定产生影响，将 §2(a)所规定的欺骗性商标与 §2(e)(1)所规定的欺骗性误导性描述商标或 §2(e)(3)所规定的地理欺骗性误导描述的商标区分开来。§2(a)所规定的欺骗性商标既不能在联邦商标登记簿也不能在补充登记簿上注册。

如果没有显示出 §2(f), 15 U.S.C. §1052(f)所规定的后天性独特性，则具有 §2(e)(1)所规定的欺骗性误导描述的商标不得在联邦商标登记簿上注册。除了以下例外情况，§2(e)(3)所规定的地理欺骗性误导描述商标既不能在联邦商标登记簿也不能

graphically deceptively misdescriptive may be registered on the Principal Register only upon a showing under §2(f) that the mark had acquired distinctiveness in connection with the applicant's goods or services before December 8, 1993. A primarily geographically misdescriptive mark may be registered on the Supplemental Register only if the mark was in lawful use in commerce before December 8, 1993. 15 U.S.C. §1091. *See* TMEP §§1210.06 *et seq*.

The determinative nature of the third inquiry, *i.e.*, the materiality of the misdescription to the purchasing decision, is indicated in the following summary by the Trademark Trial and Appeal Board:

> The Board has held that a mark is deceptive within the meaning of Section 2(a) of the Act, 15 U.S.C. 1052(a), if it misdescribes the goods, purchasers are likely to believe the misrepresentation, and the misrepresentation would materially affect their decision to purchase the goods. *See In re Quady Winery Inc*., 221 USPQ 1213 (TTAB 1984). If the mark misdescribes the goods, and purchasers are likely to believe the misrepresentation, but the misrepresentation is not material to the purchasing decision, then the mark is deceptively misdescriptive (citation omitted).
>
> In the same vein, if a mark is the name of a place known generally to the public, purchasers who encounter goods bearing the mark would think that the goods originate in that place [*i.e.*, purchasers would make a "goods-place association" (citation omitted)], the goods do not come from the named place, and the deception is material to the purchasing decision, the mark is deceptive under Section 2(a); if the deception is not material to the purchasing decision, the mark is primarily geographically deceptively misdescriptive under Section [2(e)(3)] of the Act.

Bureau National Interprofessionnel Du Cognac v. International Better Drinks Corp., 6 USPQ2d 1610, 1615 (TTAB 1988).

To establish that a misdescription would be likely to affect the decision to purchase, the examining attorney should provide evidence that the misdescriptive

在补充登记簿上注册。只有当商标在1993年12月8日之前用于与申请者的商品或服务相关而显示出具有§2(f)所规定的获得性独特性时,一项主要的地理欺骗性误导描述的商标方可在联邦商标登记簿上注册。如果一项地理欺骗性描述的商标在1993年12月8日之前进入合法的商业使用,则可以在联邦商标补充登记簿上注册。见15 U.S.C.§1091。*参见* TMEP §§1210.06 及以下。

关于第三项调查的决定因素,即误导性描述对于购买决定的重要性,商标评审及上诉委员会作了如下归纳:

> 委员会认为,如果一项商标对商品进行了误导性描述,购买者可能相信这种误导性描述,而且该误导性描述会影响购买商品的决定,那么该商标就符合《商标法》第2(a)节,15 U.S.C.1052(a)对于欺骗性商标的定义。*参见 Quady Winery Inc.*, 221 USPQ 1213 (TTAB 1984)。如果商标对商品进行了误导性描述,而且购买者也可能相信这种误导性描述,但是该误导性描述并没有实质影响到购买决定,那么该商标就属于欺骗性误导描述商标。(引注略)同样地,如果某项商标是一个为公众所熟知的地名,那么看到该商品所携带商标的购买者就会认为商品的原产地就是该地[即,购买者会产生一种"商品—地点联系"(引注略)],而该商品实际上并非来自此地,如此就对购买决定造成了实质性影响,根据第2(a)节的规定,该商标就是欺骗性的;如果这种欺骗性对于购买决定并未造成实质性影响,那么根据该法[2(e)(3)]节的规定,该商标就是地理欺骗性误导描述商标。

Bureau National Interprofessionnel Du Cognac v. International Better Drinks Corp., 6 USPQ2d 1610, 1615 (TTAB 1988)。

要证实一种误导性描述可能对购买决定产生影响,审查员应当提供证据,证明误

quality or characteristic would make the product or service more appealing or desirable to prospective purchasers. *In re Juleigh Jeans Sportswear Inc*., 24 USPQ2d 1694 (TTAB 1992).

It may often be appropriate for the examining attorney to refuse registration of a mark of this type under both §2(a) and the appropriate subsection of §2(e), because it may be difficult to determine whether misdescriptive matter would materially affect a decision to purchase. *See*, *e.g*., *Gold Seal Co. v. Weeks*, 129 F. Supp. 928, 105 USPQ 407 (D. D. C. 1955), *aff'd sub nom. S. C. Johnson & Son, Inc. v. Gold Seal Co*., 230 F. 2d 832, 108 USPQ 400 (D. C. Cir. 1956) (per curiam), *cert. denied*, 352 U.S. 829, 111 USPQ 467 (1956).

See also R. Neumann & Co. v. Overseas Shipments, Inc., 326 F. 2d 786, 140 USPQ 276 (C. C. P. A. 1964), and *Stabilisierungsfonds fur Wein v. Peter Meyer Winery GmbH*, 9 USPQ2d 1073 (TTAB 1988), in which third parties filed oppositions based on both statutory sections.

See TMEP §1210.05(b) regarding geographical indications that, when used on or in connection with wines or spirits, identify a place other than the origin of the goods.

1203.02(b) Deceptive Matter: Case References [R-2]

In the following cases, proposed marks were determined to be deceptive, under §2(a): *In re Budge Mfg. Co. Inc*., 857 F. 2d 773, 8 USPQ2d 1259 (Fed. Cir. 1988), *aff'g* 8 USPQ2d 1790 (TTAB 1987) (LOVEE LAMB held deceptive for seat covers not made of lambskin); *In re Phillips-Van Heusen Corp*., 63 USPQ2d 1047 (TTAB 2002) (SUPER SILK held deceptive for "clothing, namely dress shirts and sport shirts made of silk-like fabric"); *In re Organik Technologies, Inc*., 41 USPQ2d 1690 (TTAB 1997) (ORGANIK deceptive for clothing and textiles made from cotton that is neither from an organically grown plant nor free of chemical processing or treatment, notwithstanding applicant's assertions that the

导性描述的质量或特点能够使产品或服务对潜在的购买者产生更大的吸引力或更合意。*Juleigh Jeans Sportswear Inc*.,24 USPQ2d 1694(TTAB 1992)。

审查员根据 §2(a)和§2(e)的相应子节对这种商标拒绝予以注册常常可能是恰当的,因为误导性描述的内容是否会对购买决定产生实质性影响也许难以判断。*参见*判例 *Gold Seal Co. v. Weeks*, 129 F. Supp. 928, 105 USPQ 407 (D. D. C. 1955), *aff'd sub nom. S. C. Johnson & Son, Inc. v. Gold Seal Co.*, 230 F. 2d 832, 108 USPQ 400 (D. C. Cir. 1956)(per curiam), *cert. denied*, 352 U. S. 829, 111 USPQ 467 (1956)。

另参见 R. Neumann & Co. v. Overseas Shipments, Inc., 326 F. 2d 786, 140 USPQ 276 (C. C. P. A. 1964)以及 *Stabilisierungsfonds fur Wein v. Peter Meyer Winery GmbH*, 9 USPQ2d 1073 (TTAB 1988),在该两案中,第三方根据上述两项法律规定提出异议。

有关用于酒类商品的地理商标识别商品原产地以外的地点的情况,*参见* TMEP §1210.05(b)。

1203.02(b) 欺骗性内容:参考案例[R-2]

在下列案件中,申请注册的商标根据 §2(a)被判定具有欺骗性:*Budge Mfg. Co. Inc.*, 857 F. 2d 773, 8 USPQ2d 1259 (Fed. Cir. 1988), *aff'g* 8 USPQ2d 1790 (TTAB 1987)(对于并非由羔羊皮制成的座椅套,"LOVEE LAMB"(可爱的羔羊)被认为具有欺骗性);*Phillips-Van Heusen Corp.*, 63 USPQ2d 1047 (TTAB 2002)(对于"由仿丝绸织物制成的正式衬衫和运动衬衫衣服","SUPER SILK"(超级丝绸)被认为具有欺骗性); *Organik Technologies, Inc.*, 41 USPQ2d 1690 (TTAB 1997)(尽管申请者声明其由棉花制成的服装及纺织品商品是经过无化学漂白工艺流程制

goods are manufactured by a process that avoids the use of chemical bleaches, because the identification of goods was broad enough to include textiles and clothing manufactured with chemical processes or dyes); *In re Juleigh Jeans Sportswear Inc*., 24 USPQ2d 1694 (TTAB 1992) (LONDON LONDON held deceptive for clothing having no connection with London); *In re Perry Mfg. Co*., 12 USPQ2d 1751 (TTAB 1989) (PERRY NEW YORK and design of New York City skyline held deceptive for clothing originating in North Carolina, in view of the renown of New York City in the apparel industry); *Stabilisierungsfonds fur Wein v. Peter Meyer Winery GmbH*, 9 USPQ2d 1073, 1075 (TTAB 1988) (GOLDENER TROPFEN held deceptive for wines, in view of evidence of the international renown of the Goldtropfchen vineyard of West Germany, the Board finding that the purchasing public would be likely to think, mistakenly, that applicant's wines were produced from grapes grown there in accordance with German wine laws and regulations); *Bureau National Interprofessionnel Du Cognac v. International Better Drinks Corp*., 6 USPQ2d 1610 (TTAB 1988) (COLAGNAC held deceptive for cola-flavored liqueur containing Spanish brandy, the Board concluding that purchasers were likely to believe that applicant's goods contained COGNAC brandy); *In re Shapely, Inc*., 231 USPQ 72 (TTAB 1986) (SILKEASE held deceptive as applied to clothing not made of silk); *In re House of Windsor, Inc*., 221 USPQ 53 (TTAB 1983), *recon. denied*, 223 USPQ 191 (TTAB 1984) (BAHIA held deceptive as applied to cigars having no connection with the Bahia province of Brazil, the record indicating that tobacco and cigars are important products in the Bahia region); *Evans Products Co. v. Boise Cascade Corp*., 218 USPQ 160 (TTAB 1983) (CEDAR RIDGE held deceptive for embossed hardboard siding not made of cedar); *In re Intex Plastics Corp*., 215 USPQ 1045 (TTAB 1982) (TEXHYDE held deceptive as applied to synthetic fabric for use in the manufacture of furniture, upholstery, luggage and the like); *Tanners' Council of America, Inc. v. Samsonite Corp*., 204 USPQ 150 (TTAB 1979) (SOFTHIDE held deceptive for imitation leather material); *In re Salem China Co*., 157 USPQ 600 (TTAB 1968) (AMERICAN LIMOGES, used on dinnerware that was neither made in Limoges, France, nor made from Limoges clay, held deceptive because of the association of

造的，但是由于其并非由有机种植的植物制成，而且仍然经过了化学工艺处理，因此“ORGANIK”（有机）仍然被认为具有欺骗性，因为所识别的商品范围覆盖了广泛的领域，足以包括经过化学漂染的纺织品和服装）；*Juleigh Jeans Sportswear Inc.*, 24 USPQ2d 1694（TTAB 1992）（对于同伦敦没有联系的服装，“LONDON LONDON”（伦敦、伦敦）被认为具有欺骗性）；*Perry Mfg. Co.*, 12 USPQ2d 1751（TTAB 1989）（由于纽约市在服装业的名声，对于原产于北卡罗来纳的服装，“PERRY NEW YORK”（派里纽约）以及纽约市轮廓的图案被认为具有欺骗性）；*Stabilisierungsfonds fur Wein v. Peter Meyer Winery GmbH*, 9 USPQ2d 1073, 1075（TTAB 1988）（由于证据表明西德的 Goldtropfchen 葡萄园享有国际声誉，委员会判定购买公众可能会错误地认为申请者的葡萄酒是采用根据德国酒类法律法规种植的葡萄生产的，因此对于葡萄酒，“GOLDENER TROPFEN”被认为具有欺骗性）；*Bureau National Interprofessionnel Du Cognac v. International Better Drinks Corp.*, 6 USPQ2d 1610（TTAB 1988）（委员会判定，购买者可能会认为申请者的产品含有“COGNAC”白兰地，因此对于含有西班牙白兰地的可乐味利口酒而言，“COLAGNAC”被认为具有欺骗性）；*Shapely, Inc.*, 231 USPQ 72（TTAB 1986）（对于并非以丝绸制成的服装，“SILKEASE”（绸爽）被认为具有欺骗性）；*House of Windsor, Inc.*, 221 USPQ 53（TTAB 1983），*recon. denied*, 223 USPQ 191（TTAB 1984）（档案表明，烟草和雪茄是 Bahia（巴伊亚）地区的重要产品，因此对于与巴西的 Bahia（巴伊亚）省没有关系的雪茄，“BAHIA”被认为具有欺骗性）；*Evans Products Co. v. Boise Cascade Corp.*, 218 USPQ 160（TTAB 1983）（对于并非以雪松制成的硬质壁板，“CEDAR RIDGE”（雪松岭）被认为具有欺骗性）；*Intex Plastics Corp.*, 215 USPQ 1045（TTAB 1982）（对于用于家具制造、室内装潢、箱包以及诸如此类的混纺织物，“TEXHYDE”（织皮）被认为具有欺骗性）；*Tanners' Council of America, Inc. v. Samsonite Corp.*, 204 USPQ 150（TTAB 1979）（对于仿皮材料，“SOFTHIDE”（软牛皮）被认为具有欺骗性）；*Salem China Co.*, 157 USPQ 600（TTAB 1968）（由于 Limoges（利摩日）同高品质瓷器的联系，对于既非法国 Limoges（利摩日）制造，又非由 Limoges 粘土制成的餐具，“AMERICAN LIMOGES”（美国 Limoges（利摩日））

Limoges with fine quality china); *Company of Cutlers of Hallamshire in the County of York v. Regent-Sheffield, Ltd.*, 155 USPQ 597 (TTAB 1967) (SHEFFIELD, used on cutlery not made in Sheffield, England, held deceptive because of the renowned status of Sheffield in relation to cutlery); *In re U.S. Plywood Corp.*, 138 USPQ 403 (TTAB 1963) (IVORY WOOD, for lumber and timber products, held deceptive since the goods were not made of ivorywood nor did they contain an ivorywood pattern).

Marks were found not to be deceptive in the following cases: *Philip Morris Inc. v. Reemtsma Cigarettenfabriken GmbH*, 14 USPQ2d 1487 (TTAB 1990) (PARK AVENUE held neither deceptive nor geographically deceptively misdescriptive as applied to applicant's cigarettes and smoking tobacco, the Board finding no goods/place association between Park Avenue in New York City, on which opposer's world headquarters was located, and tobacco products); *In re Fortune Star Products Corp.*, 217 USPQ 277 (TTAB 1982) (NIPPON, for radios, televisions and the like, found not deceptive in relation to the goods because, although the applicant was an American firm, the goods were actually made in Japan); *In re Sweden Freezer Mfg. Co.*, 159 USPQ 246, 249 (TTAB 1968) (SWEDEN and design, for which registration was sought under §2(f) for external artificial kidney units, held not deceptive, the Board finding the case to be in the category "where a geographical trademark may involve a degree of untruth but the deception may be perfectly innocent, harmless or negligible"); *A. F. Gallun & Sons Corp. v. Aristocrat Leather Products, Inc.*, 135 USPQ 459 (TTAB 1962) (COPY CALF, for wallets and billfolds of synthetic and plastic material made to simulate leather, found not deceptive, the Board noting that the mark, as an obvious play on the expression "copy cat," suggested to purchasers that the goods were imitations of items made of calf skin).

1203.03 Matter which May Disparage, Falsely Suggest a Connection, or Bring into Contempt or Disrepute

Section 2(a) of the Trademark Act, 15 U.S.C. §1052(a), bars the registration on

被认为具有欺骗性)；*Company of Cutlers of Hallamshire in the County of York v. Regent-Sheffield, Ltd.*, 155 USPQ 597 (TTAB 1967)(由于 Sheffield 以餐具著称，用于不在英国 Sheffield 制造的餐具上的“SHEFFIELD”被认为具有欺骗性)；*U. S. Plywood Corp.*, 138 USPQ 403 (TTAB 1963)(由于既不是以象牙木制成，又不带有象牙木图案，因此对于木料及木制品而言，“IVORY WOOD”(象牙木)被认为具有欺骗性)。

在下列案件中，商标被判定不具有欺骗性：*Philip Morris Inc. v. Reemtsma Cigarettenfabriken GmbH*, 14 USPQ2d 1487 (TTAB 1990)(委员会认为，异议人全球总部所在地纽约市帕克大道与烟草产品之间并不存在商品与地点的联系，因此用于申请人烟草的“PARK AVENUE”(公园路)被认为既非欺骗性也非地理欺骗性误导描述)；*Fortune Star Products Corp.*, 217 USPQ 277 (TTAB 1982)(“NIPPON”(日本)对于收音机、电视之类而言，被认为不具有欺骗性，因为虽然申请者是美国公司，但产品实际都是在日本生产的)；*Sweden Freezer Mfg. Co.*, 159 USPQ 246, 249 (TTAB 1968)(根据 §2(f)的规定，为外用人造肾脏申请注册的“SWEDEN”(瑞典)及图案，被认为不具有欺骗性，委员会认为该案属于“尽管地理商标涉嫌具有一定程度的虚假性，但这种虚假性可能是完全无辜、无害或可以忽略的”。)；*A. F. Gallun & Sons Corp. v. Aristocrat Leather Products, Inc.*, 135 USPQ 459 (TTAB 1962)(用于人造及塑料材料制成的钱包和皮夹的“COPY CALF”(复制牛皮)被认为不具欺骗性，委员会认为，该商标明显仿照习语“copy cat”(复制者)，向购买者表明了该商品系仿牛皮制品)。

1203.03 可能贬损、虚假地暗示某种关系或导致不光彩或不名誉的内容

《商标法》第2(a)节，15U. S. C. §1052(a)严禁在联邦商标登记簿或补充登记簿

either the Principal or the Supplemental Register of a designation that consists of or comprises matter which, with regard to persons, institutions, beliefs, or national symbols, does any of the following: (1) disparages them, (2) falsely suggests a connection with them, (3) brings them into contempt, or (4) brings them into disrepute.

Section 2(a) is distinctly different from §2(d), 15 U.S.C. §1052(d), for which the relevant test is likelihood of confusion. In *University of Notre Dame du Lac v. J.C. Gourmet Food Imports Co., Inc.*, 703 F.2d 1372, 1375-76, 217 USPQ 505, 508-09 (Fed. Cir. 1983), *aff'g* 213 USPQ 594 (TTAB 1982), the Court of Appeals for the Federal Circuit noted as follows:

> A reading of the legislative history with respect to what became §2(a) shows that the drafters were concerned with protecting the name of an individual or institution which was not a technical "trademark" or "trade name" upon which an objection could be made under §2(d)...
>
> Although not articulated as such, it appears that the drafters sought by §2(a) to embrace concepts of the right to privacy, an area of the law then in an embryonic state (footnote omitted). Our review of case law discloses that the elements of a claim of invasion of one's privacy have emerged as distinctly different from those of trademark or trade name infringement. There may be no likelihood of such confusion as to the source of goods even under a theory of "sponsorship" or "endorsement," and, nevertheless, one's right of privacy, or the related right of publicity, may be violated.

The right to privacy protects a party's control over the use of its identity or "persona." A party acquires a protectible interest in a name or equivalent designation under §2(a) where the name or designation is unmistakably associated with, and points uniquely to, that party's personality or "persona." A party's interest in a name or designation does not depend upon adoption and use as a technical trademark or trade name. *University of Notre Dame du Lac v. J. C. Gourmet Food Im-*

上注册包含对有关个人、机构、信仰以及国家象征存在如下情况的内容:(1)对其进行侮辱,(2)虚假地暗示同其存在某种关系,(3)使其不光彩或(4)不名誉。

第 2(a)节的规定与 §2(d),15 U.S.C.§1052(d)显然不同,但各自的相关判别标准可能产生混淆。在 *University of Notre Dame du Lac v. J. C. Gourmet Food Imports Co., Inc.*, 703 F.2d 1372, 1375-76, 217 USPQ 505, 508-09 (Fed. Cir. 1983), *aff'g* 213 USPQ 594 (TTAB 1982)一案中,联邦巡回上诉法院作了如下论述:

> 仔细地阅读立法发展史可以发现,制定 §2(a)条款的原因是,立法者要保护那些在技术上并非"商标"或"商号"的个人或机构的名称,因为可以根据 §2(d)的规定对这些名称提出异议……。
>
> 尽管没有如此明确地表示,但是立法者似乎想通过 §2(a)来采纳隐私权的概念,而当时这一领域的法律仍处于萌芽状态(脚注略)。通过对判例法的回顾,我们揭示了构成隐私侵犯的要素与商标及商号侵权的要素截然不同。即使在"赞助"或"背书"的理论下,对商品的来源也不太可能产生混淆,不过,一个人的隐私权或者相关的名声权却可能遭到侵犯。

隐私权保护当事人对于使用其身份或"人格"的控制。根据 §2(a)的规定,只要该名字或名称明白无误地与该当事人的人格相联系并且唯一地指向该当事人的人格,当事人对于名字或名称就享有可受保护的权益。当事人对于名字或名称的权益并不取决于是否将其采用并用作一种技术性商标或商号。*University of Notre Dame du*

ports Co., Inc., 703 F.2d at 1376-77, 217 USPQ at 509; *Buffett v. Chi-Chi's, Inc.*, 226 USPQ 428, 429 (TTAB 1985).

See TMEP §§1203.03(c) and 1203.03(d) regarding disparagement, bringing into contempt and bringing into disrepute, and TMEP §§1203.03(e) and 1203.03(f) regarding false suggestion of a connection.

See Carson v. Here's Johnny Portable Toilets, Inc., 698 F.2d 831, 218 USPQ 1 (6th Cir. 1983), concerning the various forms of identity which have been protected under the rights of privacy and publicity.

1203.03(a) "Persons" Defined

Section 2(a) of the Trademark Act, 15 U.S.C. §1052(a), protects, *inter alia*, "persons, living or dead."

Section 45 of the Act, 15 U.S.C. §1127, defines "person" and "juristic person" as follows:

> The term "person" and any other word or term used to designate the applicant or other entitled to a benefit or privilege or rendered liable under the provisions of this Act includes a juristic person as well as a natural person. The term "juristic person" includes a firm, corporation, union, association, or other organization capable of suing and being sued in a court of law.
>
> The term "person" also includes the United States, any agency or instrumentality thereof, or any individual, firm, or corporation acting for the United States and with the authorization and consent of the United States. The United States, any agency or instrumentality thereof, and any individual, firm, or corporation acting for the United States and with the authorization and consent of the United States, shall be subject to the provisions of this Act in the same manner and to the same extent

Lac v. J. C. Gourmet Food Imports Co., Inc., 703 F.2d 1376－77, 217 USPQ 509; *Buffett v. Chi-Chi's, Inc.*, 226 USPQ 428, 429 (TTAB 1985)。

有关贬损、导致不光彩和不名誉的情况，*参见* TMEP §§1203.03(c)和1203.03(d)；有关虚假地暗示某种关系的情况，*参见* §§1203.03(e)和1203.03(f)。

有关隐私权和名誉权所保护的各种身份形式，*参见* Carson v. Here's Johnny Portable Toilets, Inc., 698 F.2d 831, 218 USPQ 1 (6th Cir. 1983)。

1203.03(a) "人"的定义

《商标法》第2(a)节，15 U.S.C. §1052(a)对"在世或去世的人"进行保护等。

《商标法》第45节，15 U.S.C. §1127，对"人"和"法人"作了如下定义：

> "人"一词和任何其他文字或术语用来指定依据本法有权获得利益或特权或者依本法承担责任的申请者或其他人，包括法人和自然人。"法人"一词包括企业、公司、联盟、联合会或其他具有诉讼能力的组织。
>
> "人"一词还包括美国及其任何部门和机构或者任何美国同意和授权、代表美国行事的个人、企业或公司。美国及其任何部门和机构，或者任何美国同意和授权、代表美国行事的个人、企业或公司，均应与任何非政府实体

as any nongovernmental entity.

The term "person" also includes any State, any instrumentality of a State, and any officer or employee of a State or instrumentality of a State acting in his or her official capacity. Any State, and any such instrumentality, officer, or employee, shall be subject to the provisions of this Act in the same manner and to the same extent as any non-governmental entity.

The term "persons" in §2(a) refers to real persons, not fictitious characters. In addition to natural persons, it includes juristic persons, *i.e.*, legally-created entities such as firms, corporations, unions, associations or any other organizations capable of suing and being sued in a court of law. *See Morehouse Mfg. Corp. v. J. Strickland & Co.*, 407 F.2d 881, 160 USPQ 715 (C.C.P.A. 1969); *Popular Merchandise Co. v. "21" Club, Inc.*, 343 F.2d 1011, 145 USPQ 203 (C.C.P.A. 1965); *John Walker & Sons, Ltd. v. American Tobacco Co.*, 110 USPQ 249 (Comm'r Pats. 1956); *Copacabana, Inc. v. Breslauer*, 101 USPQ 467 (Comm'r Pats. 1954).

With respect to natural persons, they may be living or dead. However, §2(a) may not be applicable with regard to a deceased person when there is no longer anyone entitled to assert a propriety right or right of privacy. *Lucien Piccard Watch Corp. v. Since 1868 Crescent Corp.*, 314 F. Supp. 329, 165 USPQ 459 (S.D.N.Y. 1970) (DA VINCI held not to falsely suggest connection with deceased artist Leonardo Da Vinci).

A juristic person's rights under §2(a) are extinguished when the juristic person ceases to exist. *In re Wielinski*, 49 USPQ2d 1754 (TTAB 1998).

Juristic persons or institutions do not have to be well known to be protected from the registration of a mark that falsely suggests a connection with or disparages them, or brings them into contempt or disrepute. *Gavel Club v. Toastmasters International*, 127 USPQ 88, 94 (TTAB 1960).

一样，以相同方式和范围，接受本法的管辖。

“人”一词还包括任何州、州的任何机构以及州或州机构的任何官员或职员。任何州和任何州机构、官员或职员应与任何非政府实体一样，以相同方式和范围，接受本法的管辖。

§2(a)中定义的“人”是指真实的人，而非虚拟的人物。除自然人外，还包括了法人，即：依法设立的实体，如企业、公司、联盟、联合会以及其他具有诉讼能力的组织。参见 *Morehouse Mfg. Corp. v. J. Strickland & Co.*, 407 F.2d 881, 160 USPQ 715 (C.C.P.A.1969)；*Popular Merchandise Co. v. "21" Club, Inc.*, 343 F.2d 1011, 145 USPQ 203 (C.C.P.A.1965)；*John Walker & Sons, Ltd. v. American Tobacco Co.*, 110 USPQ 249 (Comm'r Pats.1956)；*Copacabana, Inc. v. Breslauer*, 101 USPQ 467 (Comm'r Pats.1954)。

至于自然人，可以是在世者或者去世者。不过，当不再有人对其财产权或隐私权拥有权利时，§2(a)就不再适用于死者了。*Lucien Piccard Watch Corp. v. Since 1868 Crescent Corp.*, 314 F. Supp. 329, 165 USPQ 459 (S.D.N.Y.1970)（“DA VINCI”被认为虚假地暗示与已故艺术家 Leonardo Da Vinci 之间的关系）。

如果法人不复存在，则 §2(a)所规定的法人权利亦消失。见 *Wielinski*, 49 USPQ2d 1754 (TTAB 1998)。

不管法人或机构是否出名，凡是虚假地暗示与他们有关系、贬损他们或使他们不光彩或不名誉的商标都不能注册，以对他们进行保护。*Gavel Club v. Toastmasters International*, 127 USPQ 88, 94 (TTAB 1960)。

It is well settled that the United States Government is a juristic person. *See NASA v. Record Chemical Co. Inc.*, 185 USPQ 563, 566 (TTAB 1975), and cases cited therein.

A mark does not have to comprise a person's full or correct name to be unregistrable; a nickname or other designation by which a person is known by the public may be unregistrable under this provision of the Act. *Buffett v. Chi-Chi's, Inc.*, 226 USPQ 428, 430 (TTAB 1985) (evidence of record "sufficient to raise a genuine issue of material fact as to whether the term 'MARGARITAVILLE' is so uniquely and unmistakably associated with opposer as to constitute opposer's name or identity such that when applicant's mark is used in connection with its [restaurant] services, a connection with opposer would be assumed").

1203.03(b) "National Symbols" Defined

A "national symbol" is subject matter of unique and special significance that, because of its meaning, appearance and/or sound, immediately suggests or refers to the country for which it stands. *In re Consolidated Foods Corp.*, 187 USPQ 63 (TTAB 1975) (noted national symbols include the bald eagle, Statue of Liberty, American flag, Presidential symbol, designation "Uncle Sam" and the unique human representation thereof, and the heraldry and shield designs used in governmental offices). National symbols include the symbols of foreign countries as well as those of the United States. *In re Anti-Communist World Freedom Congress, Inc.*, 161 USPQ 304 (TTAB 1969).

The Trademark Act does not prohibit registration of marks comprising national symbols; it only prohibits registration of matter that may disparage national symbols, falsely suggest a connection with them, or hold them up to contempt or disrepute. *Liberty Mutual Insurance Co. v. Liberty Insurance Co. of Texas*, 185 F. Supp. 895, 908, 127 USPQ 312, 323 (E.D. Ark. 1960) (marks comprising portion of the Statue of Liberty found not to disparage, bring into contempt or disrepute, or falsely suggest a connection with the Statue of Liberty or the United States gov-

已经明确地确定，美国政府是一个法人。参见 *NASA v. Record Chemical Co. Inc.*, 185 USPQ 563, 566 (TTAB 1975)，以及所引用的判例。

不管商标是否由某人的全名或真名组成，都可能是不可注册的；根据《商标法》的本项规定，绰号或此人为公众所知的其他名称都是不可注册的。*Buffett v. Chi-Chi's, Inc.*, 226 USPQ 428, 430 (TTAB 1985)（"有充分的"记录证据"可以提出一个真实的事实问题，即'MARGARITAVILLE'一词是否唯一、明白无误地与异议人相关联，申请者的商标中所使用的异议人的名字或身份使商标在与其[餐馆]服务"相关时，是否可以认为与异议者发生了关系）。

1203.03(b) "国家象征"的定义

"国家象征"是具有独特和特殊意义的标的物，因为其涵义、外观和/或声音可以立即暗示或意指该象征所代表的国家。见 *Consolidated Foods Corp.*, 187 USPQ 63 (TTAB 1975)（认为，国家象征包括秃鹰、自由女神像、星条旗、总统符号、"山姆大叔"字样及独特的人物形象，以及政府部门所使用的纹章和盾形图案）。国家象征包括美国和外国的象征。见 *Anti-Communist World Freedom Congress, Inc.*, 161 USPQ 304 (TTAB 1969)。

《商标法》并不禁止含有国家象征的商标注册；而只是禁止可能贬损国家象征、虚假地暗示与其有某种关系或者使其不光彩或不名誉的标的物的注册。见 *Liberty Mutual Insurance Co. v. Liberty Insurance Co. of Texas*, 185 F. Supp. 895, 908, 127 USPQ 312, 323 (E.D. Ark. 1960)（包含部分自由女神像的商标被判定并没有贬损女神像或美国政府、虚假地暗示与其有某种关系或者使其不光彩或不名誉，而法庭

ernment, the Court "[a]ssuming without deciding" that the statue is a national symbol).

Designations have been held to be national symbols within the meaning of §2(a) in the following cases: *In re Anti-Communist World Freedom Congress, Inc.*, 161 USPQ 304 (TTAB 1969) (representation of a hammer and sickle held to be a national symbol of the Union of Soviet Socialist Republics (U.S.S.R.)); *In re National Collection & Credit Control, Inc.*, 152 USPQ 200, 201 n.2 (TTAB 1966) ("The American or bald eagle with wings extended is a well-known national symbol or emblem of the United States"); *In re Teasdale Packing Co., Inc.*, 137 USPQ 482 (TTAB 1963) (U.S. AQUA and design held unregistrable under §2(a) on the ground that purchasers of applicant's canned drinking water would be misled into assuming approval or sponsorship by the United States government in view of the nature of the mark, including a red, white and blue shield design, and the nature of the goods, the Board noting a program for stocking emergency supplies of water in fallout shelters and the setting of standards for drinking water by United States government agencies).

Designations have been held not to be national symbols in the following cases: *W.H. Snyder and Sons, Inc. v. Ladd*, 227 F.Supp.185, 140 USPQ 647 (D.D.C. 1964) (HOUSE OF WINDSOR held not to be a national symbol of England, but merely the name of its present reigning family); *NASA v. Bully Hill Vineyards, Inc.*, 3 USPQ2d 1671 (TTAB 1987) (SPACE SHUTTLE found not to constitute a national symbol on the evidence of record, the Board also finding "shuttle" to be a generic term for a space vehicle or system); *Jacobs v. International Multifoods Corp.*, 211 USPQ 165, 170-71 (TTAB 1981), *aff'd on other grounds*, 668 F.2d 1234, 212 USPQ 641 (C.C.P.A. 1982) ("[H]istorical events such as the 'BOSTON TEA PARTY'..., although undoubtedly associated with the American heritage, do not take on that unique and special significance of a 'national symbol' designed to be equated with and associated with a particular country."); *In re General Mills, Inc.*, 169 USPQ 244 (TTAB 1971) (UNION JACK, which applicant was using on packages of frozen fish marked "English cut cod" and in its res-

"不经裁判即推定"女神像是一种国家象征)。

在下列案件中,商标被认定属于 §2(a)中定义的国家象征:*Anti-Communist World Freedom Congress, Inc.*, 161 USPQ 304 (TTAB 1969)(镰刀铁锤图案被认为是前苏联(U.S.S.R.)的国家象征);*National Collection & Credit Control, Inc.*, 152 USPQ 200, 201 n.2 (TTAB 1966)("展翅翱翔的美洲鹰或称秃鹰是众所周知的美国国家象征");*Teasdale Packing Co., Inc.*, 137 USPQ 482 (TTAB 1963)("U.S. AQUA"被认为不能按 §2(a)的规定进行注册,因为申请者的罐装饮用水的购买者会由于该商标的特点——包括红白蓝三色盾形图案——以及该商品的特点而误以为是由美国政府批准或赞助的,为此委员会引用了美国政府部门制定的一项关于在核武器掩体中储备紧急淡水供应以及设置的饮用水标准的计划)。

在下列案件中,商标被认定不属于 §2(a)中定义的国家象征:*W. H. Snyder and Sons, Inc. v. Ladd*, 227 F. Supp. 185, 140 USPQ 647 (D.D.C. 1964)("HOUSE OF WINDSOR"(温莎宫)被认为不是英格兰的国家象征,而只是在位王室的名称);*NASA v. Bully Hill Vineyards, Inc.*, 3 USPQ2d 1671 (TTAB 1987)(根据档案证据,"SPACE SHUTTLE"(太空梭)被认为不构成国家象征,委员会同时还判定"shuttle"一词只是空间交通工具或系统的一般术语);*Jacobs v. International Multifoods Corp.*, 211 USPQ 165, 170-71 (TTAB 1981), *aff'd on other grounds*, 668 F.2d 1234, 212 USPQ 641 (C.C.P.A. 1982)("诸如'BOSTON TEA PARTY'(波士顿茶业事件)之类的历史事件……尽管无疑地与美国传统存在联系,但是并不构成与特定国家相联系的'国家象征'的独特和特殊的重要意义。");*General Mills, Inc.*, 169 USPQ 244 (TTAB 1971)(申请者将 "UNION JACK"用于标有"英国产鳕鱼"冰冻鱼

taurant near representations of the British national flag, found not to suggest a particular country, the Board noting that it could consider only the matter for which registration was sought); *In re Horwitt*, 125 USPQ 145, 146 (TTAB 1960) (U.S. HEALTH CLUB found registrable for vitamin tablets. "Considering both the nature of the mark and the goods, it is concluded that the purchasing public would not be likely to mistakenly assume that the United States Government is operating a health club, that it is distributing vitamins, or that it has approved applicant's goods.")

The name of a country is not a national symbol within the meaning of §2(a) of the Trademark Act, *In re Sweden Freezer Mfg. Co.*, 159 USPQ 246, 248-249 (TTAB 1968), nor does use of the name of a country as a mark, by itself, amount to deception, disparagement, or a "false connection" under §2(a). *In re Fortune Star Products Corp.*, 217 USPQ 277 (TTAB 1982).

The acronyms for, and names of, government agencies and bureaus are not considered to be national symbols. *Consolidated Foods Corp.*, 187 USPQ at 64 (OSS, acronym for the Office of Strategic Services, held not to be a national symbol, but merely to designate a particular (and long defunct) government agency, the Board contrasting national symbols with names and acronyms of government agencies. "'National symbols' ... are more enduring in time, ... and immediately conjure up the image of the country as a whole. Symbols of a country take on a special meaning and significance and are not so numerous as to dilute the special meaning and significance that each has.")

"National symbols" cannot be equated with the "insignia" of nations. As noted in *Liberty Mutual Insurance Co.*, 185 F. Supp. at 908, 127 USPQ at 323:

> The Act ... does not put national symbols on a par with the flag, coat of arms, or other insignia of the United States, which may not in any event be made the subject matter of a trade or service mark. With regard to national symbols the statute provides merely that they shall not be disparaged or held up to contempt or disrepute, and shall not be used as falsely

肉包装以及在附近展示英国国旗的餐馆，该商标被认为并没有代表了某一特定国家，委员会指出，可以认为它是要申请注册的内容）；*Horwitt*，125 USPQ 145，146（TTAB 1960）（“U.S. HEALTH CLUB”（美国健康俱乐部）被判定可以作为维他命药片的商标注册。“综合考虑该商标和商品的性质，我们得出结论，购买公众不太可能错误地推出美国政府正在经营一家经销维他命的健康俱乐部，或者政府批准认可了申请者的商品。”）。

国名并不是《商标法》§2(a)所规定的国家象征，见 *Sweden Freezer Mfg. Co.*，159 USPQ 246，248－249（TTAB 1968），将国家作为商标使用本身也并不产生 §2(a)所规定的欺骗性、贬损或者“虚假的关系”。见 *Fortune Star Products Corp.*，217 USPQ 277（TTAB 1982）。

政府部门或办事处的缩写和名称不被认为是国家象征。见 *Consolidated Foods Corp.*，187 USPQ at 64（委员会比较了国家象征和政府部门的名称及缩写，认为“OSS”，即战略服务处的缩写，不属于国家象征，而只是指一个特定的（且废止已久的）政府部门。“‘国家象征’……是更能经受时间考验的……而且能立刻同国家的整体形象联系起来。国家象征拥有特别的含义和意义，而且数量不多，不至于冲淡每一个国家象征的特别含义和意义。”）。

“国家象征”并不等同于各国的“标记”。正如 *Liberty Mutual Insurance Co.*，185 F.Supp.908，127 USPQ 323 一案中所说的：

> 法律……并没有将国家象征等同于旗帜、盾徽或其他美国的商标，这些商标并不是在任何情况下都可以成为商标或服务商标的内容。对于国家象征，法律只规定他们不应是贬损性的，或者会导致不光彩或不名誉，并且也

to suggest a connection between the holder of the mark and the symbol.

See TMEP §1204 regarding insignia.

While the prohibition of §2(a) against the registration of matter that may disparage or falsely suggest a connection with national symbols, or bring them into contempt or disrepute, may not be applicable to a particular designation, many names, acronyms, titles, terms, and symbols are protected by other statutes or rules. *See* TMEP §1205.01.

1203.03(c) Disparagement, Bringing into Contempt and Bringing into Disrepute

Section 2(a) prohibits the registration of a mark that consists of or comprises matter that may disparage, or bring into contempt or disrepute, persons, institutions, beliefs or national symbols. *See* TMEP §1203.03(a) regarding persons, and TMEP §1203.03(b) regarding national symbols.

In sustaining an opposition on this ground, the Trademark Trial and Appeal Board stated as follows:

> Disparagement is essentially a violation of one's right of privacy — the right to be "let alone" from contempt or ridicule. See, *Carson v. Here's Johnny Portable Toilets, Inc.*, 698 F. 2d 831, 218 USPQ 1 (6th Cir. 1983). It has been defined as the publication of a statement which the publisher intends to be understood, or which the recipient reasonably should understand, as tending "to cast doubt upon the quality of another's land, chattels, or intangible things." Restatement (Second) of Torts §629 (1977). The two elements of such a claim are (1) that the communication reasonably would be understood as referring to the plaintiff; and (2) that the communication is disparaging, that is, would be considered offensive or objectionable by a reasonable person of ordinary sensibilities. *Id.* (citations omitted).

不应用于虚假地表示商标持有人同该象征之间存在某种关系。

有关国家标记的信息，*参见* TMEP §1204。

虽然 §2(a)禁止对可能贬损国家象征或虚假地暗示与国家象征有某种关系，或者使国家象征不光彩或不名誉的内容予以注册，但此项规定并不适用于其他法律法规所保护的特定名称、许多名字、缩写、头衔、术语和符号。*参见* TMEP §1205.01。

1203.03(c) 贬损、导致不光彩和不名誉

第 2(a)节禁止对包含对有关个人、机构、信仰以及国家象征进行贬损、虚假地暗示与其有关系或者使其不光彩或不名誉的内容予以注册。有关个人方面，*参见* TMEP §1203.03(a)；有关国家象征，*参见* TMEP §1203.03(b)。

在支持一项以此为理由的异议中，商标评审及上诉委员会论述如下：

> 贬损本质上是对个人的隐私权——不受侮辱奚落“侵扰”的权利——的侵犯。*参见 Carson v. Here's Johnny Portable Toilets, Inc.*, 698 F.2d 831, 218 USPQ 1 (6th Cir.1983)。它已经被定义为一种声明的发布，声明发布者意在其能被理解为或者声明的收受者照理应能理解为，“对他人的土地、动产或无形财产的性质表示怀疑”的意向。见《侵权法(第二次)重述》§629 (1977)。这一主张的两个要素是：(1)所传递的信息照理会被理解为是指原告；以及(2)信息是贬损性的，也就是说，拥有一般情感的讲道理的人都会认为是无礼的或不快的。*同前*(引注略)。

Greyhound Corp. v. Both Worlds Inc., 6 USPQ2d 1635, 1639 (TTAB 1988).

With regard to the first element set forth, the Board found that the applicant's design of a dog defecating strongly resembled the opposer's running dog symbol and that the evidence of record established that the symbol "points uniquely and unmistakably to opposer's persona." *Id.* at 1640.

With regard to the second element, the Board noted the negative nature of the design and stated as follows:

> As it relates to opposer, ... the offensiveness of the design becomes even more objectionable because it makes a statement about opposer itself, and holds opposer up to ridicule and contempt.

Id.

1203.03(d) Disparagement, Bringing into Contempt and Bringing into Disrepute: Case References

See Boswell v. Mavety Media Group Ltd., 52 USPQ2d 1600 (TTAB 1999) (BLACK TAIL used on adult entertainment magazines, found not to be disparaging of women in general, or African-American women in particular, nor to bring those groups into contempt or disrepute); *Order Sons of Italy in America v. Memphis Mafia Inc.*, 52 USPQ2d 1364 (TTAB 1999) (THE MEMPHIS MAFIA for entertainment services found not to be matter that disparages Italian-Americans or bring them into contempt or disrepute); *Harjo v. Pro Football Inc.*, 50 USPQ2d 1705 (TTAB 1999) (REDSKINS, used in connection with presentation of professional football contests, found to be matter that may disparage Native Americans and bring them into contempt or disrepute, but not scandalous matter); *In re In Over Our Heads Inc.*, 16 USPQ2d 1653, 1654 (TTAB 1990) (MOONIES and design incorporating a "buttocks caricature," for dolls whose pants can be dropped, held not to be disparaging matter which would be unregistrable under §2(a), the Board finding that the mark "would, when used on a doll, most likely be per-

Greyhound Corp. v. Both Worlds Inc., 6 USPQ2d 1635, 1639 (TTAB 1988)。

关于第一项要素,委员会认为,申请者的狗正在大便的图案与异议人的奔跑狗符号极其相似,并且档案证据表明,该商标"唯一、明白无误地指向异议人的人格"。*同前*1640。

关于第二个要素,委员会对于该图案的消极性质陈述如下:

> 由于图案与异议人有关,……图案的无礼程度变得更令人不快,因为它提到了异议人本人,使异议人受到嘲笑和贬损。

同前。

1203.03(d) 贬损、导致不光彩和不名誉:参考案例

Boswell v. Mavety Media Group Ltd., 52 USPQ2d 1600 (TTAB 1999)(用于成人娱乐杂志的"BLACK TAIL"(黑尾)被认为并没有在一般意义上侮辱妇女,或者特别侮辱非裔妇女,同时也没有给这些人群带来不光彩或不名誉);*Order Sons of Italy in America v. Memphis Mafia Inc.*, 52 USPQ2d 1364 (TTAB 1999)(用于娱乐服务的"THE MEMPHIS MAFIA"(孟菲斯黑手党)被认为并非贬损意大利裔美国人,也不是使其不光彩或不名誉的内容);*Harjo v. Pro Football Inc.*, 50 USPQ2d 1705 (TTAB 1999)(用于职业橄榄球大赛的"REDSKINS"(红皮),被认为可能是贬损美国土著、令其不光彩或不名誉的内容,但不是令人反感的内容);*In Over Our Heads Inc.*, 16 USPQ2d 1653, 1654 (TTAB 1990)(在裤子可以脱下的娃娃上使用的"MOONIES"和含有"屁股漫画"的图案被认为并不属于 §2(a)所规定的不可注册的贬损性内容,委员会判定该商标"在娃娃上使用时,最可能被认知为表示该娃娃的'光

ceived as indicating that the doll 'moons,' and would not be perceived as referencing members of The Unification Church."); *Greyhound Corp. v. Both Worlds Inc.*, 6 USPQ2d 1635, 1639-40 (TTAB 1988) (design of dog defecating, for clothing, held to disparage, and bring into contempt or disrepute, opposer's running dog symbol, the Board finding the evidence of record "sufficient to show prima facie that this design [the running dog symbol] is, in effect, an alter ego of opposer which points uniquely and unmistakably to opposer's persona."); *In re Anti-Communist World Freedom Congress, Inc.*, 161 USPQ 304 (TTAB 1969) (design of an "X" superimposed over a hammer and sickle held to disparage, and hold in contempt and disrepute, a national symbol of the U.S.S.R.).

1203.03(e) False Suggestion of a Connection

Section 2(a) prohibits the registration of a mark that consists of or comprises matter that may falsely suggest a connection with persons, institutions, beliefs or national symbols. *See* TMEP §1203.03(a) regarding persons, TMEP §1203.03(b) regarding national symbols, and TMEP §1203.03 for information about the legislative history of §2(a).

To establish that a proposed mark falsely suggest a connection with a person or an institution, it must be shown that: (1) the mark is the same as, or a close approximation of, the name or identity of a person or institution; (2) the mark would be recognized as such, in that it points uniquely and unmistakably to that person or institution; (3) the person or institution named by the mark is not connected with the activities performed by applicant under the mark; and (4) the fame or reputation of the person or institution is such that, when the mark is used with the applicant's goods or services, a connection with the person or institution would be presumed. *In re Nuclear Research Corp.*, 16 USPQ2d 1316, 1317 (TTAB 1990); *Buffett v. Chi-Chi's, Inc.*, 226 USPQ 428, 429 (TTAB 1985); *In re Cotter & Co.*, 228 USPQ 202, 204 (TTAB 1985).

In *In re Sloppy Joe's International Inc.*, 43 USPQ2d 1350, 1353-34 (TTAB 1997),

屁股'，而不太可能被认为是指联合教团的成员。"）；*Greyhound Corp. v. Both Worlds Inc.*，6 USPQ2d 1635，1639－40（TTAB 1988）（服装上的狗正在大便的图案被认为贬损了异议人的奔跑狗符号，并使其不光彩或不名誉，委员会判定档案证据"足以初步确立，该图案［奔跑狗符号］实际上是异议人的一种第二自我，并唯一、明白无误地指向异议人的人格。"）；*Anti-Communist World Freedom Congress，Inc.*，161 USPQ 304（TTAB 1969）（铁锤镰刀交叉叠加的图案被认为贬损了前苏联的国家象征，并使其不光彩和不名誉）。

1203.03(e)　虚假地暗示某种关系

第2(a)节禁止对由虚假地暗示与某人、机构、信仰以及国家象征有某种关系的内容组成的商标予以注册。有关人的方面，*参见* TMEP §1203.03(a)；有关国家象征的情况，*参见* TMEP §1203.03(b)；有关§2(a)立法史的情况，*参见* TMEP §1203.03。

要确立申请注册的商标虚假地暗示与某人或某机构有某种关系，必须表明：(1)商标与某人或机构的名字或标记相同，或者非常接近；(2)商标会被认知为唯一、明白无误地指向该人或该机构；(3)商标所提及的人或机构与申请人以商标所进行的活动没有关联；以及(4)由于该人或该机构的名誉及声誉，商标用于申请人的商品或服务时，会造成同该人或机构存在某种关系的推定。*参见 Nuclear Research Corp.*，16 USPQ2d 1316，1317（TTAB 1990）；*Buffett v. Chi-Chi's，Inc.*，226 USPQ 428，429（TTAB 1985）；*In re Cotter & Co.*，228 USPQ 202，204（TTAB 1985）。

在 *Sloppy Joe's International Inc.*，43 USPQ2d 1350，1353－34（TTAB 1997） the Trademark Trial and Appeal Board held that Ernest Hemingway's friendship with the original owner of applicant's bar, his frequenting the bar and his use of the back room as an office is not the kind of "connection" contemplated by §2(a). Rather, a commercial connection, such as an ownership interest or commercial endorsement or sponsorship of applicant's services would be necessary to entitle the applicant to registration.

If it is unclear whether the person or institution is connected with the goods sold or services performed by the applicant, the examining attorney should make an explicit inquiry under 37 C.F.R. §2.61(b).

A refusal on this basis requires, by implication, that the person or institution with which a connection is falsely suggested must be the prior user. *In re Nuclear Research Corp.*, 16 USPQ2d at 1317; *In re Mohawk Air Services Inc.*, 196 USPQ 851, 854-55 (TTAB 1977).

Intent to identify a party or trade on its goodwill is not a required element of a §2(a) claim of false suggestion of an association with such party. *S & L Acquisition Co. v. Helene Arpels, Inc.*, 9 USPQ2d 1221, 1224 (TTAB 1987); *Consolidated Natural Gas Co. v. CNG Fuel Systems, Ltd.*, 228 USPQ 752, 754 (TTAB 1985). However, evidence of such an intent could be highly persuasive that the public would make the intended false association. *University of Notre Dame du Lac v. J. C. Gourmet Food Imports Co., Inc.*, 703 F.2d 1372, 1377, 217 USPQ 505, 509 (Fed. Cir. 1983), *aff'g* 213 USPQ 594 (TTAB 1982).

1203.03(f) False Suggestion of a Connection: Case References

See University of Notre Dame du Lac v. J. C. Gourmet Food Imports Co., Inc., 703 F.2d 1372, 1377, 217 USPQ 505, 509 (Fed. Cir. 1983), *aff'g* 213 USPQ 594 (TTAB 1982) (NOTRE DAME and design, for cheese, held not to falsely suggest a connection with the University of Notre Dame. "As the board noted, 'Notre Dame' is not a name solely associated with the University. It serves to identify a

一案中，商标评审及上诉委员会认为，Ernest Hemingway 与申请者酒吧原始所有人的友谊、他经常出入该酒吧并将酒吧后屋用作办公室的事实，并不属于 §2(a)所指的"关系"。相反地，一种商业关系，例如对申请者的服务拥有所有权利益或进行商业背书或赞助，即可以使申请者获得注册的资格。

如果不清楚此人或机构是否与申请者出售的商品或提供的服务有关系，审查员就应当根据 37 C.F.R.§2.61(b)的规定进行明确的调查。

不言而喻，以此理由拒绝注册，要求虚假地暗示与其有关系的该人或该机构必须是以前的用户。见 *Nuclear Research Corp.*, 16 USPQ2d at 1317; *Mohawk Air Services Inc.*, 196 USPQ 851, 854–55 (TTAB 1977)。

意图识别某一方或以某一方的信誉进行贸易并不是 §2(a)所规定的主张虚假地暗示与该方的联系的一个必要因素。见 *S & L Acquisition Co. v. Helene Arpels, Inc.*, 9 USPQ2d 1221, 1224 (TTAB 1987); *Consolidated Natural Gas Co. v. CNG Fuel Systems, Ltd.*, 228 USPQ 752, 754 (TTAB 1985)。不过，这种意图的证据可能非常有说服力，表明公众会产生这种意图中的错误联系。见 *University of Notre Dame du Lac v. J. C. Gourmet Food Imports Co., Inc.*, 703 F.2d 1372, 1377, 217 USPQ 505, 509 (Fed. Cir. 1983), *aff'g* 213 USPQ 594 (TTAB 1982)。

1203.03(f)　虚假地暗示某种关系：参考案例

参见 University of Notre Dame du Lac v. J. C. Gourmet Food Imports Co., Inc., 703 F.2d 1372, 1377, 217 USPQ 505, 509 (Fed. Cir. 1983), *aff'g* 213 USPQ 594 (TTAB 1982)(在奶酪上使用的"NOTRE DAME"(圣母院)及图案被认为并没有虚假地暗示与 Notre Dame (圣母)大学有某种关系。"正如委员会所指出的，'Notre Dame'二字并非只与该大学有联系。它可以用来识别著名和神圣的圣像，以

famous and sacred religious figure and is used in the names of churches dedicated to Notre Dame, such as the Cathedral of Notre Dame in Paris, France. Thus it cannot be said that the only 'person' which the name possibly identifies is the University and that the mere use of NOTRE DAME by another appropriates its identity."); *In re Sauer*, 27 USPQ2d 1073 (TTAB 1993), *aff'd*, 26 F.3d 140 (Fed. Cir. 1994) (registration of BO BALL for oblong shaped leather ball with white stitching properly refused under §2(a), since use of "Bo" would be recognized by purchasers as reference to football and baseball player Bo Jackson, and there was no connection between Jackson and applicant); *In re Urbano*, 51 USPQ2d 1776 (TTAB 1999) (SYDNEY 2000, used for advertising and business services and communication services, falsely suggests connection with Olympic Games, since general public would recognize phrase as referring unambiguously to Olympic Games to be held in Sydney, Australia, in 2000; entire organization that comprises Olympic games qualifies as "institution."); *In re North American Free Trade Association*, 43 USPQ2d 1282 (TTAB 1997) (NAFTA, used on "promotion of trade and investment" services, falsely suggests connection with North American Free Trade Agreement; NAFTA qualifies as institution because it encompasses treaty, supplemental agreements, and various commissions, committees and offices created by those documents); *In re Sloppy Joe's International Inc.*, 43 USPQ2d 1350 (TTAB 1997) (use of mark SLOPPY JOE'S, with design that includes portrait of Ernest Hemingway, falsely suggests connection with deceased writer); *Internet Inc. v. Corporation for National Research Initiatives*, 38 USPQ2d 1435 (TTAB 1996) (cancellation petitioners failed to state claim for relief where they have not alleged, and cannot reasonably allege, that term INTERNET points uniquely and unmistakably to their own identity or persona); *Ritz Hotel Ltd. v. Ritz Closet Seat Corp.*, 17 USPQ2d 1466, 1471 (TTAB 1990) (RIT-Z in stylized form, for toilet seats, held not to falsely suggest a connection with opposer, the Board observing that there was "no evidence of record directed to showing a connection of applicant's mark with opposer corporation, The Ritz Hotel Limited"); *In re Nuclear Research Corp.*, 16 USPQ2d 1316 (TTAB 1990) (NRC and design, for radiation and chemical agent monitors, electronic testers and nuclear gauges,

及用于献给圣墓的教堂名称，比如法国的巴黎圣母院大教堂。因此不能说该名所可能识别的唯一的一个‘人’就是该大学，或者说他人只要使用 NOTRE DAME，就具有这一身份）；*Sauer*，27 USPQ2d 1073（TTAB 1993），*aff'd*，26 F.3d 140（Fed. Cir. 1994）（为白线缝制的椭圆形皮球注册“BO BALL”，根据 §2(a)的规定被正当地驳回，因为使用“Bo”一词会使购买者联想到橄榄球和棒球运动员 Bo Jackson，而 Jackson 与申请者之间没有任何联系）；*Urbano*，51 USPQ2d 1776（TTAB 1999）（用于广告、商业服务和通讯服务的“SYDNEY（悉尼）2000”虚假地暗示与奥运会有联系，因为一般公众会毫无疑问地将这些文字与 2000 年在悉尼举办的奥运会相联系；构成奥运会的整个组织是一个“机构”）；*North American Free Trade Association*，43 USPQ2d 1282（TTAB 1997）（用于“贸易和投资促销活动的”“NAFTA”虚假地暗示了与北美自由贸易协议的关系；NAFTA 是一个机构，因为它包含了条约、补充协议以及各种由这些文件所设立的调查团、委员会和官员）；*Sloppy Joe's International Inc.*，43 USPQ2d 1350（TTAB 1997）（使用含有 Ernest Hemingway（恩斯特·海明威）肖像的“SLOPPY JOE'S”标识及图案，虚假地暗示了与这位已故作家的联系）；*Internet Inc. v. Corporation for National Research Initiatives*，38 USPQ2d 1435（TTAB 1996）（请求撤销注册“INTERNET”之人没有宣称或者不能合理地宣称“INTERNET”一字唯一并明白无误地指向其身份及人格，因此没有申述要求救济的主张）；*Ritz Hotel Ltd. v. Ritz Closet Seat Corp.*，17 USPQ2d 1466，1471（TTAB 1990）（用于马桶圈的固定样式的“RIT-Z”被认为并没有虚假地暗示与异议人的关系，委员会认为“没有档案证据直接地表明申请者的商标与异议人的公司——Ritz Hotel Limited——存在联系”）；*Nuclear Research Corp.*，16 USPQ2d 1316（TTAB 1990）（用于放射物和化合物监测器、电子测试仪以及核子测量仪的“NRC”及图案，

held not to falsely suggest a connection with the U. S. Nuclear Regulatory Commission in view of applicant's use of NRC long prior to the inception of that agency); *NASA v. Bully Hill Vineyards, Inc.*, 3 USPQ2d 1671, 1676 (TTAB 1987) (opposition to the registration of SPACE SHUTTLE for wines dismissed, the Board finding "shuttle" to be a generic term for a space vehicle or system. "Where a name claimed to be appropriated does not point uniquely and unmistakably to that party's personality or 'persona,' there can be no false suggestion."); *Board of Trustees of University of Alabama v. BAMA-Werke Curt Baumann*, 231 USPQ 408 (TTAB 1986) (petition to cancel registration of BAMA, for shoes, slippers, stockings, socks and insoles, granted, the Board finding that the evidence of record indicated that BAMA points uniquely to the University of Alabama and thus falsely suggests a connection with the University); *In re Cotter & Co.*, 228 USPQ 202 (TTAB 1985) (WESTPOINT, for shotguns and rifles, held to falsely suggest a connection with an institution, the United States Military Academy). For examples of findings of false suggestion of a connection prior to the decision of the Court of Appeals for the Federal Circuit in *Notre Dame*, *supra*, *see In re U. S. Bicentennial Society*, 197 USPQ 905 (TTAB 1978) (U. S. BICENTENNIAL SOCIETY, for ceremonial swords, held to falsely suggest a connection with the American Revolution Bicentennial Commission and the United States government); *In re National Intelligence Academy*, 190 USPQ 570 (TTAB 1976) (NATIONAL INTELLIGENCE ACADEMY, for educational and instructional services in intelligence gathering for law enforcement officers, held to falsely suggest a connection with the United States government).

1204 Refusal on Basis of Flag, Coat of Arms or Other Insignia of United States, State or Municipality, or Foreign Nation

Extract from 15 U. S. C. §1052. No trademark by which the goods of the applicant may be distinguished from the goods of others shall be refused registration on the principal register on account of its nature unless it ... (b) Consists of or comprises the flag or coat of arms or other insignia of the United States, or of any State or

被认为并没有虚假地暗示与美国原子能管理委员会的关系，因为在该机构设立以前很久，申请者就已经在使用该商标了）；*NASA v. Bully Hill Vineyards, Inc.*, 3 USPQ2d 1671, 1676 (TTAB 1987)（对注册“SPACE SHUTTLE”提出的异议遭到驳回，委员会判定“shuttle”只是一个用于空间交通工具或系统的一般术语。“如果声称被盗用的名称并没有唯一和明白无误地指向某当事人的人格，那就不存在虚假的暗示。”）；*Board of Trustees of University of Alabama v. BAMA-Werke Curt Baumann*, 231 USPQ 408 (TTAB 1986)（请求撤销在鞋、拖鞋、长袜、短袜机鞋垫上使用的“BAMA”商标被获准，因为委员会判定，档案证据显示 BAMA 唯一地指向 Alabama 大学，因此虚假地暗示了与该大学的联系）；*Cotter & Co.*, 228 USPQ 202 (TTAB 1985)（在霰弹枪和来复枪上使用的“WESTPOINT”（西点）商标被认为虚假地暗示了与美国陆军学校有联系）。有关在上述联邦巡回上诉法院 *Notre Dame* 一案之前判定虚假暗示联系的例子，请参见 *U.S. Bicentennial Society*, 197 USPQ 905 (TTAB 1978)（纪念宝剑上的“U.S. BICENTENNIAL SOCIETY”（美国二百周年学会）被判定虚假地暗示了与美国革命二百周年委员会和美国政府有联系）；*National Intelligence Academy*, 190 USPQ 570 (TTAB 1976)（为执法官员收集情报进行教育和指导服务的“NATIONAL INTELLIGENCE ACADEMY”（国家情报研究院）被认为虚假地暗示了与美国政府有联系）。

1204 以含有美国、州及自治市或者外国的旗帜、盾徽或其他徽记为由拒绝注册

摘自 15 U.S.C.§1052。凡用来将申请者商品与他人商品区分开来的商标均可以在联邦商标登记簿上注册，除非——(b)其包含美国、任何州或自治市或者任何外国的旗帜、盾徽或其他徽记或任何此类象征的模拟物。

municipality, or of any foreign nation, or any simulation thereof.

Section 2(b) of the Trademark Act, 15 U.S.C. §1052(b), bars the registration on either the Principal Register or the Supplemental Register of marks that consist of or comprise (whether consisting solely of, or having incorporated in them) the flag, coat of arms, or other insignia of the United States, of any state or municipality, or of any foreign nation. Section 2(b) also bars the registration of marks that consist of or comprise any simulation of such symbols.

Section 2(b) differs from the provision of §2(a) regarding national symbols (*see* TMEP §1203.03(b)) in that §2(b) requires no additional element, such as disparagement or a false suggestion of a connection, to preclude registration.

Flags and coats of arms are specific designs formally adopted to serve as emblems of governmental authority. The wording "other insignia" should not be interpreted broadly, but should be considered to include only those emblems and devices that also represent such authority and that are of the same general class and character as flags and coats of arms. The Trademark Trial and Appeal Board has construed the statutory language as follows:

> [T]he wording "or other insignia of the United States" must be restricted in its application to insignia of the same general class as "the flag or coats of arms" of the United States. Since both the flag and coat of arms are emblems of national authority it seems evident that other insignia of national authority such as the Great Seal of the United States, the Presidential Seal, and seals of government departments would be equally prohibited registration under Section 2(b). On the other hand, it appears equally evident that department insignia which are merely used to identify a service or facility of the Government are not insignia of national authority and that they therefore do not fall within the general prohibitions of this section of the Statute.

In re U.S. Department of the Interior, 142 USPQ 506, 507 (TTAB 1964) (logo

《商标法》第2(b)节，15 U.S.C.§1052(b)禁止由美国、任何州及自治市或者任何外国的旗帜、盾徽或其他徽记构成或组成(无论是全部由其构成，还是与其合并而成)的商标在联邦商标登记簿或补充登记簿上注册。第2(b)节同时也禁止任何包含此类象征的模拟物的商标注册。

第2(b)节的规定与关于国家象征的§2(a)的规定不同(参见§1203.03(b))，§2(b)的拒绝注册并不需要其他因素，例如贬损或者虚假地暗示某种关系。

旗帜和盾徽是正式用作政府权威象征的特定符号。对“其他徽记”一词不应作广义的解释，而应认为只包括那些也代表了此类权威并与那些旗帜和盾徽属于同类和相同性质的象征和图案。商标评审及上诉委员会对法律语言作了如下解释：

> “美国的其他徽记”一语必须限于与美国的“旗帜或盾徽”属于同一类别的徽记。由于旗帜和盾徽是国家权威的象征，很显然其他国家权威徽记，例如美国国玺、总统印鉴以及政府部门的公章，根据2(b)节的规定显然也同样被禁止注册。另一方面，同样显然的是，仅仅用于识别某种政府服务或机构的部门徽记不属于国家权威的徽记，因此不属于此项法律一般禁止的范围。

见 *U.S. Department of the Interior*, 142 USPQ 506, 507 (TTAB 1964)(由

comprising the words "NATIONAL PARK SERVICE" and "Department of the Interior," with depiction of trees, mountains and a buffalo, surrounded by an arrowhead design, held not to be an insignia of the United States).

Letters that merely identify people and things associated with a particular agency or department of the United States government, instead of representing the authority of the government or the nation as a whole, are generally not considered to be "insignia of the United States" within the meaning of §2(b). The Board, in dismissing an opposition to the registration of "USMC" in a stylized presentation, for prostheses, fracture braces and orthopedic components, discussed the meaning of "insignia" under §2(b), as follows:

> The letters "USMC" are nothing like a flag or coat of arms. These types of insignia are pictorial in nature, they can be described, but cannot be pronounced. Even if the letters could be construed to be an insignia, opposer has not shown that they would be seen as an insignia of the United States.

U.S. Navy v. U.S. Mfg. Co., 2 USPQ2d 1254, 1256 (TTAB 1987). As a result of the enactment of Public Law 98-525 on October 19, 1984, the initials, seal and emblem of the United States Marine Corps are "deemed to be insignia of the United States," under 10 U. S. C. §7881, pertaining to unauthorized use of Marine Corps insignia. However, "USMC" was not so protected when the applicant began using its stylized version of those letters as a mark. In view of the provision in Public Law 98-525 that the amendments adding Chapter 663 (10 U. S. C. §7881) shall not affect rights that vested before the date of its enactment, the majority of the Board found that enactment of the law did not adversely affect the mark's registrability, stating that "opposer has not shown that applicant's mark was an insignia of the United States prior to the law making it one, or that the law effectively bars registration to applicant." *Id*. at 1260. (*See* TMEP §1205. 01 regarding subject matter which is protected by statute.)

See also Liberty Mutual Insurance Co. v. Liberty Insurance Co. of Texas, 185 F.

“NA- TIONAL PARK SERVICE”（国家公园服务署）和“Department of the Interior”（内务部）字样以及箭头图案环绕的树木、山脉和一头野牛的图样共同构成的徽标被认为不是一种美国的徽记）。

仅仅用来识别与美国政府特定机关或部门相联系的人或物而并非代表整个政府或国家的权威的字母，通常不被认为是 §2(b)所定义的“美国的徽记”。对于一项以固定格式显示、用于修复假体、骨折吊带和整形外科元件的“USMC”注册商标，有人提出异议，委员会在驳回该异议的过程中讨论了 §2(b)所规定的“徽记”的含义，结论如下：

> 字母“USMC”与旗帜或盾徽截然不同。此类徽标为图片性质，可以进行描述，但无法读出来。即使这些字母能够构成一种徽记，但异议者仍然未能证明它们可以被视为一种美国的徽记。

U.S. Navy v. U.S. Mfg. Co., 2 USPQ2d 1254, 1256 (TTAB 1987)。由于1984 年 10 月 19 日颁布了《公共法》98－525，美国海军陆战队的首字母、印章和商标都被“认为”是“美国的徽记”，根据 10 U.S.C.§7881 的规定，属于未经授权使用陆战队徽记。不过，当申请人开始使用固定格式的“USMC”作为商标时，这些字母并不属于此项规定所保护的对象。《公共法》98－525 规定，在修正案中增加了第 663 章(10 U.S.C.§7881)不应影响《公共法》实施以前已经存在的权利，因此委员会的多数意见认为，《公共法》的实施并不能影响该商标的可注册性，并论述道：“异议人未能证明，申请者的商标在《公共法》使之成为美国徽记之前就已经是一种美国徽记或者《公共法》有效地禁止了申请人注册该商标。”*同前*。1260。（有关受法律保护的标的物，*参见* TMEP §1205.01。）

另参见 Liberty Mutual Insurance Co. v. Liberty Insurance Co. of Texas, 185

Supp. 895, 908, 127 USPQ 312, 323 (E. D. Ark. 1960) ("That the Statue of Liberty is not a part of the 'insignia of the United States' is too clear to require discussion.")

As stated above, marks that consist of or comprise any simulation of the flag, coat of arms, or other insignia of the United States, of any state or municipality, or of any foreign nation are also unregistrable under §2(b). "Simulation," as contemplated by §2(b), refers to "something that gives the appearance or effect or has the characteristics of an original item." *In re Waltham Watch Co.*, 179 USPQ 59, 60 (TTAB 1973) (mark consisting of wording and the design of a globe and six flags for watches found registrable, the Board stating, "[A]lthough the flags depicted in applicant's mark incorporate common elements of flag designs such as horizontal or vertical lines, crosses or stars, they are readily distinguishable from any of the flags of the nations alluded to by the examiner. In fact, applicant's mark would be regarded as nothing more than a conglomeration of nondescript flags utilized to symbolize the significance of the globe design and the slogan 'TIMING THE WORLD' appearing thereon.") Whether a mark comprises a simulation must be determined from a visual comparison of the mark vis-à-vis replicas of the flag, coat of arms or other insignia in question. *Id*.

The determination of whether a proposed mark consists of or comprises a flag, coat of arms or other insignia must be made "without a careful analysis and side-by-side comparison." *In re Advance Industrial Security, Inc.*, 194 USPQ 344, 346 (TTAB 1977) (ADVANCE SECURITY and design consisting of an eagle on a triangular shield, in gold and brown, for detective and investigative services and providing security systems and services, found registrable, the Board stating, "When the mark of the applicant and the Coat of Arms or Great Seal of the United States are compared in their entireties, it is adjudged that applicant's mark does not consist of or comprise the Coat of Arms of the United States or any simulation thereof ...") The public should be considered to retain only a general or overall, rather than specific, recollection of the various elements or characteristics of design marks. *Id*.

F. Supp. 895, 908, 127 USPQ 312, 323 (E. D. Ark. 1960)("自由女神像不是'美国的徽记'的一部分,这点显而易见,无需加以讨论")。

如上所述,由美国、任何州及自治市,或者任何外国的旗帜、盾徽或其他徽记的模拟物构成或组成的商标根据 §2(b)的规定,不能注册。"模拟物",根据 §2(b)的规定,是指"表现出原物的外观或效果,或者具有其特点的物体"。见 *Waltham Watch Co.*, 179 USPQ 59, 60 (TTAB 1973)(由文字以及地球和六面旗帜图案构成的商标被判定作为手表的商标可以注册,委员会称:"尽管申请者商标中展示的旗帜带有旗帜图案的共同要素,诸如水平和垂直的线条、十字及星形等,但是审查者还是很容易就能将其同任何国旗区分开来。实际上,可以认为申请者的商标只是一些不具特征的旗帜的混合,用以表现地球图案以及所附的'TIMING THE WORLD'口号")。某项商标是否由模拟物组成必须通过该商标与所涉旗帜、盾徽或其他徽记复制品的视觉对比来加以判断。*同前*。

判断拟注册的商标是否由一种旗帜、盾徽或其他徽记构成或组成必须是在"不加仔细分析和各方面逐一对比"的情况下作出的。见 *Advance Industrial Security, Inc.*, 194 USPQ 344, 346。(TTAB 1977)(用于侦探和调查服务以及提供保安系统及服务的"ADVANCE SECURITY"(高级保安)以及包含三角盾上的老鹰图案被判定可以注册,委员会认为:"将申请人的商标与美国盾徽及国玺进行整体对比时,可以判定申请人的商标并非由美国盾徽或其模拟物构成或组成……。")我们应当考虑到公众对图案商标所保留的印象仅仅是一般或总体的印象,而非对商标的各个要素或特点具有具体的记忆。*同前*。

The incorporation in a mark of individual or distorted features that are merely suggestive of flags, coats of arms or other insignia does not bar registration under §2(b). *See Knorr-Nahrmittel A. G. v. Havland International, Inc.*, 206 USPQ 827, 833 (TTAB 1980) (While applicant originally may have intended to include the flags of the Scandinavian countries in the mark, NOR-KING and design, "[a]ll that the record reflects is that the mark contains a representation of certain flags, but not the flag or flags of any particular nation." Opposer's cause of action under §2(b) found to be without merit; opposition sustained on other grounds); *In re National Van Lines, Inc.*, 123 USPQ 510 (TTAB 1959) (mark comprising words and the design of a shield with vertical stripes held registrable, the Board finding the design to be readily distinguishable from the shield of the Great Seal of the United States and, therefore, not a simulation of the seal or any portion thereof); *In re American Box Board Co.*, 123 USPQ 508 (TTAB 1959) (design mark comprising an eagle and shield held registrable, the Board finding that it did not involve a simulation of the Great Seal of the United States because the eagle and shield of applicant's mark differed substantially from those on the seal in both appearance and manner of display).

See TMEP §§1205 *et seq*. regarding matter that is protected by statute or by Article 6*ter* of the Paris Convention.

To overcome a refusal under §2(a) or §2(b), deletion of the unregistrable matter is sometimes permitted. *See* TMEP §807.15 regarding removal of matter from drawings.

1205 Refusal on Basis of Matter Protected by Statute or Convention

1205.01 Statutory Protection

Various federal statutes and regulations prohibit or restrict the use of certain words, names, symbols, terms, initials, marks, emblems, seals, insignia, badges, decorations, medals and characters adopted by the United States government

商标中含有仅仅暗示旗帜、盾徽或其他徽记的个别或失真的特征，并不属于 §2(b)所规定的拒绝予以注册的范围。*参见 Knorr-Nahrmittel A. G. v. Havland International, Inc.*, 206 USPQ 827, 833 (TTAB 1980)(尽管申请者最初可能想在商标中加入斯堪的纳维亚国家的国旗、"NOR-KING"及图案，"但是所有的档案表明，该商标包含了某种旗帜图案，而非任何特定国家的旗帜。"异议人根据 §2(b)提出的诉讼理由被判定没有道理；因此异议被驳回)；*National Van Lines, Inc.*, 123 USPQ 510 (TTAB 1959)(由文字和带有垂直条文盾形图案组成的商标被认为可以注册，委员会判定该图案可以明显地与美国国玺的盾形区分开来，因此，不属于国玺或其任何部分的模拟)；*American Box Board Co.*, 123 USPQ 508 (TTAB 1959)(由老鹰和盾形的图案组成的商标被认为可以注册，委员会判定，该商标并不包含美国国玺的模拟物，因为申请人商标中的鹰和盾在外观和表现方式两方面都与国玺中的存在实质性差异)。

有关受到法律或《巴黎公约》第 6 条之三保护的标的物，*参见* TMEP §§1205 及以下。

为了克服根据 §2(a)或 §2(b)作出的拒绝注册决定，有时可允许删除不可注册的内容。有关从附图去除内容的信息，*参见* TMEP §807.15。

1205　以标的物受到法律或公约保护为理由拒绝予以注册

1205.01　法律保护

各种联邦法律法规禁止或限制使用美国政府或特定国内国际组织所采用的文字、名称、符号、术语、首字母、商标、象征、图章、标记、徽记、装饰、纪念章以及字符。这

or particular national and international organizations. These designations are reserved for the specific purposes prescribed in the relevant statute and must be free for use in the prescribed manner. *See* the listings of citations to sections of the United States Code and the Code of Federal Regulations in Appendix C of this Manual.

For example, Congress has created about 70 statutes that grant exclusive rights to use certain designations to federally created private corporations and organizations. Violation of some of these statutes may be a criminal offense, *e.g.*, 18 U. S.C. §§705 (regarding badges, medals, emblems or other insignia of veterans' organizations); 706 ("Red Cross," "Geneva Cross," and emblem of Greek red cross); 707 (4-H Club); 708 (coat of arms of the Swiss Confederation); 711 ("Smokey Bear"); and 711a ("Woodsy Owl" and slogan, "Give a Hoot, Don't Pollute"). Other statutes provide for civil enforcement, *e.g.*, 36 U.S.C. §§153104 (National Society of the Daughters of the American Revolution); 30905 (Boy Scouts); 80305 (Girl Scouts); 130506 (Little League); and 21904 (The American National Theater and Academy).

The following are examples of the protection of words and symbols by statute.

(1) The Copyright Act of 1976 includes provisions regarding the use of appropriate notices of copyright. These include provisions concerning the use of the letter "C" in a circle - ©, the word "Copyright" and the abbreviation "Copr." to identify visually perceptible copies (17 U.S.C. §401); the use of the letter "P" in a circle to indicate phonorecords of sound recordings (17 U.S.C. §402); and the use of the words "mask work," the symbol *M* and the letter "M" in a circle to designate mask works (17 U.S.C. §909). The Act designates these symbols to perform the function of indicating that the user of the symbol is asserting specific statutory rights.

(2) Use of the Greek red cross other than by the American National Red Cross is proscribed by statute. 18 U.S.C. §706. Use of the coat of arms

些名称符号留作相关法律所规定的特定用途，必须能够以规定的方式自由使用。参见本手册附录 C 中《美国法典》以及《联邦法规法典》章节引用列表。

例如，国会已经制定了约 70 部法律，授予联邦设立的私人公司和组织使用某些名称符号的专属权利。违反其中的一些法律可能构成犯罪，例如，18 U.S.C.§§705（关于退伍军人组织的徽记、纪念章、象征及其他徽记）；706（“Red Cross”（红十字）、“Geneva Cross”（日内瓦十字）以及希腊红十字的象征）；707（“4－H Club”）（4－H 俱乐部）；708（瑞士联邦的盾徽）；711（“Smokey Bear”）（吸烟熊）；以及 711a（“Woodsy Owl”（森林猫头鹰）及口号，“Give a Hoot, Don't Pollute”（大声疾呼，不要污染））。违反另外一些法律则只处以民事制裁，例如，36 U.S.C.§§153104（美国革命女儿全国协会）；30905（童子军）；80305（女童子军）；130506（少年棒球联盟）；以及 21904（美国国家剧院学会）。

以下是法律规定受保护的文字和符号的例子。

(1) 《1976 年著作权法》包括了有关使用适当著作权告知的规定。这些规定是关于使用带圈的字母“C”即©，“Copyright”一词以及缩写“Copr.”以识别可视的复制品（17 U.S.C.§401）；使用带圈的字母“P”以表示录音唱片（17 U.S.C.§402）；以及使用“mask work”字样，符号*M*以及带圈的字母“M”表示掩膜作品（17 U.S.C.§909）。著作权法指定将这些符号用作表明符号的使用者拥有特定的法定权利。

(2) 法律禁止美国国家红十字会以外的人使用希腊红十字。18 U.S.C.§706。

of the Swiss Confederation for trade or commercial purposes is proscribed by statute. 18 U. S. C. §708. *See In re Health Maintenance Organizations, Inc.*, 188 USPQ 473 (TTAB 1975) (mark comprising a dark cross with legs of equal length on which a caduceus is symmetrically imposed (representation of caduceus disclaimed) held registrable, the Board finding the mark readily distinguishable from the Greek red cross (on white background) and the Swiss confederation coat of arms (white cross on red background)).

(3) False advertising or misuse of names to indicate a federal agency is proscribed by 18 U. S. C. §709. For example, this provision prohibits knowing use, without written permission of the Director of the Federal Bureau of Investigation, of the words "Federal Bureau of Investigation," the initials "F. B. I." or any colorable imitation, in various formats "in a manner reasonably calculated to convey the impression that such advertisement, ... publication, ... broadcast, telecast, or other production, is approved, endorsed, or authorized by the Federal Bureau of Investigation." Thus, an examining attorney must refuse to register such matter, pursuant to 18 U. S. C. §709, if its use is reasonably calculated to convey an approval, endorsement or authorization by the Federal Bureau of Investigation.

(4) Section 110 of the Amateur Sports Act of 1978, 36 U. S. C. §220506, protects various designations associated with the Olympics. Under 36 U. S. C. §220506(a), the United States Olympic Committee has the exclusive right to use the name "United States Olympic Committee," its symbol and emblem, and the words "Olympic," "Olympiad," "Citius Altius Fortius," "Pan American," "Paralympiad," "America Espirito Sport Fraternite," or any combination thereof. The United States Supreme Court has held that the grant by Congress to the United States Olympic Committee of the exclusive right to use the word "Olympic" does not violate the First Amendment. *San Francisco Arts & Athletics*,

法律禁止为贸易或商业目的使用瑞士联邦的盾徽。18U.S.C.§708。*参见 Health Maintenance Organizations, Inc.*, 188 USPQ 473（TTAB 1975）（商标由上有对称蛇杖图样的等长黑色十字（放弃了蛇杖图样）组成，被认为可以注册，委员会认为该商标与希腊红十字（白底）和瑞士联邦盾徽（红底白十字）明显不同）。

(3) 18 U.S.C.§709 禁止标示联邦机构的虚假广告和名称滥用。例如，该规定禁止未经联邦调查局局长书面准许，有意地使用各种形式的"联邦调查局"、"F.B.I."缩写或任何有色模拟物，"从而照理可以给人一种此类广告、……出版物、……广播、电视广播或其他产品是由联邦调查局批准、背书或授权的印象"。因此，如果标的物的使用照理可以给人一种得到联邦调查局批准、背书或授权的印象，就必须依照 18 U.S.C.§709 的规定拒绝该标的物注册。

(4) 《1978 年业余体育法》第 110 节，36 U.S.C.§220506 保护各种与奥林匹克相联系的标识。根据 36 U.S.C.§220506(a)，美国奥委会拥有专属权利使用"美国奥委会"名称、符号和象征，以及"Olympic"、"Olympiad"、"Citius Altius Fortius"、"Pan American"、"Paralympiad"、"America Espirito Sport Fraternite"等字样以及以上的任何组合的专属权利。美国联邦最高法院判定，国会授予美国奥委会使用"Olympic"一词的专属权利并不违

Inc. v. U.S. Olympic Committee, 483 U.S. 522, 3 USPQ2d 1145 (1987) (concerning petitioner's use of "Gay Olympic Games"). Under 36 U.S.C. §220506(c), a person is subject to suit in a civil action by the Committee if such person, without the Committee's consent, uses for the purpose of trade, to induce the sale of goods or services, or to promote any theatrical exhibition, athletic performance, or competition, a designation noted above (listed in §220506(a)) or "any trademark, trade name, sign, symbol, or insignia falsely representing association with, or authorization by, the International Olympic Committee or ... [the United States Olympic Committee]" or any simulation of the words "Olympic," "Olympiad" or "Citius Altius Fortius" "tending to cause confusion, to cause mistake, to deceive, or to falsely suggest a connection with ... [the United States Olympic Committee] or any Olympic activity."

See U.S. Olympic Committee v. Toy Truck Lines Inc., 237 F.3d 1331, 57 USPQ2d 1380 (Fed. Cir. 2001); *O-M Bread, Inc. v. U.S. Olympic Committee.*, 65 F.3d 933, 36 USPQ2d 1041 (Fed. Cir. 1995); *U.S. Olympic Committee v. Intelicense Corp., S.A.*, 737 F.2d 263, 222 USPQ 766 (2d Cir. 1984), *cert. denied* 469 U.S. 982 (1984); *U.S. Olympic Committee v. Union Sport Apparel*, 220 USPQ 526 (E.D. Va. 1983); *U.S. Olympic Committee v. International Federation of Body Builders*, 219 USPQ 353 (D.D.C. 1982); *Stop the Olympic Prison v. U.S. Olympic Committee*, 489 F. Supp. 1112, 207 USPQ 237 (S.D.N.Y. 1980).

(5) In chartering the Blinded Veterans Association, Congress granted it the sole right to use its name and such seals, emblems and badges as it may lawfully adopt. 36 U.S.C. §30306. This protection of its exclusive right to use "Blinded Veterans Association" does not extend to the term "blinded veterans," which has been found generic. *Blinded Veterans Association v. Blinded American Veterans Foundation*, 872 F.2d 1035, 10 USPQ2d 1432 (D.C. Cir. 1989).

反宪法第一修正案。*San Francisco Arts & Athletics, Inc. v. U.S. Olympic Committee*，483 U.S.522，3 USPQ2d 1145（1987)（关于申诉人使用"Gay Olympic Games"一案）。根据 36 U.S.C.§220506(c)的规定，任何人，如果未经委员会同意，将上述标识（列于 §220506(a)中）用于商业目的、促进商品及服务的销售或促销任何舞台展示、体育表演及竞赛，或者使用"任何虚假地表示与国际奥委会或……[美国奥委会]有联系或经其授权的商标、商号、记号、象征或标记"，或者对"Olympic"、"Olympiad"及"Citius Altius Fortius"任何的模仿，"试图混淆、误解、欺骗或虚假表示与……[美国奥委会]或任何奥林匹克活动有联系"的行为，都将遭到奥委会的民事起诉。

参见 *U.S. Olympic Committee v. Toy Truck Lines Inc.*，237 F.3d 1331，57 USPQ2d 1380（Fed. Cir. 2001）；*O-M Bread, Inc. v. U.S. Olympic Committee.*，65 F.3d 933，36 USPQ2d 1041（Fed. Cir. 1995）；*U.S. Olympic Committee v. Intelicense Corp., S.A.*，737 F.2d 263，222 USPQ 766（2d Cir. 1984），*cert. denied* 469 U.S. 982（1984）；*U.S. Olympic Committee v. Union Sport Apparel*，220 USPQ 526（E.D. Va. 1983）；*U.S. Olympic Committee v. International Federation of Body Builders*，219 USPQ 353（D.D.C. 1982）；*Stop the Olympic Prison v. U.S. Olympic Committee*，489 F. Supp. 1112，207 USPQ 237（S.D.N.Y. 1980）。

(5) 在组建"失明退伍军人联合会"期间，国会授予其合法使用其名称及印章、象征和徽章的独占权利。36 U.S.C.§30306。保护"失明退伍军人联合会"的专属使用权并不扩展到"失明退伍军人"这一词语，因为这一词语是一般用语。*Blinded Veterans Association v. Blinded American Veterans Foundation*，872 F.2d 1035，10 USPQ2d 1432（D.C. Cir. 1989）。

Usually the statute will define the appropriate use of a designation and will prescribe criminal penalties or civil remedies for improper use. However, the statutes themselves do not provide the basis for refusal of trademark registration. To determine whether registration should be refused in a particular application, the examining attorney should consult the relevant statute to determine the function of the designation and its appropriate use. If a statute provides that a specific party or government agency has the exclusive right to use a designation, and a party other than that specified in the statute has applied to register the designation, the examining attorney must refuse registration on the ground that the mark is not in lawful use in commerce, citing §§1 and 45 of the Trademark Act, 15 U.S.C. §§1051 and 1127, in addition to the relevant statute.

Depending on the nature and use of the mark, other sections of the Trademark Act may also bar registration and must be cited where appropriate. For example, it may be appropriate for the examining attorney to refuse registration under §2(a) of the Trademark Act, 15 U.S.C. §1052(a), on the ground that the mark comprises matter that may falsely suggest a connection with a national symbol, institution or person specified in the statute (*e.g.*, the United States Olympic Committee). *See* TMEP §1203.03(e). Other §2(a) bases for refusal could also apply. *See* TMEP §§1203 *et seq*. It may be appropriate to refuse registration under §2(b), 15 U.S.C. §1052(b), for matter that comprises a flag, coat of arms or other similar insignia. *See* TMEP §1204. It may be appropriate to refuse registration under §2(d), 15 U.S.C. §1052(d), if the party specified in the statute owns a registration for a mark that is the same or similar. *Cf. U.S. Olympic Committee v. Olymp-Herrenwaschefabriken Bezner GmbH & Co.*, 224 USPQ 497. (TTAB 1984) (opposition to the registration of OLYMP sustained on ground of likelihood of confusion with opposer's registered mark OLYMPIC under §2(d), the Board finding that the evidence of record did not show that OLYMP falsely suggests a connection with opposer under §2(a), and that the remedies provided in 36 U.S.C. §220506(c) for misuse of Olympic designations are not pertinent to opposition proceedings).

通常法律会对标识的适当使用作出界定，并规定不适当使用的刑事惩罚以及民事救济。不过，法律本身并没有规定驳回商标注册申请的理由。为了判断是否应当拒绝某项特定申请的注册，审查员应当参考相关法律以判断该商标的功能及其适当使用。如果某项法律规定某具体当事人或政府机构享有专属使用某一名称或符号的权利，而非法定专用权利者提出申请注册该名称或符号，则审查员可以援引该项法律以及《商标法》§§1 和 45，15 U.S.C.§§1051 和 1127 的规定，以商标不能在商业中合法使用为理由拒绝予以注册。

根据商标的性质和具体的使用，《商标法》的其他条款也可能禁止对商标进行注册，并可以被相应地引用。例如，审查员也可以根据《商标法》§2(a)，15 U.S.C.§1052(a)的规定，以商标包含可能虚假地暗示与国家象征有联系的内容或与法律特别规定的机构或人有联系（例如，美国奥委会）的内容为理由，拒绝予以注册。*参见* TMEP §1203.03(e)。也可以根据 §2(a)规定的其他理由拒绝予以注册。*参见* TMEP §§1203 及以下。对于包含旗帜、盾徽或其他类似徽记的内容，可以根据 §2(b)，15 U.S.C.§1052(b)的规定，拒绝予以注册。*参见* TMEP §1204。如果要注册的商标与某法定当事人拥有的商标相同或相似，可以根据 §2(d)，15 U.S.C.§1052(d)的规定，拒绝予以注册。比较 *U.S.Olympic Committee v.Olymp-Herrenwaschefabriken Bezner GmbH & Co.*，224 USPQ 497。(TTAB 1984)（根据 §2(d)的规定，由于与异议人的注册商标“OLYMPIC”相似，故支持对注册“OLYMP”的异议，委员会认为，档案证据并没有显示“OLYMP”存在 §2(a)所规定的虚假暗示联系，因此 36 U.S.C.§220506(c)中所规定的有关奥林匹克商标滥用的救济不适用于异议诉讼）

In some instances, it may be appropriate for the examining attorney to refuse registration pursuant to §§1, 2 (preamble) and 45 of the Trademark Act, 15 U.S.C. §§1051, 1052 and 1127, on the ground that the subject matter would not be perceived as a trademark. (For service mark applications, §3 of the Act, 15 U.S.C. §1053, should also be cited in this type of refusal).

To determine what action is appropriate, the examining attorney should look to the particular use of a symbol or term by the applicant. For example, where it is evident that the applicant has merely included a copyright symbol in the drawing of the mark inadvertently, and the symbol is not a material portion of the mark, the examining attorney should indicate that the symbol is not part of the mark and require that the applicant amend the drawing to remove the symbol, instead of issuing statutory refusals of the types noted above.

Examining attorneys should also consider whether registration of matter as a trademark by the applicant may be prohibited by Article 6*ter* of the Paris Convention. *See* TMEP §1205.02.

1205.02 Article 6*ter* of the Paris Convention

The United States is a member of the Paris Convention for the Protection of Industrial Property, as revised at Stockholm on July 14, 1967, the members of which constitute a Union for the protection of industrial property.

Under Article 6*ter* of the Paris Convention, the contracting countries have agreed to refuse or to invalidate the registration, and to prohibit the unauthorized use, as trademarks or as elements of trademarks, of armorial bearings, flags, and other State emblems of the member countries, official signs and hallmarks indicating control and warranty adopted by member countries, and any imitation from a heraldic point of view. The provision applies equally to armorial bearings, flags, other emblems, abbreviations and names of international intergovernmental organizations of which one or more countries of the Union are members, except for

在某些情况下，审查员可以根据《商标法》§§1，2（导言）和 45，15 U.S.C. §§1051，1052 和 1127 的规定，以提交注册的标的物无法被认知为商标为理由拒绝予以注册。（在这种类型的拒绝予以注册的决定中，对于服务商标申请，则应引用《商标法》§3，15 U.S.C.§1053。）

为了判断何种诉讼是适当的，审查员应考察申请者对符号或术语的具体使用。例如，如果很明显申请者不经意地在商标附图中加入了一个著作权符号，该符号就不是商标的实质部分，审查员应指出该符号不是商标的一部分，并要求申请者修改附图以去除该符号，而不是作出前述的拒绝予以注册的决定。

审查员还应当考察，申请人作为商标提交注册的内容是否为《巴黎公约》第 6 条之三所禁止。参见 TMEP §1205.02。

1205.02　《巴黎公约》第 6 条第三款

美国是 1967 年 7 月 14 日修订的《保护工业产权巴黎公约》的成员，该公约的成员组成了保护工业产权的联盟。

根据《巴黎公约》第 6 条第三款的规定，各缔约国同意，应拒绝或取消以及禁止非授权使用成员国的徽章、国旗和国家的象征符号、各成员国用以表明控制和保证的官方符号和标记或从纹章的角度对以上的任何模仿作为商标或商标的组成元素使用。此项规定同样适用于有一个或多个成员国参加的政府间的国际性组织的徽章、旗

those that are already the subject of international agreements in force, intended to ensure their protection (*e.g.*, "Red Cross" and emblems protected by the Geneva Convention of August 12, 1949).

Under Article 6*ter*, each member country shall communicate the list of emblems, official signs and hallmarks that it wishes to protect, and all subsequent modifications of its list, to the International Bureau of Intellectual Property (International Bureau), who will transmit the communications to the other member countries. Within twelve months from receipt of the notification, a member country may transmit its objections, through the International Bureau.

When the United States Patent and Trademark Office receives requests for protection under Article 6*ter* from the International Bureau, they are assigned serial numbers in the "89" series code, *i.e.*, serial numbers beginning with the digits "89," and are sometimes referred to as "non-registrations." No file wrapper is created, and the requests are not examined. Copies of the designations are filed in the paper records of the Trademark Search Library. Pertinent information is entered in the automated search records of the Office and should be discovered in an examining attorney's search. However, some of the images of these entries are not currently available in the Office's automated database and can be found only in the Search Library.

Refusal Of Marks Because of an Article 6ter Designation

The Paris Convention requires that the United States refuse to register designations that have been deposited pursuant to Article 6*ter* and to which the United States has transmitted no objections. Depending on the nature and use of the mark, §§2(a) and 2(b) of the Trademark Act, 15 U.S.C. §§1052(a) and 1052(b), may bar registration of these marks. A refusal under §2(d) of the Trademark Act is ***not*** appropriate. The issue is not whether the marks are confusingly similar, but whether registration of the mark would violate §§2(a) or 2(b) of the Trademark Act.

帜、象征符号、缩写和名称，但已成为现行国际协定的对象（例如，“红十字”就是1949年8月12日《日内瓦公约》所保护的标识）除外，这些国际协定的目的是确保对所规定的对象进行保护。

根据第6条第三款，各成员国应通过知识产权国际局（国际局），相互通知各自希望或今后希望完全地或在一定限度内受本条保护的象征符号、官方符号和标识的清单，以及以后对这项清单的任何修正。成员国如有异议，可在收到通知后十二个月内通过国际局向有关国家或政府间国际组织提出。

当美国专利和商标局收到国际局要求按第6条第三款的规定予以保护的请求时，应给这些要求保护的项目分配“89”系列码中的序列号，即以阿拉伯数字“89”开头的序列号，这些序列号有时称为“非注册项”。如果提出的请求无文件封面，则不予审查。商标的副本归入“商标搜索资料库”的书面档案中。相关信息则输入商标局的自动化搜索档案中，审查员搜索时应当可以找到这些信息。不过，目前这些信息的部分图片尚未输入商标局的自动化数据库中，而只能在“搜索资料库”中找到。

由于属于第6条第三款所规定的标识而拒绝注册为商标

《巴黎公约》规定美国对按第6条第三款的规定而保留的商标应拒绝予以注册，对此美国没有提出异议。根据商标的性质和使用情况，《商标法》§§2(a)和2(b)，15 U.S.C.§§1052(a)和1052(b)的规定可以阻止此类商标的注册。以《商标法》§2(d)的规定为拒绝理由是不适当的。问题的关键并不在于商标是否具有混淆相似性，而在于商标的注册是否违反《商标法》§§2(a)或2(b)的规定。

For example, it may be appropriate for the examining attorney to refuse registration under §2(a) of the Act on the ground that the mark comprises matter that may falsely suggest a connection with a national symbol of a member country or an international intergovernmental organization. *See* TMEP §1203.03(e). Other §2(a) bases for refusal could also apply. *See* TMEP §§1203 *et seq*. It may be appropriate to refuse registration under §2(b) of the Act if the proposed mark comprises a flag, coat of arms or other similar insignia. *See* TMEP §1204. In some instances, it may be appropriate to refuse registration under §§1, 2 (preamble) and 45 of the Trademark Act, 15 U.S.C. §§1051, 1052 and 1127, on the ground that the subject matter would not be perceived as a trademark. (For service mark applications, §3 of the Act, 15 U.S.C. §1053, should also be cited when making this type of refusal.)

1206 Refusal on Basis of Name, Portrait or Signature of Particular Living Individual or Deceased U.S. President Without Consent

Extract from 15 U.S.C.§1052. No trademark by which the goods of the applicant may be distinguished from the goods of others shall be refused registration on the principal register on account of its nature unless it ... (c) Consists of or comprises a name, portrait, or signature identifying a particular living individual except by his written consent, or the name, signature, or portrait of a deceased President of the United States during the life of his widow, if any, except by the written consent of the widow.

Section 2(c) of the Trademark Act, 15 U.S.C. §1052(c), bars the registration of a mark that consists of or comprises (whether consisting solely of, or having incorporated in the mark) a name, portrait or signature that identifies a particular living individual, or a deceased United States president during the life of his widow, except by the written consent of the individual or the president's widow.

Section 2(c) absolutely bars the registration of these marks on both the Principal Register and the Supplemental Register.

例如，审查员可以根据《商标法》§2(a)的规定，以商标包含可虚假地暗示与商标所象征的成员国或国际性政府间组织有联系的内容为理由，拒绝予以注册。*参见* TMEP §1203.03(e)。也可以以违反 §2(a)的规定为拒绝予以注册的理由。*参见* TMEP §§1203 及以下。如果提出申请的商标包含旗帜、盾徽或其他类似的徽记，可以根据《商标法》§2(b)的规定拒绝予以注册。*参见* TMEP §1204。在某些情况下，审查员可以根据《商标法》§§1，2(导言)和 45，15 U.S.C.§§1051，1052 和 1127 的规定，以提交注册的标的物无法被认知为商标为理由拒绝予以注册。(在这种类型的拒绝予以注册决定中，对于服务商标申请，还应引用《商标法》§3，15 U.S.C.§1053。)

1206 以未经同意使用某在世个人或已故美国总统的名字、肖像或签名为理由拒绝予以注册

摘自 15 U.S.C.§1052。凡用于将申请者商品同他人商品区分开来的商标均可以在联邦商标登记簿上注册，除非——(c)其包含识别某特定在世个人的名字、肖像或签名——除非经其本人书面同意，或者包含识别遗孀尚健在的已故美国总统的名字、签名或肖像——除非经其遗孀的书面同意。

《商标法》第 2(c)节，15 U.S.C.§1052(c)规定对由特定在世个人的名字、肖像或签名构成或组成(无论是全部由其构成，还是与其合并而成)的商标，以及在其遗孀在世期间使用已故美国总统的名字、签名或肖像的商标禁止注册，除非经该个人或该遗孀的书面同意。

第 2(c)绝对禁止此类商标在联邦商标登记簿和补充登记簿上注册。

The purpose of requiring the consent of a living individual to the registration of his or her name, signature or portrait is to protect rights of privacy and publicity that living persons have in the designations that identify them. *University of Notre Dame du Lac v. J. C. Gourmet Food Imports Co., Inc.*, 703 F.2d 1372, 1376, 217 USPQ 505, 509 (Fed. Cir. 1983), *aff'g* 213 USPQ 594 (TTAB 1982); *Canovas v. Venezia 80 S. R. L.*, 220 USPQ 660, 661 (TTAB 1983). *See* TMEP §1203.03 for a discussion of the right to control the use of one's identity, which underlies part of §2(a) as well as §2(c).

See TMEP §813 regarding when it is necessary for an examining attorney to inquire of the applicant as to whether a name, signature or portrait in a mark identifies a particular living individual, and regarding the entry of pertinent statements in the record for printing in the *Official Gazette* and on a registration certificate.

1206.01 Name, Portrait or Signature

Section 2(c) explicitly pertains to any name, portrait or signature that identifies a particular living individual, or a deceased president of the United States during the life of the president's widow.

To identify a particular living individual, a name does not have to be the person's full name. *See Ross v. Analytical Technology Inc.*, 51 USPQ2d 1269 (TTAB 1999) (registration of opposer's surname without consent prohibited by §2(c), where the record showed that because of opposer's reputation as an inventor in the field of electrochemical analysis, the relevant public would associate the goods so marked with opposer); *In re Steak and Ale Restaurants of America, Inc.*, 185 USPQ 447 (TTAB 1975) (PRINCE CHARLES found to identify a particular living individual whose consent was not of record); *Laub v. Industrial Development Laboratories, Inc.*, 121 USPQ 595 (TTAB 1959) (LAUB, for flowmeters, found to identify the holder of a patent for flowmeters, whose written consent was not of record); *Reed v. Bakers Engineering & Equipment Co.*, 100 USPQ 196, 199 (PO

在世个人名字、签名或肖像注册时征得其同意的目的在于保护该个人的隐私权及其在识别其的商标中的名声。见 *University of Notre Dame du Lac v. J. C. Gourmet Food Imports Co., Inc.*, 703 F.2d 1372, 1376, 217 USPQ 505, 509 (Fed. Cir. 1983), *aff'g* 213 USPQ 594 (TTAB 1982); *Canovas v. Venezia 80 S. R. L.*, 220 USPQ 660, 661 (TTAB 1983)。有关控制某人身份使用权方面的讨论，*参见* TMEP §1203.03，该条奠定了§2(a)和§2(c)的部分基础。

有关审查员有必要就商标中的名称、签名或肖像是否识别了某特定个人而对申请者进行调查的情况，以及有关在档案中输入相关声明，以便印在《公报》和注册证书上的情况，*参见* TMEP §813。

1206.01 名字、肖像或签名

第 2(c)节明确地适用于一切识别特定在世个人，以及在其遗孀在世期间识别某位已故美国总统的名字、肖像及签名。

要识别某特定在世个人，不一定需要此人的全名。*参见* *Ross v. Analytical Technology Inc.*, 51 USPQ2d 1269 (TTAB 1999)(§2(c)禁止未经异议人的同意注册其姓氏，因为档案显示由于异议人作为发明家在电气化学分析领域享有盛誉，相关公众会将带有该商标的商品与异议人相联系)；*Steak and Ale Restaurants of America, Inc.*, 185 USPQ 447 (TTAB 1975)("PRINCE CHARLES"(查尔斯王子)被认为识别了一位特定的在世个人，其档案中并无此人的同意)；*Laub v. Industrial Development Laboratories, Inc.*, 121 USPQ 595 (TTAB 1959)(申请注册流量器上使用的"LAUB"被认为识别了流量器的专利持有人，且档案中并无此人的书面同意)；*Reed v. Bakers Engineering & Equipment Co.*, 100 USPQ 196, 199 (PO Ex. Ch. 1954)(未

Ex. Ch. 1954) (registration of REED REEL OVEN, for ovens, held to be barred by §2(c) without written consent of the designer and builder of the ovens, Paul N. Reed. "'Name' in §2(c) is not restricted to the full name of an individual but refers to any name regardless of whether it is a full name, or a surname or given name, or even a nickname, which identifies a particular living individual ..."). *Cf. Société Civile Des Domaines Dourthe Frères v. S. A. Consortium Vinicole De Bordeaux Et De La Gironde*, 6 USPQ2d 1205, 1209 (TTAB 1988) ("Section 2(c) does not apply to surnames except in those cases where a particular individual is known by a surname alone.")

Cases involving portraits include *In re McKee Baking Co.*, 218 USPQ 287 (TTAB 1983) (mark comprising a sign on which the portrait of a young girl appears below the words LITTLE DEBBIE); *In re Masucci*, 179 USPQ 829 (TTAB 1973) (mark comprising name and portrait of a deceased president of the United States, President Eisenhower); *Garden v. Parfumerie Rigaud, Inc.*, 34 USPQ 30 (Comm'r Pats. 1937) (marks comprising name and portrait of Mary Garden).

1206.02 Particular Living Individual or Deceased U. S. President

Section 2(c) applies to marks that comprise matter that identify living individuals; it does not apply to marks that comprise matter that identifies deceased persons, except for a deceased president of the United States during the life of the president's widow. *See McGraw-Edison Co. v. Thomas Edison Life Insurance Co.*, 160 USPQ 685 (TTAB 1969), *vacated on other grounds*, 162 USPQ 372 (N.D. Ill. 1969) (opposition to the registration of THOMAS EDISON dismissed, the Board finding §2(c) inapplicable, as the particular individual whom the name identifies is deceased); *In re Masucci*, 179 USPQ 829 (TTAB 1973) (affirming refusal to register mark consisting of the name EISENHOWER, a portrait of President Dwight D. Eisenhower and the words PRESIDENT EISENHOWER REGISTERED PLATINUM MEDALLION #13, for greeting cards, on the ground that the mark comprises the name, signature or portrait of a deceased United States

获得这种烤箱的设计者兼制造者 *Paul N. Reed* 的书面同意而为烤箱注册“REED REEL OVEN”名称，被认为应当根据 §2(c)的规定驳回）。“§2(c)所规定的‘名字’并不限于某人的全名，而是指一切名字，无论是全名、姓氏还是教名，甚至是绰号，只要能够识别特定的在世个人……”。比较 *Société Civile Des Domaines Dourthe Frères v. S. A. Consortium Vinicole De Bordeaux Et De La Gironde*，6 USPQ2d 1205，1209 (TTAB 1988)（“第 2(c)节不适用于姓氏，除非单凭姓氏就能知道特定的个人是谁”）。

涉及肖像的案例包括：*McKee Baking Co.*，218 USPQ 287 (TTAB 1983)（商标包含了一幅图画，画中有一幅女孩子的肖像，位于“LITTLE DEBBIE”字样下方）；*Masucci*，179 USPQ 829 (TTAB 1973)（商标中包含已故美国总统 Eisenhower（艾森豪威尔）的名字和肖像）；*Garden v. Parfumerie Rigaud，Inc.*，34 USPQ 30 (Comm'r Pats. 1937)（商标中包含 *Mary Garden* 的名字和肖像）。

1206.02 特定在世个人或已故美国总统

第 2(c)节适用于包含识别在世个人的内容的商标；而不适用于包含识别已故个人的内容的商标，除非是在总统遗孀在世期间识别已故美国总统。*参见 McGraw-Edison Co. v. Thomas Edison Life Insurance Co.*，160 USPQ 685 (TTAB 1969)，*因其他原因而失效*，162 USPQ 372 (N. D. Ill. 1969)（对于注册“THOMAS EDISON”提出的异议遭到驳回，委员会认为此处不适用 §2(c)，因为所识别的特定个人已经去世了）；*Masucci*，179 USPQ 829 (TTAB 1973)（对于申请在问候卡片上使用的、由 EISENHOWER 名字、Dwight D. Eisenhower 总统的肖像和“PRESIDENT EISENHOWER REGISTERED PLATINUM MEDALLION ＃13”字样组成的商标，根据 §2(c) 维持拒绝予以注册的决定，理由是该商标包含了已故美国总统的名字、签名或

president without the written consent of his widow, under §2(c)).

The fact that a name appearing in a mark may actually be the name of more than one person does not negate the requirement for a written consent to registration, if the mark identifies, to the relevant public, a particular living individual or deceased United States president whose spouse is living. *In re Steak and Ale Restaurants of America, Inc.*, 185 USPQ 447 (TTAB 1975) (affirming refusal to register PRINCE CHARLES, for meat, in the absence of consent to register by Prince Charles, a member of the English royal family. "Even accepting the existence of more than one living 'Prince Charles,' it does not follow that each is not a particular living individual.")

If it appears that a name, portrait or signature in a mark may identify a particular living individual but in fact the applicant devised the matter as fanciful, or believes it to be fanciful, a statement to that effect should be placed in the record. If appropriate, the statement that a name, portrait or signature does not identify a particular living individual will be printed in the *Official Gazette* and on the registration certificate. *See* TMEP §813. Additional relevant circumstances should also be explained. For example, if the matter identifies a certain character in literature, or a deceased historical person, then a statement of these facts in the record may be helpful; however, this information should not be printed in the *Official Gazette* or on a registration certificate.

Although a mark may have been devised to be fanciful or arbitrary and not to identify a particular living individual, it nevertheless may name or otherwise identify one or more living individuals. Whether a consent to registration is required depends on whether the public would recognize and understand the mark as identifying the person. Therefore, if the person is not generally known, or well known in the field relating to the relevant goods or services, it may be that the mark would not constitute the identification of a particular person under §2(c), and consent would not be required. The Trademark Trial and Appeal Board noted as follows in *Martin v. Carter Hawley Hale Stores, Inc.*, 206 USPQ 931, 933

肖像，而未取得其遗孀的书面同意）。

如果商标中的名字实际上可能是多人的名字，只要该商标使相关公众识别了某特定在世个人，或是在遗孀在世期间识别了已故美国总统，都需要获得相关个人的书面同意才能注册。*参见 Steak and Ale Restaurants of America, Inc.*, 185 USPQ 447 (TTAB 1975)（维持拒绝将“PRINCE CHARLES”作为肉类商标注册的决定，因为并未获得查尔斯王子——英格兰王室成员之一——的同意。“即使我们承认活着的人中有多位名字叫‘查尔斯王子’的，也不能说，每一位就不是特定的活着的个人”）。

如果表面看来商标中的名字、肖像或签名可能识别某特定在世者，但实际上申请者所设计的内容是虚构的或者自认为是虚构的，那么应在档案中加入对这种效果的声明。如果适当，关于某名字、肖像或签名并不识别某特定在世者的声明将印在《公报》和注册证书上。*参见* TMEP §813。此外相关的情况应一并解释。例如，如果该内容识别了文学作品中的某个任务，或是已故的历史人物，那么在档案中加入相应的声明将有所助益；不过这种信息不会印在《公报》或注册证书上。

尽管商标在设计时可能是虚构或任意性的，并不识别某特定在世者，但它仍然可能指出或者识别了一个或更多的在世者。是否要求获得同意方可注册，取决于公众是否会将该商标认知并理解为识别了该个人。因此，如果该个人并非普遍为人所知，或者在相关商品或服务的领域内并不著名，那么商标就可能不构成 §2(c)所规定识别某特定个人，也就不需要获得同意。商标评审及上诉委员会在 *Martin v. Carter Hawley Hale Stores, Inc.*, 206 USPQ 931, 933 (TTAB 1979)一案中作了如下说明：

(TTAB 1979):

> [Section] 2(c) was not designed to protect every person from having a name which is similar or identical to his or her name registered as a trademark. Such a scope of protection would practically preclude the registration of a trademark consisting of a name since in most cases there would be someone somewhere who is known by the name and who might be expected to protest its registration. Rather, the Statute was intended to protect one who, for valid reasons, could expect to suffer damage from another's trademark use of his name. That is, it is more than likely that any trademark which is comprised of a given name and surname will, in fact, be the name of a real person. But that coincidence, in and of itself, does not give rise to damage to that individual in the absence of other factors from which it may be determined that the particular individual bearing the name in question will be associated with the mark as used on the goods, either because that person is so well known that the public would reasonably assume the connection or because the individual is publicly connected with the business in which the mark is used.

See also Fanta v. Coca-Cola Co., 140 USPQ 674 (TTAB 1964) (dismissing a petition to cancel registrations of FANTA, for soft drinks and syrup concentrate, the Board noting no use by the petitioner, Robert D. Fanta, of his name in connection with the sale of soft drinks, nor any indication that petitioner had attained recognition in that field); *DeCecco v. Wright*, 120 USPQ 20 (TTAB 1958) ("The question whether the name 'DECECCO' as used by applicant in connection with his goods serves to identify opposer is a matter for proof."); *Brand v. Fairchester Packing Co.*, 84 USPQ 97 (Comm'r Pats. 1950) (affirming dismissal of a petition to cancel the registration of ARNOLD BRAND, for fresh tomatoes, the Commissioner finding nothing in the record to indicate that the mark identified the petitioner, Arnold Brand, an attorney specializing in patent and trademark matters, with the tomato business, or that use of the mark would lead the public to make such a connection).

第 2(c)节的意图并不是保护每一个人,使与每个人的名字相似或相同的名字都不能作为商标注册。如果是这样一种保护范围,那么实际上由名字构成的商标就不能注册了,因为在大多数情况下,总是存在叫这个名字的人并且此人可能会对注册提出抗议。确切地说,法律的原意是保护那些有合法理由预期,会因为他人将其名字注册为商标而受到损害的人。也就是说,很有可能一切由名或姓构成的商标,实际上,都会是某个真人的名字。如果没有其他因素致使以所涉名字为名的特定个人会在商标用于商品时与其发生联系,无论是因为此人很著名而使公众合理地推定这种联系,还是因为公众将该个人与使用商标而从事的商业活动相联系,那么这种巧合本身并不会对该个人造成损害。

另参见 Fanta v. Coca-Cola Co., 140 USPQ 674 (TTAB 1964)(驳回撤销用于软饮料和果汁原汁的"FANTA"注册商标的请求,委员会认为,申诉人 *Robert D. Fanta* 并未将其名字同软饮料的销售活动联系使用,也没有任何迹象表明申诉人在该领域很有名。);*DeCecco v. Wright*, 120 USPQ 20 (TTAB 1958)("关于申请者在其商品上使用的'DECECCO'名称是否可以识别异议人的问题仍有待证实。");*Brand v. Fairchester Packing Co.*, 84 USPQ 97 (Comm'r Pats. 1950)(驳回撤销用于新鲜西红柿的"ARNOLD BRAND"注册商标的请求,本委员认为,档案中没有证据显示该商标识别了申诉人 *Arnold Brand*——系专业从事专利和商标事务的律师——从事西红柿生意,也没有显示该商标的使用会使公众产生这样一种联系)。

1206.03 Consent of Individual or President's Widow Required

1206.03(a) Consent Must Be Written Consent to Registration

When a name, portrait or signature in a mark identifies a particular living individual, or a deceased president of the United States during the life of his widow, the mark can be registered only if the written consent of the individual, or of the president's widow, is filed in the application.

The consent must be a written consent to the registration of the identifying matter as a trademark. *See Reed v. Bakers Engineering & Equipment Co.*, 100 USPQ 196, 199 (PO Ex. Ch. 1954) ("Consent to register must be distinguished from consent to use. There may very well be consent to use without any consent to register. And neither is consent to register sufficient under the statute unless it is a written consent to register as specified in the statute.") Permission to use a mark in connection with specific goods without specific written consent to also register that mark does not give a party the right to register the subject matter as a trademark. *Garden v. Parfumerie Rigaud, Inc.*, 34 USPQ 30, 31 (Comm'r Pats. 1937) (granting petition to cancel registrations of marks that named and portrayed the petitioner, Mary Garden, who, although she had consented to the use of her name and portrait in connection with a particular perfume, had not given written consent to register the marks for perfumes and other cosmetic items. "Permission to use one's name and portrait in connection with a specified item of merchandise falls far short of consent to register one's name and portrait as a trade mark for such merchandise generally.") Consent to *register* a mark that makes no reference to consent to *use* is acceptable; the Office has no authority to regulate use of a mark.

Written consents for minors may be given by their guardians.

1206.03(b) Implicit Consent

When a particular individual identified by matter in a mark is also the person who

1206.03 要求获得个人或总统遗孀的同意

1206.03(a) 同意必须是书面同意注册

如果商标中的名字、肖像或签名识别了某特定在世者，或是其遗孀尚健在的已故美国总统，那么该商标只有获得了该本人或该遗孀的书面同意书，并随同申请书提交，方可注册。

同意必须是书面同意书将该识别性内容作为商标注册。参见 *Reed v. Bakers Engineering & Equipment Co.*, 100 USPQ 196, 199 (PO Ex. Ch. 1954)（"同意注册必须与同意使用区别。可能存在很多同意使用但不同意注册的情况。而且根据法律规定，即使同意注册也还是不充分的，还必须是法律所特别规定的同意注册的书面同意书"。）准许将某商标用于特定的商品，而并没有特别的书面同意书准许注册该商标，则当事人并不享有将该内容注册为商标的权利。见 *Garden v. Parfumerie Rigaud, Inc.*, 34 USPQ 30, 31 (Comm'r Pats. 1937)（准许撤销提及并描绘了申诉人的注册商标，因为，尽管申诉人 *Mary Garden* 同意将其名字和肖像用于某种香水，但并未书面同意将其注册为香水和其他化妆品的商标。"准许将某人的名字及肖像同特定商品联系使用，与同意将此人的名字和肖像作为此类商品商标进行注册截然有别。"）同意*注册*商标，而没有提及同意*使用*是可以的，因为商标局没有权力管理商标的使用。

未成年人的书面同意可以由其监护人作出。

1206.03(b) 默许

如果商标所识别的特定个人与提出申请的个人是同一人，那么可以推定他同意

signed the application, then his or her consent to registration will be presumed. *Alford Mfg. Co. v. Alfred Electronics*, 137 USPQ 250 (TTAB 1963), *aff'd*, 333 F.2d 912, 142 USPQ 168 (C.C.P.A.1964) ("The written consent to the registration of the mark 'ALFORD' by Andrew Alford, the individual, is manifested by the fact that said person executed the application ..."); *Ex parte Dallioux*, 83 USPQ 262, 263 (Comm'r Pats. 1949) ("By signing the application, the applicant here obviously consents ...").

An implied consent to register has been found in certain other limited situations. *Compare*, *In re D. B. Kaplan Delicatessen*, 225 USPQ 342, 344 (TTAB 1985) (consent to the use and registration of the mark D. B. KAPLAN'S DELICATESSEN, for restaurant services, found to be implicit in the terms of the "buy-out" agreement which relinquished all property rights in the name and forbade its use by the named party in any subsequent business) *with*, *In re New John Nissen Mannequins*, 227 USPQ 569 (TTAB 1985) (consent to register not implied from appearance of the name "John Nissen" in a deed of incorporation of applicant's predecessor, nor from existence of foreign registrations incorporating the name).

An applicant does not have to submit a new consent if a consent to register is already part of the record in the file of a valid registration for a mark comprised in whole or in part of the same name, portrait or signature for the same goods or services. In this situation, the applicant only has to claim ownership of that existing registration. If an applicant has submitted a consent to register in an application that has not matured to registration, a new consent is not required for pertinent co-pending applications, but a copy of the consent must be placed in each pending application. *In re McKee Baking Co.*, 218 USPQ 287 (TTAB 1983) (applicant's claim of ownership of a prior registration that includes a consent to register in the record held sufficient for purposes of complying with the consent requirement of the Act).

See TMEP §813 regarding a statement of consent of a living individual to the registration of his or her name or likeness.

注册。*Alford Mfg. Co. v. Alfred Electronics*，137 USPQ 250（TTAB 1963），*aff'd*，333 F.2d 912，142 USPQ 168（C. C. P. A. 1964）（"Andrew Alford 对于注册'ALFORD'商标的书面同意书，可以通过此人签署申请书的事实而表明……"）；*Dallioux*，83 USPQ 262，263（Comm'r Pats. 1949）（"通过签署申请书，申请者在此明白地同意……"）。

在某些有限的情况下，也可以认为存在默许。比较：*D. B. Kaplan Delicatessen*，225 USPQ 342，344（TTAB 1985）（同意使用和注册用于餐饮服务的"D. B. KAPLAN'S DELICATESSEN"商标，被认为在"整体收购"协议的条款中默许，在该协议中，有关该名称的一切财产权利都被放弃，并且禁止原来使用该名称的当事人在以后的一切业务中使用该商标。）与 *New John Nissen Mannequins*，227 USPQ 569（TTAB 1985）（在申请者继承人的组成公司交易中使用的"John Nissen"以及存在包含该名字的外国注册，均不能表明对注册的默许）。

如果一项有效的注册商标档案中已经包含了对用于同一商品或服务的同一名字、肖像或签名全部或部分同意，则申请者无须重新提交新的同意书。在这种情况下，申请者只需要声明对该现存注册商标享有所有权。如果申请者在一项尚未获得注册的申请中已经提交了一份同意书，则相关的等待批准的申请中并不要求新的同意书，但在每项等待批准的申请中均须有该同意书的复印件。见 *McKee Baking Co.*，218 USPQ 287（TTAB 1983）（申请者声明对一项包含有注册同意书的先前注册商标享有所有权，被认为符合《商标法》对同意注册的要求）。

有关在世者同意将其名字或其他类似物注册为商标的声明，参见 TMEP §813。

1207 Refusal on Basis of Likelihood of Confusion, Mistake or Deception

Extract from 15 U.S.C.§1052. No trademark by which the goods of the applicant may be distinguished from the goods of others shall be refused registration on the principal register on account of its nature unless it ... (d) Consists of or comprises a mark which so resembles a mark registered in the Patent and Trademark Office, or a mark or trade name previously used in the United States by another and not abandoned, as to be likely, when used on or in connection with the goods of the applicant, to cause confusion, or to cause mistake, or to deceive ...

Section 2(d) of the Trademark Act, 15 U.S.C. §1052(d), is the statutory basis for a refusal to register due to likelihood of confusion with another mark. Section 2(d) applies to both the Principal and the Supplemental Register.

1207.01 Likelihood of Confusion [R-2]

In the *ex parte* examination of a trademark application, a refusal under §2(d) is normally based on the examining attorney's conclusion that the applicant's mark, as used on or in connection with the specified goods or services, so resembles a *registered* mark as to be likely to cause confusion. (*See* TMEP §1207.02 concerning §2(d) refusals to register marks that so resemble another mark as to be likely to deceive, and TMEP §1207.03 concerning §2(d) refusals based on unregistered marks. *Note*: Refusals based on unregistered marks are not issued in *ex parte* examination.)

The examining attorney must conduct a search of Office records to determine whether the applicant's mark so resembles any registered mark(s) as to be likely to cause confusion or mistake, when used on or in connection with the goods or services identified in the application. The examining attorney also searches pending applications for conflicting marks with earlier effective filing dates. *See* TMEP

1207 以可能存在混淆、错误或欺骗为理由拒绝注册

摘自 15 U.S.C.§1052。凡用于将申请者商品同他人商品区分开来的商标都可以在联邦商标登记簿上注册，除非——(d)其包含类似于已在专利商标局登记注册商标的商标，或者他人以前在美国使用的商标或商号，现在仍未抛弃的，因为当这样的商标用于申请者的商品时，可能导致混淆、错误或构成欺骗……

《商标法》第 2(d)节，15 U.S.C.§1052(d)是以可能与其他商标混淆为理由而拒绝注册的法律依据。第 2(d)节同时适用于联邦商标登记簿和补充登记簿。

1207.01 混淆的可能性［R-2］

在对商标申请的单方审查中，依据 §2(d)作出的拒绝予以注册决定通常是基于审查员判定，申请者的商标用于特定商品或服务时，与某已注册商标近似，而可能导致混淆。(有关根据 §2(d)的规定拒绝注册与另一商标近似而可能产生欺骗的商标，*参见* TMEP §1207.02；有关 §2(d)所规定的根据未注册的商标拒绝予以注册，*参见* TMEP §1207.03。注：在单方审查中，不存在根据未注册的商标拒绝予以注册这一问题。)

审查员必须搜索商标局档案，以判断申请者的商标是否与任何已注册商标相似，并可能在用于申请所识别的商品及服务时导致混淆或错误。审查员还要搜索正在申请的商标，检查是否存在有效备案日期较早、与之有冲突的商标。有关冲突商标的

§§1208 *et seq*. regarding conflicting marks. The examining attorney must place a copy of the search strategy in the file.

If the examining attorney determines that there is a likelihood of confusion between applicant's mark and a previously registered mark, the examining attorney refuses registration under §2(d). Before citing a registration, the examining attorney must check the automated records of the Office to confirm that any registration that is the basis for a §2(d) refusal is an active registration. *See* TMEP §716.02(e). Also, if Office records indicate that an assignment of the conflicting registration has been recorded, the examining attorney should check the Assignment Historical Database (*i.e.*, the automated records of the Assignment Services Division of the Office) to determine whether the conflicting mark has been assigned to applicant.

See TMEP §716.02(e) regarding suspension pending cancellation of a cited registration under §8 of the Act or expiration of a cited registration for failure to renew under §9 of the Act.

In *In re E. I. du Pont de Nemours & Co.*, 476 F.2d 1357, 177 USPQ 563 (C.C.P.A. 1973), the Court of Customs and Patent Appeals discussed the factors relevant to a determination of likelihood of confusion.

In *ex parte* examination, the issue of likelihood of confusion typically revolves around the similarity or dissimilarity of the marks and the relatedness of the goods or services. The other factors listed in *du Pont* may be considered only if relevant evidence is contained in the record. *See In re Majestic Distilling Co.*, 315 F.3d 1311, 1315, 65 USPQ2d 1201, 1204 (Fed. Cir. 2003) ("Not all of the *DuPont* factors may be relevant or of equal weight in a given case, and 'any one of the factors may control a particular case,'" quoting *In re Dixie Restaurants, Inc.*, 105 F.3d 1405, 1406-07, 41 USPQ2d 1531, 1533 (Fed. Cir. 1997)); *In re National Novice Hockey League, Inc.*, 222 USPQ 638, 640 (TTAB 1984). In an *ex parte* case, the following factors are usually the most relevant:

情况，参见 TMEP §§1208 及以下。审查员必须在文件中加入搜索策略的复印件。

如果审查员判定，申请商标与某已注册商标存在混淆的可能性，则审查员应根据 §2(d)拒绝予以注册。在引用一项现有注册之前，审查员必须检查商标局自动化档案，以确认所引用的任何注册作为依据按 §2(d)的规定拒绝予以注册是有效的。参见 TMEP §716.02(e)。同样，如果档案显示，存在冲突注册的转让记录，则审查员应当审查转让历史数据库（即商标局转让服务处的自动化档案）以判断该冲突商标是否已经转让给了申请者。

有关《商标法》§8 规定的暂缓撤销引用注册的情况，以及《商标法》§9 规定的因未续展而导致引用注册到期的情况，参见 TMEP §716.02(e)。

在 *E.I. du Pont de Nemours & Co.*, 476 F.2d 1357, 177 USPQ 563 (C.C.P.A. 1973)一案中，关税及专利上诉法院讨论了判定混淆可能性的相关因素。

在单方审查中，混淆可能性的问题通常涉及商标的相似性或不相似性以及与商品或服务的相关性。在 *du Pont* 中列出的其他因素只有在档案中包含相关证据的情况下才加以考虑。参见 *Majestic Distilling Co.*, 315 F.3d 1311, 1315, 65 USPQ2d 1201, 1204 (Fed. Cir. 2003)（"并非所有 *Du Pont* 因素都与具体的案件相关或具有同等的重要性，而且'这些因素中的任何一个都可以控制某特定案件'"，引自 *Dixie Restaurants, Inc.*, 105 F.3d 1405, 1406-07, 41 USPQ2d 1531, 1533 (Fed. Cir. 1997); *National Novice Hockey League, Inc.*, 222 USPQ 638, 640 (TTAB 1984)。在一个单方案件中，通常与下列因素最相关：

- The similarity or dissimilarity of the marks in their entireties as to appearance, sound, connotation and commercial impression.

- The relatedness of the goods or services as described in an application or registration or in connection with which a prior mark is in use.

- The similarity or dissimilarity of established, likely-to-continue trade channels.

- The conditions under which and buyers to whom sales are made, *i. e.* "impulse" vs. careful, sophisticated purchasing.

- The number and nature of similar marks in use on similar goods.

- A valid consent agreement between the applicant and the owner of the previously registered mark.

The Court of Appeals for the Federal Circuit has provided the following guidance with regard to determining and articulating likelihood of confusion:

> The basic principle in determining confusion between marks is that marks must be compared in their entireties and must be considered in connection with the particular goods or services for which they are used (citations omitted). It follows from that principle that likelihood of confusion cannot be predicated on dissection of a mark, that is, on only part of a mark (footnote omitted). On the other hand, in articulating reasons for reaching a conclusion on the issue of confusion, there is nothing improper in stating that, for rational reasons, more or less weight has been given to a particular feature of a mark, provided the ultimate conclusion rests on consideration of the marks in their entireties (footnote omitted). Indeed, this type of analysis appears to be unavoidable.

In re National Data Corp., 753 F. 2d 1056, 1058, 224 USPQ 749, 750-51 (Fed. Cir. 1985).

- 商标外观、声音、含义和商业印象在总体上的相似性或不相似性。

- 申请书或注册记录中所描述的商品或服务的相关性或与先前注册的在用商标的关系。

- 已确立并可能继续的销售渠道的相似性或不相似性。

- 销售的状况以及购买者向何人购买，即“心血来潮”与仔细、深思熟虑的购买之间的对比。

- 当前在类似商品上使用的类似商标的数量和性质。

- 申请者与先前注册的商标的所有人之间的有效同意协议。

联邦巡回上诉法院已经对判断和衡量混淆可能性提出了以下指导原则：

> 判断商标间混淆可能性的基本原则是，必须对总体商标进行比较，并且必须与其所用于的特定商品及服务联系起来考虑(引注略)。根据此原则，不能把商标分割开来考虑，即不能根据商标的一部分来预测混淆可能性(脚注略)。另一方面，在阐述关于混淆性问题结论的理由时，以合理的理由对商标的某一特定特征进行不同轻重的衡量是允许的，只要最终结论是对商标整体的考虑而得出的(脚注略)。实际上，这类分析似乎是不可避免的。

见 *National Data Corp*., 753 F.2d 1056, 1058, 224 USPQ 749, 750 - 51 (Fed. Cir. 1985)。

There is no mechanical test for determining likelihood of confusion. The issue is not whether the actual goods are likely to be confused but, rather, whether there is a likelihood of confusion as to the *source* of the goods. *In re Shell Oil Co.*, 992 F.2d 1204, 1208, 26 USPQ2d 1687, 1690 (Fed. Cir. 1993), and cases cited therein. Each case must be decided on its own facts.

The determination of likelihood of confusion under §2(d) in an intent-to-use application does not differ from the determination in any other type of application.

1207.01(a) Relatedness of the Goods or Services

If the marks of the respective parties are identical, the relationship between the goods or services need not be as close to support a finding of likelihood of confusion as would be required in a case where there are differences between the marks. *Amcor, Inc. v. Amcor Industries, Inc.*, 210 USPQ 70, 78 (TTAB 1981).

In some instances, because of established marketing practices, the use of identical marks on seemingly unrelated goods and services could result in a likelihood of confusion. *See In re Phillips-Van Heusen Corporation*, 228 USPQ 949, 951 (TTAB 1986) ("The licensing of commercial trademarks for use on 'collateral' products (such as clothing, glassware, linens, etc.), that are unrelated in nature to those goods or services on which the marks are normally used, has become a common practice in recent years.")

1207.01(a)(i) Goods or Services Need Not Be Identical

The goods or services do not have to be identical or even competitive in order to determine that there is a likelihood of confusion. The inquiry is whether the goods are related, not identical. The issue is not whether the goods will be confused with each other, but rather whether the public will be confused about their source. *See Safety-Kleen Corp. v. Dresser Indus., Inc.*, 518 F.2d 1399, 1404, 186 USPQ 476, 480 (C.C.P.A. 1975). It is sufficient that the goods or services of the applicant

对于混淆可能性的判断,不存在机械的衡量标准。问题并不在于是否可能混淆实际的商品,而是在于,是否可能对商品的*来源*产生混淆。*参见*相关判例:*Shell Oil Co*., 992 F.2d 1204, 1208, 26 USPQ2d 1687, 1690 (Fed. Cir. 1993),及其所引用的判例。每个案件都必须根据其自身的情况进行裁决。

在意图使用申请中,根据 §2(d)进行的混淆可能性判断与其他类型的申请的判断并无不同。

1207.01(a)　　商品或服务的相关性

如果各方当事人的商标是完全相同的,那么二者商品或服务之间的关系不必很接近即可判定存在混淆的可能性,而在商标存在差异的情况下,则要求二者的商品或服务具有较接近的关系。见 *Amcor, Inc. v. Amcor Industries, Inc*., 210 USPQ 70, 78 (TTAB 1981)。

在某些情况下,由于已确立的市场做法,相同的商标即便用在似乎不相关的商品和服务上仍然可以导致混淆的可能性。*参见 Phillips-Van Heusen Corporation*, 228 USPQ 949, 951 (TTAB 1986)("商标使用许可允许商标用在性质与其通常使用的商品和服务无关的'平行'产品(诸如服装、玻璃制品、亚麻布制品等等)上,最近几年这已成为一种普遍的做法。")。

1207.01(a)(i)　　商品或服务不必是相同的

在判断存在混淆可能的过程中,商品或服务不必是相同的,甚至不必是竞争性的。问题在于商品是否相关,而非相同。问题不在于商品是否会彼此混淆,而在于公众是否会混淆其来源。*参见 Safety-Kleen Corp. v. Dresser Indus., Inc*., 518 F.2d 1399, 1404, 186 USPQ 476, 480 (C.C.P.A. 1975)。如果申请者和注册者的商品

and the registrant are so related that the circumstances surrounding their marketing are such that they are likely to be encountered by the same persons under circumstances that would give rise to the mistaken belief that they originate from the same source. *See*, *e.g.*, *On-line Careline Inc. v. America Online Inc.*, 229 F.3d 1080, 56 USPQ2d 1471 (Fed. Cir. 2000) (ON-LINE TODAY for Internet connection services held likely to be confused with ONLINE TODAY for Internet content); *In re Martin's Famous Pastry Shoppe, Inc.*, 748 F.2d 1565, 223 USPQ 1289 (Fed. Cir. 1984) (MARTIN'S for wheat bran and honey bread held likely to be confused with MARTIN'S for cheese); *In re Corning Glass Works*, 229 USPQ 65 (TTAB 1985) (CONFIRM for a buffered solution equilibrated to yield predetermined dissolved gas values in a blood gas analyzer held likely to be confused with CONFIRMCELLS for diagnostic blood reagents for laboratory use); *In re Jeep Corp.*, 222 USPQ 333 (TTAB 1984) (LAREDO for land vehicles and structural parts therefor held likely to be confused with LAREDO for pneumatic tires).

Conversely, if the goods or services in question are not related or marketed in such a way that they would be encountered by the same persons in situations that would create the incorrect assumption that they originate from the same source, then, even if the marks are identical, confusion is not likely. *See*, *e.g.*, *Local Trademarks, Inc. v. Handy Boys Inc.*, 16 USPQ2d 1156 (TTAB 1990) (LITTLE PLUMBER for liquid drain opener held not confusingly similar to LITTLE PLUMBER and design for advertising services, namely the formulation and preparation of advertising copy and literature in the plumbing field); *Quartz Radiation Corp. v. Comm/Scope Co.*, 1 USPQ2d 1668 (TTAB 1986) (QR for coaxial cable held not confusingly similar to QR for various products (*e.g.*, lamps, tubes) related to the photocopying field).

1207.01(a)(ii) Goods May Be Related to Services

It is well recognized that confusion is likely to occur from the use of the same or

或服务存在关联，从而在市场营销条件下，可能出现二者的商品或服务被同一人遇到，并且会造成该人误以为二者的商品或服务来自同一来源，只要存在这种情况就足以判定存在混淆可能。参见判例 *On-line Careline Inc. v. America Online Inc.*, 229 F.3d 1080, 56 USPQ2d 1471 (Fed. Cir. 2000)(用于因特网接入服务的“ON-LINE TODAY”被认为可能会与用于因特网内容的“ONLINE TODAY”相混淆); *Martin's Famous Pastry Shoppe, Inc.*, 748 F.2d 1565, 223 USPQ 1289 (Fed. Cir. 1984)(用于麦麸蜂蜜面包的“MARTIN'S”被认为可能会与用于奶酪的“MARTIN'S”相混淆); *Corning Glass Works*, 229 USPQ 65 (TTAB 1985)(用于血液气体分析器平衡预先溶解气体数值的缓冲溶液的“CONFIRM”商标被认为可能与用于实验室用血液鉴定剂的“CONFIRMCELLS”商标相混淆); *Jeep Corp.*, 222 USPQ 333 (TTAB 1984)(用于陆地车辆及结构部件的“LAREDO”被认为可能与用于充气轮胎的“LAREDO”相混淆)。

相反地，如果涉及的商品或服务并不存在可能出现二者的商品或服务被同一人遇到，并且会造成该人误以为二者的商品或服务来自同一来源的这种关联或市场运作，如果是属于这种情况，那么即使商标完全相同，也不可能发生混淆。*参见*判例：*Local Trademarks, Inc. v. Handy Boys Inc.*, 16 USPQ2d 1156 (TTAB 1990)(用于液体排放开启器的“LITTLE PLUMBER”被认为不会与用于广告服务，即在铅管业领域进行广告制作和文字编写的类似商标“LITTLE PLUMBER”及图案发生混淆); *Quartz Radiation Corp. v. Comm/Scope Co.*, 1 USPQ2d 1668 (TTAB 1986)(用于同轴电缆的“QR”被认为不会与用于影印领域各种产品(例如，灯、管)的“QR”因相似而发生混淆)。

1207.01(a)(ii) 商品可能与服务发生关联

众所周知，如果类似的商标一方面用于商品，另一方面又用于该商品涉及的服

similar marks for goods, on the one hand, and for services involving those goods, on the other. *See, e.g., In re Hyper Shoppes (Ohio) Inc.*, 837 F.2d 463, 6 USPQ2d 1025 (Fed. Cir. 1988) (BIGG'S (stylized) for retail grocery and general merchandise store services held likely to be confused with BIGGS and design for furniture); *In re H.J. Seiler Co.*, 289 F.2d 674, 129 USPQ 347 (C.C.P.A. 1961) (SEILER for catering services held likely to be confused with SEILER'S for smoked and cured meats); *In re Azteca Restaurant Enterprises, Inc.*, 50 USPQ2d 1209 (TTAB 1999) (AZTECA MEXICAN RESTAURANT for restaurant services held likely to be confused with AZTECA for Mexican food products); *In re Golden Griddle Pancake House Ltd.*, 17 USPQ2d 1074 (TTAB 1990) (GOLDEN GRIDDLE PANCAKE HOUSE for restaurant services held likely to be confused with GOLDEN GRIDDLE for table syrup); *In re Mucky Duck Mustard Co. Inc.*, 6 USPQ2d 1467 (TTAB 1988) (MUCKY DUCK and duck design for mustard held likely to be confused with THE MUCKY DUCK and duck design for restaurant services); *In re U.S. Shoe Corp.*, 229 USPQ 707 (TTAB 1985) (CAREER IMAGE (stylized) for retail women's clothing store services and clothing held likely to be confused with CREST CAREER IMAGES (stylized) for uniforms); *In re United Service Distributors, Inc.*, 229 USPQ 237 (TTAB 1986) (design for distributorship services in the field of health and beauty aids held likely to be confused with design for skin cream); *In re Phillips-Van Heusen Corp.*, 228 USPQ 949 (TTAB 1986) (21 CLUB for various items of men's, boys', girls' and women's clothing held likely to be confused with THE "21" CLUB (stylized) for restaurant services and towels); *Steelcase Inc. v. Steelcare Inc.*, 219 USPQ 433 (TTAB 1983) (STEELCARE INC. for refinishing of furniture, office furniture, and machinery held likely to be confused with STEELCASE for office furniture and accessories); *Corinthian Broadcasting Corporation v. Nippon Electric Co., Ltd.*, 219 USPQ 733 (TTAB 1983) (TVS for transmitters and receivers of still television pictures held likely to be confused with TVS for television broadcasting services); *In re Industrial Expositions, Inc.*, 194 USPQ 456 (TTAB 1977) (POLLUTION ENGINEERING EXPOSITION for programming and conducting of industrial trade shows held likely to be confused with POLLUTION ENGINEERING for a periodical

务，也可能导致混淆的发生。*参见*判例：*Hyper Shoppes*（*Ohio*）*Inc*.，837 F.2d 463，6 USPQ2d 1025（Fed.Cir.1988）（用于零售杂货店以及一般商店服务的“BIGG’S（风格化）”被认为可能与用于家具的“BIGGS”及图案相混淆）；*H.J.Seiler Co*.，289 F.2d 674，129 USPQ 347（C.C.P.A.1961）（用于承办酒席服务的“SEILER”被认为可能与用于腌熏肉类的“SEILER’S”相混淆）；*Azteca Restaurant Enterprises*，*Inc*.，50 USPQ2d 1209（TTAB 1999）（用于餐饮服务的“AZTECA MEXICAN RESTAURANT”被认为可能与用于墨西哥食品的“AZTECA”相混淆）；*Golden Griddle Pancake House Ltd*.，17 USPQ2d 1074（TTAB 1990）（用于餐饮服务的“GOLDEN GRIDDLE PANCAKE HOUSE”被认为可能与用于餐用糖浆的“GOLDEN GRIDDLE”相混淆）；*Mucky Duck Mustard Co.Inc*.，6 USPQ2d 1467（TTAB 1988）（用于芥末的“MUCKY DUCK”及鸭子图案被认为可能与用于餐饮服务的“MUCKY DUCK”及鸭子图案相混淆）；*U.S.Shoe Corp*.，229 USPQ 707（TTAB 1985）[用于女装零售商店服务的“CAREER IMAGE（风格化）”被认为可能与用于制服的“CREST CAREER IMAGES（风格化）”相混淆]；*United Service Distributors*，*Inc*.，229 USPQ 237（TTAB 1986）（用于健康美容业经销服务的图案被认为可能与用于护肤霜的图案相混淆）；*Phillips-Van Heusen Corp*.，228 USPQ 949（TTAB 1986）[用于各式服装的“21 CLUB”被认为可能与用于餐饮服务和毛巾的“THE‘21’CLUB（风格化）”相混淆]；*Steelcase Inc.v.Steelcare Inc*.，219 USPQ 433（TTAB 1983）（用于家具、办公家具和机械修整服务的“STEELCARE INC.”被认为可能与用于办公家具及用品的“STEELCASE”相混淆）；*Corinthian Broadcasting Corporation v.Nippon Electric Co*.，*Ltd*.，219 USPQ 733（TTAB 1983）（用于静态电视图像传输接收器的“TVS”被认为可能与用于电视广播服务的“TVS”相混淆）；*Industrial Expositions*，*Inc*.，194 USPQ 456（TTAB 1977）（用于工业贸易展览安排管理服务的“POLLUTION ENGINEERING EXPOSITION”被认为可能与用于某期刊的

magazine).

1207.01(a)(iii) Reliance on Identification of Goods/Services in Registration and Application [R-2]

The nature and scope of a party's goods or services must be determined on the basis of the goods or services recited in the application or registration. *See, e.g., Hewlett-Packard Co. v. Packard Press Inc.*, 281 F.3d 1261, 62 USPQ2d 1001 (Fed. Cir. 2002); *In re Shell Oil Co.*, 992 F.2d 1204, 26 USPQ2d 1687, 1690 n.4 (Fed. Cir. 1993); *J & J Snack Foods Corp. v. McDonald's Corp.*, 932 F.2d 1460, 18 USPQ2d 1889 (Fed. Cir. 1991); *Octocom Systems Inc. v. Houston Computer Services Inc.*, 918 F.2d 937, 16 USPQ2d 1783 (Fed. Cir. 1990); *Canadian Imperial Bank of Commerce, N.A. v. Wells Fargo Bank*, 811 F.2d 1490, 1 USPQ2d 1813 (Fed. Cir. 1987); *Paula Payne Products Co. v. Johnson Publishing Co.*, 473 F.2d 901, 177 USPQ 76 (C.C.P.A. 1973).

If the cited registration describes goods or services broadly, and there is no limitation as to the nature, type, channels of trade or class of purchasers, it is presumed that the registration encompasses all goods or services of the type described, that they move in all normal channels of trade, and that they are available to all classes of purchasers. Therefore, if the cited registration has a broad identification of goods or services, an applicant does not avoid likelihood of confusion merely by more narrowly identifying its related goods. *See, e.g., In re Linkvest S.A.*, 24 USPQ2d 1716 (TTAB 1992) (where a registrant's goods are broadly identified as "computer programs recorded on magnetic disks," without any limitation as to the kind of programs or the field of use, it is necessary to assume that the registrant's goods encompass all such computer programs, and that they travel in the same channels of trade and are available to all classes of prospective purchasers of those goods); *In re Diet Center Inc.*, 4 USPQ2d 1975 (TTAB 1987) (VEGETABLE SVELTES for wheat crackers sold through franchised outlets offering weight reduction services held likely to be confused with SVELTE for low calorie frozen

"POLLUTION ENGINEERING"相混淆)。

1207.01(a)(iii) 取决于对所申请和注册的商品/服务的识别[R-2]

当事人的商品或服务的性质和范围必须根据申请或注册中所述的商品或服务来判定。*参见*判例:*Hewlett-Packard Co. v. Packard Press Inc.*, 281 F.3d 1261, 62 USPQ2d 1001 (Fed. Cir. 2002); *Shell Oil Co.*, 992 F.2d 1204, 26 USPQ2d 1687, 1690 n.4 (Fed. Cir. 1993); *J & J Snack Foods Corp. v. McDonald's Corp.*, 932 F.2d 1460, 18 USPQ2d 1889 (Fed. Cir. 1991); *Octocom Systems Inc. v. Houston Computer Services Inc.*, 918 F.2d 937, 16 USPQ2d 1783 (Fed. Cir. 1990); *Canadian Imperial Bank of Commerce, N. A. v. Wells Fargo Bank*, 811 F.2d 1490, 1 USPQ2d 1813 (Fed. Cir. 1987); *Paula Payne Products Co. v. Johnson Publishing Co.*, 473 F.2d 901, 177 USPQ 76 (C.C.P.A. 1973)。

如果所引用的注册对商品或服务进行了广泛的描述,并且对于性质、类型、销售渠道或购买人群都没有限定,那么可以推定该注册包括所指的一切类型的商品或服务,适用于一切通常的销售渠道,并且向一切购买人群供应。因此,如果所引用的注册对商品或服务的识别非常广泛,那么申请者就不能通过对其商品作更狭窄的识别而避免混淆的可能性。*参见*相关判例:*Linkvest S. A.*, 24 USPQ2d 1716 (TTAB 1992)(注册者的商品广泛地识别为"记录于磁盘的计算机程序",而对于程序种类及使用领域均无任何限制,那么就必须推定注册者的商品包括了所有此类计算机程序,以同样的销售渠道经营,并向此类商品所有的潜在购买者供应);*Diet Center Inc.*, 4 USPQ2d 1975 (TTAB 1987)(用于通过特许商店出售小麦饼干提供减肥服务的"VEGETABLE SVELTES"被认为可能与用于低热量冰冻甜点的"SVELTE"相混

dessert); *In re Uncle Sam Chemical Co., Inc.*, 229 USPQ 233 (TTAB 1986) (SPRAYZON for cleaning preparations and degreasers for industrial and institutional use held likely to be confused with SPRA-ON and design for preparation for cleaning woodwork and furniture). Similarly, there is a likelihood of confusion if an applicant identifies its goods or services so broadly that the identification encompasses the goods or services identified in the registration of a similar mark. *See, e.g., In re Americor Health Services*, 1 USPQ2d 1670 (TTAB 1986) (RESOLVE for corporate employee assistance services, namely, providing confidential mental health counseling services, held likely to be confused with RESOLVE for counseling services in the field of infertility); *In re Equitable Bancorporation*, 229 USPQ 709 (TTAB 1986) (RESPONSE for banking services held likely to be confused with RESPONSE CARD for banking services rendered through 24-hour teller machines).

An applicant may not restrict the scope of its goods and/or the scope of the goods covered in the registration by extrinsic argument or evidence, for example, as to the quality or price of the goods. *See, e.g., In re Bercut-Vandervoort & Co.*, 229 USPQ 763, 764 (TTAB 1986).

In the situation where the terminology in the identification is unclear, the Trademark Trial and Appeal Board has permitted an applicant to provide extrinsic evidence to show that the registrant's identification has a specific meaning to members of the trade. The Board noted that in light of such evidence it is improper to consider the identification in a vacuum and attach all possible interpretations to it. *In re Trackmobile Inc.*, 15 USPQ2d 1152, 1154 (TTAB 1990).

1207.01(a)(iv) No "Per Se" Rule

The facts in each case vary and the weight to be given each factor may be different in light of the varying circumstances; therefore, there can be no rule that certain goods or services are *per se* related, such that there must be a likelihood of confusion from the use of similar marks in relation thereto. *See, e.g., Informa-*

淆)；*Uncle Sam Chemical Co*., *Inc*., 229 USPQ 233 (TTAB 1986)(用于工业及机构用清洁及除油服务的"SPRAYZON"被认为可能与用于清洁木制品及家具服务的"SPRA-ON"及图案相混淆)。类似地，如果申请者对其商品或服务进行了广泛的识别，识别的范围包括了某相似商标的申请中所识别的商品或服务，也会导致混淆的可能。*参见* 相关判例：*Americor Health Services*, 1 USPQ2d 1670 (TTAB 1986)(用于公司雇员辅助服务，即提供机密精神健康咨询服务的"RESOLVE"被认为可能与用于提供不孕症咨询服务的"RESOLVE"相混淆)。*Equitable Bancorporation*, 229 USPQ 709 (TTAB 1986)(用于银行服务的"RESPONSE"被认为可能与用于24小时语音银行服务的"RESPONSE CARD"相混淆)。

申请者不能通过外在的(例如商品的质量或价格)抗辩或证据，对自己商品的范围和/或对注册所包含的商品的范围进行限制。*参见* 判例：*Bercut-Vandervoort & Co*., 229 USPQ 763, 764 (TTAB 1986)。

在识别的意义不明的情况下，商标评审及上诉委员会允许申请者提供外在的证据，表明注册者的识别对所在行业的成员具有某种具体的含义。委员会指出，有此类证据为根据，认为识别处于真空中并且可以给它附加一切可能的解释是不适当的。见 *Trackmobile Inc*., 15 USPQ2d 1152, 1154 (TTAB 1990)。

1207.01(a)(iv) 不存在"本身"规则

根据不同的情况，每个案件具有不同的事实，每个因素所占的分量也不相同；因此，不存在某些商品或服务本身关联而导致相关的相似商标的使用必定产生混淆可

tion Resources Inc. v. X Press Information Services*, 6 USPQ2d 1034, 1038 (TTAB 1988) (regarding computer hardware and software); *Hi-Country Foods Corp. v. Hi Country Beef Jerky*, 4 USPQ2d 1169, 1171 (TTAB 1987) (regarding food products); *In re Quadram Corp.*, 228 USPQ 863, 865 (TTAB 1985) (regarding computer hardware and software); *In re British Bulldog, Ltd.*, 224 USPQ 854, 855-56 (TTAB 1984) and cases cited therein (regarding clothing).

1207.01(a)(v) Expansion of Trade Doctrine

The examining attorney must consider any goods or services in the registrant's normal fields of expansion to determine whether the registrant's goods or services are related to the applicant's identified goods or services under §2(d). *In re General Motors Corp.*, 196 USPQ 574 (TTAB 1977). A trademark owner is entitled to protection against the registration of a similar mark on products that might reasonably be expected to be produced by him in the normal expansion of his business. The test is whether purchasers would believe the product or service is within the registrant's logical zone of expansion. *CPG Products Corp. v. Perceptual Play, Inc.*, 221 USPQ 88 (TTAB 1983).

1207.01(a)(vi) Evidence Showing Relatedness of Goods or Services [R-2]

The examining attorney must provide evidence showing that the goods and services are related to support a finding of likelihood of confusion. Evidence of relatedness might include news articles and/or evidence from computer databases showing that the relevant goods or services are used together or used by the same purchasers; advertisements showing that the relevant goods or services are advertised together or sold by the same manufacturer or dealer; or copies of prior use-based registrations of the same mark for both applicant's goods and services and the goods and services listed in the cited registration. *See* TMEP §1207.01(d)(iii) and cases cited therein regarding the probative value of third party registrations.

能的规则。*参见*判例：*Information Resources Inc. v. X * Press Information Services*，6 USPQ2d 1034，1038（TTAB 1988）（关于计算机硬件和软件）；*Hi-Country Foods Corp. v. Hi Country Beef Jerky*，4 USPQ2d 1169，1171（TTAB 1987）（关于食品）；*Quadram Corp.*，228 USPQ 863，865（TTAB 1985）（关于计算机硬件和软件）；*British Bulldog, Ltd.*，224 USPQ 854，855－856（TTAB 1984）以及所引用的判例（关于服装）。

1207.01(a)(v) 贸易扩张原理

审查员必须考虑注册者正常扩张领域内的一切商品或服务，以判断注册者的商品或服务是否同申请者根据 §2(d)识别的商品或服务相关联。见 *General Motors Corp.*，196 USPQ 574（TTAB 1977）。商标所有者有权要求用于可合理预见在其业务正常扩张后可能生产的产品的类似商标不得注册。考察的标准是，购买者是否会认为该产品或服务属于注册者的合理扩张领域。*CPG Products Corp. v. Perceptual Play, Inc.*，221 USPQ 88（TTAB 1983）。

1207.01(a)(vi) 表明商品或服务相关性的证据［R－2］

审查员必须提供证据，表明商品和服务相关，可支持混淆可能性的判定。相关性的证据可以包括，表明相关商品或服务在一起使用或由相同的购买者使用的新闻文章和/或来自计算机数据库的证据；表明相关商品或服务一起做广告或由相同的制造商或经销商进行销售的广告；或者，申请者的商品和服务以及被引用的注册中列出的商品和服务所使用的同一商标的先前使用注册的注册复印件。有关第三方注册的证明价值，参见 TMEP §1207.01(d)(iii)以及所引用的判例。

The identification of goods/services in the subject application and the cited registration(s) may in itself constitute evidence of the relatedness of the goods or services. *Hewlett-Packard Co. v. Packard Press Inc.*, 281 F.3d 1261, 1267, 62 USPQ2d 1001, 1004 (Fed. Cir. 2002) (Board erred in finding that there was insufficient evidence of relatedness, "because the Board did not consider the important evidence already before it, namely the ITU application and [opposer's multiple] registrations").

1207.01(b)　　Similarity of the Marks [R-2]

If it appears that confusion may be likely as a result of the contemporaneous use of similar marks by the registrant and the applicant with the identified goods or services, the next step is to evaluate the marks themselves, in relation to the goods and services. The test of likelihood of confusion is not whether the marks can be distinguished when subjected to a side-by-side comparison, but whether the marks are sufficiently similar that there is a likelihood of confusion as to the source of the goods or services. When considering the similarity of the marks, "[a]ll relevant facts pertaining to the appearance and connotation must be considered." *Recot, Inc. v. M. C. Becton*, 214 F.3d 1322, 1329, 54 USPQ2d 1894, 1897 (Fed. Cir. 2000). In evaluating the similarities between marks, the emphasis must be on the recollection of the average purchaser who normally retains a general, rather than specific, impression of trademarks. *Sealed Air Corp. v. Scott Paper Co.*, 190 USPQ 106, 108 (TTAB 1975).

Where the goods are identical, "the degree of similarity [between the marks] necessary to support a conclusion of likely confusion declines." *Century 21 Real Estate Corp. v. Century Life of America*, 970 F. 2d 874, 877, 23 USPQ2d 1698, 1701 (Fed. Cir. 1992), *cert. denied* 506 U.S. 1034 (1992); *ECI Division of E-Systems, Inc. v. Environmental Communications Inc.*, 207 USPQ 443 (TTAB 1980).

1207.01(b)(i)　　Word Marks

The points of comparison for a word mark are appearance, sound, and meaning or connotation. Similarity of the marks in one respect — sight, sound or meaning—

提交的申请和被引用的注册对商品/服务的识别本身可以构成商品或服务的相关性的证据。见 *Hewlett-Packard Co. v. Packard Press Inc.*, 281 F.3d 1261, 1267, 62 USPQ2d 1001, 1004 (Fed. Cir. 2002)(委员会错误地判定缺乏证明相关性的充分证据,"因为委员会没有考虑到就在眼前的重要证据,即 ITU 申请和[异议人的多项]注册")。

1207.01(b) 商标的相似性 [R-2]

如果由于注册者和申请者同时使用类似的商标识别商品或服务时似乎可能产生混淆,那么下一步就是要与商品和服务联系起来对商标本身进行评价。判断混淆可能性的标准并不在于商标是否能够通过逐方面的比较区分开来,而在于商标是否充分地相似,从而导致对商品或服务来源的混淆可能。在考虑商标相似性时,"一切与外观和内涵有关的事实都要加以考虑。"*Recot, Inc. v. M. C. Becton*, 214 F.3d 1322, 1329, 54 USPQ2d 1894, 1897 (Fed. Cir. 2000)。在评价商标间的相似性时,重点必须放在一般购买者所保留的记忆上,一般购买者通常对商标只有一般的印象,而没有很具体的印象。*Sealed Air Corp. v. Scott Paper Co.*, 190 USPQ 106, 108 (TTAB 1975)。

如果商品完全相同,"对于支持可能存在混淆的结论所必需的[商标间的]相似程度要求就降低了"。*Century 21 Real Estate Corp. v. Century Life of America*, 970 F.2d 874, 877, 23 USPQ2d 1698, 1701 (Fed. Cir. 1992), *cert. denied* 506 U.S. 1034 (1992); *ECI Division of E-Systems, Inc. v. Environmental Communications Inc.*, 207 USPQ 443 (TTAB 1980)。

1207.01(b)(i) 文字商标

对文字商标进行对比的要点在于对比外观、声音以及含义或内涵。商标在某一个方面相似——视觉、声音或含义——并不自动得出存在混淆可能性的结论,即使商

will not automatically result in a finding of likelihood of confusion even if the goods are identical or closely related. Rather, the rule is that taking into account all of the relevant facts of a particular case, similarity as to one factor alone *may* be sufficient to support a holding that the marks are confusingly similar. *In re Lamson Oil Co.*, 6 USPQ2d 1041, 1043 (TTAB 1987).

1207.01(b)(ii) Similarity In Appearance

Similarity in appearance is one factor in determining whether there is a likelihood of confusion between marks. Marks may be confusingly similar in appearance despite the addition, deletion or substitution of letters or words. *See, e.g.*, *Weiss Associates Inc. v. HRL Associates, Inc.*, 902 F.2d 1546, 14 USPQ2d 1840 (Fed. Cir. 1990) (TMM held confusingly similar to TMS, both for systems software); *Canadian Imperial Bank of Commerce, N. A., v. Wells Fargo Bank*, 811 F.2d 1490, 1 USPQ2d 1813 (Fed. Cir. 1987) (COMMCASH held likely to be confused with COMMUNICASH, both for banking services); *In re Lamson Oil Co.*, 6 USPQ2d 1041 (TTAB 1987) (TRUCOOL for synthetic coolant held likely to be confused with TURCOOL for cutting oil); *In re Curtice-Burns, Inc.*, 231 USPQ 990 (TTAB 1986) (MCKENZIE'S (stylized) for processed frozen fruits and vegetables held likely to be confused with McKenzie for canned fruits and vegetables); *In re Pix of America, Inc.*, 225 USPQ 691 (TTAB 1985) (NEWPORTS for women's shoes held likely to be confused with NEWPORT for outer shirts); *In re Pellerin Milnor Corp.*, 221 USPQ 558 (TTAB 1983) (MILTRON for microprocessor used in commercial laundry machines held likely to be confused with MILLTRONICS (stylized) for electronic control devices for machinery); *In re BASF A.G.*, 189 USPQ 424 (TTAB 1975) (LUTEXAL for resinous chemicals used in dyeing textiles held likely to be confused with LUTEX for non-resinous chemicals used in the textile industry).

1207.01(b)(iii) Comparing Marks That Contain Additional Matter [R-2]

It is a general rule that likelihood of confusion is not avoided between otherwise

品完全相同或密切相关。相反地，原则是要考虑具体案件的所有相关事实，某一因素的相似性*可能*充分支持商标之间存在可混淆的相似性的结论。见 *Lamson Oil Co.*, 6 USPQ2d 1041, 1043 (TTAB 1987)。

1207.01(b)(ii) 外观相似性

在判断商标之间是否存在混淆可能性时，外观相似性是需要考虑的因素之一。即使增删替换了某些字母或字，商标在外观上还可能具有引起混淆的相似性。*参见*判例：*Weiss Associates Inc. v. HRL Associates, Inc.*, 902 F.2d 1546, 14 USPQ2d 1840 (Fed. Cir. 1990)（"TMM"被认为与"TMS"存在会混淆的相似性，二者都是用于系统软件）；*Canadian Imperial Bank of Commerce, N.A., v. Wells Fargo Bank*, 811 F.2d 1490, 1 USPQ2d 1813 (Fed. Cir. 1987)（"COMMCASH"被认为可能与"COMMUNICASH"相混淆，二者都是用于银行服务）；*Lamson Oil Co.*, 6 USPQ2d 1041 (TTAB 1987)（用于合成冷冻剂的"TRUCOOL"被认为可能与用于切削油的"TURCOOL"相混淆）；*Curtice-Burns, Inc.*, 231 USPQ 990 (TTAB 1986)［用于后加工冷冻水果和蔬菜的"MCKENZIE'S（风格化）"被认为可能与用于罐头水果和蔬菜的"McKenzie"相混淆］；*Pix of America, Inc.*, 225 USPQ 691 (TTAB 1985)（用于女鞋的"NEWPORTS"被认为可能与用于外套的"NEWPORT"相混淆）；*Pellerin Milnor Corp.*, 221 USPQ 558 (TTAB 1983)［用于商业洗衣房机械微处理器的"MILTRON"被认为可能与用于机械电子控制装置的"MILLTRONICS（风格化）"相混淆］；*BASF A.G.*, 189 USPQ 424 (TTAB 1975)（用于织物印染树脂化合物的"LUTEXAL"被认为可能与用于纺织业无树脂化合物的"LUTEX"相混淆）。

1207.01(b)(iii) 比较含有附加内容的商标［R－2］

一般规则是，如果只是对描述或暗示所指的商品或服务的公司标识或内容进行

confusingly similar marks merely by adding or deleting a house mark or matter that is descriptive or suggestive of the named goods or services. Sometimes the rule is expressed in terms of the dominance of the common term. Therefore, if the dominant portion of both marks is the same, then confusion may be likely notwithstanding peripheral differences. *See*, *e*. *g*., *Hewlett-Packard Co*. *v*. *Packard Press Inc*., 281 F.3d 1261, 62 USPQ2d 1001 (Fed. Cir. 2002) (even though applicant's mark PACKARD TECHNOLOGIES (with "TECHNOLOGIES" disclaimed) does not incorporate every feature of opposer's HEWLETT PACKARD marks, similar overall commercial impression is created); *In re El Torito Restaurants Inc*., 9 USPQ2d 2002 (TTAB 1988) (MACHO COMBOS (with "COMBOS" disclaimed) held likely to be confused with MACHO (stylized), both for food items as a part of restaurant services); *In re Computer Systems Center Inc*., 5 USPQ2d 1378 (TTAB 1987) (CSC ADVANCED BUSINESS SYSTEMS for retail computer stores held likely to be confused with CSC for computer time sharing and computer programming services); *In re Equitable Bancorporation*, 229 USPQ 709 (TTAB 1986) (RESPONSE held likely to be confused with RESPONSE CARD (with "CARD" disclaimed), both for banking services); *In re The U*. *S*. *Shoe Corp*., 229 USPQ 707 (TTAB 1985) (CAREER IMAGE (stylized) for clothing held likely to be confused with CREST CAREER IMAGES (stylized) for uniforms); *In re Apparel Ventures*, *Inc*., 229 USPQ 225 (TTAB 1986) (SPARKS BY SASSAFRAS (stylized) for clothing held likely to be confused with SPARKS (stylized) for footwear); *In re Corning Glass Works*, 229 USPQ 65 (TTAB 1985) (CONFIRM for a buffered solution equilibrated to yield predetermined dissolved gas values in a blood gas analyzer held likely to be confused with CONFIRMCELLS for diagnostic blood reagents for laboratory use); *In re Energy Images*, *Inc*., 227 USPQ 572 (TTAB 1985) (SMART-SCAN (stylized) for optical line recognition and digitizing processors held likely to be confused with SMART for remote data gathering and control systems); *In re Riddle*, 225 USPQ 630 (TTAB 1985) (RICHARD PETTY'S ACCU TUNE and design for automotive service stations held likely to be confused with ACCUTUNE for automotive testing equipment); *In re Denisi*, 225 USPQ 624 (TTAB 1985) (PERRY'S PIZZA held likely

一些增删,并不能避免具有混淆相似性的商标之间产生混淆的可能性。有时这一规则被称为"共用词语的统治性"。因此,如果两个商标的统治性部分是相同的,那么尽管存在表面差异,还是可能存在混淆。*参见* 判例:*Hewlett-Packard Co. v. Packard Press Inc.*, 281 F.3d 1261, 62 USPQ2d 1001 (Fed. Cir. 2002)[即使申请者的商标"PACKARD TECHNOLOGIES"("TECHNOLOGIES"撤回)并不包含异议人"HEWLETT PACKARD"商标的所有特征,但在整体上已经可以造成近似的商业印象了]; *El Torito Restaurants Inc.*, 9 USPQ2d 2002 (TTAB 1988)["MACHO COMBOS"("COMBOS"撤回)被认为可能与"MACHO(风格化)"发生混淆,二者都用于作为餐饮服务一部分的食物];*Computer Systems Center Inc.*, 5 USPQ2d 1378 (TTAB 1987)(用于计算机零售店的"CSC ADVANCED BUSINESS SYSTEMS"被认为可能与用于计算机分时技术及编程服务的"CSC"相混淆);*Equitable Bancorporation*, 229 USPQ 709 (TTAB 1986)["RESPONSE"被认为可能与"RESPONSE CARD"("CARD"撤回)相混淆,二者均用于银行服务];*The U.S. Shoe Corp.*, 229 USPQ 707 (TTAB 1985)[用于服装的"CAREER IMAGE(风格化)"被认为可能与用于制服的"CREST CAREER IMAGES(风格化)"相混淆]; *Apparel Ventures, Inc.*, 229 USPQ 225 (TTAB 1986)[用于服装的"SPARKS BY SASSAFRAS(风格化)"被认为可能与用于鞋类的"SPARKS(风格化)"相混淆];*Corning Glass Works*, 229 USPQ 65 (TTAB 1985)(用于血液气体分析器平衡预先溶解气体数值的缓冲溶液的"CONFIRM"商标被认为可能与用于实验室用血液鉴定剂的"CONFIRMCELLS"商标相混淆);*Energy Images, Inc.*, 227 USPQ 572 (TTAB 1985)[用于光学条形码识别及数字化处理器的"SMART-SCAN(风格化)"被认为可能与用于远程数据收集及控制系统的"SMART"相混淆];*Riddle*, 225 USPQ 630 (TTAB 1985)(用于汽车服务站的"RICHARD PETTY'S ACCU TUNE"及图案被认为可能与用于汽车测试设备的"ACCUTUNE"相混淆); *Denisi*, 225 USPQ 624 (TTAB 1985)

to be confused with PERRY'S, both for restaurant services); *In re Collegian Sportswear Inc.*, 224 USPQ 174 (TTAB 1984) (COLLEGIAN OF CALIFORNIA and design (with "CALIFORNIA" disclaimed) held likely to be confused with COLLEGIENNE, both for items of clothing); *In re Pierre Fabre S. A.*, 188 USPQ 691 (TTAB 1975) (PEDI-RELAX for foot cream held likely to be confused with RELAX for antiperspirant).

Exceptions to the above stated general rule regarding additions or deletions to marks may arise if: (1) the marks in their entireties convey significantly different commercial impressions, or (2) the matter common to the marks is not likely to be perceived by purchasers as distinguishing source because it is merely descriptive or diluted. *See, e.g., In re Farm Fresh Catfish Co.*, 231 USPQ 495 (TTAB 1986) (CATFISH BOBBERS (with "CATFISH" disclaimed) for fish held not likely to be confused with BOBBER for restaurant services); *In re Shawnee Milling Co.*, 225 USPQ 747 (TTAB 1985) (GOLDEN CRUST for flour held not likely to be confused with ADOLPH'S GOLD'N CRUST and design (with "GOLD'N CRUST" disclaimed) for coating and seasoning for food items); *In re S. D. Fabrics, Inc.*, 223 USPQ 54 (TTAB 1984) (DESIGNERS/FABRIC (stylized) for retail fabric store services held not likely to be confused with DAN RIVER DESIGNER FABRICS and design for textile fabrics).

1207.01(b)(iv) Similarity in Sound—Phonetic Equivalents

Similarity in sound is one factor in determining whether there is a likelihood of confusion between marks. There is no "correct" pronunciation of a trademark because it is impossible to predict how the public will pronounce a particular mark. Therefore, "correct" pronunciation cannot be relied on to avoid a likelihood of confusion. *See, e.g., Kabushiki Kaisha Hattori Tokeiten v. Scuotto*, 228 USPQ 461 (TTAB 1985) (SEYCOS and design for watches held likely to be confused with SEIKO for watches and clocks); *In re Great Lakes Canning, Inc.*, 227 USPQ 483 (TTAB 1985) (CAYNA (stylized) for soft drinks held likely to be confused

(“PERRY’S PIZZA”被认为可能与“PERRY’S”相混淆，二者均用于餐饮服务)；*Collegian Sportswear Inc*., 224 USPQ 174 (TTAB 1984)[“COLLEGIAN OF CALIFORNIA”及图案(“CALIFORNIA”撤回)被认为可能与“COLLEGIENNE”相混淆，二者均用于服装]；*Pierre Fabre S.A*., 188 USPQ 691 (TTAB 1975)(用于护足霜的“PEDI-RELAX”被认为可能与用于止汗剂的“RELAX”相混淆)。

在以下情况下，可能出现对上述关于商标增删的一般规则的例外情况：(1)商标在整体上传达了明显不同的商业印象，或(2)商标的共同部分不可能使购买者产生区分来源的感觉，因为这一部分仅仅是描述性的或已经淡化。*参见* 判例：*Farm Fresh Catfish Co*., 231 USPQ 495 (TTAB 1986)[用于鱼肉的“CATFISH BOBBERS”(“CATFISH”撤回)被认为可能与用于餐饮服务的“BOBBER”相混淆]；*Shawnee Milling Co*., 225 USPQ 747 (TTAB 1985)[用于面粉的“GOLDEN CRUST”被认为可能与用于食物佐料的“ADOLPH’S GOLD’N CRUST”及图案(“GOLD’N CRUST”撤回)相混淆]；*S. D. Fabrics, Inc*., 223 USPQ 54 (TTAB 1984)[用于零售纺织品商店服务的“DESIGNERS/FABRIC(风格化)”被认为可能与用于纺织品的“DAN RIVER DESIGNER FABRICS”及图案相混淆]。

1207.01(b)(iv) 声音相似性——发音相同

在判断商标间是否存在混淆可能时，声音相似性是需要考虑的因素之一。对于某项商标而言，不存在“正确的”发音，因为无法预测公众会怎样读某特定商标。因此，不能依赖“正确的”发音来避免混淆的可能。*参见* 判例：*Kabushiki Kaisha Hattori Tokeiten v. Scuotto*, 228 USPQ 461 (TTAB 1985)(用于手表的“SEYCOS”及图案被认为可能与用于钟表的“SEIKO”相混淆)；*Great Lakes Canning, Inc*., 227 USPQ 483(TTAB 1985)[用于软饮料的“CAYNA(风格化)”被认为可能与用于罐装冷冻水

with CANA for, *inter alia*, canned and frozen fruit and vegetable juices); *In re Energy Telecommunications & Electrical Association*, 222 USPQ 350 (TTAB 1983) (ENTELEC and design for association services in the telecommunication and energy industries held likely to be confused with INTELECT for conducting expositions for the electrical industry); *In re Cresco Mfg. Co.*, 138 USPQ 401 (TTAB 1963) (CRESCO and design for leather jackets held likely to be confused with KRESSCO for hosiery).

1207.01(b)(v) Similarity in Meaning

Similarity in meaning or connotation is another factor in determining whether there is a likelihood of confusion between marks. The focus is on the recollection of the average purchaser who normally retains a general, rather than specific, impression of trademarks. *See, e.g., In re M. Serman & Company, Inc.*, 223 USPQ 52 (TTAB 1984) (CITY WOMAN held likely to be confused with CITY GIRL, both for clothing); *Gastown Inc., of Delaware v. Gas City, Ltd.*, 187 USPQ 760 (TTAB 1975) (GAS CITY (with "GAS" disclaimed) held likely to be confused with GASTOWN, both for gasoline); *Watercare Corp. v. Midwesco-Enterprise, Inc.*, 171 USPQ 696 (TTAB 1971) (AQUA-CARE (stylized) held likely to be confused with WATERCARE (stylized), both for water conditioning products).

The meaning or connotation of a mark must be determined in relation to the named goods or services. Even marks that are identical in sound and/or appearance may create sufficiently different commercial impressions when applied to the respective parties' goods or services so that there is no likelihood of confusion. *See, e.g., In re Sears, Roebuck and Co.*, 2 USPQ2d 1312 (TTAB 1987) (CROSS-OVER for bras held not likely to be confused with CROSSOVER for ladies' sportswear, the Board finding that the term was suggestive of the construction of applicant's bras, but was likely to be perceived by purchasers either as an entirely arbitrary designation or as being suggestive of sportswear that "crosses over" the

果蔬菜的“CANA”相混淆]；*Energy Telecommunications & Electrical Association*，222 USPQ 350（TTAB 1983）（用于电信及能源业联络服务的“ENTELEC”及图案被认为可能与用于提供电子业展览会服务的“INTELECT”相混淆）；*Cresco Mfg. Co.*，138 USPQ 401（TTAB 1963）（用于皮夹克的“CRESCO”及图案被认为可能与用于针织品的“KRESSCO”相混淆）。

1207.01(b)(v)　　含义相似性

在判断商标之间是否存在混淆可能时，含义相似性是需要考虑的因素之一。重点应放在一般购买者的记忆，因为一般购买者通常对商标只有一般的印象，而没有具体的印象。参见判例：*M. Serman & Company, Inc.*，223 USPQ 52（TTAB 1984）（“CITY WOMAN”被认为可能与“CITY GIRL”相混淆，二者均用于服装）；*Gastown Inc., of Delaware v. Gas City, Ltd.*，187 USPQ 760（TTAB 1975）[“GAS CITY”（“GAS”撤回）被认为可能与“GASTOWN”相混淆，二者均用于煤气]；*Watercare Corp. v. Midwesco-Enterprise, Inc.*，171 USPQ 696（TTAB 1971）[“AQUA-CARE（风格化）”被认为可能与“WATERCARE（风格化）”相混淆，二者均用于水软化处理产品]。

商标的含义或内涵必须同相关商品或服务联系起来进行判断。即使是声音和/或外观完全相同的商标，用于各方当事人的商品或服务时也可能造成泾渭分明的商业印象，如此就不存在混淆的可能。参见判例：*Sears, Roebuck and Co.*，2 USPQ2d 1312（TTAB 1987）（用于文胸的“CROSS-OVER”被认为不可能与用于女式运动装的“CROSSOVER”相混淆，委员会认为，该词暗示了申请者文胸的结构，而用于女式运动装时，购买者可能以为只是一种完全任意的标识，或者暗示了该运动装“跨越”了

line between informal and more formal wear when applied to ladies' sportswear); *In re British Bulldog, Ltd.*, 224 USPQ 854 (TTAB 1984) (PLAYERS for men's underwear held not likely to be confused with PLAYERS for shoes, the Board finding that the term PLAYERS implies a fit, style, color and durability adapted to outdoor activities when applied to shoes, but "implies something else, primarily indoors in nature" when applied to men's underwear); *In re Sydel Lingerie Co., Inc.*, 197 USPQ 629 (TTAB 1977) (BOTTOMS UP for ladies' and children's underwear held not likely to be confused with BOTTOMS UP for men's clothing, the Board finding that the term connotes the drinking phrase "Drink Up" when applied to men's suits, coats and trousers, but does not have this connotation when applied to ladies' and children's underwear).

1207.01(b)(vi) Doctrine of Foreign Equivalents

Under the doctrine of foreign equivalents, a foreign word (from a language familiar to an appreciable segment of American consumers) and the English equivalent may be found to be confusingly similar. *See, e.g., Continental Nut Co. v. Cordon Bleu, Ltee*, 494 F.2d 1397, 181 USPQ 647 (C.C.P.A. 1974); *In re American Safety Razor Co.*, 2 USPQ2d 1459 (TTAB 1987) (BUENOS DIAS for soap held likely to be confused with GOOD MORNING and design for latherless shaving cream); *In re Ithaca Industries, Inc.*, 230 USPQ 702 (TTAB 1986) (LUPO for men's and boys' underwear held likely to be confused with WOLF and design for various items of clothing); *In re Hub Distributing, Inc.*, 218 USPQ 284 (TTAB 1983) (EL SOL for clothing and footwear held likely to be confused with SUN and design for footwear).

Compare the following decisions involving marks found not confusingly similar, based on consideration of factors such as the overall appearance and pronunciation of the marks, the extent to which the terms are "equivalent," and the relatedness of the named goods and/or services: *In re Sarkli Ltd.*, 721 F.2d 353, 220 USPQ 111 (Fed. Cir. 1983) (REPECHAGE for various skin care products held not

非正式与更正式服装的界限)；*British Bulldog, Ltd.*, 224 USPQ 854 (TTAB 1984)(用于男式内衣的"PLAYERS"被认为不可能与用于鞋类的"PLAYERS"相混淆，委员会认定，PLAYERS 一词用于鞋类时暗示了适合户外活动的装备、风格、色彩以及耐久力，但是用于男式内衣时，则"暗示其它的东西，主要是室内性的")；*Sydel Lingerie Co., Inc.*, 197 USPQ 629 (TTAB 1977)(用于女式及儿童内衣的"BOTTOMS UP"被认为不可能与用于男装的"BOTTOMS UP"相混淆，委员会认定，该词用于男式套装、上装及长裤时意味着饮酒的习语"Drink Up"，但用于女式及儿童内衣时则没有这种内涵)。

1207.01(b)(vi) 外语对等原则

根据外语对等原则，一个外语词(来自于一种相当数量的美国消费者熟悉的语言)与其英语同义词可以被认为具有混淆的相似性。*参见* 判例：*Continental Nut Co. v. Cordon Bleu, Ltee*, 494 F.2d 1397, 181 USPQ 647 (C.C.P.A. 1974)；*American Safety Razor Co.*, 2 USPQ2d 1459 (TTAB 1987)(用于肥皂的"BUENOS DIAS"被认为可能与用于无沫剃须膏的"GOOD MORNING"相混淆)；*Ithaca Industries, Inc.*, 230 USPQ 702 (TTAB 1986)(用于男式内衣的"LUPO"被认为可能与用于各式服装的"WOLF"及图案相混淆)；*Hub Distributing, Inc.*, 218 USPQ 284 (TTAB 1983)(用于服装和鞋类的"EL SOL"被认为可能与用于鞋类的"SUN"及图案相混淆)。

比较下列判决，涉及了被判定为不存在混淆相似性的商标，其考虑因素包括整体外观以及商标的发音、词语"等效"的程度以及所指商品和/或服务的相关性：*参见* 判例：*Sarkli Ltd.*, 721 F.2d 353, 220 USPQ 111 (Fed. Cir. 1983)(用于各种皮肤护理

likely to be confused with SECOND CHANCE for face creams and other toiletries); *In re Buckner Enterprises Corp*., 6 USPQ2d 1316 (TTAB 1987) (DOVE and design for solid fuel burning stoves and furnaces held not likely to be confused with PALOMA for various forms of gas heating apparatus); *In re L'Oreal S.A*., 222 USPQ 925 (TTAB 1984) (HAUTE MODE for hair coloring cream shampoo held not likely to be confused with HI-FASHION SAMPLER (with "SAMPLER" disclaimed) for finger nail enamel); *In re Tia Maria, Inc*., 188 USPQ 524 (TTAB 1975) (TIA MARIA for restaurant services held not likely to be confused with AUNT MARY'S for canned fruits and vegetables).

The doctrine of foreign equivalents is not normally invoked if the marks alleged to be confusingly similar are both foreign words. *See Safeway Stores Inc. v. Bel Canto Fancy Foods Ltd*., 5 USPQ2d 1980, 1982 (TTAB 1987) ("[T]his Board does not think it proper to take the French expression 'bel air' and the Italian expression 'bel aria' and then convert both into English and compare the English translations ... "). However, application of the doctrine of foreign equivalents is not barred in every case where the respective marks consist of terms from different foreign languages. *Miguel Torres S.A. v. Casa Vinicola Gerardo Cesari S.R.L*., 49 USPQ2d 2018 (TTAB 1998) (likelihood of confusion found between the Italian DUE TORRI and design for wines, and the Spanish TORRES and design for wines and brandy and TRES TORRES for brandy).

While foreign words are generally translated into English for trademark comparison purposes, works from dead or obscure languages may be so unfamiliar to the American buying public that they should not be translated into English. *See Enrique Bernat F.S.A. v. Guadalajara Inc*., 210 F.3d 439, 54 USPQ2d 1497 (5th Cir.2000), *reh'g denied* 218 F.3d 745 (2000). The test is whether, to those American buyers familiar with the foreign language, the word would denote its English equivalent. *See In re Zazzara*, 156 USPQ 348 (TTAB 1967). The determination of whether a language is "dead" must be made on a case-by-case basis, based upon the meaning that the term would have to the relevant purchasing public.

产品的"REPECHAGE"被认为不可能与用于面霜及其他化妆品的"SECOND CHANCE"相混淆);*Buckner Enterprises Corp.*, 6 USPQ2d 1316 (TTAB 1987)(用于固体燃料炉的"DOVE"及图案被认为不可能与用于各种气体加热设备的"PALOMA"相混淆);*L'Oreal S.A.*, 222 USPQ 925 (TTAB 1984)[用于染发护理香波的"HAUTE MODE"被认为不可能与用于指甲油的"HI-FASHION SAMPLER"("SAMPLER"撤回)相混淆];*Tia Maria, Inc.*, 188 USPQ 524 (TTAB 1975)(用于餐饮服务的"TIA MARIA"被认为不可能与用于罐头水果和蔬菜的"AUNT MARY'S"相混淆)。

如果被宣称具有混淆相似性的商标都是外来文字,则外语对等原则通常不适用。*参见 Safeway Stores Inc. v. Bel Canto Fancy Foods Ltd.*, 5 USPQ2d 1980, 1982 (TTAB 1987)("委员会认为不应取出法语'bel air'一词和意大利语'bel aria'一词,然后将二者译成英语并比较其译文……。"不过,并不是所有相关商标包含不同外语语的案件都排除了外语对等原则的适用。见 *Miguel Torres S.A. v. Casa Vinicola Gerardo Cesari S.R.L.*, 49 USPQ2d 2018 (TTAB 1998)(用于葡萄酒的意大利语"DUE TORRI"及图案被认为可能与用于葡萄酒和白兰地的西班牙语"TORRES"及图案以及用于白兰地的"TRES TORRES"相混淆)。

尽管为了进行商标比较,外国文字一般要翻译成英语,但如果文字是来自已死或晦涩的语言,美国购买公众非常不熟悉,则不应再译成英语。*参见 Enrique Bernat F. S.A. v. Guadalajara Inc.*, 210 F.3d 439, 54 USPQ2d 1497 (5th Cir.2000), *reh'g denied* 218 F.3d 745 (2000)。判断标准在于,对于熟悉该外语的美国购买者而言,该字是否表示了其英语同义字的含义。*参见 In re Zazzara*, 156 USPQ 348 (TTAB 1967)。判断某种语言是否是"死亡的",必须根据每个个案的具体情况作出,要根据该词对于相关购买公众所表示的含义。

Example: Latin is generally considered a dead language. However, if there is evidence that a Latin term is still in use by the relevant purchasing public (*e.g.*, if the term appears in current dictionaries or news articles), then a Latin term is not considered dead. The same analysis should be applied to other uncommon languages.

1207.01(b)(vii) Transposition of Terms

Where the primary difference between marks is the transposition of the elements that compose the marks and where this transposition does not change the overall commercial impression, there may be a likelihood of confusion. *See*, *e.g.*, *In re Wine Society of America Inc.*, 12 USPQ2d 1139 (TTAB 1989) (THE WINE SOCIETY OF AMERICA and design, for "wine club membership services including the supplying of printed materials, sale of wines to members, conducting wine tasting sessions and recommending specific restaurants offering wines sold by applicant," held likely to be confused with AMERICAN WINE SOCIETY 1967 and design, for a newsletter, bulletin and journal of interest to members of the registrant); *In re Nationwide Industries Inc.*, 6 USPQ2d 1882 (TTAB 1988) (RUST BUSTER (with "RUST" disclaimed) for rust-penetrating spray lubricant held likely to be confused with BUST RUST for penetrating oil); *In re General Tire & Rubber Co.*, 213 USPQ 870 (TTAB 1982) (SPRINT STEEL RADIAL (with "STEEL" and "RADIAL" disclaimed) for tires held likely to be confused with RADIAL SPRINT (with "RADIAL" disclaimed) for tires).

However, if the transposed mark creates a distinctly different commercial impression, then confusion is not likely. *See*, *e.g.*, *In re Best Products Co.*, *Inc.*, 231 USPQ 988 (TTAB 1986) (BEST JEWELRY and design (with "JEWELRY" disclaimed) for retail jewelry store services held not likely to be confused with JEWELERS' BEST for jewelry).

1207.01(b)(viii) Marks Consisting of Multiple Words

When assessing the likelihood of confusion between compound word marks, one

例如：拉丁语通常被认为是一种死语言。不过，如果有证据证明某拉丁词语仍然为相关购买公众所使用（例如，如果该词语出现在现代词典或新闻文章中），则该拉丁词语就不能认为是已经死亡的。同样的分析应适用于其他罕见语言。

1207.01(b)(vii)　词语的变换

如果商标之间的主要区别变换了组成要素的次序，而这种次序的变换并没有改变整体的商业印象，那么就存在混淆的可能性。*参见* 判例：*Wine Society of America Inc.*, 12 USPQ2d 1139 (TTAB 1989)（用于"葡萄酒俱乐部会员服务，包括提供印刷材料、向会员出售葡萄酒、举办品酒会以及推荐申请者所出售的特别餐馆用酒等"的"THE WINE SOCIETY OF AMERICA"及图案被认为可能与用于向注册者会员提供的新闻通讯、期刊及杂志的"AMERICAN WINE SOCIETY 1967"及图案相混淆）；*Nationwide Industries Inc.*, 6 USPQ2d 1882 (TTAB 1988)［用于除锈喷雾润滑剂的"RUST BUSTER"（"RUST"撤回）被认为可能与用于润滑油的"BUST RUST"相混淆］；*General Tire & Rubber Co.*, 213 USPQ 870 (TTAB 1982)［用于轮胎的"SPRINT STEEL RADIAL"（"STEEL"和"RADIAL"撤回）被认为可能与用于轮胎的"RADIAL SPRINT"（"RADIAL"撤回）相混淆］。

不过，如果申请注册的商标造成了一种截然不同的商业印象，就可能不存在混淆。*参见* 判例：*Best Products Co., Inc.*, 231 USPQ 988 (TTAB 1986)［用于零售珠宝商店的"BEST JEWELRY"及图案（"JEWELRY"撤回）被认为不可能与用于珠宝的"JEWELERS' BEST"相混淆］。

1207.01(b)(viii)　由多个文字组成的商标

在评价多字混合的商标之间的混淆可能性时，必须判断文字商标的某一部分是

must determine whether there is a portion of the word mark that is dominant in terms of creating a commercial impression. Although there is no mechanical test to select a "dominant" element of a compound word mark, consumers would be more likely to perceive a fanciful or arbitrary term rather than a descriptive or generic term as the source-indicating feature of the mark. Accordingly, if two marks for related goods or services share the same dominant feature and the marks, when viewed in their entireties, create similar overall commercial impressions, then confusion is likely. *See In re J. M. Originals Inc.*, 6 USPQ2d 1393 (TTAB 1987) (JM ORIGINALS (with "ORIGINALS" disclaimed) for various items of apparel held likely to be confused with JM COLLECTABLES for "knitwear — namely, sport shirts").

If the common element of two marks is "weak" in that it is generic, descriptive or highly suggestive of the named goods or services, consumers typically will be able to avoid confusion unless the overall combinations have other commonality. *See, e.g., In re Bed & Breakfast Registry*, 791 F. 2d 157, 229 USPQ 818 (Fed. Cir. 1986) (BED & BREAKFAST REGISTRY for making lodging reservations for others in private homes held not likely to be confused with BED & BREAKFAST INTERNATIONAL for room booking agency services); *The U. S. Shoe Corp. v. Chapman*, 229 USPQ 74 (TTAB 1985) (COBBLER'S OUTLET for shoes held not likely to be confused with CALIFORNIA COBBLERS (stylized) for shoes); *In re Istituto Sieroterapico E Vaccinogeno, Toscano "SCLAVO" S. p. A.*, 226 USPQ 1035 (TTAB 1985) (ASO QUANTUM (with "ASO" disclaimed) for diagnostic laboratory reagents held not likely to be confused with QUANTUM I for laboratory instrument for analyzing body fluids).

In a sense the public can be said to rely more on the nondescriptive portions of each mark. On the other hand, this does not mean that the public looks only at the differences, or that the descriptive words play no role in creating confusion. *In re National Data Corp.*, 753 F. 2d 1056, 224 USPQ 749 (Fed. Cir. 1985) (THE CASH MANAGEMENT EXCHANGE (with "CASH MANAGEMENT" disclaimed) for computerized cash management services held likely to be confused

否在造成商业印象中占有统治地位。尽管没有什么机械的方法可以从多字混合的商标中选出一个“占统治地位的”元素，但是消费者更可能将某一虚构或任意性词语看作是商标的来源识别特征，而比较不可能将一个描述性或一般性的词语看作是商标的来源识别特征。因此，如果用于相关的商品或服务的两个商标都使用了同样的具有统治地位的特征，且商标在整体上造成了类似的商业印象，那么就可能存在混淆。*参见* *J. M. Originals Inc.*, 6 USPQ2d 1393 (TTAB 1987)［用于各种服饰的“JM ORIGINALS”(“ORIGINALS”撤回)被认为可能与用于“针织衫——即运动衫”的“JM COLLECTABLES”相混淆］。

如果两个商标的共同元素很“弱”，即它是对所指商品或服务的一般性、描述性或高度暗示性词语，那么消费者通常能够避免混淆，除非整体的结合具有了其他共同性。*参见*判例：*Bed & Breakfast Registry*, 791 F.2d 157, 229 USPQ 818 (Fed. Cir. 1986)(用于私人住宅住宿预定服务的“BED & BREAKFAST REGISTRY”被认为不可能与用于订房代理服务的“BED & BREAKFAST INTERNATIONAL”相混淆)；*The U. S. Shoe Corp. v. Chapman*, 229 USPQ 74 (TTAB 1985)［用于鞋类的“COBBLER'S OUTLET”被认为不可能与用于鞋类的“CALIFORNIA COBBLERS(风格化)”相混淆］；*Istituto Sieroterapico E Vaccinogeno, Toscano "SCLAVO" S. p. A.*, 226 USPQ 1035 (TTAB 1985)(用于医学实验室试剂的“ASO QUANTUM”被认为不可能与用于实验室体液分析设备的“QUANTUM”相混淆)。

从某种意义上说，可以认为，公众更依赖于每个商标的非描述性部分。另一方面，这并不意味着公众只关注差异，或者在导致混淆方面描述性词汇完全没有作用。见 *National Data Corp.*, 753 F.2d 1056, 224 USPQ 749 (Fed. Cir. 1985)［用于计算机化现金管理服务的“THE CASH MANAGEMENT EXCHANGE”(“CASH MANAGEMENT”撤回］被认为可能与用于各种金融服务的“CASH MANAGEMENT

with CASH MANAGEMENT ACCOUNT for various financial services).

1207.01(b)(ix) Weak or Descriptive Marks

The Trademark Trial and Appeal Board and the courts have recognized that merely descriptive and weak designations may be entitled to a narrower scope of protection than an entirely arbitrary or coined word. *In re Central Soya Company, Inc.*, 220 USPQ 914 (TTAB 1984). However, even a weak mark is entitled to protection against the registration of a similar mark for closely related goods or services. *King Candy Co. v. Eunice King's Kitchen, Inc.*, 496 F.2d 1400, 182 USPQ 108 (C.C.P.A.1974).

In *In re Hunke & Jochheim*, 185 USPQ 188, 189 (TTAB 1975), the Board stated:

> [R]egistration on the Supplemental Register may be considered to establish prima facie that, at least at the time of registration, the registered mark possessed a merely descriptive significance. (citation omitted.) This is significant because it is well established that the scope of protection afforded a merely descriptive or even a highly suggestive term is less than that accorded an arbitrary or coined mark. That is, terms falling within the former category have been generally categorized as "weak" marks, and the scope of protection extended to these marks has been limited to the substantially identical notation and/or to the subsequent use and registration thereof for substantially similar goods.

However, even marks that are registered on the Supplemental Register may be cited under §2(d). *In re Clorox Company*, 578 F.2d 305, 198 USPQ 337 (C.C.P.A.1978).

1207.01(b)(x) Parody Marks

Parody is not a defense to a likelihood of confusion refusal . There are confusing

ACCOUNT"相混淆)。

1207.01(b)(ix) 弱商标或描述性商标

商标评审及上诉委员会和法院都认为,仅为描述性和弱的符号商标的保护范围与完全任意性或臆造的文字商标的保护范围相比,更为狭窄。见 *Central Soya Company, Inc.*, 220 USPQ 914 (TTAB 1984)。但是,即使是弱商标,也有权受到保护,用于紧密相关的商品或服务的类似商标,禁止注册。*King Candy Co. v. Eunice King's Kitchen, Inc.*, 496 F.2d 1400, 182 USPQ 108 (C.C.P.A.1974)。

在 *Hunke & Jochheim*, 185 USPQ 188, 189 (TTAB 1975)一案中,委员会指出:

> 在联邦商标补充登记簿上的注册可以被认为初步地证明:至少在注册当时,该注册商标拥有仅仅描述性的意义。(引注略)这一点很重要,因为早已确立,仅仅是描述性或高度暗示性的词语所受的保护范围比任意性或臆造性商标要小。也就是说,属于前一范畴的词语通常被归为"弱"商标类,此类商标的保护范围限于实质相同的含义和/或以后在实质相似的商品上的使用和注册。

不过,即使是在联邦商标补充登记簿上注册的商标,也可以根据 §2(d)被引用。见 *Clorox Company*, 578 F.2d 305, 198 USPQ 337 (C.C.P.A.1978)。

1207.01(b)(x) 滑稽模仿商标

滑稽模仿不能抗辩以混淆性为理由拒绝予以注册的决定。滑稽模仿包括混淆性

parodies and non-confusing parodies. *See* 3 J. McCarthy, *McCarthy on Trademarks and Unfair Competition*, §31.153 (4th ed. 2000). A true parody actually decreases the likelihood of confusion because the effect of the parody is to create a distinction in the viewer's mind between the actual product and the joke. While a parody must call to mind the actual product to be successful, the same success also necessarily distinguishes the parody from the actual product. *Mutual of Omaha Insurance Co. v. Novak*, 648 F. Supp. 905, 231 USPQ 963 (D. Neb. 1986).

Another example of parody can be found in *Columbia Pictures Industries Inc., v. Miller*, 211 USPQ 816 (TTAB 1981) (CLOTHES ENCOUNTERS held likely to be confused with CLOSE ENCOUNTERS OF THE THIRD KIND, for men's and women's clothing); *Cf., Jordache Enterprises, Inc. v. Hogg Wyld, Inc.*, 828 F. 2d 1482, 4 USPQ2d 1216 (10th Cir. 1987) (LARDASHE for pants was not an infringement of the JORDACHE mark).

1207.01(c) Design Marks

When the marks at issue are both design marks, the issue of the similarity of the marks must be decided primarily on the basis of visual similarity. In this situation, consideration must be given to the fact that a purchaser's recollection of design marks is often of a general and hazy nature. *See, e.g., Red Carpet Corp. v. Johnstown American Enterprises Inc.*, 7 USPQ2d 1404 (TTAB 1988) (stylized house design for service of management of real estate properties for others held not likely to be confused with stylized house design for real estate brokerage services); *In re United Service Distributors, Inc.*, 229 USPQ 237 (TTAB 1986) (silhouette of two profiles facing right within a teardrop background for distributorship services in the field of health and beauty aids held likely to be confused with silhouette of two profiles facing left within an oval background for skin cream); *Ocean Spray Cranberries, Inc. v. Ocean Garden Products, Inc.*, 223 USPQ 1027 (TTAB 1984) (abstract circular design mark for seafood held not likely to be confused with oval breaking wave design for various food items including juices and

和非混淆性两种。参见 3 J. McCarthy, *McCarthy on Trademarks and Unfair Competition*, §31.153 (4th ed. 2000)。真正的滑稽模仿实际上降低了混淆的可能性,因为滑稽模仿的效果是在观众的脑海中产生了实际产品与笑话的区别。尽管滑稽模仿要获得成功必须使人联想到实际的产品,但同样还必须能够将笑话与实际产品区分开来。*Mutual of Omaha Insurance Co. v. Novak*, 648 F. Supp. 905, 231 USPQ 963 (D. Neb. 1986)。

另一个滑稽模仿的例子是 *Columbia Pictures Industries Inc., v. Miller*, 211 USPQ 816 (TTAB 1981)("CLOTHES ENCOUNTERS"被认为可能与用于男女服装的"CLOSE ENCOUNTERS OF THE THIRD KIND"相混淆);比较:*Jordache Enterprises, Inc. v. Hogg Wyld, Inc.*, 828 F.2d 1482, 4 USPQ2d 1216 (10th Cir. 1987)(用于长裤的"LARDASHE"并不构成对"JORDACHE"商标的侵权)。

1207.01(c)　　图案商标

如果所涉及的商标都是图案商标,那么商标的相似性问题主要就根据视觉相似性来判定。在这种情况下,必须考虑到购买者对图案商标的记忆通常是一般性和模糊性的。参见 判例:*Red Carpet Corp. v. Johnstown American Enterprises Inc.*, 7 USPQ2d 1404 (TTAB 1988)(用于不动产管理服务的风格化的房屋图案被认为不可能与用于不动产经纪服务的风格化的房屋图案相混淆);*United Service Distributors, Inc.*, 229 USPQ 237 (TTAB 1986)(用于健康美容领域批发销售服务的泪珠状背景里两个面向右的侧面轮廓像被认为可能与用于护肤霜的椭圆形背景里两个面向左的侧面轮廓像相混淆);*Ocean Spray Cranberries, Inc. v. Ocean Garden Products, Inc.*, 223 USPQ 1027 (TTAB 1984)(用于海鲜的抽象圆形图案被认为不可能与用于各种食品,包括果汁和水果的椭圆形碎波图案相混淆); *Steury Corp.*, 189

fruits); *In re Steury Corp.*, 189 USPQ 353 (TTAB 1975) (design comprised of three generally horizontal bars for boats and camper trailers held likely to be confused with design comprised of two generally horizontal bars for boats and campers); *Matsushita Electric Industrial Co., Ltd. v. Sanders Associates, Inc.*, 177 USPQ 720 (TTAB 1973) (triangular arrow design within a square border for various items of electrical and electronic equipment held likely to be confused with triangular arrow design for various items of electrical and electronic components and equipment).

1207.01(c)(i) Legal Equivalents—Comparison of Words and Their Equivalent Designs

Under the doctrine of legal equivalents, a pictorial representation and its literal equivalent may be found to be confusingly similar. This doctrine is based on a recognition that a pictorial depiction and equivalent wording are likely to impress the same mental image on purchasers. *See, e.g., In re Rolf Nilsson AB*, 230 USPQ 141 (TTAB 1986) (design comprising the silhouette of the head of a lion and the letter "L" for shoes held likely to be confused with LION for shoes); *Puma-Sportschuhfabriken Rudolf Dassler KG v. Garan, Inc.*, 224 USPQ 1064 (TTAB 1984) (designs of mountain lion, for shirts and tops, held confusingly similar to PUMA, for items of clothing; the design of a puma, for items of sporting goods and clothing; and PUMA and design, for T-shirts); *In re Duofold Inc.*, 184 USPQ 638 (TTAB 1974) (design of eagle lined for the color gold, for various items of sports apparel, held likely to be confused with GOLDEN EAGLE and design of an eagle, for various items of clothing).

1207.01(c)(ii) Composite Marks Consisting of Both Words and Designs

Often, the examining attorney must determine whether a likelihood of confusion exists between composite marks that consist of a design element as well as words

USPQ 353 (TTAB 1975)(用于小船和露营拖车的包含三条水平条纹的图案被认为可能与用于小船和露营拖车的包含两条水平条纹的图案相混淆); *Matsushita Electric Industrial Co., Ltd. v. Sanders Associates, Inc.*, 177 USPQ 720 (TTAB 1973)(用于各种电气设备的正方形表框内的三角形箭头状图案被认为可能与用于各种电气组件及设备的三角形箭头状图案相混淆)。

1207.01(c)(i) 法律对等——文字与其等效图案的比较

根据法律对等原则,一种图形表达和与其等效的文字表达可能被认为构成混淆相似性。这一原则的依据是,我们认为一种图形描述和与其等效的文字表达可能在购买者脑海中造成相同的印象。*参见*判例: *Rolf Nilsson AB*, 230 USPQ 141 (TTAB 1986)(用于鞋类的由狮头形象和字母"L"构成的图案被认为可能与用于鞋类的"LION"相混淆); *Puma-Sportschuhfabriken Rudolf Dassler KG v. Garan, Inc.*, 224 USPQ 1064 (TTAB 1984)(用于衬衣和上装的美洲狮图案被认为与用于服装的"PUMA"、用于运动品及服装的美洲狮图案、用于T恤衫的"PUMA"及图案具有混淆相似性); *Duofold Inc.*, 184 USPQ 638 (TTAB 1974)(用于各种运动服饰的金色勾勒的老鹰图案被认为与用于服装的"GOLDEN EAGLE"及图案相混淆)。

1207.01(c)(ii) 由文字和图案构成的复合商标

审查员经常必须判定由图案与文字和/或字母构成的复合商标之间是否存在混

and/or letters. Frequently the marks at issue are similar in only one element. Although it is not proper to dissect a mark, if one feature of a mark is more significant than another feature, greater weight may be given to the dominant feature for purposes of determining likelihood of confusion. *Giant Food, Inc. v. Nation's Foodservice, Inc.*, 710 F.2d 1565, 218 USPQ 390 (Fed. Cir. 1983). However, the fundamental rule in this situation is that the marks must be considered in their entireties. *See Massey Junior College, Inc. v. Fashion Institute of Technology*, 492 F.2d 1399, 181 USPQ 272 (C.C.P.A. 1974).

If a mark comprises both a word and a design, greater weight is often given to the word, because it is the word that purchasers would use to refer to or request the goods or services. *In re Appetito Provisions Co. Inc.*, 3 USPQ2d 1553, 1554 (TTAB 1987) (APPETITO and design of two broad stripes lined for the colors red and green, for Italian sausage, held likely to be confused with A APPETITO'S and design and A APPETITO'S INC. and design of a sandwich (with "INC." and sandwich design disclaimed), both for restaurant services). The Court of Appeals for the Federal Circuit has cautioned, however, that "[t]here is no general rule as to whether letters or designs will dominate in composite marks; nor is the dominance of letters or design dispositive of the issue." *In re Electrolyte Laboratories Inc.*, 929 F.2d 645, 647, 16 USPQ2d 1239, 1240 (Fed. Cir. 1990) (K + and design for dietary potassium supplement held not likely to be confused with K + EFF (stylized) for dietary potassium supplement).

The comparison of composite marks must be done on a case-by-case basis without reliance on mechanical rules of construction. *See, e.g., Specialty Brands, Inc. v. Coffee Bean Distributors, Inc.*, 748 F.2d 669, 223 USPQ 1281 (Fed. Cir. 1984) (finding a likelihood of confusion between SPICE VALLEY and SPICE ISLANDS, both for tea); *Spice Islands, Inc. v. The Frank Tea & Spice Co.*, 505 F.2d 1293, 184 USPQ 35 (C.C.P.A. 1974) (SPICE TREE and tree design held not confusingly similar to SPICE ISLANDS and tree design, both for spices); *In re Sun Supermarkets, Inc.*, 228 USPQ 693 (TTAB 1986) (SUN SUPERMARKETS and design of sun held likely to be confused with SUNSHINE and design of

淆可能性。通常涉案商标只在某一元素上相似。尽管将一项商标拆解开来是不适当的,但如果某商标的一个特征比其他部分更重要,那么在判断混淆可能性的时候,对于这项占统治地位的特征就要给予更多的关注。*Giant Food, Inc. v. Nation's Foodservice, Inc.*, 710 F.2d 1565, 218 USPQ 390 (Fed. Cir. 1983)。不过,在这种情况下,基本的规则仍然是在总体上对这些商标进行考虑。*参见 Massey Junior College, Inc. v. Fashion Institute of Technology*, 492 F.2d 1399, 181 USPQ 272 (C.C.P.A. 1974)。

如果一项商标同时包含文字和图案,通常应更关注文字,因为购买者通常是使用文字指称或申请购买商品或服务。见 *Appetito Provisions Co. Inc.*, 3 USPQ2d 1553, 1554 (TTAB 1987)(用于意大利香肠的"APPETITO"以及两条红绿色的宽条纹图案被认为可能与"A APPETITO'S"及图案以及"A APPETITO'S INC."及三明治图案("INC."和三明治图案撤回)相混淆,二者均用于餐饮服务)。不过,联邦巡回上诉法院警告说:"关于是字母还是图案在复合商标中占有统治地位并没有一般规则;对于这个问题,字母或图案的统治地位也并不是决定性因素。"见 *Electrolyte Laboratories Inc.*, 929 F.2d 645, 647, 16 USPQ2d 1239, 1240 (Fed. Cir. 1990)(用于食用钾元素补充的"K+"及图案被认为可能与用于食用钾元素补充的"K+EFF(风格化)"相混淆)。

对于复合商标的比较必须根据每个个案的具体情况进行,而不能依赖机械的解释规则。*参见*判例 *Specialty Brands, Inc. v. Coffee Bean Distributors, Inc.*, 748 F.2d 669, 223 USPQ 1281 (Fed. Cir. 1984)(判定均用于茶的"SPICE VALLEY"和"SPICE ISLANDS"之间存在混淆可能);*Spice Islands, Inc. v. The Frank Tea & Spice Co.*, 505 F.2d 1293, 184 USPQ 35 (C.C.P.A. 1974)("SPICE TREE"及树木图案被认为并不与" SPICE ISLANDS"及树木图案混淆性相似,二者均用于香料);*Sun Supermarkets, Inc.*, 228 USPQ 693 (TTAB 1986)("SUN SUPERMARKETS"和太阳图案被认为可能与"SUNSHINE"和太阳图案,以及"SUNRISE"和太阳图案

sun and SUNRISE and design of sun, all for retail grocery store services).

1207.01(c)(iii) Comparison of Typed Marks and Special Form Marks [R-2]

If a mark (in either an application or a registration) is presented in typed form, the owner of the mark is not limited to any particular depiction. The rights associated with a mark in typed form reside in the wording (or other literal element, *e.g.*, letters, numerals, punctuation) and not in any particular display. Therefore, an applicant cannot, by presenting its mark in special form, avoid likelihood of confusion with a mark that is registered in typed form because the marks presumably could be used in the same manner of display. *See*, *e.g.*, *In re Melville Corp.*, 18 USPQ2d 1386, 1388 (TTAB 1991); *In re Pollio Dairy Products Corp.*, 8 USPQ2d 2012, 2015 (TTAB 1988); *Sunnen Products Co. v. Sunex International Inc.*, 1 USPQ2d 1744, 1751 (TTAB 1987); *In re Hester Industries, Inc.*, 231 USPQ 881, 883, n.6 (TTAB 1986).

1207.01(d) Miscellaneous Considerations

1207.01(d)(i) Doubt Resolved in Favor of Registrant

If there is any doubt as to whether there is a likelihood of confusion, that doubt must be resolved in favor of the prior registrant. *In re Shell Oil Co.*, 992 F.2d 1204, 26 USPQ2d 1687 (Fed. Cir. 1993); *In re Hyper Shoppes (Ohio), Inc.* 837 F.2d 463, 6 USPQ2d 1025 (Fed. Cir. 1988).

1207.01(d)(ii) Absence of Actual Confusion

It is well settled that the relevant test is *likelihood of confusion*, not actual confusion. It is unnecessary to show actual confusion to establish likelihood of confusion. *Weiss Associates Inc. v. HRL Associates Inc.*, 902 F.2d 1546, 1549, 14 US-

相混淆，三者均用于百货零售服务）。

1207.01(c)(iii)　印刷字体商标与特殊格式商标的比较［R-2］

如果商标（无论是一项申请还是一项注册）以印刷字体表现，商标的所有人在表现商标时不受具体表现形式的限制。与印刷字体形式的商标相关的权利驻留于文字中（或其他文字元素，例如字母、数字、标点）而不驻留于任何特定的显示形式。因此，申请者无法通过以特殊形式表现其商标的方法，避免与一个已经注册的印刷字体格式的商标产生混淆的可能性，因为可推测这些商标都可能以同样的显示方式使用。*参见*判例：*Melville Corp.*，18 USPQ2d 1386，1388（TTAB 1991）；*Pollio Dairy Products Corp.*，8 USPQ2d 2012，2015（TTAB 1988）；*Sunnen Products Co. v. Sun-ex International Inc.*，1 USPQ2d 1744，1751（TTAB 1987）；*Hester Industries, Inc.*，231 USPQ 881，883，n.6（TTAB 1986）。

1207.01(d)　其他考虑因素

1207.01(d)(i)　以有利于注册者的方式解决疑问

如果对于是否存在混淆可能性有任何疑问，必须以有利于先注册者的方式解答疑问。*参见*判例：*Shell Oil Co.*，992 F.2d 1204，26 USPQ2d 1687（Fed. Cir. 1993）；*Hyper Shoppes（Ohio），Inc.* 837 F.2d 463，6 USPQ2d 1025（Fed. Cir. 1988）。

1207.01(d)(ii)　缺乏实际混淆

早已确立的是，相关的判断标准是*混淆的可能*性，而非实际的混淆。证明混淆可能性时，不必确立实际的混淆。见 *Weiss Associates Inc. v. HRL Associates Inc.*，902 F.2d 1546，1549，14 USPQ2d 1840，1842-1843（Fed. Cir. 1990）及其引用的判例。

PQ2d 1840, 1842-43 (Fed. Cir. 1990), and cases cited therein.

1207.01(d)(iii) Third-Party Registrations [R-1]

Generally, the existence of third-party registrations cannot justify the registration of another mark that is so similar to a previously registered mark as to create a likelihood of confusion, or to cause mistake, or to deceive. Third-party registrations may be relevant to show that the mark or a portion of the mark is descriptive, suggestive, or so commonly used that the public will look to other elements to distinguish the source of the goods or services. *See, e.g., AMF Inc. v. American Leisure Products, Inc.*, 474 F.2d 1403, 1406, 177 USPQ 268, 269-70 (C.C.P.A. 1973); *Plus Products v. Star-Kist Foods, Inc.*, 220 USPQ 541, 544 (TTAB 1983). Properly used in this limited manner, third party registrations are similar to dictionaries showing how language is generally used. *See, e.g., Specialty Brands, Inc. v. Coffee Bean Distributors, Inc.*, 748 F.2d 669, 675, 223 USPQ 1281, 1285-86 (Fed. Cir. 1984); *Tektronix, Inc. v. Daktronics, Inc.*, 534 F.2d 915, 917, 189 USPQ 693, 694-95 (C.C.P.A. 1976); *In re Melville Corp.*, 18 USPQ2d 1386, 1388 (TTAB 1991); *In re Dayco Products-Eaglemotive Inc.*, 9 USPQ2d 1910, 1911 (TTAB 1988); *In re J. M. Originals Inc.*, 6 USPQ2d 1393, 1394 (TTAB 1987); *United Foods Inc. v. J. R. Simplot Co.*, 4 USPQ2d 1172, 1174 (TTAB 1987).

Third-party registrations that cover a number of different goods or services have some probative value to the extent that they may serve to suggest that goods or services are of a type that may emanate from a single source, if the registrations are based on use in commerce. However, registrations issued under 15 U.S.C. §1126(e), based on a foreign registration, have very little, if any, persuasive value. *In re Albert Trostel & Sons Co.*, 29 USPQ2d 1783 (TTAB 1993); *In re Mucky Duck Mustard Co. Inc.*, 6 USPQ2d 1467 (TTAB 1988).

The submission of a list of registrations or a copy of a search report is not proper evidence of third-party registrations. To make registrations of record, soft copies

1207.01(d)(iii) 第三方注册［R-1］

一般而言，第三方注册的存在不能成为注册另一个与先注册的商标相似、能够造成混淆可能性或引起错误或欺骗的理由。第三方注册可能可以用来表明商标或其一部分是描述性、暗示性的或者被普遍地使用而致使公众需要通过其他元素来区分商品或服务的来源。*参见* 判例 *AMF Inc. v. American Leisure Products, Inc.*, 474 F.2d 1403, 1406, 177 USPQ 268, 269-270 (C.C.P.A.1973); *Plus Products v. Star-Kist Foods, Inc.*, 220 USPQ 541, 544 (TTAB 1983)。以这种受限制的方式适当地使用时，第三方注册类似于一本说明语言通常是如何使用的词典。*参见* 判例：*Specialty Brands, Inc. v. Coffee Bean Distributors, Inc.*, 748 F.2d 669, 675, 223 USPQ 1281, 1285-1286 (Fed. Cir. 1984); *Tektronix, Inc. v. Daktronics, Inc.*, 534 F.2d 915, 917, 189 USPQ 693, 694-695 (C.C.P.A.1976); *Melville Corp.*, 18 USPQ2d 1386, 1388 (TTAB 1991); *Dayco Products-Eaglemotive Inc.*, 9 USPQ2d 1910, 1911 (TTAB 1988); *J. M. Originals Inc.*, 6 USPQ2d 1393, 1394 (TTAB 1987); *United Foods Inc. v. J. R. Simplot Co.*, 4 USPQ2d 1172, 1174 (TTAB 1987)。

如果第三方注册包括了许多不同的商品或服务，则具有一些证明价值，如果注册是基于在商业活动中使用，它们可以用来表明商品或服务可能来自于单一的来源。不过，根据 15 U.S.C. §1126(e)的规定以外国注册为由核准的注册只具有极少的（如果有的话）证明价值。见 *Albert Trostel & Sons Co.*, 29 USPQ2d 1783 (TTAB 1993); *Mucky Duck Mustard Co. Inc.*, 6 USPQ2d 1467 (TTAB 1988)。

提交一份注册清单或者一份搜索报告并不是证明第三方注册的适当证据。要制

of the registrations or the electronic equivalent thereof (*i. e.*, printouts of the registrations taken from the electronic search records of the United States Patent and Trademark Office) must be submitted. *Raccioppi v. Apogee Inc.*, 47 USPQ2d 1368 (TTAB 1998); *In re Smith & Mehaffey*, 31 USPQ2d 1531, 1532 n.3 (TTAB 1994); *Weyerhaeuser Co. v. Katz*, 24 USPQ2d 1230 (TTAB 1992); *In re Hub Distributing, Inc.*, 218 USPQ 284 (TTAB 1983). *See* TMEP §710.03.

1207.01(d)(iv) Collateral Attack on Registration Improper in *Ex Parte* Proceeding [R-2]

Section 7(b) of the Trademark Act, 15 U.S.C. §1057(b), provides that a certificate of registration on the Principal Register shall be *prima facie* evidence of the validity of the registration, of the registrant's ownership of the mark and of the registrant's exclusive right to use the mark in commerce in connection with the goods or services specified in the certificate. During *ex parte* prosecution, an applicant will not be heard on matters that constitute a collateral attack on the cited registration (*e.g.*, a registrant's nonuse of the mark). *See In re Dixie Restaurants*, 105 F.3d 1405, 41 USPQ2d 1531 (Fed. Cir. 1997); *Cosmetically Yours, Inc. v. Clairol Inc.*, 424 F.2d 1385, 1387, 165 USPQ 515, 517 (C.C.P.A. 1970); *In re Peebles Inc.* 23 USPQ2d 1795, 1797 n.5 (TTAB 1992); *In re Pollio Dairy Products Corp.*, 8 USPQ2d 2012, 2014-15 (TTAB 1988).

It is also inappropriate for the applicant to place the burden of showing a likelihood of confusion on the owner of the cited registration. *In re Majestic Distilling Co.*, 315 F.3d 1311, 1318, 65 USPQ2d 1201, 1206 (Fed. Cir. 2003) ("[I]t is the duty of the PTO and this court to determine whether there is a likelihood of confusion between two marks ... [I]t is no answer for the applicant to ask that the application be passed to publication to see whether the owner of the cited mark will oppose the registration.," quoting *Dixie Restaurants*, *supra*, 105 F.3d at 1408, 41 USPQ2d at 1535.)

作注册记录,必须提交注册的软拷贝或者其电子版等价物(即从美国专利局和商标局的电子搜索记录中打印出来的注册)。*Raccioppi v. Apogee Inc.*, 47 USPQ2d 1368 (TTAB 1998); *Smith & Mehaffey*, 31 USPQ2d 1531, 1532 n.3 (TTAB 1994); *Weyerhaeuser Co. v. Katz*, 24 USPQ2d 1230 (TTAB 1992); *Hub Distributing, Inc.*, 218 USPQ 284 (TTAB 1983)。*参见* TMEP §710.03。

1207.01(d)(iv)　在单方诉讼中不得附带攻击注册 [R-2]

《商标法》第7(b)节,15 U.S.C. §1057(b)规定,一项在联邦商标登记簿上注册的注册证书应是注册有效性、注册者对所属商标的所有权以及注册者享有在商业活动中将所属商标用于证书上所列的商品或服务的专属权利的确凿证据。在单方诉讼中,将不审理申请者对被引用的注册进行附带攻击的内容。*参见 Dixie Restaurants*, 105 F.3d 1405, 41 USPQ2d 1531 (Fed. Cir. 1997); *Cosmetically Yours, Inc. v. Clairol Inc.*, 424 F.2d 1385, 1387, 165 USPQ 515, 517 (C.C.P.A.1970); *Peebles Inc.* 23 USPQ2d 1795, 1797 n.5 (TTAB 1992); *Pollio Dairy Products Corp.*, 8 USPQ2d 2012, 2014-2015 (TTAB 1988)。

申请者也不可以将证明混淆可能性的责任转移给被引用的注册的所有人。见 *Majestic Distilling Co.*, 315 F.3d 1311, 1318, 65 USPQ2d 1201, 1206 (Fed. Cir. 2003)("判断两个商标之间是否存在混淆可能性是 PTO 和本法庭的责任……不同意申请人提出的将其申请刊登出来以察看被引用的商标的所有人是否对此项注册提出异议的要求",引自 *Dixie Restaurants, supra*, 105 F.3d at 1408, 41 USPQ2d at 1535)。

1207.01(d)(v) Classification of Goods/Services

The classification of goods and services has no bearing on the question of likelihood of confusion. Rather, it is the manner in which the applicant and/or registrant have identified their goods or services that is controlling. *Jean Patou Inc. v. Theon Inc.*, 9 F.3d 971, 29 USPQ2d 1771 (Fed. Cir. 1993); *National Football League v. Jasper Alliance Corp.*, 16 USPQ2d 1212, 1216 n.5 (TTAB 1990).

1207.01(d)(vi) Prior Decisions of Examining Attorneys

Each case must be decided on its own merits. Previous decisions by examining attorneys in approving other marks are without evidentiary value and are not binding on the agency or the Board. *In re Sunmarks Inc.*, 32 USPQ2d 1470 (TTAB 1994); *In re National Novice Hockey League, Inc.*, 222 USPQ 638, 641 (TTAB 1984).

1207.01(d)(vii) Sophisticated Purchasers

The fact that purchasers are sophisticated or knowledgeable in a particular field does not necessarily mean that they are immune from source confusion. *See In re Decombe*, 9 USPQ2d 1812 (TTAB 1988); *In re Pellerin Milnor Corp.*, 221 USPQ 558 (TTAB 1983). However, circumstances suggesting care in purchasing may tend to minimize likelihood of confusion.

1207.01(d)(viii) Consent Agreements

The term "consent agreement" generally refers to an agreement in which a party (*e.g.*, a prior registrant) consents to the use and/or registration of a mark by another party (*e.g.*, an applicant for registration of the same mark or a similar mark), or in which each party consents to the use and/or registration of the same

1207.01(d)(v)　商品/服务的分类

商品和服务的类别与混淆可能性问题没有关系。而申请者和/或注册者识别其商品或服务的方式则是控制因素。见 *Jean Patou Inc. v. Theon Inc.*, 9 F.3d 971, 29 USPQ2d 1771（Fed. Cir. 1993）；*National Football League v. Jasper Alliance Corp.*, 16 USPQ2d 1212, 1216 n.5（TTAB 1990）。

1207.01(d)(vi)　审查员以前的裁决

每个案件都必须根据其自身的情况进行裁决。审查员以前所作的支持其他商标的裁决不具有证据价值，对本机构或委员会没有约束力。见 *Sunmarks Inc.*, 32 USPQ2d 1470（TTAB 1994）；*National Novice Hockey League, Inc.*, 222 USPQ 638, 641（TTAB 1984）。

1207.01(d)(vii)　经验丰富的购买者

购买者在某一领域富有经验或知识渊博并不必然意味着他们不会混淆来源。参见 *Decombe*, 9 USPQ2d 1812（TTAB 1988）；*Pellerin Milnor Corp.*, 221 USPQ 558（TTAB 1983）。不过，如果所处的条件提醒要谨慎购买，则可能降低混淆的可能性。

1207.01(d)(viii)　同意协议

"同意协议"一词通常是指，一方（例如先前的注册者）同意另一方（例如申请注册相同或类似商标的申请人）使用和/或注册某一商标的协议，或者一方当事人同意另一方当事人使用和/或注册相同或类似商标的协议。

mark or a similar mark by the other party.

A consent agreement may be submitted by the applicant to overcome a refusal of registration under §2(d) of the Act, or in anticipation of a refusal to register. When a consent agreement is submitted, the examining attorney will consider the agreement, and all other evidence in the record, to determine likelihood of confusion. The examining attorney should not solicit a consent agreement.

Consents come in different forms and under circumstances in infinite variety. They are, however, but one factor to be taken into account with all of the other relevant circumstances bearing on the likelihood of confusion referred to in §2(d). *In re N. A. D. Inc.*, 754 F.2d 996, 224 USPQ 969 (Fed. Cir. 1985).

In *In re E. I. du Pont de Nemours & Co.*, 476 F.2d 1357, 1363, 177 USPQ 563, 568 (C.C.P.A. 1973), the Court of Customs and Patent Appeals stated as follows:

> [W]hen those most familiar with use in the marketplace and most interested in precluding confusion enter agreements designed to avoid it, the scales of evidence are clearly tilted. It is at least difficult to maintain a subjective view that confusion will occur when those directly concerned say it won't. A mere *assumption* that confusion is likely will rarely prevail against uncontroverted evidence from those on the firing line that it is not.

A consent agreement that is not merely a "naked" consent typically details reasons why no likelihood of confusion exists and/or arrangements undertaken by the parties to avoid confusing the public. *In re Permagrain Products, Inc.*, 223 USPQ 147 (TTAB 1984) (consent agreement found to be "naked" because the agreement did not restrict the markets in such a way as to avoid confusion).

The Court of Appeals for the Federal Circuit has made it clear that consent agreements should be given great weight, and that the Office should not substitute its judgment concerning likelihood of confusion for the judgment of the real parties

申请者可以提交一份同意协议，以克服根据《商标法》§2(d)作出或即将作出的拒绝予以注册的决定。如果提交了同意协议，审查员将根据该协议以及所有其他记录证据，来判断混淆的可能性。审查员不得促使达成同意协议。

同意可以在各种情况下以不同的形式作出。不过，它们只不过是与 §2(d)中提及的所有其他对混淆可能性有影响的因素一起考虑的一个因素。见 *N.A.D. Inc.*, 754 F.2d 996, 224 USPQ 969 (Fed. Cir. 1985)。

在 *E.I. du Pont de Nemours & Co.*, 476 F.2d 1357, 1363, 177 USPQ 563, 568 (C.C.P.A. 1973)一案中，关税及专利上诉法院阐述如下：

> 当那些最熟悉市场使用和最希望排除混淆的人签订了专门用来避免混淆的协议，证据的天平就明显地倾斜了。如果直接相关的人说不会发生混淆，那么至少是很难保持会发生混淆的主观看法。如果最直接使用和消费的人们所提供的无可辩驳的证据表明不会发生混淆，那么仅仅*推论*可能发生就很难与之抗衡了。

一项并非"无证据的"同意的协议通常会详细地列举为何不存在混淆可能的理由，和/或各方当事人所采取的避免公众混淆的方法。见 *Permagrain Products, Inc.*, 223 USPQ 147 (TTAB 1984)(由于协议未对市场作出避免混淆的限制，故同意协议被判定是"无证据的")。

联邦巡回上诉法院明确指出，应当给予同意协议很大的分量，因此，如没有充分理由，商标局不应以混淆可能性的判断代替具有真正利害关系的当事人的判断，也就

in interest without good reason, that is, unless the other factors clearly dictate a finding of likelihood of confusion. *Amalgamated Bank of New York v. Amalgamated Trust & Savings Bank*, 842 F.2d 1270, 6 USPQ2d 1305 (Fed. Cir. 1988); *Bongrain International (American) Corp. v. Delice de France Inc.*, 811 F.2d 1479, 1 USPQ2d 1775 (Fed. Cir. 1987); and *In re N.A.D. Inc.*, 754 F.2d 996, 224 USPQ 969 (Fed. Cir. 1985).

Compare In re Mastic Inc., 829 F.2d 1114, 4 USPQ2d 1292 (Fed. Cir. 1987) (refusal to register affirmed even with a consent to register where applicant had not used the mark in commerce and consent agreement contained contradictory statements).

The examining attorney should give great weight to a proper consent agreement. The examining attorney should not interpose his or her own judgment concerning likelihood of confusion when an applicant and registrant have entered into a *credible* consent agreement and, *on balance*, the other factors do not dictate a finding of likelihood of confusion.

A consent agreement is not the same as a "concurrent use" agreement. The term "concurrent use" is a term of art that refers to a geographical restriction on the registration. *See* TMEP §§1207.04 *et seq.* regarding concurrent use.

1207.01(d)(ix) Fame of Mark [R-2]

The fame of a registered mark is a factor to be considered in determining likelihood of confusion. *In re E. I. du Pont de Nemours & Co.*, 476 F.2d 1357, 1361, 177 USPQ 563, 567 (C.C.P.A. 1973). Famous marks enjoy a wide latitudc of legal protection because they are more likely to be remembered and associated in the public mind than a weaker mark. *Bose Corp. v. QSC Audio Products Inc.*, 293 F.3d 1367, 63 USPQ2d 1303 (Fed. Cir. 2002) (Trademark Trial and Appeal Board erred in discounting the fame of opposer's marks ACOUSTIC WAVE and WAVE); *Recot, Inc. v. M. C. Becton*, 214 F. 3d 1322, 1327, 54 USPQ2d 1894,

是说，除非有其他因素明显地表明存在混淆可能性。相关判例：*Amalgamated Bank of New York v. Amalgamated Trust & Savings Bank*，842 F. 2d 1270，6 USPQ2d 1305（Fed. Cir. 1988）；*Bongrain International*（*American*）*Corp. v. Delice de France Inc.*，811 F. 2d 1479，1 USPQ2d 1775（Fed. Cir. 1987）；*N. A. D. Inc.*，754 F. 2d 996，224 USPQ 969（Fed. Cir. 1985）。

比较：*Mastic Inc.*，829 F. 2d 1114，4 USPQ2d 1292（Fed. Cir. 1987）（由于申请者并未将商标用于商业活动，而且同意协议中含有相反的声明，因此尽管有注册同意书，还是维持拒绝予以注册的决定）。

审查员应充分注意正当的同意协议。如果申请者和注册者已经达成了*可信的*同意协议，而且*总体而言*，并没有其它因素表明存在混淆可能性，审查员不应插入自己对于混淆可能性的判断。

同意协议与"同时使用"协议不同。"同时使用"是一个专门术语，是指对注册的地理限制。有关同时使用的内容，*参见* TMEP §§1207.04 及以下。

1207.01(d)(ix) 商标的声誉［R-2］

已注册商标的声誉也是判断混淆可能性的一个考虑因素。见 *E. I. du Pont de Nemours & Co.*，476 F. 2d 1357，1361，177 USPQ 563，567（C. C. P. A. 1973）。驰名商标享有广泛的法律保护，因为它们相比较弱的商标更可能为公众所记忆并形成联系。相关判例：*Bose Corp. v. QSC Audio Products Inc.*，293 F. 3d 1367，63 USPQ2d 1303（Fed. Cir. 2002）（商标评审及上诉委员会错误地低估了异议人商标"ACOUSTIC WAVE"和"WAVE"的声誉）；*Recot, Inc. v. M. C. Becton*，214 F. 3d 1322，1327，54 USPQ2d 1894，1897（Fed. Cir. 2000）（委员会错误地限制给予异议

1897 (Fed. Cir. 2000) (Board erred in limiting the weight accorded to the fame of opposer's FRITO-LAY mark); *Kenner Parker Toys Inc. v. Rose Art Industries, Inc.*, 963 F.2d 350, 352, 22 USPQ2d 1453, 1456 (Fed. Cir. 1992), *cert. denied*, 506 U.S. 862 (1992) (Board erred in discounting the fame of opposer's mark PLAY-DOH). The Court of Appeals for the Federal Circuit has stated:

> [A] mark with extensive public recognition and renown deserves and receives more legal protection than an obscure or weak mark.
>
> Achieving fame for a mark in a marketplace where countless symbols clamor for public attention often requires a very distinct mark, enormous advertising investments, and a product of lasting value. After earning fame, a mark benefits not only its owner, but the consumers who rely on the symbols to identify the source of a desired product. Both the mark's fame and the consumer's trust in that symbol, however, are subject to exploitation by free riders.

Kenner Parker Toys, 963 F.2d at 353, 22 USPQ2d at 1456.

When present, the fame of the mark is "a dominant factor in the likelihood of confusion analysis for a famous mark, independent of the consideration of the relatedness of the goods." *Recot, Inc. v. M. C. Becton*, 214 F. 3d 1322, 1328, 54 USPQ2d 1894, 1898. However, like the other *du Pont* factors, the fame of a mark may be considered only if there is relevant evidence of record. *See* TMEP §1207.01 and cases cited therein.

Direct evidence of consumer recognition of a mark is not necessary. The "fame of a mark may be measured indirectly, among other things, by the volume of sales and advertising expenditures of the goods traveling under the mark, and by the length of time those indicia of commercial awareness have been evident." *See Bose*, 293 F.3d at 1371, 63 USPQ2d at 1371, and cases cited therein. It is important to consider the context of how the proposed mark is presented in sales and advertising materials. In *Bose*, the Court found that evidence of extensive sales

人“FRITO-LAY”商标的分量)；*Kenner Parker Toys Inc. v. Rose Art Industries, Inc.*, 963 F.2d 350, 352, 22 USPQ2d 1453, 1456 (Fed. Cir. 1992), *cert. denied*, 506 U.S. 862 (1992)(委员会错误地低估了异议人商标“PLAY-DOH”的声誉)。联邦巡回上诉法院阐述道：

> 相比一项模糊的或弱商标，拥有广泛公众认可和声望的商标应当获得也获得了更多的法律保护。
>
> 商标要在一个充满无数试图吸引公众注意的符号的市场中获得声誉，需要一种非常独特的商标、大量的广告投资以及具有持久价值的产品。在获得声誉之后，一项商标不但有利于其所有人，而且依赖该商标识别所需产品来源的消费者也从中受益。但是，商标的声誉和消费者对该标记的信任都会遭到搭便车者的剥削。
>
> *Kenner Parker Toys*, 963 F.2d at 353, 22 USPQ2d 1456。

如果存在，商标的声誉“在分析驰名商标的混淆可能性中，是一个具有统治地位的因素，独立于商品相关性考虑”。*Recot, Inc. v. M. C. Becton*, 214 F.3d 1322, 1328, 54 USPQ2d 1894, 1898。不过，就像其他 *du Pont* 因素一样，商标的声誉只有在存在相关档案证据的情况下才加以考虑。参见 TMEP §1207.01 及其引用的判例。

并不需要消费者认知某一商标的直接证据。“商标的声誉可以通过使用该商标的商品的销售量和广告支出，以及该商标获得明确商业认可的时间长度，进行间接的衡量。”参见 *Bose*, 293 F.3d at 1371, 63 USPQ2d 1371，以及所引用的判例。对申请注册的商标如何在销售和广告材料中展现的背景情况进行考虑很重要。在 *Bose* 案中，

and advertising expenses established the fame of opposer's WAVE and ACOUSTIC WAVE marks, noting that opposer's sales literature, advertisements, and promotional materials included frequent and prominent references to the marked product separate and apart from the house mark BOSE.

In *Tiffany & Broadway v. Commissioner*, 167 F. Supp. 2d 949 (S. D. Tex. 2001), the fame of four registered marks cited against the applicant was a significant factor in finding a likelihood of confusion between applicant's TIFFANY for ladies' dress shoes and registrant's TIFFANY and TIFFANY & CO. for a variety of goods, including jewelry, china, silverware, glassware, leather goods, belt buckles, ties, scarves, clocks, watches, brushes and lamps, and for retail store services specializing in the sale of jewelry, watches, clocks, and gift items. The *ex parte* record included excerpts from 18 news articles where the registrant Tiffany & Company was identified as a famous business; citations to three published decisions in which the fame of the TIFFANY mark had been judicially recognized; and evidence that the registrant's goods were sold at over 60 Tiffany locations worldwide—including 34 in the United States—and through independently-owned retail stores and mail order outlets.

1207.01(d)(x) Conflicting Marks Owned by Different Parties

During the examination of an application, the examining attorney should consider separately each registration found in a search of the marks registered in the Office that may bar registration of the applicant's mark under §2(d). If the examining attorney finds registrations that appear to be owned by more than one registrant, he or she should consider the extent to which dilution may indicate that there is no likelihood of confusion. However, the examining attorney must cite all the marks that are considered to be a bar against registration of the mark presented in the application, even if they are owned by different parties. The examining attorney should always explain the reason that the mark in each cited registration is grounds for refusal under §2(d).

法庭判定，大量的销售和广告支出证据证明了异议人“WAVE”和“ACOUSTIC WAVE”商标的声誉，并引用了异议人的销售记录、广告以及促销材料，这些促销材料包括了独立于公司专用标识“BOSE”之外，经常且突出地提到使用商标的产品。

在 *Tiffany & Broadway v. Commissioner*, 167 F. Supp. 2d 949 (S. D. Tex. 2001)一案中，在判定申请人用于女装鞋的“TIFFANY”与注册者用于各种商品——包括珠宝、瓷器、银器、玻璃器皿、皮革制品、皮带扣、领带、围巾、钟表、刷子和灯具，以及专营珠宝、钟表和礼品的零售商店服务——的“TIFFANY”和“TIFFANY & CO.”之间存在混淆的裁决中，被引用来对抗申请者的四项已注册商标是一个重要的因素。单方档案包括来自于 18 篇新闻文章的关于注册者 Tiffany & Company 被认为是一家著名企业的摘录；引用三项已出版的、依法承认 TIFFANY 商标声誉的判决；以及注册者的商品通过全球 60 多家 Tiffany 专卖店——其中 34 家在美国——和自营零售店以及邮购方式进行销售的证据。

1207.01(d)(x) 不同当事人拥有的冲突商标

在审查申请的过程中，审查员应当分别考虑在商标局注册商标中搜索到的、可能导致根据 §2(d)的规定驳回申请者商标注册的每一项先前注册。如果审查员发现某项注册具有不止一个注册者，就应当考虑淡化程度可以表明不存在混淆可能性。不过，审查员必须引用所有被认为可能阻碍拟注册的商标的注册的商标，即使这些商标为不同的当事人所有。审查员应当解释所引用的每项注册中的商标构成 §2(d)所规定的拒绝予以注册的原因。

1207.02 Marks That Are Likely to Deceive

In addition to referring to a mark that so resembles another mark as to be likely to cause confusion or mistake, §2(d) refers to a mark being likely "to deceive." As a practical matter, this provision is rarely applied in examination, because deceptiveness involves intent and would be difficult to prove in an *ex parte* proceeding.

1207.03 Marks Previously Used in United States but Not Registered

As a basis for refusal, §2(d) refers not only to registered marks but also to "a mark or trade name previously used in the United States by another and not abandoned." Refusal on the basis of an unregistered mark or trade name has sometimes been referred to as refusal on the basis of a "known mark." This provision is not applied in *ex parte* examination because of the practical difficulties with which an examining attorney is faced in attempting to locate "previously used" marks and attempting to determine whether anyone has rights in them and whether they are "not abandoned."

1207.04 Concurrent Use Registration

1207.04(a) Concurrent Use—In General [R-1]

Section 2(d) of the Trademark Act, 15 U.S.C. §1052(d), contains a proviso under which an eligible applicant may request issuance of a registration concurrent with the registration of a conflicting mark.

In a concurrent use application, the applicant normally requests a geographically restricted registration. The applicant seeks registration for a specified geographical area of the United States and lists one or more parties who concededly have

1207.02 可能具有欺骗性的商标

§2(d)除了涉及因为与另一商标极其类似而可能造成混淆或错误的商标之外，还涉及可能“具有欺骗性”的商标。不过作为实践性事项，在审查过程中此项规定极少适用，因为欺骗牵涉到故意，因此很难在单方程序中证明。

1207.03 先前已在美国使用但未注册的商标

作为拒绝予以注册的法律依据，§2(d)不仅涉及业已注册的商标，而且还涉及“他人以前在美国使用且尚未放弃的商标或商号”。以存在未注册的商标或商号为由拒绝予以注册有时被称为以存在“已知商标”而拒绝予以注册。此项规定不适用于单方审查，因为审查员在查明“以前使用的”商标以及判断是否有人对该商标享有权利、该商标是否属“尚未放弃”的实践过程中面临诸多困难。

1207.04 同时使用注册

1207.04(a) 同时使用——概述［R-1］

《商标法》第2(d)节，15 U.S.C.§1052(d)包含一个附带条件，规定符合条件的申请者可以要求核准一项与某冲突商标注册同时使用的注册。

在一项同时使用申请中，申请者通常会要求进行地理性限制注册。申请人寻求在美国某特定地区注册商标，并列出在美国其他地区对该商标享有确定无疑的权利

rights in the mark in other geographical areas of the United States. These other parties may own applications or registrations, or they may have common law rights in a mark, but no application or registration. "Incontestable" registrations (*i.e.*, where the registrant's right to use the mark has become incontestable pursuant to 15 U.S.C. §1065) are subject to concurrent use registration proceedings. *See Holiday Inn v. Holiday Inns, Inc.*, 534 F.2d 312, 189 USPQ 630 (C.C.P.A. 1976); *Thriftimart, Inc. v. Scot Lad Foods, Inc.*, 207 USPQ 330 (TTAB 1980). However, registrations and applications to register on the Supplemental Register and registrations under the Act of 1920 (*see* TMEP §1601.05) are not subject to concurrent use registration proceedings. 37 C.F.R. §2.99(g).

Concurrent use registration is requested by the applicant; it should not be suggested or initiated by the examining attorney.

1207.04(b) Filing Basis of Application Seeking Concurrent Use

In an application based on use in commerce under 15 U.S.C. §1051(a), the applicant may seek concurrent use registration at the time the application is filed or in a subsequent amendment. *See* 37 C.F.R. §2.73(a).

An applicant who files solely under §44, 15 U.S.C. §1126, may not seek a concurrent use registration.

In an application based on a bona fide intent to use the mark in commerce under 15 U.S.C. §1051(b), the applicant may not amend to seek concurrent use registration until the applicant files an acceptable amendment to allege use or statement of use. 37 C.F.R. §§2.73(b) and 2.99(g).

1207.04(c) Basis for Concurrent Use Registration

If an applicant requests a concurrent use registration, the examining attorney must first determine the basis for seeking such a registration. An application for

的一方或多方当事人。这些其他当事人可能拥有注册申请或注册，或者可能对某商标享有普通法上的权利，但并未提出申请或获得注册。“无可争辩”的注册（即根据 15 U.S.C.§1065 的规定，注册者使用商标的权利无可争辩）应按同时使用注册程序执行。*参见 Holiday Inn v. Holiday Inns, Inc.*, 534 F.2d 312, 189 USPQ 630（C.C.P.A.1976）; *Thriftimart, Inc. v. Scot Lad Foods, Inc.*, 207 USPQ 330（TTAB 1980）。不过，根据《1920 年商标法》（*参见* TMEP §1601.05）的规定而获得或申请在联邦商标补充登记簿上注册，并不按同时使用注册程序执行。37 C.F.R.§2.99(g)。

要求同时使用注册应由申请者提出；审查员不得建议或主动提出进行这种注册。

1207.04(b) 提出同时使用申请的依据

在根据 15 U.S.C.§1051(a)的规定，提出商业使用申请时，在提交申请或事后提交修正书时，申请者可以寻求同时使用注册。*参见* 37 C.F.R.§2.73(a)。

仅以 §44, 15 U.S.C.§1126 为依据提出申请的申请者，不得寻求获得同时使用注册。

在根据 15 U.S.C.§1051(b)的规定，以在商业活动中存在使用商标的真实意图为由提出申请时，申请者不得进行修改以寻求获得同时使用注册，除非申请者提交可接受的宣称使用修正书或者使用声明书。37 C.F.R.§§2.73(b)和 2.99(g)。

1207.04(c) 同时使用注册的依据

如果申请者要求获得同时使用注册，审查员必须首先判断寻求该项注册的依据。

registration as a concurrent user is either: (1) subject to a concurrent use registration proceeding before the Trademark Trial and Appeal Board, or (2) pursuant to the final determination by a court of competent jurisdiction of the concurrent rights of the parties to use the same or similar marks in commerce. *See* 15 U.S.C. §1052(d); 37 C.F.R. §2.99.

1207.04(d) Determining Eligibility for Concurrent Use

An applicant is eligible to request a registration subject to concurrent use if it meets one or more of the following criteria:

(1) The concurrent use request is sought pursuant to a decree of a court of competent jurisdiction reflecting its final determination of the rights of the concurrent user;

(2) The owner of the registration consents to the grant of a concurrent use registration to the applicant; or

(3) The applicant's date of first use in commerce is before the *filing date* of the pending applications or of any registrations issued under the Trademark Act of 1946. When a party specified as an excepted user does not own an application or registration, the applicant's date of first use in commerce is before the filing date of any application to register the mark that may be filed by the excepted user.

The applicant has the burden of proving that it is entitled to a concurrent use registration. 37 C.F.R. §2.99(e).

1207.04(d)(i) Requirements for All Concurrent Use Applications

An application for registration as a lawful concurrent user is generally examined in the same manner as any other application for registration. 37 C.F.R. §2.99(a). The examining attorney must examine the application to determine whether it

作为同时使用者提出的注册申请可以:(1)执行由商标审判及上诉委员会审理的同时使用注册程序,也可以根据(2)管辖法院对当事人同时在商业中使用相同或相似商标的权利的最终判决执行。*参见* 15 U.S.C.§1052(d);37 C.F.R.§2.99。

1207.04(d)　　判断同时使用是否适格

只要符合下列条件中的一项或多项,申请者可以申请同时使用注册:

(1) 根据管辖法院作出的、反映其对同时使用者的权利的最终判决,寻求同时使用注册;

(2) 该项注册的所有人同意授予申请者同时使用注册;或者

(3) 申请者首次在商业中使用该商标的日期先于待核准申请或任何根据《1946年商标法》的规定颁发的注册的*申请*日期。当被指定为除外使用者的一方当事人不拥有申请或注册时,申请者在商业中首次使用商标的日期应先于该除外使用者提出注册该商标的任何申请的申请日期。

申请者对于其有权获得同时使用注册负有证明责任。37 C.F.R.§2.99(e)。

1207.04(d)(i)　　同时使用申请的必备要求

合法同时使用者注册申请的审查方式与其他一切注册申请相同。37 C.F.R. §2.99(a)。审查员必须审查该申请,以判断是否符合非限制申请的相关要求(*参见* 37

complies with the relevant requirements for a non-restricted application (*see* 37 C.F.R.§§2.32-2.41). Additionally, the application must comply with the following requirements for a concurrent use application:

(1) The applicant must specify the goods and the geographic area for which the applicant seeks registration of the mark. 15 U.S.C. §1051(a)(3)(D); 37 C.F.R. §2.42. The applicant must also set forth the mode of use. 15 U.S.C. §1052(d); 37 C.F.R. §2.42.

(2) The applicant must specify, to the extent of its knowledge, the exceptions to its claim of exclusive use, listing any concurrent use by others and the relevant goods, geographic areas and periods of this use. 15 U.S.C. §1051(a)(3)(D); 37 C.F.R. §2.42.

(3) The applicant must also list the names and addresses of the concurrent users, the registrations issued to or applications filed by them (if any), and the mode of such use. 37 C.F.R. §2.42.

The applicant does not have to insert the stated exceptions in the verification or declaration; the exceptions may be set forth in the statement portion of the application.

In addition to the requirements noted above, which apply to all applications for concurrent use registration, concurrent use applications must meet other conditions, depending on whether the application is subject to a concurrent use before the Board (*see* TMEP §§1207.04(e) *et seq.*) or pursuant to the decree of a court (*see* TMEP §§1207.04(f) *et seq.*).

1207.04(e) Applications Subject to Concurrent Use Proceeding Before the Trademark Trial and Appeal Board

If an application for concurrent use registration complies with the above requirements and it appears that the applicant is entitled to registration but for the ques-

C.F.R.§§2.32－2.41)。此外,同时使用申请还必须符合下列要求:

(1) 申请者必须指定使用申请注册的商标的商品和地理区域。15 U.S.C. §1051(a)(3)(D);37 C.F.R.§2.42。申请者还必须说明使用的方式。15 U.S.C.§1052(d);37 C.F.R.§2.42。

(2) 申请者必须根据已知情况明确其所主张的专属使用的除外情况,列明一切由他人实施的同时使用以及相关商品、地区和使用期间。15 U.S.C. §1051(a)(3)(D);37 C.F.R.§2.42。

(3) 申请者还必须列明同时使用者的姓名地址、其提交的申请或已获得的注册(如有)以及使用方式。37 C.F.R.§2.42。

申请者无须在确认书或声明书中加入前述例外情况;该例外情况可以在申请书的陈述部分表明。

除了上述一切同时使用注册申请的必备要求以外,同时使用申请还必须满足其他条件,具体取决于该同时使用是按委员会(*参见* TMEP §§1207.04(e)及以下)审理程序执行还是按法院的判决执行(*参见* TMEP §§1207.04(f)及以下)。

1207.04(e) 按商标评审及上诉委员会的同时使用审理程序执行的申请

如果某项同时使用注册申请符合上述要求,而且申请者似乎除了同时使用权利

tion of concurrent rights, the examining attorney will approve the application for publication subject to a concurrent use registration proceeding. 15 U. S. C. §1062 (a).

Ordinarily, the examining attorney should not require an applicant for concurrent use registration to submit evidence in support of its claim to concurrent rights. However, the examining attorney should refuse registration under §2(d) if the applicant has requested a concurrent use registration and information in the record suggests that the applicant has not met the basic requirements for concurrent use registration (*e.g.*, if the application indicates that the applicant adopted and used the mark with knowledge of the rights of a person specified as an excepted user, or that actual confusion has resulted from the concurrent use of the marks of the parties in their respective geographic areas). *See In re Place for Vision, Inc.*, 196 USPQ 267, 269-70 (TTAB 1977). *Gray v. Daffy Dan's Bargaintown*, 823 F.2d 522, 3 USPQ2d 1306 (Fed. Cir. 1987), *aff'g* 229 USPQ 474 (TTAB 1986).

1207.04(e)(i) Preparing the File for Publication

When the examining attorney determines that the mark in an application that is subject to a concurrent use proceeding is ready for publication, the examining attorney should prepare the file as follows:

(1) The file must contain as many copies of the written application, specimens and drawing as may be necessary for the preparation of notices for each party specified as a concurrent user in the application. 37 C.F.R. §2.99(b). The copies are used by the Board to notify the concurrent users of the institution of the concurrent use proceeding.

(2) The application must contain a concurrent use statement that will be printed in the *Official Gazette*. The statement may be submitted by the applicant or prepared by the examining attorney. The statement must be in the following form:

问题以外，并无其他问题妨碍其获得注册的资格，审查员将批准申请按同时使用注册程序进行公布。15 U.S.C.§1062(a)。

一般情况下，对于一项同时使用注册申请，审查员不会要求提交其同时使用主张的证据。不过，如果申请人已经申请同时使用注册，而档案资料表明申请者不符合同时使用注册的基本要求(例如，如果申请书显示申请者是在得知存在除外使用者权利的情况下采用和使用该商标，或者各当事方在各自地区同时使用商标导致了实际的混淆)，就应根据 §2(d)的规定拒绝予以注册。*参见 Place for Vision, Inc.*, 196 USPQ 267, 269－270 (TTAB 1977)。*Gray v. Daffy Dan's Bargaintown*, 823 F.2d 522, 3 USPQ2d 1306 (Fed. Cir. 1987), *aff'g* 229 USPQ 474 (TTAB 1986)。

1207.04(e)(i) 准备公布的文件

如果审查员判定，需按同时使用程序执行的正在申请的商标已经具备了公布的条件，审查员应准备下列文件：

(1) 文件必须包括与申请书中所列的同时使用者数量相同的书面申请、样本以及附图的副本，以备向各当事方进行公告。*参见* 37 C.F.R.§2.99(b)。委员会使用此副本通知同时使用程序中的同时使用者。

(2) 申请书必须包括一份同时使用声明书，该声明书将刊登于《公报》上。该声明书可以由申请者提交，或由审查员准备。声明书必须符合以下格式：

Subject to Concurrent Use Proceeding with ________ [specifying the application serial number(s) or registration number(s), if any, of each other party; otherwise, the name and address of each other party].

Applicant claims the exclusive right to use the mark in the area comprising ________ [specifying the area for which the applicant seeks registration].

(3) To aid in the preparation of the file by the Legal Instruments Examiner (LIE), the examining attorney should prepare a one-page summary of the relevant concurrent use information. The information on the summary page should be set forth in the following manner:

CONCURRENT USE SUMMARY

Applicant:

Address:

Mark:

Goods or services:

Other Reg. or Serial Nos.:

Dates of use:

Areas of use:

EXCEPTIONS TO EXCLUSIVE USE

Name:

Address:

Mark:

Goods or Services:

与____________［如各对方当事人有申请序列号或注册号，则在此列明；如无，列明其姓名地址］同时获得注册。

申请人主张在下述地区享有使用该商标的专属权利，包括：____________［列明申请者寻求注册的地区］。

(3) 为了协助法律文件审查员(LIE)准备文件，审查员须准备一份一页的相关同时使用信息摘要。信息摘要需符合下列格式：

同时使用信息摘要

申请人：

地址：

商标：

商品或服务：

对方的注册号或序列号：

使用日期：

使用地区：

专属使用的除外情况

姓名：

地址：

商标：

商品或服务：

Reg. or Serial No.:

Dates of Use:

Area of use:

This summary should be attached to the front of the file.

After publication, if no opposition is filed, or if any opposition that is filed is dismissed or withdrawn, the Trademark Trial and Appeal Board will institute the concurrent use proceeding. The Board will consider and determine concurrent use rights only in the context of a concurrent use registration proceeding. 37 C. F. R. §2.99(h). *See* 37 C. F. R. §2.99; TMEP §1506.

See, *generally*, *Trademark Trial and Appeal Board Manual of Procedure* (TBMP) Chapter 1100 (1st ed. Sept. 1995).

1207. 04(f) Application for Concurrent Use Registration Pursuant to Court Decree

Under the last two sentences of §2(d), the Office may issue a concurrent use registration pursuant to the final determination of a court of competent jurisdiction that more than one person is entitled to use the same or similar marks in commerce. An applicant who seeks a concurrent use registration on the basis of a court determination does not have to claim use in commerce prior to the specified dates or obtain the consent of the owner of the involved mark, and the registration may be issued notwithstanding the possibility of public confusion. *See Holiday Inn v. Holiday Inns, Inc.*, 534 F. 2d 312, 189 USPQ 630 (C. C. P. A. 1976). *Cf. Alfred Dunhill of London, Inc. v. Dunhill Tailored Clothes, Inc.*, 293 F. 2d 685, 130 USPQ 412 (C. C. P. A. 1961), *cert. denied*, 369 U. S. 864, 133 USPQ 702 (1962).

When examining an application for concurrent use registration pursuant to the decree of a court, the examining attorney must determine whether the application complies with the specific requirements for concurrent use applications (*see*

注册号或序列号：

使用日期：

使用地区：

此摘要应附于文件首页。

公布之后，如果没有人提出异议，或者提出的异议遭到驳回或被撤回，商标评审及上诉委员会就会启动同时使用程序。委员会只在同时使用注册申请程序中考虑并裁判同时使用权利。37 *C.F.R.*§2.99(h)。*参见* 37 *C.F.R.*§2.99；*TMEP* §1506。

一般参见：*Trademark Trial and Appeal Board Manual of Procedure*（TBMP）Chapter 1100（1st ed. Sept. 1995）。

1207.04(f) 根据法院判决提出的同时使用注册申请

根据 §2(d)最后两句的规定，商标局可以依据具有管辖权法院有关一人以上都有权在商业活动中使用该相同或相似商标的最终裁判，核准一项同时使用注册。根据法院裁判申请同时使用注册的申请人不必主张在商业活动中使用在先，或者获得了相关商标所有人的同意，并且，无论是否可能引起公众混淆，都可以获得注册。*参见 Holiday Inn v. Holiday Inns, Inc.*，534 F.2d 312，189 USPQ 630（C.C.P.A. 1976）. 比较：*Alfred Dunhill of London, Inc. v. Dunhill Tailored Clothes, Inc.*，293 F.2d 685，130 USPQ 412（C.C.P.A. 1961），*cert. denied*，369 U.S. 864，133 USPQ 702（1962）。

在审查一项根据法院裁决提出的同时使用注册申请的过程中，审查员必须判断该申请是否符合同时使用申请的必备要求（*参见* TMEP §§1207.04(d)和(d)(i)），以

TMEP §§1207.04(d) and (d)(i)) and the requirements that would apply to an unrestricted application.

In addition, under 37 C.F.R. §2.99(f), all of the following conditions must be met, or a concurrent use proceeding before the Board must be prepared and instituted:

(1) The applicant is entitled to registration subject only to the concurrent lawful use of a party to the court proceeding;

(2) The court decree specifies the rights of the parties;

(3) A true copy of the court decree is submitted to the examining attorney;

(4) The concurrent use application complies fully and exactly with the court decree; and

(5) The excepted use specified in the concurrent use application does not involve a registration, or any involved registration has been restricted by the Director in accordance with the court decree.

If any of the above conditions are *not* satisfied, the examining attorney will approve the application for publication subject to a concurrent use registration proceeding (*see* TMEP §§1207.04(e) and (e)(i)), rather than pursuant to the court decree. 37 C.F.R. §2.99(f).

1207.04(f)(i) Preparing the File for Publication

If the application complies with all of the conditions listed in TMEP §1207.04(f) and all other relevant requirements, and is otherwise entitled to registration, the examining attorney will approve the application for publication of the mark. The examining attorney should prepare the file as follows:

The application must contain a concurrent use statement to be printed in the *Official Gazette*. The statement may be submitted by the applicant or prepared by the

及适用于非限制申请的其他要求)。

此外,根据 37 C.F.R.§2.99(f)的规定,必须符合下列所有条件,否则就必须准备并启动委员会的同时使用程序:

(1) 在法院程序中,申请者只有根据合法的同时使用才有权进行注册;

(2) 法院判决确定了各方当事人的权利;

(3) 向审查员提交法院判决的正式副本;

(4) 该同时使用申请完全并准确地符合法院的判决;以及

(5) 同时使用申请中所确定的除外使用不涉及某项注册,或者任何涉及的注册根据法院判决受到了局长的限制。

如果上述条件中任何一项不能满足,审查员就将同意根据同时使用注册程序(参*见* TMEP §§1207.04(e)和(e)(i))将该申请公布,而不是照法院判决办事。37 C.F.R.§2.99(f)。

1207.04(f)(i) 准备公布的文件

如果申请满足 TMEP §1207.04(f)所列出的所有条件,并且符合其他相关要求,那么就有权注册,审查员将会同意公布该商标的申请。审查员须准备下列文件:

申请书必须包括一份同时使用声明书,将会被印于《公报》。该声明可以由申请

examining attorney. The statement will delineate the concurrent rights of the parties as determined by the court, in the following form:

Registration limited to the area comprising __________ [specifying the area granted to the applicant by the court and any other restriction designated by the court] pursuant to the decree of ______________ [specifying the name of the court, proceeding number and date of the decree].

Concurrent registration with ______________ [specifying the application serial number(s) or registration number(s), if any, of each other party; otherwise, the name and address of each other party].

After publication, if no opposition is filed, or if any opposition that is filed is dismissed or withdrawn, the application will mature into a registration.

1208 Conflicting Marks in Pending Applications

37 C.F.R.§2.83. Conflicting marks.

(a) Whenever an application is made for registration of a mark which so resembles another mark or marks pending registration as to be likely to cause confusion or mistake or to deceive, the mark with the earliest effective filing date will be published in the "Official Gazette" for opposition if eligible for the Principal Register, or issued a certificate of registration if eligible for the Supplemental Register.

(b) In situations in which conflicting applications have the same effective filing date, the application with the earliest date of execution will be published in the "Official Gazette" for opposition or issued on the Supplemental Register.

(c) Action on the conflicting application which is not published in the Official Gazette for opposition or not issued on the Supplemental Register will be suspended by the Examiner of Trademarks until the published or issued application is registered or abandoned.

者提交,或由审查员准备。声明书须叙述法院所判定的各方当事人所享有的同时使用权利,并须符合下列格式:

根据______的判决[列明法院名称、案号和判决作出日期],注册限于下列地区:______[列明法院准许申请者进行使用的地区,以及法院作出的其他任何限制]。

与______[如各对方当事人有申请序列号或注册号,则在此列明;如无,列明其姓名地址]同时获得注册。

公布之后,如果无人提出异议,或者一切提出的异议均遭到驳回或者被撤回,该申请就将核准成为注册。

1208 未决申请中的冲突商标

37 C.F.R.§2.83。冲突商标。

(a)如果一项注册申请的商标与其他正在申请中的商标极其相似,以至于可能导致混淆、错误或欺骗,若适合在联邦商标登记簿注册,有效归档在先的商标就会被刊登在《公报》上以供他人提出异议,若适合在补充登记簿注册,则就会签发注册证书。

(b)在冲突申请归档日期相同的情况下,首先签署的申请将被公布在《公告》上以供他人提出异议,或者即在补充登记簿核准注册。

(c)针对未在《公告》上公布以供异议,或者未在补充登记簿注册的冲突申请提出的诉请将遭到商标审查员的禁止,直至公布或者提交的申请被注册或放弃。

1208.01 Priority for Publication or Issue Based on Effective Filing Date

In *ex parte* examination, priority among conflicting pending applications is determined based on the effective filing dates of the applications, without regard to whether the dates of use in a later-filed application are earlier than the filing date or dates of use of an earlier-filed application, whether the applicant in a later-filed application owns a registration for a mark that would be considered a bar to registration of the earlier-filed application, or whether an application was filed on the basis of use of the mark in commerce or a bona fide intent to use the mark in commerce.

When two or more applications contain marks that are conflicting, the mark in the application that has the *earliest effective filing date* will be published for opposition if it is eligible for registration on the Principal Register, or will be registered if it is eligible for registration on the Supplemental Register. 37 C. F. R. §2.83(a). *See* TMEP §§206 *et seq*. regarding effective filing dates.

The examining attorney cannot refuse registration under §2(d) of the Trademark Act based on an earlier-filed application for a conflicting mark until the mark registers. Therefore, when the examining attorney has examined the later-filed application and determined that it is in condition to be approved for publication or issue or in condition for a final refusal, except for the conflict between the marks, the examining attorney will *suspend* action on the later-filed application until the earlier-filed application matures into a registration or is abandoned. 37 C. F. R. §2.83(c); TMEP §§716.02(c) and 1208.02(c).

1208.01(a) What Constitutes Conflict Between Pending Applications

Marks in applications filed by different parties are in conflict when the registration of one of the marks would be a bar to the registration of the other under

1208.01 基于有效归档日期的公布及核准优先权

在部分审查中，存在冲突的未决申请之间的优先权是根据有效归档日期先后来判定的，而不考察后归档申请的使用日期是否先于其归档日期或先归档申请的使用日期，不考察后归档申请的申请者是否拥有一项可以被认为妨碍先归档申请获得注册的注册商标，也不考察申请是否是基于在商业活动中使用该商标还是在商业活动中存在善意使用该商标的意图而获得归档的。

当两项或两项以上的申请包含冲突商标时，具有*最早有效归档日期*的申请中的商标将被公布以供异议，只要其符合在联邦商标登记簿注册的条件，或者，如果符合条件，就可以在联邦商标补充登记簿注册。37 C.F.R.§2.83(a)。有关有效归档日期的内容，*参见* TMEP §§206 及以下。

审查员不能根据《商标法》第§2(d)节的规定，以存在先归档的冲突商标申请为由拒绝注册，直至该冲突商标获得注册。因此，如果审查员已经对后归档申请进行了审查，并判定其符合公布或核准的条件，或者符合最终拒绝的条件，那么除了商标间冲突的原因，审查员将暂停对后归档申请提出的诉请，直至先归档申请获得注册或被放弃。37 C.F.R.§2.83(c)；TMEP §§716.02(c)和 1208.02(c)。

1208.01(a) 什么构成了未决申请间的冲突

如果某一项商标根据《商标法》第§2(d)，15U.S.C.§1052(d)的规定，构成了其

§2(d) of the Trademark Act, 15 U.S.C.§1052(d). Therefore, the term "conflicting application" refers to an application to register a mark that so resembles the mark in another application as to be likely to cause confusion. *See* TMEP §702.03(b). *See* TMEP §§1207 *et seq*. regarding likelihood of confusion. There may be several conflicting pending applications.

1208.01(b) What Constitutes Effective Filing Date

The *filing date* of an application is the date when all the elements designated in 37 C.F.R.§2.21(a) are received at the Office. While this is generally the *effective filing date* for purposes of determining priority among conflicting applications, in certain situations another date is treated as the effective filing date. *See* TMEP §§206 *et seq*. For example, in an application claiming priority under §44(d) of the Trademark Act based on a foreign application, the effective filing date is the date of filing the foreign application. TMEP §206.02. In a §1(b) application that is amended to the Supplemental Register on the filing of an acceptable allegation of use, the effective filing date is the date of filing the amendment to allege use or the statement of use. TMEP §206.01.

If two or more applications conflict, the application with the earliest effective filing date will be approved for publication for opposition or for issuance of a registration on the Supplemental Register, as appropriate. 37 C.F.R.§2.83(a); TMEP §1208.01.

If conflicting applications have the same effective filing date, the application with the earliest date of execution will be published for opposition or issued on the Supplemental Register. 37 C.F.R.§2.83(b). An application that is unexecuted will be treated as having a later date of execution.

Occasionally, conflicting applications will have the same date of filing and execution. If this situation occurs, the application with the lowest serial number will have priority for publication or issuance. When determining which serial number

他商标注册的障碍,那么不同当事人申请中的商标就会产生冲突。因此,"冲突申请"一词是指某项申请,其注册商标与其他申请提出的商标极其相似从而可能导致混淆。*参见* TMEP §702.03(b)。有关混淆可能性的内容,*参见* TMEP §§1207 及以下。可能存在若干项互相冲突的未决申请。

1208.01(b) 什么构成了有效归档日

申请的*归档日*是指商标局收到所有 37 C.F.R.§2.21(a)所规定材料的日期。尽管通常*有效归档日*是判断各申请之间优先权的标准,但在某些情况下,其他日期会被认作有效归档日。*参见* TMEP §§206 及以下。例如,某申请主张《商标法》§44(d)所规定的基于外国申请的优先权,那么有效归档日就是该外国申请归档的日期。TMEP §206.02。在一项根据§1(b)提出,并通过提交可接受的使用证明修正,而向联邦商标补充登记簿注册的申请中,有效归档日期就是提交宣称使用修正书或者使用声明书的日期。TMEP §206.01。

如果两项或更多的申请之间发生冲突,那么有效归档日最早的申请会相应地被同意公布以供异议,或在补充登记簿核准注册。37 C.F.R. §2.83(a); TMEP §1208.01。

如果冲突申请的归档日期相同,首先签署的申请将被公布在《公告》上以供他人提出异议,或者即在补充登记簿核准注册。37 C.F.R.§2.83(b)。未签署的申请会被视为签署之日在后。

偶然地,冲突申请的归档和签署日都相同。如果发生这种情况,序列号在前的申请拥有公布及核准的优先权。在判断那个序列号在前时,审查员应忽略序列码(例如,

is the lowest, the examining attorney should disregard the series code (*e.g.*, "76" or "78") and look only to the six digit serial number.

1208.01(c) Change in Effective Filing Date During Examination

If the effective filing date in an application containing a conflicting mark changes, the examining attorney should review all the application(s) involved to determine which application has the earliest effective filing date as a result of the change.

The examining attorney should conduct a new search of the mark whenever the effective filing date of an application changes to a date that is later than the original filing date.

1208.01(d) Examination of Conflicting Marks After Reinstatement or Revival

When an abandoned application is revived or reinstated (*see* TMEP §§1712.01, 1713 and 1714 *et seq.*), the examining attorney must conduct a new search to determine whether any later-filed applications for conflicting marks have been approved for publication or registration, and place the search strategy in the file.

If a later-filed application has been approved, the examining attorney should inform the examining attorney who approved the later-filed application that the earlier-filed application has been revived, if necessary. If the later-filed application has been published, the examining attorney handling that application should request jurisdiction (*see* TMEP §1504.04(a)) and suspend the application pending disposition of the earlier-filed application that was revived or reinstated.

If a later-filed application for a conflicting mark has matured into registration, the examining attorney must refuse registration of the revived or reinstated application under §2(d), even though the application for the registered mark was filed

“76”或“78”)，而只审查六位阿拉伯数字序列号。

1208.01(c) 审查过程中有效归档日的改变

如果包含冲突商标的申请的有效归档日发生了变化，审查员应当重新审查所有相关的申请，以判断发生变化后哪一项申请的有效归档日为最先。

只要某申请的有效归档日变更后晚于其原始归档日，审查员就应当进行新的商标查询。

1208.01(d) 恢复或重新生效后对于冲突商标的审查

如果被放弃的申请重新生效或恢复(*参见* TMEP §§1712.01，1713 和 1714 及以下)，审查员必须重新查询以判断是否有后归档的冲突商标申请已经被批准公布或注册，并且将查询策略附于档案中。

如果后归档的申请已经获得批准，如有必要，审查员应通知批准该后归档申请的审查员，告知其先归档的申请已经重新生效。如果后归档的申请已经公布，负责该申请的审查员应请求管辖权(*参见* TMEP §1504.04(a))并且暂停办理该重新生效或恢复的先归档申请。

如果冲突商标的后归档申请已经核准注册，审查员必须根据 §2(d)的规定，拒绝重新生效或恢复的申请注册，即使该已注册的商标的申请日期后于申请重新生效或

after the revived or reinstated application. The Office does not have the authority to cancel the registration.

1208. 02 Conflicting Applications Examination Procedure

1208. 02(a) Examination of Application with Earliest Effective Filing Date

When the application with the earliest effective filing date is first reviewed for action, the examining attorney should approve the application for publication or for issuance of a registration on the Supplemental Register, if appropriate. 37 C. F. R. §2.83(a).

If the application with the earliest effective filing date is not in condition for publication or issue, the examining attorney should issue an Office action that includes all relevant refusals and requirements.

The Office does not notify applicants of potentially conflicting later-filed applications.

See TMEP §§206 *et seq*. and 1208. 01(b) regarding what constitutes an effective filing date.

1208. 02(b) Action on Later-Filed Application: Giving Notice of the Earlier Application or Applications

If, when the later-filed conflicting application is first reviewed for action, it is not in condition for publication or issue, the examining attorney should, in addition to treating other matters, send with the Office action a copy of the drawing or a printout from the Office's automated search system of the information for the mark in each earlier-filed application. The examining attorney's letter should also advise the applicant that the earlier application, if and when it matures into a registration, may be ci-

恢复的申请日期。商标局没有撤销注册的权力。

1208.02 冲突申请审查程序

1208.02(a) 对于有效归档日在先的申请的审查

有效归档日在先的申请首先经过审查之后，审查员就应当相应地批准该申请进行公布或在补充登记簿注册。37 C.F.R.§2.83(a)。

如果有效归档日在先的申请不符合公布或核准的条件，审查员就应当签发包括一切相关驳回及要求的审查决定书。

商标局不向申请人通报可能发生冲突的后归档申请的情况。

有关什么构成了有效的归档日期，参见 TMEP §§206 及以下，以及 1208.01(b)。

1208.02(b) 对于后归档申请的决定:关于在先申请的通知

如果后归档的冲突申请首先进行了审查以作出决定，却不符合公布或核准的条件，那么审查员就应当在处理其他事务之外，于发出决定书的同时随同发出附图的复印件，或者是商标局自动化查询系统中有关各先归档申请商标信息的输出文本。审查员的信函应当同时建议申请者，如果在先申请一旦注册成功，可能会被引用来对抗

ted against the applicant's later-filed application. The applicant should be notified of all conflicting applications with earlier effective filing dates.

See TMEP §1208.02(c) regarding suspension of later-filed conflicting applications that are otherwise in condition to be approved for publication or issue.

1208.02(c) Suspension of Later-Filed Application [R-1]

When the later-filed application is in condition for publication or issue except for the conflicting mark in an earlier-filed application, either because no action was necessary on the application as filed or because examination on other matters has been brought to a conclusion, the examining attorney should suspend the later-filed application until the mark in the earlier-filed application is registered or the earlier-filed application is abandoned. 37 C.F.R. §2.83(c). *In re Direct Access Communications (M.C.G.) Inc.*, 30 USPQ2d 1393 (Comm'r Pats. 1993). If the examining attorney discovers that a previously-filed pending application was abandoned, but that a petition to revive is pending, the examining attorney should suspend the later-filed application pending disposition of the petition to revive.

Action on the later-filed application should also be suspended when the application is in condition for a final action but for the conflict with the earlier-filed application. The letter of suspension should repeat the outstanding issues, but these issues should not be made final.

If the Office action informing the applicant of the suspension is the first action in the case, the examining attorney should include a copy of the drawing or a print-out from the Office automated search system of the information for the mark in each earlier-filed conflicting application.

1208.02(d) Action on Later-Filed Application upon Disposition of the Earlier Application or Applications

If all conflicting earlier-filed applications have either matured into registrations or

申请者的在后申请。所有具备在先有效归档日期的冲突申请均应向申请者通知。

有关中止审查符合公布或核准条件的后核准冲突申请的情况，参见 TMEP §1208.02(c)。

1208.02(c) 后归档申请的停审处理[R-1]

如果后归档申请除了与先归档申请存在冲突以外符合其他公布或注册的条件，那么或者是因为对该归档申请无须作出决定，或者是因为对于其他事项的审查已经得出了结论，审查员应当对后归档申请作停审处理，直至先归档申请所提交的商标获得注册，或者先归档申请被放弃。37 C.F.R. §2.83(c)。相关判例：*Direct Access Communications* (*M.C.G.*) *Inc.*, 30 USPQ2d 1393 (Comm'r Pats. 1993)。如果审查员发现先归档未决申请已被放弃，但是恢复申请正在进行中，审查员应当对后归档申请作停审处理，等待恢复申请的结果。

如果除了与先归档申请冲突之外，申请符合其他进行最终决定的条件，那么对于后归档申请的决定也应当暂停处理。停审函应当重申大致的要点，但这些要点不应被确定为最终决定。

如果商标局通知申请者停审处理的决定是该案的初步决定，那么审查员就应当随同发出附图的复印件，或者是商标局自动化查询系统中有关各先归档申请商标信息的输出文本。

1208.02(d) 根据在先申请最终决定对后归档申请的决定

如果所有的先归档申请都已经要么获得注册、要么被放弃，并且不存在其他停

become abandoned, and there are no other grounds for suspension, the examining attorney should remove the later-filed application from suspension and take appropriate action as follows.

The examining attorney should cite the registration or registrations that issued from the earlier-filed conflicting application or applications, if there is a likelihood of confusion. This will be a first refusal under §2(d) of the Trademark Act, 15 U.S.C. §1052(d). Any other outstanding issues should be repeated at this time.

If all earlier-filed applications have become abandoned, the examining attorney should either approve the later-filed application for publication or issue, or repeat and make final any remaining issues, as appropriate.

If some, but not all of the earlier-filed conflicting applications have matured into registrations, the examining attorney will normally not issue a refusal of registration until the remaining conflicting application(s) are registered or abandoned, in order to avoid issuing piecemeal refusals.

1208.02(e) Applicant's Argument on Issues of Conflict

If an applicant with a later-filed application argues that there is no conflict in relation to the application with the earlier effective filing date, the examining attorney should consider the merits of that argument and determine whether or not the earlier-filed application constitutes a potential bar to registration under §2(d) of the Act.

If the examining attorney concludes that the earlier-filed application is not a potential bar, the examining attorney should remove the application from suspension and take appropriate action on any other outstanding issues.

However, if the examining attorney concludes that the earlier-filed application is a potential bar, the examining attorney should issue an action for the later-filed application (*e.g.*, a letter of suspension if there are no other issues that are not in

审事由，那么审查员就应当取消对后归档申请的停审处理，采取下列适当的程序。

如果存在混淆可能，审查员应引用由先归档冲突申请核准的注册。这将构成《商标法》§2(d)，15 U.S.C.§1052(d)所规定的初步拒绝。任何其他要点均应于此时重申。

如果先归档申请已经撤回，那么审查员就应当相应地批准后归档申请进行公布或注册，或者重申一切既有问题并作出最终裁定。

如果一些，而非全部先归档冲突申请获得了注册，审查员通常不会作出拒绝予以注册的决定，直至仍然存在冲突的申请获得注册或被放弃，以避免作出大量单独的拒绝决定。

1208.02(e) 申请者关于冲突问题的抗辩

如果后归档申请的申请者抗辩称，与拥有在先有效归档日期的申请并无冲突，审查员就应当考虑该抗辩的是非曲直，判断先归档申请是否构成《商标法》§2(d)所规定的潜在注册阻碍。

如果审查员判定先归档申请并不构成潜在阻碍，就应当取消该申请的停审处理决定，并根据其他要点采取相应的程序。

不过，如果审查员判定先归档申请存在潜在阻碍，那么就应当就后归档申请签发决定(例如，一封停审函——如果并不存在其他不符合最终决定的问题)，对于申请者

condition for final action), in which the examining attorney explains why the applicant's argument is not persuasive. *See* TMEP §716.03 regarding requests for removal of applications from suspension.

1208.02(f) Conflicting Mark Mistakenly Published or Approved for Issuance on the Supplemental Register

If a later-filed conflicting mark is mistakenly published for opposition, it may be necessary for the examining attorney to obtain jurisdiction of the application to take appropriate action. *See* TMEP §§1504 *et seq*. concerning obtaining jurisdiction of an application after publication.

The examining attorney does not lose jurisdiction of an application forwarded for issuance on the Supplemental Register until the day of issuance of the registration.

1208.03 Procedure Relating to Possibility of Interference

An interference will not be declared except upon petition to the Director. The Director will declare an interference only upon a showing of extraordinary circumstances that would result in a party being unduly prejudiced without an interference. These cases are extremely rare. In ordinary circumstances, the availability of an opposition or cancellation proceeding is deemed to remove any undue prejudice. 37 C.F.R. §2.91(a). Interferences are generally limited to situations where a party would otherwise be required to engage in a series of opposition or cancellation proceedings, and where the issues are substantially the same. *See* TMEP §1208.03(b). The potential need to file two notices of opposition that could be consolidated if the issues were sufficiently similar, is not considered an extraordinary circumstance that will unduly prejudice a petitioner without an interference.

All petitions, or requests for interference are to be forwarded to the Commissioner for Trademarks for decision. The examining attorney does not make a determination on a request for interference.

的抗辩为何不成立进行解释。有关取消申请停审决定的信息，*参见* TMEP §716.03。

1208.02(f) 错误地公布或在补充登记簿注册了冲突商标

如果某项后归档冲突商标被错误地公布以供异议，审查员可能就需要获得该申请的管辖权以采取相应的措施。了解有关公布之后取得某项申请管辖权的内容，*参见* TMEP §§1504 及以下。

审查员一直拥有针对送交补充登记簿注册的申请的管辖权，直至注册核准之日。

1208.03 关于介入干涉可能的程序

只有向局长提出申诉，才有可能实施介入干涉。只有证明出现了特别状况，如不干涉可能导致一方当事人遭到不正当的损害，局长才会宣布进行介入干涉。此类案件极其罕见。在通常情况下，启动异议或撤销程序被认为足以弥补一切不正当的损害。37 C.F.R.§2.91(a)。介入干涉通常仅限于如不实施一方当事人就会被要求进行一系列的异议或撤销程序，而所涉问题实质上是同样的。*参见* TMEP §1208.03(b)。如果所涉问题充分相似，可能须将两份异议通知合并处理的情况，并不被认为是如不干涉会导致一方不正当受损的特殊情况。

所有的申诉，或干涉请求都被转交商标专员进行裁决。审查员无须对干涉请求作出裁定。

See TBMP Chapter 1000.

1208.03(a) Procedures on Request for Interference

The request for interference should be in a separate paper in the form of a petition, and should be captioned as a petition. The petition fee indicated in 37 C.F.R. §2.6 should accompany the request. A petition to declare an interference should not be filed before the application has been examined and the mark has been found to be registrable but for the existence of one or more conflicting pending applications.

If the examining attorney receives a petition or request for interference, the examining attorney should forward it, with the file, to the Office of the Commissioner for Trademarks.

A request for interference does not make an application "special" or alter the normal order of examination.

See TBMP Chapter 1000.

1208.03(b) Decision on Request for Interference

Section 16 of the Trademark Act, 15 U.S.C. §1066, states that, upon petition showing extraordinary circumstances, the Director may declare that an interference exists when application is made for the registration of a mark that so resembles a mark previously registered by another, or for the registration of which another has previously applied, as to be likely, when used on or in connection with the goods or services of the applicant, to cause confusion or mistake or to deceive. No interference shall be declared between an application and a registration that has become incontestable.

The Director will declare an interference only upon a showing of extraordinary circumstances that would result in a party being unduly prejudiced in the absence

参见 TBMP Chapter 1000。

1208.03(a) 请求介入干涉的程序

干涉的请求应当以申诉的形式用独立的文件提出,并应注明是申诉。提出请求时即应同时缴付 37 C.F.R.§2.6 所规定的申诉费用。干涉申诉应在申请审查之前提起,而且该商标已被判定只是因为存在未决冲突申请而不能注册。

审查员一旦收到介入干涉的申诉或请求,即应将其随同有关档案转交商标专员办公室。

介入干涉的请求并不导致一种"特殊的"申请,或者改变正常的审查程序。

参见 TBMP Chapter 1000。

1208.03(b) 请求介入干涉的裁决

《商标法》第 16 节,15 U.S.C.§1066 规定,根据申诉所表明的特别状况,如果申请注册的标记与他人先前注册或申请的商标极其相似,从而在用于申请人的商品或服务时可能导致混淆、错误或欺骗,那么局长可以宣布实施介入干涉。在一项申请与一项无可争辩的注册之间不应进行介入干涉。

只有证明出现了特别状况,如不干涉可能导致一方当事人遭到不正当的损害,局

of an interference. 37 C.F.R. §2.91(a). The availability of opposition and cancellation procedures provides a remedy and ordinarily precludes the possibility of undue prejudice to a party. The request for interference must show that there is some extraordinary circumstance that would make the remedy of opposition or cancellation inadequate or prejudicial to the party's rights. *See In re Family Inns of America, Inc.*, 180 USPQ 332 (Comm'r Pats. 1974).

The fact that an earlier-filed application based on intent to use the mark in commerce under §1(b) or based on §44 has been cited against a later-filed application based on use in commerce under §1(a) is not an extraordinary circumstance that warrants declaration of an interference. An opposition proceeding is the proper forum for determining priority between an applicant and another party. Priority for purposes of examination of an application is determined by filing date.

Although §16 of the Act permits the declaration of an interference between an application and a registration, the practice of declaring an interference in these cases has been discontinued. The reason is that the applicant cannot obtain a registration if the interfering registration remains on the register. Therefore, even if the applicant prevailed in the interference, the applicant would still have to petition to cancel the interfering registration. *See In re Kimbell Foods, Inc.*, 184 USPQ 172 (Comm'r Pats. 1974); *Ex parte H. Wittur & Co.*, 153 USPQ 362 (Comm'r Pats. 1966); 37 C.F.R. §2.96.

See TBMP Chapter 1000.

1208.03(c) Procedure When Interference Is to be Declared

If the Director grants a petition requesting an interference, the examining attorney must determine that each mark is registrable but for the interfering mark before the interference will be instituted. 37 C.F.R. §2.92.

All marks must be published for opposition before interference proceedings are instituted; if possible, the marks should be published simultaneously.

长才会宣布进行介入干涉。37 C.F.R.§2.91(a)。如果启动异议和撤销程序能够提供救济途径,通常就排除了给一方造成不正当损害的可能性。介入干涉的请求必须证明,存在某些特殊情况,使得对于一方的权利而言异议或撤销的救济不足或可能导致损害。*参见 Family Inns of America, Inc.*, 180 USPQ 332 (Comm'r Pats.1974)。

基于§1(b)规定的在商业活动中意图使用的先归档申请被引用来对抗一项基于§1(a)规定的在商业活动中使用的后归档申请,不是导致宣布干涉介入的特别状况。异议程序是解决申请者与他方之间优先权问题的适当方式。在申请审查过程中,对于优先权的判断通过归档日期进行。

尽管《商标法》§16 允许在一项申请和一项注册之间实施干涉,但在此类案件中实际上已经废止了进行干涉的做法。原因在于如果受到干涉的注册仍然登记在册,申请者就不能获得注册。因此,即使申请者在干涉中获得支持,申请者仍然不得不进行申诉以撤销遭到干涉的注册。*参见 Kimbell Foods, Inc.*, 184 USPQ 172 (Comm'r Pats.1974);*H. Wittur & Co.*, 153 USPQ 362 (Comm'r Pats.1966);37 C.F.R.§2.96。

参见 TBMP Chapter 1000。

1208.03(c) 宣布进行介入干涉后的程序

如果局长同意了请求予以干涉的申诉,审查员必须在启动干涉程序之前,判断除了引起干涉的商标之外,其他每个商标均为可注册。37 C.F.R.§2.92。

在干涉程序启动之前,所有商标都必须公布以供异议;如果可能,商标应当同时公布。

Each application that is to be the subject of an interference must contain the following statement to be printed in the *Official Gazette*:

This application is being published subject to declaration of interference with:

Serial No.:
Filed:
Applicant:
(Address, if there is no attorney)
Attorney and Address:
Mark:

The examining attorney should prepare the statement.

If an application that is published subject to declaration of interference is opposed by a party other than the applicant(s) in the interfering application(s), the opposition will be determined first. If still necessary and appropriate, the interference will be instituted. If an opposition is filed by the applicant in the interfering application, the interference proceeding will not be instituted. The rights of the parties will be determined in the opposition proceeding.

If, during the pendency of an interference, another application appears involving substantially the same registrable subject matter, the examining attorney may request suspension of the interference for the purpose of adding that application. If the application is not added, the examining attorney should suspend further action on the application pending termination of the interference proceeding. 37 C.F.R. §2.98.

See TBMP Chapter 1000.

1209 Refusal on Basis of Descriptiveness

Extract from 15 U.S.C.§1052. No trademark by which the goods of the applicant

涉及干涉程序的各申请必须提供以下声明书，刊登在《公告》上：

根据介入干涉的决定，兹公布本申请：

序列号：
归档：
申请人：
（如无代理人，须注明地址）

代理人及其地址：
商标：

审查员应准备该声明书。

如果根据干涉决定公布的申请遭到干涉申请人以外他方的异议，则首先要对该异议进行裁决。如果仍然有必要并且适当，介入干涉程序就将启动。如果在干涉申请中，申请者提出了异议书，则不会启动干涉。各当事方的权利将在异议程序中进行裁判。

如果，在干涉程序进行期间，出现另一项实质内容相同的申请，则审查员可以要求暂停干涉程序，以加入该申请。如果该申请未被加入，审查员应在干涉程序终止前，暂停对该申请作进一步处理。*37 C.F.R.§2.98*。

参见 *TBMP Chapter 1000*。

1209 以描述性为由拒绝予以注册

摘自15 U.S.C.§1052。由于其性质，用于区别申请者商品与他人商品的商标

may be distinguished from the goods of others shall be refused registration on the principal register on account of its nature unless it ... (*e*) *Consists of a mark which*, (1) *when used on or in connection with the goods of the applicant is merely descriptive or deceptively misdescriptive of them* ...

Matter that "merely describes" the goods or services on or in connection with which it is used is not registrable on the Principal Register. As noted in *In re Abcor Development Corp.*, 588 F. 2d 811, 813, 200 USPQ 215, 217 (C. C. P. A. 1978):

> The major reasons for not protecting such marks are: (1) to prevent the owner of a mark from inhibiting competition in the sale of particular goods; and (2) to maintain freedom of the public to use the language involved, thus avoiding the possibility of harassing infringement suits by the registrant against others who use the mark when advertising or describing their own products.

1209.01 Distinctiveness/Descriptiveness Continuum

With regard to trademark significance, matter may be categorized along a continuum, ranging from marks that are highly distinctive to matter that is a generic name for the goods or services. The degree of distinctiveness — or, on the other hand, descriptiveness — of a designation can be determined only by considering it in relation to the specific goods or services. *Remington Products, Inc. v. North American Philips Corp.*, 892 F. 2d 1576, 13 USPQ2d 1444, 1448 (Fed. Cir. 1990) (the mark must be considered in context, *i.e.*, in connection with the goods).

At one extreme are marks that, when used in relation to the goods or services, are completely arbitrary or fanciful. Next on the continuum are suggestive marks, followed by merely descriptive matter. Finally, generic terms for the goods or services are at the opposite end of the continuum from arbitrary or fanciful marks. As stated in *H. Marvin Ginn Corp. v. International Association of Fire Chiefs, Inc.*,

均可以在联邦商标登记簿注册，除非——(e)包含一项商标，该商标(1)用于申请者的商品时只是描述性的，或者存在欺骗性的错误描述……

“只是描述”商品或服务的内容不能在联邦商标登记簿注册。正如*Abcor Development Corp.*, 588 F.2d 811, 813, 200 USPQ 215, 217 (C.C.P.A.1978)一案中所述：

> 不保护此类商标的主要原因在于：(1)为了防止商标所有人限制某一特定商品的竞争；以及(2)保持公众使用所涉语言的自由，以避免注册者对在广告或产品描述中使用到该商标的其他人提起冗长的侵害诉讼。

1209.01 独特性/描述性的连续区域

关于商标的意义，其内容范围可能存在一种连续区域，从高度独特性的商标到属于商品或服务一般名称的内容。某项标识独特性的程度——或者，从另一方面说，描述性的程度——只能通过与特定商品或服务联系起来考虑才能进行判定。参见*Remington Products, Inc. v. North American Philips Corp.*, 892 F.2d 1576, 13 USPQ2d 1444, 1448 (Fed.Cir.1990)(商标必须在其应用环境中进行考虑，即与商品联系起来考虑)。

商标的一个极端是，当商标与商品或服务相关地使用时，是完全任意性或臆造性的。其次是暗示性商标，再其次是仅具描述性的商标。最后，与任意性或臆造性商标相对的另一个极端是，使用一般词语作为商品或服务的商标。正如*H. Marvin Ginn Corp. v. International Association of Fire Chiefs, Inc.*, 782 F.2d 987, 989, 228

782 F.2d 987, 989, 228 USPQ 528, 530 (Fed. Cir. 1986), "[t]he generic name of a thing is in fact the ultimate in descriptiveness."

Fanciful, arbitrary and suggestive marks, often referred to as "inherently distinctive" marks, are registrable on the Principal Register without proof of acquired distinctiveness. *See* TMEP §1209.01(a).

Marks that are merely descriptive of the goods or services may not be registered on the Principal Register absent a showing of acquired distinctiveness under 15 U.S.C. §1052(f). *See* TMEP §1209.01(b) regarding merely descriptive marks, and TMEP §§1212 *et seq*. regarding acquired distinctiveness. Merely descriptive marks may be registrable on the Supplemental Register. 15 U.S.C. §1091.

Matter that is generic for the goods or services is not registrable on either the Principal or the Supplemental Register under any circumstances. *See* TMEP §§1209.01(c) *et seq*.

1209.01(a) Fanciful, Arbitrary and Suggestive Marks

Fanciful marks comprise terms that have been invented for the sole purpose of functioning as a trademark or service mark. Such marks comprise words that are either unknown in the language (*e.g.*, PEPSI, KODAK, EXXON) or are completely out of common usage (*e.g.*, FLIVVER).

Arbitrary marks comprise words that are in common linguistic use but, when used to identify particular goods or services, do not suggest or describe a significant ingredient, quality or characteristic of the goods or services (*e.g.*, APPLE for computers; OLD CROW for whiskey).

Suggestive marks are those that, when applied to the goods or services at issue, require imagination, thought or perception to reach a conclusion as to the nature of those goods or services. Thus, a suggestive term differs from a descriptive term, which immediately tells something about the goods or services. *See In re*

USPQ 528, 530 (*Fed. Cir.* 1986)一案中所述:"事物的一般名称事实上是描述性的极点。"

臆造性、任意性和暗示性的商标,通常被称为"固有独特性"的商标,无须独特性证明就可以在联邦商标登记簿上注册。*参见 TMEP* §1209.01(*a*)。

根据 15 U.S.C.§1052(f)的规定,仅对商品或服务具有描述性的商标,若无获得性独特性的证明,不得在联邦商标登记簿上注册。有关仅具描述性的商标的情况,参见 TMEP §1209.01(b)。有关获得性独特性的情况,*参见* TMEP §§1212 及以下。仅具描述性的商标可以在联邦商标补充登记簿上注册。15 U.S.C.§1091。

商品或服务的一般性内容在任何情况下都不得在联邦商标登记簿或补充登记簿上注册。*参见* TMEP §§1209.01(c)及以下。

1209.01(a) 臆造性、任意性和暗示性的商标

臆造性商标由发明仅作为商标或服务商标使用的词语构成。此类商标包括语言中不存在的词语(例如,PEPSI, KODAK, EXXON)以及通常完全不再使用的词语(例如 FLIVVER)。

任意性商标包括通常语言中仍然使用,但是用于识别特定商品或服务时,并不暗示或描述该商品或服务主要成分、品质或特性的词语(例如,用于电脑的 APPLE;用于威士忌的 OLD CROW)。

暗示性商标是指,在用于所涉商品或服务时,通过想象,或者感觉,以得出某种关于商品或服务性质的结论的商标。因此,暗示性词语不同于描述性词语,后者即时表达了关于商品或服务的某些信息。*参见 Shutts*, 217 USPQ 363 (TTAB 1983)("SNO-

Shutts, 217 USPQ 363 (TTAB 1983) (SNO-RAKE held not merely descriptive of a snow removal hand tool). *See also In re Quik-Print Copy Shop, Inc.*, 203 USPQ 624 (TTAB 1979), *aff'd*, 616 F. 2d 523, 205 USPQ 505 (C. C. P. A. 1980) (QUIK-PRINT held merely descriptive of printing services); *In re Aid Laboratories, Inc.*, 223 USPQ 357 (TTAB 1984) (BUG MIST held merely descriptive of insecticide). Suggestive marks, like fanciful and arbitrary marks, are registrable on the Principal Register without proof of secondary meaning. Therefore, a designation does not have to be devoid of all meaning in relation to the goods and services to be registrable.

1209.01(b) Merely Descriptive Marks

To be refused registration on the Principal Register under §2(e)(1) of the Trademark Act, 15 U.S.C. §1052(e)(1), a mark must be merely descriptive or deceptively misdescriptive of the goods or services to which it relates. A mark is considered merely descriptive if it describes an ingredient, quality, characteristic, function, feature, purpose or use of the specified goods or services. *See In re Gyulay*, 820 F.2d 1216, 3 USPQ2d 1009 (Fed. Cir. 1987) (APPLE PIE held merely descriptive of potpourri); *In re Bed & Breakfast Registry*, 791 F.2d 157, 229 USPQ 818 (Fed. Cir. 1986) (BED & BREAKFAST REGISTRY held merely descriptive of lodging reservations services); *In re MetPath Inc.*, 223 USPQ 88 (TTAB 1984) (MALE-P. A. P. TEST held merely descriptive of clinical pathological immunoassay testing services for detecting and monitoring prostatic cancer); *In re Bright-Crest, Ltd.*, 204 USPQ 591 (TTAB 1979) (COASTER-CARDS held merely descriptive of a coaster suitable for direct mailing).

The determination of whether or not a mark is merely descriptive must be made in relation to the goods or services for which registration is sought, not in the abstract. This requires consideration of the context in which the mark is used or intended to be used in connection with those goods or services, and the possible significance that the mark would have to the average purchaser of the goods or serv-

RAKE"被认为对于除雪工具仅具描述性)。另参见 *Quik-Print Copy Shop, Inc.*, 203 USPQ 624 (TTAB 1979), *aff'd*, 616 F.2d 523, 205 USPQ 505 (C.C.P.A. 1980)("QUIK-PRINT"被认为对于打印服务而言仅具描述性);*Aid Laboratories, Inc.*, 223 USPQ 357 (TTAB 1984)("BUG MIST"被认为对于杀虫剂而言仅具描述性)。与臆造性和任意性商标一样,暗示性商标如无次要含义的证明,即可在联邦商标登记簿注册。因此,一项标识不必排斥有关注册商品和服务的一切含义。

1209.01(b) 仅具描述性的商标

如果是根据《商标法》§2(e)(1),15 U.S.C.§1052(e)(1)的规定而拒绝在联邦商标登记簿注册,那么对于相关的商品或服务商标必须仅具描述性或者存在欺骗性的错误描述。如果某商标描述了特定商品或服务的成分、品质、特性、功能、特征、目的或用途,就会被认为仅具描述性。参见 *Gyulay*, 820 F.2d 1216, 3 USPQ2d 1009 (Fed.Cir.1987)("APPLE PIE"被认为对于杂烩菜而言仅具描述性);*Bed & Breakfast Registry*, 791 F.2d 157, 229 USPQ 818 (Fed.Cir.1986)("BED & BREAKFAST REGISTRY"被认为对于住宿预订服务而言仅具描述性);*MetPath Inc.*, 223 USPQ 88 (TTAB 1984)("MALE-P.A.P. TEST"被认为对于临床病理免疫测试服务而言仅具描述性);*Bright-Crest, Ltd.*, 204 USPQ 591 (TTAB 1979)("COASTER-CARDS"被认为对于适合直邮销售的杯垫而言仅具描述性)。

商标是否仅具描述性必须与申请注册的商品或服务联系起来,而不是抽象地进行判断。这就要求考虑商标用于或意图用于商品或服务时的上下文环境,以及该商标对于该商品或服务的一般市场购买者可能造成的意义。参见 *Omaha National Corp.*,

ices in the marketplace. *See In re Omaha National Corp*., 819 F.2d 1117, 2 USPQ2d 1859 (Fed. Cir. 1987); *In re Abcor Development Corp*., 588 F.2d 811, 200 USPQ 215 (C.C.P.A. 1978); *In re Venture Lending Associates*, 226 USPQ 285 (TTAB 1985).

It is not necessary that a term describe all of the purposes, functions, characteristics or features of a product to be considered merely descriptive; it is enough if the term describes one significant function, attribute or property. *In re H.U.D.D.L.E*., 216 USPQ 358 (TTAB 1982); *In re MBAssociates*, 180 USPQ 338 (TTAB 1973).

The great variation in facts from case to case prevents the formulation of specific rules for specific fact situations. Each case must be decided on its own merits. *See In re Ampco Foods, Inc*., 227 USPQ 331 (TTAB 1985); *In re Venturi, Inc*., 197 USPQ 714 (TTAB 1977).

See TMEP §§1209.03(a) through (s) regarding factors that often arise in determining whether a mark is merely descriptive or generic.

See also TMEP §§1213 *et seq*. concerning disclaimer of merely descriptive matter within a mark.

1209.01(c) Generic Terms

Generic terms are terms that the relevant purchasing public understands primarily as the common or class name for the goods or services. *In re Dial-A-Mattress Operating Corp*., 240 F.3d 1341, 57 USPQ2d 1807, 1811 (Fed. Cir. 2001); *In re American Fertility Society*, 188 F.3d 1341, 1346, 51 USPQ2d 1832, 1836 (Fed. Cir. 1999). These terms are incapable of functioning as registrable trademarks denoting source, and are not registrable on the Principal Register under §2(f) or on the Supplemental Register.

1209.01(c)(i) Test [R-2]

There is a two-part test used to determine whether a designation is generic: (1)

819 F.2d 1117，2 USPQ2d 1859（Fed. Cir. 1987）；*Abcor Development Corp.*，588 F.2d 811，200 USPQ 215（C. C. P. A. 1978）；*Venture Lending Associates*，226 USPQ 285（TTAB 1985）。

某一词语不必描述产品所有的目的、功能、特性或特征，就可以被认为仅具描述性；只要该词语描述了一项重要的功能、特征或性质即可。*参见 H. U. D. D. L. E.*，216 USPQ 358（TTAB 1982）；*MBAssociates*，180 USPQ 338（TTAB 1973）。

个案事实的巨大差异使得确定事实情况的特定规则无法形成公式。每个案件都必须根据其自身的情况进行裁决。*参见 Ampco Foods，Inc.*，227 USPQ 331（TTAB 1985）；*Venturi，Inc.*，197 USPQ 714（TTAB 1977）。

有关在判断商标是属于仅具描述性还是一般词语的过程中经常发生的情况，*参见* TMEP §§1209.03(a)至（s）。

有关撤回商标中仅具描述性的内容的情况，另*参见* TMEP §§1213 及以下。

1209.01(c) 一般词语

一般词语是指被相关购买公众主要理解为商品或服务通用或种类名称的词语。*参见 Dial-A-Mattress Operating Corp.*，240 F. 3d 1341，57 USPQ2d 1807，1811（Fed. Cir. 2001）；*American Fertility Society*，188 F. 3d 1341，1346，51 USPQ2d 1832，1836（Fed. Cir. 1999）。这些词语不具有注册商标标示来源的功能，不能根据§2(f)在联邦商标登记簿注册，或者在补充登记簿注册。

1209.01(c)(i) 检验［R-2］

有一种两步骤的检验方式，用于判断某标识是否是一般性的：(1)涉案商品或服

What is the class of goods or services at issue? and (2) Does the relevant public understand the designation primarily to refer to that class of goods or services? *H. Marvin Ginn Corp. v. International Association of Fire Chiefs, Inc.*, 782 F.2d 987, 990, 228 USPQ 528, 530 (Fed. Cir. 1986). The test turns upon the primary significance that the term would have to the relevant public.

The examining attorney has the burden of proving that a term is generic by clear evidence. *In re Merrill Lynch, Pierce, Fenner & Smith Inc.*, 828 F.2d 1567, 4 USPQ2d 1141 (Fed. Cir. 1987). Evidence of the public's understanding of a term can be obtained from any competent source, including dictionary definitions, research databases, newspapers and other publications. *See In re Northland Aluminum Products, Inc.*, 777 F.2d 1556, 227 USPQ 961 (Fed. Cir. 1985) (BUNDT, a term that designates a type of cake, held generic for ring cake mix); *In re Analog Devices Inc.*, 6 USPQ2d 1808 (TTAB 1988), *aff'd*, 871 F.2d 1097, 10 USPQ2d 1879 (Fed. Cir. 1989) (ANALOG DEVICES held generic for devices having analog capabilities).

When a term is a compound word, the examining attorney may establish that a term is generic by producing evidence that each of the constituent words is generic, and that the separate words retain their generic significance when joined to form a compound that has "a meaning identical to the meaning common usage would ascribe to those words as a compound." *In re Gould Paper Corp.*, 834 F.2d 1017, 5 USPQ2d 1110, 1111-1112 (Fed. Cir. 1987) (SCREENWIPE held generic as applied to premoistened antistatic cloths for cleaning computer and television screens).

However, the Court of Appeals for the Federal Circuit has expressly limited the holding in *Gould* to "compound terms formed by the union of words" where the public understands the individual terms to be generic for a genus of goods or services, and the joining of the individual terms into one compound word lends "no additional meaning to the term." *In re Dial-A-Mattress Operating Corp.*, 240 F.3d 1341, 57 USPQ2d 1807, 1810 (Fed. Cir. 2001) (citing *In re American Fertility So-*

务的种类是什么？以及(2)相关公众是否将该标识理解为主要是用于表示商品或服务的种类？见 *H. Marvin Ginn Corp. v. International Association of Fire Chiefs, Inc.*，782 F.2d 987，990，228 USPQ 528，530（Fed. Cir. 1986）。该检验方式将表明词语对于相关公众的主要意义。

审查员负有以清晰的证据证明词语具有一般性的责任。见 *Merrill Lynch, Pierce, Fenner & Smith Inc.*，828 F.2d 1567，4 USPQ2d 1141（Fed. Cir. 1987）。公众对于某词语理解的证据可以采自一切适合的来源，包括词典定义、查询数据库、报纸和其他出版物等。*参见 Northland Aluminum Products, Inc.*，777 F.2d 1556，227 USPQ 961（Fed. Cir. 1985）（标识某种蛋糕的词语"BUNDT"被认为是婚礼蛋糕混合料的一般名称）；*Analog Devices Inc.*，6 USPQ2d 1808（TTAB 1988），*aff'd*，871 F.2d 1097，10 USPQ2d 1879（Fed. Cir. 1989）（"ANALOG DEVICES"被认为是模拟装置的一般名称）。

如果是一个复合词，审查员可以通过提出证据证明构成该词的各词语是一般名称，并且这些独立的词语在构成"其含义与组成部分进行复合时所具有的一般意义相同的"复合词时，保持了各自的一般意义，从而证明该复合词是一般词语。*见 Gould Paper Corp.*，834 F.2d 1017，5 USPQ2d 1110，1111－1112（Fed. Cir. 1987）（"SCREENWIPE"（屏幕擦）用于电子计算机及电视屏幕预湿防静电织物时被认为属于一般词语）。

不过，联邦巡回区上诉法院明确将 *Gould* 案中的观点限于"由词语联合组成的复合词语"，该词语由公众理解为商品或服务种类的一般单词构成，并且这些单词组合为一个复合词时"未对该词增添其他含义"。*参见 Dial-A-Mattress Operating Corp.*，240 F.3d 1341，57 USPQ2d 1807，1810（Fed. Cir. 2001）（引用 *American Fertility*

ciety, 188 F.3d 1341, 51 USPQ2d 1832, 1837 (Fed. Cir. 1999)). Where the mark is a phrase, the examining attorney cannot simply cite definitions and generic uses of the individual components of the mark, but must provide evidence of the meaning of the composite mark as a whole.

In *American Fertility Society*, the court held that evidence that the components "Society" and "Reproductive Medicine" were generic was not enough to establish that the composite phrase SOCIETY FOR REPRODUCTIVE MEDICINE was generic for association services in the field of reproductive medicine. The court held that the examining attorney must show: (1) the genus of services that the applicant provides; and (2) that the relevant public understands the proposed composite mark to primarily refer to that genus of services. 51 USPQ2d at 1836-37.

In *Dial-A-Mattress*, the court held that an alphanumeric phone number "bears closer conceptual resemblance to a phrase than a compound word." 57 USPQ2d at 1811. The court found that 1-888-M-A-T-R-E-S-S was not generic as applied to "telephone shop-at-home retail services in the field of mattresses," because there was no evidence of record that the public understood the term to refer to shop-at-home telephone mattress retailers. Therefore, to establish that a mnemonic phone number is generic, the examining attorney must show that the relevant public would understand the mark as a whole to have generic significance.

With respect to top level domain indicators (TLDs), the Trademark Trial and Appeal Board held that, unlike an alphanumeric telephone number, a generic term combined with a TLD "cannot be characterized as a mnemonic phrase." The Board stated:

> [The designation CONTAINER. COM] is instead a compound word, a generic term combined with the top level domain indicator, ".COM." In proving genericness, the Office may satisfy its burden by showing that these separate generic words have a meaning identical to the meaning common usage would ascribe to those words as a compound. *In re Gould Paper Corp.*, 834 F.2d 1017, 5 USPQ2d 1110 (Fed. Cir. 1987). In a simi-

Society，188 F.3d 1341，51 USPQ2d 1832，1837（Fed. Cir. 1999））。如果商标是一个短语，审查员就不能简单地引用定义解释和构成该商标组成部分单词的一般性用途，而必须提供有关该复合商标整体含义的证据。

在 *American Fertility Society* 一案中，法庭认为证明组成部分"Society"（学会）和"Reproductive Medicine"（生殖医学）一般性的证据不足以证明由其构成的短语"SOCIETY FOR REPRODUCTIVE MEDICINE"（生殖医学学会）用于生殖医学领域联络服务时属于一般词语。法庭认为审查员必须证明：(1)申请者所提供的服务的种类；以及(2)相关公众认为该申请注册的复合商标主要是用来表示服务种类。51 USPQ2d at 1836－1837。

在 *Dial-A-Mattress* 一案中，法庭认为一种混编电话号码"在概念上与短语而非复合词近似"。57 USPQ2d at 1811。法庭判定"1－888－M-A-T-R-E-S-S"用于"床垫电话订购服务"时不属于一般性名称，因为没有档案证据表明，公众将该词理解为指代床垫电话订购零售商的词语。因此，为了证明一种有助记忆的电话号码属于一般词语，审查员必须表明相关公众会在整体上将该商标理解为具有一般意义。

至于顶级域名标识（TLD），商标评审及上诉委员会认为，与混编电话号码不同，与 TLD 结合的一般词语"不能被认为是有助记忆的短语"。委员会称：

> ［标识 CONTAINER. COM］不是复合词语，而是与顶级域名标识".COM."相结合的一般词语。为了证明其一般性，商标局可以通过表明这些独立的一般词语具有与构成复合词后通常使用意义同样的含义来完成其证明责任。*Gould Paper Corp.*，834 F.2d 1017，5 USPQ2d 1110（Fed.

lar sense, neither the generic term nor the domain indicator has the capability of functioning as an indication of source, and combining the two does not result in a compound term that has somehow acquired this capability.

In re Martin Container, Inc., 65 USPQ2d 1058, 1061 (TTAB 2002). *Accord, In re CyberFinancial. Net, Inc.*, 65 USPQ2d 1789 (TTAB 2002) (the designation BONDS.COM, used in an offer of services, held generic for providing information regarding financial products and services via the Internet). *See also* TMEP §§1209.03(m) and 1215.05.

When examining an application which includes a TLD, the examining attorney must include evidence such as dictionary definitions to establish that the TLD lacks trademark significance.

1209.01(c)(ii) Terminology

As specifically amended by the Trademark Law Revision Act of 1988, §14 of the Trademark Act provides for the cancellation of a registration of a mark at any time if the mark "becomes the generic name for the goods or services, or a portion thereof, for which it is registered ..."15 U.S.C. §1064(3). Previously, that provision had pertained to a mark that "becomes the common descriptive name of an article or substance ..."Cases previously distinguished between generic names and "apt or common descriptive names," which referred to matter that, while not characterized as "generic," had become so associated with the product that it was recognized in the applicable trade as another name for the product, serving as a term of art for all goods of that description offered by different manufacturers rather than identifying the goods of any one producer. *See Questor Corp. v. Dan Robbins & Associates, Inc.*, 199 USPQ 358, 364 (TTAB 1978), *aff'd*, 599 F.2d 1009, 202 USPQ 100 (C.C.P.A. 1979). In addition, the Trademark Law Revision Act of 1988 amended §15 of the Trademark Act to adopt the term "generic name" to refer to generic designations. 15 U.S.C. §1065(4). In view of the amendment of

Cir. 1987)。从类似的意义上说，该一般词语与域名标识均不具有标示来源的功能，而此二者的结合也不会导致一个具有此种功能的复合词。

Martin Container, Inc., 65 USPQ2d 1058, 1061 (TTAB 2002)。与此一致：*CyberFinancial.Net, Inc.*, 65 USPQ2d 1789 (TTAB 2002)(用于提供服务的标识"BONDS.COM"，被认为属于通过因特网提供有关金融产品咨询服务的一般词语)。*另参见* TMEP §§1209.03(m)和 1215.05。

在审查包含 TLD 的申请时，审查员必须使用诸如词典定义之类的证据以证明该 TLD 缺乏商标意义。

1209.01(c)(ii) 术语

作为《1988 年商标法修正法》的特别修订，《商标法》§14 规定，一旦"商标成为所注册商品或服务的一般名称，或其一部分，得以注册……"，那么随时都可以撤销该商标的注册登记。15 U.S.C. §1064(3)。先前，该规定则是适用于"成为某商品或物的描述性名称……"的商标。以前的判例区分了一般名称和"适当或通常的描述性名称"，后者是指某些内容，尽管不属于"一般"，但由于与产品密切联系而在相关行业中被认为是该产品的另一名称，从而成为所描述的一切由不同制造商提供的商品的术语，而不是用来识别某一供应商的货物。*参见 Questor Corp. v. Dan Robbins & Associates, Inc.*, 199 USPQ 358, 364 (TTAB 1978), *aff'd*, 599 F.2d 1009, 202 USPQ 100 (C.C.P.A. 1979)。此外，《1988 年商标法修正法》还修订了《商标法》§15，采用了"一般名称"一词以指代一般性的标识。15U.S.C. §1065(4)。根据对

§§14 and 15, a distinction between "generic" names and "apt or common descriptive" names should not be made. Rather, the terminology of the Act should be consistently used, *e.g.*, in refusals to register matter that is a generic name for the goods or services, or a portion thereof. *See In re K-T Zoe Furniture Inc.*, 16 F. 3d 390, 29 USPQ2d 1787 (Fed. Cir. 1994).

Similarly, cases have distinguished between "generic" terms and terms that were deemed "so highly descriptive as to be incapable of exclusive appropriation as a trademark." *See In re Harcourt Brace Jovanovich, Inc.*, 222 USPQ 820 (TTAB 1984) (LAW & BUSINESS held so highly descriptive as to be incapable of distinguishing applicant's services of arranging and conducting seminars in the field of business law); *In re Industrial Relations Counselors, Inc.*, 224 USPQ 309 (TTAB 1984) (INDUSTRIAL RELATIONS COUNSELORS, INC. held an apt name or so highly descriptive of educational services in the industrial relations field that it is incapable of exclusive appropriation and registration, notwithstanding *de facto* source recognition capacity). Regarding current practice for refusing registration of such matter, the Trademark Trial and Appeal Board noted as follows in In *re Women's Publishing Co. Inc.*, 23 USPQ2d 1876, 1877 n.2 (TTAB 1992):

> The Examining Attorney's refusal that applicant's mark is "so highly descriptive that it is incapable of acting as a trademark" is not technically a statutory ground of refusal. Where an applicant seeks registration on the Principal Register, the Examining Attorney may refuse registration under Section 2(e)(1) of the Act, 15 USC 1052(e)(1), on the basis that the mark sought to be registered is generic (citations omitted). Alternatively, an Examining Attorney may refuse registration under the same section if he or she believes that the mark is merely descriptive and that applicant's showing of acquired distinctiveness is unpersuasive of registrability.

In essence, the Board was merely emphasizing the need to use precise statutory language in stating grounds for refusal. While the decision does not explicitly bar

§§14 和 15 的修正，不应认为“一般”名称和“适当或通常的描述性”名称有所不同。更进一步说，《商标法》的术语应当前后统一地使用，例如，在拒绝商品或服务一般名称或其一部分注册的决定中。参见 *K-T Zoe Furniture Inc.*, 16 F.3d 390, 29 USPQ2d 1787 (Fed. Cir. 1994)。

类似地，判例还区分了“一般”词语和被视为“高度描述性以至于不能专门用作商标的”词语。参见 *Harcourt Brace Jovanovich, Inc.*, 222 USPQ 820 (TTAB 1984) (“LAW & BUSINESS”(法与商)被认为具有高度描述性以至于不能区分申请者提供组织举办商法研讨会的服务)；*Industrial Relations Counselors, Inc.*, 224 USPQ 309 (TTAB 1984) (“INDUSTRIAL RELATIONS COUNSELORS, INC.” (工业关系顾问公司)被认为是一个通用词语，对于劳资关系教育服务而言具有高度的描述性，因而不能用于专门用途和注册，尽管在事实上具有标示来源的功能)。关于当前拒绝此类内容注册的实践，商标评审及上诉委员会在 *Women's Publishing Co. Inc.*, 23 USPQ2d 1876, 1877 n.2 (TTAB 1992)一案中陈述如下：

> 审查员以“具有高度描述性，以至于不具备商标功能”为由拒绝注册申请者的商标在技术上并非具有法律依据的拒绝。如果某申请寻求在联邦商标登记簿注册，审查员就可以根据《商标法》第 2(e)(1)节，15 USC 1052(e)(1)的规定，以该申请注册的商标具有一般性为由拒绝予以注册(引注略)。或者，如果审查员确信该商标仅具描述性，并且申请者对于获得性独特性的证明不符合注册要求，那么也可以根据同一法律规定拒绝予以注册。

其实，委员会只是强调在陈述拒绝予以注册决定的理由时，需要运用准确的法律语言。尽管该判决并未明确禁止在所有情况下均禁止使用“具有高度描述性以至于

the use of the terminology "so highly descriptive that it is incapable of acting as a trademark" under all circumstances, the case illustrates that the use of this terminology may lead to confusion and should be avoided. It is particularly important in this context to use the precise statutory language to avoid doctrinal confusion. *See generally* McLeod, *The Status of So Highly Descriptive and Acquired Distinctiveness*, 82 Trademark Rep. 607 (1992). Therefore, examining attorneys should not state that a mark is "so highly descriptive that it is incapable of acting as a trademark" in issuing refusals. Rather, in view of the amendments of the Trademark Act noted above, the terminology "generic name for the goods or services" should be used in appropriate refusals, and use of the terminology "so highly descriptive" should be discontinued when referring to incapable matter.

This does not mean that designations that might formerly have been categorized as "so highly descriptive" should not be regarded as incapable. The Court of Appeals for the Federal Circuit has specifically stated that "a phrase or slogan can be so highly laudatory and descriptive as to be incapable of acquiring distinctiveness as a trademark." *In re Boston Beer Co. L. P.*, 198 F. 3d 1370, 53 USPQ2d 1056, 1058 (Fed. Cir. 1999) (THE BEST BEER IN AMERICA for beer and ale held to be "so highly laudatory and descriptive of the qualities of [applicant's] product that the slogan does not and could not function as a trademark to distinguish Boston Beer's goods and serve as a indication of origin").

The Court of Appeals for the Federal Circuit has stated that "[t]he critical issue in genericness cases is whether members of the relevant public primarily use or understand the term sought to be registered to refer to the genus of goods or services in question." *H. Marvin Ginn Corp. v. International Association of Fire Chiefs, Inc.*, 782 F. 2d 987, 989-990, 228 USPQ 528, 530 (Fed. Cir. 1986). Also note that it is entirely appropriate to consider whether a particular designation is "highly descriptive" in evaluating registrability under §2(f), or in similar circumstances.

The expression "generic name for the goods or services" is not limited to noun forms but also includes "generic adjectives," that is, adjectives that refer to a ge-

不具有商标功能"的术语，但是判例表明了使用此种术语可能导致的混淆，以及应当加以避免的态度。在此种情况下，尤其重要的是使用精确的法律语言以避免理论上的混淆。*一般*参见 McLeod，*The Status of So Highly Descriptive and Acquired Distinctiveness*，82 Trademark Rep. 607 (1992)。因此，在作出拒绝决定时，审查员不应称某商标为"具有高度描述性以至于不具有商标功能"。此外，根据上述对《商标法》的修正，应当在适当的拒绝决定中使用"用于商品或服务的一般名称"，而"高度描述性的"一词不应继续在涉及不能注册的内容时使用。

这并不意味着以前可能被归为"高度描述性的"标识不应再被认为不能注册。联邦巡回区上诉法院特别阐述道："某句短语或口号可以是高度赞美性和描述性的，以至于不具有商标所需的独特性"。见 *Boston Beer Co. L. P.*，198 F.3d 1370，53 USPQ2d 1056，1058 (Fed. Cir. 1999)（用于啤酒和麦芽酒的"THE BEST BEER IN AMERICA"（美国最佳啤酒）被认为"对于[申请人的]产品具有高度的赞美性和描述性，以至于该口号无法具有商标功能，不能区分 Boston Beer 的商品和服务，也不能标示来源"）。

联邦巡回区上诉法院阐述道："涉及一般性案件的要点在于，相关公众是否主要将该申请注册词语用于或理解为是指称相关商品或服务的种类。"见 *H. Marvin Ginn Corp. v. International Association of Fire Chiefs, Inc.*，782 F.2d 987，989－990，228 USPQ 528，530 (Fed. Cir. 1986)。另外需要注意的是，在根据 §2(f) 评价注册性时，或者相似的情况下，考虑某特定标识是否属于"高度描述性"是完全正确的。

"用于商品或服务的一般名称"的说法并不限于名词形式，还包括了"一般性的

nus, species, category or class of goods or services. *In re Reckitt & Colman, North America Inc.*, 18 USPQ2d 1389 (TTAB 1991) (PERMA PRESS generic for soil and stain removers for use on permanent press products).

1209.01(c)(iii) Generic Matter: Case References [R-2]

In the following cases, the matter sought to be registered was found generic: *In re Boston Beer Co. L. P.*, 198 F.3d 1370, 53 USPQ2d 1056, 1058 (Fed. Cir. 1999) (THE BEST BEER IN AMERICA for beer and ale held to be "so highly laudatory and descriptive of the qualities of [applicant's] product that the slogan does not and could not function as a trademark to distinguish Boston Beer's goods and serve as a indication of origin"); *In re Gould Paper Corp.*, 834 F.2d 1017, 5 USPQ2d 1110 (Fed. Cir. 1987) (SCREENWIPE held generic as applied to premoistened antistatic cloths for cleaning computer and television screens); *In re Northland Aluminum Products, Inc.*, 777 F.2d 1556, 227 USPQ 961 (Fed. Cir. 1985) (BUNDT, a term that designates a type of cake, held generic for ring cake mix); *In re American Institute of Certified Public Accountants*, 65 USPQ2d 1972 (TTAB 2003) (CPA EXAMINATION held generic for "printed matter, namely, practice accounting examinations; accounting exams; accounting exam information booklets; and prior accounting examination questions and answers"); *In re American Academy of Facial Plastic and Reconstructive Surgery*, 64 USPQ2d 1748 (TTAB 2002) (FACIAL PLASTIC SURGERY held generic for training, association, and collective membership services, where evidence showed that the phrase "facial plastic surgery" is a recognized field of surgical specialization); *In re A La Vieille Russie, Inc.*, 60 USPQ2d 1895 (TTAB 2001) (RUSSIANART generic for dealership services in the field of fine art, antiques, furniture and jewelry); *Continental Airlines Inc. v. United Airlines Inc.*, 53 USPQ2d 1385 (TTAB 1999) (E-TICKET generic for computerized reservation and ticketing of transportation services); *In re Log Cabin Homes Ltd.*, 52 USPQ2d 1206 (TTAB 1999) (LOG CABIN HOMES generic for architectural design of buildings and retail outlets selling kits for building log homes); *In re Web Communications*, 49 USPQ2d 1478 (TTAB

形容词”,亦即指称商品或服务某一种类、品种、类别或级别的形容词。见 *Reckitt & Colman, North America Inc.*, 18 USPQ2d 1389 (TTAB 1991)(“PERMA PRESS”属于耐久定形品用污渍清洗液的一般名称)。

1209.01(c)(iii)　一般性内容:参考案例[R-2]

在下列判例中,申请注册的内容被认为是一般性的: *Boston Beer Co. L. P.*, 198 F.3d 1370, 53 USPQ2d 1056, 1058 (Fed. Cir. 1999)(用于啤酒和麦芽酒的“THE BEST BEER IN AMERICA”(美国最佳啤酒)被认为“对于(申请人的)产品具有高度的赞美性和描述性,以至于该口号无法具有商标功能,不能区分 Boston Beer 的商品和服务,也不能标示来源”); *Gould Paper Corp.*, 834 F.2d 1017, 5 USPQ2d 1110 (Fed. Cir. 1987)(用于清洁电子计算机及电视屏幕的预湿防静电织物的“SCREENWIPE”(屏幕擦)被认为是一般性词语); *Northland Aluminum Products, Inc.*, 777 F.2d 1556, 227 USPQ 961 (Fed. Cir. 1985)(用于标示一种蛋糕的“BUNDT”一词被认为是婚礼蛋糕混合配料的一般词语); *American Institute of Certified Public Accountants*, 65 USPQ2d 1972 (TTAB 2003)(“CPA EXAMINATION”(注册会计师考试)被认为是用于“印刷品,即:实习会计考试试卷;会计考试试卷;会计考试资料册;以及历年会计考试的试题和答案”的一般词语); *American Academy of Facial Plastic and Reconstructive Surgery*, 64 USPQ2d 1748 (TTAB 2002)(“FACIAL PLASTIC SURGERY”(面部整容)被认为是用于培训、联络以及集体会员服务的一般词语,因为证据显示短语“facial plastic surgery”(面部整容)是一种公认的外科手术专业领域); *A La Vieille Russie, Inc.*, 60 USPQ2d 1895 (TTAB 2001)(“RUSSIANART”(俄罗斯艺术)被认为是用于艺术品、古董、家具以及珠宝领域代理经销服务的一般词语); *Continental Airlines Inc. v. United Airlines Inc.*, 53 USPQ2d 1385 (TTAB 1999)(“E-TICKET”(电子票)被认为是用于运输服务电脑预订及订票的一般词语); *Log Cabin Homes Ltd.*, 52 USPQ2d 1206 (TTAB 1999)(“LOG CABIN HOMES”(木屋)被认为是用于出售原木屋建筑工具的零售商店和大楼建筑设计的

1998) (WEB COMMUNICATIONS generic for consulting services to businesses seeking to establish sites on a global computer network); *In re Central Sprinkler Co.*, 49 USPQ2d 1194 (TTAB 1998) (ATTIC generic for sprinklers installed primarily in attics); *In re Stanbel Inc.*, 16 USPQ2d 1469 (TTAB 1990), *aff'd*, 20 USPQ2d 1319 (Fed. Cir. 1991) (ICE PAK for reusable ice substitute for use in food and beverage coolers held generic; even assuming a contrary holding, evidence submitted by applicant deemed insufficient to establish acquired distinctiveness); *In re The Paint Products Co.*, 8 USPQ2d 1863 (TTAB 1988) (PAINT PRODUCTS CO. for "interior and exterior paints and coatings, namely, alkyd, oil, latex, urethane and epoxy based paints and coatings" held so highly descriptive as to be incapable of becoming distinctive; even assuming the term could function as a mark, applicant's evidence deemed insufficient to establish acquired distinctiveness); *In re Analog Devices Inc.*, 6 USPQ2d 1808 (TTAB 1988), *aff'd*, 871 F.2d 1097, 10 USPQ2d 1879 (Fed. Cir. 1989) (ANALOG DEVICES held generic for devices having analog capabilities); *In re Mortgage Bankers Association of America*, 226 USPQ 954 (TTAB 1985) (CERTIFIED MORTGAGE BANKER ("MORTGAGE BANKER" disclaimed) for "educational services, namely providing qualifying examinations, testing and grading in the field of real estate finance" held so highly descriptive as to be incapable of functioning as a mark notwithstanding evidence of acquired distinctiveness); *In re Half Price Books, Records, Magazines, Inc.*, 225 USPQ 219, 222 (TTAB 1984) (HALF PRICE BOOKS RECORDS MAGAZINES for retail book and record store services "is incapable of designating origin and any evidence of secondary meaning can only be viewed as 'de facto' in import and incapable of altering the inability of the subject matter for registration to function as a service mark").

In the following cases, the matter sought to be registered was found not to be generic: *In re Dial-A-Mattress Operating Corp.*, 240 F.3d 1341, 57 USPQ2d 1807 (Fed. Cir. 2001) (1-888-M-A-T-R-E-S-S not generic for "telephone shop-at-home retail services in the field of mattresses"); *In re American Fertility Society*, 188 F.3d 1341, 51 USPQ2d 1832 (Fed. Cir. 1999) (SOCIETY FOR REPRODUCTIVE

一般词语）；*Web Communications*，49 USPQ2d 1478（TTAB 1998）（“WEB COMMUNICATIONS”（网上沟通）被认为是用于全球网站建设业务咨询服务的一般词语）；*Central Sprinkler Co*.，49 USPQ2d 1194（TTAB 1998）（“ATTIC”（顶楼）被认为是用于屋内喷淋装置的一般词语）；*Stanbel Inc*.，16 USPQ2d 1469（TTAB 1990），*aff'd*，20 USPQ2d 1319（Fed. Cir. 1991）（“ICE PAK”（冰块）被认为是用于取代食品和饮料冷却器的可再用冰块的一般词语；即使假设此点判决相反，申请者提交的证据也被认为不足以证明获得性独特性）；*The Paint Products Co*.，8 USPQ2d 1863（TTAB 1988）（用于“内外油漆涂料，即醇酸树脂、润滑油、乳胶、尿烷以及环氧油漆涂料”的“PAINT PRODUCTS CO.”（油漆产品公司）被认为具有高度的描述性而不具有独特性；即使假设该词可以用作商标，申请者的证据也不足以证明获得性独特性）；*Analog Devices Inc*.，6 USPQ2d 1808（TTAB 1988），*aff'd*，871 F.2d 1097，10 USPQ2d 1879（Fed. Cir. 1989）（“ANALOG DEVICES”（模拟装置）被认为是用于模拟装置的一般词语）；*Mortgage Bankers Association of America*，226 USPQ 954（TTAB 1985）（用于“教育服务，即：提供不动产金融领域资格考试、测验以及评级”的“CERTIFIED MORTGAGE BANKER”（注册房屋贷款银行人员）（“MORTGAGE BANKER”撤回）被认为具有高度的描述性以至于不具有商标的功能，尽管证据表明其已经具备了独特性）；*Half Price Books, Records, Magazines, Inc*.，225 USPQ 219，222（TTAB 1984）（用于书籍唱片零售服务的“HALF PRICE BOOKS RECORDS MAGAZINES”（半价书、唱片、杂志）“无法标示来源，而一切次要含义的证据只被视为具有‘事实上’的意义，无法改变该内容不能作为服务商标注册的状况”）。

在下列判例中，申请注册的内容被认为不具有一般性：*Dial-A-Mattress Operating Corp*.，240 F.3d 1341，57 USPQ2d 1807（Fed. Cir. 2001）（对于“床垫电话销售服务”而言“1-888-M-A-T-R-E-S-S”不具有一般性）；*American Fertility Society*，188 F.3d 1341，51 USPQ2d 1832（Fed. Cir. 1999）（对于生殖药物联系服务而言，

MEDICINE not generic for association services in the field of reproductive medicine); *In re Merrill Lynch, Pierce, Fenner & Smith Inc.*, 828 F.2d 1567, 4 USPQ2d 1141 (Fed. Cir. 1987) (CASH MANAGEMENT ACCOUNT for "stock brokerage services, administration of money market fund services, and providing loans against securities services" held merely descriptive, rather than generic, and remanded to Board to consider sufficiency of §2(f) evidence); *H. Marvin Ginn Corp. v. International Association of Fire Chiefs, Inc.*, 782 F.2d 987, 228 USPQ 528 (Fed. Cir. 1986) (FIRE CHIEF not generic for publications); *In re Federated Dept. Stores Inc.*, 3 USPQ2d 1541 (TTAB 1987) (THE CHILDREN'S OUTLET "OUTLET" disclaimed), while merely descriptive of applicant's "retail children's clothing store services," held capable of functioning as a mark, with evidence submitted by applicant sufficient to establish acquired distinctiveness pursuant to §2(f)); *Hunter Publishing Co. v. Caulfield Publishing Ltd.*, 1 USPQ2d 1996 (TTAB 1986) (SYSTEMS USER for periodic trade journal held merely descriptive, rather than generic, and applicant's evidence held sufficient to establish acquired distinctiveness pursuant to §2(f)); *In re Failure Analysis Associates*, 1 USPQ2d 1144 (TTAB 1986) (FAILURE ANALYSIS ASSOCIATES, for "consulting services in the field of mechanical, structural, metallurgical, and metal failures, fires and explosions; engineering services in the field of mechanical design and risk analysis" and "consulting engineering services in the metallurgical field," found to be merely descriptive of applicant's services rather than incapable of distinguishing them from those of others; evidence submitted by applicant held sufficient to demonstrate acquired distinctiveness under §2(f)).

1209.02 Procedure for Descriptiveness and/or Genericness Refusal [R-1]

The examining attorney must consider the evidence of record to determine whether a mark is merely descriptive or whether it is suggestive or arbitrary. *See In re Noble Co.*, 225 USPQ 749, 750 (TTAB 1985). The examining attorney may request that the applicant submit additional explanations or materials to clarify the

"SOCIETY FOR REPRODUCTIVE MEDICINE"（生殖医学学会）不具有一般性）；*Merrill Lynch, Pierce, Fenner & Smith Inc.*, 828 F.2d 1567, 4 USPQ2d 1141 (Fed. Cir. 1987)（用于"股票经纪服务，货币市场基金管理服务，以及提供针对证券的借贷服务"的"CASH MANAGEMENT ACCOUNT"（现金管理账户）被认为仅具描述性，而非一般性，并且要求委员会重新考虑有关§2(f)所规定的证据的充分性）；*H. Marvin Ginn Corp. v. International Association of Fire Chiefs, Inc.*, 782 F.2d 987, 228 USPQ 528 (Fed. Cir. 1986)（对于出版物而言，"FIRE CHIEF"（消防主管）不具有一般性）；*Federated Dept. Stores Inc.*, 3 USPQ2d 1541 (TTAB 1987)（尽管对于申请人的"童装零售服务"而言，"THE CHILDREN'S OUTLET"（"OUTLET"撤回）仅具描述性，但由于申请人提交的证据足以证明其获得了 §2(f)所规定的独特性，因而被认为具有商标的功能）；*Hunter Publishing Co. v. Caulfield Publishing Ltd.*, 1 USPQ2d 1996 (TTAB 1986)（用于商业期刊的"SYSTEMS USER"被认为仅具描述性，而非一般性，且申请人提交的证据被认为足以证明其获得了 §2(f)所规定的独特性。）；*Failure Analysis Associates*, 1 USPQ2d 1144 (TTAB 1986)（用于"机械、建筑、冶金、金属缺陷、火灾及爆炸领域；机械设计和风险分析领域工程服务"以及"冶金领域工程咨询服务"的"FAILURE ANALYSIS ASSOCIATES"（故障分析师）被认为对于申请者的服务仅具描述性，而非不能将其与他人的服务区分开来；而申请人提交的证据被认为足以证明其获得了 §2(f)所规定的独特性）。

1209.02　以描述性和/或一般性为由拒绝注册的程序［R-1］

审查员必须考虑档案证据以判断商标是否仅具描述性，或者是否属于暗示性或任意性。参见 *Noble Co.*, 225 USPQ 749, 750 (TTAB 1985)。审查员可以要求申请者提交其他解释或者材料以澄清商品或服务的性质。37 C.F.R. §2.61(b)；TMEP

nature of the goods or services. 37 C.F.R. §2.61(b); TMEP §814. The examining attorney should also do any necessary research to determine the nature of the use of the designation in the marketplace. If the examining attorney refuses registration, he or she should support the refusal with appropriate evidence.

In all cases the examining attorney should try to make the Office action as complete as possible, so that the applicant may respond appropriately.

A designation that is merely descriptive should be refused registration under §2(e)(1) of the Trademark Act, 15 U.S.C. §1052(e)(1). When issuing any refusal under §2(e)(1), if the designation appears to be a generic name for the goods or services, the examining attorney should provide an advisory statement that the subject matter appears to be a generic name for the goods or services, in conjunction with the refusal on the ground that the matter is merely descriptive. If, on the other hand, the mark appears to be capable, the examining attorney should provide appropriate advice concerning a possible amendment to the Supplemental Register or assertion of a claim of acquired distinctiveness. *See* TMEP §1102.03 concerning ineligibility of the proposed mark in a §1(b) application for the Supplemental Register prior to filing an acceptable amendment to allege use under 15 U.S.C. §1051(c) or statement of use under 15 U.S.C. §1051(d). If the record is unclear as to whether the designation is capable of functioning as a mark, the examining attorney should refrain from giving any advisory statement. In general, the Office should make every effort to apprise applicants as early as possible of the prospects for registration through appropriate amendments, if feasible.

An examining attorney should not issue a refusal in an application for the Principal Register on the ground that a mark is a generic name for the goods or services unless the applicant asserts that the mark has acquired distinctiveness under 15 U.S.C. §1052(f). Even if it appears that the mark is generic, the proper basis for refusal is §2(e)(1). If there is strong evidence that the proposed mark is generic, a statement that the subject matter appears to be a generic name for the goods or services can be included as part of the §2(e)(1) refusal. It has been said that a ge-

§814。审查员还应当作一切必要的查询，以判断在市场中对该标识进行使用的性质。如果审查员拒绝予以注册，必须有适当的证据佐证。

在所有情况下，审查员均应尽可能作出完整的决定，如此申请者可以做出相应的反应。

对于仅具描述性的标识应当根据《商标法》§2(e)(1)，15 U.S.C.§1052(e)(1)的规定拒绝注册。在根据§2(e)(1)作出任何拒绝予以注册决定的情况下，如果该标识看来是商品或服务的一般名称，则审查员应当提供一份意见陈述，告知该内容看来是商品或服务的一般名称，与以该内容仅具描述性为由作出的拒绝予以注册决定一并发出。另一方面，如果该商标看来可以注册，则审查员应当提供相应的建议，告知可以提出修正书以注册于联邦商标补充登记簿，或者提交关于获得性独特性主张的声明书。有关在提交 15 U.S.C.§1051(c)所规定的可接受的宣称使用修正书，或 15 U.S.C.§1051(d)所规定的使用声明书之前，根据 §1(b)提出注册申请的商标在补充登记册注册的不适格性，*参见* TMEP §1102.03。如果档案关于该标识是否具有商标功能的内容不明，则审查员应当避免再给予任何意见陈述。通常，如果可能，商标局应当尽力尽早地通过适当的修正书将有关注册的前景状况通知申请者。

在申请于联邦商标登记簿注册的申请中，审查员不应以商标属于商品或服务的一般名称为由驳回，除非申请者根据 15 U.S.C.§1052(f)主张该商标已具备了独特性。即使看来商标具有一般性，拒绝予以注册的适当依据也应为 §2(e)(1)。如果存在强有力的证据表明，申请注册的商标具有一般性，可以在根据§2(e)(1)作出的驳回决定中加入关于该内容看来属于商品或服务的一般名称的声明书。已经提到过，一

neric term is "the ultimate in descriptiveness." *H. Marvin Ginn Corp. v. International Association of Fire Chiefs, Inc.*, 782 F.2d 987, 989, 228 USPQ 528, 530 (Fed. Cir. 1986).

If, in response to a first-action refusal under §2(e)(1), the applicant merely argues that the mark is registrable on the Principal Register without claiming acquired distinctiveness or amending to the Supplemental Register, the examining attorney should issue a final refusal under §2(e)(1), on the ground that the proposed mark is merely descriptive, if he or she is not persuaded by the applicant's arguments.

If the applicant responds to a §2(e)(1) refusal by amending its application to the Supplemental Register, this amendment presents a new issue requiring consideration by the examining attorney (unless the amendment is irrelevant to the outstanding refusal—*see* TMEP §714.05(a)(i)). If the examining attorney determines that the designation is a generic name for the applicant's goods or services, the examining attorney should then refuse registration on the Supplemental Register. The statutory basis for such a refusal is §23 of the Trademark Act, 15 U.S.C. §1091. This action must be nonfinal. *See* TMEP §§815 *et seq.* and 816 *et seq.* concerning applications for registration on the Supplemental Register.

If the applicant amends an application to assert acquired distinctiveness under §2(f), this raises a new issue. *See* TMEP §1212.02(h). If the examining attorney determines that the designation is a generic name for the applicant's goods or services, the examining attorney should continue the refusal of registration on the Principal Register under §2(e)(1). The examining attorney should also explain why the showing of acquired distinctiveness is insufficient. The action must be nonfinal. *See* TMEP §§1212 *et seq.* regarding distinctiveness under §2(f), and TMEP §1212.02(i) regarding assertion of §2(f) claims with respect to generic matter.

To the fullest extent possible, the examining attorney will examine §1(b) intent-to-use applications for registrability under §2(e)(1) according to the same procedures and

般词语是“描述性的终点”。见 *H. Marvin Ginn Corp. v. International Association of Fire Chiefs, Inc.*, 782 F.2d 987, 989, 228 USPQ 528, 530 (Fed. Cir. 1986)。

如果在针对根据§2(e)(1)作出的初步驳回决定提出的答辩中,申请者仅抗辩称无须主张获得性独特性或修正向补充登记簿申请注册,商标就可以在联邦商标登记簿注册,则只要审查员认为申请者的抗辩并不成立,就应当根据§2(e)(1)以该申请注册商标仅具描述性为由作出最终驳回决定。

如果申请者通过将其申请修正为向补充登记簿申请注册,对基于§2(e)(1)作出的不予注册决定提出反应,则此项修正即提出了一个需要审查员考虑的新问题(除非与未生效的拒绝决定不相关——*参见* TMEP §714.05(a)(i))。如果审查员判定该标识是申请者商品或服务的一般名称,则审查员即应拒绝在补充登记簿注册。此类拒绝决定的法律依据是《商标法》§23,15 U.S.C. §1091。此项决定必须是非终局性的。关于申请在补充登记簿注册的内容,*参见* TMEP §§815 及以下和§§816 及以下。

如果申请者修正申请,主张已经具备了 §2(f)所规定的独特性,那么就产生了一个新问题。*参见* TMEP §1212.02(h)。如果审查员判定该标识是申请者商品或服务的一般名称,则审查员即应继续根据 §2(e)(1)拒绝在补充登记簿注册。审查员也应解释为何对于获得性独特性的证明不够充分。此项决定必须是非终局性的。有关§2(f)所规定的独特性,参见 TMEP §§1212 及以下;关于 §2(f)所规定的有关一般性内容的证明,*参见* TMEP §1212.02(i)。

如有最大范围的可能,审查员须依照与任何其他申请同样的程序和标准,审查

standards that apply to any other application. *See In re American Psychological Association*, 39 USPQ2d 1467 (Comm'r Pats. 1996); TMEP §§1102 and 1102.01.

1209.03 Considerations Relevant to Determination of Descriptiveness

The following sections discuss factors and situations that often arise during a determination of whether a mark is descriptive or generic.

1209.03(a) Third-Party Registrations

Third-party registrations are not conclusive on the question of descriptiveness. Each case must stand on its own merits, and a mark that is merely descriptive should not be registered on the Principal Register simply because other such marks appear on the register. *In re Scholastic Testing Service, Inc.*, 196 USPQ 517 (TTAB 1977) (SCHOLASTIC held merely descriptive of devising, scoring and validating tests for others). The question of whether a mark is merely descriptive must be determined based on the evidence of record at the time registration is sought. *See In re Nett Designs Inc.*, 236 F.3d 1339, 57 USPQ2d 1564 (Fed. Cir. 2001); *In re Sun Microsystems Inc.*, 59 USPQ2d 1084 (TTAB 2001) (AGENTBEANS held merely descriptive of computer software for use in development and deployment of application programs on a global computer network).

1209.03(b) No Dictionary Listing

The fact that a term is not found in a dictionary is not controlling on the question of registrability if the examining attorney can show that the term has a well understood and recognized meaning. *See In re Orleans Wines, Ltd.*, 196 USPQ 516 (TTAB 1977) (BREADSPRED held merely descriptive of jellies and jams).

1209.03(c) First or Only User

The fact that an applicant may be the first and only user of a merely descriptive or

根据 §1(b)提出的意图使用申请,以确定 §2(e)(1)所规定的可注册性。参见 *American Psychological Association*, 39 USPQ2d 1467 (Comm'r Pats. 1996); TMEP §§1102 和 1102.01。

1209.03 判断描述性时的相关考虑

以下各节将讨论判断商标属于描述性还是一般性时经常发生的因素和情况。

1209.03(a) 第三方注册

第三方注册不是描述性问题的决定性因素。每个案件都必须根据其自身的情况来作判断,而仅具描述性的商标不应在联邦商标登记簿注册,原因只是在于其他此类商标已经获得了注册。见 *Scholastic Testing Service, Inc.*, 196 USPQ 517 (TTAB 1977)(对于为他人提供的设计、评分及验证服务而言,"SCHOLASTIC"被认为仅具描述性)。商标是否仅具描述性的问题必须根据提出注册申请时的档案证据加以判断。参见 *Nett Designs Inc.*, 236 F.3d 1339, 57 USPQ2d 1564 (Fed. Cir. 2001); *Sun Microsystems Inc.*, 59 USPQ2d 1084 (TTAB 2001)("AGENTBEANS"被认为对于研发全球网络应用程序所用的电脑软件而言仅具描述性)。

1209.03(b) 无词典条目

如果审查员能够证明词语具有一种得到充分公认的含义,那么对于可注册性问题,该词未列于词典之中就并非决定因素。参见 *Orleans Wines, Ltd.*, 196 USPQ 516 (TTAB 1977)("BREADSPRED"被认为对于果冻和果酱而言仅具描述性)。

1209.03(c) 首先及唯一使用者

如果词语所表达的唯一意义仅具描述性,那么申请者可能是该仅具描述性或一

generic designation does not justify registration if the only significance conveyed by the term is merely descriptive. *See In re National Shooting Sports Foundation, Inc.*, 219 USPQ 1018 (TTAB 1983) (SHOOTING, HUNTING, OUTDOOR TRADE SHOW AND CONFERENCE held apt descriptive name for conducting and arranging trade shows in the hunting, shooting and outdoor sports products field). *See also* TMEP §1212.06(e)(i) and cases cited therein.

1209.03(d) Combined Terms [R-2]

When two descriptive terms are combined, the determination of whether the composite mark also has a descriptive significance turns upon the question of whether the combination of terms evokes a new and unique commercial impression. If each component retains its descriptive significance in relation to the goods or services, the combination results in a composite that is itself descriptive. *In re Tower Tech, Inc.*, 64 USPQ2d 1314 (TTAB 2002) (SMARTTOWER merely descriptive of "commercial and industrial cooling towers and accessories therefor, sold as a unit"); *In re Sun Microsystems Inc.*, 59 USPQ2d 1084 (TTAB 2001) (AGENTBEANS merely descriptive of computer software for use in development and deployment of application programs on global computer network); *In re Putman Publishing Co.*, 39 USPQ2d 2021 (TTAB 1996) (FOOD & BEVERAGE ON-LINE held to be merely descriptive of news and information service for the food processing industry); *In re Copytele Inc.*, 31 USPQ2d 1540 (TTAB 1994) (SCREEN FAX PHONE merely descriptive of "facsimile terminals employing electrophoretic displays"); *In re Entenmann's Inc.*, 15 USPQ2d 1750 (TTAB 1990), *aff'd per curiam*, 928 F.2d 411 (Fed. Cir. 1991) (OATNUT held to be merely descriptive of bread containing oats and hazelnuts); *In re Serv-A-Portion Inc.*, 1 USPQ2d 1915 (TTAB 1986) (SQUEEZE N SERV held to be merely descriptive of ketchup and thus subject to disclaimer); *In re Wells Fargo & Co.*, 231 USPQ 95 (TTAB 1986) (EXPRESSERVICE held to be merely descriptive of banking and trust services); *In re Uniroyal, Inc.*, 215 USPQ 716 (TTAB 1982) (STEELGLAS BELTED RADIAL held merely descriptive of vehicle tires contai-

般性标识首先和唯一使用者的事实并不能导致其获得可注册性。参见 *National Shooting Sports Foundation*, *Inc*., 219 USPQ 1018 (TTAB 1983)[对于策划举办狩猎、设计及户外运动产品展览会的服务而言,"SHOOTING, HUNTING, OUTDOOR TRADE SHOW AND CONFERENCE"(室外展销会)被认为仅具描述性]。参见 TMEP §1212.06(e)(i)以及所引用的判例。

1209.03(d) 组合词语 [R-2]

如果两个描述性词语组合在一起,那么对于该复合商标是否也具有描述性意义的判断就会导致这种词语的组合是否能够引起一种全新和独特的商业印象的问题。如果各组成部分仍然保有其对于商品或服务的描述性质,那么组合形成的复合词本身也是描述性的。参见 *Tower Tech*, *Inc*., 64 USPQ2d 1314 (TTAB 2002)(对于"配套出售的工商用冷却塔及附件"而言,"SMARTTOWER"仅具描述性);*Sun Microsystems Inc*., 59 USPQ2d 1084 (TTAB 2001)(对于研发全球网络应用程序所用的电脑软件而言,"AGENTBEANS"仅具描述性);*Putman Publishing Co*., 39 USPQ2d 2021 (TTAB 1996)("FOOD & BEVERAGE ONLINE"被认为对于食品加工工业新闻资讯服务而言仅具描述性);*Copytele Inc*., 31 USPQ2d 1540 (TTAB 1994)(对于"采用电泳显示的传真终端"而言,"SCREEN FAX PHONE"仅具描述性);*Entenmann's Inc*., 15 USPQ2d 1750 (TTAB 1990), *aff'd per curiam*, 928 F.2d 411 (Fed. Cir. 1991)("OATNUT"被认为对于燕麦榛果面包而言仅具描述性);*Serv-A-Portion Inc*., 1 USPQ2d 1915 (TTAB 1986)("SQUEEZE N SERV"被认为对于番茄沙司而言仅具描述性,并因此而撤回);*Wells Fargo & Co*., 231 USPQ 95 (TTAB 1986)("EXPRESSERVICE"被认为对于银行及信托服务而言仅具描述性);*Uniroyal*, *Inc*., 215 USPQ 716 (TTAB 1982)("STEELGLAS BELTED RADIAL"被认为对于含有钢及玻璃带的汽车轮胎而言仅具描述性);*Bright-Crest*, *Ltd*., 204 USPQ

ning steel and glass belts); *In re Bright-Crest, Ltd.*, 204 USPQ 591 (TTAB 1979) (COASTER-CARDS held merely descriptive of coasters suitable for direct mailing).

However, a mark comprising a combination of merely descriptive components is registrable if the combination of terms creates a unitary mark with a unique, non-descriptive meaning, or if the composite has a bizarre or incongruous meaning as applied to the goods. *See In re Colonial Stores Inc.*, 394 F.2d 549, 157 USPQ 382 (C.C.P.A.1968) (SUGAR & SPICE held not merely descriptive of bakery products); *In re Shutts*, 217 USPQ 363 (TTAB 1983) (SNO-RAKE held not merely descriptive of a snow removal hand tool).

When there is evidence that the composite mark itself has been used together to form a phrase that is descriptive of the goods or services, it is unnecessary to engage in an analysis of each individual component. *In re Shiva Corp.*, 48 USPQ2d 1957 (TTAB 1998) (TARIFF MANAGEMENT merely descriptive of computer hardware and computer programs to control, reduce and render more efficient wide area network usage).

The Trademark Trial and Appeal Board has held that the addition of the prefix "e" does not change the merely descriptive significance of a term in relation to goods or services sold or rendered electronically, where the record showed that the "e" prefix has become commonly recognized as a designation for goods or services sold and/or delivered electronically. *In re SPX Corp.*, 63 USPQ2d 1592 (TTAB 2002) (EAUTODIAGNOSTICS merely descriptive of an "electronic engine analysis system comprised of a hand-held computer and related computer software"); *In re Styleclick.com Inc.*, 57 USPQ2d 1445 (TTAB 2000) (E FASHION merely descriptive of software used to obtain beauty and fashion information, and for electronic retailing services); *Continental Airlines Inc. v. United Airlines Inc.*, 53 USPQ2d 1385 (TTAB 1999) (E-TICKET generic for computerized reservation and ticketing of transportation services). Similarly, the prefix "i" or "I" would be understood by purchasers to signify Internet, when used in rela-

591 (TTAB 1979)(“COASTER-CARDS”被认为对于适合直邮销售的杯垫而言仅具描述性)。

但是,如果词语的组合造成了一种具有独特、非描述性含义的单一商标,或者适用于商品时具有独特或不一致的含义,那么由仅具描述性的组成部分构成的商标可以注册。*参见 Colonial Stores Inc.*, 394 F.2d 549, 157 USPQ 382 (C.C.P.A.1968) (“SUGAR & SPICE”被认为对于面包糕点产品而言并非仅具描述性); *Shutts*, 217 USPQ 363 (TTAB 1983)(“SNO-RAKE”被认为对于除雪工具而言并非仅具描述性)。

如果有证据表明,复合商标本身被一起用于构成某一对商品或服务进行描述的短语,那么就不必再对各单独组成部分进行分析了。见 *Shiva Corp.*, 48 USPQ2d 1957 (TTAB 1998)(对于电脑硬件以及管理、降低和实施更有效率的广域网所用的电脑程序而言,“TARIFF MANAGEMENT”被认为仅具描述性)。

商标评审及上诉委员会判定,附加前缀“e”并不能改变一个用于电子化销售或提供商品及服务的词语仅具描述性意义的性质,因为档案表明,前缀“e”已经被普遍公认为电子化销售和/或交付商品及服务的一种标识。*参见* SPX Corp., 63 USPQ2d 1592 (TTAB 2002)(对于“由手提电脑及相关软件组成的电子引擎分析系统”而言,“EAUTODIAGNOSTICS”仅具描述性); Styleclick. com Inc., 57 USPQ2d 1445 (TTAB 2000)(对于用于获取美容及时尚咨询的软件,以及电子零售服务而言,“E FASHION”仅具描述性); *Continental Airlines Inc. v. United Airlines Inc.*, 53 USPQ2d 1385 (TTAB 1999)(对于电脑化运输预订及订票服务而言,“E-TICKET”属于一般词语)。类似地,前缀“i”以及“I”在用于因特网相关的产品或服务时,会被购买

tion to Internet-related products or services. *See In re Zanova, Inc*., 59 USPQ2d 1300 (TTAB 2000) (ITOOL merely descriptive of computer software for use in creating web pages, and custom designing websites for others).

The addition of an entity designator (*e.g*., Corporation, Corp., Co., Inc., Ltd., etc.) to a descriptive term does not alter the term's descriptive significance, because an entity designation has no source-indicating capacity. *See In re Taylor & Francis [Publishers] Inc*., 55 USPQ2d 1213, 1215 (TTAB 2000) ("PRESS," as applied to a printing or publishing establishment, "is in the nature of a generic entity designation which is incapable of serving a source-indicating function"); *In re The Paint Products Co*., 8 USPQ2d 1863, 1866 (TTAB 1988) ("'PAINT PRODUCTS CO.' is no more registrable for goods emanating from a company that sells paint products than it would be as a service mark for the retail paint store services offered by such a company."); *In re Packaging Specialists, Inc*., 221 USPQ 917, 919 (TTAB 1984) (the element 'INC.' [in PACKAGING SPECIALISTS, INC.] has "no source indication or distinguishing capacity"). *See* TMEP §1213.03(d) regarding disclaimer of entity designators.

1209.03(e) More Than One Meaning

The fact that a term may have meanings other than the one relevant to a particular application is not controlling, because descriptiveness must be determined in relation to the goods or services for which registration is sought. *See In re Chopper Industries*, 222 USPQ 258 (TTAB 1984); *In re Bright-Crest, Ltd*., 204 USPQ 591 (TTAB 1979); *In re Champion International Corp*., 183 USPQ 318 (TTAB 1974).

See TMEP §1213.05(c) regarding wording that constitutes a "double entendre."

1209.03(f) Picture or Illustration

A visual representation that consists merely of an illustration of the goods, or of an article that is an important feature or characteristic of the goods or services, is

者理解为表示因特网。参见 *Zanova, Inc.*, 59 USPQ2d 1300（TTAB 2000)（对用于创建网页以及他人自定义设计网站的电脑软件而言,"ITOOL"仅具描述性）。

对描述性词语附加实体标示（例如,Corporation, Corp., Co., Inc., Ltd.,等等）并不能改变该词语的描述性质,因为实体标识不具有标示来源的功能。参见 *Taylor & Francis [Publishers] Inc.*, 55 USPQ2d 1213, 1215（TTAB 2000)（"PRESS"用于打印或出版公司时,"只具有一般实体标识的性质,不具有来源标示的功能"）; *The Paint Products Co.*, 8 USPQ2d 1863, 1866（TTAB 1988)（"'PAINT PRODUCTS CO.'不能再作为销售油漆产品的公司所出产商品的注册商标,而只能用作该公司提供的油漆零售服务的服务商标"）; *Packaging Specialists, Inc.*, 221 USPQ 917, 919（TTAB 1984)（"PACKAGING SPECIALISTS, INC."中的要素"INC."不具有"标示或区分来源的功能"）。有关撤回实体标识的情况,参见 TMEP §1213.03(d)。

1209.03(e)　　具有一种以上的含义

某词语除了与特定申请相关的含义之外另有其他含义,并不是决定性的,因为描述性必须与注册申请的商品或服务联系起来进行判断。参见 *Chopper Industries*, 222 USPQ 258（TTAB 1984）; *Bright-Crest, Ltd.*, 204 USPQ 591（TTAB 1979）; *Champion International Corp.*, 183 USPQ 318（TTAB 1974）。

有关构成"双关语"的构词,参见 TMEP §1213.05(c)。

1209.03(f)　　图片及图表

仅由商品,或是由构成商品及服务重要特性之事物的图示所构成的视觉表达,

merely descriptive under §2(e)(1) of the Act. *See In re Society for Private and Commercial Earth Stations*, 226 USPQ 436 (TTAB 1985) (representation of satellite dish held merely descriptive of services of an association promoting the interests of members of the earth station industry); *In re Underwater Connections, Inc.*, 221 USPQ 95 (TTAB 1983) (pictorial representation of a compressed air gas tank held merely descriptive of travel tour services involving underwater diving). *But see In re LRC Products Ltd.*, 223 USPQ 1250 (TTAB 1984) (stylized hand design found not merely an illustration of the goods, *i.e.*, gloves; thus not merely descriptive).

1209.03(g) Foreign Equivalents/Dead or Obscure Languages

The foreign equivalent of a merely descriptive English word is no more registrable than the English word itself. Words from modern languages are translated into English to determine descriptiveness or genericness. *In re Northern Paper Mills*, 64 F.2d 998, 17 USPQ 492 (C.C.P.A.1933). The test is whether, to those American buyers familiar with the foreign language, the word would have a descriptive or generic connotation. *In re Zazzara*, 156 USPQ 348 (TTAB 1967) (PIZZA FRITTE, the Italian equivalent of "fried buns," held incapable for fried dough). *See In re Oriental Daily News, Inc.*, 230 USPQ 637 (TTAB 1986) (Chinese characters that translate as ORIENTAL DAILY NEWS held merely descriptive of newspapers); *In re Geo. A. Hormel & Co.*, 227 USPQ 813 (TTAB 1985) (SAPORITO, an Italian word meaning "tasty," held merely descriptive because it describes a desirable characteristic of applicant's dry sausage); *In re Optica International*, 196 USPQ 775 (TTAB 1977) (OPTIQUE, a French word meaning "optic," held merely descriptive of eyeglass frames).

While foreign words are generally translated into English for purposes of determining descriptiveness, foreign words from dead or obscure languages may be so unfamiliar to the American buying public that they should not be translated into English for descriptiveness purposes. *See Enrique Bernat F. S. A. v. Guadalajara*

根据《商标法》§2(e)(1),属于仅具描述性的内容。参见 *Society for Private and Commercial Earth Stations*, 226 USPQ 436 (TTAB 1985)(卫星天线的图像被认为对于卫星地面站行业成员联合促销服务而言仅具描述性);*Underwater Connections, Inc.*, 221 USPQ 95 (TTAB 1983)(压缩空气储气罐的图像被认为对于涉及潜水的旅游服务而言仅具描述性)。不过,另请参见 *LRC Products Ltd.*, 223 USPQ 1250 (TTAB 1984)(风格化的手形图案被认为不仅仅是商品——即手套——的一种图示;因此并非仅具描述性)。

1209.03(g) 外语同义词/废弃或晦涩的语言

仅具描述性的英语词的外语同义词并不比该英语词本身更具可注册性。取自现代语言的词语会被译成英语以判断是否具有描述性或一般性。见 *Northern Paper Mills*, 64 F.2d 998, 17 USPQ 492 (C.C.P.A.1933)。判断标准在于,对于熟悉该外语的美国购买者,该词是否具有描述性或一般性的含义。见 *Zazzara*, 156 USPQ 348 (TTAB 1967)("fried buns"的意大利语同义词"PIZZA FRITTE"被认为不能注册为油炸面圈的商标)。参见 *Oriental Daily News, Inc.*, 230 USPQ 637 (TTAB 1986)(译为英文"ORIENTAL DAILY NEWS"的中文字被认为对于报纸而言仅具描述性);*Geo. A. Hormel & Co.*, 227 USPQ 813 (TTAB 1985)(意为"好味道"的意大利词"SAPORITO"被认为仅具描述性,因为它只是描述了申请者的干香肠的一种诱人特征);*Optica International*, 196 USPQ 775 (TTAB 1977)(意为"视觉"的法语词"OPTIQUE"被认为对于镜框而言仅具描述性)。

尽管判断描述性时,外语词语一般要译成英语,但如果词语是来自已经废弃或晦涩的语言,以至于美国购买公众非常不熟悉,就不应再为描述性之目的译成英语了。

Inc., 210 F.3d 439, 54 USPQ2d 1497 (5th Cir. 2000), *reh'g denied* 218 F.3d 745 (2000); *cf*. *General Cigar Co. Inc. v. G. D. M. Inc*., 988 F. Supp. 647, 45 USPQ2d 1481 (S.D.N.Y. 1997). The determination of whether a language is "dead" must be made on a case-by-case basis, based upon the meaning that the term would have to the relevant purchasing public.

Example: Latin is generally considered a dead language. However, if there is evidence that a Latin term is still in use by the relevant purchasing public (*e.g*., if the term appears in current dictionaries or news articles), then a Latin term is not considered dead. The same analysis should be applied to other uncommon languages.

1209.03(h) Incongruity

Arbitrary and incongruous combinations of English terms with terms from a foreign language have been found registrable. *See In re Johanna Farms Inc*., 8 USPQ2d 1408 (TTAB 1988) (LA YOGURT for yogurt held registrable on Principal Register under §2(f), with a disclaimer of "YOGURT"); *In re Universal Package Corp*., 222 USPQ 344 (TTAB 1984) (LE CASE held not merely descriptive of jewelry boxes and gift boxes and, therefore, registrable with a disclaimer of "CASE").

1209.03(i) Intended Users

A term that identifies a group to whom the applicant directs its goods or services is merely descriptive. *See Hunter Publishing Co. v. Caulfield Publishing Ltd*., 1 USPQ2d 1996 (TTAB 1986) (SYSTEMS USER found merely descriptive of a trade journal directed toward users of large data processing systems; evidence sufficient to establish distinctiveness under §2(f)); *In re Camel Mfg. Co., Inc*., 222 USPQ 1031 (TTAB 1984) (MOUNTAIN CAMPER held merely descriptive of retail mail order services in the field of outdoor equipment and apparel).

参见 Enrique Bernat F.S.A. v. Guadalajara Inc.，210 F.3d 439，54 USPQ2d 1497（5th Cir.2000），*reh'g denied* 218 F.3d 745（2000）；比较：*General Cigar Co. Inc. v. G.D.M. Inc.*，988 F.Supp.647，45 USPQ2d 1481（S.D.N.Y.1997）。判断某种语言是否是"死亡的"，必须基于个案的情况进行，考察该词语对于相关购买公众所能表示的含义。

> *例如*：拉丁语通常被认为是一种死语言。不过，如果有证据证明某拉丁词语仍然为相关购买公众所使用（例如，如果该词出现在现代词典或新闻文章中），则该拉丁词语就不被认为是已经死亡的。同样的分析应适用于其他非常用语言。

1209.03(h)　　不一致性

英语词语与外语词语任意和不一致的组合被判定可以注册。*参见 Johanna Farms Inc.*，8 USPQ2d 1408（TTAB 1988）（用于酸奶酪的"LA YOGURT"在撤回"YOGURT"后，被认为可以根据 §2(f) 在联邦商标登记簿注册）；*Universal Package Corp.*，222 USPQ 344（TTAB 1984）（"LE CASE"，"CASE"撤回申请后，被认为对于珠宝盒和礼物盒而言并非仅具描述性，因而可以注册）。

1209.03(i)　　意图使用者

识别申请者商品及服务指向群体的词语仅具描述性。*参见 Hunter Publishing Co. v. Caulfield Publishing Ltd.*，1 USPQ2d 1996（TTAB 1986）（指向大型数据处理系统用户的"SYSTEMS USER"被认为对于一份商业期刊而言仅具描述性；而有充分证据证明 §2(f) 所规定的独特性）；*Camel Mfg. Co., Inc.*，222 USPQ 1031（TTAB 1984）（"MOUNTAIN CAMPER"（山地露营者）被认为对于室外器材服装零售邮购服务而言仅具描述性）。

1209.03(j) Phonetic Equivalent

A slight misspelling of a word will not turn a descriptive or generic word into a non-descriptive mark. *See C-Thru Ruler Co. v. Needleman*, 190 USPQ 93 (E.D. Pa. 1976) (C-THRU held to be the equivalent of "see-through" and therefore merely descriptive of transparent rulers and drafting aids); *In re Hubbard Milling Co.*, 6 USPQ2d 1239 (TTAB 1987) (MINERAL-LYX held generic for mineral licks for feeding livestock).

1209.03(k) Laudatory Terms

Laudatory terms, those that attribute quality or excellence to goods or services, are merely descriptive under §2(e)(1). *See In re Nett Designs Inc.*, 236 F.3d 1339, 57 USPQ2d 1564 (Fed. Cir. 2001) (THE ULTIMATE BIKE RACK found to be merely descriptive and therefore subject to disclaimer); *In re Boston Beer Co. L. P.*, 198 F. 3d 1370, 53 USPQ2d 1056 (Fed. Cir. 1999) (THE BEST BEER IN AMERICA so highly laudatory and descriptive as applied to beer and ale that it is incapable of acquiring distinctiveness); *In re Best Software Inc.*, 58 USPQ2d 1314 (TTAB 2001) (the words BEST and PREMIER in mark BEST! SUPPORTPLUS PREMIER held merely descriptive of computer consultation and support services and thus subject to disclaimer); *In re Dos Padres Inc.*, 49 USPQ2d 1860 (TTAB 1998) (QUESO QUESADILLA SUPREME merely descriptive of cheese); *In re Consolidated Cigar Co.*, 35 USPQ2d 1290 (TTAB 1995) (SUPER BUY held merely descriptive of tobacco products); *General Foods Corp. v. Ralston Purina Co.*, 220 USPQ 990 (TTAB 1984) (ORIGINAL BLEND held merely descriptive of cat food).

1209.03(l) Telephone Numbers

If an applicant applies to register a designation that consists of a merely descriptive term with numerals in the form of an alphanumeric telephone number (*e.g.*, 800, 888 or 900 followed by a word), the examining attorney should refuse regis-

1209.03(j) 同音词

对词语拼写进行轻微的调整无法将一个描述性或一般性的词语变为一项非描述性的商标。参见 *C-Thru Ruler Co. v. Needleman*, 190 USPQ 93 (E.D.Pa.1976)("C-THRU"被认为等同于"see-through",因而对于透明的尺和制图辅助设备而言仅具描述性);*Hubbard Milling Co.*, 6 USPQ2d 1239 (TTAB 1987)("MINERAL-LYX"被认为属于牲畜饲养矿物添加剂的一般名称)。

1209.03(k) 赞美性词语

称赞商品或服务品质及优点的赞美性词语,根据§2(e)(1)属于仅具描述性的词语。参见 *Nett Designs Inc.*, 236 F.3d 1339, 57 USPQ2d 1564 (Fed. Cir. 2001)("THE ULTIMATE BIKE RACK"被判定仅具描述性,因此而被撤回);*Boston Beer Co. L. P.*, 198 F.3d 1370, 53 USPQ2d 1056 (Fed. Cir. 1999)("THE BEST BEER IN AMERICA"(美国最佳啤酒)用于啤酒和麦芽酒时被认为具有高度赞美性和描述性,因此不具备独特性);*Best Software Inc.*, 58 USPQ2d 1314 (TTAB 2001)("BEST! SUPPORTPLUS PREMIER"商标中的词语"BEST"(最佳)和"PREMIER"(优质)被认为对于电脑支持及咨询服务而言仅具描述性,因而被撤回);*Dos Padres Inc.*, 49 USPQ2d 1860 (TTAB 1998)(对于奶酪而言"QUESO QUESADILLA SUPREME"仅具描述性);*Consolidated Cigar Co.*, 35 USPQ2d 1290 (TTAB 1995)(对于烟草制品而言"SUPER BUY"仅具描述性);*General Foods Corp. v. Ralston Purina Co.*, 220 USPQ 990 (TTAB 1984)(对于猫食而言"ORIGINAL BLEND"被认为仅具描述性)。

1209.03(l) 电话号码

如果申请者申请注册的标识包含以混编电话号码形式出现的仅具描述性的数字和词语(例如,800, 888或900,后面加上某词语),审查员应当根据§2(e)(1)拒绝注册。

tration under §2(e)(1). *See In re Page*, 51 USPQ2d 1660 (TTAB 1999) (888 PATENTS merely descriptive of patent-related legal services). The fact that a designation is in the form of a telephone number is insufficient, by itself, to render it distinctive.

If the relevant term is merely descriptive, but not generic, the mark may be registered on the Principal Register with a proper showing of acquired distinctiveness under §2(f), or on the Supplemental Register. *See Express Mortgage Brokers Inc. v. Simpson Mortgage Inc.*, 31 USPQ2d 1371 (E. D. Mich. 1994) (369-CASH held merely descriptive but shown to have acquired distinctiveness as applied to mortgage brokering and mortgage-related services). Of course, the designation must also be used in the manner of a mark. *See* TMEP §§1202 *et seq*. regarding use as a mark.

If the proposed mark is generic, the designation is unregistrable on either the Principal or the Supplemental Register. However, to support a refusal of registration on the ground that a telephone number is generic, the Court of Appeals for the Federal Circuit has held that it is not enough to show that the telephone number consists of a non-source-indicating area code and a generic term. The examining attorney must show evidence of the meaning the relevant purchasing public accords the proposed alphanumeric mark as a whole. *In re Dial-A-Mattress Operating Corp.*, 240 F.3d 1341, 57 USPQ2d 1807, 1811 (Fed. Cir. 2001). *See also Dial-A-Mattress Franchise Corp. v. Page*, 880 F. 2d 675, 11 USPQ2d 1644 (2d Cir. 1989) (use of confusingly similar telephone number enjoined). *But see Dranoff-Perlstein Associates v. Sklar*, 967 F. 2d 852, 23 USPQ2d 1174, 1178 (3d Cir. 1992) ("[W]e decline to adopt the position espoused by the Second Circuit that telephone numbers which correlate to generic terms may be protectible as trademarks ... If telephone numbers that correlate to generic terms were granted protection, the first firm in a given market to obtain such a telephone number would, merely by winning the race to the telephone company, gain an unfair advantage over its competitors.") (footnotes omitted); 800 *Spirits Inc. v. Liquor By Wire, Inc.*, 14 F. Supp. 2d 675 (D. N. J. 1998) (800 SPIRITS generic for "gift delivery service of

参见 *Page*，51 USPQ2d 1660 (TTAB 1999)（“888 PATENTS”对于专利方面的法律服务而言仅具描述性）。以电话号码形式出现的标识本身不具有独特性。

如果相关词语仅具描述性，而不是一般性的，那么通过适当的证明该商标已经获得了 §2(f)所规定的独特性，就可以在联邦商标登记簿注册，或者直接在补充登记簿注册。参见 *Express Mortgage Brokers Inc. v. Simpson Mortgage Inc.*，31 USPQ2d 1371 (E.D. Mich. 1994)（用于抵押经纪以及抵押相关服务的“369-CASH”被认为仅具描述性，但是证明了已经具备独特性）。当然，该标识必须也是以商标的方式进行使用的。有关作为商标使用的内容，参见 TMEP §§1202 及以下。

如果申请注册的商标是一般性的，则该标识不得在联邦商标登记簿和补充登记簿注册。不过，在支持一项以电话号码具有一般性为由作出的拒绝予以注册决定时，联邦巡回区上诉法院认为，这不足以证明电话号码是由一个非来源标示性地区代码和一个一般性词语组成的。审查员必须提出相关购买公众在整体上所理解的该混编商标含义的证据。见 *Dial-A-Mattress Operating Corp.*，240 F.3d 1341，57 USPQ2d 1807，1811 (Fed. Cir. 2001)。另参见 *Dial-A-Mattress Franchise Corp. v. Page*，880 F.2d 675，11 USPQ2d 1644 (2d Cir. 1989)（禁止使用容易引起混淆的相似电话号码）。不过，请参见 *Dranoff-Perlstein Associates v. Sklar*，967 F.2d 852，23 USPQ2d 1174，1178 (3d Cir. 1992)（“我们不能采用第二巡回区法院所赞成的立场，即：涉及一般词语的电话号码也可以获得商标保护……如果涉及一般词语的电话号码获得了保护，那么首先在某一确定市场中获得此类电话号码的公司，仅仅通过赢得与电话公司竞赛的胜利，就可以获得针对其他竞争者的不公平优势。”）（脚注略）；800 *Spirits Inc. v. Liquor By Wire, Inc.*，14 F. Supp. 2d 675 (D.N.J. 1998)（对于“酒精饮料礼品送货服务”而言“800 SPIRITS”属于一般词语）。

alcohol beverages").

1209.03(m) Domain Names [R-2]

Internet domain names raise some unique trademark issues. A mark comprised of an Internet domain name is registrable as a trademark or service mark only if it functions as an identifier of the source of goods or services. Portions of the uniform resource locator (URL) including the beginning, ("http://www.") and the top level Internet domain name (TLD) (*e.g.*, ".com," ".org," ".edu,") function to indicate an address on the World Wide Web, and therefore generally serve no source-indicating function. *See* TMEP §§1215 *et seq*. regarding marks comprising domain names. TLDs may also signify abbreviations for the type of entity for whom use of the cyberspace has been reserved. For example, the TLD ".com" signifies to the public that the user of the domain name constitutes a commercial entity. *In re Martin Container, Inc.*, 65 USPQ2d 1058, 1060-1061 (TTAB 2002) ("[T]o the average customer seeking to buy or rent containers, "CONTAINER. COM" would immediately indicate a commercial web site on the Internet which provides containers."). *See also Goodyear's India Rubber Glove Mfg. Co. v. Goodyear Rubber Co.*, 128 U.S. 598, 602 (1888) ("The addition of the word 'Company' [to an otherwise generic mark] only indicates that parties have formed an association or partnership to deal in such goods ..." and does not render the generic mark registrable).

If a proposed mark includes a TLD such as ".com", ".biz", ".info", the examining attorney must provide evidence that the term is a TLD, and, if available, evidence of the significance of the TLD as an abbreviation (*e.g.* ".edu" signifies an educational institution, ".biz" signifies a business).

Because TLDs generally serve no source-indicating function, their addition to an otherwise unregistrable mark typically cannot render it registrable. *In re CyberFinancial.Net, Inc.*, 65 USPQ2d 1789, 1792 (TTAB 2002) ("Applicant seeks to register the generic term 'bonds,' which has no source-identifying significance in

1209.03(m)　　域名 [R-2]

因特网域名引发了一些特殊的商标问题。只有在具备商品或服务来源标示功能时,由因特网域名构成的商标才可以注册为商标或服务商标。统一资源定位符(URL)的部分,包括首部("http://www")以及标示万维网地址的因特网顶级域名(TLD)(例如,".com"、".org"、".edu"),因此通常不具有来源标示的功能。参见 TMEP §§1215 及以下,了解有关包含域名的商标的内容。TLD 也可以表示使用该电脑空间实体的类型缩写。例如,TLD ".com"向公众表示该域名的使用者由某商业实体构成。见 *Martin Container, Inc.*, 65 USPQ2d 1058, 1060-1061 (TTAB 2002)("对于希望购买或租赁集装箱的一般消费者而言,'CONTAINER.COM'立即表明了一个供应集装箱的因特网商业站点")。另参见 *Goodyear's India Rubber Glove Mfg. Co. v. Goodyear Rubber Co.*, 128 U.S. 598, 602 (1888)("[在一般性的商标上]加上'公司'一词,只能表示当事人已经成立了一个联合会或合伙组织以从事此类商品的交易……。"并不能使该一般性商标获得可注册性)。

如果申请注册的商标包含诸如".com"、".biz"、".info"之类的 TLD,审查员必须提出证据表明该词是一个 TLD,并且,如果可以,提出该 TLD 作为一种缩写的含义(例如,".edu"表示一所教育机构,".biz"表示一种商业活动)。

因为 TLD 一般不具有来源标示功能,所以附加于一项不可注册的商标时并不会使之具备可注册性。见 *CyberFinancial. Net, Inc.*, 65 USPQ2d 1789, 1792 (TTAB 2002)("申请者希望注册用于其服务时不具有来源识别作用的一般词语

connection with applicant's services, in combination with the top level domain indicator ".com," which also has no source-identifying significance. And combining the two terms does not create a term capable of identifying and distinguishing applicant's services."); *In re Martin Container*, 65 USPQ2d at 1061 ("[N]either the generic term nor the domain indicator has the capability of functioning as an indication of source, and combining the two does not result in a compound term that has somehow acquired this capability."). *See also Goodyear*, 128 U.S. at 602 (the incorporation of a term with no source-indicating function into an otherwise generic mark cannot render it registrable). For example, if a proposed mark is composed of merely descriptive term(s) combined with a TLD, the examining attorney must refuse registration on the Principal Register under Trademark Act §2(e)(1), 15 U.S.C. §1052(e)(1), on the ground that the mark is merely descriptive. *See* TMEP §1215.04.

Similarly, if a proposed mark is composed of generic term(s) for the applicant's goods or services and a TLD, the examining attorney must refuse registration on the ground that the mark is generic. *See* TMEP §§1209.01(c)(i) and 1215.05.

1209.03(n) "America" or "American"

If "AMERICA" or "AMERICAN" appears in a phrase or slogan, the examining attorney must evaluate the entire mark to determine whether it is merely descriptive as laudatory or even incapable. *In re Boston Beer Co. L. P.*, 198 F.3d 1370, 53 USPQ2d 1056 (Fed. Cir. 1999) (THE BEST BEER IN AMERICA so highly laudatory and descriptive as applied to beer and ale that it is incapable of acquiring distinctiveness); *In re Carvel Corp.*, 223 USPQ 65 (TTAB 1984) (AMERICA'S FRESHEST ICE CREAM held incapable); *In re Wileswood, Inc.*, 201 USPQ 400 (TTAB 1978) (AMERICA'S FAVORITE POPCORN held merely descriptive). Typically these marks primarily extol the quality or popularity of the goods or services and secondarily denote geographic origin. The examining attorney must look at each mark to determine whether it is capable, considering all relevant cir-

'bonds',与同样不具有来源标示意义的顶级域名标识'.com'构成的组合词。这两个词语的组合无法创造出一个能够识别并区分申请者服务的词语");*Martin Container*, 65 USPQ2d at 1061("无论是一般词语还是域名标识均不具有来源标示的功能,而这两者的组合也无法构成一个能够获得此种功能的复合词")。另参见 *Goodyear*, 128 U.S. at 602(不具来源标示功能的词语与另一个一般商标的结合不能使之具备可注册性)。例如,如果一项申请注册的商标有仅具描述性的词语和一个 TLD 构成,则审查员必须根据《商标法》§2(e)(1), 15 U.S.C. §1052(e)(1)的规定,以该商标仅具描述性为由拒绝在联邦商标登记簿注册。参见 TMEP §1215.04。

类似地,如果一项申请注册的商标由申请者商品或服务的一般名称和一个 TLD 构成,审查员也必须以该商标属于一般性名称为理由拒绝予以注册。参见 TMEP §§1209.01(c)(i)和 1215.05。

1209.03(n) "美国"及"美国的"

如果短语或口号中出现了"美国"或"美国的"字样,则审查员必须对整个商标进行评价,以判断其是否仅具描述性而属于赞美之辞,甚或不具商标功能。见 *Boston Beer Co. L. P.*, 198 F.3d 1370, 53 USPQ2d 1056 (Fed. Cir. 1999)("THE BEST BEER IN AMERICA"(美国最佳啤酒)用于啤酒和麦芽酒时具有高度赞美性和描述性,并因此无法具备独特性);*Carvel Corp.*, 223 USPQ 65 (TTAB 1984)("AMERICA'S FRESHEST ICE CREAM"(美国最新鲜奶油)被判定不得注册);*Wileswood, Inc.*, 201 USPQ 400 (TTAB 1978)("AMERICA'S FAVORITE POPCORN"(美国最受欢迎的爆米花)被认为仅具描述性)。通常此类商标主要是赞美商品的质量或受欢迎程度,而次要含义才是产地。审查员必须考察每个商标的情况,考虑所有相关

cumstances and case law. *See* TMEP §1210.02(c) and cases cited therein regarding use of terms such as "AMERICA," "AMERICAN," and "USA" in a way that is primarily geographically descriptive under 15 U.S.C. §1052(e)(2), primarily geographically deceptively misdescriptive under 15 U.S.C. §1052(e)(3), or deceptive under 15 U.S.C. §1052(a).

1209.03(o) "National" or "International"

The terms "NATIONAL" and "INTERNATIONAL" have been held to be merely descriptive of services that are international or nationwide in scope. *See Jefferson Bankshares Inc. v. Jefferson Savings Bank*, 14 USPQ2d 1443 (W.D. Va. 1989) (NATIONAL BANK merely descriptive of banking services); *National Automobile Club v. National Auto Club, Inc.*, 365 F.Supp.879, 180 USPQ 777 (S.D.N.Y.1973), *aff'd*, 502 F.2d 1162 (2d Cir. 1974) (NATIONAL merely descriptive of auto club services); *In re Institutional Investor, Inc.*, 229 USPQ 614 (TTAB 1986) (INTERNATIONAL BANKING INSTITUTE for organizing seminars for bank leaders of major countries held incapable); *In re Billfish International Corp.*, 229 USPQ 152 (TTAB 1986) (BILLFISH INTERNATIONAL CORPORATION merely descriptive of corporation involved with billfish on an international scale); *In re National Rent A Fence, Inc.*, 220 USPQ 479 (TTAB 1983) (NATIONAL RENT A FENCE merely descriptive of nationwide fence rental services); *BankAmerica Corp. v. International Travelers Cheque Co.*, 205 USPQ 1233 (TTAB 1979) (INTERNATIONAL TRAVELERS CHEQUE merely descriptive of financial consulting services that are international in scope); *National Fidelity Life Insurance v. National Insurance Trust*, 199 USPQ 691 (TTAB 1978) (NATIONAL INSURANCE TRUST merely descriptive of services of handling administrative matters in locating suitable insurance coverage for attorneys).

1209.03(p) Function or Purpose

Terms that identify the function or purpose of a product or service may be merely

环境以及判例法，以判断其是否可以注册。关于根据 15 U.S.C.§1052(e)(2)的规定，主要以地理描述性方式使用“AMERICA”、“AMERICAN”以及“USA”之类词语的情况，以及根据 15 U.S.C.§1052(e)(3)的规定，主要以地理欺骗性方式使用“AMERICA”、“AMERICAN”以及“USA”之类词语的情况，以及根据 15 U.S.C.§1052(a)的规定，以欺骗方式使用“AMERICA”、“AMERICAN”以及“USA”之类词语的情况，*参见* TMEP §1210.02(c)以及所引用的判例。

1209.03(o)　“国家的”及“国际的”

“国家的”和“国际的”两词被认为对于国际或全国范围的服务而言仅具描述性。*参见 Jefferson Bankshares Inc. v. Jefferson Savings Bank*, 14 USPQ2d 1443 (W.D. Va. 1989)(“NATIONAL BANK”对于银行服务而言仅具描述性)；*National Automobile Club v. National Auto Club, Inc.*, 365 F. Supp. 879, 180 USPQ 777 (S.D.N.Y. 1973), *aff'd*, 502 F.2d 1162 (2d Cir. 1974)(“NATIONAL”(全国)对于汽车俱乐部服务而言仅具描述性)；*Institutional Investor, Inc.*, 229 USPQ 614 (TTAB 1986)(“INTERNATIONAL BANKING INSTITUTE”(国际银行研究所)被判定不得为主要国家银行领导人组织讨论会的服务注册)；*Billfish International Corp.*, 229 USPQ 152 (TTAB 1986)(“BILLFISH INTERNATIONAL CORPORATION”对于涉及国际金枪鱼业务的公司而言仅具描述性)；*National Rent A Fence, Inc.*, 220 USPQ 479 (TTAB 1983)(“NATIONAL RENT A FENCE”对于全国范围栅栏租赁服务而言仅具描述性)；*BankAmerica Corp. v. International Travelers Cheque Co.*, 205 USPQ 1233 (TTAB 1979)(“INTERNATIONAL TRAVELERS CHEQUE”对于国际范围金融咨询服务而言仅具描述性)；*National Fidelity Life Insurance v. National Insurance Trust*, 199 USPQ 691 (TTAB 1978)(“NATIONAL INSURANCE TRUST”(全国保险信托)对于向律师提供确定适当保险范围的管理事务服务而言仅具描述性)。

1209.03(p)　功能及用途

根据15U.S.C.§1051(e)(1)的规定，识别产品或服务功能或用途的词语可能

descriptive or generic under 15 U.S.C. §1051(e)(1). *In re Gould Paper Corp.*, 834 F.2d 1017, 5 USPQ2d 1110 (Fed. Cir. 1987) (SCREENWIPE held generic for an anti-static cloth used for cleaning computer and television screens); *In re Central Sprinkler Co.*, 49 USPQ2d 1194 (TTAB 1998) (ATTIC generic for sprinklers installed primarily in attics); *In re Reckitt & Colman, North America Inc.*, 18 USPQ2d 1389 (TTAB 1991) (PERMA PRESS generic for soil and stain removers for use on permanent press products); *In re Wallyball, Inc.*, 222 USPQ 87 (TTAB 1984) (WALLYBALL held descriptive of sports clothing and game equipment); *In re National Presto Industries, Inc.*, 197 USPQ 188 (TTAB 1977) (BURGER held merely descriptive of cooking utensils); *In re Orleans Wines, Ltd.*, 196 USPQ 516 (TTAB 1977) (BREADSPRED held merely descriptive of jams and jellies).

1209.03(q) Source or Provider of Goods or Services

Terms that identify the source or provider of a product or service may be merely descriptive under 15 U.S.C. §1051(e)(1) or generic. *In re Major League Umpires*, 60 USPQ2d 1059 (TTAB 2001) (MAJOR LEAGUE UMPIRE merely descriptive of clothing, face masks, chest protectors and skin guards); *In re Taylor & Francis [Publishers] Inc.*, 55 USPQ2d 1213 (TTAB 2000) (PSYCHOLOGY PRESS merely descriptive of books in field of psychology); *In re The Paint Products Co.*, 8 USPQ2d 1863 (TTAB 1988) (PAINT PRODUCTS COMPANY incapable for paint); *In re The Phone Co., Inc.*, 218 USPQ 1027 (TTAB 1983) (THE PHONE COMPANY merely descriptive of telephones).

1209.03(r) Retail Store and Distributorship Services

A term that is generic for goods is descriptive of retail store services featuring those goods, when the goods are not a significant item typically sold in the type of store in question. *In re Pencils Inc.*, 9 USPQ2d 1410 (TTAB 1988) (PENCILS held merely descriptive of office supply store services). However, where the mat-

仅具描述性或者属于一般性。参见 *Gould Paper Corp.*, 834 F.2d 1017, 5 USPQ2d 1110 (Fed. Cir. 1987)（"SCREENWIPE"被认为对于清洁电脑及电视屏幕用的防静电织物而言属于一般词语）; *Central Sprinkler Co.*, 49 USPQ2d 1194 (TTAB 1998)（"ATTIC"对于室内喷淋装置而言属于一般词语）; *Reckitt & Colman, North America Inc.*, 18 USPQ2d 1389 (TTAB 1991)（"PERMA PRESS"对于耐久定形品用污渍清洗液而言属于一般名称）; *Wallyball, Inc.*, 222 USPQ 87 (TTAB 1984)（"WALLYBALL"被认为对于运动服装和比赛用品而言仅具描述性）; *National Presto Industries, Inc.*, 197 USPQ 188 (TTAB 1977)（"BURGER"被认为对于烹调器具而言仅具描述性）; *Orleans Wines, Ltd.*, 196 USPQ 516 (TTAB 1977)（"BREADSPRED"被认为对于果酱和果冻而言仅具描述性）。

1209.03(q) 商品或服务的来源及供应商

根据 15 U.S.C. §1051(e)(1)的规定，识别产品或服务来源及供应商的词语可能仅具描述性或者属于一般性。参见 *Major League Umpires*, 60 USPQ2d 1059 (TTAB 2001)（"MAJOR LEAGUE UMPIRE"对于服装、面具、护胸及皮肤防护装置而言仅具描述性）; *Taylor & Francis [Publishers] Inc.*, 55 USPQ2d 1213 (TTAB 2000)（"PSYCHOLOGY PRESS"（心理学出版社）对于心理学领域的书籍而言仅具描述性）; *The Paint Products Co.*, 8 USPQ2d 1863 (TTAB 1988)（"PAINT PRODUCTS COMPANY"（油漆产品公司）不得注册为油漆商标）; *The Phone Co., Inc.*, 218 USPQ 1027 (TTAB 1983)（"THE PHONE COMPANY"（电话公司）对于电话而言仅具描述性）。

1209.03(r) 零售商店及批发服务

如果商品并不是涉案商店通常所销售的重要物品，则该商品的一般名称对于经营该商品的零售商店而言就仅具描述性。见 *Pencils Inc.*, 9 USPQ2d 1410 (TTAB 1988)（"PENCILS"（铅笔）被认为对于办公用品商店服务而言仅具描述性）。但是，

ter sought to be registered identifies the primary articles of a store or distributorship service, the term is considered generic. *In re A La Vieille Russie, Inc.*, 60 USPQ2d 1895 (TTAB 2001) (RUSSIANART generic for dealership services in the field of fine art, antiques, furniture and jewelry); *In re Log Cabin Homes Ltd.*, 52 USPQ2d 1206 (TTAB 1999) (LOG CABIN HOMES generic for retail outlets selling kits for building log homes); *In re Bonni Keller Collections Ltd.*, 6 USPQ2d 1224 (TTAB 1987) (LA LINGERIE held generic for retail stores specializing in the sale of lingerie); *In re Wickerware, Inc.*, 227 USPQ 970 (TTAB 1985) (WICKERWARE generic for mail order and distributorship services in the field of products made of wicker); *In re Half Price Books, Records, Magazines, Inc.*, 225 USPQ 219 (TTAB 1984) (HALF PRICE BOOKS RECORDS MAGAZINES generic for retail book and record store services). The examining attorney, therefore, must analyze the term in relation to the services recited, the context in which it is used and the possible significance it would have to the recipient of the services. *Pencils*, 9 USPQ2d at 1411.

1209.03(s) Slogans

Slogans that are considered to be merely informational in nature or to be common laudatory phrases or statements that would ordinarily be used in business or in the particular trade or industry are not registrable. *In re Boston Beer Co. L. P.*, 198 F.3d 1370, 53 USPQ2d 1056 (Fed. Cir. 1999) (THE BEST BEER IN AMERICA so highly laudatory and descriptive as applied to beer and ale that it is incapable of acquiring distinctiveness). *See* TMEP §1202.04 and cases cited therein.

1209.04 Deceptively Misdescriptive Marks

Section 2(e)(1) of the Trademark Act, 15 U.S.C. §1052(e)(1), also prohibits registration of designations that are deceptively misdescriptive of the goods or services to which they are applied. The examining attorney must consider the mark in relation to the applicant's goods or services to determine whether a mark

如果申请注册的内容识别了商店的主要商品或者批发服务，该词会就被认为是一般性的。相关判例：*A La Vieille Russie*，*Inc*.，60 USPQ2d 1895（TTAB 2001）（"RUSSIANART"属于精美艺术品、古董、家具以及珠宝商店服务的一般词语）；*Log Cabin Homes Ltd*.，52 USPQ2d 1206（TTAB 1999）（"LOG CABIN HOMES"（木屋）属于经营原木屋建筑工具零售商店的一般词语）；*Bonni Keller Collections Ltd*.，6 USPQ2d 1224（TTAB 1987）（"LA LINGERIE"被认为属于专营女士紧身内衣零售商店的一般词语）；*Wickerware*，*Inc*.，227 USPQ 970（TTAB 1985）（"WICKERWARE"属于柳条制品邮购及批发服务的一般词语）；*Half Price Books*，*Records*，*Magazines*，*Inc*.，225 USPQ 219（TTAB 1984）（"HALF PRICE BOOKS RECORDS MAGAZINES"（搬家书籍、唱片、杂志）属于书籍和唱片零售商店服务的一般词语）。因此，审查员必须将所述服务、使用的环境以及可能对服务接受者造成的意义结合起来对该词语进行分析。见 *Pencils*，9 USPQ2d at 1411。

1209.03(s)　　　口号

被认为仅具有信息性的口号，或者通常用于商业或特定行业中的普通赞美之词或陈述不得注册。见 *Boston Beer Co*. *L*. *P*.，198 F. 3d 1370，53 USPQ2d 1056（Fed. Cir. 1999）（"THE BEST BEER IN AMERICA"（美国最佳啤酒）用于啤酒和麦芽酒时具有高度的赞美性和描述性，导致无法具备独特性）。*参见* TMEP §1202.04 以及所引用的判例。

1209.04　　　欺骗性虚假描述商标

《商标法》第 2(e)(1)节，15 U.S.C.§1052(e)(1)，同时对所适用商品及服务进行欺骗性错误描述的标识禁止注册。审查员必须将商标与申请者的商品及服务联系起来考虑，以判断某项商标是否属于欺骗性错误描述。

is deceptively misdescriptive.

The examining attorney must first determine whether a term is misdescriptive as applied to the goods or services. A term that conveys an immediate idea of an ingredient, quality, characteristic, function or feature of the goods or services with which it is used is merely descriptive. *See* TMEP §1209.01(b). If a term immediately conveys such an idea but the idea is false, although plausible, then the term is deceptively misdescriptive and is unregistrable under §2(e)(1). *See In re Woodward & Lothrop Inc.*, 4 USPQ2d 1412 (TTAB 1987) (CAMEO held deceptively misdescriptive of jewelry); *In re Ox-Yoke Originals, Inc.*, 222 USPQ 352 (TTAB 1983) (G.I. held deceptively misdescriptive of gun cleaning patches, rods, brushes, solvents and oils).

The Trademark Act does not prohibit the registration of misdescriptive terms unless they are deceptively misdescriptive, that is, unless persons who encounter the mark, as used on or in connection with the goods or services in question, are likely to believe the misrepresentation. *See Binney & Smith Inc. v. Magic Marker Industries, Inc.*, 222 USPQ 1003 (TTAB 1984) (LIQUID CRAYON held neither common descriptive name, nor merely descriptive, nor deceptively misdescriptive of coloring kits or markers).

As explained in the case of *In re Quady Winery Inc.*, 221 USPQ 1213, 1214 (TTAB 1984):

> The test for deceptive misdescriptiveness has two parts. First we must determine if the matter sought to be registered misdescribes the goods. If so, then we must ask if it is also deceptive, that is, if anyone is likely to believe the misrepresentation. *Gold Seal Co. v. Weeks*, 129 F. Supp. 928 (D.D.C. 1955), *aff'd sub nom. S. C. Johnson & Son v. Gold Seal Co.*, 230 F. 2d 832 (D. C. Cir.) (*per curiam*), *cert. denied*, 352 U. S. 829 (1956). A third question, used to distinguish between marks that are deceptive under Section 2(a) and marks that are deceptively misdescriptive under Section 2(e)(1), is whether the misrepresentation would material-

审查员必须首先判断某词语用于商品及服务时是否存在错误描述。传达了所适用商品及服务成分、质量、特性、功能或特征的即时印象的词语仅具有描述性。*参见* TMEP §1209.01(b)。如果某词语即时传达了这样一种印象，尽管这种印象似是而非，但却是错误的，那么该词语就存在欺骗性错误描述，并且根据 §2(e)(1)不得注册。*参见* 相关判例：*Woodward & Lothrop Inc.*, 4 USPQ2d 1412 (TTAB 1987) ("CAMEO"被认为是对于珠宝的欺骗性错误描述)；*Ox-Yoke Originals, Inc.*, 222 USPQ 352 (TTAB 1983)("G.I."被认为是对清洗枪支用的布片、杆棒、刷子、溶剂及润滑油的欺骗性错误描述)。

《商标法》并没有禁止错误描述性词语的注册，除非它们属于欺骗性错误描述，也就是说，除非在用于涉案商品或服务时，看到该商标的人可能相信这种错误表达。*参见 Binney & Smith Inc. v. Magic Marker Industries, Inc.*, 222 USPQ 1003 (TTAB 1984)("LIQUID CRAYON"(液体蜡笔)被认为对于染色工具或器具而言，既不属于普通描述性名称，也不是仅具描述性，也不属于欺骗性错误描述)。

正如在 *Quady Winery Inc.*, 221 USPQ 1213, 1214 (TTAB 1984)一案中所解释的：

> 对于欺骗性错误描述的检验分为两步。首先我们必须判断申请注册的内容是否对商品进行了错误描述。如果是，那么我们必须追问，它是否也是欺骗性的，也就是说，是否有人可能相信此种错误表达。*参见* 判例：*Gold Seal Co. v. Weeks*, 129 F. Supp. 928 (D.D.C. 1955), *aff'd sub nom. S.C. Johnson & Son v. Gold Seal Co.*, 230 F.2d 832 (D.C. Cir.)(*per curiam*), *cert. denied*, 352 U.S. 829 (1956)。第三个问题，用来区分第 2(a)节规定的欺骗性商标，和第 2(e)(1)节所规定的欺骗性错误描述商标，就是

ly affect the decision to purchase the goods. *Cf. In re House of Windsor, Inc.*, 221 USPQ 53 (TTAB 1983).

If the misdescription represented by the mark is material to the decision to purchase the goods or use the services, then the mark should be refused registration under §2(a) of the Trademark Act, 15 U.S.C. §1052(a). *See* TMEP §1203.02 regarding deceptive marks, and 1203.02(a) regarding the distinction between deceptive marks and deceptively misdescriptive marks.

The examining attorney should consider and make of record, or require the applicant to make of record, all available information that shows the presence or absence, and the materiality, of a misrepresentation. The mere fact that the true nature of the goods or services is revealed by other matter on the labels, advertisements or other materials to which the mark is applied does not preclude a determination that a mark is deceptively misdescriptive. *See R. Neumann & Co. v. Overseas Shipments, Inc.*, 326 F.2d 786, 140 USPQ 276 (C.C.P.A. 1964) (DURA-HYDE held deceptive and deceptively misdescriptive of plastic material of leather-like appearance made into shoes); *In re Woolrich Woolen Mills Inc.*, 13 USPQ2d 1235 (TTAB 1989) (WOOLRICH for clothing not made of wool found not to be deceptive under §2(a)); *Tanners' Council of America, Inc. v. Samsonite Corp.*, 204 USPQ 150 (TTAB 1979) (SOFTHIDE held deceptive within the meaning of §2(a) for imitation leather material).

See also Northwestern Golf Co. v. Acushnet Co., 226 USPQ 240 (TTAB 1985); *R. J. Reynolds Tobacco Co. v. Brown & Williamson Tobacco Corp.*, 226 USPQ 169 (TTAB 1985); and *American Speech-Language-Hearing Association v. National Hearing Aid Society*, 224 USPQ 798 (TTAB 1984) regarding the issue of deceptive misdescriptiveness.

Marks that have been refused registration pursuant to §2(e)(1) on the ground of deceptive misdescriptiveness may be registrable under §2(f) upon a showing of acquired distinctiveness, or on the Supplemental Register. 15 U.S.C. §§1052(f) and 1091. Marks that are deceptive under §2(a) are not registrable on either the Prin-

该错误表达是否会实质影响到购买该商品的决定。比较：*House of Windsor, Inc.*, 221 USPQ 53 (TTAB 1983)。

如果商标所表达的错误描述对于购买商品或使用服务的决定具有实质影响，那么就应当根据《商标法》§2(a)，15 U.S.C. §1052(a)的规定驳回该商标的注册申请。关于欺骗性商标的情况，*参见* §1203.02；关于欺骗性商标和欺骗性错误描述商标之间的区别，*参见* 1203.02(a)。

审查员应当考虑并解释档案，或者要求申请者解释档案中一切证明错误表达是否存在及其实质性的可用资料。商标所适用的商品或服务的真实性质系通过标签、广告或其他材料中的其他内容才得以表现，并不能就此得出该商标不属于欺骗性错误描述的判断。*参见 R. Neumann & Co. v. Overseas Shipments, Inc.*, 326 F.2d 786, 140 USPQ 276 (C.C.P.A. 1964)("DURA-HYDE"被认为对于塑料仿皮鞋面材料存在欺骗和欺骗性错误描述)；*Woolrich Woolen Mills Inc.*, 13 USPQ2d 1235 (TTAB 1989)(用于非羊毛制服装的"WOOLRICH"被判定并不具有§2(a)所规定的欺骗性)；*Tanners' Council of America, Inc. v. Samsonite Corp.*, 204 USPQ 150 (TTAB 1979)(用于仿皮材料的"SOFTHIDE"被认为具有 §2(a)所述的欺骗性)。

另参见 Northwestern Golf Co. v. Acushnet Co., 226 USPQ 240 (TTAB 1985)；*R.J. Reynolds Tobacco Co. v. Brown & Williamson Tobacco Corp.*, 226 USPQ 169 (TTAB 1985)；有关欺骗性错误描述的情况，*参见 American Speech-Language-Hearing Association v. National Hearing Aid Society*, 224 USPQ 798 (TTAB 1984)。

根据§2(e)(1)，以欺骗性错误描述为理由不予注册的商标，如能表明具备了独特性，可以根据 §2(f)准予注册，或者可以直接向联邦商标补充登记簿注册。15 U.S.C. §§1052(f) 和1091。具有§2(a)所规定的欺骗性的商标，在任何情况下，都不得在

cipal Register or the Supplemental Register under any circumstances.

1210 Refusal on Basis of Geographic Significance

Extract from 15 U.S.C.§1052. No trademark by which the goods of the applicant may be distinguished from the goods of others shall be refused registration on the principal register on account of its nature unless it—

(*a*) *Consists of or comprises ... deceptive ... matter; ... or a geographical indication which, when used on or in connection with wines or spirits, identifies a place other than the origin of the goods and is first used on or in connection with wines or spirits by the applicant on or after* [*January 1, 1996*].

...

(*e*) *Consists of a mark which ...* (*2*) *when used on or in connection with the goods of the applicant is primarily geographically descriptive of them, except as indications of regional origin may be registrable under section 4,* (*3*) *when used on or in connection with the goods of the applicant is primarily geographically deceptively misdescriptive of them ...*

Section 2(e)(2) of the Trademark Act, 15 U.S.C.§1052(e)(2), prohibits registration on the Principal Register of a mark that is primarily geographically descriptive of the goods or services named in the application. *See* TMEP §1210.01(a).

Section 2(e)(3) of the Trademark Act, 15 U.S.C.§1052(e)(3), prohibits registration of a mark that is primarily geographically deceptively misdescriptive of the goods or services named in the application. *See* TMEP §1210.01(b). Prior to the amendment of the Trademark Act on January 1, 1994, by the North American Free Trade Agreement Implementation Act, Public Law 103-182, 107 Stat.2057, the statutory basis for refusal to register primarily geographically deceptively misdescriptive marks was §2(e)(2).

Section 2(a) of the Trademark Act, 15 U.S.C.§1052(a), prohibits registration of

联邦商标登记簿或补充登记簿注册。

1210　以地理含义为理由拒绝予以注册

摘自 15 U.S.C.§1052。由于其性质,用于区别申请者商品与他人商品的商标均可以在联邦商标登记簿注册,除非——

(a)含有……欺骗性的……内容;……或一种地理标示,该标示用于葡萄酒或白酒时,识别了某一商品原产地以外的地理位置,并且申请者是在[1996 年 1 月 1 日]之时或以后首次将其用于葡萄酒或白酒。

……

(e)包含一种商标……(2)该商标用于申请者的商品时主要是一种地理性描述,除了作为原产地标识根据第 4 节可以注册,(3)该商标用于申请人的商品时,主要是对其的地理欺骗性错误描述……

《商标法》2(e)(2)节,15 U.S.C.§1052(e)(2),禁止主要是对申请中所述商品或服务进行地理描述的商标向联邦商标登记簿注册登记。*参见* TMEP §1210.01(a)。

《商标法》2(e)(3)节,15 U.S.C.§1052(e)(3),禁止主要是对申请中所述商品或服务进行欺骗性地理描述的商标注册登记。*参见* TMEP §1210.01(b)。在《北美自由贸易协议实施法》,Public Law 103-182, 107 Stat.2057 于 1994 年 1 月 1 日对《商标法》作出修正之前,对主要属地理性虚假描述商标拒绝予以注册的法律依据是§2(e)(2)。

《商标法》第2(a)节,15U.S.C.§1052(a)对包含欺骗性内容的标识,以及用于

a designation that consists of or comprises deceptive matter, as well as geographical indications which, when used on or in connection with wines or spirits, identifies a place other than the origin of the goods. *See* TMEP §§1210.01(c), 1210.05(a) and 1210.05(b).

See TMEP §1210.06(a) regarding the registrability of geographic terms on the Supplemental Register, TMEP §1210.06(b) regarding the registrability of geographic terms on the Principal Register under §2(f), and TMEP §1210.08 regarding disclaimer of geographic terms.

1210.01 Elements

1210.01(a) Geographically Descriptive Marks—Test

If a mark identifies the geographic origin of the goods or services, the issue is whether or not the mark is primarily geographically descriptive of the goods or services within the meaning of §2(e)(2) of the Trademark Act, 15 U.S.C. §1052(e)(2).

To establish a *prima facie* case for refusal to register a mark as primarily geographically descriptive, the examining attorney must show that:

(1) the primary significance of the mark is geographic (*see* TMEP §1210.02(b));

(2) purchasers would be likely to make a goods/place or services/place association, *i.e.*, to think that the goods or services originate in the geographic place identified in the mark (*see* TMEP §§1210.04 *et seq.*); and

(3) the mark identifies the geographic origin of the goods or services (*see* TMEP §1210.03).

A mark that is found to be primarily geographically descriptive within the mean-

葡萄酒及白酒时识别商品原产地以外地理位置的地理标识，禁止注册。*参见* TMEP §§1210.01(c)，1210.05(a)和1210.05(b)。

有关地理词语在联邦商标补充登记簿的可注册性，*参见* TMEP §1210.06(a)；关于地理词语根据 §2(f)在联邦商标登记簿的可注册性，*参见* TMEP §1210.06(b)；关于撤回地理词语的情况，*参见* TMEP §1210.08。

1210.01 各项原则

1210.01(a) 地理描述性商标——检验

如果一项商标识别了商品或服务的原产地，那么问题就在于，根据《商标法》§2(e)(2)，15 U.S.C.§1052(e)(2)所规定的含义，该商标是否主要是对商品或服务的地理描述。

为了初步证明可以主要属于地理描述为理由拒绝注册商标，审查员必须表明：

(1) 该商标的主要含义是地理性的(*参见* TMEP §1210.02(b))；

(2) 购买者可能会达成一种商品/地点或服务/地点的联系，亦即，认为商品或服务来源于商标所识别的地点(*参见* TMEP §§1210.04 及以下)；以及

(3) 该商标识别了商品或服务的原产地(*参见* TMEP §1210.03)。

一项商标如被判定符合§2(e)(2)所述的含义，主要属于地理描述，那么就可以

ing of §2(e)(2) may be registrable on the Principal Register under §2(f), or on the Supplemental Register. *See* TMEP §§1210.06(a) and (b).

1210.01(b) Geographically Deceptively Misdescriptive Marks—Test

If a mark identifies a place other than the place where the goods or services originate, the issue is: (1) whether the mark is primarily geographically deceptively misdescriptive of the goods or services within the meaning of §2(e)(3) of the Trademark Act, 15 U.S.C. §1052(e)(3); or (2) whether the mark is deceptive of the goods or services within the meaning of §2(a) of the Trademark Act, 15 U.S.C. §1052(a). *See* TMEP §§1210.01(c) and 1210.05(a) *et seq*. regarding geographically deceptive marks.

To support a refusal to register a mark as primarily geographically deceptively misdescriptive, the examining attorney must show that:

(1) the primary significance of the mark is geographic (*see* TMEP §1210.02(b));

(2) purchasers would be likely to make a goods/place or services/place association, *i.e.*, to think that the goods or services originate in the geographic place identified in the mark (*see* TMEP §§1210.04 *et seq*.); and

(3) the goods or services do not originate in the place identified in the mark (*see* TMEP §1210.03).

In re Save Venice New York Inc., 259 F.3d 1346, 59 USPQ2d 1778 (Fed. Cir. 2001); *In re Wada*, 194 F.3d 1297, 52 USPQ2d 1539 (Fed. Cir. 1999); *Institut National Des Appellations D'Origine v. Vintners Int'l Co. Inc*., 958 F.2d 1574, 22 USPQ2d 1190 (Fed. Cir. 1992); *In re Nantucket, Inc*., 677 F.2d 95, 213 USPQ 889 (C.C.P.A. 1982).

A mark that is primarily geographically deceptively misdescriptive may not be

根据 §2(f)在联邦商标登记簿注册，或者直接在补充登记簿注册。*参见* TMEP §§1210.06(a)和(b)。

1210.01(b) 地理欺骗性错误描述商标——检验

如果一项商标识别了某一商品或服务原产地以外的地点，那么问题就在于：(1)该商标是否在《商标法》§2(e)(3)，15 U.S.C. §1052(e)(3)所述含义下属于对商品或服务的地理欺骗性错误描述；或者(2)该商标是否在《商标法》§2(a)，15 U.S.C. §1052(a)所述含义下对商标或服务存在欺骗性。关于地理欺骗性商标的情况，*参见* TMEP §§1210.01(c)和 1210.05(a)及以下。

为了支持一项对地理欺骗性描述商标拒绝予以注册的决定，审查员必须证明：

(1) 该商标的主要含义是地理性的(*参见* TMEP §1210.02(b))；

(2) 购买者可能会达成一种商品/地点或服务/地点的联系，亦即，认为商品或服务来源于商标所识别的地点(*参见* TMEP §§1210.04 及以下)；以及

(3) 商品或服务并不来源于商标所识别的地点(*参见* TMEP §1210.03)。

相关判例：*Save Venice New York Inc.*, 259 F.3d 1346, 59 USPQ2d 1778 (Fed.Cir.2001)；*In re Wada*, 194 F.3d 1297, 52 USPQ2d 1539 (Fed.Cir.1999)；*Institut National Des Appellations D'Origine v. Vintners Int'l Co. Inc.*, 958 F.2d 1574, 22 USPQ2d 1190 (Fed.Cir.1992)；*Nantucket, Inc.*, 677 F.2d 95, 213 USPQ 889 (C.C.P.A.1982)。

主要属于地理欺骗性错误描述的商标不得在联邦商标补充登记簿注册，除非该

registered on the Supplemental Register unless the mark has been in lawful use in commerce since before December 8, 1993, and may not be registered on the Principal Register under §2(f) unless the mark became distinctive of the goods or services in commerce before December 8, 1993. TMEP §§1210.06(a) and (b). A mark that includes a primarily geographically deceptively misdescriptive term is unregistrable even with a disclaimer. *See* TMEP §1210.08.

1210.01(c) Geographically Deceptive Marks—Test

To support a refusal of registration on the ground that a geographic term is deceptive under §2(a), the examining attorney must show that:

(1) the primary significance of the mark is geographic (*see* TMEP §1210.02(b));

(2) the goods or services do not originate in the place identified in the mark (*see* TMEP §1210.03);

(3) purchasers would be likely to make a goods/place or services/place association, *i.e.*, to believe that the goods or services originate in the geographic place identified in the mark (*see* TMEP §§1210.04 *et seq.*); and

(4) a purchaser's erroneous belief as to the geographic origin of the goods or services would materially affect the purchaser's decision to buy the goods or use the services.

See Institut National des Appellations D'Origine v. Vintners Int'l Co., Inc., 958 F.2d 1574, 1580, 22 USPQ2d 1190, 1195 (Fed. Cir. 1992) (evidence showing that Chablis is name of region in France insufficient to establish that CHABLIS WITH A TWIST is geographically deceptive of wine under §2(a), where evidence showed that the term "Chablis" would be perceived by consumers in the United States as the generic name for a type of wine with the general characteristics of

商标于 1993 年 12 月 8 日之前已经合法地用于商业活动，而且，该商标不得根据§2(f)在联邦商标登记簿注册，除非该商标于 1993 年 12 月 8 日之前已经在商业活动中对其商品或服务具备了独特性。TMEP §§1210.06(a)和(b)。即使部分撤回，包含了主要属于地理欺骗性错误描述词语的商标也不得注册。*参见* TMEP §1210.08。

1210.01(c) 地理欺骗性商标——检验

为了支持一项以地理词语具有§2(a)所规定的欺骗性为理由作出的拒绝予以注册决定，审查员必须证明：

(1) 该商标的主要含义是地理性的(*参见* TMEP §1210.02(b))；

(2) 商品或服务并不来源于商标所识别的地点(*参见* TMEP §1210.03)。

(3) 购买者可能会达成一种商品/地点或服务/地点的联系，亦即，认为商品或服务来源于商标所识别的地点(*参见* TMEP §§1210.04 及以下)；以及

(4) 购买者对于商品或服务原产地的错误相信会实质性影响到购买者购买商品或使用服务的决定。

参见 Institut National des Appellations D'Origine v. Vintners Int'l Co., Inc., 958 F.2d 1574, 1580, 22 USPQ2d 1190, 1195 (Fed. Cir. 1992)（证据表明"Chablis"是一个法国地名，并不足以证明"CHABLIS WITH A TWIST"对于葡萄酒构成了 §2(a)所述的地理性欺骗，因为证据表明"Chablis"一词会被美国的消费者认作某种具有法国 chablis 酒普遍特性葡萄酒的一般名称）。

French chablis).

Section 2(a) is an absolute bar to registration on either the Principal or Supplemental Register. *See* TMEP §§1210.06(a) and (b). A disclaimer of the deceptive matter will not overcome a refusal under §2(a). *See* TMEP §1210.08.

See TMEP §§1210.05(a) *et seq*. for additional information about geographically deceptive marks.

1210.02 Primarily Geographic Significance

A mark is primarily geographic if it identifies a real and significant geographic location, and the primary meaning of the mark is the geographic meaning.

1210.02(a) Geographic Locations

A geographic location may be any term identifying a country, city, state, continent, locality, region, area or street.

The adjectival form of the name of a geographic location, a geographic nickname, or an abbreviation or other variant of the name of a geographic location is treated the same as the actual name of the geographic location if it is likely to be perceived as such by the purchasing public. *See In re Jack's Hi-Grade Foods, Inc.*, 226 USPQ 1028 (TTAB 1985) (NEAPOLITAN held primarily geographically deceptively misdescriptive of sausage emanating from the United States, where the term is defined as "of or pertaining to Naples in Italy").

A map or outline of a geographic area is treated the same as the actual name of the geographic location if it is likely to be perceived as such by the purchasing public. *See In re Canada Dry Ginger Ale, Inc.*, 86 F.2d 830, 32 USPQ 49 (C.C.P.A.1936) (map of Canada held to be the equivalent of the word "Canada"). *Cf. In re Texsun Tire and Battery Stores, Inc.*, 229 USPQ 227 (TTAB 1986) (indicating that if the depiction of a map is fanciful or so integrated with other elements of a

第 2(a)节构成了在联邦商标登记簿以及补充登记簿注册的绝对障碍。*参见* TMEP §§1210.06(a)和(b)。将欺骗性内容撤回并不能推翻根据 §2(a)作出的拒绝予以注册决定。*参见* TMEP §1210.08。

关于地理欺骗性商标的其他情况,参见 TMEP §§1210.05(a)及以下。

1210.02 主要地理含义

如果一项商标识别了一个真实且重要的地理位置,那么该商标就主要是地理性的,并且该商标的主要含义就是该地理含义。

1210.02(a) 地理位置

一种地理位置可以是识别某一国家、城市、州、大陆、地方、地区、区域或街道的任何词语。

如果同样可能被购买公众所认知,那么地理位置的形容词形式、地理昵称,或者是地理位置的缩写或其他名称变体都与该地理位置的实际名称一样对待。*参见 Jack's Hi-Grade Foods, Inc*., 226 USPQ 1028 (TTAB 1985)(对于产自美国的香肠,"NEAPOLITAN"被认为主要属于地理欺骗性错误描述,因为该词被定义为"属于或关于意大利那不勒斯的")。

如果同样可能被购买公众所认知,那么地理区域的地图或略图都与该地理位置的实际名称一样对待。*参见 Canada Dry Ginger Ale, Inc*., 86 F.2d 830, 32 USPQ 49 (C.C.P.A.1936)(加拿大地图被认为等同于"加拿大"一词)。比较:*Texsun Tire and Battery Stores, Inc*., 229 USPQ 227 (TTAB 1986)(指出,如果地图的形象是臆造的,或者与商标其他要素紧密结合而造成了单一的整体,那么该地图就不应被认为

mark that it forms a unitary whole, then the map should not be considered primarily geographically descriptive).

Vague geographic terms (*e. g.*, "Global," "National," "International," or "World") are *not* considered to be primarily geographic, though they may be merely descriptive or deceptively misdescriptive under §2(e)(1). *See* TMEP §1209.03(o).

See also In re Pebble Beach Co., 19 USPQ2d 1687 (TTAB 1991) (17 MILE DRIVE not a geographic term, where it refers to a specific location wholly owned by applicant, and was coined by applicant to refer both to applicant's services and the place where the services were performed).

1210.02(b) Primary Significance

To support a refusal to register geographic matter, the Trademark Act requires that the mark be *primarily* geographic, that is, that its primary significance be that of a geographic location. 15 U.S.C. §§1052(e)(2) and (3). *See*, *e.g.*, *In re Wada*, 194 F.3d 1297, 52 USPQ2d 1539 (Fed. Cir. 1999) (primary significance of NEW YORK held to geographic; Court was not persuaded by assertions that the composite NEW YORK WAYS GALLERY evokes a gallery that features New York "ways" or "styles"); *Scotch Whisky Ass'n v. U.S. Distilled Products Co.*, 952 F.2d 1317, 21 USPQ2d 1145 (Fed. Cir. 1991) (not necessary to show that term is "primarily recognized as a geographic term in and of itself" in order to state a claim under §2(a); allegations that Scottish surname MCADAMS is strongly associated by the United States public with Scotland, that it is a common practice to market Scotch whisky in the United States under marks comprising Scottish surnames, and that such marks have come to be understood by the United States public to identify the geographic origin of such goods found sufficient to state a claim under §2(a)); *In re Societe Generale des Eaux Minerales de Vittel S.A.*, 824 F.2d 957, 3 USPQ2d 1450 (Fed. Cir. 1987) (evidence insufficient to establish that public in United States would perceive VITTEL as the name of a place where cos-

主要是地理欺骗性的)。

含混的地理词语(例如,"全球的"、"全国的"、"国际的"及"世界的")*不被*认为主要是地理性的,尽管它们可能是仅具描述性或 §2(e)(1)所规定的欺骗性错误描述的。*参见* TMEP §1209.03(o)。

另参见 Pebble Beach Co., 19 USPQ2d 1687 (TTAB 1991)("17 MILE DRIVE"不是一个地理词语,而是指申请者完全所有的某特定地点,并且申请者创造了这个词以指称其服务以及提供服务的场所)。

1210.02(b) 主要含义

为了支持一项拒绝注册地理内容的决定,《商标法》规定商标须主要为地理性的,也就是说,其主要含义是指称某一地理位置。15 U.S.C.§§1052(e)(2)和(3)。*参见*判例:*Wada*, 194 F.3d 1297, 52 USPQ2d 1539 (Fed. Cir. 1999)("NEW YORK"的主要含义被认为是地理性的;法庭没有采纳词组"NEW YORK WAYS GALLERY"会使人想到一家带有纽约"方式"或"风格"画廊的主张);*Scotch Whisky Ass'n v. U.S. Distilled Products Co.*, 952 F.2d 1317, 21 USPQ2d 1145 (Fed. Cir. 1991)(不必表明该词语是"本身主要被认知为一个地理词语"以提出 §2(a)所规定的主张;认为,美国公众将苏格兰姓氏"MCADAMS"与苏格兰紧密联系,因此美国的市场惯例是以含有苏格兰姓氏的商标经营苏格兰威士忌酒,所以此类商标已经被美国公众理解为识别了此类商品的原产地,因而有充分理由根据§2(a)提出主张); *Societe Generale des Eaux Minerales de Vittel S.A.*, 824 F.2d 957, 3 USPQ2d 1450 (Fed. Cir. 1987)(证据不足以证明美国公众会将"VITTEL"认作化妆品产地的地名;法国地名 Vittel

metic products originate; Vittel, France found to be obscure); *In re Cotter & Co.*, 228 USPQ 202 (TTAB 1985) (WESTPOINT held not primarily geographically deceptively misdescriptive of various types of guns that are not produced in West Point, New York, the Board observing that the primary significance of WESTPOINT is as the name of the United States Military Academy rather than the town in New York); *In re Norfolk Wallpaper, Inc.*, 216 USPQ 903 (TTAB 1983) (THE NORFOLK PLAN held not primarily geographically descriptive of "installation of wallpaper and retail wallpaper store services," the Board noting that the examining attorney failed to make the necessary threshold showing of the relevant geographic place to which descriptiveness is attributed).

The fact that the mark has meaning or usage other than as a geographic term does not necessarily alter its primarily geographic significance. Thus, if a geographic term has another meaning, the examining attorney must determine whether the *primary* significance is geographic. If so, refusal of registration under §2(e)(2) or §2(e)(3) is appropriate. *See, e.g., In re Opryland USA Inc.*, 1 USPQ2d 1409, 1413 (TTAB 1986) (THE NASHVILLE NETWORK held primarily geographically descriptive of television program production and distribution services, the Board finding that the primary significance of the term was Nashville, Tennessee, and not that of a particular style of music); *In re Cookie Kitchen, Inc.*, 228 USPQ 873, 874 (TTAB 1986) (the fact that MANHATTAN identifies an alcoholic cocktail does not alter the primary significance of that term as a borough of New York City); *In re Jack's Hi-Grade Foods, Inc.*, 226 USPQ 1028, 1029 (TTAB 1985) (the fact that NEAPOLITAN identifies, among other things, a type of ice cream does not alter the primary significance of that term as meaning "of or pertaining to Naples in Italy").

However, if the most prominent meaning or significance of the mark is not geographic, or if the mark creates a separate readily understood meaning that is not geographic, then a refusal under §2(e)(2) or §2(e)(3) is not appropriate. *See Hyde Park Clothes, Inc. v. Hyde Park Fashions, Inc.*, 93 USPQ 250 (S.D.N.Y. 1951), *aff'd*, 204 F.2d 223, 97 USPQ 246 (2d Cir. 1953), *cert. denied*, 346 U.S.

被认为意义含混)；*Cotter & Co*., 228 USPQ 202 (TTAB 1985)(对于纽约西点镇生产的各种枪支,“WESTPOINT”被认为并不构成主要属地理欺骗性错误描述,委员会认为,“WESTPOINT”的主要含义是用作美国陆军学院的名称,而不是纽约的这个镇)；*Norfolk Wallpaper, Inc*., 216 USPQ 903 (TTAB 1983)(对于“墙纸铺设和零售商店服务”,“THE NORFOLK PLAN”被认为并非主要是地理描述性的,委员会称,审查员未能达到证明描述所指向的相关地点的最低要求)。

商标存在地理词语以外其他含义或用途的事实并不能必然改变其主要的地理性含义。因此,如果一个地理词语存在其他含义,审查员必须判断其主要含义是否是地理性的。如果是,那么就可以根据§2(e)(2)或§2(e)(3)拒绝予以注册。*参见*判例:*Opryland USA Inc*., 1 USPQ2d 1409, 1413 (TTAB 1986)(“THE NASHVILLE NETWORK”被认为对于电视节目制作和经销服务而言主要属于地理性欺骗,委员会判定该词的主要含义是田纳西州的Nashville,而不是某种特定风格的音乐)；*Cookie Kitchen, Inc*., 228 USPQ 873, 874 (TTAB 1986)(“MANHATTAN”识别了某种鸡尾酒的事实并不能改变该词是纽约市一个区的主要含义)；*Jack's Hi-Grade Foods, Inc*., 226 USPQ 1028, 1029 (TTAB 1985)(“NEAPOLITAN”除了识别其他事物以外,还识别了一种冰淇淋的事实并不能改变其“属于或关于意大利那不勒斯”的主要含义)。

不过,如果商标最显著的含义或意义并不是地理性的,或者如果该商标造成了一种独立的、易于理解的非地理性含义,那么就不能根据§2(e)(2)或§2(e)(3)拒绝予以注册。*参见 Hyde Park Clothes, Inc. v. Hyde Park Fashions, Inc*., 93 USPQ 250 (S.D.N.Y.1951), *aff'd*, 204 F.2d 223, 97 USPQ 246 (2d Cir.1953), *cert.denied*,

827, 99 USPQ 491 (1953) (primary significance of HYDE PARK for men's suits is to suggest that the product is stylish or of high quality rather than to provide information about geographic origin); *In re International Taste Inc*., 53 USPQ2d 1604, 1605-06 (TTAB 2000) (because of other prominent, significant meaning of HOLLYWOOD as referring to the entertainment industry in general, doubt about the primary significance of HOLLYWOOD was resolved in favor of the applicant); *In re Urbano*, 51 USPQ2d 1776, 1780 (TTAB 1999) (primary significance of SYDNEY 2000, used for advertising and business services and communication services, is as a reference to the Olympic Games, not to the name of a place within the meaning of §§2(e)(2) and 2(e)(3)); *In re Jim Crockett Promotions Inc*., 5 USPQ2d 1455, 1456 (TTAB 1987) (primary significance of THE GREAT AMERICAN BASH for promoting, producing and presenting professional wrestling matches, is to suggest something of desirable quality or excellence rather than to describe the geographic origin of the services); *In re Dixie Insurance Co*., 223 USPQ 514, 516 (TTAB 1984) (DIXIE held not primarily geographically descriptive of property and casualty underwriting services, where the examining attorney provided no evidence to show that the geographical significance of DIXIE was its primary significance). *See also In re Municipal Capital Markets Corp*., 51 USPQ2d 1369, 1371 (TTAB 1999) (COOPERSTOWN held not to be primarily geographically deceptively misdescriptive of restaurant services, the majority finding that the primary significance of COOPERSTOWN is that of "an institution, namely, the Baseball Hall of Fame" rather than a geographic location).

The fact that the mark identifies more than one geographic location does not necessarily detract from the term's primary geographic significance. *See, e.g., In re Loew's Theatres, Inc*., 769 F.2d 764, 226 USPQ 865, 868 (Fed. Cir. 1985) (DURANGO held primarily geographically deceptively misdescriptive of chewing tobacco not grown in Durango, Mexico, where the evidence of record showed that tobacco is a crop produced and marketed in that area, even though there is more than one place named Durango); *In re Cambridge Digital Systems*, 1 USPQ2d 1659, 1662 (TTAB 1986) (CAMBRIDGE DIGITAL and design ("DIGITAL" dis-

346 U.S.827，99 USPQ 491（1953）（对于男士套装，“HYDE PARK”的主要含义是暗示该产品紧跟潮流或者品质优良，而不是提供关于原产地的信息）；*International Taste Inc*.，53 USPQ2d 1604，1605－1606（TTAB 2000）（由于“HOLLYWOOD”一般指称娱乐业时所具有的突出、重要的含义，对于“HOLLYWOOD”主要含义的质疑最终通过支持申请者而加以解决）；*Urbano*，51 USPQ2d 1776，1780（TTAB 1999）（用于广告及商业服务和通讯服务时，“SYDNEY 2000”的主要含义是指奥运会，而不是指§§2(e)(2)和2(e)(3)所规定的地名）；*Jim Crockett Promotions Inc*.，5 USPQ2d 1455，1456（TTAB 1987）（用于促销、生产和展示职业摔跤比赛的“THE GREAT AMERICAN BASH”的主要含义是暗示某些诱人的品质或优点，而不是描述服务的原产地）；*Dixie Insurance Co*.，223 USPQ 514，516（TTAB 1984）（“DIXIE”被认为对于财产及事故保险服务而言并非主要属于地理性描述，因为审查员没有证据表明“DIXIE”的地理含义是其首要含义）。另参见 *Municipal Capital Markets Corp*.，51 USPQ2d 1369，1371（TTAB 1999）（“COOPERSTOWN”被认为对于餐饮服务而言并不主要属于地理欺骗性错误描述，多数意见判定，“COOPERSTOWN”的主要含义是“一种机构，即，棒球名人堂”，而不是一种地理位置）。

商标识别了一个以上的地理位置并不必然减损其主要地理含义。参见判例：*Loew's Theatres*，*Inc*.，769 F.2d 764，226 USPQ 865，868（Fed.Cir.1985）（“DURANGO”被认为主要是对非墨西哥Durango出产嚼烟的地理欺骗性错误描述，因为档案证据表明烟草是当地出产和交易的作物，即使有不止一个地方叫做Durango）；*Cambridge Digital Systems*，1 USPQ2d 1659，1662（TTAB 1986）（“CAMBRIDGE

claimed) held primarily geographically descriptive of computer system and parts thereof, where applicant's place of business is Cambridge, Massachusetts, even though there is more than one Cambridge).

When two geographical terms are combined in the same mark, the primary significance of the composite may still be geographic, if purchasers would believe that the goods or services originate from or are rendered in both of the locations named in the mark. *See In re Narada Productions, Inc.*, 57 USPQ2d 1801, 1803 (TTAB 2001) (CUBA L. A. primarily geographically deceptively misdescriptive of musical recordings and live musical performances that do not originate in Cuba or Los Angeles, the Board finding that purchasers would understand the composite as a reference to the two places named rather than to "some mythical place called 'Cuba L. A.'"); *In re London & Edinburgh Insurance Group Ltd.*, 36 USPQ2d 1367, 1369-70 (TTAB 1995) (LONDON & EDINBURGH INSURANCE primarily geographically descriptive of insurance and underwriting services that are rendered or originate in the cities of London and Edinburgh).

When a geographic term is combined with additional matter (*e.g.*, wording and/or a design element), the examining attorney must determine the primary significance of the composite. *See In re Bacardi & Co. Ltd.*, 48 USPQ2d 1031, 1034 (TTAB 1997) (HAVANA SELECT, HAVANA CLASICO, OLD HAVANA, HAVANA PRIMO, and HAVANA CLIPPER primarily geographically deceptively misdescriptive of rum, the Board finding that the added terms do not detract from primarily geographic significance). *See* TMEP §§1210.07 *et seq.* regarding composite marks that include geographic terms.

Generally, the addition of a highly descriptive or generic term to the name of a geographic place does not alter its primarily geographic significance. *See, e.g. In re JT Tobacconists*, 59 USPQ2d 1080, 1083 (TTAB 2001); *In re Carolina Apparel*, 48 USPQ2d 1542, 1543 (TTAB 1998); *In re Chalk's International Airlines Inc.*, 21 USPQ2d 1637, 1639 (TTAB 1991); *In re Wine Society of America Inc.*, 12 USPQ2d 1139, 1141-42 (TTAB 1989); *In re Cambridge Digital Systems, su-*

DIGITAL”及图案(“DIGITAL”撤回)被认为主要是对电脑系统及其组件的地理性描述,因为申请者的营业地位于马萨诸塞州的 Cambridge,尽管有不止一个“Cambridge”)。

如果同一商标中存在两个地理词语,则该组合的主要含义仍然可能是地理性的,只要购买者可能相信商品或服务同时来源或提供于该商标所述的地点。*参见 Narada Productions, Inc.*, 57 USPQ2d 1801, 1803 (TTAB 2001)(对于并非来源于古巴或洛杉矶的音乐录音制品以及现场表演,“CUBA L.A.”就主要是地理欺骗性错误描述,委员会判定购买者可能会将该词组理解为指代这两个地方,而不是“什么叫做‘Cuba L.A.’的传说中的地方”);*London & Edinburgh Insurance Group Ltd.*, 36 USPQ2d 1367, 1369 - 1370 (TTAB 1995)(“LONDON & EDINBURGH INSURANCE”主要属于对来源于伦敦及爱丁堡的保险承销服务的地理性描述)。

如果一个地理词语与其他内容(例如,文字和/或图案要素)组合在一起,审查员就必须判断该合成词的主要含义。*参见 Bacardi & Co. Ltd.*, 48 USPQ2d 1031, 1034 (TTAB 1997)(“HAVANA SELECT”、“HAVANA CLASICO”、“OLD HAVANA”、“HAVANA PRIMO”以及“HAVANA CLIPPER”主要是对朗姆酒的地理欺骗性错误描述,委员会判定附加词语并不能减损其主要地理含义)。有关包含地理词语的复合商标的情况,*参见* TMEP §§1210.07 及以下。

一般说来,在地名上加以高度描述性或一般性的词语,并不能改变其主要的地理性含义。*参见*判例:*In re JT Tobacconists*, 59 USPQ2d 1080, 1083 (TTAB 2001); *Carolina Apparel*, 48 USPQ2d 1542, 1543 (TTAB 1998); *Chalk's International Airlines Inc.*, 21 USPQ2d 1637, 1639 (TTAB 1991); *Wine Society of America Inc.*, 12 USPQ2d 1139, 1141 - 1142 (TTAB 1989); *Cambridge Digital Systems*, *案卷号同前*。

pra.

See TMEP §1210.04(d) regarding obscure or remote geographic marks.

1210.02(c) "America" or "American" and Similar Terms in Marks

When terms such as "AMERICA," "AMERICAN" and "USA" appear in marks, the determination as to whether the term or the entire mark should be considered geographic can be a particularly difficult one. There is no simple or mechanical answer to the question of how to treat "AMERICA" or "AMERICAN" in a mark. The examining attorney must evaluate each mark on a case-by-case basis. The examining attorney must consider the entire context, the type of goods or services at issue, the geographic origin of the goods or services and, most importantly, the overall commercial impression engendered by the mark at issue. The following principles, developed in the case law, should provide guidance in reaching a judgment in a given case.

(1) If "AMERICA" or "AMERICAN" is used in a way that primarily denotes the United States origin of the goods or services, then the term is primarily geographically descriptive. *See, e.g., American Diabetes Association, Inc. v. National Diabetes Association*, 533 F. Supp. 16, 214 USPQ 231 (E.D. Pa. 1981), *aff'd*, 681 F.2d 804 (3d Cir. 1982) (AMERICAN DIABETES ASSOCIATION held primarily geographically descriptive); *In re Monograms America, Inc.*, 51 USPQ2d 1317 (TTAB 1999) (MONOGRAMS AMERICA primarily geographically descriptive of consultation services for owners of monogramming shops); *In re BankAmerica Corp.*, 231 USPQ 873 (TTAB 1986) (BANK OF AMERICA held primarily geographically descriptive); *American Paper & Plastic Products, Inc. v. American Automatic Vending Corp.*, 152 USPQ 117 (TTAB 1966) (AMERICAN AUTOMATIC VENDING held primarily geographically descriptive). One commentator refers to such

有关含混或偏远地理性商标的情况，参见 TMEP §1210.04(d)。

1210.02(c)　商标中的“美国”或“美国的”及类似词语

如果商标中出现诸如“AMERICA”、“AMERICAN”以及“USA”的词语，则对于该词语以及整个商标是否应被认为是地理性的判断可能会异常困难。对于如何对待商标中的“美国”以及“美国的”的问题并没有简单或机械的答案。审查员必须根据个案情况对每个商标进行评估。审查员必须考虑整体环境、涉及的商品或服务的类型、该商品或服务的原产地，以及最重要的是涉案商标造成的整体商业印象。判例法所发展起来的下列原则，应在对特定案件作出判决的过程中起到指导作用。

(1)　如果“美国”及“美国的”的使用方式主要表明该商品或服务原产于美国，则该词语就主要是地理描述性的。参见 判例：*American Diabetes Association*, *Inc*. *v*. *National Diabetes Association*, 533 F. Supp. 16, 214 USPQ 231 (E. D. Pa. 1981), *aff'd*, 681 F. 2d 804 (3d Cir. 1982)（“AMERICAN DIABETES ASSOCIATION”被认为主要属于地理性描述）；*Monograms America*, *Inc*., 51 USPQ2d 1317 (TTAB 1999)（“MONOGRAMS AMERICA”对于为交织字母刺绣商店所有人提供的咨询服务而言，主要属于地理性描述）；*BankAmerica Corp*., 231 USPQ 873 (TTAB 1986)（“BANK OF AMERICA”被认为主要属于地理性描述）；*American Paper & Plastic Products*, *Inc*. *v*. *American Automatic Vending Corp*., 152 USPQ 117 (TTAB 1966)（“AMERICAN AUTOMATIC VENDING”被认为主要属于地理性描述）。一位阐释者将此类商标称为展示某种对“美

marks as exhibiting an "unadorned" use of "AMERICA" or "AMERICAN." 2 J. McCarthy, *McCarthy on Trademarks and Unfair Competition*, §14:11 (4th ed. 2000). Many service marks (*e.g.*, association-type marks) fall squarely into this category. *See also In re U.S. Cargo, Inc.*, 49 USPQ2d 1702 (TTAB 1998) (U.S. CARGO primarily geographically descriptive of towable trailers carrying cargo and vehicles).

(2) If a composite mark does not primarily convey geographic significance overall, or if "AMERICA" or "AMERICAN" is used in a nebulous or suggestive manner, then it is inappropriate to treat "AMERICA" or "AMERICAN" as primarily geographically descriptive. *See, e.g.*, *Hamilton-Brown Shoe Co. v. Wolf Brothers & Co.*, 240 U.S. 251 (1916) (THE AMERICAN GIRL held not primarily geographically descriptive for shoes); *American Plan Corp. v. State Loan & Finance Corp.*, 365 F.2d 635, 150 USPQ 767 (3d Cir. 1966), *cert. denied*, 385 U.S. 1011, 152 USPQ 844 (1967) (AMERICAN PLAN CORPORATION held not primarily geographically descriptive); *Wilco Co. v. Automatic Radio Mfg. Co., Inc.*, 255 F. Supp. 625, 151 USPQ 24 (D. Mass. 1966) (ALL AMERICAN held not primarily geographically descriptive); *In re Jim Crockett Promotions Inc.*, 5 USPQ2d 1455 (TTAB 1987) (THE GREAT AMERICAN BASH held not primarily geographically descriptive of wrestling exhibitions). The introduction of a nuance, even a subtle one, may remove a mark from the primarily geographically descriptive category. This area calls for the most difficult analysis. The examining attorney must determine whether the overall commercial impression is something other than primarily geographic — for example, due to double meanings or shades of suggestive meanings.

(3) If "AMERICA" or "AMERICAN" is used in virtually any manner with goods or services that are not from the United States, then the examining attorney should treat the term as primarily geographically deceptively misdescriptive under §2(e)(3) or even deceptive under §2(a), if

国”及“美国的”，“不加装饰的”使用。见：2 J. McCarthy，*McCarthy on Trademarks and Unfair Competition*，§14:11 (4th ed. 2000)。许多服务商标（例如，联合商标）完全属于此类别。*另参见* *U. S. Cargo，Inc.*，49 USPQ2d 1702 (TTAB 1998)（“U.S. CARGO”对于装载货物及车辆的拖车，主要属于地理性描述）。

(2) 如果一项符合商标在整体上主要表达的并不是地理含义，或者如果“美国”及“美国的”是以某种含混或暗示的方式使用，那么就不能认为“美国”及“美国的”主要是一种地理性描述。*参见* 判例：*Hamilton-Brown Shoe Co. v. Wolf Brothers & Co.*，240 U. S. 251 (1916)（“THE AMERICAN GIRL”；*American Plan Corp. v. State Loan & Finance Corp.*，365 F. 2d 635，150 USPQ 767 (3d Cir. 1966)，*cert. denied*，385 U. S. 1011，152 USPQ 844 (1967)（“AMERICAN PLAN CORPORATION”被认为主要并不是地理性描述）；*Wilco Co. v. Automatic Radio Mfg. Co., Inc.*，255 F. Supp. 625，151 USPQ 24 (D. Mass. 1966)（“ALL AMERICAN”被认为主要并不是地理性描述）；*Jim Crockett Promotions Inc.*，5 USPQ2d 1455 (TTAB 1987)（“THE GREAT AMERICAN BASH”被认为主要并不是对摔跤表演的地理性描述）。如果存在细微差别，甚至是极细小的那种，也可以将一项商标从主要属于地理性描述的范畴中划出。这一部分就会导致最艰难的分析。审查员必须判断，整体的商业印象是否不属于主要地理性——例如，由于双重含义或暗示含义的差别。

(3) 如果“美国”及“美国的”无论以何种方式用于实际上并非出自美国的商品或服务，那么审查员就可以相应地根据§2(e)(3)判定其为主要属地理欺骗

appropriate. *See*, *e. g.*, *Singer Mfg. Co. v. Birginal-Bigsby Corp.*, 319 F.2d 273, 138 USPQ 63 (C. C. P. A. 1963) (AMERICAN BEAUTY held primarily geographically deceptively misdescriptive when used on Japanese-made sewing machines); *In re Biesseci S. p. A.*, 12 USPQ2d 1149 (TTAB 1989) (AMERICAN SYSTEM and design ("AMERICAN" disclaimed) held deceptive for clothing manufactured in Italy). *Cf. In re Salem China Co.*, 157 USPQ 600 (TTAB 1968) (AMERICAN LIMOGES held deceptive under §2(a) when used on china not made in Limoges, France). In this situation, even marks that arguably convey a non-geographic commercial impression must be viewed with great skepticism. The cases indicate that if there is any likelihood that the inclusion of "AMERICA" or "AMERICAN" in a mark may mislead the public as to the national origin of the goods or services, the mark should be treated as at least geographically deceptively misdescriptive.

(4) If "AMERICA" or "AMERICAN" appears in a phrase or slogan, the examining attorney must evaluate the entire mark to determine whether it is merely descriptive as laudatory, or even incapable. *In re Boston Beer Co. L. P.*, 198 F. 3d 1370, 53 USPQ2d 1056 (Fed. Cir. 1999) (THE BEST BEER IN AMERICA so highly laudatory and descriptive as applied to beer and ale that it is incapable of acquiring distinctiveness); *In re Carvel Corp.*, 223 USPQ 65 (TTAB 1984) (AMERICA'S FRESHEST ICE CREAM held incapable); *In re Wileswood, Inc.*, 201 USPQ 400 (TTAB 1978) (AMERICA'S FAVORITE POPCORN held merely descriptive); *Kotzin v. Levi Strauss & Co.*, 111 USPQ 161 (Comm'r Pats. 1956) (AMERICA'S FINEST JEANS and AMERICA'S FINEST for overalls held not confusingly similar and incapable by inference). Typically these marks primarily extol the quality or popularity of the goods or services and secondarily denote geographic origin. *See* TMEP §1209.03(n) regarding use of terms such as "AMERICA" and "AMERICAN" in a way that is merely descriptive or generic.

性错误描述，甚或根据§2(a)判定其具有欺骗性。*参见* 判例：*Singer Mfg. Co. v. Birginal-Bigsby Corp.*, 319 F.2d 273, 138 USPQ 63 (C.C.P.A. 1963)(用于日本产缝纫机时，"AMERICAN BEAUTY"被认为主要属于地理欺骗性错误描述)；*Biesseci S.p.A.*, 12 USPQ2d 1149 (TTAB 1989)("AMERICAN SYSTEM"及图案("AMERICAN"撤回)用于意大利产服装时被认为存在欺骗性)。比较：*Salem China Co.*, 157 USPQ 600 (TTAB 1968)("AMERICAN LIMOGES"用于非法国 Limoges 产瓷器时被认为具有欺骗性)。在这种情况下，即使对于可以抗辩称其传达的是非地理性商业印象的商标，也必须用极其怀疑的态度进行审视。判例表明，如果存在任何可能，可以得出结论说商标中"美国"及"美国的"可能在商品或服务的原产国方面误导公众，那么该商标即应被至少视为属于地理欺骗性错误描述。

(4) 如果短语或口号中出现了"美国"或"美国的"字样，则审查员必须对整个商标进行评价，以判断其是否仅具描述性而属于赞美之辞，甚或不具商标功能。见 *Boston Beer Co. L. P.*, 198 F.3d 1370, 53 USPQ2d 1056 (Fed. Cir. 1999)("THE BEST BEER IN AMERICA"(美国最佳啤酒)用于啤酒和麦芽酒时具有高度赞美性和描述性，并因此无法具备独特性)；*Carvel Corp.*, 223 USPQ 65 (TTAB 1984)("AMERICA'S FRESHEST ICE CREAM"被判定不得注册)；*Wileswood, Inc.*, 201 USPQ 400 (TTAB 1978)("AMERICA'S FAVORITE POPCORN"被认为仅具描述性)；*Kotzin v. Levi Strauss & Co.*, 111 USPQ 161 (Comm'r Pats. 1956)("AMERICA'S FINEST JEANS"(美国最精美牛仔裤)和"AMERICA'S FINEST"(美国最精美)用于外衣时，通过介入干涉程序而被判定不属于混淆性相似，可以注册)。通常此类商标主要是赞美商品的质量或受欢迎程度，而次要含义才是产地。有关以某种仅具描述性或一般性的方式使用诸如"美国"以及"美国的"的词语，*参见* TMEP §1209.03(n)。

1210.02(d) Non-Geographic Characteristics of Goods or Services Conveyed by Geographic Terms

Geographic matter may serve to designate a kind or type of goods or services, or to indicate a style or design that is a feature of the goods or services, rather than to indicate their geographic origin. For example, the geographic components in terms such as "dotted swiss," "Boston baked beans," "Swiss cheese," "Early American design" and "Italian spaghetti" are not understood as indicating geographic origin of the goods but, rather, a particular type or style of product regardless of where it is produced. *See Forschner Group Inc. v. Arrow Trading Co. Inc.*, 30 F.3d 348, 31 USPQ2d 1614 (2d Cir. 1994) (SWISS ARMY KNIFE); *Hyde Park Clothes, Inc. v. Hyde Park Fashions, Inc.*, 93 USPQ 250 (S.D.N.Y. 1951), *aff'd*, 204 F.2d 223, 97 USPQ 246 (2d Cir. 1953), *cert. denied*, 346 U.S. 827, 99 USPQ 491 (1953) (primary significance of HYDE PARK for men's suits is to suggest that the product is stylish or of high quality rather than to provide information about geographic origin).

When geographic terms are used in circumstances in which it is clear that they are meant to convey some meaning other than geographic origin, registration should not be refused on the basis of geographical descriptiveness or misdescriptiveness. However, there may be some other basis for refusal; for example, the terms may be merely descriptive or deceptively misdescriptive of the goods or services under §2(e)(1) of the Act, 15 U.S.C. §1052(e)(1). *In re Busch Entertainment Corp.*, 60 USPQ2d 1130 (TTAB 2000) (EGYPT merely descriptive of subject matter or motif of amusement park services).

If it is unclear whether the primary significance of the term is geographic or merely descriptive or deceptively misdescriptive, the examining attorney may refuse registration on both grounds in the alternative.

1210.03 Geographic Origin of the Goods or Services

The question of whether a term is primarily geographically descriptive under

1210.02(d) 地理词语所表达的商品或服务的非地理特性

地理性内容也可以用来标示商品或服务的种类或类型，或者标示商品或服务的某种式样或设计，而不是标示其原产地。例如，词语中的地理组成部分，诸如“dotted swiss”（细点瑞士布）、“Boston baked beans”（波士顿烤豆）、“Swiss cheese”（瑞士奶酪）、“Early American design”（早期美国设计）以及“Italian spaghetti”（意大利通心面）等不会被理解为标示了商品的原产地，而是标示产品的某种特定类型或式样，无论它是在哪里生产的。*参见* 相关判例：*Forschner Group Inc. v. Arrow Trading Co. Inc.*, 30 F.3d 348, 31 USPQ2d 1614 (2d Cir. 1994)（“SWISS ARMY KNIFE”）；*Hyde Park Clothes, Inc. v. Hyde Park Fashions, Inc.*, 93 USPQ 250 (S.D.N.Y. 1951), *aff'd*, 204 F.2d 223, 97 USPQ 246 (2d Cir. 1953), *cert. denied*, 346 U.S. 827, 99 USPQ 491 (1953)（用于男装的“HYDE PARK”的主要含义是暗示该产品紧跟潮流或品质优良，而不是提供有关原产地的信息）。

如果地理词语使用的环境清楚地表明，它们是传达一些原产地以外的含义，那么就不能以地理性描述或错误描述为理由拒绝予以注册。不过，仍可以以其他理由拒绝予以注册；例如，根据《商标法》，15 U.S.C. §1052(e)(1)，该词语可能对于商品仅具描述性，或者存在欺骗性错误描述。见 *Busch Entertainment Corp.*, 60 USPQ2d 1130 (TTAB 2000)（对于游乐园服务的主题或主要内容，“EGYPT”仅具描述性）。

如果不清楚词语的主要含义是地理性的，还是仅具描述性，还是欺骗性错误描述，审查员可以同时以可采用的理由拒绝予以注册。

1210.03 商品或服务的原产地

词语是主要属于§2(e)(2)所规定的地理性描述，还是主要属于§2(e)(3)所规定

§2(e)(2) or primarily geographically deceptively misdescriptive under §2(e)(3) depends on whether or not the mark identifies the place from which the goods or services originate. Goods or services may be said to "originate" from a geographic location if, for example, they are manufactured, produced or sold there. *See Fred Hayman Beverly Hills Inc. v. Jacques Bernier Inc.*, 38 USPQ2d 1691 (TTAB 1996) (RODEO DRIVE held primarily geographically deceptively misdescriptive of perfume, where opposer's evidence showed that a significant number of Rodeo Drive retailers sell "prestige" fragrances, and that the public would be likely to make the requisite goods/place association between perfume and Rodeo Drive). *Cf. In re Jacques Bernier Inc.*, 894 F.2d 389, 13 USPQ2d 1725 (Fed. Cir. 1990) (RODEO DRIVE held not primarily geographically deceptively misdescriptive of perfume because of the lack of persuasive evidence of a goods/place association in the *ex parte* record).

Goods and services do not always originate from the applicant's place of business. *See In re Nantucket Allserve Inc.*, 28 USPQ2d 1144 (TTAB 1993) (NANTUCKET NECTARS held primarily geographically descriptive of soft drinks, even though the goods were manufactured elsewhere, where the record showed that applicant's headquarters and research and development division were on Nantucket, the distributor of the goods was located on Nantucket, the specimens indicated that the goods were "born" or "created" on Nantucket, and the goods were sold in the applicant's store on Nantucket); *In re Chalk's International Airlines Inc.*, 21 USPQ2d 1637 (TTAB 1991) (PARADISE ISLAND AIRLINES held primarily geographically descriptive of the transportation of passengers and goods by air, because the applicant's services included flights to and from Paradise Island, Bahamas, even though the flights were not based there); *In re Fortune Star Products Corp.*, 217 USPQ 277 (TTAB 1982) (NIPPON held not deceptive of, *inter alia*, radios and televisions because, although the applicant is an American corporation, the goods are made in Japan). *Cf. In re Gale Hayman Inc.*, 15 USPQ2d 1478 (TTAB 1990) (SUNSET BOULEVARD held not primarily geographically descriptive of perfume and cologne, the Board holding that the mere fact that appli-

的地理欺骗性错误描述，这一问题取决于该商标是否识别了商品或服务的产地。商品或服务可以被称为“产”自某一地点，如果，距离来说，它们是在那里制造、生产或销售的。参见 *Fred Hayman Beverly Hills Inc. v. Jacques Bernier Inc.*, 38 USPQ2d 1691 (TTAB 1996)(“RODEO DRIVE”被认为对于香水而言主要属于地理欺骗性错误描述，因为异议者的证据表明，相当数量的 Rodeo Drive 零售商出售“声誉卓著的”芳香剂，因此公众可能会认为香水和 Rodeo Drive 之间存在必然的商品/地点联系)。比较：*Jacques Bernier Inc.*, 894 F.2d 389, 13 USPQ2d 1725 (Fed. Cir. 1990)(“RODEO DRIVE”被认为对于香水而言不属于地理欺骗性错误描述，因为在单方档案中没有可靠证据表明存在商品/地点联系)。

商品和服务并不总是产自申请者的营业地。参见 *Nantucket Allserve Inc.*, 28 USPQ2d 1144 (TTAB 1993)(“NANTUCKET NECTARS”被认为对于软饮料而言主要属于地理性描述，即使该商品是在他处生产的，因为档案表明申请者的总部和研发部门位于楠塔基特(Nantucket)，商品批发商位于楠塔基特，样本显示该商品是在楠塔基特“出生”或“被创造”的，而且申请者在楠塔基特的商店也出售该商品)；*Chalk's International Airlines Inc.*, 21 USPQ2d 1637 (TTAB 1991)(“PARADISE ISLAND AIRLINES”被认为对于客货空运而言主要属于地理性描述，因为申请者的服务包括帕拉代斯岛(Paradise Island)和巴哈马(Bahamas)的来往航班，即使航班基地并不设在那里)；*Fortune Star Products Corp.*, 217 USPQ 277 (TTAB 1982)(“NIPPON”(日本)被认为对于电台和电视而言不存在欺骗性，因为，尽管申请者是一家美国公司，但商品是在日本制造的)。比较：*Gale Hayman Inc.*, 15 USPQ2d 1478 (TTAB 1990)(“SUNSET BOULEVARD”(日落大道)被认为对于香水和古龙水而言主要不属于地理性描述，委员会认为仅仅由于申请者的主要办事处位于日落

cant's principal offices are in Century City, close to Sunset Boulevard, does not mandate a finding that a goods/place association should be presumed, determining that the public would not make a goods/place association, and noting that there was no evidence that any perfume or cologne is manufactured or produced on Sunset Boulevard or that applicant's goods are sold there).

When the goods or services may be said to originate both in the geographic place named in the mark and outside that place, registration will normally be refused on the ground that the mark is primarily geographically descriptive under §2(e)(2) of the Trademark Act. *In re California Pizza Kitchen Inc.*, 10 USPQ2d 1704, 1706 n.2 (TTAB 1988) (CALIFORNIA PIZZA KITCHEN for restaurant services held primarily geographically descriptive, where the services were rendered both in California and elsewhere).

1210.04 Goods/Place or Services/Place Association

Refusal of registration under §2(e)(2) (primarily geographically descriptive), §2(e)(3) (primarily geographically deceptively misdescriptive), or §2(a) (deceptive) requires that there be a goods/place or services/place association such that the public is likely to believe that the goods or services originate in the place identified in the mark.

1210.04(a) Place Does Not Have to be Well Known for the Goods or Services

It is not necessary to show that the place identified in the mark is well known or noted for the goods or services to establish a goods/place or services/place association in support of a refusal under §2(e)(2) or §2(e)(3). *In re Broyhill Furniture Industries, Inc.*, 60 USPQ2d 1511 (TTAB 2001) (TOSCANA primarily geographically deceptively misdescriptive of furniture not originating in Tuscany, Italy); *In re JT Tobacconists*, 59 USPQ2d 1080 (TTAB 2001) (MINNESOTA CI-

大道附近的世纪城(Century City),不能得出结论认为应当假设存在一种商品/地点联系,判定公众不会产生某种商品/地点联系,并且解释道,没有证据证明有任何香水或古龙水是在日落大道制造或生产的,或者申请者的商品在该地销售)。

如果可以认为商品或服务同时产自商标中所提及的地点和其他地方,通常会根据《商标法》§2(e)(2)的规定,以该商标主要属于地理性描述为理由拒绝予以注册。见 *California Pizza Kitchen Inc.*, 10 USPQ2d 1704, 1706 n.2 (TTAB 1988)(用于餐饮服务的"CALIFORNIA PIZZA KITCHEN "被认为主要属于地理性描述,因为同时在加利福尼亚和其他地方提供了服务)。

1210.04　商品/地点或服务/地点联系

根据§2(e)(2)(主要属地理性描述)、§2(e)(3)(主要属地理欺骗性错误描述)、§2(a)(欺骗性)作出的拒绝予以注册决定要求存在某种商品/地点或服务/地点联系,以至于公众可能会相信商品或服务产自商标所识别的地点。

1210.04(a)　对于商品或服务而言,地点不必是著名的

要证明存在某种商品/地点或服务/地点以支持根据§2(e)(2)或 §2(e)(3)作出的拒绝予以注册的决定,并不需要表明商标所识别的地点对于商品或服务而言是著名或驰名的。相关判例:*Broyhill Furniture Industries, Inc.*, 60 USPQ2d 1511 (TTAB 2001)("TOSCANA"对于并非意大利托斯卡纳(Tuscany)出产的家具而言主要属于地理欺骗性描述);*JT Tobacconists*, 59 USPQ2d 1080 (TTAB 2001)("MINNESO-

GAR COMPANY primarily geographically descriptive of cigars); *In re California Pizza Kitchen Inc.*, 10 USPQ2d 1704 (TTAB 1988) (CALIFORNIA PIZZA KITCHEN held primarily geographically descriptive of restaurant services). The examining attorney "must show only a reasonable basis for concluding that the public is likely to believe the mark identifies the place from which the goods [or services] originate ..." *In re Loew's Theatres, Inc.*, 769 F.2d 764, 768, 226 USPQ 865, 868 (Fed. Cir. 1985) (evidence from a gazeteer and dictionary showing that tobacco is a crop produced and marketed in Durango, Mexico held sufficient to establish a *prima facie* goods/place association). *See* TMEP §1210.04(c) and cases cited therein.

If the place identified in the mark is well known or noted for the goods or services specified and the applicant's goods or services do not originate from that place, the mark is likely to be deceptive under §2(a). *Id.*, 769 F.2d at 768 n.6, 226 USPQ at 868 n.6. *See* TMEP §§1210.05(a) *et seq.* regarding deceptive geographical marks.

1210.04(b) Geographically Descriptive Marks—Association Presumed Unless Applicant Raises Genuine Issue as to Whether Primary Significance of Term is Geographic or Place is Obscure or Remote

When the geographic significance of a term is its primary significance and the geographic place is neither obscure nor remote, the goods/place or services/place association may ordinarily be presumed from the fact that the applicant's goods or services originate in the place named in the mark. *In re JT Tobacconists*, 59 USPQ2d 1080 (TTAB 2001) (MINNESOTA CIGAR COMPANY primarily geographically descriptive of cigars); *In re U. S. Cargo, Inc.*, 49 USPQ2d 1702 (TTAB 1998) (U. S. CARGO primarily geographically descriptive of towable trailers carrying cargo and vehicles); *In re Carolina Apparel*, 48 USPQ2d 1542 (TTAB 1998) (CAROLINA APPAREL primarily geographically descriptive of

TA CIGAR COMPANY"对于雪茄而言主要属于地理描述性)；*California Pizza Kitchen Inc.*，10 USPQ2d 1704 (TTAB 1988)("CALIFORNIA PIZZA KITCHEN"被认为对于餐饮服务而言主要属于地理性描述)。审查员"必须证明存在合理依据，以得出结论认为，公众可能相信该商标识别了商品[或服务]的产地……"见*Loew's Theatres, Inc.*，769 F.2d 764，768，226 USPQ 865，868 (Fed. Cir. 1985)(来自地名词典和字典的证据表明，烟草是墨西哥杜兰戈(Durango)生产销售的作物，被认为足以初步证明存在一种商品/地名联系)。*参见* TMEP §1210.04(c)以及所引用的判例。

如果商标所识别的地点对于所涉的商品或服务而言是驰名或著名的，而申请者的商品或服务并非产自该地点，则根据§2(a)该商标可能就是欺骗性的。*同前*，769 F.2d at 768 n.6，226 USPQ at 868 n.6。有关欺骗性地理商标的内容，*参见* TMEP §§1210.05(a)及以下。

1210.04(b) 地理描述性商标——推定联系，除非申请者提出真正的问题，涉及该词语的主要含义是否是地理性的，或者地点是否是含混或偏远的

如果词语的地理含义是其主要含义，并且该地点既非含混又非偏远，那么只要申请者的商品或服务产自该商标所述的地点，一般就可推定存在商品/地点或服务/地点联系。相关判例：*JT Tobacconists*，59 USPQ2d 1080 (TTAB 2001)("MINNESOTA CIGAR COMPANY"对于雪茄主要属于地理性描述)；*U.S. Cargo, Inc.*，49 USPQ2d 1702 (TTAB 1998)("U.S.CARGO"对于装载货物及车辆的拖车而言主要属于地理性描述)；*Carolina Apparel*，48 USPQ2d 1542 (TTAB 1998)("CAROLINA APPAREL"对于服装店零售服务而言主要属于地理性描述)；*Chalk's International Airlines Inc.*，21 USPQ2d 1637 (TTAB 1991)("PARADISE ISLAND

retail clothing store services); *In re Chalk's International Airlines Inc.*, 21 USPQ2d 1637 (TTAB 1991) (PARADISE ISLAND AIRLINES held primarily geographically descriptive of the transportation of passengers and goods by air); *In re California Pizza Kitchen Inc.*, 10 USPQ2d 1704 (TTAB 1988) (CALIFORNIA PIZZA KITCHEN held primarily geographically descriptive of restaurant services where applicant's services originate in California).

However, if the applicant provides information that creates a genuine issue as to whether the primary significance of the term is geographic or whether the place is obscure or remote, the examining attorney must submit evidence to establish the goods/place association. The Trademark Trial and Appeal Board has stated:

> We believe that, where the refusal to register is based on the Trademark Examining Attorney's finding that a mark is primarily geographically descriptive of the goods (that is, the goods actually come from the geographical place designated in the mark), the Trademark Examining Attorney would need to submit evidence to establish a public association of the goods with that place if, for example, a genuine issue is raised that (1) the place named in the mark may be so obscure or remote that purchasers would fail to recognize the term as indicating the geographical source of the goods to which the mark is applied or (2) an admittedly well-recognized geographical term may have other meanings, such that the term's geographical significance may not be the primary significance to prospective purchasers. Where, on the other hand, there is no genuine issue that the geographical significance of a term is its primary significance and where the geographical place is neither obscure nor remote, a public association of the goods with the place may ordinarily be presumed from the fact that the applicant's own goods come from the geographical place named in the mark.

In re Handler Fenton Westerns, Inc., 214 USPQ 848, 849-50 (TTAB 1982) (DENVER WESTERNS held primarily geographically descriptive of western-style

AIRLINES”被认为对于客货空运而言主要属于地理性描述)；*California Pizza Kitchen Inc.*，10 USPQ2d 1704（TTAB 1988)(“CALIFORNIA PIZZA KITCHEN”被认为对于餐饮服务而言主要属于地理性描述，因为申请者的服务来源自加利福尼亚)。

不过，如果申请者提供信息产生一个真正的争议，即，关于该词语的主要含义是否是地理性的，或者该地点是否是含混或偏远的，那么审查员就必须提出证据对商品/地点联系进行证明。商标评审及上诉委员会阐述道：

> 我们认为，如果由于商标审查员判定某商标主要属于对商品的地理性描述(亦即，商品实际来自于该商标所标示的地点)，从而做出拒绝予以注册的决定，那么，如果，例如，就(1)商标所指称的地点可能过于含混或偏远，以至于购买者无法识别该词语系标示该商标所适用商品的产地，或者(2)一个受到广泛承认的可识别地理词语可能有其他含义，如此该词语的地理含义对于潜在的购买者而言可能并非其主要含义产生争议，商标审查员则需要提出证据证明商品与该地点之间存在公众联想。另一方面，如果词语的首要含义是地理性含义，并且该地点既不含混也不偏远，对此并不存在真正的争议，那么一般可以根据申请者自己的产品来自于商标中所称的地点这一事实推定存在商品与地点的公众联想。

见 *Handler Fenton Westerns, Inc.*，214 USPQ 848，849－850（TTAB 1982)(“DENVER WESTERNS”被认为对于产自丹佛(Denver)的西式衬衫而言主要属于

shirts originating in Denver).

Thus, if a mark identifies the geographic origin of the goods or services, the examining attorney must determine: (1) whether there is a genuine issue as to whether the place identified in the mark is obscure or remote (*see* TMEP §1210.04(d)); and (2) whether the primary meaning of the mark is geographic (*see* TMEP §1210.02(b)). If there is no issue as to these considerations, a goods/place association may ordinarily be presumed from the fact that the applicant's own goods come from the geographic place identified in the mark.

However, if there is a genuine issue as to whether the place identified in the mark is obscure or remote, or whether the mark has a primary meaning that is not geographic, the examining attorney must provide evidence to establish an association between the goods or services and the place named in the mark. *In re John Harvey & Sons Ltd.*, 32 USPQ2d 1451 (TTAB 1994) (HARVEYS BRISTOL CREAM not primarily geographically descriptive of cakes flavored with sherry wine); *In re Gale Hayman Inc.*, 15 USPQ2d 1478 (TTAB 1990) (SUNSET BOULEVARD held not primarily geographically descriptive of perfume and cologne, the Board holding that the mere fact that applicant's principal offices are in Century City, close to Sunset Boulevard, does not mandate a finding that a goods/place association should be presumed). *See* TMEP §1210.04(c).

1210.04(c) Establishing Goods/Place or Services/Place Association

As noted in TMEP §1210.04(b), the examining attorney must submit evidence to establish a goods/place or services/place association if: (1) the goods or services do not originate in the place named in the mark; or (2) the goods or services originate in the place named in the mark, but there is a genuine issue as to whether the place is obscure or remote, or whether the primary significance of the place is geographic.

There is no requirement that the place identified in the mark be well known or

地理描述性)。

因此,如果一项商标识别了商品或服务的原产地,那么审查员就必须判断:(1)关于商标所识别的地点是否属于含混或偏远是否存在真正的争议(*参见* TMEP §1210.04(d));以及(2)该商标的主要含义是否是地理性的(*参见* TMEP §1210.02(b))。如果关于这些考虑均不存在争议,那么一般可以根据申请者自己的产品来自于商标中所识别地点这一事实推定存在商品/地点联系。

不过,如果关于商标所识别的地点是否是含混或偏远的,或者该词语的主要含义是否是地理性的存在真正的争议,那么审查员就必须提出证据证明在商品或服务与商标所指称地点之间存在联系。相关判例:*John Harvey & Sons Ltd*., 32 USPQ2d 1451 (TTAB 1994)("HARVEYS BRISTOL CREAM"用于雪利酒蛋糕时并非主要属于地理性描述);*Gale Hayman Inc*., 15 USPQ2d 1478 (TTAB 1990)("SUNSET BOULEVARD"被认为并非主要是对于香水和古龙水的地理性描述,委员会认为仅仅由于申请者的主要机构位于日落大道附近的世纪城这一事实,并不能得出结论认为可以推定存在一种商品/地点联系)。*参见* TMEP §1210.04(c)。

1210.04(c) 证明商品/地点或服务/地点联系

正如 TMEP §1210.04(b)所述,审查员必须提出证据证明存在商品/地点或服务/地点联系,只要:(1)商品或服务并非产自商标所指称的地点;或者(2)商品或服务来自商标所指称的地点,但关于该地点是否属于含混或偏远,或者该地点的首要含义是否是地理性的存在真正的争议。

要证明存在某种商品/地点或服务/地点以支持根据§2(e)(2)或§2(e)(3)作出

noted for the goods or services to find the existence of a goods/place or services/place association under §2(e)(2) or §2(e)(3). *See* TMEP §1210.04(a). The Court of Appeals for the Federal Circuit has held that to establish a goods/place or services/place association, the examining attorney must "show only a reasonable basis for concluding that the public is likely to believe the mark identifies the place from which the goods [or services] originate ..." *In re Loew's Theatres, Inc.*, 769 F.2d 764, 768, 226 USPQ 865, 868 (Fed. Cir. 1985) (evidence from a gazeteer and dictionary showing that tobacco is a crop produced and marketed in Durango, Mexico held sufficient to establish a *prima facie* goods/place association). *See In re Save Venice New York Inc.*, 259 F.3d 1346, 59 USPQ2d 1778 (Fed. Cir. 2001) (THE VENICE COLLECTION and design held primarily geographically deceptively misdescriptive of products that do not originate in Venice, Italy, where an atlas and a gazetteer showed that Venice was a large metropolitan area where fine art objects, glassware and decorative items had been made and sold for centuries, and a popular tourist destination); *In re Wada*, 194 F.3d 1297, 52 USPQ2d 1539 (Fed. Cir. 1999) (NEW YORK WAYS GALLERY held primarily geographically deceptively misdescriptive where manufacturing listings and Nexis® excerpts showed that handbags and luggage are designed and manufactured in New York); *In re Boyd Gaming Corp.*, 57 USPQ2d 1944 (TTAB 2000) (HAVANA RESORT & CASINO and ROYAL HAVANA RESORT & CASINO held primarily geographically deceptively misdescriptive of wearing apparel, beauty products and perfume that do not come from Havana, Cuba, where the record showed that Havana produces a variety of goods, including clothing and cosmetic items); *In re Bacardi & Co. Ltd.*, 48 USPQ2d 1031 (TTAB 1997) (HAVANA SELECT, HAVANA CLASICO, OLD HAVANA, HAVANA PRIMO, and HAVANA CLIPPER all held primarily geographically deceptively misdescriptive of rum that does not originate in Havana, Cuba, where the evidence showed that Havana is a major city and rum is a significant product); *In re Pan-O-Gold Baking Co.*, 20 USPQ2d 1761 (TTAB 1991) (NEW ENGLAND primarily geographically deceptively misdescriptive of bread and rolls that do not come from the New England area).

的拒绝予以注册的决定，并不需要表明商标所识别的地点对于商品或服务而言是著名或驰名的。参见 TMEP §1210.04(a)。联邦巡回区上诉法院已经确定，为了证明存在商品/地点或服务/地点联系，审查员必须"证明存在合理依据，以得出结论认为，公众可能相信该商标识别了商品[或服务]的产地……"见 *Loew's Theatres, Inc.*, 769 F.2d 764, 768, 226 USPQ 865, 868 (Fed. Cir. 1985)(来自地名词典和字典的证据表明，烟草是墨西哥杜兰戈生产销售的作物，被认为足以初步证明存在一种商品/地名联系)。参见相关判例：*Save Venice New York Inc.*, 259 F.3d 1346, 59 USPQ2d 1778 (Fed. Cir. 2001)("THE VENICE COLLECTION"及图案被认为对于并非来自于意大利威尼斯的产品而言主要属于地理性描述，因为地图集和地名词典表明，威尼斯是一个大城市，数百年来出产精美艺术品、玻璃器皿以及装饰物，并且是一个著名的旅游点)；*Wada*, 194 F.3d 1297, 52 USPQ2d 1539 (Fed. Cir. 1999)("NEW YORK WAYS GALLERY"被认为主要属于地理欺骗性错误描述，因为制造业列表以及 Nexis® (摘录表明，纽约有大量厂商设计制造各种手提包和行李箱)；*Boyd Gaming Corp.*, 57 USPQ2d 1944 (TTAB 2000)("HAVANA RESORT & CASINO"以及"ROYAL HAVANA RESORT & CASINO"被认为对于并非产自古巴哈瓦那的服饰、美容产品以及香水而言主要属于地理欺骗性错误描述，因为档案表明哈瓦那出产各种商品，包括服装和化妆品)；*Bacardi & Co. Ltd.*, 48 USPQ2d 1031 (TTAB 1997)("HAVANA SELECT"、"HAVANA CLASICO"、"OLD HAVANA"、"HAVANA PRIMO"以及"HAVANA CLIPPER"对于并非产于古巴哈瓦那的朗姆酒而言主要属于地理欺骗性错误描述，因为证据表明哈瓦那是一个大城市，且朗姆酒是其主要产品)；*Pan-O-Gold Baking Co.*, 20 USPQ2d 1761 (TTAB 1991) ("NEW ENGLAND"对于并非产自新英格兰地区的面包和面包卷而言主要属于地理欺骗性错误描述)。

In *Save Venice*, the Court noted that in the modern marketing context, geographic regions that are noted for certain products or services are likely to expand from their traditional goods or services into related goods or services, and that this would be expected by consumers. Accordingly, the could held that "the registrability of a geographic mark may be measured against the public's association of that region with both its traditional goods and any related goods or services that the public is likely to believe originate there." 259 F. 3d at 1355, 59 USPQ2d at 1784.

However, a showing that the geographic place is known to the public and could be the source of the goods or services may not be enough in itself to establish a goods/place or services/place association in all cases. *See In re Municipal Capital Markets Corp*., 51 USPQ2d 1369, 1371 (TTAB 1999) (COOPERSTOWN *not* primarily geographically deceptively misdescriptive of restaurant services; "the Examining Attorney must present evidence that does something more than merely establish that services as ubiquitous as restaurant services are offered in the pertinent geographic location"); *In re Venice Maid Co., Inc*., 222 USPQ 618, 619 (TTAB 1984) (VENICE MAID held *not* primarily geographically deceptively misdescriptive of canned foods, including, *inter alia*, lasagna and spaghetti, where the evidence of a goods/place association was found insufficient; "we are unwilling to sustain the refusal to register in this case simply on the basis that Venice is a large Italian city that could, conceivably, be the source of a wide range of goods, including canned foods").

The question of whether there is a goods/place or services/place association is determined on a case-by-case basis, based on the evidence in the record. *Compare Fred Hayman Beverly Hills Inc. v. Jacques Bernier Inc*., 38 USPQ2d 1691 (TTAB 1996) (RODEO DRIVE held primarily geographically deceptively misdescriptive of perfume, where opposer's evidence showed that a significant number of Rodeo Drive retailers sell "prestige" fragrances, and that the public would be likely to make the requisite goods/place association between perfume and Rodeo Drive) *with In re Jacques Bernier Inc*., 894 F. 2d 389, 13 USPQ2d 1725 (Fed. Cir. 1990)

在 *Save Venice* 案中，法庭阐述说，在现代市场环境中，用来标注特定产品或服务的地理区域可能从其传统的商品或服务扩展到关联商品或服务领域中去，而且消费者对此并不感到意外。因此，法庭认为“公众可能将地区与其传统产品，以及一切公众可能认为产自该地的关联产品或服务都进行联系，于是对于一项地理商标的可注册性的衡量就可能有悖于这种公众联想”。259 F.3d 1355，59 USPQ2d 1784。

不过，证明地点为公众所知晓并可以是商品或服务的来源，本身可能并不足以证明在一切情况下均存在一种商品/地点或服务/地点联系。*参见* 相关判例：*Municipal Capital Markets Corp*.，51 USPQ2d 1369，1371（TTAB 1999）（“COOPERSTOWN”对于餐饮服务并非主要属于地理欺骗性错误描述；“审查员必须提出证据，而不是仅仅证明此种服务像所有餐饮服务一样在相关的地点提供”）；*Venice Maid Co*.，*Inc*.，222 USPQ 618，619（TTAB 1984）（“VENICE MAID”被认为对于罐头食品——其中包括卤汁面条和意大利细面条——而言并非主要属于地理欺骗性错误描述，因为商品/地点的证据被判定不足；“在本案中，我们不愿意简单地以威尼斯是个意大利大城市，因此必然是许多商品，包括罐头食品的产地为理由而维持不予注册的决定”）。

是否存在商品/地点或服务/地点联系的问题应根据个案的不同情况，基于档案证据加以判断。比较 *Fred Hayman Beverly Hills Inc*. *v*. *Jacques Bernier Inc*.，38 USPQ2d 1691（TTAB 1996）（“RODEO DRIVE”被认为用于香水时主要属于地理欺骗性错误描述，因为异议者的证据表明，相当数量的 Rodeo Drive 零售商出售“声誉卓著的”芳香剂，因此公众可能会认为香水和 Rodeo Drive 之间存在必然的商品/地点联系。）与 *Jacques Bernier Inc*.，894 F.2d 389，13 USPQ2d 1725（Fed. Cir. 1990）

(RODEO DRIVE held not primarily geographically deceptively misdescriptive of perfume because of the lack of persuasive evidence of a goods/place association in the *ex parte* record). *See also Philip Morris Inc. v. Reemtsma Cigarettenfabriken GmbH*, 14 USPQ2d 1487 (TTAB 1990) (PARK AVENUE held neither deceptive nor geographically deceptively misdescriptive as applied to cigarettes and smoking tobacco, the Board finding no goods/place association between tobacco products and Park Avenue in New York City, on which opposer's world headquarters was located).

To establish a goods/place or services/place association, the examining attorney may provide such evidence as excerpts from telephone directories, gazetteers, encyclopedias, geographic dictionaries, or the LEXIS-NEXIS® database. The examining attorney should also examine the specimen(s) and any other evidence in the record that shows the context in which the applicant's mark is used.

1210.04(d) Obscure or Remote Geographic Marks

As noted in TMEP §1210.04(b), if there is a genuine question as to whether the place identified in the mark is obscure or remote, or whether the term has a primary meaning that is not geographic, the examining attorney must provide evidence to establish the goods/place or services/place association. *See, e.g., In re John Harvey & Sons Ltd.*, 32 USPQ2d 1451 (TTAB 1994) (HARVEYS BRISTOL CREAM not primarily geographically descriptive of cakes flavored with sherry wine); *In re Bavaria St. Pauli Brauerei AG*, 222 USPQ 926 (TTAB 1984) (reversing examining attorney's requirement for disclaimer of "JEVER" in application to register JEVER and design for beer originating in Jever, West Germany, where the sole evidence of a goods/place association was an entry from a 32-year-old geographic index); *In re Brauerei Aying Franz Inselkammer KG*, 217 USPQ 73 (TTAB 1983) (AYINGER BIER ("BIER" disclaimed) held not primarily geographically descriptive of beer emanating from Aying, West Germany, a hamlet of 500 inhabitants, where the examining attorney's evidence of a goods/place as-

（“RODEO DRIVE”被认为对于香水而言不属于地理欺骗性错误描述，因为在单方档案中没有可靠证据表明存在商品/地点联系）。*另参见 Philip Morris Inc. v. Reemtsma Cigarettenfabriken GmbH*，14 USPQ2d 1487（TTAB 1990）（用于烟卷和烟草时，“PARK AVENUE”被认为既不带有欺骗性，也并非地理欺骗性错误描述，委员会判定烟草产品和异议者总部所在地纽约市 Park 大街之间并不存在商品/地点联系）。

为了证明某种商品/地点或服务/地点联系，审查员可以提供诸如来自于电话地址名录、地名词典、百科全书、地理学词典，或者 LEXIS-NEXIS® 数据库的摘录以作为证据。审查员还应当审查样本和其他一切表明申请者商标使用环境的档案证据。

1210.04(d) 含混或偏远的地理商标

正如 TMEP §1210.04(b)所述，如果关于商标所识别的地点是否是含混或偏远的，或者该词语的主要含义是否是地理性的存在真正的争议，那么审查员就必须提出证据证明存在商品/地点或服务/地点联系。*参见*判例：*John Harvey & Sons Ltd.*，32 USPQ2d 1451（TTAB 1994）（“HARVEYS BRISTOL CREAM”用于雪利酒蛋糕时并非主要属于地理性描述）；*Bavaria St. Pauli Brauerei AG*，222 USPQ 926（TTAB 1984）（对于为产自西德耶弗尔（Jever）的啤酒注册“JEVER”及图案的申请，维持审查员要求撤回“JEVER”的决定，因为商品/地点联系的唯一证据来自一本有 32 年历史的地理学索引中的条目）；*Brauerei Aying Franz Inselkammer KG*，217 USPQ 73（TTAB 1983）（对于产自西德阿伊因（Aying）——一个只有 500 名居民的小镇——的啤酒，“AYINGER BIER”（“BIER”撤回）被认为并非主要属于地理性描述，因为审查员关于商品/地点联系的证据是将 Aying 识别为原产地的样本标签）。

sociation was the specimen label identifying Aying as the place of origin).

Geographic matter may be so obscure or remote that it would not be recognized as an indication of the geographic source of the goods or services. In such a case, the mark is treated as an arbitrary designation (*see* TMEP §1210.04(e)) because its geographic meaning is likely to be lost on consumers and not perceived as its primary significance. *See ConAgra Inc. v. Saavedra*, 4 USPQ2d 1245 (TTAB 1987) (TAPATIO held not primarily geographically deceptively misdescriptive of meatless hot sauce, despite the fact that the mark is a Spanish term meaning "of or pertaining to Guadalajara, Mexico" and the goods did not originate from Guadalajara).

Remoteness or obscurity is determined from the perspective of the average American consumer. *See In re Societe Generale des Eaux Minerales de Vittel, S.A.*, 824 F.2d 957 3 USPQ2d 1450 (Fed. Cir. 1987) (VITTEL and design held not primarily geographically descriptive of cosmetic products because of lack of goods/place association between the goods and the applicant's place of business in Vittel, France). However, the examining attorney does not have to show that the nationwide general public would associate the mark with the place. The significance of the term is determined not in the abstract, but from the point of view of the consumers of the particular goods or services identified in the application. *In re MCO Properties Inc.*, 38 USPQ2d 1154 (TTAB 1995) (FOUNTAIN HILLS held primarily geographically descriptive of real estate development services rendered in Fountain Hills, Arizona, where the record showed that Fountain Hills was the name of the town where the applicant was located and rendered its services, and that the purchasers who came in contact with the mark would associate that place with the services).

1210.04(e) Arbitrary Use of Geographic Terms

The name of a geographic location that has no significant relation to commercial activities or the production of the relevant goods or services, such as ALASKA for

地理性内容可能过于含混或偏远，以至于不会被识别为一种对于商品或服务的原产地标示。在这样的情况下，商标会被看作是任意性标识(*参见* TMEP §1210.04(e))，因为其地理性含义对于消费者不起作用，并且不会被认为是其主要含义。*参见* *ConAgra Inc. v. Saavedra*，4 USPQ2d 1245 (TTAB 1987)(“TAPATIO”用于净素辣沙司时被认为并非主要属于地理欺骗性描述，尽管该商标是一个西班牙语词语，意为“属于或关于于墨西哥的瓜达拉哈拉(Guadalajara)”，而该商品并非产自瓜达拉哈拉)。

偏远性或含混性需根据一般美国消费者的看法来判断。*参见* *Societe Generale des Eaux Minerales de Vittel, S.A.*, 824 F.2d 957 3 USPQ2d 1450 (Fed. Cir. 1987)(用于化妆品时，“VITTEL”及图案被认为并非主要属于地理性描述，因为商品与申请人的营业地法国维泰勒(Vittel)之间缺乏商品/地点联系)。不过，审查员不必证明全国范围的一般公众都会将该地点与商标相联系。词语的含义不能抽象地进行判断，而必须从消费者对于申请所识别的特定商品或服务的观点出发。见 *MCO Properties Inc.*, 38 USPQ2d 1154 (TTAB 1995)(对于在亚利桑那州方廷希尔(Fountain Hills)提供的房地产开发服务而言，“FOUNTAIN HILLS”被认为主要属于地理性描述，因为档案显示方廷希尔是申请者住所地和服务提供地所在镇的名称，而且与该商标发生联系的购买者会将地点与该服务相联系)。

1210.04(e) 对地理性词语的任意使用

与相关商品或服务的商业活动及生产无关的地名，例如用于香蕉的ALASKA，

bananas, is treated as an arbitrary mark because it is unlikely that consumers would believe that the mark identifies the place from which the goods originate. *See In re Nantucket, Inc.*, 677 F.2d 95, 105, 213 USPQ 889, 897 (C.C.P.A. 1982) (Nies, J., concurring) (construing use of "the names of places devoid of commercial activity" as "arbitrary usage").

See TMEP 1210.07(e) regarding arbitrary, fanciful or suggestive composite marks.

1210.05 Geographically Deceptive Marks

1210.05(a) Deceptive Geographical Marks—in General

See TMEP §1210.01(c) regarding the test for determining whether a geographic term is deceptive under 15 U.S.C. §1052(a).

The distinction between marks that are primarily geographically deceptively misdescriptive under 15 U.S.C. §1052(e)(3) and those that are deceptive under §2(a) is whether the fact that the mark identifies a place from which the goods or services do not originate is likely to be material to consumers' decision to purchase the goods or use the services. If so, the mark is deceptive within the meaning of §2(a); if not, the mark is primarily geographically deceptively misdescriptive within the meaning of §2(e)(3). *See In re House of Windsor, Inc.*, 221 USPQ 53 (TTAB 1983), *recon. denied*, 223 USPQ 191 (TTAB 1984), in which the Trademark Trial and Appeal Board provided the following guidance in assessing whether the deception is material:

> In embracing a "materiality" test to distinguish marks that fall within the proscription of Section [2(e)(3)] from those that fall also within the proscription of Section 2(a), we are really saying no more than that we must look to the evidence that has been presented about the probable reaction of purchasers to a particular geographical term when it is applied

被视为任意商标，因为消费者不可能认为该商标识别了商品产地。参见 *Nantucket*，*Inc*.，677 F.2d 95，105，213 USPQ 889，897（C.C.P.A.1982）（Nies，J.，concurring）（分析了以"任意使用方式"对"缺乏商业活力的地名"进行使用的情况）。

关于任意性、臆造性以及暗示性复合商标，参见 TMEP 1210.07(e)。

1210.05　　地理欺骗性商标

1210.05(a)　　欺骗地理性商标——概述

有关判断一个地理性词语是否带有 15 U.S.C. §1052(a)所规定的欺骗性的检验标准，参见 TMEP §1210.01(c)。

15 U.S.C. §1052(e)(3)所规定的主要属于地理欺骗性错误描述的商标与§2(a)所规定的欺骗性商标的区别在于，该商标所识别的非商品或服务原产地的地点对于消费者购买该商品或采用该服务的决定是否存在实质影响。如果是，那么该商标就是§2(a)所指的欺骗性商标；如果不是，那么该商标就存在§2(e)(3)所述的主要属于地理欺骗性错误描述。参见 *House of Windsor*，*Inc*.，221 USPQ 53（TTAB 1983），*recon*.*denied*，223 USPQ 191（TTAB 1984），在该案中，商标评审及上诉委员会为判断欺骗是否属于实质性提出了下列指导原则：

> 在采用某种"实质性"检验标准以区分第 2(e)(3)节所禁止的商标和同时为第 2(a)节所禁止的商标时，我们只能说，我们必须审查有关购买者对于某特定地理性词语用于特定商品时可能出现的反应的证据。如果证据表

to particular goods. If the evidence shows that the geographical area named in the mark is an area sufficiently renowned to lead purchasers to make a goods-place association but the record does not show that goods like applicant's or goods related to applicant's are a principal product of that geographical area, then the deception will most likely be found not to be material and the mark, therefore, not deceptive. On the other hand, if there is evidence that goods like applicant's or goods related to applicant's are a principal product of the geographical area named by the mark, then the deception will most likely be found material and the mark, therefore, deceptive.

221 USPQ at 57 (BAHIA held deceptive of cigars that do not originate in the Bahia province of Brazil, where the evidence of record was "unequivocal" that tobacco and cigars are important products in the Bahia region).

If a mark comprises geographic matter that is deceptive within the meaning of §2(a) combined with additional matter, the mark as a whole is unregistrable. *See In re Perry Mfg. Co.*, 12 USPQ2d 1751 (TTAB 1989) (PERRY NEW YORK and design ("NEW YORK" disclaimed) held deceptive for various items of clothing that originate in North Carolina, and have no connection with New York, because of the renown of New York in the apparel industry); *In re Biesseci S.p.A.*, 12 USPQ2d 1149 (TTAB 1989) (AMERICAN SYSTEM and design ("AMERICAN" disclaimed), for clothing manufactured in Italy, held deceptive).

If a composite mark comprises geographic matter that is deceptive, the mark is subject to strict scrutiny and may be held to be deceptive even if the mark as a whole is not perceived as identifying a geographic origin. *See In re Danish Maid Cultured Products, Inc.*, 156 USPQ 430 (TTAB 1967) (DANISH MAID CULTURED PRODUCTS and design depicting the world famous mermaid statue in Copenhagen, Denmark held deceptive for consulting and advisory services relating to dairy products that do not originate in Denmark); *In re Richemond*, 131 USPQ 441 (TTAB 1961) (MAID IN PARIS held deceptive for perfume manufac-

明，商标所指称的地区对于首要购买者群体而言够著名，可以由此得出一种商品－地点联系，但是档案并未显示申请者的商品或与申请者相关的商品是该地区的主要产品，那么很有可能就要判定这种欺骗并不是实质性的，该商标也就因而不具有欺骗性。另一方面，如果有证据表明申请者的商品或与其相关的商品确属商标所示地区的主要产品，那么就很可能判定这种欺骗属于实质性，因而该商标也就是欺骗性的。

221 USPQ at 57（“BAHIA”被认为对于并非产自巴西巴伊亚（Bahia）省的雪茄而言是欺骗性的，因为档案证据“毫不含糊地”表明，烟草和雪茄是巴伊亚地区的主要产品）。

如果某项商标包含了§2(a)所规定的欺骗性地理内容，而与其他内容组合在一起，那么该商标整体也是不可注册的。*参见 Perry Mfg. Co.*，12 USPQ2d 1751（TTAB 1989）（对于产自北卡罗莱纳而与纽约无关的各种服装而言，“PERRY NEW YORK”及图案（“NEW YORK”撤回）被认为具有欺骗性，因为纽约在服装业享有盛誉）；*Biesseci S.p.A.*，12 USPQ2d 1149（TTAB 1989）（对于意大利产的服装而言，“AMERICAN SYSTEM”及图案（“AMERICAN”撤回）被认为具有欺骗性）。

如果某项复合商标包含了欺骗性的地理内容，那么该商标就必须接受严格审查，并且可能被认为是欺骗性的，即使该商标作为整体并没有被认为是在对原产地进行识别。*参见 Danish Maid Cultured Products, Inc.*，156 USPQ 430（TTAB 1967）（对于并非来自于丹麦的有关乳制品的咨询服务，表现世界著名的丹麦哥本哈根美人鱼雕像的“DANISH MAID CULTURED PRODUCTS”及图案被认为具有欺骗性）；*Richemond*，131 USPQ 441（TTAB 1961）（对于美国制造的香水，“MAID IN PARIS”

tured in the United States); *National Lead Co. v. Michigan Bulb Co.*, 120 USPQ 115 (Comm'r Pats. 1959) (DUTCH BOY held deceptive for flower bulbs that do not originate in Holland).

A disclaimer of the deceptive matter will not overcome a §2(a) refusal. *See* TMEP §1210.08. A mark that is deceptive under §2(a) may not be registered on either the Principal Register or the Supplemental Register. *See* TMEP §§1210.06(a) and 1210.06(b).

See also TMEP §§1203.02 *et seq*. regarding deceptive marks, and TMEP §1210.05(b) regarding geographical designations used on or in connection with wines or spirits that identify a place other than the origin of the goods.

1210.05(b) Wines and Spirits

Section 2(a) of the Trademark Act, 15 U.S.C. §1052(a), prohibits the registration of a designation that consists of or comprises "a geographical indication which, when used on or in connection with wines or spirits, identifies a place other than the origin of the goods and is first used on or in connection with wines or spirits by the applicant on or after [January 1, 1996]." This provision was added by the Uruguay Round Agreements Act, implementing the Trade Related Intellectual Property (TRIPs) portions of the General Agreement on Tariffs and Trade (GATT). It applies only to geographic indications that were first used in commerce on or after January 1, 1996, one year after the effective date of the legislation implementing GATT.

The examining attorney must refuse registration under §2(a) of any geographical designation that was first used in commerce on or in connection with wines or spirits on or after January 1, 1996, if it identifies a place other than the origin of the goods. Section 2(a) is an absolute bar to the registration of these geographical designations on either the Principal Register or the Supplemental Register. Neither a disclaimer of the geographical designation nor a claim that it has acquired

被认为具有欺骗性）；*National Lead Co. v. Michigan Bulb Co.*, 120 USPQ 115 (Comm'r Pats. 1959)（对于并非产自荷兰的花鳞茎，"DUTCH BOY"被认为具有欺骗性）。

将欺骗性内容撤回并不能推翻根据 §2(a)作出的拒绝予以注册决定。*参见* TMEP §1210.08。§2(a)所规定的欺骗性商标既不能在联邦商标登记簿也不能在补充登记簿注册。*参见* TMEP §§1210.06(a)和 1210.06(b)。

另，有关欺骗性商标的内容，*参见* TMEP §1203.02 及以下；有关用于或联系于葡萄酒或白酒时，能够识别商品原产地以外地点的地理商标，*参见* TMEP §1210.05(b)。

1210.05(b) 葡萄酒和白酒

《商标法》第 2(a)节，15 U.S.C. §1052(a)对含有"用于葡萄酒或白酒时，识别了某一商品原产地以外的地点，并且申请者是在[1996 年 1 月 1 日]之时或以后首次将其用于葡萄酒或白酒的地理标示"禁止注册。此项规定是根据实施《关税与贸易总协议》(GATT)中《相关贸易的知识产权》(TRIPs)部分的《乌拉圭回合协议法》附加的。该规定仅适用于 1996 年 1 月 1 日——实施 GATT 的立法生效日期一年以后——当时或之后首次用于商业活动的地理标识。

对任何在 1996 年 1 月 1 日以后首次在商业活动中用于葡萄酒或白酒的地理标识，只要该标识识别了商品产地以外的地点，审查员都必须根据 §2(a)拒绝予以注册。第 2(a)节构成了地理标识在联邦商标登记簿以及补充登记簿注册的绝对阻碍。如果商标包含了识别葡萄酒或白酒原产地以外地点的地理标识，那么无论是撤回该

distinctiveness under §2(f) can obviate a §2(a) refusal if the mark consists of or comprises a geographical indication that identifies a place other than the origin of the wines or spirits.

1210.06 Supplemental Register and Section 2(f)

1210.06(a) Registrability of Geographic Terms on the Supplemental Register

Primarily Geographically Descriptive Marks. A term that is primarily geographically descriptive of the goods or services under §2(e)(2), 15 U.S.C. §1052(e)(2), may be registered on the Supplemental Register, if it is not barred by other section(s) of the Act.

Primarily Geographically Deceptively Misdescriptive Marks. A mark that is found to be primarily geographically deceptively misdescriptive under §2(e)(3), 15 U.S.C. §2(e)(3), may not be registered on the Supplemental Register unless the mark has been in lawful use in commerce since before December 8, 1993, the date of enactment of the North American Free Trade Agreement Implementation Act, Public Law 103-182, 107 Stat. 2057. 15 U.S.C. §1091(a).

Geographically Deceptive Marks. A mark that is deceptive under §2(a), 15 U.S.C. §1052(a), may not be registered on the Supplemental Register. *In re Juleigh Jeans Sportswear Inc.*, 24 USPQ2d 1694 (TTAB 1992).

1210.06(b) Registrability of Geographic Terms Under Section 2(f)

Primarily Geographically Descriptive Marks. A term that is primarily geographically descriptive of the goods or services under §2(e)(2), 15 U.S.C. §1052(e)(2), may be registered on the Principal Register if it is shown to have acquired distinctiveness under §2(f), 15 U.S.C. §1052(f). *See* TMEP §§1212 *et seq*. regarding §2(f).

Primarily Geographically Deceptively Misdescriptive Marks. A mark that is primari-

地理标识，还是根据 §2(f)主张已经具备了独特性，都不能推翻根据§2(a)做出的不予注册的决定。

1210.06　联邦商标补充登记簿和第 2(f)节

1210.06(a)　地理词语在联邦商标补充登记簿的可注册性

主要属于地理描述性的商标 如果根据§2(e)(2)，15 U.S.C.§1052(e)(2)，某词语主要属于对商品或服务的地理性描述，那么如果《商标法》其他部分并未禁止，则该词语就可以在联邦商标补充登记簿注册。

主要属于地理欺骗性错误描述的商标 一项商标根据§2(e)(3)，15 U.S.C.§2(e)(3)被判定主要属于地理欺骗性错误描述，那么就不能在补充登记簿注册，除非该商标自 1993 年 12 月 8 日——《北美自由贸易协定实施法》，Public Law 103 - 182，107 Stat.2057.，15 U.S.C.§1091(a)生效之日——起就已经合法地在商业活动中进行使用了。

地理欺骗性商标 根据§2(a)，15 U.S.C.§1052(a)的规定具有欺骗性的商标，不能在补充登记簿注册。*Juleigh Jeans Sportswear Inc.*，24 USPQ2d 1694（TTAB 1992）。

1210.06(b)　第 2(f)节所规定的地理词语的可注册性

主要属于地理描述性的商标 如果根据§2(e)(2)，15 U.S.C.§1052(e)(2)，某词语主要属于对商品或服务的地理性描述，那么如果可以证明已经获得了§2(f)所规定的独特性，则该词语就可以在联邦商标登记簿注册。有关 §2(f)的内容，*参见* TMEP §§1212 及以下。

主要属于地理欺骗性错误描述的商标 一项商标根据§2(e)(3)，15 U.S.C.§2(e)

ly geographically deceptively misdescriptive under §2(e)(3), 15 U.S.C.§1052(e)(3), may not be registered under §2(f) unless the mark became distinctive of the goods or services in commerce before December 8, 1993, the date of enactment of the North American Free Trade Agreement Implementation Act. *See In re Boyd Gaming Corp*., 57 USPQ2d 1944 (TTAB 2000); *Fred Hayman Beverly Hills Inc. v. Jacques Bernier Inc*., 38 USPQ2d 1691 (TTAB 1996).

Geographically Deceptive Marks. A mark that is deceptive under 15 U. S. C. §1052(a) may not be registered on the Principal Register even under §2(f).

Section 2(f) in Part. An applicant may claim that a geographic component of a mark has acquired distinctiveness under §2(f). *See* TMEP §1212.02(f) regarding claims of acquired distinctiveness as to a portion of a mark. Thus, if the examining attorney requires a disclaimer of matter that is primarily geographically descriptive under §2(e)(2), the applicant may seek to overcome the disclaimer requirement by submitting a showing that the geographic component has acquired distinctiveness under §2(f). If the applicant is able to establish to the satisfaction of the examining attorney that the geographic component has acquired distinctiveness, the examining attorney will approve the mark for publication with a notation that there is a claim of distinctiveness under §2(f) as to the geographic component. *See* TMEP §1210.08 for additional information about disclaimer of geographic terms.

1210.07 Geographic Terms Combined With Additional Matter

A geographic composite mark is one composed of geographic matter coupled with additional matter (*e.g*., wording and/or a design element). When examining such a mark, the examining attorney must determine the primary significance of the composite. *See In re Save Venice New York Inc*., 259 F.3d 1346, 59 USPQ2d 1778 (Fed.Cir.2001) (THE VENICE COLLECTION and SAVE VENICE INC. with an image of the winged Lion of St. Mark, for various goods, held primarily geographically deceptively misdescriptive of products that do not originate in Venice,

(3)被判定主要属于地理欺骗性错误描述,那么就不能根据§2(f)注册;除非该商标自1993年12月8日——《北美自由贸易协定实施法》,Public Law 103-182,107 Stat.2057.,15 U.S.C.§1091(a)生效之日——起就已经在商业活动中对于商品或服务具备了独特性。*参见 Boyd Gaming Corp.*,57 USPQ2d 1944(TTAB 2000);*Fred Hayman Beverly Hills Inc. v. Jacques Bernier Inc.*,38 USPQ2d 1691(TTAB 1996)。

地理欺骗性商标 根据 §2(a),15 U.S.C.§1052(a)的规定具有欺骗性的商标,不能在联邦商标登记簿注册。

部分的第2(f)节。申请人可以主张商标的某一地理性组成部分已经具备了 §2(f)所规定的独特性。*参见* TMEP §1212.02(f),了解有关主张商标的某一部分已经具备独特性的内容。因此,如果审查员要求撤回 §2(e)(2)所规定的主要属于地理性描述的内容,申请者可以通过提交证据表明该地理性组成部分已经具备了 §2(f)所规定的独特性,从而寻求克服该撤回要求。如果申请者能够令审查员满意地证明该地理性组成部分已经具备了独特性,那么审查员就会批准该商标公布,同时附注关于该地理性组成部分存在 §2(f)所规定的独特性主张。*参见* TMEP §1210.08,了解其他有关撤回地理性词语的信息。

1210.07 地理性词语与其他内容相结合

地理复合商标是由地理性内容和其他内容(例如,文字和/或图案因素)共同组成的商标。在审查此类商标时,审查员必须判断复合词的主要含义。*参见*判例:*Save Venice New York Inc.*,259 F.3d 1346,59 USPQ2d 1778(Fed.Cir.2001)(用于各种商品的"THE VENICE COLLECTION"和"SAVE VENICE INC."以及一幅圣马可的双翼飞狮像被认为对于并非产自意大利威尼斯的商品而言主要属于地理欺骗性

Italy); *In re Wada*, 194 F.3d 1297, 52 USPQ2d 1539 (Fed. Cir. 1999) (NEW YORK WAYS GALLERY ("NEW YORK" disclaimed) held primarily geographically deceptively misdescriptive of backpacks, handbags, purses and similar items); *In re Bacardi & Co. Ltd.*, 48 USPQ2d 1031 (TTAB 1997) (HAVANA SELECT, HAVANA CLASICO, OLD HAVANA, HAVANA PRIMO, and HAVANA CLIPPER primarily geographically deceptively misdescriptive of rum). *See* TMEP §1210.02(b) regarding the "primary" significance of geographic terms.

Depending on the primary significance of the composite, the examining attorney will handle the geographic issue in a geographic composite mark in one of the following ways:

(1) If the examining attorney finds that the mark, when viewed as a whole, is arbitrary, fanciful or suggestive, he or she will approve the mark for publication without evidence that the mark has acquired distinctiveness under §2(f);

(2) If the examining attorney finds that the mark is primarily geographically descriptive under §2(e)(2) without a showing of acquired distinctiveness, primarily geographically deceptively misdescriptive under §2(e)(3), or deceptive under §2(a), he or she will refuse registration of the mark as a whole; or

(3) If the examining attorney finds that the geographic matter is a separable part of the mark, the examining attorney's action will depend on whether the matter is primarily geographically descriptive, primarily geographically deceptively misdescriptive, or deceptive. *See* TMEP §1210.08 regarding disclaimer of geographic terms, and TMEP §1210.06(b) regarding claims of acquired distinctiveness as to a geographic component of a mark.

See TMEP §§1210.07(a) through 1210.07(e) for guidelines regarding the examination of an application to register a mark comprising a geographic term com-

错误描述)；*Wada*，194 F.3d 1297，52 USPQ2d 1539（Fed. Cir. 1999)(对于背包、手提包、钱包和类似物品而言，“NEW YORK WAYS GALLERY”(“NEW YORK”撤回)被认为主要属于地理欺骗性错误描述)；*Bacardi & Co. Ltd.*，48 USPQ2d 1031（TTAB 1997)(“HAVANA SELECT”、“HAVANA CLASICO”、“OLD HAVANA”、“HAVANA PRIMO”以及“HAVANA CLIPPER”对于朗姆酒主要属于地理欺骗性错误描述)。有关地理词语“主要”含义的情况，参*见* TMEP §1210.02(b)。

根据复合词的首要含义，审查员可以以下列方式之一处理地理复合商标中的地理性问题：

(1) 如果审查员判定，作为总体看来，该商标是任意、臆造或暗示性的，并且没有证据表明商标具备了 §2(f)所规定的独特性，那么他就可以批准商标公布；

(2) 如果审查员判定，该商标主要属于§2(e)(2)所规定的地理性描述，并且没有证据表明其具备了独特性；主要属于 §2(e)(3)所规定的地理欺骗性错误描述；或是具有§2(a)所规定的欺骗性，那么他就可以拒绝该商标整体注册；或者

(3) 如果审查员判定，地理性内容是该商标的一个独立部分，那么审查员的决定取决于该内容是否主要属于地理性描述、地理欺骗性错误描述，还是具有欺骗性。有关撤回地理词语的情况，参*见* TMEP §1210.08；有关商标的地理性组成部分已经具备独特性的主张的情况，参*见* TMEP §1210.06(b)。

由地理词语和其他内容构成商标注册申请的审查指导原则，参*见* TMEP §§1210.07(a)至 1210.07(e)。

bined with additional matter.

1210.07(a) Geographic Terms Combined With Descriptive Matter

Generally, the addition of a highly descriptive or generic term to the name of a geographic place does not alter its primarily geographic significance. *In re JT Tobacconists*, 59 USPQ2d 1080 (TTAB 2001) (MINNESOTA CIGAR COMPANY primarily geographically descriptive of cigars); *In re Carolina Apparel*, 48 USPQ2d 1542 (TTAB 1998) (CAROLINA APPAREL primarily geographically descriptive of retail clothing store services); *In re Chalk's International Airlines Inc.*, 21 USPQ2d 1637 (TTAB 1991) (PARADISE ISLAND AIRLINES held primarily geographically descriptive of the transportation of passengers and goods by air); *In re Wine Society of America Inc.*, 12 USPQ2d 1139 (TTAB 1989) (THE WINE SOCIETY OF AMERICA held primarily geographically descriptive of wine club membership services); *In re California Pizza Kitchen Inc.*, 10 USPQ2d 1704 (TTAB 1988) (CALIFORNIA PIZZA KITCHEN ("PIZZA KITCHEN" disclaimed) held primarily geographically descriptive of restaurant services); *In re Cambridge Digital Systems*, 1 USPQ2d 1659 (TTAB 1986) (CAMBRIDGE DIGITAL and design ("DIGITAL" disclaimed) held primarily geographically descriptive of computer systems and parts thereof).

1210.07(b) Marks That Include Primarily Geographically Descriptive Terms Combined With Additional Matter

If a composite mark comprises a geographic term that is primarily geographically descriptive of the goods or services under §2(e)(2), and the mark as a whole would be likely to be perceived as indicating the geographic origin of the goods or services, then the examining attorney must consider: (1) whether the geographic term is a separable element in the mark, and (2) the nature of the additional matter that makes up the composite mark.

If the geographic term is a separable element and the additional matter making up the mark is inherently distinctive as applied to the goods or services (*i.e.*,

1210.07(a) 地理性词语与描述性内容相结合

一般说来，在地名上加以高度描述性或一般性的词语，并不能改变其主要的地理性含义。相关判例：*JT Tobacconists*，59 USPQ2d 1080（TTAB 2001）（“MINNESOTA CIGAR COMPANY”对于雪茄主要属于地理性描述）；*Carolina Apparel*，48 USPQ2d 1542（TTAB 1998）（“CAROLINA APPAREL”对于服装零售店服务主要属于地理性描述）；*Chalk's International Airlines Inc.*，21 USPQ2d 1637（TTAB 1991）（“PARADISE ISLAND AIRLINES”被认为对于客货空运而言主要属于地理性描述）；*Wine Society of America Inc.*，12 USPQ2d 1139（TTAB 1989）（“THE WINE SOCIETY OF AMERICA”被认为对于葡萄酒俱乐部会员服务而言主要属于地理性描述）；*California Pizza Kitchen Inc.*，10 USPQ2d 1704（TTAB 1988）（“CALIFORNIA PIZZA KITCHEN”（“PIZZA KITCHEN”撤回）被认为对于餐饮服务而言主要属于地理性描述）；*Cambridge Digital Systems*，1 USPQ2d 1659（TTAB 1986）（“CAMBRIDGE DIGITAL”及图案被认为对于电脑系统及组件而言主要属于地理性描述）。

1210.07(b) 包含主要属地理性描述词语与其他内容组合的商标

如果一项符合商标包含根据§2(e)(2)主要属于对商品或服务的地理性描述的词语，并且该商标整体可能会被认为标示了商品或服务的原产地，那么审查员就必须考虑：(1)该地理词语是否属于该商标的独立要素，以及(2)其他共同构成该商标的内容的性质。

如果该地理词语是一种独立要素，并且其他共同构成商标的内容适用于商品或

coined, arbitrary, fanciful or suggestive), the applicant may either: (1) register the mark on the Principal Register with a disclaimer of the geographic term, or (2) establish that the geographic term has acquired distinctiveness under §2(f). *See* TMEP §1210.08 regarding disclaimer of geographic terms, and TMEP §§1210.06(b) and 1212.02(f) regarding §2(f) claims as to a portion of the mark.

However, if the geographic term is not a separable element or if none of the additional matter that makes up the composite mark is inherently distinctive (*e.g.*, it is merely descriptive or incapable), then the examining attorney should refuse registration of the entire mark on the Principal Register pursuant to §2(e)(2).

1210.07(c) Marks That Include Primarily Geographically Deceptively Misdescriptive Terms Combined With Additional Matter

If a composite mark comprises matter that is primarily geographically deceptively misdescriptive within the meaning of §2(e)(3), and the mark as a whole would be likely to be perceived as indicating the geographic origin of the goods or services, then the examining attorney should refuse registration of the mark as a whole under §2(e)(3), unless the applicant has established that the primarily geographically deceptively misdescriptive matter acquired distinctiveness under §2(f) before December 8, 1993. A disclaimer of the geographic matter will not overcome the §2(e)(3) refusal. *In re Save Venice New York Inc.*, 259 F.3d 1346, 59 USPQ2d 1778 (Fed. Cir. 2001); *In re Wada*, 194 F.3d 1297, 52 USPQ2d 1539 (Fed. Cir. 1999). *See* TMEP §1210.08 regarding disclaimer of geographic terms, and TMEP §1210.06(b) regarding §2(f).

1210.07(d) Marks That Include Geographically Deceptive Terms Combined With Additional Matter

If a composite mark comprises geographic matter that is deceptive within the

服务时具有固有独特性(亦即,属于被创造的、任意的、臆造的或暗示性的内容),则申请者可以:(1)撤回该地理词语,在联邦商标登记簿注册该商标,或(2)证明该地理词语已经具备了 §2(f)所规定的独特性。有关撤回地理词语的情况,参见 TMEP §1210.08;有关商标的组成部分的主张,*参见* TMEP §1210.06(b)和 1212.02(f)。

不过,如果地理词语并不是独立的因素,或者其他构成复合商标的内容并不具有固有独特性(例如,只具有独特性,或者不得注册),那么审查员就应当根据 §2(e)(2)拒绝整个商标在联邦标记登记簿注册。

1210.07(c)　　包含主要属地理欺骗性错误描述词语与其他内容组合的商标

如果符合商标包含 §2(e)(3)所述的主要属于地理欺骗性错误描述的内容,并且该商标整体可能被认为是对商品或服务原产地的标识,那么审查员就应当根据 §2(e)(3)拒绝该商标的整体注册,除非申请者证明在 1993 年 12 月 8 日以前,该主要属地理欺骗性错误描述的内容已经具备了 §2(f)所规定的独特性。撤回该地理性内容并不能推翻根据 §2(e)(3)作出的不予注册的决定。见 *Save Venice New York Inc.*, 259 F.3d 1346, 59 USPQ2d 1778 (Fed. Cir. 2001); *Wada*, 194 F.3d 1297, 52 USPQ2d 1539 (Fed. Cir. 1999)。有关撤回地理性词语的内容,*参见* TMEP §1210.08;有关 §2(f)的情况,*参见* TMEP §1210.06(b)。

1210.07(d)　　包含地理欺骗性词语与其他内容组合的商标

如果一项符合商标包含§2(a)所述的地理欺骗性内容,并且该商标整体可能被认

meaning of §2(a), and the mark when viewed as a whole would be likely to be perceived as indicating geographic origin, the examining attorney should refuse registration of the mark as a whole under §2(a). *See* TMEP §1210.05(a) and cases cited therein for further information about geographically deceptive marks.

Composite marks that are geographically deceptive cannot be registered on either the Principal or the Supplemental Register, even with a disclaimer of the geographic component. *See* TMEP §§1210.06(a), 1210.06(b) and 1210.08.

1210.07(e) Arbitrary, Fanciful or Suggestive Composite Marks

If, when viewed as a whole, a composite mark would not be likely to be perceived as identifying the geographic origin of the goods or services (*i.e.*, the mark as a whole is not primarily geographically descriptive, primarily geographically deceptively misdescriptive, or deceptive), then the mark is regarded as arbitrary, fanciful or suggestive. *See National Lead Co. v. Wolfe*, 223 F.2d 195, 105 USPQ 462 (9th Cir.1955), *cert. denied*, 350 U.S.883, 107 USPQ 362 (1955) (DUTCH BOY for paint); *In re Sharky's Drygoods Co.*, 23 USPQ2d 1061 (TTAB 1992) (PARIS BEACH CLUB, applied to T-shirts and sweatshirts, not deceptive under §2(a)); *In re Yardley of London, Inc.*, 165 USPQ 272 (TTAB 1970) (LONDON LASHES for brush-on lash lengthener); *In re International Minerals & Chemical Corp.*, 147 USPQ 262 (TTAB 1965) (KENTUCKY TURF for fertilizer).

1210.08 Disclaimer of Geographic Terms in Composite Marks

Primarily Geographically Descriptive Marks

When appropriate, the applicant will be required to disclaim a separable component of a mark that is primarily geographically descriptive under §2(e)(2). A disclaimer is appropriate in this situation if the geographic component is a separable feature of the mark, and the composite mark includes an inherently distinctive, non-disclaimed component (*e.g.*, coined, arbitrary, fanciful or suggestive word-

为是对原产地的标示，那么审查员就应当根据§2(a)拒绝该商标整体注册。*参见* TMEP §§1210.05(a)及所引用的判例，进一步了解关于地理欺骗性商标的情况。

具有地理欺骗性的复合商标既不能在联邦商标登记簿也不能在补充登记簿注册，即使撤回该地理性组成部分。*参见* TMEP §§1210.06(a)，1210.06(b)和1210.08。

1210.07(e) 任意性、臆造性及暗示性复合商标

如果从整体角度观察，某复合商标不可能被认为是对商品或服务原产地的识别(亦即，该商标整体上并非主要属于地理性描述、地理欺骗性错误描述，或具有欺骗性)，则该商标可以被认为是任意性、臆造性或暗示性的。*参见* *National Lead Co. v. Wolfe*, 223 F.2d 195, 105 USPQ 462 (9th Cir. 1955), *cert. denied*, 350 U.S. 883, 107 USPQ 362 (1955)(用于油漆的"DUTCH BOY")；*Sharky's Drygoods Co.*, 23 USPQ2d 1061 (TTAB 1992)(用于T恤衫和运动衫，且不具有§2(a)所规定的欺骗性的"PARIS BEACH CLUB")；*Yardley of London, Inc.*, 165 USPQ 272 (TTAB 1970)(用于睫毛增长器的"LONDON LASHES")；*International Minerals & Chemical Corp.*, 147 USPQ 262 (TTAB 1965)(用于肥料的"KENTUCKY TURF")。

1210.08 撤回复合商标中的地理词语

主要属于地理描述性的商标

如果可以，申请人将会被要求撤回商标中主要属于§2(e)(2)所规定的地理描述性组成内容。如果地理性组成部分是该商标的独立部分，并且该复合商标包含固有独特性、未撤回的组成部分(例如，被创造的、任意的、臆造的或暗示性的文字或图

ing or design).

The composite mark must include a nondisclaimed component because a mark cannot be registered if all the components have been disclaimed. *See* TMEP §1213.06. *See, e.g., In re Wine Society of America Inc.*, 12 USPQ2d 1139, 1142 (TTAB 1989).

A unitary mark should not be broken up or divided for purposes of disclaiming the parts. A unitary mark is one in which the registrable and unregistrable elements are so integrated or merged together that they cannot be regarded as separable units, for example, a mark formed by combining or hyphenating two terms, one of which would be unregistrable by itself; or where a registrable term and an unregistrable term are joined together to form a mark that has a distinctive nondescriptive meaning of its own; or where the words that have been put together function as a unit, with each relating to the other rather than directly to the goods. *See In re Interstate Bakeries Corp.*, 156 USPQ 702 (TTAB 1968) (requirement for disclaimer of "DANISH" reversed in application to register DANISH VILLAGE for bread). *See* TMEP §§1213.05 *et seq*. regarding unitary marks.

When the examining attorney requires a disclaimer of primarily geographically descriptive matter, the applicant may seek to overcome the disclaimer requirement by submitting a showing that the geographic term has become distinctive under §2(f). *See* TMEP §§1210.06(b) and 1212.02(f).

Primarily Geographically Deceptively Misdescriptive and Deceptive Marks

A mark that includes matter that is primarily geographically deceptively misdescriptive under §2(e)(3) or deceptive under §2(a) is not registrable even with a disclaimer. *See* TMEP §§1210.01(b) and 1210.05(a). *In re Save Venice New York Inc.*, 54 USPQ2d 1106, 1110 (TTAB 2000), *aff'd*, 259 F.3d 1346, 59 USPQ2d 1778 (Fed. Cir. 2001) (THE VENICE COLLECTION and design held primarily geographically deceptively misdescriptive of products that do not originate in Venice, Italy); *In re Wada*, 194 F. 3d 1297, 52 USPQ2d 1539, 1541-42 (Fed.

案)，那么在这种情况下就可以撤回该部分内容。

该复合商标必须包含未撤回的组成部分，因为如果所有的部分都被撤回，商标也就不能注册了。*参见* TMEP §1213.06。*参见* *Wine Society of America Inc*., 12 USPQ2d 1139, 1142 (TTAB 1989)。

单一商标不得为撤回部分内容之目的而进行拆解或分割。单一商标是指，在该商标中可注册和不可注册的要素紧密结合在一起，以至于不能被认为是独立的部分，例如，某商标是由两个词语通过连接符结合起来的，其中之一本身不可注册；或者，由可注册词语与不可注册词语结合构成的商标本身具有显著的非描述性含义；或者，各词语组合在一起作为一体起作用，各部分之间相互关联，而非直接与商品关联。*参见* *Interstate Bakeries Corp*., 156 USPQ 702 (TTAB 1968)(对于为面包注册"DANISH VILLAGE"商标的申请，撤回"DANISH"的要求遭到撤销)。有关单一商标的内容，*参见* TMEP §§1213.05 及以下。

如果审查员要求撤回主要属于地理性描述的内容，申请者可以通过提交证据证明该地理性词语已经具备了 §2(f)所规定的独特性，以寻求克服撤回要求。*参见* TMEP §§1210.06(b)和 1212.02(f)。

主要属于地理欺骗性错误描述以及欺骗性的商标

包含§2(e)(3)所规定的主要属地理欺骗性错误描述，以及§2(a)所规定的欺骗性内容的商标不得注册，即使部分撤回。*参见* TMEP §§1210.01(b)和 1210.05(a)。相关判例：*Save Venice New York Inc*., 54 USPQ2d 1106, 1110 (TTAB 2000), *aff'd*, 259 F.3d 1346, 59 USPQ2d 1778 (Fed. Cir. 2001)("THE VENICE COLLECTION"被认为对于并非产自意大利威尼斯的产品主要属于地理欺骗性错误描述)； *Wada*, 194 F.3d 1297, 52 USPQ2d 1539, 1541－1542 (Fed. Cir. 1999)("NEW

Cir. 1999) (NEW YORK WAYS GALLERY ("NEW YORK" disclaimed) held primarily geographically deceptively misdescriptive of backpacks, handbags, purses and similar items); *In re Perry Mfg. Co.*, 12 USPQ2d 1751, 1751-52 (TTAB 1989) (PERRY NEW YORK and design ("NEW YORK" disclaimed) held deceptive for clothing that originates in North Carolina and has no connection with New York, because of the renown of New York in the apparel industry).

Matter that is deceptive or primarily geographically deceptively misdescriptive may be omitted or deleted from the drawing of a mark in appropriate cases. *See* TMEP §807.15.

See TMEP §§1213 *et seq.* for more information about disclaimers.

1210.09 Geographic Certification Marks

Under certain circumstances the name of the place from which goods or services originate may function as a certification mark. When geographic terms are used to certify regional origin, registration of certification marks should not be refused and, in applications to register composite certification marks, disclaimers of these geographic terms should *not* be required on the ground of geographical descriptiveness. *See* TMEP §§1306.02 *et seq.* concerning procedures for registration of certification marks that certify regional origin.

When a geographical term used in a composite certification mark is not used to certify regional origin, appropriate refusals and requirements should be made.

1211 Refusal on Basis of Surname

Extract from 15 U.S.C.§1052. No trademark by which the goods of the applicant may be distinguished from the goods of others shall be refused registration on the principal register on account of its nature unless it ... (e) Consists of a mark which ... (4) is primarily merely a surname.

YORK WAYS GALLERY”(“NEW YORK”撤回)被认为对于背包、手提包、钱包和类似物品而言主要属于地理欺骗性错误描述);*Perry Mfg. Co.*, 12 USPQ2d 1751, 1751－1752 (TTAB 1989)(对于产自北卡罗莱纳而与纽约无关的各种服装而言,“PERRY NEW YORK”及图案(“NEW YORK”撤回)被认为具有欺骗性,因为纽约在服装业享有盛誉)。

在相关案件中,欺骗性的或主要属于地理欺骗性错误描述的内容可以从商标附图中省略或删除。*参见* TMEP §807.15。

有关撤回的更多情况,*参见* TMEP §§1213 及以下。

1210.09 地理证明商标

在特定情况下,商品或服务产地的名称可以用作证明商标。如果地理词语被用于证明产地,对证明商标的注册申请就不应驳回,并且,在复合证明商标的注册申请中,不应以地理描述性为由要求撤回这些地理词语。有关注册验证产地的证明商标的注册程序,*参见* TMEP §§1306.02 及以下。

如果用于复合证明商标中的地理词语并不是用来证明产地,那么就应当相应地驳回申请或提出要求。

1211 以姓氏为理由拒绝予以注册

摘自 15 U. S. C. §1052。由于其性质,用区别申请者商品与他人商品的商标均可以在联邦商标登记簿注册,除非——(e)包含一种商标……(4)主要只是一个姓氏。

Under §2(e)(4) of the Trademark Act, 15 U.S.C. §1052(e)(4), a mark that is primarily merely a surname is not registrable on the Principal Register absent a showing of acquired distinctiveness under §2(f), 15 U.S.C. §1052(f). *See* TMEP §§1212 *et seq*. regarding acquired distinctiveness. Formerly §2(e)(3) of the Act, this section was designated §2(e)(4) when the North American Free Trade Agreement Implementation Act, Public Law 103 182, took effect on January 1, 1994. A mark that is primarily merely a surname may be registrable on the Supplemental Register.

The Trademark Act, in §2(e)(4), reflects the common law that exclusive rights in a surname *per se* cannot be established without evidence of long and exclusive use that changes its significance to the public from that of a surname to that of a mark for particular goods or services. The common law also recognizes that surnames are shared by more than one individual, each of whom may have an interest in using his surname in business; and, by the requirement for evidence of distinctiveness, the law, in effect, delays appropriation of exclusive rights in the name. *In re Etablissements Darty et Fils*, 759 F.2d 15, 17, 225 USPQ 652, 653 (Fed. Cir. 1985).

The question of whether a mark is primarily merely a surname depends on the mark's *primary* significance to the purchasing public. *See, e.g., Ex parte Rivera Watch Corp*., 106 USPQ 145, 149 (Comm'r Pats. 1955). Each case must be decided on its own facts, based upon the evidence in the record.

1211.01 "Primarily Merely a Surname"

The legislative history of the Trademark Act of 1946 indicates that the word "primarily" was added to the existing statutory language "merely" with the intent to exclude registration of names such as "Johnson" or "Jones," but not registration of names such as "Cotton" or "King" which, while surnames, have a primary significance other than as a surname. *See Sears, Roebuck & Co. v. Watson*, 204 F.2d 32, 33-34, 96 USPQ 360, 362 (D.C. Cir. 1953), *cert. denied*, 346 U.S. 829, 99

根据《商标法》§2(e)(4)，15 U.S.C.§1052(e)(4)的规定，如果尚未证明商标已经具备了 §2(f)，15 U.S.C.§1052(f)所规定的独特性，那么主要只是姓氏的商标不得在联邦商标登记簿注册。有关获得性独特性的内容，*参见* TMEP §§1212 及以下。此节在原《商标法》中是 §2(e)(3)，1994 年 1 月 1 日《北美自由贸易协定实施法》，Public Law 103－182，生效后，即转为 §2(e)(4)。

《商标法》§2(e)(4)反映了在普通法上，如果缺乏长时期专属使用的证据，其对于公众的含义就不能从姓氏转变为用于特定商品或服务的商标，于是对于姓氏本身也就不存在专属权利。普通法同样认识到，姓氏可以为一个以上的个人所有，每个人将其姓氏用于商业时都可能存在某种利益；并且，法律通过对独特性证据的要求，实际上迟延了对姓名中专属权利的占用。*参见 Etablissements Darty et Fils*，759 F.2d 15，17，225 USPQ 652，653（Fed.Cir.1985）.

商标是否是主要仅为姓氏的问题取决于该商标对于购买公众的*首要*含义。*参见*判例：*Rivera Watch Corp.*，106 USPQ 145，149（Comm'r Pats.1955）。每一个案件都必须根据其自身情况，基于档案证据进行裁判。

1211.01　　“主要仅为姓氏”

《1946 年商标法》的立法史表明，在既有的法律语言“仅仅”之上加以“主要”一词的意图在于排斥诸如“Johnson”或“Jones”的姓名注册，但是并不排斥诸如“Cotton”或“King”的姓名，因为尽管后者也是姓氏，但其主要含义却并非姓氏。*参见 Sears，Roebuck & Co.v.Watson*，204 F.2d 32，33－34，96 USPQ 360，362（D.C.Cir.1953），*cert.denied*，346 U.S.829，99 USPQ 491（1953）；*Rivera Watch Corp.*，106 USPQ 145，149（Comm'r Pats.1955）。

USPQ 491 (1953); *Ex parte Rivera Watch Corp*., 106 USPQ 145, 149 (Comm'r Pats. 1955).

The question of whether a term is primarily merely a surname depends on the primary, not the secondary, significance to the purchasing public. The Trademark Trial and Appeal Board has identified five factors to be considered in making this determination:

(1) whether the surname is rare;

(2) whether the term is the surname of anyone connected with the applicant;

(3) whether the term has any recognized meaning other than as a surname;

(4) whether it has the "look and feel" of a surname; and

(5) whether the stylization of lettering is distinctive enough to create a separate commercial impression.

In re Benthin Management GmbH, 37 USPQ2d 1332, 1333-1334 (TTAB 1995).

1211.01(a) Non-Surname Significance

Often a word will have a meaning or significance in addition to its significance as a surname. The examining attorney must determine the primary meaning of the term to the public. *See* TMEP §§1211.01(a)(i) through 1211.01(a)(vi) regarding considerations that often arise in determining whether a term is primarily merely a surname.

1211.01(a)(i) Ordinary Language Meaning

If there is a readily recognized meaning of a term, apart from its surname significance, such that the primary significance of the term is not that of a surname, registration should be granted on the Principal Register without evidence of ac-

商标是否是主要仅为姓氏的问题取决于该商标对于购买公众的*首要*，而非第二含义。商标评审及上诉委员会已经确定了在此种判断过程中需要考虑的五种因素：

（1） 该姓氏是否稀有；

（2） 该词语是否是与申请者有联系的某人的姓氏；

（3） 该词语在作为姓氏之外是否存在其他含义；

（4） 该词语是否具有姓氏的“外观和感觉”；以及

（5） 对于字体的风格化是否充分显著，从而能够造成一种独立的商业印象。

见 *Benthin Management GmbH*，37 USPQ2d 1332，1333 - 1334（TTAB 1995）。

1211.01(a) 非姓氏含义

一个词语在其姓氏含义之外，经常会具有一种其他的含义或意义。审查员必须判别该词语对于公众的首要含义。有关在判断词语是否主要仅为姓氏的过程中经常需要考虑的问题，*参见* TMEP §§1211.01(a)(i)至 1211.01(a)(vi)。

1211.01(a)(i) 一般语义

如果除了姓氏含义之外，词语还存在获得普遍认可的含义，那么该词语的主要含义就不是姓氏，不经获得性独特性证明即可在联邦商标登记簿核准注册。*参见*判例：

quired distinctiveness. *See In re United Distillers plc*, 56 USPQ2d 1220 (TTAB 2000) (the relatively rare surname HACKLER held not primarily merely a surname, in light of dictionary meaning); *Fisher Radio Corp. v. Bird Electronic Corp.*, 162 USPQ 265 (TTAB 1969) (BIRD held not primarily merely a surname despite surname significance); *In re Hunt Electronics Co.*, 155 USPQ 606 (TTAB 1967) (HUNT held not primarily merely a surname despite surname significance). However, this does not mean that an applicant only has to uncover a non-surname meaning of the proposed mark to obviate a refusal under §2(e)(4). *See In re Nelson Souto Major Piquet*, 5 USPQ2d 1367, 1368 (TTAB 1987) (N. PIQUET (stylized) held primarily merely a surname despite significance of the term "piquet" as "the name of a relatively obscure card game").

1211.01(a)(ii) Phonetic Equivalent of Term With Ordinary Language Meaning

A term may be primarily merely a surname even if it is the phonetic equivalent of a word that has an ordinary meaning (*e.g.*, Byrne/burn; Knott/not or knot; Chappell/chapel). *See In re Pickett Hotel Co.*, 229 USPQ 760 (TTAB 1986) (PICKETT SUITE HOTEL held primarily merely a surname despite applicant's argument that PICKETT is the phonetic equivalent of the word "picket"). *Cf. In re Monotype Corp. PLC*, 14 USPQ2d 1070, 1071 (TTAB 1989) (CALISTO held not primarily merely a surname, the Board characterizing the telephone directory evidence of surname significance as "minimal" and in noting the mythological significance of the name "Callisto," stating that it is common knowledge that there are variations in the rendering of mythological names transliterated from the Greek alphabet (distinguishing *In re Pickett Hotel Co., supra*)). Similarly, the fact that a word which has surname significance is also a hybrid or derivative of another word having ordinary language meaning is insufficient to overcome the surname significance unless the perception of non-surname significance would displace the primary surname import of the word. *See In re Etablissements Darty et Fils*, 759 F.2d 15, 225 USPQ 652 (Fed. Cir. 1985) (DARTY held primarily mere-

United Distillers plc, 56 USPQ2d 1220 (TTAB 2000)(根据词典定义,相对罕见的姓氏"HACKLER"被认为主要不仅是一个姓氏);*Fisher Radio Corp. v. Bird Electronic Corp.*, 162 USPQ 265 (TTAB 1969)(尽管具有姓氏含义,"BIRD"还是被认为主要不仅是一个姓氏);*Hunt Electronics Co.*, 155 USPQ 606 (TTAB 1967)(尽管具有姓氏含义,"HUNT"还是被认为主要不仅是一个姓氏)。不过,这并不意味着申请者只要揭示申请注册的商标具有非姓氏含义就可以免遭根据 §2(e)(4)作出的不予注册的决定。*参见 Nelson Souto Major Piquet*, 5 USPQ2d 1367, 1368 (TTAB 1987)(尽管"piquet"一词具有"一种相对冷僻的纸牌游戏的名称"的含义,但"N. PIQUET(风格化)"还是被认为主要仅为一个姓氏)。

1211.01(a)(ii) 具有一般语义的同音词

即使一个词的同音词具有一般含义(例如,Byrne/burn; Knott/not 或 knot; Chappell/chapel),它仍然可能主要仅为一个姓氏。*参见 Pickett Hotel Co.*, 229 USPQ 760 (TTAB 1986)(尽管申请者抗辩称"PICKETT"是"picket"一词的同音词,但"PICKETT SUITE HOTEL"还是被认为主要仅为一个姓氏)。比较:*Monotype Corp. PLC*, 14 USPQ2d 1070, 1071 (TTAB 1989)("CALISTO"被认为并非主要仅为一个姓氏,委员会认为姓氏含义的证据电话号码簿意义"最小",并且在引用"Callisto"名字的神话含义时称,采用音译自希腊字母表的神话姓名时存在各种变体属于常识(区别于 *Pickett Hotel Co.*, *案卷号同前*))。类似地,如果具有姓氏含义的词语同时是另一个具有一般语义词语的混合词或派生词,并不足以克服其姓氏含义,除非非姓氏含义取代了该词的主要姓氏意义。*参见 Etablissements Darty et Fils*, 759 F. 2d 15, 225 USPQ 652 (Fed. Cir. 1985)(尽管申请者抗辩称该商标是"dart"一词文字

ly a surname despite applicant's argument that the mark is a play on the word "dart"); *In re Petrin Corp.*, 231 USPQ 902 (TTAB 1986) (PETRIN held primarily merely a surname despite applicant's argument that the mark represents an abbreviation of "petroleum" and "insulation").

1211.01(a)(iii) Geographical Significance

A term with surname significance may not be primarily merely a surname if that term also has a well-known geographical meaning. *In re Colt Industries Operating Corp.*, 195 USPQ 75 (TTAB 1977) (FAIRBANKS held not primarily merely a surname because the geographical significance of the mark was determined to be just as dominant as its surname significance). However, the fact that a term is shown to have some minor significance as a geographical term will not dissipate its primary significance as a surname. *In re Hamilton Pharmaceuticals Ltd.*, 27 USPQ2d 1939, 1943 (TTAB 1993) (HAMILTON held primarily merely a surname).

1211.01(a)(iv) Historical Place or Person [R-2]

A term with surname significance may not be primarily merely a surname if that term also identifies a historical place or person. *See Lucien Piccard Watch Corp. v. Since* 1868 *Crescent Corp.*, 314 F. Supp. 329, 165 USPQ 459 (S.D.N.Y. 1970) (DA VINCI found not primarily merely a surname because it primarily connotes Leonardo Da Vinci); *In re Pyro-Spectaculars, Inc.*, 63 USPQ2d 2022, 2024 (TTAB 2002) (SOUSA for fireworks and production of events and shows featuring pyrotechnics held not primarily merely a surname, where the evidence showed present day recognition and continuing fame of John Philip Sousa as a composer of patriotic music, and the applicant's goods and services were of a nature that "would be associated by potential purchasers with patriotic events such as the Fourth of July, patriotic figures, and patriotic music"); *Michael S. Sachs Inc. v. Cordon Art B.V.*, 56 USPQ2d 1132 (TTAB 2000) (primary significance of M. C. ESCHER is that of famous deceased Dutch artist). *Cf. In re Pickett Hotel Co.*,

游戏的结果，但"DARTY"还是被认为主要仅为一个姓氏）；*Petrin Corp*.，231 USPQ 902（TTAB 1986）（尽管申请者抗辩称该商标表示"petroleum"和"insulation"二词的缩写，但"PETRIN"还是被认为主要仅为一个姓氏）。

1211.01(a)(iii)　地理含义

如果具有姓氏含义的词语同时具有著名的地理含义，则该词也可能并非主要仅属姓氏。*In re Colt Industries Operating Corp*.，195 USPQ 75（TTAB 1977）（"FAIRBANKS"被认为并非仅是姓氏，因为该商标的地理含义被判定与其姓氏含义同样重要）。不过，若某词作为地理词语只表现出一些次要的含义，那么就不能改变其主要含义的姓氏性质。*参见 Hamilton Pharmaceuticals Ltd*.，27 USPQ2d 1939，1943（TTAB 1993）（"HAMILTON"被认为主要仅是一个姓氏）。

1211.01(a)(iv)　历史地点或人物［R-2］

如果具有姓氏含义的词语同时识别了一个历史地点或人物，则该词也可能并非主要仅属姓氏。*参见 Lucien Piccard Watch Corp*. *v*. *Since* 1868 *Crescent Corp*.，314 F.Supp.329，165 USPQ 459（S.D.N.Y.1970）（"DA VINCI"被认为并非仅是一个姓氏，因为其意为 Leonardo Da Vinci）；*Pyro-Spectaculars*，*Inc*.，63 USPQ2d 2022，2024（TTAB 2002）（用于烟火以及使用烟火的集会和表演产品的"SOUSA"被认为并非仅是一个姓氏，因为证据表明 John Philip Sousa 作为一名爱国音乐作曲家享誉已久，并且在当今时代仍然得到公认，而申请者的商品和服务的性质"会被潜在购买者与爱国集会活动，诸如 7 月 4 日、爱国图画以及爱国音乐相联系"）；*Michael S*. *Sachs Inc*. *v*. *Cordon Art B*. *V*.，56 USPQ2d 1132（TTAB 2000）（"M.C.ESCHER"的主要含义是著名的已故荷兰艺术家）。比较：*Pickett Hotel Co*.，229 USPQ 760

229 USPQ 760 (TTAB 1986) (PICKETT SUITE HOTEL held primarily merely a surname despite applicant's evidence that PICKETT was the name of a famous Civil War general); *In re Champion International Corp.*, 229 USPQ 550 (TTAB 1985) (McKINLEY held primarily merely a surname despite being the name of a deceased president).

1211.01(a)(v) Rare Surnames

The rarity of a surname is a factor to be considered in determining whether a term is primarily merely a surname. *In re Benthin Management GmbH*, 37 USPQ2d 1332 (TTAB 1995) (the fact that BENTHIN was a rare surname found to be a factor weighing against a finding that the term would be perceived as primarily merely a surname); *In re Sava Research Corp.*, 32 USPQ2d 1380 (TTAB 1994) (SAVA not primarily merely a surname, where there was evidence that the term had other meaning, no evidence that the term was the surname of anyone connected with applicant, and the term's use as a surname was very rare); *In re Garan Inc.*, 3 USPQ2d 1537 (TTAB 1987) (GARAN held not primarily merely a surname). However, the fact that a surname is rare does not *per se* preclude a finding that a term is primarily merely a surname. Even a rare surname may be held primarily merely a surname if its primary significance to purchasers is that of a surname. *See In re Etablissements Darty et Fils*, 759 F.2d 15, 225 USPQ 652 (Fed. Cir. 1985) (DARTY held primarily merely a surname); *In re Rebo High Definition Studio Inc.*, 15 USPQ2d 1314 (TTAB 1990) (REBO held primarily merely a surname); *In re Pohang Iron & Steel Co., Ltd.*, 230 USPQ 79 (TTAB 1986) (POSTEN held primarily merely a surname). Regardless of the rarity of the surname, the test is whether the primary significance of the term to the purchasing public is that of a surname.

1211.01(a)(vi) "Look And Feel" of a Surname

There are some names which by their very nature have only a surname signifi-

(TTAB 1986)(尽管申请者提供的证据表明“PICKETT”是内战中著名将领的名字，“PICKETT SUITE HOTEL”被认为主要仅是一个姓氏)；*Champion International Corp.*, 229 USPQ 550 (TTAB 1985)(“McKINLEY”被认为仅是一个姓氏,尽管这也是已故总统的名字)。

1211.01(a)(v)　罕见姓氏

在判断一个词语是否主要是一个姓氏的过程中,姓氏的罕见程度是一个需要考虑的因素。相关判例：*Benthin Management GmbH*, 37 USPQ2d 1332 (TTAB 1995)(“BENTHIN”属于罕见姓氏这一情况,被认为在衡量针对该词会被认为主要属于一个姓氏的观点提出的抗辩时,属于需要考虑的因素之一)；*Sava Research Corp.*, 32 USPQ2d 1380 (TTAB 1994)(“SAVA”被认为并非主要属于一个姓氏,因为证据表明该词具有其他含义,而并没有证据证明该词是任何与申请者有关者的姓氏,而且该词作为姓氏使用极为罕见)；*Garan Inc.*, 3 USPQ2d 1537 (TTAB 1987)(“GARAN”被认为并非主要是一个姓氏)。不过,罕见姓氏这一性质本身并不能导致判定该词并非主要是一个姓氏。即使是一个罕见姓氏,也可能被认为主要是一个姓氏,只要它对于购买者的主要含义是该姓氏。参见 *Etablissements Darty et Fils*, 759 F.2d 15, 225 USPQ 652 (Fed. Cir. 1985)(“DARTY”被认为主要仅是一个姓氏)；*Rebo High Definition Studio Inc.*, 15 USPQ2d 1314 (TTAB 1990)(“REBO”被认为主要仅是一个姓氏)；*Pohang Iron & Steel Co., Ltd.*, 230 USPQ 79 (TTAB 1986)(“POSTEN”被认为主要仅是一个姓氏)。不管姓氏的罕见性如何,检验的标准是该词对于购买公众的主要含义是否是该姓氏。

1211.01(a)(vi)　姓氏的“外观和感受”

有一些名字,尽管属于罕见姓氏,但由于其特殊性质仍然只具有姓氏含义。

cance even though they are rare surnames. *See In re Industrie Pirelli Societa per Azioni*, 9 USPQ2d 1564, 1566 (TTAB 1988), *aff'd*, 883 F.2d 1026 (Fed. Cir. 1989) (PIRELLI held primarily merely a surname, the Board stating that "certain rare surnames look like surnames and certain rare surnames do not and ... 'PIRELLI' falls into the former category ..."); *In re Petrin Corp.*, 231 USPQ 902 (TTAB 1986) (PETRIN held primarily merely a surname). Conversely, there is a category of surnames that are so rare that they do not even have the appearance of surnames. Where these are involved, even in the absence of non-surname significance, a reasonable application of the test of "primary significance to the purchasing public" could result in a finding that such a surname, when used as a mark, would be perceived as arbitrary or fanciful. *In re United Distillers plc*, 56 USPQ2d 1220 (TTAB 2000) (HACKLER does not have the look and feel of a surname).

1211.01(b) Surname Combined with Additional Matter

Often a mark will be comprised of a word that, standing by itself, would be primarily merely a surname, coupled with additional matter (*e.g.*, letters, words, designs). The question remains whether the mark sought to be registered would be perceived by the public primarily merely as a surname. *In re Hutchinson Technology Inc.*, 852 F.2d 552, 7 USPQ2d 1490 (Fed. Cir. 1988). *See* TMEP §§1211.01(b)(i) through 1211.01(b)(vii) for additional information about surnames combined with additional matter.

1211.01(b)(i) Double Surnames

A combination of two surnames is not primarily merely a surname, within the meaning of §2(e)(4), unless there is evidence of record showing that the combination would be perceived by the public primarily merely as a surname. *See In re Standard Elektrik Lorenz A. G.*, 371 F.2d 870, 152 USPQ 563 (C. C. P. A. 1967) (SCHAUB-LORENZ held not primarily merely a surname, the Court noting that

参见 *Industrie Pirelli Societa per Azioni*, 9 USPQ2d 1564, 1566 (TTAB 1988), *aff'd*, 883 F.2d 1026 (Fed. Cir. 1989)("PIRELLI"被认为主要仅是一个姓氏,委员会称:"某些罕见姓氏看起来像是姓氏,另一些则并非如此,而且……'PIRELLI'就属于前者……");*Petrin Corp*., 231 USPQ 902 (TTAB 1986)("PETRIN"被认为主要仅是一个姓氏)。与此相反,有一种姓氏太过罕见以至于外观上都不像是姓氏。如果涉及此类姓氏,即使缺乏非姓氏含义,合理申请对"对于购买公众的主要含义"进行检验的结果仍然会是判定该姓氏用作商标时会被认为是任意性或臆造性的。见:*United Distillers plc*, 56 USPQ2d 1220 (TTAB 2000)("HACKLER"不具有姓氏的外观和感受)。

1211.01(b) 姓氏与其他内容的组合

一项商标经常由本身属于主要仅是姓氏的词语,加上其他内容构成(例如:字母、文字、图案)。申请注册的商标是否会被公众认为主要是一个姓氏的问题仍然存在。*Hutchinson Technology Inc*., 852 F.2d 552, 7 USPQ2d 1490 (Fed. Cir. 1988)。有关姓氏与其他内容组合的其他情况,*参见* TMEP §§1211.01(b)(i)至 1211.01(b)(vii)。

1211.01(b)(i) 双重姓氏

根据 §2(e)(4),两个姓氏的组合并非主要是一个姓氏,除非有档案证据表明该组合会被公众认为主要仅是姓氏。*参见 Standard Elektrik Lorenz A.G*., 371 F.2d 870, 152 USPQ 563 (C.C.P.A. 1967)("SCHAUB-LORENZ"被认为并非主要仅是

there was no evidence submitted that the mark sought to be registered was primarily merely a surname; that the only evidence of surname significance related to the individual "SCHAUB" and "LORENZ" portions of the mark; and that the mark must be considered in its entirety rather than dissected).

1211.01(b)(ii) Stylization or Design Element

A mark comprised of a word that, standing by itself, would be considered primarily merely a surname, but which is coupled with a distinctive stylization or design element, is not considered primarily merely a surname. *In re Benthin Management GmbH*, 37 USPQ2d 1332 (TTAB 1995) (stylized display of term BENTHIN found to be a factor weighing against a finding that the term would be perceived as primarily merely a surname). However, the addition of a nondistinctive design element or stylization to a term that, standing by itself, is primarily merely a surname does not remove the term from that category. The primary significance of the mark, in its entirety, would be merely that of a surname. *See In re Pickett Hotel Co.*, 229 USPQ 760, 763 (TTAB 1986) (PICKETT SUITE HOTEL held primarily merely a surname despite the stylization of the lettering, which was considered "insignificant, in that it is clearly not so distinctive as to create any separate commercial impression in the minds of purchasers of appellant's services").

The display of a term in lower-case lettering does not detract from its surname significance. *In re Directional Marketing Corp.*, 204 USPQ 675 (TTAB 1979).

1211.01(b)(iii) Surname Combined with Initials

The addition of initials to a term that, standing by itself, is primarily merely a surname does not remove the term from that category. In fact, the use of the first name initial followed by a surname has been held to reinforce, rather than diminish, the surname significance of a term. *See In re I. Lewis Cigar Mfg. Co.*, 205 F.2d 204, 98 USPQ 265 (C.C.P.A. 1953) (S. SEIDENBERG & CO'S. held primarily

一个姓氏，法庭解释说，提交的证据并没有能够证明申请注册的商标主要仅是一个姓氏；姓氏含义仅有的证据是关于该商标的“SCHAUB”和“LORENZ”部分；因此对于该商标必须从其整体而不是分解的意义上去考虑）。

1211.01(b)(ii) 风格化或图案因素

如果某项商标包含本身属于主要仅是姓氏的词语，但是同时附随显著的风格化或图案因素，那么就不被认为主要仅为姓氏。见：*Benthin Management GmbH*，37 USPQ2d 1332（TTAB 1995）（“BENTHIN”一词的风格化展示被判定，在衡量针对该词会被认为主要属于一个姓氏的观点提出的抗辩时，属于需要考虑的因素之一）。不过，在一个本身属于主要仅为姓氏的词语上加以不具独特性的图案因素或进行风格化，并不能改变该词的性质。该商标在整体上的主要含义，会被认为仅仅是一个姓氏。*参见 Pickett Hotel Co*.，229 USPQ 760，763（TTAB 1986）（“PICKETT SUITE HOTEL”被认为主要仅为姓氏，尽管对于字母拼法进行了风格化，但这种风格化被认为是“可以忽略，因为很明显对于申请者的服务，并没有在购买者的脑海中显著地造成任何独立的商业印象”）。

以较小的字体展示词语，无法减损其姓氏含义。*见 Directional Marketing Corp*.，204 USPQ 675（TTAB 1979）。

1211.01(b)(iii) 与首字母大写词组合的姓氏

在本身主要仅为姓氏的词语上加以首字母大写并不能改变该词的性质。实际上，在姓氏之前冠以首字母大写被认为是加强，而非削弱了该词的姓氏含义。*参见 I. Lewis Cigar Mfg. Co*.，205 F.2d 204，98 USPQ 265（C.C.P.A.1953）（“S.SEIDEN-

merely a surname); *In re Nelson Souto Major Piquet*, 5 USPQ2d 1367 (TTAB 1987) (N. PIQUET held primarily merely a surname); *In re Taverniti*, SARL, 225 USPQ 1263 (TTAB 1985), *recon. denied* 228 USPQ 975 (TTAB 1985) (J. TAVERNITI held primarily merely a surname); *Ex parte Sears, Roebuck & Co.*, 87 USPQ 400 (PO Ex. Ch. 1950) (J. C. HIGGINS held primarily merely a surname).

1211.01(b)(iv) Surname Combined with Title

A title, such as "Mr.," "Mrs." or "Mlle.," does not diminish the surname significance of a term; rather, it may enhance the surname significance of a term. *In re Revillon*, 154 USPQ 494 (TTAB 1967) (MLLE. REVILLON held primarily merely a surname). *Cf. In re Hilton Hotels Corp.*, 166 USPQ 216 (TTAB 1970) (LADY HILTON held not primarily merely a surname because it suggests a person or lady of nobility).

1211.01(b)(v) Surname in Plural or Possessive Form

The surname significance of a term is not diminished by the fact that the term is presented in its plural or possessive form. *See In re Woolley's Petite Suites*, 18 USPQ2d 1810 (TTAB 1991) (WOOLLEY'S PETITE SUITES for hotel and motel services held primarily merely a surname); *In re McDonald's Corp.*, 230 USPQ 304, 306 (TTAB 1986) (MCDONALD'S held primarily merely a surname based on a showing of surname significance of "McDonald," the Board noting that "it is clear that people use their surnames in possessive and plural forms to identify their businesses or trades"); *In re Luis Caballero, S. A.*, 223 USPQ 355 (TTAB 1984) (BURDONS held primarily merely a surname based in part on telephone listings showing surname significance of "Burdon"); *In re Directional Marketing Corp.*, 204 USPQ 675 (TTAB 1979) (DRUMMONDS held primarily merely a surname based on a showing of surname significance of "Drummond").

1211.01(b)(vi) Surname Combined with Wording

The treatment of marks that include wording in addition to a term that, standing

BERG & CO'S."被认为主要仅为姓氏);*Nelson Souto Major Piquet*,5 USPQ2d 1367(TTAB 1987)("N. PIQUET"被认为主要仅为姓氏);*Taverniti*,SARL,225 USPQ 1263(TTAB 1985),*recon. denied* 228 USPQ 975(TTAB 1985)("J. TAVERNITI"被认为主要仅为姓氏);*Sears*,*Roebuck & Co.*,87 USPQ 400(PO Ex. Ch. 1950)("J.C. HIGGINS"被认为主要仅为姓氏)。

1211.01(b)(iv) 与称谓组合的姓氏

称谓,诸如"Mr."、"Mrs."及"Mlle."等不会减弱词语的姓氏含义;甚至会强化该词的姓氏含义。见 *Revillon*,154 USPQ 494(TTAB 1967)("MLLE. REVILLON"被认为主要仅为姓氏)。比较:*Hilton Hotels Corp.*,166 USPQ 216(TTAB 1970)("LADY HILTON"被认为并非主要仅为姓氏,因为该词暗示了一位贵族人物或夫人)。

1211.01(b)(v) 复数及所有格形式的姓氏

以复数或所有格形式出现并不能减弱词语的姓氏含义。参见 *Woolley's Petite Suites*,18 USPQ2d 1810(TTAB 1991)(用于宾馆及汽车旅馆的"WOOLLEY'S PETITE SUITES"被认为主要仅为姓氏);*McDonald's Corp.*,230 USPQ 304,306(TTAB 1986)(由于证明了其姓氏含义,"MCDONALD'S"被认为主要仅为姓氏,委员会称"很明显人们以复数和所有格形式使用其姓氏以识别其业务");*Luis Caballero*,*S.A.*,223 USPQ 355(TTAB 1984)(部分基于电话簿所表明"Burdon"的姓氏含义,"BURDONS"被认为主要仅为姓氏);*Directional Marketing Corp.*,204 USPQ 675(TTAB 1979)(基于证明了"Drummond"的姓氏含义,"DRUMMONDS"被认为主要仅为姓氏)。

1211.01(b)(vi) 与措辞组合的姓氏

对于在本身主要仅为姓氏的词语以外附加措辞而构成的商标所采取的处理方

by itself, is primarily merely a surname, depends on the significance of the non-surname wording.

If the wording combined with the surname is incapable of functioning as a mark (*i.e.*, a generic name for the goods or services), the examining attorney should refuse registration on the ground that the entire mark is primarily merely a surname under §2(e)(4). If the policy were otherwise, one could evade §2(e)(4) by the easy expedient of adding the generic name of the goods or services to a word that is primarily merely a surname. *In re Hamilton Pharmaceuticals Ltd.*, 27 USPQ2d 1939 (TTAB 1993) (HAMILTON PHARMACEUTICALS for pharmaceutical products held primarily merely a surname); *In re Cazes*, 21 USPQ2d 1796, 1797 (TTAB 1991) (BRASSERIE LIPP held primarily merely a surname where "'brasserie' is a generic term for applicant's restaurant services"); *In re Woolley's Petite Suites*, 18 USPQ2d 1810 (TTAB 1991) (WOOLLEY'S PETITE SUITES for hotel and motel services held primarily merely a surname); *In re Possis Medical, Inc.*, 230 USPQ 72, 73 (TTAB 1986) (POSSIS PERFUSION CUP held primarily merely a surname, the Board finding that "[a]pplicant's argument that PERFUSION CUP is not a generic name for its goods ... is contradicted by the evidence the Examining Attorney has pointed to"); *In re E. Martinoni Co.*, 189 USPQ 589, 590-591 (TTAB 1975) (LIQUORE MARTINONI (stylized) for liqueur held primarily merely a surname, with "liquore" being the Italian word for "liqueur").

If the wording combined with the surname is capable of functioning as a mark (*i.e.*, matter that is arbitrary, suggestive or merely descriptive of the goods or services), the mark is not considered to be primarily merely a surname under §2(e)(4). However, if the additional wording is merely descriptive or the equivalent, and a disclaimer is otherwise proper, the examining attorney should require a disclaimer of the additional wording. *See In re Hutchinson Technology Inc.*, 852 F.2d 552, 7 USPQ2d 1490 (Fed. Cir. 1988) (HUTCHINSON TECHNOLOGY for computer components held not primarily merely a surname when the mark is considered as a whole, the Court remanding the case for entry of a disclaimer of

法，取决于该非姓氏措辞。

如果与形式组合的措辞不具有商标功能（亦即，是商品或服务的一般名称），那么审查员就应当根据§2(e)(4)的规定，以该商标整体主要仅为姓氏为理由拒绝予以注册。如果不采取这种方针，人们就可以简单地通过在主要仅为姓氏的词上加以商品或服务的一般名称而规避§2(e)(4)的规定。相关判例：*Hamilton Pharmaceuticals Ltd.*, 27 USPQ2d 1939 (TTAB 1993)（用于药品的"HAMILTON PHARMACEUTICALS"被认为主要仅为姓氏）；*Cazes*, 21 USPQ2d 1796, 1797 (TTAB 1991)（"BRASSERIE LIPP，因为"'brasserie'是申请者所提供的餐饮服务的一般词语"）；*Woolley's Petite Suites*, 18 USPQ2d 1810 (TTAB 1991)（用于宾馆和汽车旅馆服务的"WOOLLEY'S PETITE SUITES"被认为主要仅为姓氏）：*Possis Medical, Inc.*, 230 USPQ 72, 73 (TTAB 1986)（"POSSIS PERFUSION CUP"被认为主要仅为姓氏，委员会判定"申请者抗辩称"PERFUSION CUP"并非其商品的一般名称……有悖于审查员所指出的证据"）；*E. Martinoni Co.*, 189 USPQ 589, 590 - 591 (TTAB 1975)（用于利口酒的"LIQUORE MARTINONI（风格化）"被认为主要仅为姓氏，因为"liquore"就是意大利语的"liqueur"）。

如果与姓氏组合的措辞具有商标功能（亦即，任意性、暗示性或仅为对商品及服务的描述），那么该商标就不能被认为是§2(e)(4)所规定的主要仅为姓氏。不过，如果附加的措辞仅具描述性或者是同义词，并且可以撤回，那么审查员应当要求撤回该措辞。参见 *Hutchinson Technology Inc.*, 852 F.2d 552, 7 USPQ2d 1490 (Fed. Cir. 1988)（用于电脑组件的"HUTCHINSON TECHNOLOGY"从商标的整体考虑被认

"TECHNOLOGY" before publication).

1211.01(b)(vii) Surname Combined With Domain Name

A surname combined with a top-level domain name (*e.g.*, JOHNSON.COM) is primarily merely a surname under §2(e)(4). *See* TMEP §1215.03

1211.02 Evidence Relating to Surname Refusal

1211.02(a) Evidentiary Burden—Generally

The burden is initially on the examining attorney to establish a *prima facie* case that a mark is primarily merely a surname. The burden then shifts to the applicant to rebut this showing. *In re Petrin Corp.*, 231 USPQ 902 (TTAB 1986). The evidence submitted by the examining attorney was found insufficient to establish a *prima facie* case in the following decisions: *In re Kahan & Weisz Jewelry Mfg. Corp.*, 508 F.2d 831, 184 USPQ 421 (C.C.P.A. 1975); *In re BDH Two Inc.*, 26 USPQ2d 1556 (TTAB 1993); *In re Raivico*, 9 USPQ2d 2006 (TTAB 1988); *In re Garan Inc.*, 3 USPQ2d 1537 (TTAB 1987).

There is no rule as to the kind or amount of evidence necessary to make out a *prima facie* showing that a term is primarily merely a surname. This question must be resolved on a case-by-case basis. *See*, *e.g.*, *In re Monotype Corp. PLC*, 14 USPQ2d 1070 (TTAB 1989); *In re Pohang Iron & Steel Co., Ltd.*, 230 USPQ 79 (TTAB 1986). The entire record is examined to determine the surname significance of a term. The following are examples of evidence that may be relevant: telephone directory listings; excerpted articles from computerized research databases; evidence in the record that the term is a surname; the manner of use on specimens; dictionary definitions of the term and evidence from dictionaries showing no definition of the term. The quantum of evidence that is persuasive in finding surname significance in one case may be insufficient in another because of

为并非仅为姓氏,法庭发回该案,要求在公布前撤回“TECHNOLOGY”)。

1211.01(b)(vii)　与域名组合的姓氏

与顶级域名组合的姓氏(例如,JOHNSON.COM)根据 §2(e)(4)主要仅为姓氏。*参见* TMEP §1215.03。

1211.02　关于以姓氏为理由拒绝予以注册的证据

1211.02(a)　举证责任——概述

首先,审查员对于商标主要仅为姓氏的初步证明负有举证责任。然后,举证责任就转到申请人一方,对这种证明进行反驳。见 *Petrin Corp*., 231 USPQ 902 (TTAB 1986)。在下列案件的判决中,审查员提交的证据被判定不足以形成初步证明:*Kahan & Weisz Jewelry Mfg. Corp*., 508 F.2d 831, 184 USPQ 421 (C.C.P.A.1975); *BDH Two Inc*., 26 USPQ2d 1556 (TTAB 1993); *Raivico*, 9 USPQ2d 2006 (TTAB 1988); *Garan Inc*., 3 USPQ2d 1537 (TTAB 1987)。

关于形成某词语主要仅为姓氏的初步证明所需的证据种类和量并没有任何规定。该问题必须根据个案的不同情况加以解决。*参见 Monotype Corp. PLC*, 14 USPQ2d 1070 (TTAB 1989); *Pohang Iron & Steel Co., Ltd*., 230 USPQ 79 (TTAB 1986)。整个档案都应加以审查以判断词语的姓氏含义。以下是可能相关的证据列举:电话地址簿列表;来自于电脑化搜索数据库的摘录文章;该词是姓氏的档案证据;样本的使用方式;词典对该词的定义以及词典表明无此词定义的证据。由于名称本身的差异,在一个案件中对于证明姓氏含义充分的证据量在另一个案件中就有可能

the differences in the names themselves. *See In re Etablissements Darty et Fils*, 759 F.2d 15, 17, 225 USPQ 652, 653 (Fed. Cir. 1985).

See TMEP §§710 *et seq*. and 1211.02(b) *et seq*. for additional information about evidence.

1211.02(b) Evidentiary Considerations

In appropriate cases, the examining attorney may present evidence that may appear contrary to his or her position, with an appropriate explanation as to why, in view of other evidence presented, this evidence was not considered controlling. In some cases, this may foreclose objections from an applicant and present a more complete picture in the event of an appeal.

See TMEP §§1211.02(b)(i) through 1211.02(b)(vi) regarding types of evidence that may be relevant to a refusal of registration under §2(e)(4).

1211.02(b)(i) Telephone Directory Listings

Telephone directory listings from telephone books or electronic databases are one type of credible evidence of the surname significance of a term. The Trademark Trial and Appeal Board has declined to hold that a minimum number of listings in telephone directories must be found to establish a *prima facie* showing that the mark is primarily merely a surname. *See*, *e.g.*, *In re Petrin Corp*., 231 USPQ 902 (TTAB 1986); *In re Wickuler-Kupper-Brauerei KGaA*, 221 USPQ 469 (TTAB 1983).

It is the American public's perception of a term that is determinative. Therefore, foreign telephone directory listings are not probative of the significance of a term to the purchasing public in the United States, regardless of whether the applicant is of foreign origin. *See*, *e.g.*, *Société Civile Des Domaines Dourthe Frères v. S. A. Consortium Vinicole De Bordeaux Et De La Gironde*, 6 USPQ2d 1205 (TTAB

证据不足。参见 *Etablissements Darty et Fils*，759 F.2d 15，17，225 USPQ 652，653（Fed. Cir. 1985）。

有关证据的其他情况，参见 TMEP §§710 及以下和 1211.02(b)及以下。

1211.02(b)　　有关证据的考虑因素

在适当的案件中，审查员可以提出与其地位相反的证据，同时说明从提交的其他证据来看，该证据为何不能被认为是决定性的。在某些案件中，这样做可以预先防止申请者提出异议并在上诉中提出某种更为复杂的解释。

有关与根据 §2(e)(4)作出不予注册决定相关的证据种类，参见 TMEP §§1211.02(b)(i)至 1211.02(b)(vi)。

1211.02(b)(i)　　电话地址簿列表

来自电话手册以及电子数据库的电话地址簿列表对于词语的姓氏含义是一种可信的证据。商标评审及上诉委员会对于商标主要仅为姓氏的初步证明，并没有确定一种电话簿列表数所需要的最小数量。参见 *Petrin Corp.*，231 USPQ 902（TTAB 1986）；*Wickuler-Kupper-Brauerei KGaA*，221 USPQ 469（TTAB 1983）。

美国公众对于词语的感知是决定性因素。因此，关于某词对于美国购买公众的含义，外国电话簿列表不具有证明力，不管申请者是否来自外国。参见 *Société Civile Des Domaines Dourthe Frères v. S. A. Consortium Vinicole De Bordeaux Et De La Gironde*，6 USPQ2d 1205（TTAB 1988）；*Stromsholmens Mekaniska Verkstad AB*，228 USPQ 968（TTAB 1986）；*Wickuler-Kupper-Brauerei*，案卷号同前。

1988); *In re Stromsholmens Mekaniska Verkstad AB*, 228 USPQ 968 (TTAB 1986); *In re Wickuler-Kupper-Brauerei*, *supra*.

1211.02(b)(ii) LEXIS-NEXIS® Research Database Evidence

Excerpted articles from the LEXIS-NEXIS® research database are one type of credible evidence of the surname significance of a term. There is no requirement that the examining attorney make of record every story found in a LEXIS-NEXIS ® search. However, the examining attorney is presumed to make the best case possible. *See In re Federated Department Stores Inc*., 3 USPQ2d 1541, 1542 n.2 (TTAB 1987). *See also In re Monotype Corp. PLC*, 14 USPQ2d 1070, 1071 (TTAB 1989) ("We must conclude that, because the Examining Attorney is presumed to have made the best case possible, the 46 stories not made of record [the search yielded 48 stories] do not support the position that CALISTO is a surname and, indeed, show that CALISTO has non surname meanings.") An Office action that includes any evidence obtained from a research data base should include a citation to the research service and a clear record of the specific search that was conducted, indicating the libraries or files that were searched and the date of the search (*e.g.*, LEXIS®, NEXIS® library, CURRNT file as of April 28, 1992). The printout summarizing the search should be made a part of the record. Relevant information not included on the printout, such as the number of documents viewed, should be stated in narrative in the Office action. *See* TMEP §710.01(a).

Since it is the American public's perception of a term that is determinative, evidence from foreign publications is given little or no weight. *See In re BDH Two Inc*., 26 USPQ2d 1556 (TTAB 1993).

1211.02(b)(iii) Surname of Person Associated with Applicant

The fact that a term is the surname of an individual associated with the applicant (*e.g.*, an officer or founder) is evidence of the surname significance of the term.

1211.02(b)(ii)　LEXIS-NEXIS® 搜索数据库证据

来自于 LEXIS-NEXIS®搜索数据库的摘录文章对于词语的姓氏含义是一种可信的证据。并不要求审查员对于从 LEXIS-NEXIS®查询到的一切情况都要进行记录。不过,审查员被假定已经作了尽量详尽的搜索。*参见 Federated Department Stores Inc.*, 3 USPQ2d 1541, 1542 n.2 (TTAB 1987)。*另参见 Monotype Corp. PLC*, 14 USPQ2d 1070, 1071 (TTAB 1989)("我们必须得出如下结论,由于审查员被假定为已经作了尽量详尽的搜索,未进入档案的 46 种情况[搜索结果得到 48 种情况]并不能支持 CALISTO 是一个姓氏的观点,而且实际上,表明了 CALISTO 不具有姓氏含义")。一项包含任何来自于搜索的证据的商标局决定,必须包含一份搜索服务引用表,以及进行特定搜索的清晰记录,标明进行搜索的资料库或文件,以及搜索的日期(例如:LEXIS®, NEXIS® 资料库,当前文件,1992 年 4 月 28 日)。档案中应包括搜索摘要的打印稿。打印稿中未涉及的相关信息,诸如所审阅文件的编号,应在商标局决定中详细说明。*参见* TMEP §710.01(a)。

由于美国公众对于词语的感知具有决定意义,因此来自于外国出版物的证据极少或者没有证明力。*参见 BDH Two Inc.*, 26 USPQ2d 1556 (TTAB 1993)。

1211.02(b)(iii)　与申请者有关之人的姓氏

某词语是与申请者有关的个人的姓氏(例如,某一名官员或者创立者),这种情况

See In re Etablissements Darty et Fils, 759 F.2d 15, 225 USPQ 652 (Fed. Cir. 1985); *In re Rebo High Definition Studio Inc.*, 15 USPQ2d 1314 (TTAB 1990); *In re Industrie Pirelli Societa per Azioni*, 9 USPQ2d 1564 (TTAB 1988), *aff'd*, 883 F.2d 1026 (Fed. Cir. 1989); *In re Taverniti, SARL*, 225 USPQ 1263 (TTAB 1985), *recon. denied*, 228 USPQ 975 (TTAB 1985).

1211.02(b)(iv) Specimens Confirming Surname Significance of Term

The fact that a term appears on the specimens of record in a manner that confirms its surname significance is evidence of the surname significance of a term. *See Société Civile Des Domaines Dourthe Frères v. S. A. Consortium Vinicole De Bordeaux Et De La Gironde*, 6 USPQ2d 1205, 1208 (TTAB 1988) (DOURTHE found primarily merely a surname, the Board noting applicant's references to "Dourthe" as the name of a particular family and finding the surname significance of the term to be reinforced by the appearance on applicant's wine labels of the name and/or signature of an individual named Pierre Dourthe); *In re Taverniti, SARL*, 225 USPQ 1263, 1264 (TTAB 1985), *recon. denied*, 228 USPQ 975 (TTAB 1985) (J. TAVERNITI held primarily merely a surname, the Board considering, among other factors, the presentation of the mark on the specimens in signature form); *In re Luis Caballero, S. A.*, 223 USPQ 355, 356-57 (TTAB 1984) (BURDONS held primarily merely a surname, the Board weighting heavily the applicant's use of "Burdon" on the specimens as a surname, albeit of a fictitious character ("John William Burdon")).

1211.02(b)(v) Negative Dictionary Evidence

Negative dictionary evidence (*i.e.* evidence that a term is absent from dictionaries or atlases) may demonstrate the lack of non-surname significance of a term. *See In re Petrin Corp.*, 231 USPQ 902 (TTAB 1986).

1211.02(b)(vi) Evidence of Fame of a Mark

Evidence of the fame of a mark (*e.g.*, evidence of consumer recognition of a

是该词语具有姓氏含义的证据。参见 *Etablissements Darty et Fils*，759 F.2d 15，225 USPQ 652（Fed. Cir. 1985）；*Rebo High Definition Studio Inc.*，15 USPQ2d 1314（TTAB 1990）；*Industrie Pirelli Societa per Azioni*，9 USPQ2d 1564（TTAB 1988），*aff'd*，883 F.2d 1026（Fed. Cir. 1989）；*Taverniti*，*SARL*，225 USPQ 1263（TTAB 1985），*recon. denied*，228 USPQ 975（TTAB 1985）。

1211.02(b)(iv)　确认词语姓氏含义的样本

某词语在档案样本中以确认其姓氏含义的形式出现，也是该词语具有姓氏含义的证据。参见 *Société Civile Des Domaines Dourthe Frères v. S. A. Consortium Vinicole De Bordeaux Et De La Gironde*，6 USPQ2d 1205，1208（TTAB 1988）（“DOURTHE”被判定主要仅为姓氏，委员会认为，申请人提到“Dourthe”时称其为某特定家族的名称，并且判定，出现在申请者葡萄酒标签上的名为“Pierre Dourthe”的人的名字和/或签名强化了该词的姓氏含义）；*Taverniti*，*SARL*，225 USPQ 1263，1264（TTAB 1985），*recon. denied*，228 USPQ 975（TTAB 1985）（“J. TAVERNITI”被认为主要仅为姓氏，委员会在考虑其他因素的同时，也考虑到样本中以签名形式出现的该商标）；*Luis Caballero*，*S. A.*，223 USPQ 355，356－357（TTAB 1984）[“BURDONS”被认为主要仅为姓氏，委员会着重考虑了申请人在样本中对“Burdon”的使用，尽管这是一个虚构角色（“John William Burdon”）]。

1211.02(b)(v)　消极的词典证据

消极词典证据（亦即，表明词典及地图册中不存在某词条目的证据）可以证明某词不具有姓氏含义。见 *Petrin Corp.*，231 USPQ 902（TTAB 1986）。

1211.02(b)(vi)　有关商标声誉的证据

有关商标声誉的证据（例如，消费者认可某商标的证据，或者对某商标进行宣传

mark, or expenditures made in promoting or advertising a mark) is not relevant unless registration is sought under §2(f). *In re McDonald's Corp.*, 230 USPQ 304, 307 (TTAB 1986) (MCDONALD'S held primarily merely a surname in spite of strong secondary meaning, with the Board stating that "the word 'primarily' refers to the primary significance of the term, that is, the ordinary meaning of the word, and not to the term's strength as a trademark due to widespread advertising and promotion of the term as a mark to identify goods and/or services.") *See also In re Industrie Pirelli Societa per Azioni*, 9 USPQ2d 1564 (TTAB 1988), *aff'd*, 883 F.2d 1026 (Fed. Cir. 1989); *In re Nelson Souto Major Piquet*, 5 USPQ2d 1367 (TTAB 1987).

1212 Acquired Distinctiveness or Secondary Meaning

15 U.S.C. §1052(f). Except as expressly excluded in subsections (a), (b), (c), (d), (e)(3), and (e)(5) of this section, nothing herein shall prevent the registration of a mark used by the applicant which has become distinctive of the applicant's goods in commerce. The Director may accept as prima facie evidence that the mark has become distinctive, as used on or in connection with the applicant's goods in commerce, proof of substantially exclusive and continuous use thereof as a mark by the applicant in commerce for the five years before the date on which the claim of distinctiveness is made. Nothing in this section shall prevent the registration of a mark which, when used on or in connection with the goods of the applicant, is primarily geographically deceptively misdescriptive of them, and which became distinctive of the applicant's goods in commerce before the date of the enactment of the North American Free Trade Agreement Implementation Act.

If a proposed mark is not inherently distinctive, it may be registered on the Principal Register only upon proof of acquired distinctiveness, or "secondary meaning," that is, proof that it has become distinctive as applied to the applicant's goods or services in commerce. If the applicant establishes, to the satisfaction of the examining attorney, that the matter in question has acquired distinctiveness as

和广告的支出证据)并不具有相关性,除非是根据 §2(f)申请注册。见 *McDonald's Corp.*, 230 USPQ 304, 307 (TTAB 1986)("MCDONALD'S"被认为主要仅为姓氏,尽管存在强有力的次要含义,委员会认为"'主要'一词是指词语的主要含义,也就是说,该词的一般含义,而不是指该词由于将其作为识别商品的商标而进行广泛的广告和宣传后作为商标的效力。")。另参见 *Industrie Pirelli Societa per Azioni*, 9 USPQ2d 1564 (TTAB 1988), *aff'd*, 883 F. 2d 1026 (Fed. Cir. 1989); *Nelson Souto Major Piquet*, 5 USPQ2d 1367 (TTAB 1987)。

1212　　获得性独特性及次要含义

15 U. S. C. §1052(f)。除本节(a)、(b)、(c)和(d)和(e)(3)小节明确排除的以外,已由申请人使用,并在商业活动中对于申请人的商品具备独特性的商标均可注册。对于在商业活动中用于申请者商品的商标已经具备独特性的证据,局长可以将其接受为对申请者主张独特性之日五年之前,申请者在商业活动中对商标所实施的实质性专属和持续使用的初步证明。本节中无其他规定禁止一项用于申请人的商品注册时,主要属于对该商品地理欺骗性错误描述的商标,以及在《北美自由贸易协定实施法案》规定之日前已经在商业活动中对于申请者具备了独特性的商标。

如果一项申请注册的商标并不具有固有独特性,那么只有证明已经具备独特性,或者具有"次要含义"——亦即:证明该商标在商业活动中适用于申请者的商品或服务时已经具备了独特性——的情况下方可在联邦商标登记簿注册。如果申请者符合审查员的要求能够证明,所涉内容已经具备了与所指称商品或服务相关联的独特性,

a mark in relation to the named goods or services, then the mark is registrable on the Principal Register under §2(f) of the Trademark Act, 15 U.S.C. §1052(f).

Within the context of the Trademark Act, §2(f) may be described as follows:

> [U]nlike the first five sections of 15 U. S. C. §1052 which define the grounds upon which a trademark registration is to be refused, Section 2(f) serves as an exception to a rejection under the provisions of one of the other sections, Section 2(e) (citation omitted). Section 2(f) permits registration of marks that, despite not qualifying for registration in light of Section 2(e), have nevertheless "become distinctive of the applicant's goods in commerce." Thus, "Section 2(f) is not a provision on which registration can be refused," ... but is a provision under which an applicant has a chance to prove that he is entitled to a federal trademark registration which would otherwise be refused.

Yamaha Int'l Corp. v. Hoshino Gakki Co. Ltd., 840 F.2d 1572, 1580, 6 USPQ2d 1001, 1007 (Fed. Cir. 1988), quoting *In re Capital Formation Counselors, Inc.*, 219 USPQ 916, 917 n.2 (TTAB 1983).

The purpose and significance of secondary meaning may be described as follows:

> A term which is descriptive ... may, through usage by one producer with reference to his product, acquire a special significance so that to the consuming public the word has come to mean that the product is produced by that particular manufacturer. 1 Nims, *Unfair Competition and Trademarks* at §37 (1947). This is what is known as secondary meaning.
>
> The crux of the secondary meaning doctrine is that the mark comes to identify not only the goods but the source of those goods. To establish secondary meaning, it must be shown that the *primary* significance of the term in the minds of the consuming public is not the product but the producer (citations omitted). This may be an anonymous producer, since consumers often buy goods without knowing the personal identity or ac-

那么该商标就可以根据《商标法》§2(f),15 U.S.C.§1052(f)的规定在联邦商标登记簿注册。

结合《商标法》的规定,对于§2(f)可以作如下阐释:

> 与规定了拒绝商标注册理由的15 U.S.C.§1052前五节不同,第2(f)节所规定的是在根据第2(e)节其他各节其中之一规定拒绝注册时的例外情况(引注略)。对尽管根据第2(e)节的规定不得注册,但却"在商业活动中对于申请者的商品具备了独特性"的商标,第2(f)节允许注册。因此,"第2(f)节所规定的并非不予注册的理由,"而是规定申请者有机会证明其对于原本应当遭到拒绝的某项联邦商标注册拥有权利。

见 *Yamaha Int'l Corp. v. Hoshino Gakki Co. Ltd.*, 840 F.2d 1572, 1580, 6 USPQ2d 1001, 1007 (Fed. Cir. 1988),引用 *Capital Formation Counselors, Inc.*, 219 USPQ 916, 917 n.2 (TTAB 1983)。

次要含义的目的和意义可以阐释如下:

> 具有描述性的词语……可以经由某生产商用于其产品,从而获得一种特殊的意义,如此就可以使该词对于消费公众而言具有指示该产品是由特定制造商所生产的含义。1 Nims, *Unfair Competition and Trademarks* at §37 (1947)。这就是所谓的次要含义。
>
> 次要含义理论的关键在于商标不仅识别了商品,而且还识别了这些商品的来源。为了证明次要含义,必须表明,该词语在消费公众脑海中的*首要*含义不是该产品,而是生产商(引注略)。这可能是一个不知名的生产商,因为消费者购买商品时经常并不了解制造商的个人身份或者真实姓名。

tual name of the manufacturer.

Ralston Purina Co. v. Thomas J. Lipton, Inc., 341 F.Supp.129, 133, 173 USPQ 820, 823 (S.D.N.Y.1972).

There are three basic types of evidence that may be used to establish acquired distinctiveness under §2(f):

(1) A claim of ownership of one or more prior registrations on the Principal Register of the same mark for goods or services that are the same as or related to those named in the pending application (*see* 37 C.F.R. §2.41 (b); TMEP §§1212.04 *et seq.*);

(2) A statement verified by the applicant that the mark has become distinctive of the applicant's goods or services by reason of substantially exclusive and continuous use in commerce by the applicant for the five years before the date when the claim of distinctiveness is made (*see* 37 C.F.R. §2.41(b); TMEP §§1212.05 *et seq.*);

(3) Actual evidence of acquired distinctiveness (*see* 37 C.F.R. §2.41(a); TMEP §§1212.06 *et seq.*).

The applicant may submit one or any combination of these types of evidence, which are discussed below. Depending on the mark and the facts in the record, the examining attorney may determine that a claim of ownership of a prior registration(s) or a claim of five years'substantially exclusive and continuous use in commerce is insufficient to establish a *prima facie* case of acquired distinctiveness. The applicant may then submit actual evidence of acquired distinctiveness.

1212.01 General Evidentiary Matters

Whether acquired distinctiveness has been established is a question of fact. *See In re Loew's Theatres, Inc.*, 769 F.2d 764, 769, 226 USPQ 865, 869 (Fed. Cir. 1985), and cases cited therein. The record must contain facts or evidence of ac-

Ralston Purina Co. v. Thomas J. Lipton, Inc., 341 F. Supp. 129, 133, 173 USPQ 820, 823 (S.D.N.Y.1972)。

有三种基本的证据种类可以用来证明 §2(f)所规定的获得性独特性：

(1) 主张在联邦商标登记簿拥有一项或更多同样的在先注册商品或服务商标，该商标与未决申请中所指称的商标相同或相关(*参见* 37 C.F.R.§2.41(b)；TMEP §§1212.04 及以下)；

(2) 一份经过申请者宣誓证明的声明书，声明由于申请者在主张独特性之日五年之前已经在商业活动中实施的实质性专属和持续使用，该商标已经具备了独特性(*参见* 37 C.F.R.§2.41(b)；TMEP §§1212.05 及以下)；

(3) 有关获得性独特性的实际证据(*参见* 37 C.F.R.§2.41(a)；TMEP §§1212.06 及以下)。

申请者可以提交一种证据，或是几种类型证据的组合，关于这一点下文再讨论。根据商标本身以及档案所揭示的情况，审查员可以判断拥有在先注册的所有权要求，或是在商业活动中五年实质性专属和持续使用的权力要求对于获得性独特性是否足以建立一种初步证明。随后申请者可以提交获得性独特性的实际证据。

1212.01 证据概述

获得性独特性能否成立是一个事实问题。*参见 Loew's Theatres, Inc.*, 769 F.2d 764, 769, 226 USPQ 865, 869 (Fed.Cir.1985)，以及所引用的判例。档案中必须包含有关获得性独特性的情况或证据。

quired distinctiveness.

The burden of proving that a mark has acquired distinctiveness is on the applicant. *See Yamaha Int'l Corp. v. Hoshino Gakki Co. Ltd.*, 840 F.2d 1572, 1578-79, 6 USPQ2d 1001, 1006 (Fed. Cir. 1988); *In re Meyer & Wenthe, Inc.*, 267 F.2d 945, 122 USPQ 372 (C.C.P.A. 1959).

The applicant may present any competent evidence to establish that a mark has acquired distinctiveness. Actual evidence of acquired distinctiveness may be submitted regardless of the length of time the mark has been used. *Ex parte Fox River Paper Corp.*, 99 USPQ 173 (Comm'r Pats. 1953).

The amount and character of evidence required to establish acquired distinctiveness depends on the facts of each case and particularly on the nature of the mark sought to be registered. *See Roux Laboratories, Inc. v. Clairol Inc.*, 427 F.2d 823, 166 USPQ 34 (C.C.P.A. 1970); *In re Hehr Mfg. Co.*, 279 F.2d 526, 126 USPQ 381 (C.C.P.A. 1960); *In re Gammon Reel, Inc.*, 227 USPQ 729 (TTAB 1985).

Typically, more evidence is required where a mark is so highly descriptive that purchasers seeing the matter in relation to the named goods or services would be less likely to believe that it indicates source in any one party. *See, e.g., In re Bongrain International Corp.*, 894 F.2d 1316, 13 USPQ2d 1727 (Fed. Cir. 1990); *In re Seaman & Associates, Inc.*, 1 USPQ2d 1657 (TTAB 1986); *In re Packaging Specialists, Inc.*, 221 USPQ 917 (TTAB 1984).

Facts based on events that occurred subsequent to the filing date of the application may be considered. Whether acquired distinctiveness has been established is determined in view of the facts that exist at the time registrability is being considered. *McCormick & Co., Inc. v. Summers*, 354 F.2d 668, 148 USPQ 272 (C.C.P.A. 1966); *General Foods Corp. v. MGD Partners*, 224 USPQ 479 (TTAB 1984); *Kaiser Aluminum & Chemical Corp. v. American Meter Co.*, 153 USPQ 419 (TTAB 1967); *In re Hoffman House Sauce Co.*, 137 USPQ 486 (TTAB 1963).

证明商标具备了获得性独特性的责任由申请者承担。*参见 Yamaha Int'l Corp. v. Hoshino Gakki Co. Ltd.*, 840 F.2d 1572, 1578－1579, 6 USPQ2d 1001, 1006 (Fed. Cir. 1988); *Meyer & Wenthe, Inc.*, 267 F.2d 945, 122 USPQ 372 (C.C.P.A. 1959)。

申请者可以提交一切适格的证据以证明商标具备了获得性独特性。无论商标已经使用了多久,都可以提交作为获得性独特性的实际证据。*Fox River Paper Corp.*, 99 USPQ 173 (Comm'r Pats. 1953)。

证明获得性独特性的证据量和性质取决于个案情况,尤其是申请注册商标的性质。*参见 Roux Laboratories, Inc. v. Clairol Inc.*, 427 F.2d 823, 166 USPQ 34 (C.C.P.A. 1970); *Hehr Mfg. Co.*, 279 F.2d 526, 126 USPQ 381 (C.C.P.A. 1960); *Gammon Reel, Inc.*, 227 USPQ 729 (TTAB 1985)。

典型而言,如果商标具有高度描述性,以至于购买者见到此类内容用于所述商品或服务时不太可能认为其任何部分标示了来源,那么就需要更多的证据。*参见 Bongrain International Corp.*, 894 F.2d 1316, 13 USPQ2d 1727 (Fed. Cir. 1990); *Seaman & Associates, Inc.*, 1 USPQ2d 1657 (TTAB 1986); *Packaging Specialists, Inc.*, 221 USPQ 917 (TTAB 1984)。

申请归档日之后所发生事件的情况也可以加以考虑。是否能够证明具备获得性独特性,须从考察可注册性当时的情况出发加以考虑。*参见 McCormick & Co., Inc. v. Summers*, 354 F.2d 668, 148 USPQ 272 (C.C.P.A. 1966); *General Foods Corp. v. MGD Partners*, 224 USPQ 479 (TTAB 1984); *Kaiser Aluminum & Chemical Corp. v. American Meter Co.*, 153 USPQ 419 (TTAB 1967); *Hoffman House Sauce Co.*, 137 USPQ 486 (TTAB 1963)。

1212.02 General Procedural Matters

1212.02(a) Situations in which a Claim of Distinctiveness under §2(f) Is Appropriate

A claim of distinctiveness by the applicant under §2(f) is usually made either in response to a statutory refusal to register or in anticipation of such a refusal. A claim of distinctiveness is appropriately made in response to, or in anticipation of, only certain statutory refusals to register. For example, it is inappropriate to assert acquired distinctiveness to contravene a refusal under §2(a), (b), (c), (d) or (e)(5), 15 U.S.C. §§1052(a), (b), (c), (d) or (e)(5). Furthermore, acquired distinctiveness may not be asserted to contravene a refusal under §2(e)(3), 15 U.S.C. §1052(e)(3), unless the mark became distinctive of the applicant's goods in commerce before December 8, 1993, the date of enactment of the North American Free Trade Agreement Implementation Act (*see* TMEP §1210.06(b)).

In *In re Soccer Sport Supply Co., Inc.*, 507 F.2d 1400, 1403 n.3, 184 USPQ 345, 347 n.3 (C.C.P.A. 1975), the Court of Customs and Patent Appeals noted as follows:

> [T]he judicially developed concept of "secondary meaning," codified by section 2(f) (15 U.S.C. 1052(f)), relates to descriptive, geographically descriptive, or surname marks which earlier had a primary meaning which did not indicate a single source and were, therefore, unregistrable because of section 2(e) (citation omitted). Additionally, section 2(f) has been applied to permit registration of a mark consisting solely of a design and, therefore, not within the purview of section 2(e).

1212.02(b) Section 2(f) Claim Is, for Procedural Purposes, a Concession that Matter Is Not Inherently Distinctive

For procedural purposes, a claim of distinctiveness under §2(f), whether made in

1212.02 程序概述

1212.02(a) 适合根据 §2(f)提出独特性主张的情况

通常,在遭到依法律规定拒绝予以注册,或者预期会遭到此类拒绝的情况下,申请者会根据 §2(f)提出独特性主张。只有以对于某些法定拒绝予以注册的决定,或其预期,所作出的答辩形式提出的独特性主张才是适当的。例如,为了抗辩根据 §2(a),(b),(c),(d)或(e)(5),15 U.S.C.§§1052(a),(b),(c),(d)或(e)(5)作出的拒绝予以注册的决定,提出获得性独特性主张就是不适当的。此外,获得性独特性主张也不能用来抗辩根据 §2(e)(3),15 U.S.C.§1052(e)(3)作出的拒绝予以注册的决定,除非该商标在 1993 年 12 月 8 日——《北美自由贸易协定实施法》生效日——之前已经在商业中成为申请者商品的独特特征(*参见* TMEP §1210.06(b))。

在 *Soccer Sport Supply Co., Inc.*, 507 F.2d 1400, 1403 n.3, 184 USPQ 345, 347 n.3 (C.C.P.A.1975)一案中,关税及专利上诉法院作了如下阐述:

> 通过司法判例发展起来的,由第 2(f)节(15 U.S.C.1052(f)法典化的"次要含义"的概念是指,早先具有首要含义,但不能标示单一来源,因而根据第 2(e)节的规定不能注册的描述性、地理描述性或姓氏商标。此外,第 2(f)节也已经被适用于准许只包含图案的商标——因而,不属于第 2(e)节规定的范围——获得注册。

1212.02(b) 出于程序目的,第 2(f)节所规定的主张是对于不具有固有独特性的内容的一种妥协

出于程序目的,§2(f)所规定的独特性主张,无论是申请归档时提出,还是事后通

the application as filed or in a subsequent amendment, may be construed as conceding that the matter to which it pertains is not inherently distinctive (and thus not registrable on the Principal Register absent proof of acquired distinctiveness). Once an applicant has claimed that matter has acquired distinctiveness under §2(f), the issue to be determined is not whether the matter is inherently distinctive but, rather, whether it has acquired distinctiveness. *See, e.g., Yamaha Int'l Corp. v. Hoshino Gakki Co. Ltd.*, 840 F.2d 1572, 1577, 6 USPQ2d 1001, 1005 (Fed. Cir. 1988); *In re Cabot Corp.*, 15 USPQ2d 1224, 1229 (TTAB 1990); *In re Professional Learning Centers, Inc.*, 230 USPQ 70, 71 (TTAB 1986); *In re Chopper Industries*, 222 USPQ 258, 259 (TTAB 1984). However, claiming distinctiveness in the alternative is *not* an admission that the proposed mark is not inherently distinctive. TMEP §1212.02(c).

For the purposes of establishing that the subject matter is not inherently distinctive, the examining attorney should not rely on this concession alone, but should rely on other appropriate evidence.

See TMEP §1212.02(d) regarding unnecessary §2(f) claims.

1212.02(c) Claiming §2(f) Distinctiveness in the Alternative

An applicant may argue the merits of an examining attorney's refusal and, in the alternative, claim that the matter sought to be registered has acquired distinctiveness under §2(f). Unlike the situation in which an applicant initially seeks registration under §2(f) or amends its application without objection, the alternative claim does not constitute a concession that the matter sought to be registered is not inherently distinctive. *See In re E S Robbins Corp.*, 30 USPQ2d 1540 (TTAB 1992); *In re Professional Learning Centers, Inc.*; 230 USPQ 70, 71 n.2 (TTAB 1986).

When an applicant claims acquired distinctiveness in the alternative, the examining attorney should treat separately the questions of (1) the underlying basis of

过修正书提出，可以被解释为对于不具有固有独特性（并因此而由于缺乏独特性证据而不能在联邦商标登记簿注册）的内容的让步。一旦申请者根据 §2(f)声称该内容具备了独特性，需要判断的问题就不再是该内容是否具有固有独特性，而是，是否具有获得性独特性。*参见*判例：*Yamaha Int'l Corp. v. Hoshino Gakki Co. Ltd.*, 840 F.2d 1572, 1577, 6 USPQ2d 1001, 1005 (Fed. Cir. 1988)；*Cabot Corp.*, 15 USPQ2d 1224, 1229 (TTAB 1990)；*Professional Learning Centers, Inc.*, 230 USPQ 70, 71 (TTAB 1986)；*Chopper Industries*, 222 USPQ 258, 259 (TTAB 1984)。不过，作为选择提出独特性主张并不等于承认该申请注册商标不具有固有独特性。TMEP §1212.02(c)。

为了证明所提交的内容不具有固有独特性，审查员不应只依赖于这种妥协，而应当依靠其他适当的证据。

有关不必要的 §2(f)主张的情况，*参见* TMEP §1212.02(d)。

1212.02(c) 作为选择对§2(f)所规定的独特性提出主张

申请者可以对审查员作出的不予注册决定的是非提出抗辩，同时也可以选择，声称申请注册的内容已经具备了 §2(f)所规定的独特性。与申请者最初根据 §2(f)申请注册，或是未遭反对时对其申请进行修正的情况不同，此种选择主张并不构成某种对于该申请注册内容不具有固有独特性的让步。*参见 E S Robbins Corp.*, 30 USPQ2d 1540 (TTAB 1992)；*Professional Learning Centers, Inc.*, 230 USPQ 70, 71 n.2 (TTAB 1986)。

如果申请者选择主张获得性独特性，审查员应当分别处理下列问题：(1)拒绝予

refusal and; (2) assuming the matter is determined to be registrable, whether acquired distinctiveness has been established. In the event of an appeal, the Board will use the same analysis, provided the evidence supporting the §2(f) claim is in the record and the alternative grounds have been considered and finally decided by the examining attorney. *In re Harrington*, 219 USPQ 854, 855 n.1 (TTAB 1983)

In *In re Capital Formation Counselors, Inc.*, 219 USPQ 916, 918 (TTAB 1983), the Board outlined its procedure in situations where the applicant maintains the position that the underlying refusal is improper and alternatively seeks registration pursuant to §2(f) in the interest of advancing the prosecution of the application:

> If we decide that the mark as applied to the services is arbitrary or suggestive of the services, as applicant claims, we must reverse the refusal of registration under Section 2(e)(1) and we need not consider any of the affidavits or other material made of record by applicant in support of its Section 2(f) claim of distinctiveness. If, on the other hand, we find the mark to be merely descriptive of the services and, in fact, so highly descriptive of them that no amount of evidence could persuade us that the mark has become distinctive, we must affirm the refusal of registration. Similarly, in this situation, we need not consider any of the affidavits or other material made of record by applicant in its Section 2(f) claim of distinctiveness. If we find that the mark is merely descriptive of the goods for purposes of Section 2(e)(1), but not so highly descriptive as to be incapable of functioning as a service mark to identify applicant's services and distinguish them from like services of others, we must determine whether the evidence in support of applicant's claim of distinctiveness is sufficient to warrant registration under the provisions of Section 2 (f) of the Trademark Act.

Similarly, the applicant may seek registration on the Principal Register under

以注册的根本原因，以及(2)假设该内容被判定可以注册，是否已经证明了具有获得性独特性。在上诉案件中，委员会将使用同样的分析方法，假设档案中的证据能够支持§2(f)所规定的主张，同时已经考虑了可选择的理由，并且最终由审查员作出了裁决。*Harrington*，219 USPQ 854，855 n.1 (TTAB 1983)。

在 *Capital Formation Counselors*，*Inc*.，219 USPQ 916，918 (TTAB 1983)一案中，委员会概述了在申请者坚持认为不予注册不正确，并且为了进一步推进申请程序选择根据§2(f)申请注册的情况下，所采用的程序：

> 如果我们判定，该商标用于服务时，如申请者所主张的属于任意性或暗示性，则我们必须推翻根据第2(e)(1)节作出的拒绝予以注册的决定，并且无需考虑宣誓书，或者申请者为了支持其根据第2(f)节提出的独特性主张而提供的其他档案材料。另一方面，如果我们判定该商标对于服务仅具描述性，并且实际上具有高度的描述性以至于没有证据能够使我们相信该商标具有独特性，我们就必须维护拒绝予以注册的决定。类似地，在这种情况下，我们也不必考虑任何宣誓书，或者申请者为了支持其根据第2(f)节提出的独特性主张而提供的其他档案材料。如果我们判定根据第2(e)(1)节该商标对于商品仅具描述性，但是并非高度描述性而导致不能识别申请者的服务并将其余他人的服务区分开来，从而不具有服务商标的功能，我们就必须判定支持申请者独特性的证据是否足以根据《商标法》第2(f)节的规定获得注册。

类似地，申请者也可以根据§2(f)申请在联邦商标登记簿注册，并且也可以选择

§2(f) and, in the alternative, on the Supplemental Register. Depending on the facts of the case, this approach may have limited practical application. If the examining attorney finds that the matter sought to be registered is not a mark within the meaning of §§1, 2, and 45 of the Trademark Act, 15 U.S.C. §§1051, 1052 and 1127 (*e.g.*, is generic or purely ornamental), the examining attorney will refuse registration on both registers.

However, if the issues are framed in the alternative (*i.e.*, whether the matter sought to be registered has acquired distinctiveness under §2(f) or, in the alternative, whether it is capable of registration on the Supplemental Register), and it is ultimately determined that the matter is a mark within the meaning of the Act (*e.g.*, that the matter is merely descriptive rather than generic), then the evidence of secondary meaning will be considered. If it is determined that the applicant's evidence is sufficient to establish that the mark has acquired distinctiveness, the application will be approved for publication on the Principal Register under §2(f). If the evidence is determined to be insufficient, the mark may be registered on the Supplemental Register.

Accordingly, the applicant may submit an amendment to the Supplemental Register, and continue to argue entitlement to registration on the Principal Register in an appeal.

If the applicant files a notice of appeal in such a case, the examining attorney should forward the application to the Trademark Trial and Appeal Board to institute the appeal. The Board will suspend action on the appeal and remand the application to the examining attorney to determine registrability on the Supplemental Register.

If the examining attorney determines that the applicant is entitled to registration on the Supplemental Register, the examining attorney will return the application to the Board to resume action on the appeal with respect to registration on the Principal Register. The examining attorney should also send a letter notifying the applicant of the acceptance of the amendment and telling the applicant that the

直接向补充登记簿注册。根据案件事实,这种方式可能限制了实际的申请。如果审查员判定,申请注册的内容不属于《商标法》§§1,2,和 45,15 U.S.C.§§1051,1052 和 1127 所规定的商标(例如,属于一般性或是纯粹装饰性),审查员就可以拒绝在两个登记簿注册。

不过,如果问题在选择过程中已经确定(亦即,申请注册的内容是否已经具备了§2(f)所规定的独特性,或者,经过选择,该内容是否能够在补充登记簿注册),并且最终判定该内容确属商标法所规定的商标(例如,该内容仅具描述性,而非属于一般性),那么就需要考虑次要含义的证据。如果判定申请人的证据足以证明该商标已经具备了独特性,那么该申请将根据 §2(f)被批准在联邦商标登记簿公布。如果证据被判定不够充分,那么该商标可以在补充登记簿注册。

相应地,申请者可以向补充登记簿提交修正书,并继续通过上诉对于在联邦商标登记簿的注册权利提出抗辩。

如果在此类案件中,申请者提交了上诉状,那么审查员就应当将该申请转送商标评审及上诉委员会以启动上诉程序。委员会将中止上诉程序,并将申请发回审查员审查其在补充登记簿的可注册性。

如果审查员判定,申请者有权在补充登记簿注册,那么审查员就会将申请交还委员会恢复有关在联邦商标登记簿注册的上诉程序。审查员还应当将接受修正书的情

application is being referred to the Board for resumption of the appeal. If the examining attorney determines that the applicant is not entitled to registration on the Supplemental Register, the examining attorney will issue a nonfinal action refusing registration on the Supplemental Register. If the applicant fails to overcome the refusal, the examining attorney will return the application to the Board to resume action on the appeal with respect to entitlement to registration on either the Principal or the Supplemental Register.

Rather than framing the issues in the alternative (*i.e.*, whether the matter has acquired distinctiveness pursuant to §2(f) or, in the alternative, whether it is capable of registration on the Supplemental Register), the applicant may amend its application between the Principal and Supplemental Registers. 37 C.F.R. §2.75. *See generally In re Educational Communications, Inc.*, 231 USPQ 787 (TTAB 1986); *In re Broco*, 225 USPQ 227 (TTAB 1984).

See TMEP §§816.02 and 1102.03 regarding amending a §1(b) application to the Supplemental Register.

1212.02(d) Unnecessary §2(f) Claims

If the applicant specifically requests registration under §2(f), but the examining attorney considers the entire mark to be inherently distinctive and the claim of acquired distinctiveness to be unnecessary, the examining attorney should so inform the applicant and inquire whether the applicant wishes to delete the statement or to rely on it.

If the applicant specifically requests registration of the entire mark under §2(f), but the examining attorney believes that part of the mark is inherently distinctive, the examining attorney should give the applicant the option of limiting the §2(f) claim to the matter that is not inherently distinctive. (*See* TMEP §1212.02(f) regarding claims of §2(f) distinctiveness as to a portion of a mark.) However, if the applicant wishes, a claim of acquired distinctiveness under §2(f) may be made as

况发函通知申请者，并告知该申请已经提交到委员会恢复上诉程序。如果审查员判定申请者无权在补充登记簿注册，那么审查员将作出非终局决定书，拒绝在联邦商标补充登记簿注册。如果申请者未能克服此项拒绝注册决定，审查员会将申请交还委员会以恢复关于在联邦商标登记簿或补充登记簿注册权利的上诉程序。

除了在选择过程中确定问题(亦即，申请注册的内容是否已经具备了 §2(f)所规定的独特性，或者，经过选择，该内容是否能够在补充登记簿注册)，申请者也可以在联邦商标登记簿和补充登记簿之间对其申请作出修正。37 C.F.R.§2.75。*一般参见 Educational Communications, Inc.*, 231 USPQ 787 (TTAB 1986)；*Broco*, 225 USPQ 227 (TTAB 1984)。

有关对根据 §1(b)提出的再补充登记簿注册的申请进行修正的情况，*参见* TMEP §§816.02 和 1102.03。

1212.02(d) 不必要的§2(f)主张

如果申请者明确要求根据 §2(f)申请注册，但是审查员认为商标整体具有固有独特性，而不必要提出获得性独特性的主张，那么审查员就应当通知申请者，并询问申请者是否希望删除该声明，或者坚持保留。

如果申请者明确要求根据 §2(f)申请注册，但是审查员认为商标部分具有固有独特性，那么审查员就应当给予申请者将该 §2(f)主张限于并不具有固有独特性内容的选择权。(有关 §2(f)所规定的主张商标某一部分已经具备独特性的内容，*参见* TMEP §1212.02(f)。)不过，如果申请者希望，就可以针对同时包含具有固有独特性和不具固有独特性内容的整个商标或者部分，提出§2(f)所规定的获得性独特性

to an entire mark or phrase that contains both inherently distinctive matter and matter that is not inherently distinctive. *In re Del E. Webb Corp.*, 16 USPQ2d 1232, 1234 (TTAB 1990).

If the application contains statements that seem to relate to acquired distinctiveness or §2(f) but do not actually amount to a request for registration under §2(f), and the examining attorney does not believe that resort to §2(f) is necessary, the examining attorney may treat the statements as surplusage. If it is necessary to communicate with the applicant about another matter, the examining attorney should inform the applicant that the statements are being treated as surplusage. If it is otherwise unnecessary to communicate with the applicant, the examining attorney may mark the statements "Do Not Print" and approve the application for publication.

1212.02(e) Disclaimers in Applications Claiming Distinctiveness under §2(f)

Section 6(a) of the Trademark Act, 15 U.S.C. §1056(a), states, in part, "The Director may require the applicant to disclaim an unregistrable component of a mark otherwise registrable." *See In re Creative Goldsmiths of Washington, Inc.*, 229 USPQ 766, 768 (TTAB 1986) ("[W]e conclude that it is within the discretion of an Examining Attorney to require the disclaimer of an unregistrable component (such as a common descriptive, or generic, name) of a composite mark sought to be registered on the Principal Register under the provisions of Section 2(f)."). *Cf. In re Wella Corp.*, 565 F.2d 143, 196 USPQ 7 (C.C.P.A. 1977).

1212.02(f) Section 2(f) Claim in Part (as to a Portion of the Mark)

A claim of acquired distinctiveness may apply to a portion of a mark. The applicant must clearly identify the portion of the mark for which distinctiveness is

主张。*Del E. Webb Corp.*, 16 USPQ2d 1232, 1234 (TTAB 1990)。

如果申请包含了看起来有关获得性独特性或§2(f),但实际上是关于§2(f)所规定的注册申请的声明,而且审查员并不认为有必要诉诸§2(f),那么审查员就可以将该声明视为冗词赘句。如果有必要就其他事项与申请者联系,审查员应当通知申请者该声明已被视为冗词赘句。如果并不需要与申请者联系,则审查员可以在该声明上标注"不必刊印",并批准该申请公布。

1212.02(e) 主张§2(f)独特性的申请中的撤回

《商标法》第6(a)节,15 U.S.C.§1056(a),其中称:"局长可以要求申请者撤回商标中不得注册的组成部分。"参见 *Creative Goldsmiths of Washington, Inc.*, 229 USPQ 766, 768 (TTAB 1986)("我们得出结论,审查员拥有自由裁量权,可以要求撤回根据第2(f)节的规定申请在联邦商标登记簿注册的复合商标中不得注册的组成部分(诸如普通描述性名称或一般名称)。")。比较 *Wella Corp.*, 565 F.2d 143, 196 USPQ 7 (C.C.P.A. 1977)。

1212.02(f) 部分第2(f)节主张(关于商标的某一部分)

获得性独特性主张亦可适用于商标的某一部分。申请人必须清晰识别独特性主

claimed. The standards for establishing acquired distinctiveness are the same whether the claim of distinctiveness pertains to the entire mark or to a portion of it. *See* TMEP §§1212.09 *et seq*. regarding claims of acquired distinctiveness in intent-to-use applications under §1(b) of the Act.

Generally, the element that is the subject of the §2(f) claim must present a distinct commercial impression apart from the other elements of the mark. That is, it must be a separable element in order for the applicant to assert that it has acquired distinctiveness as a mark.

If the examining attorney determines that the claim of distinctiveness as to a portion of the mark is appropriate, the examining attorney should ensure that the record reflects that the §2(f) claim applies to the mark "in part" and that the relevant portion of the mark is identified.

If a claim of distinctiveness applies to only part of a mark and the examining attorney determines (1) that the claimed portion of the mark is unregistrable even under §2(f) (*e.g*., because it is generic or functional), or (2) that, although the claimed portion is registrable, the applicant has failed to establish acquired distinctiveness, the examining attorney may require a disclaimer of that portion of the mark, if a disclaimer is otherwise appropriate. *See In re Lillian Vernon Corp*., 225 USPQ 213 (TTAB 1985) (requirement for disclaimer of PROVENDER affirmed in application to register PROVENDER and design for "mail order services in the gourmet, bath and gift item field," "provender" meaning "food" (claim of §2(f) distinctiveness in part held unacceptable)). *Cf*. *In re Chopper Industries*, 222 USPQ 258 (TTAB 1984) (requirement for disclaimer of CHOPPER reversed in application to register CHOPPER 1 and design for wood log splitting axes (claim of §2(f) distinctiveness in part held acceptable)).

1212.02(g) Examining Attorney's Role in Suggesting §2(f) or Appropriate Kind/Amount of Evidence

In a first action refusing registration, the examining attorney should suggest,

张所针对的商标部分。无论独特性主张针对商标整体还是部分,证明获得性独特性的标准相同。有关根据 §1(b)提出的意图使用申请中的获得性独特性主张,参见 TMEP §§1212.09 及以下。

通常,属于 §2(f)主张的要素必须表明其具有与该商标其他要素不同的商业印象。也就是说,申请者如要主张其具备了作为商标的独特性,那么就必定存在一种独立的要素。

如果审查员判定对于商标某一部分提出的独特性主张是适当的,那么审查员就应当确保档案能够反映出该 §2(f)主张是用于商标的"部分",并且商标的该相关部分已经识别。

如果一项独特性主张仅适用于商标的某一部分,而且审查员判定(1)商标的该部分甚至根据 §2(f)不得注册(例如,因为是属于一般性或功能性内容),或(2)尽管所主张的部分可以注册,但是申请者未能证明其具备独特性,那么只要可以撤回,审查员就可以要求撤回商标的这一部分。参见 *Lillian Vernon Corp.*, 225 USPQ 213 (TTAB 1985)(在"PROVENDER"以及用于"美食、浴具和礼品领域邮购服务"的图案的注册申请中,维持了撤回"PROVENDER"的要求,因为"provender"意为"食品"(根据 §2(f)提出的部分独特性主张未被接受))。比较:*Chopper Industries*, 222 USPQ 258 (TTAB 1984)(在"CHOPPER 1"以及原木斧图案的注册申请中,撤回"CHOPPER"的要求被推翻(根据 §2(f)提出的部分独特性主张被接受))。

1212.02(g) 审查员在建议适用§2(f)以及适当证据种类/量过程中的地位

在拒绝予以注册的初步决定中,如果可以,审查员应当建议申请者修正其申请以

where appropriate, that the applicant amend its application to seek registration under §2(f). For example, this should be done as a matter of course, if otherwise appropriate, in cases where registration is refused under §2(e)(4), on the ground that the mark is primarily merely a surname, and the applicant has recited dates of use that indicate that the mark has been in use in commerce for at least five years.

If the examining attorney determines that an applicant's evidence is insufficient to establish that the mark has acquired distinctiveness, the examining attorney should suggest, where appropriate, that the applicant submit additional evidence. *See In re Half Price Books, Records, Magazines, Inc.*, 225 USPQ 219, 220 n.2 (TTAB 1984) (Noting that applicant was specifically invited to seek registration pursuant to §2(f) but, after amending its application to do so, was refused registration on the ground that the mark was incapable of acquiring distinctiveness, the Board stated that, in fairness to applicant, this practice should be avoided where possible).

The examining attorney should not "require" that the applicant submit evidence of secondary meaning. There would be no practical standard for a proper response to this requirement; nor would there be a sound basis for appeal from the requirement. *See In re Capital Formation Counselors, Inc.*, 219 USPQ 916, 917 n.2 (TTAB 1983) ("Section 2(f) is not a provision on which registration can be refused.").

The examining attorney should not specify the kind or the amount of evidence sufficient to establish that a mark has acquired distinctiveness. It is the responsibility of the applicant to submit evidence to establish that the mark has acquired distinctiveness. *See* TMEP §1212.01. However, the examining attorney may make a suggestion as to a course of action if the examining attorney believes this would further the prosecution of the application.

1212.02(h) Non-Final and Final Refusals

If an application is filed under §2(f) of the Trademark Act and the examining at-

寻求根据§2(f)注册。例如,在根据§2(e)(4)的规定,以商标主要仅为姓氏为由作出了拒绝予以注册的决定,并且申请者已经陈述了使用日期,表明该商标用于商业活动已逾五年的情况下,如果可以,这种建议就应当是一种程序事项。

如果审查员判定申请者的证据不足以证明该商标具备了独特性,那么如果可以,审查员就应当建议申请者提交其他证据。*参见 Half Price Books, Records, Magazines, Inc.*, 225 USPQ 219, 220 n.2 (TTAB 1984)(尽管申请者受特别要求根据 §2(f)寻求注册,但是在按此修改了申请之后,以该商标不具备独特性为由被拒绝注册,委员会称,为了对申请者公平起见,应尽可能避免这种做法)。

审查员不应"要求"申请者提交次要含义的证据。对于此种要求的适当答复,并不存在实践的标准;由此要求而提出上诉也不存在正当的理由。*参见 Capital Formation Counselors, Inc.*, 219 USPQ 916, 917 n.2 (TTAB 1983)("第 2(f)节并非可以用来拒绝予以注册的规定")。

审查员不应确定充分证明商标具备独特性所需的证据种类或量。申请者有责任提交证据证明商标具备了独特性。*参见* TMEP §1212.01。不过,如果审查员认为可以进一步推进申请程序,可以建议所采取的行动步骤。

1212.02(h) 非终局和终局性拒绝予以注册的决定

如果申请是根据《商标法》§2(f)提出,并且审查员判定(1)该商标不具有固有

torney determines that (1) the mark is not inherently distinctive, and (2) the applicant's evidence of secondary meaning is insufficient to establish that the mark has acquired distinctiveness, the examining attorney will issue a non-final action refusing registration on the Principal Register pursuant to the appropriate section of the Trademark Act (*e.g.*, §2(e)(1)), with a finding that the applicant's evidence of secondary meaning is insufficient to overcome the stated refusal. The examining attorney should suggest, where appropriate, that the applicant submit additional evidence. *See* TMEP §1212.02(g) concerning the examining attorney's role in suggesting a claim of distinctiveness under §2(f).

If an application is not filed under §2(f) and the examining attorney determines that the mark is not inherently distinctive, the examining attorney should issue a non-final action refusing registration on the Principal Register under the appropriate section of the Act (*e.g.*, §2(e)(1)). The examining attorney should suggest, where appropriate, that the applicant amend its application to claim distinctiveness under §2(f).

Thereafter, if the applicant amends its application to seek registration under §2(f), a new issue is raised as to the sufficiency of the applicant's evidence of secondary meaning (*see* TMEP §714.05(a)(1)). The underlying statutory basis for refusal remains the same (*e.g.*, §2(e)(1)), but the issue changes from whether the underlying refusal is warranted to whether the matter has acquired distinctiveness. If the examining attorney is persuaded that a *prima facie* case of acquired distinctiveness has been established, the examining attorney will approve the application for publication under §2(f). If the examining attorney determines that the applicant's evidence is insufficient to establish that the matter has acquired distinctiveness, the examining attorney will issue a second non-final action repeating the underlying statutory basis for refusal (*e.g.*, §2(e)(1)), and explaining that the applicant's evidence is insufficient to overcome the stated refusal.

The examining attorney cannot issue a final refusal on the underlying statutory basis of the original refusal, upon an applicant's initial assertion of a §2(f) claim.

独特性，以及(2)申请者关于次要含义的证据不足以证明商标具备了获得性独特性，那么审查员就会根据《商标法》的相关章节(例如，§2(e)(1))作出拒绝在联邦商标登记簿注册的非终局性决定，同时判定申请者关于次要含义的证据不足以推翻上述拒绝决定。如果可以，审查员应当建议申请者提交其他证据。有关审查员在建议§2(f)所规定独特性主张过程中的地位，*参见* TMEP §1212.02(g)。

如果申请并非根据§2(f)提出，而且审查员判定该商标不具有固有独特性，那么审查员就应当根据《商标法》的相关章节(例如，§2(e)(1))作出拒绝在联邦商标登记簿注册的非终局性决定。如果可以，审查员应当建议申请者修正其申请，以根据§2(f)提出独特性主张。

随后，如果申请者修改了其申请以寻求根据§2(f)获得注册，那么就产生了申请者关于次要含义的证据是否充分的问题(*参见* TMEP §714.05(a)(1))。拒绝注册的根本法律依据仍然保持不变(例如，§2(e)(1))，但是问题从是否作出根本拒绝决定转变为该内容是否具备了独特性。如果审查员认为已经能够对获得性独特性作出初步证明，那么审查员就会根据§2(f)批准申请公布。如果审查员判定申请者的证据不足以证明该内已经具备了独特性，那么审查员就会作出第二份非终局性决定，重申拒绝予以注册的决定的根本法律理由(例如，§2(e)(1))，并解释申请者的证据不足以推翻上述拒绝决定。

对于申请者提出的§2(f)主张，审查员不能以最初拒绝决定的根本法律理由做

The mere assertion of distinctiveness under §2(f) raises a new issue. *See In re Educational Communications, Inc.*, 231 USPQ 787, 787 n. 2 (TTAB 1986). Even if the applicant has submitted, in support of the §2(f) claim, a statement of five years'use that is technically defective (*e. g.*, not verified or comprising incorrect language), the assertion of §2(f) distinctiveness still constitutes a new issue.

> *Exception*: The examining attorney may issue a final refusal upon an applicant's initial assertion of a §2(f) claim if the amendment is irrelevant to the outstanding refusal. *See* TMEP §714.05(a)(1). *See also* TMEP §§1212.02(a) and 1212.02(i) regarding situations where it is and is not appropriate to submit a claim of acquired distinctiveness to overcome a refusal.

After the examining attorney has issued a non-final action refusing registration on the Principal Register with a finding that the applicant's evidence of secondary meaning is insufficient to overcome the stated refusal, the applicant may elect to submit additional arguments and/or evidence regarding secondary meaning. If, after considering this submission, the examining attorney is persuaded that the applicant has established a *prima facie* case of acquired distinctiveness, the examining attorney will approve the application for publication under §2(f). If the examining attorney is not persuaded that the applicant has established a *prima facie* case of acquired distinctiveness, and the application is otherwise in condition for final refusal, the examining attorney will issue a final refusal pursuant to the appropriate section of the Act (*e. g.*, §2(e)(1)), with a finding that the applicant's evidence of acquired distinctiveness is insufficient to overcome the stated refusal. *See In re Capital Formation Counselors, Inc.*, 219 USPQ 916, 917 n. 2 (TTAB 1983) ("Section 2(f) is not a provision on which registration can be refused ...").

In any action in which the examining attorney indicates that the evidence of record is insufficient to establish that the mark has acquired distinctiveness, the examining attorney should specify the reasons for this determination. *See In re Interstate Folding Box Co.*, 167 USPQ 241, 242 (TTAB 1970); *In re H. A. Friend &*

出最终拒绝决定。根据 §2(f)提出的独特性主张引发了新的问题。*参见 Educational Communications, Inc.*, 231 USPQ 787, 787 n.2 (TTAB 1986)。即使申请者为了支持其 §2(f)主张提交了技术上存在瑕疵的(例如,未经宣誓证明或者含有不当措辞)五年使用声明书,对于 §2(f)所规定独特性的主张仍然构成了新的问题。

> *例外*:如果修正与未决的拒绝决定并不相关,那么对于申请者提出的 §2(f)主张,审查员可以作出终局拒绝决定。*参见* TMEP §714.05(a)(1)。
>
> 有关适合及不适合提出获得性独特性主张以推翻拒绝决定的情况,另*参见* TMEP §§1212.02(a)和 1212.02(i)。

审查员判定申请者关于次要含义的证据不足以推翻所述拒绝决定,并作出拒绝在联邦商标登记簿注册的非终局性决定后,申请者可以选择提交其他抗辩和(或)有关次要含义的证据。如果对提交的材料进行审查后,审查员认为已经能够对获得性独特性作出初步证明,那么审查员就会根据§2(f)批准申请公布。如果审查员认为未能对获得性独特性作出初步证明,该申请符合终局性拒绝的条件,那么审查员就会判定申请者关于获得性独特性的证据不足以推翻所述拒绝决定,并根据《商标法》相关章节(例如,§2(e)(1))做出终局性拒绝决定。*参见 Capital Formation Counselors, Inc.*, 219 USPQ 916, 917 n.2 (TTAB 1983)("第 2(f)节并非可以用来拒绝注册的规定……。")。

在一切程序中,如果审查员表示档案证据不足以证明商标具备了独特性,那么审查员应当对此种判断的理由作出说明。*参见 Interstate Folding Box Co.*, 167 USPQ 241, 242 (TTAB 1970);*H.A. Friend & Co., Inc.*, 158 USPQ 609 (TTAB 1968)。

Co., *Inc.*, 158 USPQ 609 (TTAB 1968).

1212.02(i) Section 2(f) Claim with Respect to Incapable Matter

If matter is generic, functional or purely ornamental, or otherwise fails to function as a mark, the matter is unregistrable. *See*, *e.g.*, *In re Bongrain International Corp.*, 894 F.2d 1316, 1317 n.4, 13 USPQ2d 1727, 1728 n.4 (Fed. Cir. 1990) ("If a mark is generic, incapable of serving as a means 'by which the goods of the applicant may be distinguished from the goods of others' ... it is not a trademark and can not be registered under the Lanham Act."); *H. Marvin Ginn Corp. v. International Association of Fire Chiefs*, 782 F.2d 987, 989, 228 USPQ 528, 530 (Fed. Cir. 1986), and cases cited therein ("A generic term ... can never be registered as a trademark because such a term is 'merely descriptive' within the meaning of §2(e)(1) and is incapable of acquiring *de jure* distinctiveness under §2(f). The generic name of a thing is in fact the ultimate in descriptiveness."). *See also In re Melville Corp.*, 228 USPQ 970, 972 (TTAB 1986) (BRAND NAMES FOR LESS, for retail store services in the clothing field, "should remain available for other persons or firms to use to describe the nature of their competitive services.").

An underlying basis of refusal common in each of the situations referred to above is the failure of the matter to function as a mark within the meaning of the Trademark Act (15 U.S.C. §§1051, 1052 and 1127). *In re Northland Aluminum Products*, *Inc.*, 777 F.2d 1556, 227 USPQ 961 (Fed. Cir. 1985).

It is axiomatic that matter may not be registered unless it is used as a mark, namely, "in a manner calculated to project to purchasers or potential purchasers a single source or origin for the goods in question." *In re Remington Products Inc.*, 3 USPQ2d 1714, 1715 (TTAB 1987). *See*, *e.g.*, *In re Melville Corp.*, 228 USPQ 970, 970 n.2 (TTAB 1986) ("If matter proposed for registration does not function as a mark, it is not registrable in accordance with Sections 1 and 2 of the Act because the preambles of those sections limit registration to subject matter within

1212.02(i) 有关不得注册内容的第2(f)节主张

如果内容属于一般性、功能性或纯粹装饰性，或者说不具备商标的功能，那么该内容就不得注册。*参见 In re Bongrain International Corp.*，894 F.2d 1316，1317 n.4，13 USPQ2d 1727，1728 n.4 (Fed.Cir.1990)（“如果一项商标是一般性的，不能用于‘将申请者的商品与他人的商品区分开来’……那它就不是商标，不能根据《兰哈姆法》获得注册。”）；*H. Marvin Ginn Corp. v. International Association of Fire Chiefs*，782 F.2d 987，989，228 USPQ 528，530 (Fed.Cir.1986)以及所引用的判例（“一般性的词语……绝不能注册为商标，因为这类词语根据 §2(e)(1)的规定属于‘仅具描述性’，并且无法具备 §2(f)所规定的法律上的独特性。事物的一般名称事实上是描述性的终点。”）。*另参见 Melville Corp.*，228 USPQ 970，972 (TTAB 1986)（用于服装行业零售商店服务的“BRAND NAMES FOR LESS”（廉价名牌）“应当维持可以为他人或企业用于描述其竞争性服务性质的状态。”）。

在上述各种情况下，拒绝予以注册一般的根本理由是该内容不具有《商标法》(15 U.S.C.§§1051，1052 和 1127)所规定的商标的功能。*Northland Aluminum Products, Inc.*，777 F.2d 1556，227 USPQ 961 (Fed.Cir.1985)。

显然，只有用作商标，也就是说“以一种向购买者或潜在的购买者表示所涉商品来源的方式”使用，该内容才可以注册。*Remington Products Inc.*，3 USPQ2d 1714，1715 (TTAB 1987)。*参见*判例：*Melville Corp.*，228 USPQ 970，970 n.2 (TTAB 1986)（“如果申请注册的商标不具有商标功能，根据《商标法》第 1 和第 2 节的规定不得注册，因为序言将注册限于商标的定义之内。”）；*Whataburger Systems, Inc.*，209

the definition of a trademark."); *In re Whataburger Systems, Inc.*, 209 USPQ 429, 430 (TTAB 1980) ("[A] designation may not be registered either as a trademark or as a service mark unless it is used as a mark, in such a manner that its function as an indication of origin may be readily perceived by persons encountering the goods or services in connection with which it is used.").

Therefore, where the examining attorney has determined that matter sought to be registered is not registrable because it is not a mark within the meaning of the Trademark Act, a claim that the matter has acquired distinctiveness under §2(f) as applied to the applicant's goods or services does not overcome the refusal. It would be logically inconsistent to find otherwise. *See, e. g., TrafFix Devices, Inc. v. Marketing Displays, Inc.*, 532 U.S. 23, 58 USPQ2d 1001, 1007 (2001) ("Functionality having been established, whether MDI'S dual spring design has acquired secondary meaning need not be considered."); *In re R.M.Smith, Inc.*, 734 F.2d 1482, 1484-85, 222 USPQ 1, 3 (Fed. Cir. 1984) ("Evidence of distinctiveness is of no avail to counter a de jure functionality rejection."); *In re Tilcon Warren, Inc.*, 221 USPQ 86, 88 (TTAB 1984) ("Long use of a slogan which is not a trademark and would not be so perceived does not, of course, transform the slogan into a trademark."); *In re Mancino*, 219 USPQ 1047, 1048 (TTAB 1983) ("Since the refusal ... was based on applicant's failure to demonstrate technical service mark use, the claim of distinctiveness under Section 2(f) was of no relevance to the issue in the case.").

As discussed above, evidence of acquired distinctiveness will not alter the determination that matter is unregistrable. Nevertheless, the evidence submitted by the applicant should be reviewed to determine whether it has any bearing on the underlying basis of refusal.

See also In re Wakefern Food Corp., 222 USPQ 76, 79 (TTAB 1984) (the Board, while finding applicant's evidence relating to public perception of WHY PAY MORE! entitled to relatively little weight, noting that the evidence is relevant to the issue of whether the slogan functions as a mark for applicant's supermarket

USPQ 429, 430 (TTAB 1980)（“除非已经被用作商标，其使用方式能够使接触、使用该商品或服务的人很容易就能联想到来源，否则标识也不得注册为商标或服务商标。”）。

因此，如果审查员已经判定，由于不属于《商标法》所规定的商标，申请注册的内容不得注册，那么根据 §2(f) 主张该内容对于申请者的商品或服务已经具备了独特性，也不能推翻该拒绝决定。如果情况相反，就不符合逻辑了。*参见*判例：*TrafFix Devices, Inc. v. Marketing Displays, Inc.*, 532 U.S. 23, 58 USPQ2d 1001, 1007 (2001)（“既然已经证明了具有功能性，那么就不必再考虑 MDI 的双条纹图案是否具备次要含义了。”）；*R.M. Smith, Inc.*, 734 F.2d 1482, 1484－1485, 222 USPQ 1, 3 (Fed. Cir. 1984)（“独特性的证据不能对抗法律功能性的拒绝决定。”）；*Tilcon Warren, Inc.*, 221 USPQ 86, 88 (TTAB 1984)（“长期使用一种不属于商标并不能被感知为商标的口号，当然也就不能将该口号转变为一种商标。”）；*Mancino*, 219 USPQ 1047, 1048 (TTAB 1983)（“由于该拒绝决定……是基于申请者未能证明技术服务商标的使用，因此根据第 2(f) 节提出的独特性主张在这种情况下与该问题无关。”）。

如上所述，获得性独特性的证据无法改变该内容不得注册的判断。不过，对于申请者提交的证据应当进行审查，以判断其是否与拒绝决定的根本理由有关。

另参见 *Wakefern Food Corp.*, 222 USPQ 76, 79 (TTAB 1984)（尽管判定申请者关于公众对“WHY PAY MORE!”（何必多付！）感知的证据相关性相对微弱，委员会还是认为，该证据与该口号是否具有申请者超市服务商标功能的问题相关）。

services).

1212.03 Evidence of Distinctiveness Under §2(f)

37 C.F.R.§2.41. Proof of distinctiveness under section 2(f).

(a) When registration is sought of a mark which would be unregistrable by reason of section 2(e) of the Act but which is said by applicant to have become distinctive in commerce of the goods or services set forth in the application, applicant may, in support of registrability, submit with the application, or in response to a request for evidence or to a refusal to register, affidavits, or declarations in accordance with §2.20, depositions, or other appropriate evidence showing duration, extent and nature of use in commerce and advertising expenditures in connection therewith (identifying types of media and attaching typical advertisements), and affidavits, or declarations in accordance with §2.20, letters or statements from the trade or public, or both, or other appropriate evidence tending to show that the mark distinguishes such goods.

(b) In appropriate cases, ownership of one or more prior registrations on the Principal Register or under the Act of 1905 of the same mark may be accepted as prima facie evidence of distinctiveness. Also, if the mark is said to have become distinctive of applicant's goods by reason of substantially exclusive and continuous use in commerce thereof by applicant for the five years before the date on which the claim of distinctiveness is made, a showing by way of statements which are verified or which include declarations in accordance with §2.20, in the application may, in appropriate cases, be accepted as prima facie evidence of distinctiveness. In each of these situations, however, further evidence may be required.

"To establish secondary meaning, a manufacturer must show that, in the minds of the public, the primary significance of a product feature or term is to identify the source of the product rather than the product itself." *Inwood Laboratories, Inc. v. Ives Laboratories, Inc.*, 456 U.S.844, 851 n.11, 214 USPQ 1, 4 n.11 (1982).

1212.03　§2(f)所规定独特性的证据

37 C. F. R. §2. 41。§2(f)所规定独特性的证据。

(a)如果提出注册申请的是一种根据《商标法》第2(e)节不得注册的商标,但是申请者称该商标已经在有关申请所述商品或服务的商业活动中具备了独特性,那么为了支持该商标具有可注册性的观点,申请者可以在提出申请的同时,或者在对证据要求以及拒绝决定提出答辩的过程中,提交宣誓书、或根据§2.20所作的声明、或其他表明商业使用期间、范围和性质以及相关广告支出(标明媒体类型并附典型的广告)的证据,以及宣誓书、或根据§2.20所作的声明、来自行业或公众的信函或陈述,或两者同时具备,或其他能够证明该商标区分了此类商品的相关证据。

(b)在适当的案件中,拥有一项或更多联邦商标登记簿在先注册,或根据《1905年商标法》获得的同一商标注册,可以被接受为独特性的初步证据。同样,如果申请者称该商标已经由于独特性主张日期之前5年的实质性专属和持续使用而具备了独特性,那么申请中所提出的认证陈述或依据§2.20所作的声明在适当案件中均可以被接受为独特性的初步证明。不过在这些情况下,还可以要求进一步的证据。

"为了证明次要含义,制造商必须表明,在公众的脑海中,某产品特征或词语的主要含义是识别产品来源,而非识别产品本身。" *Inwood Laboratories, Inc. v. Ives Laboratories, Inc.*, 456 U.S.844, 851 n.11, 214 USPQ 1, 4 n.11 (1982)。

1212.04 Prior Registrations as Proof of Distinctiveness

Trademark Rule 2.41(b), 37 C.F.R. §2.41(b), provides that the examining attorney may accept, as *prima facie* evidence of acquired distinctiveness, ownership by the applicant of one or more prior registrations of the same mark on the Principal Register or under the Act of 1905. *See* TMEP §1212.04(b) as to what constitutes the "same mark," and TMEP §§1212.09 *et seq*. concerning §1(b) applications.

The rule states that ownership of existing registrations to establish acquired distinctiveness "may" be considered acceptable in "appropriate cases," and that the Office may, at its option, require additional evidence of distinctiveness. *In re Dial-A-Mattress Operating Corp*., 240 F.3d 1341, 57 USPQ2d 1807 (Fed. Cir. 2001); *In re Loew's Theatres, Inc*., 769 F.2d 764, 226 USPQ 865 (Fed. Cir. 1985).

The following are general guidelines regarding claiming ownership of prior registrations as a method of establishing acquired distinctiveness.

1212.04(a) Sufficiency of Claim vis-à-vis Nature of the Mark

The examining attorney has the discretion to determine whether the nature of the mark sought to be registered is such that a claim of ownership of a prior registration for the same or similar goods or services is enough to establish acquired distinctiveness. For example, if the mark sought to be registered is deemed to be highly descriptive or misdescriptive of the goods or services named in the application, the examining attorney may require additional evidence of acquired distinctiveness. *See In re Loew's Theatres, Inc*., 769 F.2d 764, 226 USPQ 865 (Fed. Cir. 1985) (claim of ownership of a prior registration held insufficient to establish acquired distinctiveness where registration was refused as primarily geographically deceptively misdescriptive); *In re Kerr-McGee Corp*., 190 USPQ 204 (TTAB 1976) (claim of ownership of prior registrations held insufficient to establish acquired distinctiveness where registration was refused on ground that the subject

1212.04　　作为独特性证据的在先注册

《商标规则》2.41(b)，37 C.F.R.§2.41(b)规定，审查员可以将申请者所拥有的在联邦商标登记簿注册或根据《1905 年商标法》注册的同一商标的在先注册接受为获得性独特性的初步证据。关于什么构成了“同一商标”，*参见* TMEP §1212.04(b)；有关 §1(b)的申请，参见 TMEP §§1212.09 及以下。

该规则规定，以既存注册的所有权证明获得性独特性在“适当的案件中”、“可以”被接受，并且商标局可以自由选择是否要求独特性的其他证据。*参见 Dial-A-Mattress Operating Corp.*，240 F.3d 1341，57 USPQ2d 1807 (Fed. Cir. 2001)；*Loew's Theatres，Inc.*，769 F.2d 764，226 USPQ 865 (Fed. Cir. 1985)。

以下是关于主张将在先注册作为一种证明获得性独特性方法的基本情况。

1212.04(a)　　主张的充分性对比商标的性质

审查员拥有自由裁量权，以判断申请注册商标的性质是否属于主张同一或类似商品或服务在先注册所有权即足以证明获得性独特性。例如，如果申请注册的商标被视为属于对申请所述商品或服务具有高度描述性或存在错误描述，那么审查员就可以要求提供获得性独特性的其他证据。*参见 Loew's Theatres，Inc.*，769 F.2d 764，226 USPQ 865 (Fed. Cir. 1985)(在注册系以主要属于地理欺骗性错误描述为由遭到拒绝的情况下，在先注册所有权的主张被认为不足以证明获得性独特性。)；*Kerr-McGee Corp.*，190 USPQ 204 (TTAB 1976)(在注册系以内容仅属装饰性边框或文字符号“载体”由遭到拒绝的情况下，在先注册所有权的主张被认为不足以证明

matter was merely an ornamental border or "carrier" for words and symbols appearing within).

1212.04(b) "Same Mark"

A proposed mark is the "same mark as a previously-registered mark for the purpose of 37 C.F.R.§2.41(b) if it is the "legal equivalent" of such a mark. A mark is the legal equivalent of another if it creates the same, continuing commercial impression such that the consumer would consider them both the same mark. *In re Dial-A-Mattress Operating Corp.*, 240 F.3d 1341, 1347, 57 USPQ2d 1807, 1812 (Fed. Cir. 2001). *See also Bausch & Lomb Inc. v. Leupold & Stevens Inc.*, 6 USPQ2d 1475, 1477 (TTAB 1988) ("The words GOLDEN RING, while they are used to describe the device, are by no means identical to or substantially identical to the gold ring device trademark."); *In re Best Products Co., Inc.*, 231 USPQ 988, 989 n.6 (TTAB 1986) ("[W]e infer in the instant case that the differences between the marks BEST & Des. and BEST JEWELRY & Des., and between the identifications of services in their respective registrations, were deemed to be immaterial differences."); *In re Loew's Theatres, Inc.*, 223 USPQ 513, 514 n.5 (TTAB 1984), *aff'd*, 769 F.2d 764, 226 USPQ 865 (Fed. Cir. 1985) ("We do not, however, agree with the Examining Attorney that a minor difference in the marks (*i.e.*, here, merely that the mark of the existing registration is in plural form) is a proper basis for excluding any consideration of this evidence under the rule."); *In re Flex-O-Glass, Inc.*, 194 USPQ 203, 205-06 (TTAB 1977) ("[P]ersons exposed to applicant's registered mark ... would, upon encountering [applicant's yellow rectangle and red circle design] ..., be likely to accept it as the same mark or as an inconsequential modification or modernization thereof ... [A]pplicant may 'tack on' to its use of the mark in question, the use of the registered mark ... and therefore may properly rely upon its registration in support of its claim of distinctiveness herein.").

See, e.g., Van Dyne-Crotty, Inc. v. Wear-Guard Corp., 926 F.2d 1156, 17 US-

获得性独特性）。

1212.04(b)　　　　“同一商标”

只要一项申请注册的商标属于在先注册商标的“法律等同物”，那么根据 37 C.F.R.§2.41(b)的规定，该商标就是“同一商标”。如果某商标造成了相同、持续的商业印象，以至于消费者会将两商标认为是同一商标，那么该商标就是另一商标的法律等同物。另参见 *Bausch & Lomb Inc. v. Leupold & Stevens Inc.*, 6 USPQ2d 1475, 1477 (TTAB 1988)（“词组 GOLDEN RING 用于描述该图案时，绝不会意味着或实际上与金环服务商标有所不同。”）；*Best Products Co., Inc.*, 231 USPQ 988, 989 n. 6 (TTAB 1986)（“我们判定在本案中，BEST & Des. 和 BEST JEWELRY & Des. 两商标以及其各自注册中所识别的服务之间，被视为并不存在实质性差异。”）；*Loew's Theatres, Inc.*, 223 USPQ 513, 514 n.5 (TTAB 1984), *aff'd*, 769 F.2d 764, 226 USPQ 865 (Fed. Cir. 1985)（“不过，根据规则，我们并不同意审查员所认为的商标之间存在微弱差异(亦即，在此，仅仅由于既存注册商标是复数形式)就可以完全不再考虑此项证据。”）；*Flex-O-Glass, Inc.*, 194 USPQ 203, 205 - 06 (TTAB 1977)（“遭遇到申请者注册商标的人们……由于看到[申请者黄色长方形和红色圆形图案]，就会……可能这是同一商标，或者是其某种任意变形或变形……申请者可以在涉案商标的使用中‘添加’注册商标的使用……因此就可以根据其注册来支持此处对于独特性的主张。”）。

有关涉及法律等同商标在先使用的“添加”概念，参见 *Van Dyne-Crotty, Inc. v. Wear-Guard Corp.*, 926 F.2d 1156, 17 USPQ2d 1866 (Fed. Cir. 1991)。

PQ2d 1866 (Fed. Cir. 1991) regarding the concept of "tacking" with reference to prior use of a legally equivalent mark.

1212. 04(c) Relatedness of Goods or Services

The examining attorney should determine whether the goods or services named in the application are sufficiently similar to the goods or services named in the prior registration(s). *See Bausch & Lomb Inc. v. Leupold & Stevens Inc.*, 6 USPQ2d 1475, 1478 (TTAB 1988) ("Applicant's almost total reliance on the distinctiveness which its gold ring device has achieved vis-à-vis rifle scopes and handgun scopes is simply not sufficient by itself to establish that the same gold ring device has become distinctive vis-à-vis binoculars and spotting scopes."); *In re Best Products Co., Inc.*, 231 USPQ 988, 989 n.6 (TTAB 1986) ("[W]e infer in the instant case that the differences between the marks BEST & Des. and BEST JEWELRY & Des., and between the identifications of services in their respective registrations ["mail order and catalog showroom services" and "retail jewelry store services"], were deemed to be immaterial differences."); *In re Owens-Illinois Glass Co.*, 143 USPQ 431, 432 (TTAB 1964) (applicant's ownership of prior registration of LIBBEY for cut-glass articles held acceptable as *prima facie* evidence of distinctiveness of identical mark for plastic tableware, the Board stating, "Cut-glass and plastic articles of tableware are customarily sold in the same retail outlets, and purchasers of one kind of tableware might well be prospective purchasers of the other."); *In re Lytle Engineering & Mfg. Co.*, 125 USPQ 308, 309 (TTAB 1960) (applicant's ownership of prior registration of LYTLE for various services, including the planning, preparation and production of technical publications, held acceptable as *prima facie* evidence of distinctiveness of identical mark for brochures, catalogues and bulletins).

1212. 04(d) Registration Must Be in Full Force and Effect and on Principal Register or under Act of 1905

Trademark Rule 2.41(b), 37 C.F.R. §2.41(b), states that ownership of a prior

1212.04(c) 与商品或服务的相关性

审查员应当判定，申请中所述的商品或服务是否与在先注册中的商品或服务充分类似。参见判例：*Bausch & Lomb Inc. v. Leupold & Stevens Inc.*, 6 USPQ2d 1475, 1478 (TTAB 1988)（"申请者几乎完全依赖通过步枪和手枪瞄准镜为其金环图案所获得的独特性，其本身显然并不能充分证明同样的金环图案对于单双筒望远镜已经具备了独特性。"）；*Best Products Co., Inc.*, 231 USPQ 988, 989 n.6 (TTAB 1986)（"我们判定在本案中，BEST & Des. 和 BEST JEWELRY & Des. 两商标以及其各自的注册（'邮购及商品陈列服务'和'珠宝零售服务'）之间，被视为并不存在实质性差异。"）；*Owens-Illinois Glass Co.*, 143 USPQ 431, 432 (TTAB 1964)（申请者所有的用于刻花玻璃器皿的"LIBBEY"在先注册被认为可以作为同样的塑料餐具商标独特性的初步证据，委员会称，"刻花玻璃和塑料餐具习惯上在同一家零售店销售，其中一种餐具的购买者也很可能是另一种餐具的潜在购买者。"）；*Lytle Engineering & Mfg. Co.*, 125 USPQ 308, 309 (TTAB 1960)（申请者所有的用于各种服务——包括策划、准备和提供技术类出版物——的在先注册"LYTLE"，被认为可以作为同样的用于小册子、目录册以及期刊的商标具有独特性的初步证据）。

1212.04(d) 注册必须完全有效，并登记于联邦商标登记簿，或根据《1905年商标法》注册

《商标规则》2.41(b)，37C.F.R.§2.41(b)规定，申请者所拥有的"在联邦商标

registration "on the Principal Register or under the Act of 1905" may be accepted as *prima facie* evidence of distinctiveness. Therefore, claims of acquired distinctiveness under §2(f) cannot be based on ownership of registrations on the Supplemental Register. *See In re Canron, Inc.*, 219 USPQ 820 (TTAB 1983).

Moreover, a claim of acquired distinctiveness cannot be based on a registration that is cancelled or expired. *See In re BankAmerica Corp.*, 229 USPQ 852, 853 (TTAB 1986). When an examining attorney considers a §2(f) claim based on ownership of one or more prior registrations, the examining attorney should confirm, in the records of the Office, that the claimed registrations were issued on the Principal Register or under the Act of 1905 and that they are in full force and effect.

1212.04(e) Form of §2(f) Claim Based on Ownership of Prior Registrations

The following language may be used to claim distinctiveness under §2(f) on the basis of ownership of one or more prior registrations:

> The mark has become distinctive of the goods (or services) as evidenced by ownership of U.S. Registration No(s). ________ on the Principal Register for the same mark for related goods or services.

37 C.F.R. §2.41(b).

If the applicant is relying solely on its ownership of one or more prior registrations as proof of acquired distinctiveness, the §2(f) claim does not have to be verified. Therefore, an applicant or an applicant's attorney may authorize amendment of an application to add such a claim through an examiner's amendment, if otherwise appropriate.

1212.05 Five Years of Use as Proof of Distinctiveness

Section 2(f) of the Trademark Act, 15 U.S.C. §1052(f), provides that "proof of

登记簿注册或根据《1905 年商标法》注册”的同一商标的在先注册,可以被接受为获得独特性的初步证据。因此,不能以拥有登记于补充登记簿的注册为由主张具备了 §2(f)所规定的获得独特性。参见 *Canron, Inc.*, 219 USPQ 820 (TTAB 1983)。

此外,也不能根据被撤销或过期的注册主张获得独特性。参见 *BankAmerica Corp.*, 229 USPQ 852, 853 (TTAB 1986)。审查员在考察基于一项或更多在先注册而提出的 §2(f)主张时,应当通过商标局档案确认所主张的注册是登记于联邦商标登记簿,或根据《1905 年商标法》获得注册的,并且完全有效。

1212.04(e) 基于在先注册提出的§2(f)主张的格式

基于一项或更多在先注册而提出 §2(f)所规定的独特性主张时,可以采用如下措辞:

> 通过为相关商品或服务注册于联邦商标登记簿的同一商标,美国注册号____________,的所有权之佐证,该商标对于商品(或服务)已经具备了独特性。

37 C.F.R.§2.41(b)。

如果申请者只依赖一项或更多在先注册作为获得独特性的证据,那么该 §2(f)主张不必经过认证。因此,如果可以,申请者或其代理人可以通过审查者的修正书对申请进行修正,以添加此种主张。

1212.05 作为独特性证据的五年使用

《商标法》第2(f)节,15U.S.C.§1052(f)规定某种标识“在主张独特性日期之

substantially exclusive and continuous use" of a designation "as a mark by the applicant in commerce for the five years before the date on which the claim of distinctiveness is made" may be accepted as *prima facie* evidence that the mark has acquired distinctiveness as used with the applicant's goods in commerce. *See also* 37 C.F.R. §2.41(b).

The Trademark Act previously required that the relevant five-year period precede the filing date of the application. The Trademark Law Revision Act of 1988, Public Law 100-667, 102 Stat. 3935, revised §2(f) of the Act to provide for a *prima facie* showing of acquired distinctiveness based on five years' use running up to the date the claim is made. Under the revised provision, any five-year claim submitted on or after November 16, 1989, is subject to the new time period. This applies even if the application was filed prior to that date.

Section 2(f) of the Act, and 37 C.F.R. §2.41(b) state that reliance on a claim of five years' use to establish acquired distinctiveness "may" be acceptable in "appropriate cases." The Office may, at its option, require additional evidence of distinctiveness. Whether a claim of five years' use will be deemed acceptable to establish that the mark has acquired distinctiveness depends largely on the nature of the mark in relation to the specified goods or services.

The following are general guidelines regarding the statutorily suggested proof of five years' use as a method of establishing acquired distinctiveness.

1212.05(a) Sufficiency of Claim Vis-à-Vis Nature of the Mark

For most surnames, the statement of five years' use will be sufficient to establish acquired distinctiveness.

The amount of evidence necessary to establish secondary meaning varies — "the greater the degree of description a term has, the heavier the burden to prove it has attained secondary meaning." *In re Bongrain International Corp.*, 894 F.2d 1316, 13 USPQ2d 1727, 1728 n.4 (Fed. Cir. 1990); *Yamaha Int'l Corp. v. Hoshi-*

前已经作为商标由申请者在商业活动中实质性专属和持续使用了五年的证据”可以被接受为该商标在商业活动中用于申请者的商品时已经具备了独特性的初步证据。另参见 37 C.F.R.§2.41(b)。

《商标法》以前曾规定有关的五年期间需在申请归档日之前计算。《1988 年商标法修订法》,Public Law 100 - 667, 102 Stat.3935,对该法 §2(f)进行了修订,规定基于五年使用而对获得独特性所作的初步证明计算到该主张提出之日。根据修订后的规定,所有在 1989 年 12 月 6 日当时及以后提交的五年主张均适用该新的期间。即使申请是在该日期之前归档的,亦适用该规定。

《商标法》第 2(f)节,以及 37 C.F.R.§2.41(b)规定,在“适当的案件中”,基于五年使用的主张证明获得独特性“可以”被接受。商标局可以,基于其自由选择,要求关于独特性的其他证据。一项五年使用主张是否会被视为能够证明该商标已经具备了独特性,很大程度上取决于该商标相关于特定商品或服务的性质。

以下是关于法律规定所示的作为获得独特性证明方法的五年使用证据的一般指导原则。

1212.05(a) 主张的充分性对比商标的性质

对于大多数姓氏,五年使用的声明可以充分证明获得独特性。

证明次要含义所必需的证据量并不确定——“词语的描述性程度越高,证明其具有次要含义的证明责任就越重。”相关判例:*Bongrain International Corp.*, 894 F.2d 1316, 13 USPQ2d 1727, 1728 n.4 (Fed. Cir. 1990); *Yamaha Int'l Corp. v. Hoshino Gakki Co. Ltd.*, 840 F.2d 1572, 1581, 6 USPQ2d 1001, 1005 (Fed. Cir. 1988)。

no Gakki Co. Ltd., 840 F.2d 1572, 1581, 6 USPQ2d 1001, 1005 (Fed. Cir. 1988).

Accordingly, for marks refused under §§2(e)(1) or 2(e)(2), whether the statement of five years' use is sufficient in and of itself to establish acquired distinctiveness depends on the degree to which the mark is descriptive or misdescriptive. If the mark is highly descriptive or misdescriptive of the goods or services named in the application, the statement of five years'use alone will be deemed insufficient to establish acquired distinctiveness. *See In re Kalmbach Publishing Co.*, 14 USPQ2d 1490 (TTAB 1989) (applicant's sole evidence of acquired distinctiveness, a claim of use since 1975, held insufficient to establish that the highly descriptive, if not generic, designation RADIO CONTROL BUYERS GUIDE had become distinctive of applicant's magazines); *In re Gray Inc.*, 3 USPQ2d 1558, 1559 (TTAB 1987) ("[T]o support registration of PROTECTIVE EQUIPMENT [for burglar and fire alarms and burglar and fire alarm surveillance services] on the Principal Register a showing considerably stronger than a prima facie statement of five years'substantially exclusive use is required."). *Cf. In re Synergistics Research Corp.*, 218 USPQ 165 (TTAB 1983) (applicant's declaration of five years'use held sufficient to support registrability under §2(f) of BALL DARTS for equipment sold as a unit for playing a target game, in view of lack of evidence that the term is highly descriptive (*e. g.*, no dictionary evidence of any meaning of BALL DARTS and no evidence of use of the term by competitors or the public)).

For matter that does not inherently function as a mark because of its nature (*e.g.*, nondistinctive product container shapes, overall color of a product, mere ornamentation), evidence of five years'use is not sufficient to show acquired distinctiveness. In such a case, actual evidence that the mark is perceived as a mark for the relevant goods or services would be required to establish distinctiveness. *See generally In re Owens-Corning Fiberglas Corp.*, 774 F.2d 1116, 227 USPQ 417 (Fed. Cir. 1985) (color pink as uniformly applied to applicant's fibrous glass residential insulation); *In re R. M. Smith, Inc.*, 734 F.2d 1482, 222 USPQ 1 (Fed. Cir. 1984) (configuration of pistol grip water nozzle for water nozzles); *Edward Weck Inc. v. IM Inc.*, 17 USPQ2d 1142 (TTAB 1990) (color green for medical in-

因此，对于根据§§2(e)(1)或§§2(e)(2)遭到拒绝的商标，五年使用声明本身是否足以证明获得性独特性，取决于该商标描述性或错误描述性的程度。如果该商标对于申请所述的商品或服务具有高度描述性或错误描述性，那么只有五年使用声明被认为并不足以证明获得独特性。*参见 Kalmbach Publishing Co.*，14 USPQ2d 1490 (TTAB 1989)(申请人对于获得性独特性的唯一证据是自 1975 年起使用的主张，被认为不足以证明该高度描述性的——如果不是一般性的话——标识"RADIO CONTROL BUYERS GUIDE"对于申请者的杂志已经具备了独特性。)；*Gray Inc.*，3 USPQ2d 1558，1559 (TTAB 1987)("为了支持 PROTECTIVE EQUIPMENT [用于匪火警报以及匪火警戒监视服务] 在联邦商标登记簿注册，要求具备相比五年实质性专属使用声明初步证据更为强有力的证明。")。比较：*Synergistics Research Corp.*，218 USPQ 165 (TTAB 1983)(申请者五年使用的声明被认为足以支持用于射击运动整体设备的"BALL DARTS"具有 §2(f)所规定的可注册性，因为缺乏该词具有高度描述性的证据(例如，不存在 BALL DARTS 含义的词典证据，也没有竞争者或公众使用该词语的证据))。

对于因其性质而不具有固有商标功能的内容(例如，不具独特性的产品容器外形、产品的整体色彩、纯粹的装饰)，五年使用的证据不足以证明获得独特性。在这种情况下，将要求提供该商标被认为是相关商品或服务的实际证据以证明独特性。*一般参见 Owens-Corning Fiberglas Corp.*，774 F.2d 1116，227 USPQ 417 (Fed. Cir. 1985)(均匀涂在申请者的纤维玻璃家用绝缘材料上的红粉色)；*R.M. Smith, Inc.*，734 F.2d 1482，222 USPQ 1 (Fed. Cir. 1984)(用于喷水管的枪柄状喷头)；*Edward Weck Inc. v. IM Inc.*，17 USPQ2d 1142 (TTAB 1990)(用于医疗器械的绿色)*Cabot*

struments); *In re Cabot Corp*., 15 USPQ2d 1224 (TTAB 1990) (configuration of a pillow-pack container for ear plugs and configuration of a pillow-pack container with trade dress (white circle surrounded by blue border) for ear plugs); *In re Star Pharmaceuticals, Inc*., 225 USPQ 209 (TTAB 1985) (color combination of drug capsule and seeds therein for methyltestosterone); *In re Craigmyle*, 224 USPQ 791 (TTAB 1984) (configuration of halter square for horse halters).

1212.05(b) "Substantially Exclusive and Continuous"

The five years of use does not have to be exclusive, but may be "substantially" exclusive. This makes allowance for use by others that may be inconsequential or infringing, which does not necessarily invalidate the applicant's claim. *L. D. Kichler Co. v. Davoil, Inc*., 192 F.3d 1349, 52 USPQ2d 1307 (Fed. Cir. 1999).

The existence of other applications to register the same mark, or other known uses of the mark, does not automatically eliminate the possibility of using this method of proof, but the examining attorney should inquire as to the nature of such use and be satisfied that it is not substantial or does not nullify the claim of distinctiveness. *See Levi Strauss & Co. v. Genesco, Inc*., 742 F.2d 1401, 1403, 222 USPQ 939, 940-41 (Fed. Cir. 1984) ("When the record shows that purchasers are confronted with more than one (let alone numerous) independent users of a term or device, an application for registration under Section 2(f) cannot be successful, for distinctiveness on which purchasers may rely is lacking under such circumstances."); *Marshall Field & Co. v. Mrs. Fields Cookies*, 11 USPQ2d 1355, 1357-58 (TTAB 1989) ("[T]he existence of numerous third party users of a mark, even if junior, might well have a material impact on the Examiner's decision to accept a party's claim of distinctiveness."); *Flowers Industries Inc. v. Interstate Brands Corp*., 5 USPQ2d 1580, 1588-89 (TTAB 1987) ("[L]ong and continuous use alone is insufficient to show secondary meaning where the use is not substantially exclusive."); *Ex parte The Kalart Co. Inc*., 88 USPQ 221 (PO Ex. Ch. 1951).

The use of the mark during the five years must be continuous, without a period of

Corp., 15 USPQ2d 1224 (TTAB 1990)(用于耳塞的枕头状容器设计以及有商品外观(环绕白色圆圈的蓝色边框)的用于耳塞的枕头状容器设计);*Star Pharmaceuticals, Inc*., 225 USPQ 209 (TTAB 1985)(用于甲基睾丸素的药物胶囊和小颗粒色彩组合);*Craigmyle*, 224 USPQ 791 (TTAB 1984)(用于马笼头的笼头板设计)。

1212.05(b) "实质性专属和持续的"

五年的使用不必是专属的,但可以是"实质性"专属的。允许他人使用本来并不必然使申请者主张归于无效的,但是这样一来就变得不合逻辑或发生违背了。*L. D. Kichler Co. v. Davoil, Inc*., 192 F. 3d 1349, 52 USPQ2d 1307 (Fed. Cir. 1999)。

同时存在针对同一商标提出的其他申请,或是其他对于商标的知名使用,并不自然消灭以此方法进行证明的可能性,但是审查员应当调查此类使用的性质,并且确信其并非属于实质性,或者并未导致独特性主张归于无效。参见 *Levi Strauss & Co. v. Genesco, Inc*., 742 F.2d 1401, 1403, 222 USPQ 939, 940 - 941 (Fed. Cir. 1984)("如果档案显示购买者面对着不止一个(更不用说大量的了)某词语或图案的独立使用者,根据 §2(f)提出的注册申请就不能获得成功,因为在这种情况下,缺乏购买者可以依赖的独特性。");*Marshall Field & Co. v. Mrs. Fields Cookies*, 11 USPQ2d 1355, 1357 - 1358 (TTAB 1989)("如果某商标存在大量第三方使用者,即使地位低微,也可能对审查员接受当事人独特性主张的决定产生实质性的影响。");*Flowers Industries Inc. v. Interstate Brands Corp*., 5 USPQ2d 1580, 1588 - 1589 (TTAB 1987)("如果使用并非实质性专属,那么长期和持续使用本身不足以证明次要含义。")。*The Kalart Co. Inc*., 88 USPQ 221 (PO Ex. Ch. 1951)。

在五年中对商标的使用必须是持续的,商标所用于的商品或服务的业务不存在

"nonuse" or suspension of trade in the goods or services in connection with which the mark is used.

1212.05(c) Use "as a Mark"

The substantially exclusive and continuous use must be "as a mark," 15 U.S.C. §1052(f). *See In re Craigmyle*, 224 USPQ 791 (TTAB 1984) (registrability under §2(f) not established by sales over a long period of time where there was no evidence that the subject matter had been used as a mark); *In re Kwik Lok Corp.*, 217 USPQ 1245, 1248 (TTAB 1983) (declarations as to sales volume and advertising expenditures held insufficient to establish acquired distinctiveness. "The significant missing element in appellant's case is evidence persuasive of the fact that the subject matter has been used *as a mark*.").

1212.05(d) Form of the Proof of Five Years' Use

If the applicant chooses to seek registration under §2(f), 15 U.S.C. §1052(f), by using the statutory suggestion of five years of use as proof of distinctiveness, the applicant should submit a claim of distinctiveness that reads as follows, if accurate:

> The mark has become distinctive of the goods (or services) through the applicant's substantially exclusive and continuous use in commerce for at least the five years immediately before the date of this statement.

The claim of five years of use is generally required to be supported by an affidavit, or a declaration in accordance with 37 C.F.R. §2.20, signed by the applicant. *See* 37 C.F.R. §2.41(b). The affidavit or declaration can be signed by a person properly authorized to sign on behalf of applicant under 37 C.F.R. §2.33(a). *See* TMEP §804.04.

The following are guidelines regarding the form and language appropriate for a

"不使用"或者停用期间。

1212.05(c)　　"作为商标"使用

实质性专属和持续使用必须是"作为商标"的使用。15 U.S.C.§1052(f)。*参见 Craigmyle*, 224 USPQ 791 (TTAB 1984)(长期销售不能证明§2(f)所规定的可注册性,因为没有证据表明提交注册的内容是作为商标使用的。);*Kwik Lok Corp.*, 217 USPQ 1245, 1248 (TTAB 1983)(关于销售量和广告支出的声明被认为不足以证明获得性独特性。"上诉人所述情况中所缺乏的重要要素是,关于提交内容作为商标使用的有说服力的证据。")。

1212.05(d)　　五年使用证据的格式

如果申请者利用法律所规定的五年使用作为独特性证据,从而选择根据§2(f), 15 U.S.C.§1052(f)寻求注册,那么申请者就应当提出独特性主张,格式如下:

> 在本声明提出之日以前,申请者已经在商业活动中对商标实施了五年以上的实质性专属和持续使用,由此该商标对于商品(或服务)具备了独特性。

五年使用主张通常还要求附有宣誓书,或者符合37 C.F.R.§2.20的规定、由申请者签署的声明书,以作为证明。*参见* 37 C.F.R.§2.41(b)。根据37 C.F.R.§2.33(a),宣誓书或声明书可以由经过适当授权的人代表申请者签署。*参见* TMEP §804.04。

以下是关于五年使用主张恰当格式和措辞的指导原则:

claim of five years of use:

(1) Use of the precise statutory wording is desirable, but variations may be accepted if they do not affect the essential allegations.

(2) The wording "substantially exclusive and continuous use in commerce" is essential.

(3) It must be clear from the record that the five years of use has been in commerce that may lawfully be regulated by Congress. *See Blanchard & Co., Inc. v. Charles Gilman & Son, Inc.*, 145 USPQ 62 (D. Mass. 1965), *aff'd*, 353 F.2d 400, 147 USPQ 263 (1st Cir. 1965), *cert. denied* 383 U.S. 968, 149 USPQ 905 (1966).

(4) The use of the mark must cover the five years before the date of the statement of five years' use. Thus wording that indicates that the use referred to is before the date of the statement is essential. Its omission can only be excused if the facts in the record clearly show that the use includes the five years before the date of the statement.

(5) The affidavit or declaration should include a statement that the mark has become distinctive or that the applicant believes that the mark has become distinctive, but absence of this statement is not fatal. *See* TMEP §1212.07 for examples of various ways in which an applicant may assert a §2(f) claim.

(6) The affidavit or declaration should contain a reference to distinctiveness as applied to the applicant's goods or services, or to use with the applicant's goods or services, because the distinctiveness created by the five years' use must relate to the goods or services specified in the application. If there is doubt that the distinctiveness pertains to either all or any of the goods or services specified in the application, the examining attorney should inquire regarding that issue. While a clarifying response does not have to be verified, a substitute statement must be verified,

(1) 尽可能使用精确的法律语言，但如不影响实质的主张，可以作一些变动。

(2) “在商业活动中的实质性专属和持续使用”一语是关键。

(3) 档案中必须明确，五年的使用乃是用于国会可以合法规制的商业活动。参见 *Blanchard & Co., Inc. v. Charles Gilman & Son, Inc.*, 145 USPQ 62 (D. Mass. 1965), *aff'd*, 353 F.2d 400, 147 USPQ 263 (1st Cir. 1965), *cert. denied* 383 U.S. 968, 149 USPQ 905 (1966)。

(4) 对于商标的使用必须覆盖五年使用声明作出日之前五年的时间。表明所指称的使用系早于声明作出之日的措辞乃是关键。只有在档案中明确表明此种使用包括了声明作出日之前五年时间的情况下，才可以省略该措辞。

(5) 宣誓书或声明书应当包含关于该商标已经具备独特性，或者申请者认为该商标已经具备独特性的陈述，但缺少该陈述并非决定性瑕疵。有关申请者可以提出§2(f)主张的各种方式的例子，*参见* TMEP §1212.07。

(6) 宣誓书或声明书应当包含有关适用于申请者商品或服务、或与申请者商品或服务联系使用时的独特性参考材料，因为五年使用所造就的独特性必须与申请所确定的商品或服务相联系。如果对于与申请中所确定的所有或部分商品或服务相联系的独特性存在疑问，那么审查员就应当对此问题进行调查。尽管一份澄清事项的答辩不必经过认证，但是一份替换的声明则

i.e., supported by an affidavit or a declaration under 37 C.F.R. §2.20, signed by the applicant.

1212.06 Establishing Distinctiveness by Actual Evidence

Under Trademark Rule 2.41(a), 37 C.F.R. §2.41(a), an applicant may, in support of registrability, submit affidavits, declarations under 37 C.F.R. §2.20, depositions or other appropriate evidence showing the duration, extent and nature of the applicant's use of a mark in commerce that may lawfully be regulated by Congress, advertising expenditures in connection with such use, letters or statements from the trade and/or public, or other appropriate evidence tending to show that the mark distinguishes the goods or services.

Establishing acquired distinctiveness by actual evidence was explained as follows in *In re Owens-Corning Fiberglas Corp.*, 774 F.2d 1116, 1125, 227 USPQ 417, 422 (Fed. Cir. 1985):

> An evidentiary showing of secondary meaning, adequate to show that a mark has acquired distinctiveness indicating the origin of the goods, includes evidence of the trademark owner's method of using the mark, supplemented by evidence of the effectiveness of such use to cause the purchasing public to identify the mark with the source of the product.

The kind and amount of evidence necessary to establish that a mark has acquired distinctiveness in relation to goods or services necessarily depends on the nature of the mark and the circumstances surrounding the use of the mark in each case. *Yamaha Int'l Corp. v. Hoshino Gakki Co. Ltd.*, 840 F.2d 1572, 6 USPQ2d 1001 (Fed. Cir. 1988); *Roux Laboratories, Inc. v. Clairol Inc.*, 427 F.2d 823, 166 USPQ 34 (C.C.P.A. 1970); *In re Hehr Mfg. Co.*, 279 F.2d 526, 126 USPQ 381 (C.C.P.A. 1960); *In re Capital Formation Counselors*, 219 USPQ 916 (TTAB 1983).

In considering a claim of acquired distinctiveness, the issue is whether acquired distinctiveness of the mark in relation to the goods or services has in fact been es-

必须经过认证，亦即，由 37 C.F.R.§2.20 所规定的、经申请者签名的宣誓书或声明书进行佐证。

1212.06 通过实际证据证明独特性

根据《商标规则》2.41(a)，37 C.F.R.§2.41(a)的规定，为了支持其可注册性，申请者可以提交 37 C.F.R.§2.20 所规定的宣誓书及声明书，宣誓证词或其他适当的证据，以表明申请者在国会可以合法规制的商业领域中对商标进行使用的期间、范围和性质，有关此类使用的广告支出，来自于业务中和(或)公众的信函或声明，或能够表明该商标区别了商品或服务的其他适当证据。

在 *Owens-Corning Fiberglas Corp.*, 774 F.2d 1116, 1125, 227 USPQ 417, 422 (Fed. Cir. 1985)一案中，对于通过实际证据证明获得性独特性作了以下解释和例证：

> 一种根据证据对于次要含义的证明意味着，能够充分表明一项商标具有能够标示商品来源的获得性独特性，包括商标所有人使用该商标方式的证据，附以此类使用能够有效地使购买公众结合产品来源识别该商标的证据。

证明一项商标已经具备有关商品或服务的独特性所必需的证据种类和量必然取决于该商标的性质，以及在各案中使用该商标的周边环境。相关判例：*Yamaha Int'l Corp. v. Hoshino Gakki Co. Ltd.*, 840 F.2d 1572, 6 USPQ2d 1001 (Fed. Cir. 1988)；*Roux Laboratories, Inc. v. Clairol Inc.*, 427 F.2d 823, 166 USPQ 34 (C.C.P.A. 1970)；*Hehr Mfg. Co.*, 279 F.2d 526, 126 USPQ 381 (C.C.P.A. 1960)；*Capital Formation Counselors*, 219 USPQ 916 (TTAB 1983)。

在考察一项获得性独特性的主张时，问题在于该商标有关商品或服务的获得性

tablished in the minds of the purchasing public, not whether the mark is capable of becoming distinctive. *In re Redken Laboratories, Inc.*, 170 USPQ 526 (TTAB 1971); *In re Fleet-Wing Corp.*, 122 USPQ 335 (TTAB 1959).

The following are some examples of different types of evidence that have been used, alone or in combination, to establish acquired distinctiveness. No single evidentiary factor is determinative. The value of a specific type of evidence and the amount necessary to establish acquired distinctiveness will vary according to the facts of the specific case.

1212.06(a) Long Use of the Mark

Long use of the mark is one relevant factor to consider in determining whether a mark has acquired distinctiveness. *See In re Uncle Sam Chemical Co., Inc.*, 229 USPQ 233 (TTAB 1986) (§ 2(f) claim of acquired distinctiveness of SPRAYZON for "cleaning preparations and degreasers for industrial and institutional use" found persuasive where applicant had submitted declaration of its president supporting sales figures and attesting to over eighteen years of substantially exclusive and continuous use); *In re Packaging Specialists, Inc.*, 221 USPQ 917, 920 (TTAB 1984) (evidence submitted by applicant held insufficient to establish acquired distinctiveness of PACKAGING SPECIALISTS, INC., for contract packaging services, notwithstanding, *inter alia*, continuous and substantially exclusive use for sixteen years, deemed "a substantial period but not necessarily conclusive or persuasive").

1212.06(b) Advertising Expenditures

Large scale expenditures in promoting and advertising goods and services under a particular mark are significant to indicate the extent to which a mark has been used. However, proof of an expensive and successful advertising campaign is not in itself enough to prove secondary meaning. *In re Boston Beer Co. L.P.*, 198 F.

独特性是否实际上已经进入购买公众的脑海,而不在于该商标是否能够具备独特性。*参见 Redken Laboratories, Inc.*, 170 USPQ 526 (TTAB 1971); *Fleet-Wing Corp.*, 122 USPQ 335 (TTAB 1959)。

以下是一些已经被单独或组合采用,以证明获得性独特性的不同证据类型的例子。单独的证据因素并不是决定性的。特定证据类型的价值以及证明获得性独特性所必需的证据量根据特定案件的事实而各不相同。

1212.06(a) 对商标的长期使用

在判断一项商标是否具有获得性独特性的过程中,对该商标的长期使用是需要考虑的相关因素之一。*参见 Uncle Sam Chemical Co., Inc.*, 229 USPQ 233 (TTAB 1986)(根据 §2(f),对用于"企事业单位用清洁准备工作及除油服务"的 SPRAYZON 提出的获得性独特性主张被判定具有说服力,因为申请者提交了总裁证明的销售数据声明书,以及超过 18 年实质性专属和持续使用的证明。); *Packaging Specialists, Inc.*, 221 USPQ 917, 920 (TTAB 1984)(申请者提交的证据被认为不足以证明用于合同包装服务的"PACKAGING SPECIALISTS, INC."的获得性独特性,尽管也存在 16 年持续和实质性专属使用,但被视为"一种实质性的期间,但是并不必然是决定性和具有说服力的"。)。

1212.06(b) 广告支出

对于使用某特定商标的商品和服务进行促销和广告的大量支出,对于体现商标使用范围而言非常重要。不过,昂贵和成功的广告活动本身并不足以证明次要含义。

3d 1370, 53 USPQ2d 1056 (Fed. Cir. 1999) (claim based on annual sales under the mark of approximately eighty-five million dollars, and annual advertising expenditures in excess of ten million dollars — two million of which were spent on promotions and promotional items which included the phrase THE BEST BEER IN AMERICA — found insufficient to establish distinctiveness, in view of the highly descriptive nature of the proposed mark); *Mattel, Inc. v. Azrak-Hamway International, Inc.*, 724 F.2d 357, 221 USPQ 302, 305 n.2 (2d Cir. 1983). The ultimate test in determining whether a designation has acquired distinctiveness is applicant's success, rather than its efforts, in educating the public to associate the proposed mark with a single source. The examining attorney must examine the advertising material to determine how the term is being used, the commercial impression created by such use, and what the use would mean to purchasers. *In re Redken Laboratories, Inc.*, 170 USPQ 526, 529 (TTAB 1971) (evidence adduced by applicant pursuant to §2(f) held insufficient to establish acquired distinctiveness of THE SCIENTIFIC APPROACH, for lectures concerning hair and skin treatment, notwithstanding ten years of use, over $500,000 in promotion and sponsorship expenses, and the staging of over 300 shows per year). *See also In re E. I. Kane, Inc.*, 221 USPQ 1203, 1206 (TTAB 1984) (refusal to register OFFICE MOVERS, INC., for moving services, affirmed notwithstanding §2(f) claim based on, *inter alia*, evidence of substantial advertising expenditures. "There is no evidence that any of the advertising activity was directed to creating secondary meaning in applicant's highly descriptive trade name."); *In re Kwik Lok Corp.*, 217 USPQ 1245 (TTAB 1983) (evidence held insufficient to establish acquired distinctiveness for configuration of bag closures made of plastic, notwithstanding applicant's statement that advertising of the closures involved several hundred thousands of dollars, where there was no evidence that the advertising had any impact on purchasers in perceiving the configuration as a mark). *Cf. In re Haggar Co.*, 217 USPQ 81, 84 (TTAB 1982) (background design of a black swatch held registrable pursuant to §2(f) for clothing where applicant had submitted, *inter alia*, evidence of "very substantial advertising and sales," the Board finding the design to be, "because of its serrated left edge, something more than a

参见 *Boston Beer Co. L. P.*, 198 F.3d 1370, 53 USPQ2d 1056 (Fed. Cir. 1999)(基于以此商标所获的约 8500 万美元的年销售额,以及超过 1000 万美元的年广告支出——其中 200 万用于包含"THE BEST BEER IN AMERICA"一语的促销活动及促销物品——被判定不足以证明独特性,因为申请注册的商标具有高度描述性的性质);*Mattel, Inc. v. Azrak-Hamway International, Inc.*, 724 F.2d 357, 221 USPQ 302, 305 n.2 (2d Cir. 1983)。判断一种标识是否具备获得性独特性的终极检验标准是申请者造成公众将该申请注册商标与单一来源相联系的成功结果,而不是其付出的努力。审查员必须对广告材料进行审查,以判断该词语是如何使用的,通过此类使用又是如何造成商业印象,以及该使用对于购买者可能造成的含义。见 *Redken Laboratories, Inc.*, 170 USPQ 526, 529 (TTAB 1971)(申请者根据§2(f)提出的证据被认为不足以证明用于头发及皮肤护理讲座的"THE SCIENTIFIC APPROACH"的获得性独特性,尽管已有 10 年的使用,超过 50 万美元的促销及赞助费用,以及每年 300 场以上的展示演出)。另参见 *E. I. Kane, Inc.*, 221 USPQ 1203, 1206 (TTAB 1984)(维持对用于搬场服务的"OFFICE MOVERS, INC."拒绝予以注册,尽管存在根据 §2(f)所提出的,以实质性广告支出为证据的主张。"没有证据表明,任何广告活动使得申请者高度描述性的商号具有了次要含义。");*Kwik Lok Corp.*, 217 USPQ 1245 (TTAB 1983)(认为证据不足以证明塑料制口袋闭包设计的获得独特性,尽管申请者称为该闭包的广告投入了数十万美元的支出,但是并没有证据证明广告活动对于购买者将此种设计认作一项商标有任何的影响)。比较 *Haggar Co.*, 217 USPQ 81, 84 (TTAB 1982)(黑色布样的背景图案被认为可以根据§2(f)为申请者所提交的服装注册,因为存在"实质性广告和销售"的证据,委员会判定该图案

common geometric shape or design").

If the applicant prefers not to specify the extent of its expenditures in promoting and advertising goods and services under the mark because this information is confidential, the applicant may indicate the types of media through which the goods and services have been advertised (*e.g.*, national television) and how frequently the advertisements have appeared.

1212.06(c) Affidavits or Declarations Asserting Recognition of Mark as Source Indicator

Affidavits or declarations that assert recognition of the mark as a source indicator are relevant in establishing acquired distinctiveness. The value of the affidavits or declarations depends on the statements made and the identity of the affiant or declarant. *In re Chemical Dynamics Inc.*, 839 F.2d 1569, 5 USPQ2d 1828 (Fed. Cir. 1988) (conclusionary declaration from applicant's vice-president held insufficient without the factual basis for the declarant's belief that the design had become distinctive). Proof of distinctiveness requires more than proof of the existence of a relatively small number of people who associate a mark with the applicant. *In re The Paint Products Co.*, 8 USPQ2d 1863, 1866 (TTAB 1988) ("Because these affidavits were sought and collected by applicant from ten customers who have dealt with applicant for many years, the evidence is not altogether persuasive on the issue of how the average customer for paints perceives the words 'PAINT PRODUCTS CO.' in conjunction with paints and coatings."). *See also In re Gray Inc.*, 3 USPQ2d 1558, 1560 (TTAB 1987) (affidavit of applicant's counsel expressing his belief that the mark has acquired secondary meaning accorded "no probative value whatsoever" because, among other reasons, the statement is subject to bias); *In re Petersen Mfg. Co.*, 2 USPQ2d 2032 (TTAB 1987) (declarations from customers which stated that designs used by applicant indicate to the declarant that the applicant is the source of the goods, but which did not refer to or identify the designs with any specificity, not considered persuasive); *In re Bose Corp.*, 216 US-

属于“由于其锯齿状的左边缘，从而不仅仅是普通的几何形状或图案。”)。

如果申请者由于信息保密，而宁愿不列明以该商标所作的商品和服务促销广告活动支出的范围，那么申请者可以说明商品和服务进行广告的媒体种类(例如，全国电视广播)以及该广告出现的频率。

1212.06(c) 主张商标作为来源标示获得公认的宣誓书或声明书

在证明获得性独特性的过程中，主张商标作为来源标示获得了公认的宣誓书或声明书属于有关因素。宣誓书或声明书的价值取决于所作的陈述以及宣誓者或声明者的身份。*参见 Chemical Dynamics Inc.*, 839 F.2d 1569, 5 USPQ2d 1828 (Fed. Cir. 1988)(申请者副总裁所作的结论性声明被认为不充分，因为声明者对于图案具有独特性的确信缺乏事实依据)。独特性证据的要求高于存在相对少数人将商标与申请者相联系的证据。见 *The Paint Products Co.*, 8 USPQ2d 1863, 1866 (TTAB 1988)(“由于这些宣誓书系由申请者采自十名与其长年联系的消费者，因此对于一般的油漆消费者如何看待联系油漆和涂料的‘PAINT PRODUCTS CO.’之问题并不具有完全的说服力。”)。另 *参见 Gray Inc.*, 3 USPQ2d 1558, 1560 (TTAB 1987)(申请者律师表示其确信该商标具有次要含义的宣誓书属于“无论如何不具有检验价值”，因为原因之一在于该陈述存在偏见。)；*Petersen Mfg. Co.*, 2 USPQ2d 2032 (TTAB 1987)(消费者所作的声明书称申请者使用的图案向声明者标示了申请者为该商品的来源，但是该声明书并未确切提到或识别该图案，因而被认为不具说服力。)；

PQ 1001, 1005 (TTAB 1983), *aff'd*, 772 F.2d 866, 227 USPQ 1 (Fed.Cir.1985) (retailer's statement that he has been in contact with many purchasers of loudspeaker systems of whom a substantial number would recognize depicted design as originating with applicant deemed competent evidence of secondary meaning); *In re Flex-O-Glass, Inc.*, 194 USPQ 203, 206 (TTAB 1977) ("[T]he fact that the affidavits may be similar in format and expression is of no particular significance ... since the affiants have sworn to the statements contained therein.").

1212.06(d) Survey Evidence, Market Research and Consumer Reaction Studies

Survey evidence, market research and consumer reaction studies are relevant in establishing acquired distinctiveness and secondary meaning. *Yankee Candle Co., Inc. v. Bridgewater Candle Co., LLC*, 259 F.3d 25, 37, 59 USPQ2d 1720, 1730 (1st Cir.2001) ("Although survey evidence is not required, 'it is a valuable method of showing secondary meaning,'" citing *I. P. Lund Trading ApS v. Kohler Co.*, 163 F.3d 27, 41, 49 USPQ2d 1225, 1235 (1st Cir.1998)).

To show secondary meaning, the survey must show that the public views the proposed mark as an indication of the source of the product or service. *Boston Beer Co. L. P. v. Slesar Bros. Brewing Co., Inc.*, 9 F.3d 175, 28 USPQ2d 1778 (1st Cir. 1993) (survey found insufficient to establish acquired distinctiveness where survey demonstrates product-place association rather than product-source association). The applicant must document the procedural and statistical accuracy of this type of evidence and carefully frame the questions contained therein. *See In re E. I. Kane, Inc.*, 221 USPQ 1203, 1206 (TTAB 1984) ("[T]he survey asked the wrong question. The issue is not whether the term 'Office Movers' identifies a specific company. Rather, it is whether the term 'OFFICE MOVERS, INC.' identifies services which emanate from a single source."); *General Foods Corp. v. Ralston Purina Co.*, 220 USPQ 990, 994 n.7 (TTAB 1984) ("[W]here ... [reports of market research, consumer reaction studies] have been conducted for marketing rea-

Bose Corp., 216 USPQ 1001, 1005 (TTAB 1983), *aff'd*, 772 F.2d 866, 227 USPQ 1 (Fed. Cir. 1985)(零售商称,他已经联系了许多扩音系统的购买者,其中相当多的人承认将所述图案认作申请者来源标示,该声明被认为是次要含义的适格证据。); *Flex-O-Glass, Inc.*, 194 USPQ 203, 206 (TTAB 1977)("各宣誓书在格式和表达方面可能相似的事实并无特别的意义……因为宣誓者已经就所包含的陈述进行了宣誓。")。

1212.06(d) 调查证据、市场调查以及消费者反应研究

在证明获得独特性的过程中,调查证据、市场调查以及消费者反应研究属于有关因素。见 *Yankee Candle Co., Inc. v. Bridgewater Candle Co., LLC*, 259 F.3d 25, 37, 59 USPQ2d 1720, 1730 (1st Cir. 2001)("尽管并不要求提供调查证据,但'对于证明次要含义仍是有价值的方法'",引用 *I. P. Lund Trading ApS v. Kohler Co.*, 163 F.3d 27, 41, 49 USPQ2d 1225, 1235 (1st Cir. 1998))。

为了证明次要含义,调查必须表明公众将申请注册的商标视为产品或服务来源的一种标识。见 *Boston Beer Co. L. P. v. Slesar Bros. Brewing Co., Inc.*, 9 F.3d 175, 28 USPQ2d 1778 (1st Cir. 1993)(调查被判定不足以证明获得性独特性,因为调查证明的是产品－地点联系,而非产品－来源联系)。申请者对于此类证据必须证明程序和统计上的准确性,并且要仔细设计所包含的问题。参见 *E. I. Kane, Inc.*, 221 USPQ 1203, 1206 (TTAB 1984)("该调查询问了错误的问题。问题并非'Office Movers'一词是否识别了某一特定的公司。而是'OFFICE MOVERS, INC.'一词是否识别了来自单一来源的服务。"); *General Foods Corp. v. Ralston Purina Co.*, 220 USPQ 990, 994 n.7 (TTAB 1984)("如果……[市场调查以及消费者反应研究 报告]是出于市场运作的目的,而并非直接协助我们在解决程序中的问题,那么

sons rather than directly to assist in resolving the issues in proceedings before us, their value will almost always depend on interpretations of their significance by witnesses or other evidence."); *Specialty Brands, Inc. v. Spiceseas, Inc.*, 220 USPQ 73, 74 n.4 (TTAB 1983) (testimony concerning survey results, unsupported by documentation, considered unreliable hearsay).

1212.06(e) Miscellaneous Considerations Regarding Evidence Submitted to Establish Distinctiveness

1212.06(e)(i) First or Only User

When the applicant is the only source of the goods or services, use alone does not automatically represent trademark recognition and acquired distinctiveness. *See*, *e.g.*, *J. Kohnstam, Ltd. v. Louis Marx & Co., Inc.*, 280 F.2d 437, 126 USPQ 362 (C.C.P.A.1960); *In re Mortgage Bankers Association of America*, 226 USPQ 954 (TTAB 1985); *In re National Shooting Sports Foundation, Inc.*, 219 USPQ 1018 (TTAB 1983); *In re Meier's Wine Cellars, Inc.*, 150 USPQ 475 (TTAB 1966); *In re G.D. Searle & Co.*, 143 USPQ 220 (TTAB 1964), *aff'd*, 360 F.2d 650, 149 USPQ 619 (C.C.P.A.1966).

1212.06(e)(ii) State Trademark Registrations

State trademark registrations are of relatively little probative value. See, *e.g.*, *In re Vico Products Mfg. Co., Inc.*, 229 USPQ 364, 370 (TTAB 1985), *recon. denied*, 229 USPQ 716 (TTAB 1986) ("While applicant's design may be registrable under the provisions of California trademark law, it is the federal trademark statute and the cases interpreting it by which we must evaluate the registrability of applicant's asserted mark."); *In re Craigmyle*, 224 USPQ 791, 794 (TTAB 1984).

1212.06(e)(iii) Design Patent

The fact that a device is the subject of a design patent does not, without more,

其价值就几乎总是取决于证人或其他证据对其含义的解释。"); *Specialty Brands, Inc. v. Spiceseas, Inc.*, 220 USPQ 73, 74 n.4 (TTAB 1983)(未经文件佐证的有关调查结果的证词被认为是不可靠的道听途说)。

1212.06(e) 关于独特性证据的其他考虑事项

1212.06(e)(i) 首先或唯一使用者

如果申请者是商品或服务的唯一来源,单独使用并不能自然表示对商标的认可以及获得独特性。*参见* 判例: *J. Kohnstam, Ltd. v. Louis Marx & Co., Inc.*, 280 F.2d 437, 126 USPQ 362 (C.C.P.A. 1960); *Mortgage Bankers Association of America*, 226 USPQ 954 (TTAB 1985); *National Shooting Sports Foundation, Inc.*, 219 USPQ 1018 (TTAB 1983); *Meier's Wine Cellars, Inc.*, 150 USPQ 475 (TTAB 1966); *G.D. Searle & Co.*, 143 USPQ 220 (TTAB 1964), *aff'd*, 360 F.2d 650, 149 USPQ 619 (C.C.P.A. 1966)。

1212.06(e)(ii) 州商标注册

州商标注册只有相对较少的检验价值。*参见* 判例: *Vico Products Mfg. Co., Inc.*, 229 USPQ 364, 370 (TTAB 1985), *recon. denied*, 229 USPQ 716 (TTAB 1986)("尽管根据加利福尼亚商标法的规定申请者的图案可以注册,但是我们必须根据联邦法律和解释联邦法律的判例对申请者声称的商标的可注册性进行评价。"); *Craigmyle*, 224 USPQ 791, 794 (TTAB 1984)。

1212.06(e)(iii) 图案专利

如果图案属于一项图案专利的内容,那么无需更多证据,就意味着它具备了商标

mean that it functions as a mark or has acquired distinctiveness. *See*, *e.g.*, *In re Vico Products Mfg. Co., Inc.*, 229 USPQ 364, 370 (TTAB 1985), *recon. denied*, 229 USPQ 716 (TTAB 1986).

1212.06(e)(iv) Acquiescence to Demands of Competitors

Acquiescence to demands of competitors to cease use of a term can be equally viewed as simply a desire to avoid litigation. *See*, *e.g.*, *In re Wella Corp.*, 565 F. 2d 143, 144 n.2, 196 USPQ 7, 8 n.2 (C.C.P.A. 1977); *In re Consolidated Cigar Corp.*, 13 USPQ2d 1481 (TTAB 1989).

1212.07 Form of Application Asserting Distinctiveness

To base a registration on acquired distinctiveness under §2(f), 15 U.S.C. §1052 (f), an applicant must indicate its intent to do so.

The indication of the applicant's intent to rely on §2(f) can take a variety of forms, for example, a statement that registration is requested under §2(f); a statement that the mark has become distinctive, or that the applicant believes the mark has become distinctive of the goods or services in commerce; the statement relating to five years' use in commerce as suggested in §2(f); or a statement that evidence is being submitted in support of acquired distinctiveness.

If it is unclear from the application whether a claim of distinctiveness under §2(f) has been made, the examining attorney should inquire whether the applicant is seeking registration under §2(f). *See* TMEP §1212.02(d) concerning unnecessary §2(f) claims.

If the statement requesting registration under §2(f) and the evidence submitted to establish acquired distinctiveness are in the application when filed, the §2(f) statement and proof are supported by the verification of the application.

If a claim of distinctiveness pursuant to §2(f) is submitted as an amendment, or if

的功能，或者已经具备了独特性。*参见* 判例：*Vico Products Mfg. Co., Inc.*, 229 USPQ 364，370（TTAB 1985），*recon. denied*, 229 USPQ 716（TTAB 1986）。

1212.06(e)(iv) 默许竞争者的要求

对竞争者停止使用某词语要求的默许平心而论可被视作只是一种希望避免诉讼的表现。*参见* 判例：*Wella Corp.*, 565 F.2d 143，144 n.2，196 USPQ 7，8 n.2（C.C.P.A. 1977）；*Consolidated Cigar Corp.*, 13 USPQ2d 1481（TTAB 1989）。

1212.07 主张独特性申请的格式

如果是基于§2(f)，15 U.S.C.§1052(f)所规定的获得性独特性提出注册申请，申请者必须表明其具有此种意图。

申请者表明其基于 §2(f)提出主张的意图可以以各种形式出现，例如：称注册申请系根据§2(f)提出的声明；商标具备独特性的声明，或申请者确信该商标在商业活动中对商品或服务具备独特性的声明；§2(f)所示的关于在商业活动中 5 年使用的声明；或者已经提交证据证明获得独特性的声明。

如果申请者提供的信息不能明确是否根据§2(f)提出了独特性主张，那么审查员就应当调查申请者是否根据 §2(f)寻求注册。有关不必要的 §2(f)主张的情况，*参见* TMEP §1212.02(d)。

如果申请归档时已经提交了根据 §2(f)申请注册的声明，以及证明获得独特性的证据，那么该§2(f)声明以及证据就已经获得了申请书的佐证。

如果根据§2(f)提出的独特性主张是以修正书形式提交的，或者如果在修正书

additional evidence is added in an amendment, the nature of the proof submitted to establish acquired distinctiveness determines whether a verification is necessary.

A claim of ownership of one or more prior registrations as proof of distinctiveness does not have to be verified. *See* TMEP §1212.04(e).

If the applicant claims that the mark has become distinctive of the applicant's goods or services through substantially exclusive and continuous use of the mark in commerce by the applicant for the five years before the date on which the claim of distinctiveness is made, the applicant must submit this claim in the form of an affidavit, or a declaration in accordance with 37 C.F.R. §2.20, signed by the applicant. 15 U.S.C. §1052(f); 37 C.F.R. §2.41(b); TMEP §1212.05(d). *See* 37 C.F.R. §2.33(a) and TMEP §804.04 regarding persons properly authorized to sign on behalf of applicant.

If an application is amended to add a §2(f) claim relying on other types of evidence, there may be considerable flexibility as to form. While statements by the applicant regarding advertising or sales figures or other facts that may show acquired distinctiveness would normally be presented in the form of affidavits, or declarations under 37 C.F.R. §2.20, signed by the applicant, verification may not be required for other types of evidence. The examining attorney will determine whether the evidence relied on is of a nature that requires that it be verified by the applicant.

1212.08 Section 44 Applications and Distinctiveness

In applications claiming a right of priority under §44(d), 15 U.S.C. §1126(d), or based on a foreign registration under §44(e), 15 U.S.C. §1126(e), registration may be sought under §2(f) on a showing that the mark has acquired distinctiveness in commerce that may lawfully be regulated by Congress. *In re Etablissements Darty et Fils*, 759 F.2d 15, 225 USPQ 652 (Fed. Cir. 1985). Dates of first use do

中提供了其他证据，那么该提交用以证明获得独特性的证据的性质将决定是否需要作出认证。

作为独特性证据的一项或更多在先注册所有权主张不必经过认证。*参见* TMEP §1212.04(e)。

如果申请者主张，通过申请者于独特性主张日之前在商业活动中对该商标实施了5年的实质性专属和持续使用，从而使该商标对于申请者的商品或服务具备了独特性，那么申请者就必须以37 C.F.R.§2.20所规定的由其签名的宣誓书或声明书的形式提出此项主张。15 U.S.C.§1052(f)；37 C.F.R.§2.41(b)；TMEP §1212.05(d)。有关经适当授权代理申请者签署之人的情况，*参见* 37 C.F.R.§2.33(a)和TMEP §804.04。

如果一项申请经过修正，加入了基于其他类型证据所提出的§2(f)主张，那么其形式可以具有相当的灵活性。不过，申请者所作的有关广告或销售数据，或其他可以证明获得独特性事实的声明，通常须以37 C.F.R.§2.20所规定的宣誓书或声明书形式提出，并由申请者签名，对于其他类型的证据则可以不要求经过认证。审查员会判断所立基的证据是否属于要求经申请者认证的性质。

1212.08　　第44节申请和独特性

在根据§44(d)，15 U.S.C.§1126(d)主张优先权，或是根据§44(e)，15 U.S.C.§1126(e)基于外国注册而提出的申请中，可以通过证明该商标已经在国会可以合法规制的商业活动中具备了独特性而申请注册。*参见 Etablissements Darty et Fils*, 759 F.2d 15, 17, 225 USPQ 652, 653 (Fed.Cir.1985)。在仅根据§44提出的申请

not have to be stated in an application based solely on §44. However, reference to length of use or information as to specific dates of use will be important as part of the evidence presented in support of the claim of acquired distinctiveness.

The applicant may not rely on use other than use in commerce that may be regulated by the United States Congress in establishing acquired distinctiveness. Use solely in a foreign country is not evidence of acquired distinctiveness in the United States. *In re Rogers*, 53 USPQ2d 1741 (TTAB 1999).

1212.09 Intent-to-Use Applications and Distinctiveness

1212.09(a) Section 2(f) Claim Requires Prior Use

Section 2(f), 15 U.S.C. §1052(f), is limited by its terms to "a mark used by the applicant." A claim of distinctiveness under §2(f) is normally not filed in a §1(b) application before the applicant files an amendment to allege use or a statement of use, because a claim of acquired distinctiveness, by definition, requires prior use.

However, an intent-to-use applicant who has used the mark on related goods or services may file a claim of acquired distinctiveness under §2(f) before filing an amendment to allege use or statement of use, if the applicant can establish that, as a result of the applicant's use of the mark on other goods or services, the mark has become distinctive of the goods or services in the intent-to-use application, and that this previously created distinctiveness will transfer to the goods and services in the intent-to-use application when use in commerce begins. *In re Dial-A-Mattress Operating Corp.*, 240 F.3d 1341, 1347, 57 USPQ2d 1807, 1812 (Fed. Cir. 2001).

The Trademark Trial and Appeal Board has set forth the requirements for showing that a mark in an intent-to-use application has acquired distinctiveness:

> The required showing is essentially twofold. First, applicant must establish, through the appropriate submission, the acquired distinctiveness of

中，不必陈述首次使用日期。不过，提及使用期间长度以及关于特定使用日期的信息，作为佐证获得性独特性主张的证据的一部分，将会非常重要。

在证明获得性独特性的过程中，申请者不能依赖可以由国会合法规制商业活动以外的使用。只在某外国使用不能作为在美国具备独特性的证据。*Rogers*，53 USPQ2d 1741 (TTAB 1999)。

1212.09 意图使用申请和独特性

1212.09(a) 第2(f)节主张要求在先使用

第2(f)节，15 U.S.C.§1052(f)，因其条款而限于"申请者所使用的商标"。根据§2(f)提出的独特性主张在申请人提交宣称使用修正书或使用声明书之前，通常不会在一项根据§1(b)提出的申请中提交，因为根据定义，一项获得性独特性主张要求在先使用。

不过，将商标用于相关商品或服务的意图使用申请者可以在提交宣称使用修正书或使用声明书之前根据 §2(f)提出获得性独特性主张，只要申请者能够证明，由于申请者将该商标用于其他商品或服务，该商标对于意图使用申请中所述商品或服务已经具备了独特性，而且，当商业活动中的使用开始时，先前造就的独特性会转移给意图使用申请中所述的商品和服务。见 *Dial-A-Mattress Operating Corp*.，240 F.3d 1341，57 USPQ2d 1807，1812 (Fed. Cir. 2001)。

商标评审及上诉委员会确定了证明意图使用申请中的商标已经具备独特性的要求：

> 所要求的证明在本质上有两方面。首先，申请者必须提交适当的材料证明，用于所述其他商品和(或)服务的同一商标在商业活动中的获得性独

the same mark in connection with specified other goods and/or services in connection with which the mark is in use in commerce. All of the rules and legal precedent pertaining to such a showing in a use-based application are equally applicable in this context ... Second, applicant must establish, through submission of relevant evidence rather than mere conjecture, a sufficient relationship between the goods or services in connection with which the mark has acquired distinctiveness and the goods or services recited in the intent-to-use application to warrant the conclusion that the previously created distinctiveness will transfer to the goods or services in the application upon use.

In re Rogers, 53 USPQ2d 1741, 1744 (TTAB 1999).

To satisfy the first element, the applicant must establish acquired distinctiveness as to the other goods or services by appropriate evidence, such as ownership of a prior registration for the same mark for related goods or services (*see* TMEP §§1212.04 *et seq.*), a *prima facie* showing of acquired distinctiveness based on five years'use of the same mark with related goods or services (*see* TMEP §§1212.05 *et seq.*), or actual evidence of acquired distinctiveness for the same mark with respect to the other goods or services (*see* TMEP §§1212.06 *et seq.*).

To satisfy the second element, applicant must submit evidence showing "the extent to which the goods or services in the intent-to-use application are related to the goods or services in connection with which the mark is distinctive, and that there is a strong likelihood that the mark's established trademark function will transfer to the related goods or services when use in commerce occurs." *In re Rogers* at 1745.

The fact that a mark is famous in connection with certain goods or services does *not* necessarily lead to the conclusion that, upon use, distinctiveness will transfer to use of the mark in connection with unrelated goods or services in an intent-to-use application. In *Rogers*, the Board stated that:

特性。有关此种基于使用提出的申请证明的一切规则和法律先例在此种情况下同样适用……。其次,申请者必须提交相关证据而非仅仅臆测,以证明,在已具备独特性商标相关的商品或服务与意图使用申请中所述的商品或服务之间存在充分的关系,以确证先前造就的独特性可以通过使用转给申请中所述的商品或服务。

Rogers, 53 USPQ2d 1741, 1744 (TTAB 1999)。

为了满足第一项要素,申请者必须以适当的证据——如,用于相关商品或服务的同一商标的在先注册所有权(*参见* TMEP §§1212.04 及以下);基于同一商标用于相关商品或服务 5 年使用对于获得独特性的初步证明(*参见* TMEP §§1212.05 及以下);或是同一商标用于其他商品或服务时具备独特性的实际证据(*参见* TMEP §§1212.06 及以下)——以证明有关其他商品或服务的获得性独特性。

为了满足第二项要素,申请者必须提出证据证明"意图使用申请中的商品或服务与独特性商标所涉商品或服务联系的范围程度,并且在商业使用发生时,该商标的商标功能极有可能会转移给相关的商品或服务"。*Rogers* at 1745。

某项商标用于特定商品或服务时声誉卓著并不会必然得出结论认为,通过使用,独特性就会转移给意图使用申请中用于相关商品或服务的商标的使用。在 *Rogers* 案中,委员会称:

> The owner of a famous mark must still establish a strong likelihood of transference of the trademark function to the goods or services identified in the intent-to-use application. This factually-based determination will still involve establishing some degree of relationship between the goods or services for which the mark is famous and the goods or services in the intent to use application.

53 USPQ2d at 1745-1746.

An applicant whose application is based on use in commerce under 15 U. S. C. §1051(a) may also base a claim of acquired distinctiveness under §2(f) on long use of the mark on related goods or services, if the applicant meets the requirements set forth above.

1212. 09(b) Claim of §2(f) "in Part" in §1(b) Application

An intent-to-use applicant may also file a claim of acquired distinctiveness under §2(f) of the Trademark Act, 15 U.S.C. §1052(f), as to part of a mark before filing an acceptable amendment to allege use or statement of use. The claim must indicate that the applicant has already used the relevant part of the mark in commerce on or in connection with the specified goods or services or other goods or services as discussed above. *See* TMEP §1212.02(f) regarding claims of §2(f) distinctiveness "in part".

Evidence in support of such a claim may consist of (1) ownership of a prior registration covering the relevant part of the mark and the same or related goods or services (*see* TMEP §§1212.04 *et seq.*); (2) a *prima facie* showing of distinctiveness based on five years' use of the relevant part of the mark with the same or related goods or services (*see* TMEP §§1212.05 *et seq.*); or (3) actual evidence of acquired distinctiveness of the relevant part of the mark with respect to the same or related goods or services (*see* TMEP §§1212.06 *et seq.*). The examining attorney should consider the claim in the same manner as any other claim under §2(f).

驰名商标的所有者仍然必须证明该商标功能既有可能会转移给意图使用申请所识别商品或服务。此项基于事实的判断仍然会涉及证明驰名商标所涉商品或服务与意图使用申请所涉商品或服务之间存在某种程度的联系。

53 USPQ2d 1745－1746。

基于 15 U.S.C.§1051(a)所规定的商业使用提出申请的申请者,也可以基于在相关商品或服务中对商标的长期使用提出获得性独特性主张以申请注册,只要申请者符合前文所述的要求。

1212.09(b)　　§1(b)申请中的"部分" §2(f)主张

意图使用申请者也可以在提出适当的宣称使用修正书或使用声明书之前,根据《商标法》§2(f),15 U.S.C.§1052(f)的规定,对商标的一部分提出获得性独特性主张。该主张必须表明,申请者早已在商业活动中将该商标的相关部分用于所述的商品或服务,或者上文所述的其他商品或服务。有关"部分"的 §2(f)独特性主张的内容,*参见* TMEP §1212.02(f)。

用来证明此种主张的证据可以包括:(1)用于相关商品或服务的同一商标的在先注册所有权(*参见* TMEP §§1212.04 及以下);(2)基于同一商标用于相关商品或服务五年使用对于获得性独特性的初步证明(*参见* TMEP §§1212.05 及以下);或是(3)同一商标用于其他商品或服务时具备独特性的实际证据(*参见* TMEP §§1212.06 及以下)。审查员应当以与其他一切根据 §2(f)提出的主张相同的方式对该主张进行考察。

If the examining attorney determines that the applicant has established acquired distinctiveness as to the relevant part of the mark, the examining attorney should withdraw any refusal related to the nondistinctive character of that part of the mark.

1212.10 Printing " § 2(f)" Notations

Currently, when a mark is registered under §2(f), the Office prints a "2(f)" notation in the *Official Gazette* and on the certificate of registration. However, there was a period of time in the past when the Office did not print this notation. Therefore, the absence of a " § 2(f)" notation on an older registration does not necessarily mean that the mark was registered without resort to §2(f).

1213 Disclaimer of Elements in Marks

15 U.S.C.§1056. Disclaimers.

(*a*) *The Director may require the applicant to disclaim an unregistrable component of a mark otherwise registrable. An applicant may voluntarily disclaim a component of a mark sought to be registered.*

(*b*) *No disclaimer, including those made under subsection* (*e*) *of section 7 of this Act, shall prejudice or affect the applicant's or registrant's rights then existing or thereafter arising in the disclaimed matter, or his right of registration on another application if the disclaimed matter be or shall have become distinctive of his goods or services.*

In a trademark application or registration, a disclaimer is a statement that the applicant or registrant does not claim the exclusive right to use a specified element or elements of the mark. A disclaimer may be included in an application as filed or may be added by amendment, *e.g.*, to comply with a requirement by the examining attorney.

如果审查员判定,申请者已经证明了该商标的相关部分的获得独特性,那么审查员就应当撤回一切关于该商标此部分不具独特性特征的拒绝予以注册的决定。

1212.10 刊印“§2(f)”符号

现在,如果某项商标根据§2(f)获得了注册,商标局就会在《公报》和注册证书上印上“2(f)”符号。不过,在过去的一段时期,商标局并不刊印此符号。因此,旧注册缺少“§2(f)”符号并不必然意味着该商标的注册没有援引§2(f)。

1213 撤回商标不能注册的内容

15 U.S.C.§1056。撤回。

(a)局长可以要求申请人撤回一个商标的不能注册的组成部分方可注册。申请人可自动撤回申请注册商标的某一组成部分。

(b)撤回的部分,包括依照本法第7节(e)款撤回的部分,不应损害或影响申请者或注册人对被撤回部分的现有的或此后发生的权利,或者,若被撤回部分成为或已成为区别其商品或服务的显著部分时,不应损害或影响其在另一申请中注册的权利。

在申请或注册某一商标中,所谓的撤回是一项声明,声明商标申请者或注册人不主张就该商标的某一或某些明确的部分享有独占的使用权。撤回可以包括在提出的申请书中,或者例如在审核员要求提交时,以修正书的形式添加。

The purpose of a disclaimer is to permit the registration of a mark that is registrable as a whole but contains matter that would not be registrable standing alone, without creating a false impression of the extent of the registrant's right with respect to certain elements in the mark. As stated in *Horlick's Malted Milk Co. v. Borden Co.*, 295 F.232, 234, 1924 C.D.197, 199 (D.C.Cir.1924):

> [T]he fact that a mark contains descriptive words is not enough to warrant a refusal to register it. Unless it consists only of such words, it may not be refused a place on the registry of the Patent Office.

The significance of a disclaimer is conveyed in the following statement:

> As used in trade mark registrations, a disclaimer of a component of a composite mark amounts merely to a statement that, in so far as that particular registration is concerned, no rights are being asserted in the disclaimed component standing alone, but rights are asserted in the composite; and the particular registration represents only such rights as flow from the use of the composite mark.

Sprague Electric Co. v. Erie Resistor Corp., 101 USPQ 486, 486-87 (Comm'r Pats. 1954).

A disclaimer may be limited to pertain to only certain classes, or to only certain goods or services.

1213.01 History of Disclaimer Practice

There was no statutory authority for disclaimer prior to 1946. As various court decisions were rendered, Office practice fluctuated from, first, registering the composite mark without a qualifying statement; later, requiring a statement in the application disclaiming the unregistrable matter in the mark; and, finally, requiring removal of the unregistrable matter from the mark on the drawing. This fluctuation ended with the decision of *Estate of P. D. Beckwith v. Comm'r of Pats.*, 252

撤回的目的是,在商标作为一个整体具有可注册性,但包含了一些在孤立的情形下无法注册的部分时准许其注册,只要其并没有产生影响注册人就该商标的这些特定的要素所享有的权利的错误印象。正如 *Horlick's Malted Milk Co. v. Borden Co.*, 295 F.232, 234, 1924 C.D.197, 199 (D.C.Cir.1924)一案中所述:

> 某一商标包含了描述性用语并不必然导致被拒绝注册的后果。除非该商标仅仅由此类用语所组成,否则专利局不能拒绝该商标的注册。

以下的阐述则揭示了撤回的重要性:

> 商标注册中所使用的撤回某一复合商标中的某一构成部分仅仅表明:就该特定注册而言,不主张对单独的、被撤回的部分的权利,但主张该部分在复合商标中的权利;而且该特定注册仅仅表示来自于使用该复合商标所具有的权利。

Sprague Electric Co. v. Erie Resistor Corp., 101 USPQ 486, 486 - 487 (Comm'r Pats.1954)。

一项撤回可以仅限于某些特定级别的,或者仅限于某些特定的商品或服务。

1213.01 撤回的实践历程

在 1946 年以前,并没有关于撤回的立法规定。专利局的实际做法也随着不同的法院的意见而摇摆不定,起初在注册复合商标的时候并不需要一份适格的声明;后来,专利局要求在申请书中声明商标所具有的不能注册的组成部分;最后,专利局要求将不能注册的部分从商标草图中剔除。这一摇摆的立场在 *Estate of P.D. Beckwith v. Comm'r of Pats.*, 252 U.S.538, 1920 C.D.471 (1920)一案的判决中得以

U.S.538, 1920 C.D.471 (1920), in which the United States Supreme Court held that to require the removal of descriptive matter from a composite mark was erroneous, and commended the practice of a statement of disclaimer. Thus the practice of disclaimer was established officially in the Office, although still without statutory support.

The Trademark Act of 1946 created a statutory basis for the practice of disclaimer in §6, 15 U.S.C. §1056.

1213.01(a) Discretion in Requiring Disclaimer

When first incorporated in the Trademark Act in 1946, §6 stated that the Director *shall* require unregistrable matter to be disclaimed. Under the impetus of the mandatory word "shall," it became customary to require a disclaimer for every occurrence, in any type of combination, of every term or symbol which by itself might be refused registration in the first instance under the 1946 Act.

In 1962, §6 was amended to state that the Director *may* require the applicant to disclaim an unregistrable component of a mark otherwise registrable. The change from "shall" to "may" justifies the exercise of greater discretion by examining attorneys in determining whether a disclaimer is necessary.

Examining attorneys should keep in mind the basic purpose of disclaimers, which is to make of record that a significant element of a composite mark is not being appropriated apart from the composite. The examining attorney should not require that an element of a mark be disclaimed when a disclaimer would be unnecessary, *e.g.*, when the form or degree of integration of an element in the composite makes it obvious that no claim is being made in any element apart from the composite.

1213.01(b) Refusal to Register Because of Failure to Disclaim

Failure to comply with a requirement to disclaim was held to be a basis for refusal

确定。在该案中美国最高法院认为，要求将复合商标中的描述性部分去掉是错误的，并推荐使用撤回商标不能注册内容的声明。如此，撤回这一做法在专利局中被正式确立，虽然仍然缺乏制定法依据。

《1946 年商标法》§6，15 U.S.C.§1056 为撤回这一做法提供了法律依据。

1213.01(a) 要求撤回的裁量权

当首次在《1946 年商标法》中出现时，§6 规定局长应当要求就不能注册部分作出撤回。在“应当”这一强制性的用词的推动下，在任何类型的组合中所包含的任何术语或符号，只要其本身根据《1946 年商标法》在初审中可能遭到拒绝注册，任何此类情况下，都要求撤回该内容，这一做法已成为一项惯例。

1962 年，§6 被修改为局长可以要求申请者撤回一个商标的不能注册的组成部分方可注册。从“应当”到“可以”这一转变使得审查员在决定是否必须提交一份撤回声明这一事项上拥有了较大的裁量权。

审查员应当将撤回声明的基本目的铭记于心，那就是对某一复合商标中的重要组成部分没有被从该整体中不当地被剥离记入档案。如果某项撤回是不必要的，例如当复合商标的某一组成部分的形式或同主体的结合程度很明显表明了，除了对复合商标以外，对于任何组成部分都不能主张权利，审查员就不应该要求对该组成部分作出撤回。

1213.01(b) 由于未撤回而拒绝注册

在《1946年商标法》以前，没有遵循作出撤回声明的要求，将被作为拒绝予以注

to register before the Act of 1946. *See In re American Cyanamid & Chemical Corp*., 99 F.2d 964, 39 USPQ 445 (C.C.P.A.1938). Failure to comply with a requirement to disclaim also was held to justify a refusal after the 1946 Act. *See In re Hercules Fasteners, Inc*., 203 F.2d 753, 97 USPQ 355 (C.C.P.A.1953); *Ex parte Knomark Mfg. Co., Inc*., 118 USPQ 182 (PO Ex.Ch.1958). Even after amendment of the pertinent language of §6 of the 1946 Act to the discretionary wording "may require the applicant to disclaim," registration may be refused if an applicant does not comply with a requirement for a disclaimer made by the examining attorney. *See In re Omaha National Corp*., 819 F.2d 1117, 2 USPQ2d 1859 (Fed. Cir.1987); *In re Richardson Ink Co*., 511 F.2d 559, 185 USPQ 46 (C.C.P.A. 1975); *In re National Presto Industries, Inc*., 197 USPQ 188 (TTAB 1977); *In re Pendleton Tool Industries, Inc*., 157 USPQ 114 (TTAB 1968).

If an applicant fails to comply with the examining attorney's requirement for a disclaimer, the examining attorney should make the requirement final if the application is otherwise in condition for a final action.

1213.01(c) Voluntary Disclaimer of Registrable or Unregistrable Matter

Section 6(a) of the Trademark Act, 15 U.S.C. §1056(a), was amended in 1962 to add the sentence, "An applicant may voluntarily disclaim a component of a mark sought to be registered." Disclaimers volunteered by applicants generally should conform to the guidelines set forth in this Manual. *See* TMEP §§1213.08 *et seq*.

In *In re MCI Communications Corp*., 21 USPQ2d 1534 (Comm'r Pats.1991), the Commissioner held that §6 of the Act permits an applicant to disclaim matter voluntarily, regardless of whether the matter is registrable or unregistrable. The Commissioner specifically overruled all previous Office authority holding otherwise. (Previous practice prohibited the entry of disclaimers of registrable components of marks.) Therefore, if an applicant offers a disclaimer of any matter in a mark, the Office will accept the disclaimer.

册的理由。参见 *American Cyanamid & Chemical Corp*., 99 F.2d 964, 39 USPQ 445 (C.C.P.A.1938)。在《1946 年商标法》颁行以后,未能遵从撤回要求也同样被认为可以作为拒绝予以注册的理由。参见 *Hercules Fasteners, Inc*., 203 F.2d 753, 97 USPQ 355 (C.C.P.A.1953); *Knomark Mfg. Co., Inc*., 118 USPQ 182 (PO Ex.Ch.1958)。甚至在用了中肯的用语对《1946 年商标法》§6 加以修正后,用了裁量性的遣词"可以要求申请者撤回"之后,如果申请者不遵循审查员所要求的作出撤回声明的要求的话,注册也可能被拒绝。参见 *Omaha National Corp*., 819 F.2d 1117, 2 USPQ2d 1859 (Fed.Cir.1987); *Richardson Ink Co*., 511 F.2d 559, 185 USPQ 46 (C.C.P.A.1975); *National Presto Industries, Inc*., 197 USPQ 188 (TTAB 1977); *Pendleton Tool Industries, Inc*., 157 USPQ 114 (TTAB 1968)。

如果申请者没有遵循审查员的要求作出撤回,而且不如此该申请就符合终局性决定的条件,审核员就应当作出一项终局性的要求。

1213.01(c) 对于可注册或不可注册内容的自愿撤回

《商标法》§6(a),15 U.S.C.§1056(a),经过了 1962 年的修正,添加了下面一句话:"申请者可以自愿撤回申请注册商标的组成部分。"申请者的自愿撤回须遵循本手册规定的指导原则。参见 TMEP §§1213.08 及以下。

在 *MCI Communications Corp*., 21 USPQ2d 1534 (Comm'r Pats.1991)一案中,专员认为商标法§6 允许申请者自愿撤回商标的内容,而不必考虑该内容是否可以注册。专员明确地推翻了以前专利局所有的意见。(以前的实践中,禁止对于商标可注册部分的撤回。)因此,如果申请者对于商标中任何一项组成部分提出撤回,商标局都将接受。

The *MCI* decision states emphatically that the entry of a voluntary disclaimer does *not* render registrable a mark that is otherwise unregistrable under relevant sections of the Trademark Act, such as §2(d) and §2(e). The examining attorney must evaluate the entire mark, including any disclaimed matter, to determine registrability. Furthermore, the decision notes that the applicant may not disclaim the entire mark. See TMEP §1213.06.

An applicant may volunteer a disclaimer in the mistaken belief that a disclaimer would be required when, in fact, Office policy would not require a disclaimer. If this appears to be the case, the examining attorney should offer the applicant the opportunity to withdraw the disclaimer.

1213.02 "Composite" Marks

A "composite" mark may consist of a word or words combined with a design or designs; it may consist solely of words, when there are separable word elements; or it may consist solely of separable design elements. An unregistrable component of a composite mark is subject to disclaimer. However, if a composite mark (or portion thereof) is "unitary," an individual component of the mark (or of the unitary portion) that would otherwise be unregistrable need not be disclaimed. *See* TMEP §§1213.05 *et seq*.

The same principles apply to disclaimer of an unregistrable component of a mark, whether the mark is a combination of wording and designs or consists entirely of wording or entirely of designs.

1213.03 Disclaimer of Unregistrable Components of Marks

1213.03(a) "Unregistrable Components" in General

Estate of P. D. Beckwith v. Comm'r of Pats., 252 U. S. 538, 1920 C. D. 471 (1920), and other disclaimer decisions before the Trademark Act of 1946 dealt

MCI 案件的判决强调了,自愿撤回的申报并不能使得可注册的商标因此根据《商标法》的相关条款,例如§2(d)和§2(e),就变得不能注册了。审查员必须对商标的整体,包括被撤回的部分进行审查,从而决定其是否可以注册。此外,该判决还表明了申请者不得撤回整个商标。参见 TMEP §1213.06。

申请者可能错误地认为必须作出一项撤回,因而自愿作出了撤回,但是事实上商标局并没有这样规定要求。如果发生此种情况,审查员应当给予申请者撤销该撤回声明的机会。

1213.02　　“复合”商标

一项“复合”商标可以是由一个或几个文字和一个或几个图案结合而成;如果这些文字要素可以单独存在,它也可以只由文字构成;或者,它也可以仅由独立的图案要素构成。复合商标中不可注册的部分必须撤回。不过,如果某一复合商标(或者其一部分)是“一体的”,那么即使该商标(或者其单一部分)的个别组成部分不能注册,但在此情况下也不必撤回。参见 TMEP §§1213.05 及以下。

同样的原则也适用于撤回商标某一不可注册的部分,无论该商标是文字和图案的组合,还是完全由文字或完全由图案构成。

1213.03　　对于商标不可注册部分的撤回

1213.03(a)　　“不可注册部分”概述

Estate of P. D. Beckwith v. Comm’r of Pats., 252 U.S. 538, 1920 C.D. 471 (1920)一案,以及其他《1946 年商标法》颁行之前的关于撤回的判决涉及了商标中描

with disclaiming descriptive or generic matter. Section 6 of the Act referred initially to "unregistrable matter" and, since the 1962 amendment, now refers to "an unregistrable component."

Typically an unregistrable component of a registrable mark is the name of the goods or services, other matter that does not indicate source, or matter that is merely descriptive or deceptively misdescriptive of the goods or services, or primarily geographically descriptive of them.

Office practice does not require disclaimer of a surname. *Ex parte Norquist Products, Inc.*, 109 USPQ 399 (Comm'r Pats. 1956) (disclaimer of "NORQUIST" found unnecessary in application to register mark comprising "NORQUIST CORONET" on an oval background featuring a coronet, for tables and chairs). In that decision, the Commissioner stated as follows:

> Section [2(e)(4)] of the statute does not contemplate the dissection of a composite mark to determine whether a word which constitutes an integral part of the mark is primarily merely a surname. Rather, it contemplates an examination of the mark in its entirety and an evaluation of the commercial impression created by the entire mark. A word which is primarily merely a surname may lose that significance when it appears in a distinctive composite.

Norquist, at 400. The addition of other registrable matter creates a composite mark with an overall impression that is not primarily merely that of a surname. If the additional matter is minimal or unregistrable, then the mark is primarily merely a surname and refusal under §2(e)(4) of the Act, 15 U.S.C. §1052(e)(4) (formerly §2(e)(3), 15 U.S.C. §1052(e)(3)), should be made. *See In re E. Martinoni Co.*, 189 USPQ 589 (TTAB 1975). *See* TMEP §§1211.01(b) *et seq.* regarding the combination of a surname with additional matter.

In cases where registration of a mark is barred under the Trademark Act (*e.g.*, under §§2(a), 2(b), 2(c), 2(d) and 2(e)(3)), a disclaimer of an unregistrable

述性或一般性内容。《商标法》第6节最初规定了“不可注册的内容”，该法经过1962年修正后，如今的规定为“一项不可注册的部分”。

一项可注册商标中的典型的不可注册部分是该商品或服务的名称，并不表明其来源的其他内容，或者对商品或服务仅具描述性或具有错误描述性的内容，以及主要仅为对商品或服务进行地理性描述的内容。

对于商标中的姓氏，商标局并没有撤回的规定要求。*参见 Norquist Products, Inc.*, 109 USPQ 399 (Comm'r Pats. 1956)（申请注册的商标是在一个椭圆形的饰有王冠的背景上写着“NORQUIST CORONET”，用于桌椅，被判定无需撤回“NORQUIST”）。在该判决中，专员阐述如下：

> 《商标法》第2(e)(4)节的意图并非将一项复合商标分解为各个部分，然后判断构成该商标整体的某一用词是否主要仅是姓氏。该条款的意图是对商标作整体上的审查，并对该完整的商标是否能给人造成商业印象作出评判。某一主要仅是姓氏的词语被用于一项具备独特性的复合商标时，就会失去其原始的姓氏意义。

参见 Norquist 书，第400页。如果附加其他可注册内容，就可以构成一项具有不仅为姓氏的整体印象的复合商标。如果这些其他的部分无足轻重或者是不能注册的，那么该商标就主要仅是一个姓氏，因而就应当根据商标法§2(e)(4)，15 U.S.C. §1052(e)(4)（以前的§2(e)(3)，15 U.S.C. §1052(e)(3)）的规定作出拒绝予以注册的决定。关于姓氏与其他部分的结合的规定，*参见* E. Martinoni Co., 189 USPQ 589 (TTAB 1975)。*参见* TMEP §§1211.01(b)及以下。

如果《商标法》禁止某项商标的注册（例如根据§§2(a)，2(b)，2(c)，2(d) and 2(e)

component will not render the mark registrable. *See*, *e.g.*, *American Speech-Language-Hearing Association v. National Hearing Aid Society*, 224 USPQ 798, 808 (TTAB 1984) ("While the disclaimer is appropriate to indicate that respondent claims no proprietary right in the disclaimed words, the disclaimer does not affect the question of whether the disclaimed matter deceives the public, since one cannot avoid the Section 2(a) deceptiveness prohibition by disclaiming deceptive matter apart from the mark as a whole."). *See* TMEP §1213.10 concerning disclaimers with regard to likelihood of confusion, and TMEP §1210.08 regarding disclaimer of geographic terms in composite marks.

1213.03(b) Generic Matter and Matter Which Does Not Function as a Mark

If a mark is comprised in part of matter that, as applied to the goods and services, is generic or does not function as a mark, the matter must be disclaimed to permit registration on the Principal Register (including registration under §2(f) of the Act) or on the Supplemental Register. If, however, matter that would otherwise be generic or would not function as a mark is part of a unitary mark or part of a separable unitary element of a mark, the examining attorney should not require a disclaimer of the matter. *See* TMEP §1213.05.

See TMEP §1212.02(e) regarding disclaimers of unregistrable components in applications to register marks on the Principal Register under §2(f). *See also In re Creative Goldsmiths of Washington, Inc.*, 229 USPQ 766, 768 (TTAB 1986) ("[I]t is within the discretion of an Examining Attorney to require the disclaimer of an unregistrable component (such as a common descriptive, or generic, name) of a composite mark sought to be registered on the Principal Register under the provisions of Section 2(f).").

Regarding disclaimers of unregistrable components in applications to register marks on the Supplemental Register, *see In re Water Gremlin Co.*, 635 F.2d 841, 845 n.6, 208 USPQ 89, 91 n.6 (C.C.P.A. 1980) ("Section 6 is equally applicable

(3)),那么即使撤回了不能注册的内容,该商标也不能就此而转化为可注册商标。*参见*判例:*American Speech-Language-Hearing Association v. National Hearing Aid Society*, 224 USPQ 798, 808 (TTAB 1984)("虽然该项撤回确实表明了答辩人对于撤回的言辞不主张所有权,但是撤回对于被撤回的内容是否对公众有欺骗性这一问题并无影响,不能因为申请者对于一项整体的商标中某些欺骗性的部分作出撤回就可以回避 §2(a)对欺骗的禁止。")。关于有关混淆可能性的撤回,*参见* TMEP §1213.10;关于对复合商标中地理词语的撤回,*参见* TMEP §1210.08。

1213.03(b) 一般性内容和不具有商标功能的内容

如果商标中包含了部分用于商品或服务时,并不具有独特性或不具有商标的功能的内容,那么无论是想在联邦商标登记簿注册(包括商标法§2(f)规定的注册),还是在补充登记簿注册,都必须先撤回这些内容。但是,如果商标中这些不具有独特性或不具有商标功能的内容是单一商标的一部分,或者是商标的可分离的单一部分的局部,审查员就不应要求撤回这些内容。*参见* TMEP §1213.05。

有关 §2(f)规定的申请在联邦商标登记簿上注册的商标必须撤回的不可注册的内容,*参见* TMEP §1212.02(e)。*参见 Creative Goldsmiths of Washington, Inc.*, 229 USPQ 766, 768 (TTAB 1986)("审查员拥有自由裁量权,可以要求撤回根据 §2(f)的规定申请在联邦商标登记簿注册的复合商标中不得注册的组成部分(诸如普通描述性名称或一般名称)。")。

关于申请在补充登记簿上注册的商标必须撤回的不可注册的内容,*参见 Water Gremlin Co.*, 635 F.2d 841, 845 n.6, 208 USPQ 89, 91 n.6 (C.C.P.A.1980)("§6

to the Supplemental Register."); *In re Wella Corp.*, 565 F.2d 143, 196 USPQ 7 (C. C. P. A. 1977) (mark comprising stylized lettering of BALSAM, with disclaimer of "BALSAM," found registrable on Supplemental Register for hair conditioner and hair shampoo); *In re Carolyn's Candies, Inc.*, 206 USPQ 356, 360 (TTAB 1980) ("Section 6 of the Trademark Act of 1946, which provides for the disclaimer of 'unregistrable matter', does not limit the disclaimer practice to marks upon the Principal Register.").

1213.03(c) Pictorial Representations of Descriptive Matter

An accurate pictorial representation of descriptive matter is equivalent to the written expression and, therefore, must be disclaimed pursuant to the same rules applicable to merely descriptive wording. *See Thistle Class Association v. Douglass & McLeod, Inc.*, 198 USPQ 504 (TTAB 1978) (thistle design found synonymous to the word "thistle," which is used in a descriptive sense to designate a class of sailboats).

No disclaimer of highly stylized pictorial representations of descriptive matter should be required because the design element creates a distinct commercial impression. *See In re LRC Products Ltd.*, 223 USPQ 1250, 1252 (TTAB 1984) (outline of two gloved hands held arbitrary and fanciful), and cases cited therein.

1213.03(d) Entity Designations

Words or abbreviations in a trade name designating the legal character of an entity (*e.g.*, Corporation, Corp., Co., Inc., Ltd., etc.) must be disclaimed because an entity designation has no source-indicating capacity. *In re Taylor & Francis [Publishers] Inc.*, 55 USPQ2d 1213, 1215 (TTAB 2000) ("PRESS," as applied to a printing or publishing establishment, "is in the nature of a generic entity designation which is incapable of serving a source-indicating function"); *In re The Paint Products Co.*, 8 USPQ2d 1863, 1866 (TTAB 1988) ("'PAINT PRODUCTS

对于申请在补充登记簿注册也同样适用”)；*Wella Corp.*，565 F.2d 143，196 USPQ 7 (C.C.P.A.1977)(包含了风格化的“BALSAM”字样商标，撤回“BALSAM”后，被判定可以在补充登记簿上注册为护发品和洗发水的商标。)；*Carolyn's Candies, Inc.*，206 USPQ 356，360 (TTAB 1980)(《1947年商标法》§6 规定了对于不可注册内容的撤回，该规定并不仅限于在联邦商标登记簿注册时的撤回)。

1213.03(c) 描述性内容的图示

对描述性内容所作的精确图示，相当于书面表述，因此，也必须根据适用于仅具描述性措辞的规定而撤回。参见 *Thistle Class Association v. Douglass & McLeod, Inc.*，198 USPQ 504 (TTAB 1978)(以描述性的意义标示某种帆船时，蓟的图案和“thistle”一词被判定是同义的)。

如果作为描述性内容的图示风格化的程度很高时，就不必撤回，因为图示的内容给人造成了独特的商业印象。参见 *LRC Products Ltd.*，223 USPQ 1250，1252 (TTAB 1984)(两只带着手套的手的轮廓，被认为是属于任意性和臆造性的)，及其所引案例。

1213.03(d) 实体标识

企业商号中用以表明企业法律性质的用语或缩略语(例如 Corporation，Corp.，Co.，Inc.，Ltd. 等等)，必须撤回，因为实体标识不能标示来源。参见 *Taylor & Francis [Publishers] Inc.*，55 USPQ2d 1213，1215 (TTAB 2000)(“PRESS”用于打印或出版公司时，“只具有一般实体标识的性质，不具有来源标示的功能。”)；*The Paint Products Co.*，8 USPQ2d 1863，1866 (TTAB 1988)(“‘PAINT PRODUCTS CO.’

CO.' is no more registrable for goods emanating from a company that sells paint products than it would be as a service mark for the retail paint store services offered by such a company"); *In re Packaging Specialists, Inc.*, 221 USPQ 917, 919 (TTAB 1984) ("the element 'INC.' [in PACKAGING SPECIALISTS, INC.] being recognized, in trademark evaluation, to have no source indication or distinguishing capacity").

The only exception to this practice is where the entity designation is used in an arbitrary manner (*e.g.*, "THE LTD." or "KIDS INC." for clothing). In this case the term has trademark significance and a disclaimer should not be required.

1213.04 Trade Names

Unregistrable components of trade names or company names shall be disclaimed pursuant to the same rules that apply generally to trademarks. *See In re Martin's Famous Pastry Shoppe, Inc.*, 221 USPQ 364 (TTAB 1984), *aff'd on other grounds*, 748 F.2d 1565, 223 USPQ 1289 (Fed. Cir. 1984).

1213.05 "Unitary" Marks

A mark or portion of a mark is considered "unitary" when it creates a commercial impression separate and apart from any unregistrable component. That is, the elements are so merged together that they cannot be divided to be regarded as separable elements. If the matter that comprises the mark or relevant portion of the mark is unitary, no disclaimer of an element, whether descriptive, generic or otherwise, is required.

For example, a descriptive word can be combined with nondescriptive wording in such a way that the descriptive significance of the word in relation to the goods is lost and the combination functions as a unit. This happens when the combination itself has a new meaning. An example is the term "Black Magic," which has a distinct meaning of its own as a whole. The word "black" is not intended to have

不能再作为销售油漆产品的公司所出产商品的注册商标，而只能用作该公司提供的油漆零售服务的服务商标。"）；*Packaging Specialists*, *Inc*., 221 USPQ 917, 919 (TTAB 1984)（"[PACKAGING SPECIALISTS, INC.]中的要素'INC.'从商标角度评估，不具有标示或区分来源的功能。"）。

在这一问题上唯一的例外，存在于以任意的方式使用实体标识之时（例如用于服装的"THE LTD." 或者"KIDS INC."）。在这种情况下，这些词语具有商标的意义，因此无需撤回。

1213.04 商号

根据普遍适用于商标的相同规则，商号或公司名称中包含的不能注册的内容必须被撤回。参见 *Martin's Famous Pastry Shoppe*, *Inc*., 221 USPQ 364 (TTAB 1984), *aff'd on other grounds*, 748 F.2d 1565, 223 USPQ 1289 (Fed. Cir. 1984)。

1213.05 "单一"商标

如果独立于其他不可注册的内容，并能够造就一种商业印象，那么一项商标或商标的某一组成部分就被认为是"单一"的。换言之，商标的各个部分结合紧密，彼此无法作为个别的部分而被分离。如果构成商标或该商标相关部分的内容是单一的，那么对于这些部分，无论其是否是描述性的、一般性的，或诸如此类，都不需要撤回。

例如，某一描述性的词语，可以通过非描述的措辞这一途径和其他词相结合，在这一过程中，该词失去了其具有的对商品进行描述的含义，而这些词的结合体则以整体的形式发挥功能。这种组合本身具有新含义时就是如此。例如，"Black Magic"这一用语的整体就具有独特的含义。"black"一词并非试图表示相关商品的颜色，因

color significance in relation to the goods, and should not be disclaimed even if the mark is applied to goods that are black in color.

In the following cases, marks were considered unitary: *B. Kuppenheimer & Co., Inc. v. Kayser-Roth Corp.*, 326 F.2d 820, 822, 140 USPQ 262, 263 (C.C.P.A. 1964) (KUPPENHEIMER and SUP-PANTS combined so that they shared the double "P," making "an indivisible symbol rather than two divisible words"); *In re Hampshire-Designers, Inc.*, 199 USPQ 383 (TTAB 1978) (DESIGNERS PLUS + for sweaters held unitary; thus, no disclaimer of "DESIGNERS" deemed necessary); *In re J. R. Carlson Laboratories, Inc.*, 183 USPQ 509 (TTAB 1974) (E GEM for bath oil containing vitamin E held unitary; thus, no disclaimer of "E").

But see the following cases, where marks were found *not* to be unitary: *Dena Corp. v. Belvedere International Inc.*, 950 F.2d 1555, 21 USPQ2d 1047 (Fed. Cir. 1991) (EUROPEAN FORMULA above a circular design on a dark square or background considered not unitary); *In re Lean Line, Inc.*, 229 USPQ 781 (TTAB 1986) (LEAN LINE for low calorie foods considered not unitary; requirement for disclaimer of "LEAN" held proper); *In re IBP, Inc.*, 228 USPQ 303 (TTAB 1985) (IBP SELECT TRIM for pork considered not unitary; refusal of registration in the absence of a disclaimer of "SELECT TRIM" affirmed); *In re Uniroyal, Inc.*, 215 USPQ 716 (TTAB 1982) (UNIROYAL STEEL/GLAS for vehicle tires considered not unitary; requirement for disclaimer of "STEEL/GLAS" deemed appropriate); *In re EBS Data Processing, Inc.*, 212 USPQ 964, 966 (TTAB 1981) (PHACTS POCKET PROFILE, for personal medication history summary and record forms, considered not unitary; refusal to register in the absence of a disclaimer of "POCKET PROFILE" affirmed. "A disclaimer of a descriptive portion of a composite mark is unnecessary only where the form or degree of integration of that element in the composite makes it obvious that no claim other than of the composite would be involved. That is, if the elements are so merged together that they cannot be regarded as separable elements, the mark is a single unitary mark and not a composite mark and no disclaimer is necessary."); *In re National Presto Industries, Inc.*, 197 USPQ 188 (TTAB 1977) (PRESTO

此，即使这一商标所标示的商品就是黑色的，也不应当要求撤回该词。

在下列案件中的商标被认为具有单一性：*B. Kuppenheimer & Co., Inc. v. Kayser-Roth Corp.*, 326 F.2d 820, 822, 140 USPQ 262, 263 (C. C. P. A. 1964)（KUPPENHEIMER 和 SUP-PANTS 结合非常紧密，它们彼此都有两个"P"在内，因此构成了"单一的符号而不是两个可以拆分的词"）；*Hampshire-Designers, Inc.*, 199 USPQ 383 (TTAB 1978)（用于毛衣的 DESIGNERS PLUS + 这一词具有单一性，因此"DESIGNERS"不必撤回）；*J. R. Carlson Laboratories, Inc.*, 183 USPQ 509 (TTAB 1974)（用 E GEM 作为含有维他命 E 成分的浴油的商标，具有单一性，因此，"E"不必撤回）。

但是，在下列案件中的商标被认为不具有单一性：*Dena Corp. v. Belvedere International Inc.*, 950 F.2d 1555, 21 USPQ2d 1047 (Fed. Cir. 1991)（在一个深色矩形或背景的圆形图案上方所标出的 EUROPEAN FORMULA 字样并不具有单一性）；*Lean Line, Inc.*, 229 USPQ 781 (TTAB 1986)（用 LEAN LINE 作为低卡路里食品的商标，不具有单一性，因此对于就该词的撤回要求被判定是正确的）；*IBP, Inc.*, 228 USPQ 303 (TTAB 1985)（用 IBP SELECT TRIM 作为猪肉的商标，不具有单一性，因此，对于"SELECT TRIM"一词没有作出撤回的注册申请遭到拒绝得到判决的支持）；*Uniroyal, Inc.*, 215 USPQ 716 (TTAB 1982)（用 UNIROYAL STEEL/GLAS 作为机动车轮胎的商标，被认为不具有单一性，因此，对"STEEL/GLAS"一词作出撤回的要求被判定是适当的）；*EBS Data Processing, Inc.*, 212 USPQ 964, 966 (TTAB 1981)（用 PHACTS POCKET PROFILE 作为个人药物治疗史摘要和记录资料的商标被认为不具有单一性，因此维持对于未撤回"POCKET PROFILE"一词的注册申请所作出的拒绝决定。"复合商标中的描述性内容不必撤回，只有在以下的条件下方能成立，即这些内容的形式，以及与该复合商标结合的程度，非常明显地表明了，除了对于该复合商标以外没有其他的权利可以得到主张。换言之，如果商标中的组成部分结合得非常紧密，以至于不能将其视为是具有独立性的部分，该商标就是一项单一商标而非复合商标，也就不必撤回了"）；*National Presto Industries, Inc.*,

BURGER for electrical cooking utensils not unitary; requirement for disclaimer of "BURGER" affirmed).

The examining attorney must exercise discretion in determining whether a mark or portion of a mark is unitary, in which case a disclaimer of a nondistinctive component should not be required. It is not always easy to articulate why matter is unitary. However, if one cannot spell out exactly why a mark is unitary, then the mark is probably not unitary and nondistinctive elements within the mark must be disclaimed. In general, a mark is unitary if the whole is something more than the sum of its parts.

See TMEP §§1213.05(a) through (f) for examples of different types of unitary marks.

1213.05(a) Compound Word Marks

A compound word mark is comprised of two or more distinct words or words and syllables that are represented as one word (*e.g.*, BOOKCHOICE, PROSHOT, MAXIMACHINE, PULSAIR). Often, in compound word marks, the words or syllables are distinguished or highlighted by capitalizing the first letter of each (*e.g.*, TimeMaster) or by presenting them in differing color, script or size (*e.g.*, RIBtype).

A compound word mark that is appropriately represented by a typed drawing may be presented as one unitary term (*e.g.*, BOOKCHOICE) or as separate words (BOOK CHOICE). The examining attorney should determine whether the mark may be presented as separate words. *See* TMEP §807.08 regarding drawings for compound word marks.

All compound word marks, as defined above, are considered unitary, and a disclaimer of a component will not be required *unless* the mark is appropriately presented in the application in a typed drawing as two or more separate words. A compound word mark that is appropriately presented in a typed drawing as two or

197 USPQ 188 (TTAB 1977)(用 PRESTO BURGER 作为电炊具的商标不具有单一性，维持撤回“BURGER”一词的要求)。

某一商标或者商标的某一部分是否具有单一性，以及在什么情况下商标的一部分即使不具有独特性也不必撤回，审查员在认定这些问题的时候必须通过自由裁量加以认定。要清楚地说明为什么有些内容是单一的并不是容易的事。但是，如果不能明确地说明一件商标是单一的，那么该商标大致上就不是单一的，该商标中的不具有独特性的内容必须被撤回。一般而言，如果某商标的整体，比之各部分的总和更有意义，那么该商标就是单一的。

关于不同类型单一商标的示例，*参见* TMEP §§1213.05(a)至(f)。

1213.05(a) 复合文字商标

复合文字商标由两个或两个以上不同的字组成或由字和以几个音节(例如，BOOKCHOICE，PROSHOT，MAXIMACHINE，PULSAIR)表示的字组成。通常，复合文字商标中的词或音节非常特别，或者是通过开头字母大写或各个字母都大写(例如，TimeMaster)，或者是通过不同的颜色、字体或字号(例如，RIBtype)加以突出。

通过适当的打印附图表现的复合文字商标，可以表现为一个单一的词语(例如，BOOKCHOICE)，也可以表现为分离的词语(例如，BOOK CHOICE)。审查员应当判断，该商标是否可以以分离词语的形式出现。关于复合文字商标附图的情况，*参见* TMEP §807.08。

所有的复合文字商标，根据上述定义，都被认为是单一的，对于其中的一个组成部分无需撤回，除非该商标在申请中以适当的附图表现为两个或多个分离的词语。如果复合文字商标通过适当的服务表现为两个或多个分离的词语，那么该商标本身

more separate words is not considered unitary per se and a disclaimer of unregistrable components may be required.

1213.05(a)(i) Telescoped Words

A telescoped mark is one that comprises two or more words that share letters (*e.g.*, HAMERICAN, ORDERECORDER, SUPERINSE, VITAMINSURANCE, POLLENERGY). *See* TMEP §807.08 regarding drawings for telescoped marks.

A telescoped word is considered unitary. Therefore, no disclaimer of an individual portion of a telescoped word is required, regardless of whether the mark is shown in a typed or special-form drawing.

However, if a telescoped word is itself unregistrable, a disclaimer of the telescoped word may be required. *See In re Omaha National Corp.*, 819 F.2d 1117, 2 USPQ2d 1859 (Fed. Cir. 1987) (affirming refusal to register FIRSTIER and design for banking services in the absence of a disclaimer of "FIRST TIER," in view of evidence that the term describes a class of banks). *See* TMEP §1213.08(c) regarding disclaimers of misspelled words in general.

1213.05(a)(ii) Compound Words Formed with Hyphen or Other Punctuation

When a compound word is formed by hyphenating two words or terms, one of which would be unregistrable alone, no disclaimer is necessary. *"X" Laboratories, Inc. v. Odorite Sanitation Service of Baltimore, Inc.*, 106 USPQ 327, 329 (Comm'r Pats. 1955) (requirement for a disclaimer of "TIRE" deemed unnecessary in application to register TIRE-X for a tire cleaner).

Word marks consisting of two terms joined by an asterisk (*e.g.*, RIB*TYPE), a slash (*e.g.*, RIB/TYPE) or a raised period (*e.g.*, RIB°TYPE) are analogous to hyphenated words. Therefore no disclaimer of portions of marks formed by aster-

就不被认为是单一的，其中不可注册的内容可能就会被要求撤回。

1213.05(a)(i) 嵌入词

嵌入词商标是指由两个或多个词组成，并且这些词共用了某些字母（例如，HAMERICAN，ORDERECORDER，SUPERINSE，VITAMINSURANCE，POLLENERGY）。关于嵌入词商标附图的情况，*参见* TMEP §807.08。

一个嵌入词被认为是单一的。因此，对于嵌入词商标的一个单独部分无须要求撤回，无论该商标是以打印还是特殊格式的附图进行展示的。

但是，如果该嵌入词本身是不可注册的，那么可能就会要求撤回该嵌入词。*参见 Omaha National Corp.*, 819 F.2d 1117, 2 USPQ2d 1859 (Fed. Cir. 1987)（在申请将"FIRSTIER"及其图案注册为银行服务的商标时，没有撤回"FIRST TIER"，由于证据表明该用语是对一类银行的一般性描述，因此该申请被拒绝，判决维持了这一决定）。有关撤回错误拼写的一般规定，*参见* TMEP §1213.08(c)。

1213.05(a)(ii) 由连字符或其他标点符号所组成的复合词

如果复合文字是通过连字符将两个词连接而构成，即使其中之一单独是不可注册的，也无须撤回。*"X" Laboratories, Inc. v. Odorite Sanitation Service of Baltimore, Inc.*, 106 USPQ 327, 329 (Comm'r Pats. 1955)（在申请将"TIRE-X"注册为某种轮胎清洗器的商标的过程中，认为不必要求撤回"TIRE"）。

由星号（例如，RIB* TYPE）、斜线符（例如，RIB/TYPE）或上标符（例如，RIB° TYPE）连接两个用语所构成的文字商标，与由连字符组成的文字商标相似。因此，

isks, slashes or raised periods is necessary. (While hyphens, asterisks and slashes may be used in typed drawings, raised periods may not. Therefore, a mark comprised in part of a raised period must be represented by a special-form drawing to depict the raised period. However, if otherwise appropriate, the mark may be represented in a typed drawing by substituting a hyphen for the raised period. *See* TMEP §§807.06 *et seq*. regarding typed drawings.)

1213.05(b) Slogans

A registrable slogan is one that is used in a trademark sense. A registrable slogan is considered unitary and should not be broken up for purposes of requiring a disclaimer.

If an unregistrable slogan is a component of a registrable mark, then the examining attorney should require that the slogan be disclaimed.

If a mark consists entirely of a slogan that is merely descriptive or that is not being used as a mark, then registration should be refused. *See In re Carvel Corp.*, 223 USPQ 65 (TTAB 1984) (AMERICA'S FRESHEST ICE CREAM for flavored ices, etc., held incapable of distinguishing applicant's goods and unregistrable on the Supplemental Register); *In re Wakefern Food Corp.*, 222 USPQ 76 (TTAB 1984) (WHY PAY MORE! held to be an unregistrable common commercial phrase).

1213.05(c) "Double Entendre"

A "double entendre" is a word or expression capable of more than one interpretation. For trademark purposes, a "double entendre" is an expression that has a double connotation or significance *as applied to the goods or services*. The mark that comprises the "double entendre" will not be refused registration as merely descriptive if one of its meanings is not merely descriptive in relation to the goods or services.

商标中由星号、斜线符或上标符组成的部分也无须撤回。(不过,连字符、星号和斜线符在打印的附图中是可以加以表现的,而上标符则可能无法表现。因此,包含有上标符的商标必须通过特殊样式的附图清楚标示该上标符。但是,如果不如此亦可,那么该商标也可以将上标符替换成连字符打印附图表示。有关打印附图的内容,*参见* TMEP §§807.06 及以下。)

1213.05(b) 口号

如果一个口号是在商标意义上使用的话,就可以注册。并且可以注册的口号被认为是单一的,不能出于要求撤回的目的而被分割。

如果一件可注册商标中含有不可注册的口号,那么审查员应当要求撤回该口号。

如果一件商标就是一个口号,并且该口号仅仅是一般性描述或者该口号不是作为商标而使用的,那么就应该拒绝予以注册。*参见 Carvel Corp.*, 223 USPQ 65 (TTAB 1984)(申请将"AMERICA'S FRESHEST ICE CREAM"注册为风味冰淇淋等的商标,被认为不能显著突出申请者的商品,因而不能在补充登记簿注册); *Wakefern Food Corp.*, 222 USPQ 76 (TTAB 1984)("WHY PAY MORE!"这一口号被认为是不能注册的一般性广告用语)。

1213.05(c) "双关语"

"双关语"是指一个单词或词组具有不止一种的解释。就商标意义而言,"双关语"是指一个在用于商品或服务时,具有双重含义或意义的词组。如果由双关语所组成的商标,其中的一层含义不是仅仅一般性描述相关的产品或服务,那么就不能以一般性描述为理由而拒绝予以注册。

A true "double entendre" is unitary by definition. An expression that is a "double entendre" should not be broken up for purposes of requiring a disclaimer. *See In re Kraft, Inc.*, 218 USPQ 571, 573 (TTAB 1983), where the Board found inappropriate a requirement for a disclaimer of "LIGHT" apart from the mark "LIGHT N' LIVELY" for reduced calorie mayonnaise, stating as follows:

> The mark "LIGHT N' LIVELY" as a whole has a suggestive significance which is distinctly different from the merely descriptive significance of the term "LIGHT" per se. That is, the merely descriptive significance of the term "LIGHT" is lost in the mark as a whole. Moreover, the expression as a whole has an alliterative lilting cadence which encourages persons encountering it to perceive it as a whole.

See also In re Symbra'ette, Inc., 189 USPQ 448 (TTAB 1975) (SHEER ELEGANCE for panty hose held to be a registrable unitary expression; thus, no disclaimer of "SHEER" considered necessary).

The following cases illustrate situations where marks were considered to be "double entendres" and, therefore, registrable unitary marks: *In re Colonial Stores Inc.*, 394 F.2d 549, 157 USPQ 382 (C.C.P.A. 1968) (SUGAR & SPICE for bakery products); *In re Simmons Co.*, 189 USPQ 352 (TTAB 1976) (THE HARD LINE for mattresses and bed springs); *In re Delaware Punch Co.*, 186 USPQ 63 (TTAB 1975) (THE SOFT PUNCH for noncarbonated soft drink); *In re National Tea Co.*, 144 USPQ 286 (TTAB 1965) (NO BONES ABOUT IT for fresh precooked ham).

The multiple interpretations that make an expression a "double entendre" must be associations that the public would make fairly readily. *See In re Wells Fargo & Co.*, 231 USPQ 95 (TTAB 1986) (EXPRESSERVICE held merely descriptive for banking services, despite applicant's argument that the term also connotes the Pony Express, the Board finding that, in the relevant context, the public would not make that association).

根据其定义，一个真正的“双关语”具有单一性。一个“双关语”不能出于要求撤回的目的而被割裂。参见 *Kraft, Inc.*, 218 USPQ 571, 573 (TTAB 1983)，在该案中，委员会认为，申请将“LIGHT N' LIVELY”注册为某种低卡路里蛋黄酱的商标中，单独将“LIGHT”从“LIGHT N' LIVELY”分离出来要求撤回是不适当的，并阐述如下：

> “LIGHT N' LIVELY”这一商标的整体具有一种暗示性的意义，而该意义和本身仅仅是一般性描述意义的“LIGHT”一词显然不同。当“LIGHT”作为“LIGHT N' LIVELY”这一商标的一部分时，就不再只是一种描述了。此外，这一词组是抑扬顿挫的开头押韵词组，这更使得看到它的人把它视为是一个整体。

另参见 Symbra'ette, Inc., 189 USPQ 448 (TTAB 1975)(某种连裤袜的商标“SHEER ELEGANCE”被认为是可以注册的单一的词组，因而无须撤回“SHEER”)。

以下的案例阐述了何种情形下的商标被认为是“双关语”，因而该商标也就是一个单一的可注册商标：*Colonial Stores Inc.*, 394 F.2d 549, 157 USPQ 382 (C.C.P.A. 1968)(用于烘焙食品的“SUGAR & SPICE ”)；*Simmons Co.*, 189 USPQ 352 (TTAB 1976)(用于床垫和床垫弹簧的“THE HARD LINE”)；*Delaware Punch Co.*, 186 USPQ 63 (TTAB 1975)(用于不含碳酸气软饮料的“THE SOFT PUNCH”)；*National Tea Co.*, 144 USPQ 286 (TTAB 1965)(用于新鲜预熟火腿的“NO BONES ABOUT IT”)。

“双关语”所具有的多重的解释必须是公众能够看到后马上能够联想到的。*参见 Wells Fargo & Co.*, 231 USPQ 95 (TTAB 1986)(“EXPRESSERVICE”被认为仅仅是对银行服务的描述，尽管申请者抗辩说该用语也同时意味着“Pony Express”，但委员会认为，公众无法从上下文中得出这一联系)。

If all meanings of a "double entendre" are merely descriptive in relation to the goods, then the mark comprising the "double entendre" should be refused registration as merely descriptive.

1213.05(d) Incongruity

If two or more terms are combined in a mark to create an incongruity (*e.g.*, URBAN SAFARI, MR. MICROWAVE, DR. GRAMMAR), the mark is unitary and no disclaimer of nondistinctive individual elements is necessary.

1213.05(e) Sound Patterns

At times a mark will form a unitary whole through a rhyming pattern, use of alliteration or some other use of sound that creates a distinctive impression. In such a case, the mark is regarded as unitary and individual elements should not be disclaimed. *See In re Kraft, Inc.*, 218 USPQ 571 (TTAB 1983) (LIGHT N' LIVELY found to be a unitary term not subject to disclaimer). *Compare In re Lean Line, Inc.*, 229 USPQ 781, 782 (TTAB 1986) (LEAN LINE not considered unitary; "there is nothing in the record to suggest that the mere fact that both words which form the mark begin with the letter 'L' would cause purchasers to miss the merely descriptive significance of the term 'LEAN' or consider the entire mark to be a unitary expression.").

1213.05(f) Display of Mark

The visual presentation of a mark may be such that the words and/or designs form a unitary whole. In such a case, disclaimer of individual nondistinctive elements is unnecessary. *See, e.g., In re Texsun Tire and Battery Stores, Inc.*, 229 USPQ 227, 229 (TTAB 1986) ("[T]he portion of the outline of the map of Texas encircled as it is with the representation of a tire and surrounded by a rectangular border results in a unitary composite mark which is unique and fanciful.").

如果"双关语"所有的含义都只是对有关的商品的描述,那么由该"双关语"所构成的商标应当以仅具描述性为由而拒绝注册。

1213.05(d)　　不一致性

如果两个或多个用语不是正常组合在一起而构成的商标(例如,URBAN SAFARI, MR. MICROWAVE, DR. GRAMMAR),这样的商标具有单一性,其中个别的不具有独特性的内容也无须撤回。

1213.05(e)　　读音

有时,商标可以使用押韵的形式——头韵或其他能给人以特殊印象的读音——而构成具有单一性的整体。在这种情况下,该商标被认为是单一的,个别部分无需撤回。*参见 Kraft, Inc.*, 218 USPQ 571 (TTAB 1983)("LIGHT N' LIVELY"被认为是单一的用语,无须撤回)。比较 *Lean Line, Inc.*, 229 USPQ 781, 782 (TTAB 1986)("LEAN LINE"被认为不具有单一性,"档案中没有证据表明,仅仅因为组成商标的两个单词的开头都有字母'L',就能够让购买者忽略了'LEAN'所具有的仅具描述性的含义,或是让购买者将该商标视为一个单一的词组")。

1213.05(f)　　商标的表示

商标的视觉表示方式可能使得该商标的文字和(或)图案构成一个单一的整体。在这种情况下,即使对于不具独特性的个别内容也无须撤回。*参见* 判例:*Texsun Tire and Battery Stores, Inc.*, 229 USPQ 227, 229 (TTAB 1986)("环绕得克萨斯州的地图轮廓,附以轮胎图案,并有长方形的边框,这一组合构成了独特和臆造的单一

1213.06 Entire Mark May Not Be Disclaimed

An entire mark may not be disclaimed. If a mark is not registrable as a whole, a disclaimer will not make it registrable. There must be something in the combination of elements in the mark, or something of sufficient substance or distinctiveness over and above the matter being disclaimed, which would make the composite registrable after the import of the disclaimer is taken into account. *See In re Anchor Hocking Corp.*, 223 USPQ 85 (TTAB 1984); *Ex parte Ste. Pierre Smirnoff Fls, Inc.*, 102 USPQ 415 (Comm'r Pats. 1954).

In Dena Corp. v. Belvedere International Inc., 950 F.2d 1555, 1560, 21 USPQ2d 1047, 1051 (Fed. Cir. 1991), the Court of Appeals for the Federal Circuit stated as follows:

> [U]nder traditional disclaimer practice, an applicant could not disclaim all elements of a composite mark. Section 1056(a) codified this policy. A mark which must be entirely disclaimed has no 'unregistrable component,' but is instead entirely nonregistrable. In other words, a mark which must be entirely disclaimed has no 'otherwise registrable' parts. Therefore, such marks do not qualify as composite marks for which the Commissioner may require a disclaimer.

1213.07 Removal Rather than Disclaimer

When it is not clear that matter forms part of a mark, the examining attorney must consider whether it is appropriate for the applicant to amend the drawing of the mark to remove the matter, rather than to disclaim it. *See* TMEP §807.15 regarding deletion of matter from the mark on a drawing. An applicant may not amend the drawing if the amendment would constitute a material alteration of the mark. 37 C.F.R. §2.72; TMEP §807.14(a).

There are circumstances under which the applicant may remove matter from the mark shown in the drawing, or may elect not to include certain matter on the

复合商标”)。

1213.06 不可撤回整个商标

不能撤回整个商标。如果某件商标整体上是不可注册的,那么即使部分撤回,该商标也并不因此就可以注册。商标中各种内容的结合体应当具有一些东西,或者除了被撤回的内容之外还应具有一些具有特定性的实质性内容,即使考虑了可能撤回的因素也足以使得该复合商标具有可注册性。参见 *Anchor Hocking Corp.*, 223 USPQ 85(TTAB 1984);*Ste. Pierre Smirnoff Fls*, *Inc.*, 102 USPQ 415(Comm'r Pats.1954)。

在 *Dena Corp. v. Belvedere International Inc.*, 950 F.2d 1555, 1560, 21 USPQ2d 1047, 1051(Fed. Cir.1991)一案中,联邦巡回区上诉法院认为:

> 在传统的撤回实践操作中,申请人不能将一件复合商标中的所有内容都予以撤回。第1056(a)节对此作了法律规定。一项必须被全部撤回的商标“不具有可以注册的内容”,换言之就是一项不可注册的商标。也就是说,一件必须被全部撤回的商标不具有“如果撤回了就可以注册”的内容。由于专员会对这类商标提出撤回的要求,因此这类商标就不是一项适格的复合商标。

1213.07 剔除而不是撤回有关内容

当商标中的有些组成部分模棱两可时,审查员应当考虑,是否应当要求申请人对商标的附图作出修正,剔除该部分内容,而不仅仅是撤回该部分内容。关于删除商标附图中部分内容的情况,参见 TMEP §807.15。不过,如果对附图的修改将导致对该商标的实质性变动,申请人也可以不作修改。37 C.F.R. §2.72;TMEP §807.14(a)。

在某些情况下,申请人可以将附图中商标的一些内容去掉,或者是在提交申请时

drawing in the application as filed, if the overall commercial impression is not altered. *See Institut National Des Appellations D'Origine v. Vintners International Co. Inc.*, 958 F.2d 1574, 1582, 22 USPQ2d 1190, 1197 (Fed. Cir. 1992); *In re Servel, Inc.*, 181 F.2d 192, 85 USPQ 257 (C. C. P. A. 1950). However, matter may not be omitted from the drawing if the omission would result in an incomplete representation of the mark, sometimes referred to as "mutilation." *See* TMEP §807.14(b). In other words, the matter presented for registration must convey a single distinct commercial impression. If a mark is not unitary in this sense, it cannot be registered. *Dena Corp. v. Belvedere International Inc.*, 950 F.2d 1555, 21 USPQ2d 1047 (Fed. Cir. 1991).

1213.08 Form of Disclaimers

1213.08(a) Wording of Disclaimer

1213.08(a)(i) Standardized Printing Format for Disclaimer

Since November 9, 1982, disclaimers for marks published for opposition and those registered on the Supplemental Register are printed in a standardized form in the *Official Gazette*, regardless of the text submitted. Disclaimers are in the standardized format in certificates of registration on the Supplemental Register issued as of that date. Disclaimers are in the standardized format in certificates of registration on the Principal Register issued as of February 1, 1983. The disclaimed matter is taken from the disclaimer of record and inserted into the standardized disclaimer format for printing and data base purposes. The standardized disclaimer text is as follows:

> No claim is made to the exclusive right to use __________, apart from the mark as shown.

See notice at 1022 TMOG 44 (September 28, 1982). *See also In re Owatonna Tool Co.*, 231 USPQ 493, 495 (Comm'r Pats. 1983) ("[T]he use of the standardized

选择一些内容不出现在附图上，只要这样做不影响到该商标总体的商业印象。*参见* *Institut National Des Appellations D'Origine v. Vintners International Co. Inc.*, 958 F.2d 1574, 1582, 22 USPQ2d 1190, 1197 (Fed. Cir. 1992); *Servel, Inc.*, 181 F.2d 192, 85 USPQ 257 (C.C.P.A. 1950)。但是，如果省略了某些内容将导致不能完整表示该商标时——这种情形有时被称作是“切断”——这些内容就不能从附图上省略。*参见* TMEP §807.14(b)。换言之，申请人提交注册的内容必须传达某种独立的商业印象。如果在此意义上某商标不具有单一性，那么该商标就不能注册。见 *Dena Corp. v. Belvedere International Inc.*, 950 F.2d 1555, 21 USPQ2d 1047 (Fed. Cir. 1991)。

1213.08　撤回的格式

1213.08(a)　撤回的措辞

1213.08(a)(i)　撤回的标准印制格式

从 1982 年 11 月 9 日开始，商标的撤回声明被公之于众以接受监督，补充登记簿注册的撤回声明，不管其提交的文本如何，都以标准印刷式样在《公报》上刊登。从该日起，补充登记簿的注册证书也开始注明标准印刷式样的撤回声明。联邦商标登记簿的注册证书上注明标准印刷式样的撤回声明始于 1983 年 2 月 1 日。出于印刷和数据库建设之目的，被撤回的内容从撤回档案中抽出，置入标准的撤回声明式样中，标准化的撤回声明文本如下：

> 除所示商标以外，对于______________部分不主张任何专属使用之权利。

参见 1022 TMOG 44 (September 28, 1982)公告。*另参见* *Owatonna Tool Co.*, 231 USPQ 493, 495 (Comm'r Pats. 1983)(“[T]之所以使用标准化的格式，仅仅是

form is solely for the purpose of printing and data base purposes, not for the limitation of registrant's rights.").

For the record only, examining attorneys continue the past practice of accepting disclaimers with additional statements pertaining to reservation of common law rights, although §6 of the Trademark Act of 1946 states that no disclaimer shall prejudice or affect the applicant's or registrant's rights then existing or thereafter arising in the disclaimed matter. Disclaimers with these additional statements can be entered by examiner's amendment. The examining attorney must inform the applicant or attorney who authorizes the amendment that the disclaimer will be printed in the standardized format.

1213.08(a)(ii) Unacceptable Wording for Disclaimer

Wording that claims matter, rather than disclaims it, is not acceptable. A disclaimer should be no more than a statement that identifies matter to which the applicant may not have exclusive rights apart from what is shown on the drawing.

Therefore, statements that the applicant "claims" certain matter in the association shown are not acceptable. The examining attorney should require correction of this wording and of variations that amount to the same thing. Likewise, a statement that the mark is "not claimed except in the association shown," or similar wording, is not acceptable, and the examining attorney should require correction. *See Textron Inc. v. Pilling Chain Co., Inc.*, 175 USPQ 621, 622 (TTAB 1972), concerning an application which included the statement, "The mark is not to be claimed except in the setting presented." The Board found this wording unacceptable, noting, "The alleged disclaimer filed by applicant is in such vague terms that it actually disclaims nothing." *Id.*

1213.08(b) Disclaimer of Unregistrable Matter in Its Entirety

Unregistrable matter must be disclaimed in its entirety. For example, when requir-

出于印刷和数据库建设的需要，而不是出于限制注册人权利的目的”)。

出于备案之目的，审查员延续了过去的一种做法，如果撤回声明中附有另外一份涉及保留对撤回部分的普通法上权利的声明，审查员也一并接受，尽管《1946年商标法》§6 规定了，撤回声明不得损害或影响申请人或注册人对被撤回部分现有或此后发生的权利。审查员可以对这些附有其他声明的撤回作出修正。审查员必须告知申请者或经授权提出修正的代理人，撤回声明将印刷为标准化的式样。

1213.08(a)(ii)　撤回声明中的不当措辞

提出而非撤回注册内容的措辞是不可接受的。撤回只不过是明确声明了，对于商标中的一些内容，申请人不享有与附图中所示的商标相独立的专属权利。

因此，申请者“提出”某些与附图相关内容的声明是不可接受的。审查员应当要求对这类措辞，以及实际上等同原内容的变更作出纠正。同样地，称商标“除了相关附图所示，并无主张”之类的声明，或者相似的措辞都是不可接受的，审查员应当要求纠正。*参见 Textron Inc. v. Pilling Chain Co., Inc.*, 175 USPQ 621, 622 (TTAB 1972)，在申请书中有这样一项声明：“除了在所示环境中，并不对该商标提出主张。”委员会认为这样的措辞是不可接受的，并阐述道：“申请者所提交的撤回声明，其意思含糊不清，以至于事实上并没有撤回任何东西。”*同前*。

1213.08(b)　对不可注册的内容应全部撤回

不可注册的内容应当被全部撤回。例如，如果要求撤回构成合乎文法或单一表

ing a disclaimer of terms which form a grammatically or otherwise unitary expression (*e.g.*, "SHOE FACTORY, INC."), the examining attorney must require that they be disclaimed in their entirety. *See*, *e.g.*, *In re Wanstrath*, 7 USPQ2d 1412, 1413 (Comm'r Pats. 1987) (denying petitioner's request to substitute separate disclaimers of "GLASS" and "TECHNOLOGY" for the disclaimer of "GLASS TECHNOLOGY" in its registration of GT GLASS TECHNOLOGY in stylized form, the Commissioner finding "GLASS TECHNOLOGY" to be a unitary expression and noting, "Disclaimers of individual components of complete descriptive phrases are improper."); *American Speech-Language-Hearing Association v. National Hearing Aid Society*, 224 USPQ 798, 804 n. 3 (TTAB 1984) ("CERTIFIED HEARING AID AUDIOLOGIST" found to be "a unitary expression that should be disclaimed in its entirety"); *In re Surelock Mfg. Co., Inc.*, 125 USPQ 23, 24 (TTAB 1960) (proposed disclaimer of "THE" and "RED" and "CUP" held unacceptable to comply with requirement for disclaimer of "THE RED CUP," the Board concluding, "A disclaimer of the individual components of the term 'THE RED CUP,' under the circumstances, is meaningless and improper.").

This standard should be construed strictly; therefore, disclaimer of individual words separately will usually be appropriate only when the words being disclaimed are separated by registrable wording.

1213.08(c) Disclaimer of Misspelled Words

Marks often comprise words that may be characterized as "misspelled." For example, marks may comprise terms that are "telescoped" (*see* TMEP §1213.05(a)(i)) or terms that are phonetic equivalents of particular words but spelled in a manner that varies from the ordinary spelling of such words.

If a mark comprises a word or words that are misspelled but nonetheless must be disclaimed, the examining attorney should require disclaimer of the word or words in the correct spelling. *See In re Omaha National Corp.*, 819 F.2d 1117, 2

达的词语(例如,“SHOE FACTORY, INC.”),审查员就必须要求撤回全部语词。*参见 Wanstrath*, 7 USPQ2d 1412, 1413 (Comm'r Pats. 1987)(申请者申请注册“GT GLASS TECHNOLOGY”这一风格化的商标,并且不愿撤回“GLASS TECHNOLOGY”,而代之以分别撤回“GLASS”和“TECHNOLOGY”,这一要求被拒绝了。专员认为“GLASS TECHNOLOGY”是一个单一的词组,并阐述道:“撤回完全属描述性短语的个别组成部分是不适当的”)。*American Speech-Language-Hearing Association v. National Hearing Aid Society*, 224 USPQ 798, 804 n.3 (TTAB 1984)(“CERTIFIED HEARING AID AUDIOLOGIST”被认为是“单一的词组,因而必须被全部撤回”);*Surelock Mfg. Co., Inc.*, 125 USPQ 23, 24 (TTAB 1960)(为了满足撤回“THE RED CUP”的要求,而提出分别撤回“THE”、“RED”和“CUP”的提议被认为是不可接受的,委员会总结道:“对于‘THE RED CUP’的各个单词分别撤回,在这种情况下是毫无意义,因而是不正确的。”)。

对于这一标准应当从严解释;因此,只有在撤回的语词被可注册的语词分隔开时,分别撤回各个单词才一般是适当的。

1213.08(c) 撤回拼写错误的单词

商标经常会包含一些可以被定性为“拼写错误”的单词。例如,商标包含有“嵌入词”(*参见* TMEP §1213.05(a)(i));或者是一些读音上虽然相同,但在拼写上却和这些单词的通常拼写形式不同的用语。

如果商标中的用词是拼写错误且必须被撤回,审查员就应当要求撤回该词或其正确的拼写形式。*参见 Omaha National Corp.*, 819 F.2d 1117, 2 USPQ2d 1859

USPQ2d 1859 (Fed. Cir. 1987); *In re Newport Fastener Co. Inc.*, 5 USPQ2d 1064, 1067 n. 4 (TTAB 1987). The entry of a disclaimer does not necessarily render registrable a mark that is otherwise unregistrable.

If the examining attorney has not required any disclaimer of misspelled wording because a disclaimer is not necessary under Office policy, the applicant may provide a disclaimer of the wording as spelled in the mark or in its correct spelling voluntarily. In such a case, the examining attorney should accept the disclaimer. Again, the disclaimer does not necessarily render an otherwise unregistrable mark registrable. The examining attorney must consider the entire mark, including the disclaimed matter, to determine whether the entire mark is registrable.

1213. 08(d) Disclaimer of Non-English Words

Non-English wording that comprises an unregistrable component of a mark is subject to disclaimer. *See Bausch & Lomb Optical Co. v. Overseas Finance & Trading Co. Inc.*, 112 USPQ 6, 8 (Comm'r Pats. 1956) (noting that "Kogaku," the transliteration of the Japanese word for "optical," was properly disclaimed).

If non-English wording that is translated must be disclaimed, the actual non-English wording should be disclaimed, not the English translation. The applicant must disclaim the wording that actually appears in the mark, not the translated version.

See TMEP §§809 *et seq.* regarding translation of non-English wording in marks.

1213. 09 Mark of Another May Not Be Registered with Disclaimer

Normally, a mark that includes a mark registered by another person must be refused registration under 15 U. S. C. §1052(d) based on likelihood of confusion. A refusal of registration under §2(d) may not be avoided by disclaiming the mark of another. *Cf. In re Franklin Press, Inc.*, 597 F. 2d 270, 201 USPQ 662 (C. C. P. A.

(Fed. Cir. 1987)；*Newport Fastener Co. Inc.*, 5 USPQ2d 1064，1067 n. 4 (TTAB 1987)。进行了一项撤回，并不必然导致一项原本不可注册的商标变得可以注册了。

如果根据商标局的政策不必撤回，因而审查员没有要求撤回拼写错误的词语，申请者也可以主动撤回该词语，而且撤回的既可以是商标所含的拼写形式，也可以是其正确的拼写形式。在这种情况下，审查员应当接受该撤回。重申，一项撤回并不必然导致一项原本不可注册的商标变得可以注册了。审查员必须考虑整体的商标，包括被撤回的部分，以判断该商标整体是否具有可注册性。

1213.08(d) 撤回非英语文字

构成商标不可注册部分的非英语文字应当撤回。*参见 Bausch & Lomb Optical Co. v. Overseas Finance & Trading Co. Inc.*, 112 USPQ 6，8 (Comm'r Pats. 1956)（"Kogaku"是日文"光学"一词的音译，对其撤回是正确的)。

如果必须撤回某经过翻译的非英语文字，则撤回的应该是其本国的文字形式，而非英文译文。申请者必须撤回商标中实际出现的语词，而不是经过翻译的版本。

关于商标中非英语文字翻译的规定，*参见* TMEP §§809 及其以下。

1213.09 他项商标不得通过撤回而获得注册

通常，如果一项商标中包含他人已经注册的商标，就必须根据 15 U.S.C. §1052 (d)的规定，以混淆可能性为理由拒绝予以注册。即使撤回他人的商标，也不能避免根据§2(d)作出的拒绝予以注册的决定。比较：*Franklin Press, Inc.*, 597 F. 2d

1979) (permitting disclaimer of informational phrase indicating that applicant's employees are represented by certain labor organizations). *See* TMEP §1213.10 regarding disclaimer in relation to likelihood of confusion.

1213.10 Disclaimer in Relation to Likelihood of Confusion

A disclaimer does not remove the disclaimed matter from the mark. The mark must still be regarded as a whole, including the disclaimed matter, in evaluating similarity to other marks. *See In re National Data Corp.*, 753 F.2d 1056, 224 USPQ 749 (Fed. Cir. 1985); *Specialty Brands, Inc. v. Coffee Bean Distributors, Inc.*, 748 F.2d 669, 672, 223 USPQ 1281, 1282 (Fed. Cir. 1984); *Giant Food, Inc. v. Nation's Foodservice, Inc.*, 710 F.2d 1565, 1570, 218 USPQ 390, 395 (Fed. Cir. 1983); *Schwarzkopf v. John H. Breck, Inc.*, 340 F.2d 978, 144 USPQ 433 (C.C.P.A. 1965); *In re MCI Communications Corp.*, 21 USPQ2d 1534, 1538-39 (Comm'r Pats. 1991).

Typically, disclaimed matter will not be regarded as the dominant, or most significant, feature of a mark. However, since the Trademark Act permits an applicant to voluntarily disclaim registrable matter (*see* TMEP §1213.01(c)), disclaimed matter may be dominant or significant in some cases. As noted in *In re MCI Communications Corp.*, 21 USPQ2d at 1539, "Examining Attorneys will continue to consider the question of likelihood of confusion, under Section 2(d) of the statute, in relation to the marks as a whole, including any voluntarily disclaimed matter."

1213.11 Acquiring Rights in Disclaimed Matter

In *Estate of P. D. Beckwith v. Comm'r of Pats.*, 252 U.S. 538, 545, 1920 C.D. 471, 477 (1920), the United States Supreme Court stated, regarding registration of a mark with a disclaimer, that "the registrant would be precluded by his disclaimer from setting up in the future any exclusive right to the disclaimed part of it." Subsequently, that principle was applied literally; registrants were prohibited

270，201 USPQ 662（C.C.P.A.1979）（商标中包含介绍性的用语，表明申请者的雇员隶属于特定的劳工组织，允许撤回此项内容）。关于混淆可能性的撤回，参见 TMEP §1213.10。

1213.10 涉及混淆可能性的撤回

撤回并没有从商标中去除该撤回的内容。在判断该商标是否可能与其他商标相类似时，仍必须将其视为一个整体，包括被撤回的内容在内。*参见* 判例：*National Data Corp.*，753 F.2d 1056，224 USPQ 749（Fed. Cir. 1985）；*Specialty Brands, Inc. v. Coffee Bean Distributors, Inc.*，748 F.2d 669，672，223 USPQ 1281，1282（Fed. Cir. 1984）；*Giant Food, Inc. v. Nation's Foodservice, Inc.*，710 F.2d 1565，1570，218 USPQ 390，395（Fed. Cir. 1983）；*Schwarzkopf v. John H. Breck, Inc.*，340 F.2d 978，144 USPQ 433（C.C.P.A.1965）；*MCI Communications Corp.*，21 USPQ2d 1534，1538 - 39（Comm'r Pats.1991）。

通常，被撤回的内容不会被视为是商标的核心或者重要内容。不过，由于《商标法》允许申请者主动撤回可注册的内容（*参见* TMEP §1213.01(c)），因此在某些情况下，被撤回的内容可能是核心的或重要的内容。正如 *MCI Communications Corp.*，21 USPQ2d at 1539 一案中所述："审查员仍将继续根据《商标法》§2(d)的规定，将商标作为一个整体，包括任何被主动撤回的部分，来考虑混淆可能性的问题。"

1213.11 对于被撤回的内容可获得的权利

在 *Estate of P.D. Beckwith v. Comm'r of Pats.*，252 U.S.538，545，1920 C.D.471，477（1920）一案中，美国最高法院就附有撤回的注册商标作了以下论述："商标的撤回排除了商标注册人可以在将来对于撤回的部分获得专属的权利。"以后，这一原则一直按照其表述的那样被不折不扣地执行着，不允许商标注册人在申请中宣

from asserting in an application that disclaimed matter had acquired secondary meaning. *See Shaler Co. v. Rite-Way Products, Inc.*, 43 USPQ 425 (6th Cir. 1939).

The situation was changed by the Trademark Act of 1946, which provided that "disclaimer shall not prejudice or affect the applicant's or owner's rights then existing or thereafter arising in the disclaimed matter, nor shall such disclaimer prejudice or affect the applicant's or owner's rights of registration on another application of later date if the disclaimed matter has become distinctive of the applicant's or owner's goods or services." In 1962, the statutory provision was amended to read, "No disclaimer ... shall prejudice or affect the applicant's or registrant's rights then existing or thereafter arising in the disclaimed matter, or his right of registration on another application if the disclaimed matter be or shall have become distinctive of his goods or services." 15 U.S.C. §1056(b).

It is now clear that, aside from generic matter, disclaimed matter is not forever barred from registration, and it can subsequently be considered for registration on either the Principal Register or the Supplemental Register. When an application is filed seeking registration of matter previously disclaimed, it should be examined in the same manner as other applications. *See Quaker Oil Corp. v. Quaker State Oil Refining Corp.*, 161 USPQ 547 (TTAB 1969), *aff'd*, 453 F.2d 1296, 172 USPQ 361 (C. C. P. A. 1972); *Victor Tool & Machine Corp. v. Sun Control Awnings, Inc.*, 299 F.Supp.868, 162 USPQ 389 (E.D. Mich. 1968), *aff'd*, 411 F.2d 792, 162 USPQ 387 (6th. Cir. 1969).

Whether or not previously disclaimed matter has become eligible for registration depends on the circumstances and the evidence adduced in the examination process. *Helena Rubinstein, Inc. v. Ladd*, 219 F. Supp. 259, 138 USPQ 106 (D. D.C. 1963), *aff'd*, 141 USPQ 623 (D.C. Cir. 1964); *Roux Distributing Co., Inc. v. Duart Mfg. Co. Ltd.*, 114 USPQ 511 (Comm'r Pats. 1957).

1214 "Phantom" Elements in Marks

In some applications, the applicant seeks to register a "phantom" element (*i.e.*,

称被撤回的内容还具有次要含义。参见 *Shaler Co. v. Rite-Way Products, Inc.*, 43 USPQ 425 (6th Cir. 1939)。

《1946 年商标法》改变了这一情形。根据该法:"撤回不应损害或影响申请者或注册人对被撤回部分的现有的或此后发生的权利;撤回也不应损害或影响申请者或商标注册人在日后另一申请中注册的权利,只要被撤回部分对于或已对于其商品或服务具备了独特性。"在 1962 年,该条规定被修改为:"撤回……不应损害或影响申请者或注册人对被撤回部分的现有的或此后发生的权利,或者不应损害或影响其在另一申请中注册的权利,只要被撤回部分对于或已对于其商品或服务具备了独特性。"15 U.S.C. §1056(b)。

现在已经明确,除非只是一般性的内容,否则被撤回的内容不会被永远禁止注册,日后该内容有可能在联邦商标登记簿注册或者补充登记簿注册。在提交的注册申请中如果有以前被撤回的内容,对于这样的申请应与其他的申请一视同仁。参见 *Quaker Oil Corp. v. Quaker State Oil Refining Corp.*, 161 USPQ 547 (TTAB 1969), *aff'd*, 453 F.2d 1296, 172 USPQ 361 (C.C.P.A. 1972); *Victor Tool & Machine Corp. v. Sun Control Awnings, Inc.*, 299 F. Supp. 868, 162 USPQ 389 (E.D. Mich. 1968), *aff'd*, 411 F.2d 792, 162 USPQ 387 (6th Cir. 1969)。

以前被撤回的内容是否已经可以注册,取决于现在的情况以及审查过程中所提出的证据。参见 *Helena Rubinstein, Inc. v. Ladd*, 219 F. Supp. 259, 138 USPQ 106 (D.D.C. 1963), *aff'd*, 141 USPQ 623 (D.C. Cir. 1964); *Roux Distributing Co., Inc. v. Duart Mfg. Co. Ltd.*, 114 USPQ 511 (Comm'r Pats. 1957)。

1214 商标中的"不定"内容

在有些申请中,申请者会寻求将"不定"的内容(例如,一个单词,一个文字数字名

a word, alpha-numeric designation, or other component that is subject to change) as part of a mark. The applicant represents the changeable or "phantom" element by inserting a blank, or by using dots, dashes, underlining, or a designation such as "XXXX."

Examples include marks incorporating a date (usually a year), a geographic location, or a model number that is subject to change. While these are some of the most common examples of the types of elements involved, there are many variations.

1214.01 Single Application May Seek Registration of Only One Mark

Where an applicant seeks registration of a mark with a changeable or "phantom" element, the examining attorney should refuse registration under §§1 and 45 of the Trademark Act, 15 U.S.C. §§1051 and 1127, on the ground that the application seeks registration of more than one mark. *See In re International Flavors & Fragrances Inc.*, 183 F.3d 1361, 51 USPQ2d 1513 (Fed. Cir. 1999); *Cineplex Odeon Corp. v. Fred Wehrenberg Circuit of Theatres Inc.*, 56 USPQ2d 1538 (TTAB 2000).

In *International Flavors*, the applicant filed three applications to register the designations "LIVING xxxx," "LIVING xxxx FLAVOR," and "LIVING xxxx FLAVORS," for essential oils, flavor substances, and fragrances. Each application included a statement that "[t]he meaning of 'xxxx' is for a specific herb, fruit, plant or vegetable." In upholding the refusal of registration, the Federal Circuit noted that under §22 of the Trademark Act, 15 U.S.C. §1072, registration serves as constructive notice to the public of the registrant's ownership of the mark and therefore precludes another user from claiming innocent misappropriation as a trademark infringement defense. To make this constructive notice meaningful, the mark as registered must accurately reflect the mark that is used in commerce, so that someone who searches the register for a similar mark will locate the regis-

称或者是其他的会改变的部分)注册为商标的一部分。申请者须插入一个空格,或者是用点、破折号、下画线或者诸如"XXXX"的标识,以表示这些可变的或"不定"的内容。

这样的例子还包括在商标中加上一个可以改变的日期(通常是一个年份)、地理位置或者型号。不过这只是一些最常见的例子,还有很多其他的变体形式。

1214.01 一商标一申请

如果申请者申请注册的商标中含有可变的或"不定"的要素,审查员应当根据《商标法》§§1 和 45,15 U.S.C.§§1051 和 1127 的规定以申请提出了对一个以上商标的注册请求为理由拒绝予以注册。参见 *International Flavors & Fragrances Inc.*, 183 F.3d 1361, 51 USPQ2d 1513 (Fed.Cir.1999); *Cineplex Odeon Corp. v. Fred Wehrenberg Circuit of Theatres Inc.*, 56 USPQ2d 1538 (TTAB 2000)。

在 *International Flavors* 一案中,申请者提交了三份申请,分别申请将"LIVING xxxx"、"LIVING xxxx FLAVOR"、"LIVING xxxx FLAVORS"注册为香精油、香料以及香水的商标。每一份申请都附加了这样的一份声明:"'xxxx'是一种特殊的草本、水果、植物或蔬菜。"联邦巡回区法院维持了拒绝注册的决定,认为,根据《商标法》§22 ,15 U.S.C.§1072 的规定,商标的注册是向公众提供一种建设性的宣告,表明注册人对于该商标拥有所有权,因而可以排除他人以善意使用作为商标侵权的抗辩理由。为了使这样的建设性宣告具有其应有的意义,被注册的商标必须和商业活动中所使用的商标充分一致,从而检索者在检索注册商标时可以找到这一注

tration. The court stated that "phantom marks" with missing elements "encompass too many combinations and permutations to make a thorough and effective search possible" and, therefore, the registration of these marks does not provide adequate notice to competitors and the public. *International Flavors*, 51 USPQ2d at 1517-18. *Cf. In re Upper Deck Co.*, 59 USPQ2d 1688 (TTAB 2001) (hologram used on trading cards in varying shapes, sizes, contents and positions constitutes more than one "device" as contemplated by §45 of the Trademark Act).

See also TMEP §807.03 regarding the requirement that an application be limited to one mark.

1214.02 Agreement of Mark on Drawing With Mark on Specimens or Foreign Registration

Where an applicant seeks registration of a "phantom mark," the examining attorney should also consider whether the mark on the drawing is a substantially exact representation of the mark as used on the specimens in a use-based application, or the mark in the home country registration in an application based on Trademark Act §44, 15 U.S.C. §1126. *See* TMEP §§807.14 and 807.14(b).

The applicant may amend the mark to overcome a refusal on the ground that the mark on the drawing does not agree with the mark as used on the specimens, or with the mark in the foreign registration, if the amendment is not a material alteration of the mark. *See* TMEP §807.14(a) regarding material alteration.

1214.03 "Phantom Marks" in Intent-to-Use Applications

In an intent-to-use application for which no allegation of use has been filed, it may be unclear whether the applicant is seeking registration of a mark with a changeable element. If an intent-to-use application indicates that the applicant is seeking registration of a "phantom mark" (*e.g.*, if the application includes a statement that "the blank line represents a date that is subject to change"), the

册。法院认为，“不定商标”中缺少了一些内容，从而可以“包括许许多多的组合和排列情况，这使得检索者不能进行穷尽和有效的检索”。因此，这些商标即使获得注册，也不能对竞争对手和公众提供足够的提醒作用。*参见 International Flavors*，51 USPQ2d at 1517－18。并比较 *Upper Deck Co*.，59 USPQ2d 1688（TTAB 2001）（成套卡片上的全息图案形状、尺寸、内容和位置多变，不符合《商标法》§45 所规定的只能是一种“图案”的要求）。

关于一商标一申请要求的论述，另*参见* TMEP §807.03。

1214.02　附图所示商标必须与样本或国外注册的商标相一致

当申请者申请注册一项“不定”商标时，如果申请者申请的是“已使用申请”，审查员应当考虑附图上的商标是否和样品上所使用的商标充分一致；当申请者是基于《商标法》§44，15 U.S.C.§1126 提出的申请，审查员则应当考虑附图上商标是否和本国注册的商标相一致。*参见* TMEP §§807.14 和 807.14(b)。

为避免由于附图上的商标和样品上所使用的商标不一致，或者由于附图上的商标和外国注册一致而被拒绝注册，申请者可以对商标加以修改，只要该修改不对商标构成实质性变动。有关实质上的更改，*参见* TMEP §807.14(a)。

1214.03　意图使用申请中的“不定商标”

在未提交使用证明的意图使用申请中，申请者想要注册的是否属于含有可变要素的商标就可能并不十分明确。如果意图使用申请已经表明了申请者想要注册一项“不定商标”（例如，如果申请中有这样的声明：“虚线处所代表的是将来会修改的日

examining attorney should issue a refusal of registration under §§1 and 45 of the Trademark Act, 15 U.S.C. §§1051 and 1127, on the ground that the application seeks registration of more than one mark, as discussed above. If it is unclear whether an applicant is seeking registration of a "phantom" mark, the examining attorney should advise the applicant that if the specimens filed with an amendment to allege use under §1(c) of the Trademark Act, 15 U.S.C. §1051(c), or a statement of use under §1(d) of the Act, 15 U.S.C. §1051(d), show that applicant is seeking registration of a mark with a changeable element, registration will be refused on the ground that the application seeks registration of more than a single mark. This is done strictly as a courtesy. If information regarding this possible ground for refusal is not provided before the applicant files an allegation of use, the Office is not precluded from refusing registration on this basis.

1215 Marks Composed, in Whole or in Part, of Domain Names

Since the implementation of the Internet domain name system, the Office has received a growing number of applications for marks composed of domain names. Although the majority of these applications are for computer services such as Internet content providers (organizations that provide web sites with information about a particular topic or field) and online ordering services, a substantial number are for marks used on other types of services or goods.

1215.01 Background

A domain name is part of a Uniform Resource Locator (URL), which is the address of a site or document on the Internet. In general, a domain name is comprised of a second-level domain, a "dot," and a top-level domain (TLD). The wording to the left of the "dot" is the second-level domain, and the wording to the right of the "dot" is the TLD.

期。”)，审查员应当根据《商标法》§1和§45，15 U.S.C.§1051和§1127的规定拒绝该申请，因为申请者所申请注册的商标，如上所述，不止一项商标。如果申请者是否寻求注册“不定”商标并不明确，在此情况下，审查员应当向申请者提出警告，如果申请者提交的样品中附加《商标法》§1(c)，15 U.S.C.§1051(c)所规定的使用证明修正书，或者是《商标法》§1(d)，15 U.S.C.§1051(d)所规定的使用声明书，表明申请者所申请的是含有可变内容的商标，该注册就将被拒绝，因为申请者申请注册的商标超过了一项。此种告诫完全是出于好心。如果在使用证明提交之前，未向申请者告知关于该可能的驳回注册理由的信息，商标局仍然可以以此为理由作出拒绝予以注册的决定。

1215 全部或部分由域名构成的商标

自从实施因特网域名系统以来，商标局收到的含有域名的商标注册申请越来越多。虽然这些申请大多数用于电脑服务，例如网上内容提供者(在网站上提供某一特定主题或领域信息的组织)和在线购物服务，在其他服务和商品上使用域名的注册申请的数量也开始有实质性的增长。

1215.01 背景

域名是统一资源定位符(URL)的一部分，URL是一个网站或文件在因特网上的地址。一般来说，一个域名是由一个二级域名、一个“点”和一个顶级域名(TLD)所构成的。“点”的左面表示的是二级域名，右面表示的是顶级域名。

Example: If the domain name is "ABC.com," the term "ABC" is a second-level domain and the term "com" is a TLD.

A domain name is usually preceded in a URL by "http://www."The "http://" refers to the protocol used to transfer information, and the "www" refers to World Wide Web, a graphical hypermedia interface for viewing and exchanging information.

Generic TLDs. The following are examples of generic TLDs that are designated for use by the public:

.com	commercial, for-profit organizations
.edu	4-year, degree-granting colleges/universities
.gov	U.S. federal government agencies
.int	international organizations
.mil	U.S. military organizations, even if located outside the U.S.
.net	network infrastructure machines and organizations
.org	miscellaneous, usually non-profit organizations and individuals

Each of the above TLDs is intended for use by a certain type of organization. For example, the TLD ".com" is for use by commercial, for-profit organizations. However, the administrator of the .com, .net, .org and .edu TLDs does not check the requests of parties seeking domain names to ensure that such parties are a type of organization that should be using those TLDs. On the other hand, .mil, .gov, and .int TLD applications are checked, and only the U.S. military, the U.S. government, or international organizations are allowed in the respective domain space.

Country Code TLDs. Country code TLDs are for use by each individual country. For example, the TLD ".ca" is for use by Canada, and the TLD ".jp" is for use by Japan. Each country determines who may use their code. For example, some countries require that users of their code be citizens or have some association with the country, while other countries do not.

例如：如果某一域名是“ABC.com”，那么“ABC”就是一个二级域名，而“com”就是一个顶级域名。

域名通常以“http://www.”冠于URL首部。“http://www.”表示的是一种信息传输协议，而“www”是指万维网，一种信息浏览和交换的图形超媒体界面。

一般顶级域名：以下是一些分配给公众使用的一般顶级域名：

.com　商业、营利组织；

.edu　四年制、具有学位授予权的学院或大学；

.gov　美国联邦政府机构；

.int　国际性组织；

.mil　美国军方组织，即使这些组织位于美国国土之外；

.net　网络基建机构和组织；

.org　其他各种组织，通常是非营利组织以及个人。

上述每一个顶级域名所代表的是一种特定类型的组织。例如，“.com”这一顶级域名的使用者是商业、营利性组织。不过，“.com”、“.net”、“.org”和“.edu”这些顶级域名的营运商并不对域名申请者进行审查以保证某一类的组织必须使用相应的顶级域名。另一方面，使用“.mil，.gov and .int”这些域名的申请者都须经过审查，并且，只有美国的军方机构、政府或国际组织方能或者使用相应的域空间。

国家代码顶级域名。国家代码顶级域名是由各个国家所使用的。例如，加拿大使用的是“.ca”这一顶级域名，日本是使用的“.jp”这一顶级域名。何人可以使用其代码由各个国家规定。例如，有些国家规定使用其代码的使用者必须是其国民或与该国有某种联系，而其他国家就没有这样的规定。

1215.02 Use as a Mark

When a trademark, service mark, collective mark or certification mark is composed, in whole or in part, of a domain name, neither the beginning of the URL ("http://www.") nor the TLD have any source-indicating significance. Instead, those designations are merely devices that every Internet site provider must use as part of its address. Today, advertisements for all types of products and services routinely include a URL for the web site of the advertiser, and the average person familiar with the Internet recognizes the format for a domain name and understands that "http," "www," and a TLD are a part of every URL.

1215.02(a) Use Applications

A mark composed of a domain name is registrable as a trademark or service mark only if it functions as a source identifier. The mark as depicted on the specimens must be presented in a manner that will be perceived by potential purchasers to indicate source and not as merely an informational indication of the domain name address used to access a web site. *See In re Eilberg*, 49 USPQ2d 1955 (TTAB 1998).

In *Eilberg*, the Trademark Trial and Appeal Board (Board) held that a term that only serves to identify the applicant's domain name or the location on the Internet where the applicant's web site appears, and does not separately identify applicant's services, does not function as a service mark. The applicant's proposed mark was WWW.EILBERG.COM, and the specimens showed that the mark was used on letterhead and business cards in the following manner:

WILLIAM H. EILBERG

ATTORNEY AT LAW

820 HOMESTEAD ROAD, P.O. BOX 7

JENKINTOWN, PENNSYLVANIA 19046

215-885-4600

FAX 215-885-4603

EMAIL WHE@EILBERG.COM

PATENTS, TRADEMARKS AND COPYRIGHTS — WWW.EILBERG.COM

1215.02 作为商标使用

如果商标、服务商标、集体商标或认证商标全部或部分是由域名构成的，无论是开头的 URL（“http://www.”）还是顶级域名，都具有表明权属的意义。相反，这些标识不过是一种设置，这种设置是每一个网站提供者的地址中都应使用的一部分。如今，所有品种的产品和服务的广告中都惯例性地加上了客户的网站 URL，熟悉因特网的普通民众都能够辨认出域名的形式，也都知道“http”、“www”和一个顶级域名是每个 URL 的一部分。

1215.02(a) 使用申请

由域名所构成的商标，只有当其具有标示来源的功能时，才能够注册为商标或服务商标。样本中商标的标示方式，必须是能够使将来的购买者认识到该商品的来源，并且不能够仅仅是提供了访问其网站的域名地址信息。*参见 Eilberg*, 49 USPQ2d 1955 (TTAB 1998)。

在 *Eilberg* 一案中，商标评审及上诉委员会（简称委员会）认为一个用于仅仅用来表示申请者网站的域名或其在因特网上的地址，并不能够单独识别申请者的服务，不能作为一项服务商标。申请者所申请的商标是“WWW.EILBERG.COM”，样本上显示了该商标用于信笺抬头和商业名片中，方式如下所示：

WILLIAM H. EILBERG

ATTORNEY AT LAW

820 HOMESTEAD ROAD, P.O. BOX 7

JENKINTOWN, PENNSYLVANIA 19046

215-885-4600

FAX 215-885-4603

EMAIL WHE@EILBERG.COM

PATENTS, TRADEMARKS AND COPYRIGHTS

WWW.EILBERG.COM

(The specimen submitted was the business card of William H. Eilberg, Attorney at Law, 820 Homestead Road, P. O. Box 7, Jenkintown, Pennsylvania 19046, 215-855-4600, email whe@eilberg.com.)

The Board affirmed the examining attorney's refusal of registration on the ground that the matter presented for registration did not function as a mark, stating that:

> [T]he asserted mark, as displayed on applicant's letterhead, does not function as a service mark identifying and distinguishing applicant's legal services and, as presented, is not capable of doing so. As shown, the asserted mark identifies applicant's Internet domain name, by use of which one can access applicant's Web site. In other words, the asserted mark WWW.EILBERG.COM merely indicates the location on the Internet where applicant's Web site appears. It does not separately identify applicant's legal services as such. *Cf. In re The Signal Companies, Inc.*, 228 USPQ 956 (TTAB 1986).
>
> This is not to say that, if used appropriately, the asserted mark or portions thereof may not be trademarks or [service marks]. For example, if applicant's law firm name were, say, EILBERG.COM and were presented prominently on applicant's letterheads and business cards as the name under which applicant was rendering its legal services, then that mark may well be registrable.

49 USPQ2d at 1957.

The examining attorney must review the specimens in order to determine how the proposed mark is actually used. It is the perception of the ordinary customer that determines whether the asserted mark functions as a mark, not the applicant's intent, hope or expectation that it does so. *See In re Standard Oil Co.*, 275 F.2d 945, 125 USPQ 227 (C.C.P.A. 1960).

If the proposed mark is used in a way that would be perceived as nothing more than an Internet address where the applicant can be contacted, registration must

(提交的样本是 William H. Eilberg 的商业名片：Attorney at Law，820 Homestead Road，P. O. Box 7，Jenkintown，Pennsylvania 19046，215 - 855 - 4600，email whe@eilberg.com.）

委员会维持了审查员以所申请注册商标不具备商标功能为由而作出的拒绝予以注册的决定，并阐述说：

> 如申请者信笺抬头所显示的声称商标，并不能作为一项服务商标识别和区分申请者所提供的法律服务，正如所提出的样式，并不具有这样的功能。如图所示，声称的商标所识别的是申请者的因特网域名，通过该域名可以访问申请者的网站。换言之，所声称的商标"WWW. EILBERG. COM"仅仅表示了申请者网站在因特网上所处的位置。无法单独识别申请者提供的法律服务。比较：*The Signal Companies，Inc.*，228 USPQ 956（TTAB 1986）。
>
> 但是这并不是说，如果使用得当，所声称的商标或其部分不可以是商标或［服务商标］。例如，如果申请者的律师事务所的名称叫做"EILBERG. COM"，并且被显著地标在申请者的信笺抬头和商业名片上，这样申请者就使得该名称成为一项法律服务，该商标也就可以注册了。

49 USPQ2d at 1957。

审查员应当仔细审查样本，以判断申请的商标实际上是如何被使用的。在判断所声称的商标是否能够作为商标使用，所依据的应当是普通顾客对商标的感觉，而不是申请者的意图、希望和期待。*参见 Standard Oil Co.*，275 F. 2d 945，125 USPQ 227（C. C. P. A. 1960）。

如果申请的商标实际的使用方式，被认为只是可以确定联系到申请者的因特网

be refused. Examples of a domain name used only as an Internet address include a domain name used in close proximity to language referring to the domain name as an address, or a domain name displayed merely as part of the information on how to contact the applicant.

> *Example*: The mark is WWW. ABC. COM for on-line ordering services in the field of clothing. Specimens of use consisting of an advertisement that states "visit us on the web at www. ABC. com" do not show service mark use of the proposed mark.
>
> *Example*: The mark is ABC. COM for financial consulting services. Specimens of use consisting of a business card that refers to the service and lists a phone number, fax number, and the domain name sought to be registered do not show service mark use of the proposed mark.

If the specimens of use fail to show the domain name used as a mark and the applicant seeks registration on the Principal Register, the examining attorney must refuse registration on the ground that the matter presented for registration does not function as a mark. The statutory bases for the refusals are §§1, 2 and 45 of the Trademark Act, 15 U.S.C. §§1051, 1052 and 1127, for trademarks; and §§1, 3 and 45 of the Act, 15 U.S.C. §§1051, 1053 and 1127, for service marks.

If the applicant seeks registration on the Supplemental Register, the examining attorney must refuse registration under Trademark Act §23, 15 U.S.C. §1091.

1215. 02(b) Advertising One's Own Products or Services on the Internet is not a Service

Advertising one's own products or services is not a service. *In re Reichhold Chemicals, Inc.*, 167 USPQ 376 (TTAB 1970). *See* TMEP §§1301.01(a)(ii) and 1301.01(b)(i). Therefore, businesses that create a web site for the sole purpose of advertising their own products or services cannot register a domain name used to identify that activity. In examination, the issue usually arises when the applicant

地址，这样的注册就必须拒绝。仅仅是因特网地址的域名的情形还包括以下情况：一个域名在语言表达上非常接近于仅仅表示因特网地址，或者域名仅仅是作为如何与申请者取得联系这一信息的一部分。

例如：WWW.ABC.COM 是某服装在线订购服务的商标。其使用样本上包括了一条广告，称："请访问我们的网站 www.ABC.com"，并没有表明申请的商标是被用作服务商标。

例如：ABC.COM 是金融咨询服务的商标。其使用的样本中有一商业名片，该名片标明了该项服务，并列出了电话号码、传真以及申请注册的域名，不过并没有表明申请注册的商标是用作服务商标。

如果使用样本没有表明域名是被用作商标，并且申请者申请在联邦商标登记簿注册，那么审查员应当拒绝注册，因为所申请注册的内容并不具备商标功能。此项拒绝决定的法律依据，对于商标是《商标法》§§1，2 和 45，15 U.S.C.§§1051，1052 和 1127；对于服务商标是《商标法》§§1，3 和 45，15 U.S.C.§§1051，1053 和 1127。

如果申请者申请在补充登记簿注册，审查员应当依据《商标法》§23，15 U.S.C. §1091 的规定驳回申请。

1215.02(b)　在因特网上宣传自己产品或服务的广告不构成一项服务

宣传自己产品或服务的广告不构成一项服务。见 *Reichhold Chemicals, Inc.*, 167 USPQ 376（TTAB 1970）。*参见* TMEP §§1301.01(a)(ii)and 1301.01(b)(i)。因此，企业所构建的网站如果只是为了为其产品或服务做广告，用以表明这样的广告

describes the activity as a registrable service, *e.g.*, "providing information about [a particular field]," but the specimens of use make it clear that the web site merely advertises the applicant's own products or services. In this situation, the examining attorney must refuse registration because the mark is used to identify an activity that does not constitute a "service" within the meaning of the Trademark Act. Trademark Act §§1, 3 and 45, 15 U.S.C.§§1051, 1053 and 1127.

1215.02(c) Agreement of Mark on Drawing with Mark on Specimens of Use

In viewing a domain name mark (*e. g.*, ABC. COM or HTTP://WWW. ABC. COM), consumers look to the second level domain name for source identification, not to the top-level domain (TLD) or the terms "http://www." or "www." Therefore, it is usually acceptable to depict only the second level domain name on the drawing page, even if the specimens of use show a mark that includes the TLD or the terms "http://www." or "www." *Cf. Institut National des Appellations D'Origine v. Vintners Int'l Co., Inc.*, 958 F. 2d 1574, 22 USPQ2d 1190 (Fed. Cir. 1992) (CHABLIS WITH A TWIST held to be registrable separately from CALIFORNIA CHABLIS WITH A TWIST as shown on labels); *In re Raychem Corp.*, 12 USPQ2d 1399 (TTAB 1989) (refusal to register TINEL-LOCK based on specimens showing "TRO6AI-TINEL-LOCK-RING" reversed). *See also* 37 C.F.R.§§2.51(a)(1) and (b)(1), and TMEP §§807.14 *et. seq*.

> *Example*: The specimens of use show the mark HTTP://WWW. ABC. COM. The applicant may elect to depict only the term "ABC" on the drawing page.

Sometimes the specimens of use fail to show the entire mark sought to be registered (*e. g.*, the drawing of the mark is HTTP://WWW. ABC. COM, but the specimens only show ABC). If the drawing of the mark includes a TLD, or the terms "http://www.," or "www.," the specimens of use must also show the mark used with those terms. Trademark Act §1(a)(3)(C), 15 U.S.C.§1051(a)(3)(C).

活动的域名就不能注册。在审查过程中,经常会碰到这样的情形,申请者把这样的广告行为描述成是一种可以注册的服务行为,例如,把这样的广告行为说成是“提供特殊领域的信息”,但是商标的使用样本却清楚地表明,这一网站只是在为申请者的产品或服务做广告。在这种情况下,审查员应拒绝予以注册,因为该商标所识别的活动并不构成《商标法》所规定的“服务”。见《商标法》§§1, 3 和 45, 15 U.S.C.§§1051, 1053 和 1127。

1215.02(c) 附图所示商标应与使用样本上的商标相一致

在审查一项域名商标(例如 ABC.COM 或 HTTP://WWW.ABC.COM)时,消费者注意的是识别来源的二级域名,而不是顶级域名(TLD),即 http://www. 或者 www. 这些前缀。因此,如果在附图中仅仅描述二级域名通常也是可以接受的,即使商标的使用样本上所显示的商标包括了 TLD,或 http://www. 或 www. 之类的词语。*参见 Institut National des Appellations D'Origine v. Vintners Int'l Co., Inc.*, 958 F.2d 1574, 22 USPQ2d 1190 (Fed. Cir. 1992)(标签上 CALIFORNIA CHABLIS WITH A TWIST 这一商标中的“CHABLIS WITH A TWIST”部分单独是可以注册的);*Raychem Corp.*, 12 USPQ2d 1399 (TTAB 1989)(由于样本显示反转的“TR6AI-TINEL-LOCK-RING”,故拒绝予以注册“TINEL-LOCK”)。另*参见* 37 C.F.R.§§2.51(a)(1)和(b)(1),*参见* TMEP §§807.14 及以下。

> *例如*:使用样本所示的商标是 HTTP://WWW.ABC.COM。申请者可以选择在附图页中只表现“ABC”这一词。

有时候,商标的使用样本没有表现完整的申请注册商标(例如,商标的附图是 HTTP://WWW.ABC.COM,但是样本上仅仅标示了 ABC)。如果商标的附图中包括了 TLD,或 http://www. 或者 www. 这样的词语,使用样本所标示的也应当是包括了这些词语的商标。《商标法》§1(a)(3)(C), 15 U.S.C.§1051(a)(3)(C)。

Example: If the drawing of the mark is ABC.COM, specimens of use that only show the term ABC are unacceptable.

See TMEP §§807.14(a) and 1215.08 through 1215.08(b) regarding material alteration.

1215.02(d) Marks Comprised Solely of TLDs for Domain Name Registry Services

If a mark is composed solely of a TLD for "domain name registry services" (*e.g.*, the services of registering .com domain names), registration should be refused under Trademark Act §§1, 3 and 45, 15 U.S.C. §§1051, 1053 and 1127, on the ground that the TLD would not be perceived as a mark. The examining attorney should include evidence from the NEXIS® database, the Internet, or other sources to show that the proposed mark is currently used as a TLD or is under consideration as a new TLD.

If the TLD merely describes the subject or user of the domain space, registration should be refused under Trademark Act §2(e)(1), 15 U.S.C. §2(e)(1), on the ground that the TLD is merely descriptive of the registry services.

1215.02(e) Intent-to-Use Applications

A refusal of registration on the ground that the matter presented for registration does not function as a mark relates to the manner in which the asserted mark is used. Generally, in an intent-to-use application, a mark that includes a domain name will not be refused on this ground until the applicant has submitted specimens of use with either an amendment to allege use under Trademark Act §1(c), or a statement of use under Trademark Act §1(d), 15 U.S.C. §1051(c) or (d). However, the examining attorney should include an advisory note in the first Office action that registration may be refused if the proposed mark, as used on the specimens, identifies only an Internet address. This is done strictly as a courtesy.

例如：如果商标的附图是“ABC.COM”，那么使用样本就不能仅仅显示“ABC”。

关于实质性改动的规定，*参见* TMEP §§807.14(a)和1215.08至1215.08(b)。

1215.02(d)　只包含域名注册服务TLD的商标

如果商标只是由一个“提供域名注册服务”（例如，提供.com域名注册服务）的TLD所构成的，根据商标法§§1，3和45，即15 U.S.C.§§1051，1053和1127，这样的注册应被拒绝，因为TLD不能被认知为商标。审查员应当从NEXIS®数据库、因特网或其他来源搜集证据，以证明所提交的商标目前是被作为TLD而使用，或可以被认为是一项新的域名。

如果TLD描述的仅仅是域的主题或者是域空间的使用者，根据商标法§2(e)(1)，15 U.S.C.§2(e)(1)，这样的注册应当拒绝，因为这样的TLD仅仅是对域名注册服务的描述。

1215.02(e)　意图使用申请

如果一项注册申请由于所提交的标的物不能作为商标而遭到拒绝，则拒绝决定与使用所声称的商标的方式有很大的关系。因此，对于一项意图使用的申请，无法以包含域名为理由拒绝予以注册，除非申请者提交使用样本以及§1(c)所规定的宣称使用修正书，或是§1(d)所规定的使用声明书，15 U.S.C.§1051(c)及(d)。不过，在商标局初步决定中，审查员应当作出警告性提示，告知如果样本所示的商标所识别的仅仅是一个因特网地址，该申请就有可能遭到拒绝。此种告诫纯属好意。如果在使

If information regarding this possible ground for refusal is not provided to the applicant prior to the filing of the allegation of use, the Office is not precluded from refusing registration on this basis.

1215.03 Surnames

If a mark is composed of a surname and a TLD, the examining attorney must refuse registration because the mark is primarily merely a surname under Trademark Act §2(e)(4), 15 U.S.C. §1052(e)(4), absent a showing of acquired distinctiveness under Trademark Act §2(f), 15 U.S.C. §1052(f). A TLD has no trademark significance. If the primary significance of a term is that of a surname, adding a TLD to the surname does not alter the primary significance of the mark as a surname. *Cf. In re I. Lewis Cigar Mfg. Co.*, 205 F.2d 204, 98 USPQ 265 (C.C.P.A. 1953) (S.SEIDENBERG & CO'S. held primarily merely a surname); *In re Hamilton Pharmaceuticals Ltd.*, 27 USPQ2d 1939 (TTAB 1993) (HAMILTON PHARMACEUTICALS for pharmaceutical products held primarily merely a surname); *In re Cazes*, 21 USPQ2d 1796 (TTAB 1991) (BRASSERIE LIPP held primarily merely a surname where "brasserie" is a generic term for applicant's restaurant services). *See also* TMEP §1211.01(b)(vi) regarding surnames combined with additional wording.

1215.04 Descriptiveness [R-2]

If a proposed mark is composed of a merely descriptive term(s) combined with a TLD, the examining attorney should refuse registration under Trademark Act §2(e)(1), 15 U.S.C. §1052(e)(1), on the ground that the mark is merely descriptive. This applies to trademarks, service marks, collective marks and certification marks.

> *Example*: The mark is SOFT.COM for facial tissues. The examining attorney must refuse registration under §2(e)(1).

用证明提交之前,未向申请者告知关于该可能的驳回注册理由的信息,商标局仍然可以以此为理由作出拒绝予以注册的决定。

1215.03 姓氏

如果商标是由姓氏和 TLD 所构成的,审查员就必须拒绝该注册,因为根据《商标法》§2(e)(4), 15 U.S.C.§1052(e)(4)的规定,该商标主要仅属姓氏,未能显示《商标法》§2(f),15 U.S.C.§1052(f)所规定的获得独特性。TLD 不具有商标的意义。如果一个用语的主要含义是一个姓氏,那么即使在该姓氏中加上了一个 TLD,也并不能改变该商标作为姓氏的主要含义。*参见 I. Lewis Cigar Mfg. Co.*, 205 F.2d 204, 98 USPQ 265 (C.C.P.A.1953)(S.SEIDENBERG & CO'S.被认为主要仅属姓氏);*Hamilton Pharmaceuticals Ltd.*, 27 USPQ2d 1939 (TTAB 1993)(以 HAMILTON PHARMACEUTICALS 作为药品的商标被认为主要仅属姓氏);*Cazes*, 21 USPQ2d 1796 (TTAB 1991)(BRASSERIE LIPP 被认为主要仅属姓氏,而"brasserie"一词只是申请者所提供服务的一般性词语)。关于由姓氏和其他的用语所构成的复合词的规定,*另参见* TMEP §1211.01(b)(vi)。

1215.04 描述性 [R-2]

如果一项申请注册的商标由仅具描述性的词语和一个 TLD 构成,则审查员必须根据《商标法》§2(e)(1), 15 U.S.C.§1052(e)(1)的规定,以该商标仅具描述性为理由拒绝在联邦商标登记簿注册。这一规则适用于商标、服务商标、集体商标和证明商标。

例如:SOFT.COM 是一种面纸的商标。审查员应当根据 §2(e)(1)的规定,拒绝该商标注册。

Example: The mark is NATIONAL BOOK OUTLET. COM for retail book store services. The examining attorney must refuse registration under §2(e)(1).

The TLD will be perceived as part of an Internet address, and does not add source identifying significance to the composite mark. *In re CyberFinancial. Net, Inc.*, 65 USPQ2d 1789, 1792 (TTAB 2002) ("The public would not understand BONDS. COM to have any meaning apart from the meaning of the individual terms combined"); *In re Martin Container, Inc.*, 65 USPQ2d 1058, 1060 (TTAB 2002) ("[T]o the average customer seeking to buy or rent containers, "CONTAINER. COM "would immediately indicate a commercial web site on the Internet which provides containers."). *Cf. In re Patent & Trademark Services Inc.*, 49 USPQ2d 1537 (TTAB 1998) (PATENT & TRADEMARK SERVICES INC. is merely descriptive of legal services in the field of intellectual property; the term "INC." merely indicates the type of entity that performs the services, and has no significance as a mark); *In re The Paint Products Co.*, 8 USPQ2d 1863 (TTAB 1988) (PAINT PRODUCTS CO. is no more registrable as a trademark for goods emanating from a company that sells paint products than it would be as a service mark for retail paint store services offered by such a company).

See also TMEP §1209.03(m).

1215.05 Generic Refusals [R-2]

If a mark is composed of a generic term(s) for the applicant's goods or services and a TLD, the examining attorney must refuse registration on the ground that the mark is generic and the TLD has no trademark significance. Marks comprised of generic terms combined with TLDs are not eligible for registration on the Supplemental Register, or on the Principal Register under Trademark Act §2(f), 15 U.S.C. §1052(f). This applies to trademarks, service marks, collective marks and certification marks. *In re CyberFinancial. Net, Inc.*, 65 USPQ2d 1789 (TTAB 2002) (BONDS. COM held generic for providing information regarding financial

例如：NATIONAL BOOK OUTLET.COM 是书店零售服务的商标。

审查员应当根据§2(e)(1)的规定，拒绝该商标注册。

TLD 会被人们视为是因特网地址的一部分，而且并不能给该复合商标带来任何识别来源的含义。*CyberFinancial. Net, Inc.*, 65 USPQ2d 1789, 1792 (TTAB 2002)("如果脱离了由单个用语所组成的整体，公众就不能从 BONDS.COM 这一用语中得到任何的含义")；*Martin Container, Inc.*, 65 USPQ2d 1058, 1060 (TTAB 2002)("对于希望购买或承租集装箱的一般顾客而言，'CONTAINER.COM'这一用语直接标示了因特网上提供集装箱的商业网站")。比较 *Patent & Trademark Services Inc.*, 49 USPQ2d 1537 (TTAB 1998)(PATENT & TRADEMARK SERVICES INC 只是对知识产权领域法律服务的描述，"INC."这一用语仅仅是表明了从事这一服务的企业的类型，并不具备商标的意义)；*The Paint Products Co.*, 8 USPQ2d 1863 (TTAB 1988)("对于一家销售涂料产品的公司所销售的产品和由这类公司所提供的零售涂料服务，两者在使用'PAINT PRODUCTS CO.'商号是否具有可注册性这一问题上，并无二致")。

另参见 TMEP §1209.03(m)。

1215.05　　一般性而拒绝予以注册 [R-2]

如果一项申请注册的商标由申请者商品或服务的一般名称和一个 TLD 构成，审查员必须以该商标属于一般性名称、不具有商标意义为理由拒绝予以注册。由一般性词语和 TLD 所构成的商标，根据《商标法》§2(f)，15 U.S.C.§1052(f)的规定，既不得在补充登记簿注册，也不得在联邦商标登记簿注册。这一规则适用于商标、服务商标、集体商标和证明商标。*CyberFinancial. Net, Inc.*, 65 USPQ2d 1789 (TTAB 2002)(用于提供有关金融产品服务和因特网电子商务服务的信息的"BONDS.COM"，被认为具有一般性，因为"bonds"一词以该商标提供的一种金融产品的名称)；*Martin Container, Inc.*, 65 USPQ2d 1058 (TTAB 2002)(用于金属运输集装箱的店面零售和电话零售特色服务以及集装箱租赁的"CONTAINER.COM"，被认

products and services and electronic commerce services rendered via the Internet, where bonds was the name of one of the financial products offered under the mark); *In re Martin Container, Inc.*, 65 USPQ2d 1058 (TTAB 2002) (CONTAINER.COM held generic for "retail store services and retail services offered via telephone featuring metal shipping containers" and "rental of metal shipping containers").

Example: TURKEY.COM for frozen turkeys is unregistrable on either the Principal or Supplemental Register.

Example: BANK. COM for banking services is unregistrable on either the Principal or Supplemental Register.

See TMEP §1209.01(c)(i) regarding the test for establishing that a term is generic.

The examining attorney generally should not issue a refusal in an application for registration on the Principal Register on the ground that a mark is a generic name for the goods or services unless the applicant asserts that the mark has acquired distinctiveness under §2(f) of the Trademark Act, 15 U.S.C. §1052(f). Absent a claim of acquired distinctiveness, the examining attorney should issue a refusal on the ground that the mark is merely descriptive of the goods or services under §2(e)(1), 15 U.S.C. §1052(e)(1), and provide an advisory statement that the matter sought to be registered appears to be a generic name for the goods or services. *See* TMEP §1209.02.

See also TMEP §§1209.03(m).

1215.06 Marks Containing Geographical Matter

The examining attorney should examine marks containing geographic matter in the same manner that any mark containing geographic matter is examined. *See generally* TMEP §§1210 *et seq*. Depending on the manner in which it is used on or

为具有一般性）。

例如：用于冷冻火鸡肉的“TURKEY.COM”既不能在联邦商标登记簿注册，也不能在补充登记簿注册。

例如：用于银行服务的“BANK.COM”既不能在联邦商标登记簿注册，也不能在补充登记簿注册。

关于如何判断某词具有一般性的情况，*参见* TMEP §1209.01(c)(i)。

在申请于联邦商标登记簿注册的申请中，审查员不应以商标属于商品或服务的一般名称为理由拒绝，除非申请者根据 15 U.S.C.§1052(f)主张该商标已具备了独特性。如申请者不主张获得性独特性，审查员就应当根据商标法§2(e)(1)，15 U.S.C.§1052(e)(1)的规定，以该商标仅具描述性为理由拒绝其注册，并且提出一项警告性声明，告知该申请注册商标属于商品或服务的一般性名称。*参见* TMEP §1209.02。

另参见 TMEP §1209.03(m)。

1215.06　包含地理内容的商标

审查员应当像审查任何包含有地理内容的商标一样，审查这些包含有地理内容的域名商标。*参见* TMEP §§1210 及以下。由于在商品或服务上使用的方式不同，以及和商品或服务的关联程度不同，申请注册的包含有地理用语的域名商标可能是

in connection with the goods or services, a proposed domain name mark containing a geographic term may be primarily geographically descriptive under §2(e)(2) of the Trademark Act, 15 U.S.C. §1052(e)(2), primarily geographically deceptively misdescriptive under §2(e)(3) of the Trademark Act, 15 U.S.C. §1052(e)(3), deceptive under 15 U.S.C. §1052(a), and/or merely descriptive or deceptively misdescriptive under §2(e)(1) of the Trademark Act, 15 U.S.C. §1052(e)(1).

When a geographic term is used as a mark for services that are provided on the Internet, sometimes the geographic term describes the subject of the service rather than the geographic origin of the service. Usually this occurs when the mark is composed of a geographic term that describes the subject matter of information services (*e.g.*, NEW ORLEANS.COM for "providing vacation planning information about New Orleans, Louisiana by means of the global computer network"). In these cases, the examining attorney should refuse registration under §2(e)(1) because the mark is merely descriptive of the services. *See* TMEP §1210.02(d).

1215.07 Disclaimers

Trademark Act §6(a), 15 U.S.C. §1056(a), provides for the disclaimer of "an unregistrable component of a mark otherwise registrable." The guidelines on disclaimer discussed in TMEP §§1213 *et. seq*. apply to domain name mark applications.

If a composite mark includes a domain name composed of unregistrable matter (*e.g.*, a merely descriptive or generic term and a TLD), disclaimer is required.

If a disclaimer is required and the domain name includes a misspelled or telescoped word, the correct spelling must be disclaimed. *See* TMEP §§1213.05(a)(i) and 1213.08(c).

A compound term composed of arbitrary or suggestive matter combined with a "dot" and a TLD is considered unitary, and therefore no disclaimer of the TLD is

《商标法》§2(e)(2),15 U.S.C.§1052(e)(2)所规定的主要属地理性描述的商标,也可能是《商标法》§2(e)(3),15 U.S.C.§1052(e)(3)所规定的主要属地理欺骗性错误描述的商标,也可能是 15 U.S.C.§1052(a)所规定的欺骗性商标,和(或)《商标法》§2(e)(1),15 U.S.C.§1052(e)(1)所规定的仅具描述性或是欺骗性错误描述的商标。

如果地理词语被用作是因特网上所提供的服务的商标,有时该地理词语说明的是该服务的内容而不是其原产地。这一情形通常发生在商标所含的地理词语是对信息服务的内容进行描述时(例如,使用 NEW ORLEANS.COM 作为是"通过全球电脑网络提供关于 New Orleans, Louisiana 的度假计划信息")。在这种情况下,审查员应当依据 §2(e)(1)拒绝予以注册,因为该商标仅仅是对服务的描述。*参见* TMEP §1210.02(d)。

1215.07　　撤回

《商标法》§6(a), 15 U.S.C.§1056(a)规定了撤回"商标中不能注册的组成部分,方可注册"。TMEP §§1213 及以下所讨论的撤回的指导原则,也适用于域名商标申请。

如果包含域名的复合商标同时包含了不可注册的内容(例如,同时包含了一项仅具描述性的或一般性的词语和一个 TLD),则必须要求撤回。

如果被要求撤回,而该域名中还有错误拼写或者有嵌入词,则所撤回的应该是该词的正确拼写形式。*参见* TMEP §§1213.05(a)(i)和 1213.08(c)。

一个由任意性、暗示性内容和一个"点"以及一个TLD所构成的复合词被认为

required. *See* examples below and TMEP §§1213. 05 *et seq*. regarding unitary marks.

Mark	*Disclaimer*
ABC BANK. COM	BANK. COM
ABC FEDERALBANK. COM	FEDERAL BANK. COM
ABC GROCERI STOR. COM	GROCERY STORE. COM
ABC. COM	no disclaimer
ABC. BANK. COM	no disclaimer
ABCBANK. COM	no disclaimer

1215. 08 Material Alteration

Amendments may not be made to the drawing of the mark if the character of the mark is materially altered. 37 C. F. R. §2. 72. In determining whether an amendment is a material alteration, the controlling question is always whether the new and old forms of the mark create essentially the same commercial impression. *See* TMEP §807.14(a).

1215. 08(a) Adding or Deleting TLDs in Domain Name Marks

Generally, an applicant may add or delete a TLD to/from the drawing of a domain name mark (*e. g.*, COOPER amended to COPPER. COM, or COOPER. COM amended to COOPER) without materially altering the mark. A mark that includes a TLD will be perceived by the public as a domain name, while a mark without a TLD will not. However, the public recognizes that a TLD is a universally used part of an Internet address. As a result, the essence of a domain name mark is created by the second level domain name, not the TLD. The commercial

是单一的，因而无须撤回该 TLD。参*见* 以下示例和 TMEP §§1213.05 及以下，了解有关单一商标的内容。

商标	*撤回*
ABC BANK.COM	BANK.COM
ABC FEDERALBANK.COM	FEDERAL BANK.COM
ABC GROCERI STOR.COM	GROCERY STORE.COM
ABC.COM	无须撤回
ABC.BANK.COM	无须撤回
ABCBANK.COM	无须撤回

1215.08 实质性变动

如果会对商标的特征性内容产生实质性的变动，则不能对商标附图进行修正。37 C.F.R.§2.72。在判定某一修改是否构成实质性变动时，决定性的问题往往是，商标的新旧两种形式事实上是否能给人以相同的商业印象。参*见* TMEP §807.14(a)。

1215.08(a) 在域名商标中增删 TLD

通常，如果不会导致商标发生实质变动，申请者可以在域名商标的附图上增删 TLD(例如，将 COOPER 修改为 COOPER.COM，或者将 COOPER.COM 修改为 COOPER)。包含了 TLD 的商标，将会被公众认为是一个域名，而没有 TLD 的商标则不会出现这样的情况。不过，公众能够认识到 TLD 通常是作为因特网地址的一部分。所以，一项域名商标的核心部分取决于其二级域名，而非TLD。无论商标

impression created by the second-level domain name usually remains the same whether the TLD is present or not.

Example: Amending a mark from PETER to PETER.COM would *not* materially change the mark because the essence of both marks is still PETER, a person's name.

Similarly, substituting one TLD for another in a domain name mark, or adding or deleting a "dot" or "http://www." or "www." to a domain name mark is generally permitted.

Example: Amending a mark from ABC.ORG to ABC.COM would *not* materially change the mark because the essence of both marks is still ABC.

1215.08(b) Adding or Deleting TLDs in Other Marks

If a mark that is not used as an Internet domain name includes a TLD, adding or deleting the TLD may be a material alteration.

Example: Deleting the term.COM from the mark ".COM ¤" used on sports magazines would materially change the mark.

1215.09 Likelihood of Confusion

When analyzing whether a domain name mark is likely to cause confusion with another pending or registered mark, the examining attorney must consider the marks as a whole, but generally should accord little weight to the TLD portion of the mark. *See* TMEP §1207.01(b)(iii).

1215.10 Marks Containing the Phonetic Equivalent of a Top-Level Domain

Marks that contain the phonetic equivalent of a TLD (*e.g.*, ABC DOTCOM) are treated in the same manner as marks composed of a TLD. If a disclaimer is neces-

中有无 TLD,该域名商标的二级域名所给人的商业印象都是一样的。

例如:将 PETER 这一商标修改为 PETER. COM 没有对该商标作出实质性修改,因为二者核心部分仍是 PETER——一个人名。

相似地,在域名商标中更换 TLD,或者增删"点"、"http://www."、"www.",一般来说也是允许的。

例如:将 ABC. ORG 这一商标修改为 ABC. COM 并没有对该商标作出实质性修改,因为二者核心部分仍是 ABC。

1215.08(b)　在其他商标中增删 TLD

如果某一商标中虽然有 TLD,但该商标并不是因特网地址,对该 TLD 作出增删可能就构成实质性变动。

例如:将用于某体育杂志". COM¤"这一商标中的 . COM 删掉,将会实质性地改变这一商标。

1215.09　混淆可能性

在分析某一域名商标是否可能与其他未决或已注册的商标相混淆时,审查员应当从该商标的整体上加以考虑,不过通常对于该商标的 TLD 部分,不应视之过重。*参见* TMEP §1207.01(b)(iii)。

1215.10　含有顶级域名同音词的商标

如果商标含有顶级域名的同音词(例如,ABC DOTCOM),则应与其他的含有顶

sary, the disclaimer must be in the form of the TLD and not the phonetic equivalent. *See* TMEP §1213.08(c) regarding disclaimer of misspelled words.

> *Example*: The mark is INEXPENSIVE RESTAURANTS DOT COM for providing information about restaurants by means of a global computer network. Registration should be refused because the mark is merely descriptive of the services under 15 U.S.C. §1052(e)(1).

> *Example*: The mark is ABC DOTCOM. The applicant must disclaim the TLD ".COM" rather than the phonetic equivalent "DOTCOM."

1216 Effect of Applicant's Prior Registrations

1216.01 Decisions Involving Prior Registrations Not Controlling

Trademark rights are not static, and eligibility for registration must be determined on the basis of the facts and evidence of record that exist at the time registration is sought. *In re Morton-Norwich Products, Inc.*, 671 F.2d 1332, 213 USPQ 9, 18 (C.C.P.A. 1982); *In re Thunderbird Products Corp.*, 406 F.2d 1389, 160 USPQ 730 (C.C.P.A. 1969); *In re Sun Microsystems Inc.*, 59 USPQ2d 1084 (TTAB 2001); *In re Styleclick.com Inc.*, 58 USPQ2d 1523 (TTAB 2001); *In re Styleclick.com Inc.*, 57 USPQ2d 1445 (TTAB 2000).

Each case must be decided on its own facts. The Office is not bound by the decisions of the examiners who examined the applications for the applicant's previously registered marks, based on different records. *See In re Merrill Lynch, Pierce, Fenner & Smith Inc.*, 828 F.2d 1567, 4 USPQ2d 1141 (Fed. Cir. 1987) (incontestable registration of CASH MANAGEMENT ACCOUNT for credit card services did not automatically entitle applicant to registration of the same mark for broader financial services); *In re Loew's Theatres, Inc.*, 769 F.2d 764, 226 USPQ 865 (Fed. Cir. 1985) (examining attorney could properly refuse registration on ground that mark DURANGO for chewing tobacco is primarily geographically deceptive-

级域名的商标一样对待。如果必须撤回，撤回的内容必须是该顶级域名而不是其同音词。有关撤回错误拼写的规定，*参见* TMEP §1213.08(c)。

例如：INEXPENSIVE RESTAURANTS DOT COM 是某一通过全球电脑网络提供餐饮信息服务的商标。该商标的注册申请应被拒绝，因为根据 15 U.S.C.§1052(e)(1)的规定，该商标仅是对于该服务的描述。

例如：商标是 ABC DOTCOM。申请者所撤回的应该是".COM"这一顶级域名，而不是同音词"DOTCOM"。

1216 申请者拥有的在先注册的效力

1216.01 涉及在先注册的裁决不具决定性

商标权并不是静态的，是否能够注册应当根据申请注册当时的事实和档案记录决定。相关判例：*Morton-Norwich Products, Inc.*, 671 F.2d 1332, 213 USPQ 9, 18 (C.C.P.A.1982)；*Thunderbird Products Corp.*, 406 F.2d 1389, 160 USPQ 730 (C.C.P.A.1969)；*Sun Microsystems Inc.*, 59 USPQ2d 1084 (TTAB 2001)；*Styleclick.com Inc.*, 58 USPQ2d 1523 (TTAB 2001)；*In re Styleclick.com Inc.*, 57 USPQ2d 1445 (TTAB 2000)。

每个案件都必须根据其自身的情况进行裁决。基于不同的档案，商标局不受审查员对先前注册的商标所作裁决的拘束。*参见 Merrill Lynch, Pierce, Fenner & Smith Inc.*, 828 F.2d 1567, 4 USPQ2d 1141 (Fed. Cir. 1987)（作为信用卡服务的 CASH MANAGEMENT ACCOUNT 这一注册商标虽然不容置疑，但是该商标并不能自动使该申请者获得将同一商标申请注册为更广泛的金融服务商标的权利）；*Loew's Theatres, Inc.*, 769 F.2d 764, 226 USPQ 865 (Fed. Cir. 1985)（由于用作咀嚼烟草商标的DURANGO主要属地理欺骗性错误描述商标，审查员拒绝该注册

ly misdescriptive, even though applicant owned incontestable registration of same mark for cigars); *In re Best Software Inc.*, 58 USPQ2d 1314 (TTAB 2001) (applicant's ownership of registration for the mark BEST! did not preclude the examining attorney from requiring a disclaimer of "Best" in applications seeking registration of BEST! SUPPORT PLUS and BEST! SUPPORT PLUS PREMIER for the same services plus additional services); *In re Sunmarks Inc.*, 32 USPQ2d 1470 (TTAB 1994) (examining attorney not precluded from refusing registration of ULTRA for "gasoline, motor oil, automotive grease, general purpose grease, machine grease and gear oil," even though applicant owned registrations of same mark for "motor oil" and "gasoline for use as automotive fuel, sold only in applicant's automotive service stations"); *In re Medical Disposables Co.*, 25 USPQ2d 1801 (TTAB 1992) (disclaimer of the unitary term "MEDICAL DISPOSABLES" required, notwithstanding applicant's ownership of a prior registration in which a piecemeal disclaimer of the words "MEDICAL" and "DISPOSABLES" was permitted); *In re Perez*, 21 USPQ2d 1075 (TTAB 1991) (likelihood of confusion found between applicant's EL GALLO for fresh tomatoes and peppers and the previously registered mark ROOSTER for fresh citrus fruit, notwithstanding applicant's ownership of an expired registration of the same mark for the same goods); *In re Lean Line, Inc.*, 229 USPQ 781 (TTAB 1986) (LEAN found merely descriptive of low-calorie foods, even though applicant had registered the term for other goods and services and a third party had registered the term "LEAN CUISINE" with no disclaimer); *In re McDonald's Corp.*, 229 USPQ 555 (TTAB 1985) (Board not bound to allow registration of APPLE PIE TREE for restaurant services merely because applicant had succeeded in registering the character and name as trademarks and the character as a service mark); *In re Harcourt Brace Jovanovich, Inc.*, 222 USPQ 820 (TTAB 1984) (LAW & BUSINESS incapable of distinguishing the services of arranging and conducting seminars in the field of business law, notwithstanding applicant's ownership of a registration on the Supplemental Register for the same mark for books, pamphlets and monographs); *In re Local Trademarks, Inc.*, 220 USPQ 728 (TTAB 1983) (refusal of registration on the ground that WHEN IT'S TIME TO ACT did not identify advertising ser-

是适当的，即使申请者对于同样的已经注册为烟草的商标拥有不容置疑的权利。）；*Best Software Inc.*，58 USPQ2d 1314（TTAB 2001）（申请者对于注册商标"BEST!"拥有所有权，但是在申请将"BEST! SUPPORT PLUS"和"BEST! SUPPORT PLUS PREMIER"注册为相同的服务以及附加升级服务的商标时，并不能避免审查员撤回"BEST"的要求）；*Sunmarks Inc.*，32 USPQ2d 1470（TTAB 1994）（即使申请者已经取得了用于"发动机机油"以及"仅于申请者的汽车服务站方有售的汽车燃料汽油"的同一商标注册，也不能排除审查员可以拒绝将 ULTRA 注册为"汽油、发动机机油、汽车润滑油、一般用途的润滑油、机械润滑油和齿轮油"的商标）；*Medical Disposables Co.*，25 USPQ2d 1801（TTAB 1992）（单一词语"MEDICAL DISPOSABLES"应当撤回，即使申请者所拥有的在先注册中被允许分别撤回"MEDICAL"和"DISPOSABLES"）；*Perez*，21 USPQ2d 1075（TTAB 1991）（申请者所使用的新鲜西红柿和辣椒的商标"EL GALLO"与先前注册为新鲜柑橘商标的"ROOSTER"存在混淆可能性，即使申请者在同样的商品上曾经注册了同样的商标，该商标只是已失效而已）；*Lean Line, Inc.*，229 USPQ 781（TTAB 1986）（"LEAN"这一词被认为只是对低卡路里食品的描述，即使申请者已将该词注册为其他商品、服务的商标，并且也有他人将"LEAN CUISINE"注册为商标且无须撤回）；*McDonald's Corp.*，229 USPQ 555（TTAB 1985）（委员会不能仅仅因为申请者已经将"APPLE PIE TREE"的图案和名称注册为其产品的商标、将图案注册为其服务的商标，就可以允许将"APPLE PIE TREE"注册为餐饮服务的商标）；*Harcourt Brace Jovanovich, Inc.*，222 USPQ 820（TTAB 1984）（LAW & BUSINESS 这一词并不能明确区分组织安排商法研讨会的服务，即使同一商标已注册为书籍、小册子和专著的商标，且申请者对该注册商标拥有所有权）；*Local Trademarks, Inc.*，220 USPQ 728（TTAB 1983）（申请注册"WHEN IT'S TIME TO ACT"，因其不能表明其识别的是广告服务而遭到拒绝，这

vices upheld; Board not bound to allow registration simply because applicant owned registrations bearing similar recitations of services); *In re Pilon*, 195 USPQ 178 (TTAB 1977) (title of chapter or section of book not registrable, even though applicant owned prior registrations of marks comprising chapter titles). *See also In re Wilson*, 57 USPQ2d 1863 (TTAB 2001) ("Reasoned decisionmaking" doctrine, which prohibits a federal agency from creating conflicting lines of precedent governing identical situations, did not entitle applicant to registration of PINE CONE BRAND for packaged fresh citrus fruit, even though Office issued registration for similar PINE CONE mark in 1933 despite then-existing registration for PINE CONE mark that was cited against applicant).

1216.02 Effect of "Incontestability" in *Ex Parte* Examination [R-2]

Section 15 of the Trademark Act, 15 U.S.C. §1065, provides a procedure by which a registrant's exclusive right to use a mark in commerce on or in connection with the goods or services covered by the registration can become incontestable. *See* TMEP §§1605 *et seq*. for information about the requirements for filing an affidavit of incontestability under §15.

In *Park 'N Fly v. Dollar Park & Fly, Inc.*, 469 U.S. 189, 224 USPQ 327 (1985), the Supreme Court held that the owner of a registered mark may rely on incontestability to enjoin infringement, and that an incontestable registration therefore cannot be challenged on the ground that the mark is merely descriptive.

In *In re American Sail Training Association*, 230 USPQ 879 (TTAB 1986), the Trademark Trial and Appeal Board held that an examining attorney could not require a disclaimer of "TALL SHIPS" in an application for registration of the mark RETURN OF THE TALL SHIPS, where the applicant owned an incontestable registration for the mark TALL SHIPS for the identical services. This would be a collateral attack on an incontestable registration. However, this applies only where both the marks and the goods or services are identical. In *American Sail Training*, the Board noted that the matter required to be disclaimed was "identical

一决定得到了维持，委员会不能仅仅因为申请者曾经在其他服务上以相似的问句形式获得了注册，就必须允许这一注册申请）；*Pilon*，195 USPQ 178（TTAB 1977）（书籍的章节名称不能注册，即使申请者拥有的在先注册的商标也含有书籍的章名）。另参见 *Wilson*，57 USPQ2d 1863（TTAB 2001）（“合理作出裁决”理论禁止联邦部门在处理相同的情况时创设相互冲突的不同先例，但是这一原则并不能使申请者获得将“PINE CONE BRAND”注册为封装新鲜柑橘商标的权利，尽管商标局在 1933 年曾不顾有人引用已注册的“PINE CONE”提出异议，而将相似的“PINE CONE”注册为商标）。

1216.02　部分审查中“不容置疑性”的效力[R-2]

《商标法》第 15 节，15 U.S.C.§1065 规定了一项程序，根据该程序，商标用于注册范围内的相关商品或服务时，商标注册人在商业活动中对注册商标拥有不容置疑的专属使用权。关于根据 §15 的规定，要求提交不容置疑性宣誓书的情况，*参见* TMEP §§1605 及以下。

在 *Park 'N Fly v. Dollar Park & Fly, Inc.*，469 U.S. 189，224 USPQ 327（1985）一案中，最高法院认为一项注册商标的所有权人可以依据其不容置疑性而要求禁止侵害，因而一项不容置疑的注册不能基于商标仅具描述性而受到质疑。

在 *American Sail Training Association*，230 USPQ 879（TTAB 1986）一案中，商标评审及上诉委员会认为，在申请注册“RETURN OF THE TALL SHIPS”时，审查员不能要求撤回“TALL SHIPS”，因为申请者在相同的服务上拥有对“TALL SHIPS”不容置疑的注册商标权。如此将构成对于不容置疑注册的间接攻击。不过，这仅适用于商标及商品、服务都相同的情况。在 *American Sail Training* 案中，委员会称，要求撤回的内容“与申请者的不容置疑注册的内容相同”，并且“申请者的申请

to the subject matter of applicant's incontestable registration," and that "the services described in applicant's application are identical to those recited in the prior incontestable registration."230 USPQ at 880.

Ownership of an incontestable registration does *not* give the applicant a right to register the same mark for different goods or services, even if they are closely related to the goods or services in the incontestable registration. *See In re Save Venice New York Inc*., 259 F.3d 1346, 59 USPQ2d 1778, 1782 (Fed. Cir. 2001) (applicant's ownership of incontestable registration of the word mark SAVE VENICE for newsletters, brochures and fundraising services did not preclude examining attorney from refusing registration of a composite mark consisting of the phrases THE VENICE COLLECTION and SAVE VENICE INC. with an image of the winged Lion of St. Mark for different goods; "[a] registered mark is incontestable only in the form registered and for the goods or services claimed."); *In re Merrill Lynch, Pierce, Fenner & Smith Inc*., 828 F.2d 1567, 4 USPQ2d 1141 (Fed. Cir. 1987)(incontestable registration of CASH MANAGEMENT ACCOUNT for credit card services did not automatically entitle applicant to registration of the same mark for broader financial services); *In re Bose Corp*., 772 F.2d 866, 227 USPQ 1, 7 n.5 (Fed. Cir. 1985) (incontestable status of registration for one speaker design did not establish non-functionality of another speaker design with shared feature); *In re Loew's Theatres, Inc*., 769 F.2d 764, 226 USPQ 865 (Fed. Cir. 1985) (examining attorney could properly refuse registration on ground that mark DURANGO for chewing tobacco is primarily geographically deceptively misdescriptive, even though applicant owned incontestable registration of same mark for cigars); *In re Best Software Inc*., 63 USPQ2d 1109, 1113 (TTAB 2002) (applicant's ownership of incontestable registration for the mark BEST! did not preclude the examining attorney from requiring a disclaimer of "BEST" in applications seeking registration of BEST! IMPERATIV HRMS "for goods which, although similar, are nevertheless somewhat different"); *In re Best Software Inc*., 58 USPQ2d 1314 (TTAB 2001) (applicant's ownership of incontestable registration for the mark BEST ! did not preclude the examining attorney from requiring a disclaimer of

中所述之服务与不容置疑的在先注册所引述的服务相同”。230 USPQ at 880。

拥有一项不容置疑的注册，并不意味着申请者就有权将相同的商标注册为其他商品或服务的商标，即使该商品或服务与不容置疑注册中所涉的存在密切联系。参见 *Save Venice New York Inc.*，259 F.3d 1346，59 USPQ2d 1778，1782（Fed. Cir. 2001）（申请者对于用于时事通讯、宣传册和资金筹集服务的文字商标“SAVE VENICE”享有不容置疑的注册权利，但是这并不影响审查员可以拒绝将包含“THE VENICE COLLECTION”、“SAVE VENICE INC.”和圣马可双翼飞狮图案的复合商标注册为其他商品的商标；“一项注册商标只有用于注册的样式和注册者所声明的商品或服务上才是不容置疑的”）；*Merrill Lynch, Pierce, Fenner & Smith Inc.*，828 F.2d 1567，4 USPQ2d 1141（Fed. Cir. 1987）（尽管“CASH MANAGEMENT ACCOUNT”是一项信用卡服务不容置疑的注册商标，但是该商标并不自动使申请者获得在更广泛的金融服务上注册相同商标的权利）；*Bose Corp.*，772 F.2d 866，227 USPQ 1，7 n.5（Fed. Cir. 1985）（某一扬声器设计的注册，其不容置疑性并不能使得其他具有相同特性的扬声器设计失去功能性）；*Loew's Theatres, Inc.*，769 F.2d 764，226 USPQ 865（Fed. Cir. 1985）（由于用作咀嚼烟草商标的 DURANGO 主要属地理欺骗性错误描述商标，审查员拒绝该注册是适当的，即使申请者对于同样的已经注册为烟草的商标拥有不容置疑的权利）；*Best Software Inc.*，63 USPQ2d 1109，1113（TTAB 2002）（申请者对于不容置疑注册商标“BEST!”拥有所有权，但是并不能排除审查员在申请者申请将“BEST! IMPERATIV HRMS”注册为“虽然相似但仍不同的商品”的商标时，要求其撤回“BEST”）；*Best Software Inc.*，58 USPQ2d 1314（TTAB 2001）（申请者对于注册商标“BEST!”拥有所有权，但是并不能排除审查员

"BEST" in applications seeking registration of BEST! SUPPORT PLUS and BEST! SUPPORT PLUS PREMIER for the same services plus additional services); *In re Industrie Pirelli Societa per Azioni*, 9 USPQ2d 1564 (TTAB 1988), *aff'd*, 883 F.2d 1026 (Fed. Cir. 1989) (examining attorney could properly refuse registration on the ground that a mark is primarily merely a surname even if applicant owned incontestable registration of same mark for unrelated goods); *In re BankAmerica Corp.*, 231 USPQ 873 (TTAB 1986) (examining attorney could refuse registration of the mark BANK OF AMERICA for computerized financial data processing services under §§2(e)(1) and 2(e)(2), despite applicant's ownership of incontestable registrations of the same mark for related services).

1217 Res Judicata

A prior adjudication against an applicant, in connection with the same mark, on the basis of the same facts and issues, constitutes a proper ground of refusal as *res judicata*. Prior adjudications include decisions of the Trademark Trial and Appeal Board or any of the reviewing courts. The refusal is appropriate only after the time for further court review has expired and no such review has been sought or, if sought, the review action has been terminated. However, the applicant may not be precluded under the doctrine of *res judicata* from again seeking registration if the facts and circumstances have changed since the adverse decision. *See In re Honeywell Inc.*, 8 USPQ2d 1600 (TTAB 1988); *In re Johanna Farms Inc.*, 8 USPQ2d 1408 (TTAB 1988); *In re Minnetonka, Inc.*, 3 USPQ2d 1711 (TTAB 1987).

When refusing registration on the basis of *res judicata*, the examining attorney also must raise all other issues that are pertinent to the application.

When all matters other than the question of *res judicata* have been attended to, but review action on the prior adjudication is not yet terminated, the examining attorney may suspend action on the application pending termination. *See* TMEP §716.02(d).

要求申请者申请将“BEST! SUPPORT PLUS”和“BEST! SUPPORT PLUS PREMIER”注册为相同的服务以及附加升级服务的商标时撤回“BEST”); *Industrie Pirelli Societa per Azioni*, 9 USPQ2d 1564 (TTAB 1988), *aff'd*, 883 F.2d 1026 (Fed. Cir.1989)(审查员可以以商标主要属于姓氏而正确地拒绝其注册,即使申请者在其他不相关的商品上就相同的商标拥有不容置疑的注册); *BankAmerica Corp.*, 231 USPQ 873 (TTAB 1986)(审查员可以根据 §§2(e)(1)和 2(e)(2)的规定,拒绝将“BANK OF AMERICA”注册为电脑化金融数据处理服务的商标,尽管申请者对在其他相关的商品上就相同的商标拥有不容置疑的注册)。

1217 定案

如果关于同一商标,先前曾经以同样的事实和理由作出过对申请者不利的裁判,那么就构成了以“定案”为理由拒绝予以注册的正当理由。先前的裁判包括商标评审及上诉委员会,或任何上诉法院的判决。只有在法庭复审期届满,以及未提出复审要求,或提出了复审要求但该程序已终止的情况下,才可以以此为理由拒绝予以注册。不过,如果该不利裁决作出之后事实和环境发生了变化,则不能根据定案原则禁止申请者再行申请。*参见 Honeywell Inc.*, 8 USPQ2d 1600 (TTAB 1988); *Johanna Farms Inc.*, 8 USPQ2d 1408 (TTAB 1988); *Minnetonka, Inc.*, 3 USPQ2d 1711 (TTAB 1987)。

以定案为理由拒绝予以注册时,审查员必须同时举出有关该申请的所有其他问题。

如果除了定案问题以外,其他所有事项均已经过审查,但对于先前裁决的复审程序尚未终结,则审查员可以中止申请程序,等待复审终结。*参见* TMEP §716.02(d)。

Chapter 1300
Examination of Different Types of Marks

The Trademark Act of 1946 provides for registration of trademarks, service marks, collective trademarks and service marks, collective membership marks and certification marks. 15 U.S.C. §§1051, 1053, and 1054. The language of this Manual is generally directed to trademarks. Procedures for trademarks usually apply to other types of marks, unless otherwise stated. This chapter is devoted to special circumstances relating to service marks, collective marks, collective membership marks, and certification marks.

1301 Service Marks

Section 45 of the Trademark Act, 15 U. S. C. §1127, defines "service mark" as follows:

> The term "service mark" means any word, name, symbol, or device, or any combination thereof—
>
> (1) used by a person, or
>
> (2) which a person has a bona fide intention to use in commerce and applies to register on the principal register established by this Act,
>
> to identify and distinguish the services of one person, including a unique service, from the services of others and to indicate the source of the services, even if that source is unknown. Titles, character names, and other distinctive features of radio or television programs may be registered as service marks notwithstanding that they, or the programs, may advertise the goods of the sponsor.

Therefore, to be registrable as a service mark, the asserted mark must function

第 1300 章
不同类型的商标审查

《1946 年商标法》对商标、服务商标、集体商标与服务商标、集体成员商标以及证明商标的注册作了规定。15 U.S.C.§§1051,1053 及 1054。本手册内容一般针对商标而言。商标所用的程序通常也适用于其他类型的商标，除非另有规定。本章专门讨论有关服务商标、集体商标、集体成员商标以及证明商标的特别情况。

1301　　服务商标

《商标法》第 45 节，15 U.S.C.§1127，对“服务商标”作如下定义：

> “服务商标”一词是指任何文字、名称、符号或图案，或以上的任何组合，它——
>
> (1) 为某人所使用，或
>
> (2) 某人真实地计划将其用于商业用途，并向注册机构申请，在依据商标法设立的联邦商标登记簿上注册，
>
> 用以识别某人的服务（包括独特的服务），与他人的服务区分开来，并表明服务来源——即使来源未知。广播电视节目的名称、人物名，以及其他独特的特征，都可以注册为服务商标，尽管这些节目可能为赞助商的商品做广告宣传。

因此，要注册为服务商标，相关商标必须具有*识别*服务并与他人的服务*区分*开来

both to *identify and distinguish* the services recited in the application from the services of others and to *indicate the source of* the recited services, even if that source is unknown. The activities recited in the identification must constitute services as contemplated by the Trademark Act. *See* TMEP §§1301.01 *et seq*.

If a proposed mark does not function as a service mark for the services recited or if the applicant is not rendering a registrable service, the statutory basis for refusal of registration on the Principal Register is §§1, 3 and 45 of the Trademark Act, 15 U.S.C. §§1051, 1053 and 1127.

See TMEP §1303 concerning collective service marks.

1301.01 What Is a Service

A service mark can only be registered for activities that constitute services as contemplated by the Trademark Act. 15 U.S.C. §§1051, 1053 and 1127. The Trademark Act defines the term "service mark," but it does not define what constitutes a service. Many activities are obviously services (*e.g.*, dry cleaning, banking, shoe repairing, transportation, and house painting).

1301.01(a) Criteria for Determining What Constitutes a Service

The following criteria have evolved for determining what constitutes a service: (1) a service must be a real activity; (2) a service must be performed to the order of, or for the benefit of, someone other than the applicant; and (3) the activity performed must be qualitatively different from anything necessarily done in connection with the sale of the applicant's goods or the performance of another service. *In re Canadian Pacific Limited*, 754 F.2d 992, 224 USPQ 971 (Fed. Cir. 1985); *In re Betz Paperchem, Inc.*, 222 USPQ 89 (TTAB 1984); *In re Integrated Resources, Inc.*, 218 USPQ 829 (TTAB 1983); *In re Landmark Communications, Inc.*, 204 USPQ 692 (TTAB 1979). These criteria are explained more fully below.

的功能，而且要指出服务的来源，即使来源未知。此种识别行为必须构成符合《商标法》规定的服务。*参见* TMEP §§1301.01 及以下。

如果申请注册的商标没有作为相关服务的商标使用，或申请者未提供可注册的服务，则根据《商标法》§§1，3 及 45，15 U.S.C. §§1051，1053 及 1127 的规定，可拒绝其在联邦商标登记簿上注册。

参见 TMEP §1303，查阅有关集体服务商标的信息。

1301.01　什么是服务

能够构成《商标法》规定的服务的行为，方可为其注册服务商标。15 U.S.C. §§1051，1053 及 1127。《商标法》对"服务商标"作了定义，但未说明什么行为能够构成一项服务。许多行为明显是服务（比如，干洗、银行服务、修鞋、运输以及房屋油漆）。

1301.01(a)　判断构成服务的标准

以下标准用于判断什么行为构成服务：(1)服务必须是真实的行为；(2)服务必须是根据申请者以外的其他人的要求或者为其他人的利益而实施的；以及(3)实施的行为必须与申请者销售商品或实施另一项服务所必需的任何行为有本质的区别。相关判例：*Canadian Pacific Limited*，754 F.2d 992，224 USPQ 971（Fed. Cir. 1985）；*Betz Paperchem*，*Inc*.，222 USPQ 89（TTAB 1984）；*Integrated Resources*，*Inc*.，218 USPQ 829（TTAB 1983）；*Landmark Communications*，*Inc*.，204 USPQ 692（TTAB 1979）。以下详细解释这些判断标准。

1301.01(a)(i) Performance of a Real Activity

A service must be a real activity. A mere idea or concept, *e.g.*, an idea for an accounting organizational format or a recipe for a baked item, is not a service. Similarly, a system, process or method is not a service. *In re Universal Oil Products Co.*, 476 F.2d 653, 177 USPQ 456 (C.C.P.A. 1973); *In re Citibank, N.A.*, 225 USPQ 612 (TTAB 1985); *In re Scientific Methods, Inc.*, 201 USPQ 917 (TTAB 1979); *In re McCormick & Company, Inc.*, 179 USPQ 317 (TTAB 1973). *See* TMEP §1301.02(e) regarding marks that identify a system or process.

The commercial context must be considered in determining whether a real service is being performed. For example, at one time the activities of grocery stores, department stores, and similar retail stores were not considered to be services. However, it is now recognized that gathering various products together, making a place available for purchasers to select goods, and providing any other necessary means for consummating purchases constitutes the performance of a service.

1301.01(a)(ii) For the Benefit of Others

To be a service, an activity must be primarily for the benefit of someone other than the applicant. While an advertising agency provides a service when it promotes the goods or services of its clients, a company that promotes the sale of its own goods or services is doing so for its own benefit rather than rendering a service for others. *In re Reichhold Chemicals, Inc.*, 167 USPQ 376 (TTAB 1970). *See* TMEP §1301.01(b)(i). Similarly, a company that sets up a personnel department to employ workers for itself is merely facilitating the conduct of its own business, while a company whose business is to recruit and place workers for other companies is performing employment agency services.

The controlling question is who *primarily* benefits from the activity for which registration is sought. If the activity is done primarily for the benefit of others,

1301.01(a)(i)　实施真实的行为

服务必须是真实的行为。如仅仅是一种创意或想法，比如：一项关于会计组织形式或糕饼配方的创意，就不是服务。类似地，体系、工序或方法也不是服务。相关判例：*Universal Oil Products Co.*, 476 F.2d 653, 177 USPQ 456（C.C.P.A. 1973）；*Citibank, N.A.*, 225 USPQ 612（TTAB 1985）；*Scientific Methods, Inc.*, 201 USPQ 917（TTAB 1979）；*McCormick & Company, Inc.*, 179 USPQ 317（TTAB 1973）。*参见* TMEP §1301.02(e)，查阅有关识别体系或工序的商标的内容。

在判断是否提供了真实的服务时，必须考虑其商业背景。例如，在某一个时期，杂货店、百货商店以及类似的零售商店的行为被认为不是服务。不过现在，将各种产品汇集一处，为买方选择商品提供场所，并为完成交易提供其他必要手段的行为，被认为是构成服务。

1301.01(a)(ii)　为他人的利益

一种行为必须主要是为申请者以外的他人的利益所为，方能构成一项服务。广告代理商为客户推销商品或服务是提供服务，而公司为推销自己的商品或服务，则属于为自己的利益而非为他人提供服务。相关判例：*Reichhold Chemicals, Inc.*, 167 USPQ 376（TTAB 1970）。*参见* TMEP §1301.01(b)(i)。类似地，某公司设立人事部门为自己雇用工人只是为了促进自身业务的开展，而某公司的业务是为其他公司招募和安排工人就业，则是提供职业介绍的服务。

问题的关键是申请注册的行为的*主要*受益者是谁？如果主要是为他人的利益而为，

the fact that applicant derives an incidental benefit is not fatal. *In re Venture Lending Associates*, 226 USPQ 285 (TTAB 1985). On the other hand, if the activity primarily benefits applicant, it is not a registrable service even if others derive an incidental benefit. *In re Dr. Pepper Co.*, 836 F.2d 508, 5 USPQ2d 1207 (Fed. Cir. 1987) (contest promoting applicant's goods not a service, even though benefits accrue to winners of contest); *In re Alaska Northwest Publishing Co.*, 212 USPQ 316 (TTAB 1981).

Collecting information for the purpose of publishing one's own periodical is not a service, because it is done primarily for applicant's benefit rather than for the benefit of others. *See* TMEP §1301.01(b)(iii).

Offering shares of one's own stock for investment is not a service, because these are routine corporate activities that primarily benefit the applicant. *See* TMEP §1301.01(b)(iv). On the other hand, offering a retirement income plan to applicant's employees was found to be a service, because it primarily benefits the employees. *American International Reinsurance Co., Inc. v. Airco, Inc.*, 570 F.2d 941, 197 USPQ 69 (C.C.P.A. 1978), *cert. denied* 439 U.S. 866, 200 USPQ 64 (1978).

Licensing intangible property has been recognized as a separate service, analogous to leasing or renting tangible property, that primarily benefits the licensee. *In re Universal Press Syndicate*, 229 USPQ 638 (TTAB 1986).

1301.01(a)(iii) Sufficiently Distinct from Activities Involved in Sale of Goods or Performance of Other Services

In determining whether an activity is sufficiently separate from an applicant's principal activity to constitute a service, the examining attorney should first ascertain what is the applicant's principal activity under the mark in question (*i.e.*, the sale of a service or the sale of a tangible product). The examining attorney then determines whether the activity identified in the application is in any mater-

那么商标申请者从中附带受益就并不重要了。相关判例：*Venture Lending Associates*，226 USPQ 285（TTAB 1985）。另一方面，如果行为的主要受益者是商标的申请者，即使他人亦从中附带受益，也不是一项可注册的服务。相关判例：*Dr. Pepper Co.*，836 F.2d 508，5 USPQ2d 1207（Fed. Cir. 1987）（以比赛的方式推销申请者的商品不是服务，即使比赛的优胜者从中受益）；*Alaska Northwest Publishing Co.*，212 USPQ 316（TTAB 1981）。

为出版自己的杂志而收集信息的行为不是服务，因为这主要是为申请者而非为他人之利益所为。*参见* TMEP §1301.01(b)(iii)。

向他人提供自己的股票作投资不属于服务，因为这属于主要使申请者受益的常规公司行为。*参见* TMEP §1301.01(b)(iv)。另一方面，向申请者的雇员提供退休收入计划被认为是服务，因为主要受益者是雇员。相关判例：*American International Reinsurance Co., Inc. v. Airco, Inc.*，570 F.2d 941，197 USPQ 69（C.C.P.A. 1978），*cert. denied* 439 U.S.866，200 USPQ 64（1978）。

无形财产的许可被认为是一个单独的服务，有形财产的租赁亦同，因为主要是被许可人获益。相关判例：*Universal Press Syndicate*，229 USPQ 638（TTAB 1986）。

1301.01(a)(iii)　与涉及销售商品或实施其他服务的行为有充分的区别

在判断一种行为与申请者的主要行为是否有充分的区别，并构成服务时，审查员应当首先确认申请者在相关商标下的主要行为是什么（也就是说，出售服务还是出售有形产品）。然后，审查员要判断：申请中确认的行为与该特定产品或服务的其他供

ial way a different kind of economic activity than what any provider of that particular product or service normally provides. *In re Landmark Communications, Inc.*, 204 USPQ 692, 695 (TTAB 1979).

For example, operating a grocery store is clearly a service. Bagging groceries for customers is not considered a separately registrable service, because this activity is normally provided to and expected by grocery store customers, and is therefore merely ancillary to the primary service.

Providing general information or instructions as to the purpose and uses of applicant's goods is merely incidental to the sale of goods, not a separate consulting service. *See* TMEP §1301.01(b)(v).

Conducting a contest to promote the sale of one's own goods or services is usually not considered a service, because it is an ordinary and routine promotional activity. *See* TMEP §1301.01(b)(i).

While the repair of the goods of others is a recognized service, an applicant's guarantee of repair of its own goods does not normally constitute a separate service because that activity is ancillary to and normally expected in the trade. *See* TMEP §1301.01(b)(ii).

However, the fact that an activity is ancillary to a principal service or to a sale of goods does not in itself mean that it is not a separately registrable service. The statute makes no distinction between primary, incidental or ancillary services. *In re Universal Press Syndicate*, 229 USPQ 638 (TTAB 1986) (licensing cartoon character found to be a separate service that was not merely incidental or necessary to larger business of magazine and newspaper cartoon strip); *In re Betz Paperchem, Inc.*, 222 USPQ 89 (TTAB 1984) (chemical manufacturer's feed, delivery and storage of liquid chemical products held to constitute separate service, because applicant's activities extend beyond routine sale of chemicals); *In re Congoleum Corp.*, 222 USPQ 452 (TTAB 1984) (awarding prizes to retailers for purchasing applicant's goods from distributors held to be sufficiently separate from the sale of

应商通常所提供的经济行为有任何质的区别。相关判例：*Landmark Communications, Inc.*, 204 USPQ 692，695（TTAB 1979）。

例如，经营一个杂货店很明显是一种服务。而为顾客所购货物装袋的行为则不是一种单独的可注册的服务，因为杂货店顾客都期待这种行为，而店方也通常会提供这种服务，因此这只是辅助主要服务的行为。

为申请者商品的用途及使用提供一般信息或说明仅仅是商品销售的辅助行为，而不是单独的咨询服务。*参见* TMEP §1301.01(b)(v)。

通过竞赛促销自己的商品或服务通常不被认为是服务，因为这只是一种普通和日常的促销活动。*参见* TMEP §1301.01(b)(i)。

修理他人的商品被认为是一种服务，但如申请者对自己的商品进行保修，通常不构成一种单独的服务，因为这是一种辅助行为，并且在交易中通常会期待这种行为。*参见* TMEP §1301.01(b)(ii)。

但是，一种行为附属于一项主要服务或商品销售，并不意味着其自身不能构成单独可注册的服务。法律并没有区分主要服务、附带和辅助服务。相关判例：*Universal Press Syndicate*, 229 USPQ 638（TTAB 1986）（许可使用卡通人物被认为是一种单独的服务，而并非仅仅是报纸杂志连环卡通画的扩大业务的附带和必要的行为）；*Betz Paperchem, Inc.*, 222 USPQ 89（TTAB 1984）（化学品制造商供给、输送以及储存液态化学品的行为构成单独的服务，因为申请者的行为已经超出了化学品日常销售的范围。）；*Congoleum Corp.*, 222 USPQ 452（TTAB 1984）（向从批发商处购买申请者商品的零售商进行奖励的行为被认为充分独立于商品销售，从而构成了向

goods to constitute a service rendered to distributors, because it confers a benefit on distributors that is not normally expected by distributors in the relevant industry); *In re C.I.T. Financial Corp.*, 201 USPQ 124 (TTAB 1978) (computerized financial data processing services rendered to applicant's loan customers held to be a registrable service, since it provides benefits that were not previously available, and is separate and distinct from the primary service of making consumer loans); *In re U.S. Home Corp. of Texas*, 199 USPQ 698 (TTAB 1978) (planning and laying out residential communities for others was found to be a service, because it goes above and beyond what the average individual would do in constructing and selling a home on a piece of land that he or she has purchased); *In re John Breuner Co.*, 136 USPQ 94 (TTAB 1963) (credit services provided by a retail store constitute a separate service, since extension of credit is neither mandatory nor required in the operation of a retail establishment).

The fact that the activities are offered only to purchasers of the applicant's primary product or service does not necessarily mean that the activity is not a service. *In re Otis Engineering Corp.*, 217 USPQ 278 (TTAB 1982) (quality control and quality assurance services held to constitute a registrable service even though the services were limited to applicant's own equipment); *In re John Breuner Co.*, *supra* (credit services offered only to customers of applicant's retail store found to be a service).

The fact that the services for which registration is sought are offered to a different class of purchasers than the purchasers of applicant's primary product or service is also a factor to be considered. *In re Forbes Inc.*, 31 USPQ2d 1315 (TTAB 1994); *In re Home Builders Association of Greenville*, 18 USPQ2d 1313 (TTAB 1990).

Another factor to be considered in determining whether an activity is a registrable service is the use of a mark different from the mark used on or in connection with the applicant's principal product or service. *See In re Mitsubishi Motor Sales of America Inc.*, 11 USPQ2d 1312 (TTAB 1989); *In re Universal Press Syndicate*,

批发商提供的服务，因为这种行为给予批发商一种在相关行业中通常不会期待得到的利益)；*C.I.T.Financial Corp.*，201 USPQ 124 (TTAB 1978)(向申请者的消费借贷客户提供财务数据电脑处理服务被认为是一种可注册的服务，因为这提供了一种以前并不存在的利益，并且独立并区别于消费借贷的服务)；*U.S.Home Corp.of Texas*，199 USPQ 698 (TTAB 1978)(为他人规划和设计住宅区布置的行为被认为是一种服务，因为这超出了一般个人在一块土地上建造和出售房屋时所可能实施的行为的范围)；*John Breuner Co.*，136 USPQ 94 (TTAB 1963)(零售商店提供的赊欠服务是单独的服务，因为延期还款既非强制规定，亦非零售企业经营所必需)。

某行为仅提供给申请者的主营产品或服务的购买者并非一定意味着这种行为不构成服务。相关判例：*Otis Engineering Corp.*，217 USPQ 278 (TTAB 1982)(质量控制和质量保证被认为构成了一种可注册的服务，即使此类服务仅限于申请者自己的设备)；*John Breuner Co.*，*见前*(仅向申请者零售店的消费者提供的赊欠服务被认为构成了一种服务)。

对于申请注册的服务，还需要考虑其是否向申请者主要产品或服务的购买者以外的不同购买者群体提供。相关案例：*Forbes Inc.*，31 USPQ2d 1315 (TTAB 1994)；*Home Builders Association of Greenville*，18 USPQ2d 1313 (TTAB 1990)。

判断一种行为是否属于可注册的服务时需要考虑的另一个因素是，是否使用与申请者主要产品或服务所使用的商标不同的商标。相关判例：*Mitsubishi Motor Sales of America Inc.*，11 USPQ2d 1312 (TTAB 1989)；*Universal Press Syndicate*， *supra*; *In re Congoleum Corp.*, *supra*; *In re C. I. T. Financial Corp.*, *supra*. However, an activity that is normally expected or routinely done in connection with sale of a product or another service is not a registrable service even if it is identified by a different mark. *In re Dr. Pepper Co.*, 836 F.2d 508, 5 USPQ2d 1207 (Fed. Cir. 1987); *In re Television Digest, Inc.*, 169 USPQ 505 (TTAB 1971). Moreover, the mark identifying the ancillary service does not have to be different from the mark identifying the applicant's goods or primary service. *Ex parte Handmacher-Vogel, Inc.*, 98 USPQ 413 (Comm'r Pats. 1953).

1301.01(b) Whether Particular Activities Constitute "Services"

1301.01(b)(i) Contests and Promotional Activities

It is well settled that the promotion of one's own goods is not a service. *In re Radio Corp. of America*, 205 F.2d 180, 98 USPQ 157 (C.C.P.A. 1953) (record manufacturer who prepares radio programs primarily designed to advertise and sell records is not rendering service); *In re SCM Corp.*, 209 USPQ 278 (TTAB 1980) (supplying merchandising aids and store displays to retailers does not constitute separate service); *Ex parte Wembley, Inc.*, 111 USPQ 386 (Comm'r Pats. 1956) (national advertising program designed to sell manufacturer's goods to ultimate purchasers is not service to wholesalers and retailers, because national product advertising is normally expected of manufacturers of nationally distributed products, and is done in furtherance of the sale of the advertised products).

However, an activity that goes above and beyond what is normally expected of a manufacturer in the relevant industry may be a registrable service, even if it also serves to promote the applicant's primary product or service. *In re U.S. Tobacco Co.*, 1 USPQ2d 1502 (TTAB 1986) (tobacco company's participating in auto race held to constitute an entertainment service, because participating in an auto race is not an activity that a seller of tobacco normally does); *In re Heavenly Creations, Inc.*, 168 USPQ 317 (TTAB 1971) (applicant's free hairstyling instruction-

见前，*In re Congoleum Corp.*，*见前*；*C.I.T. Financial Corp.*，*见前*。但是，即使使用了不同的商标，一种通常被期待或与产品销售或另一项服务有关的日常行为不是一种可注册的服务。相关判例：*Dr. Pepper Co.*，836 F.2d 508，5 USPQ2d 1207（Fed. Cir. 1987）；*Television Digest*，*Inc.*，169 USPQ 505（TTAB 1971）。此外，识别辅助服务的商标并不一定要有别于识别申请者的商品或主要服务的商标。相关判例：*Handmacher-Vogel*，*Inc.*，98 USPQ 413（Comm'r Pats. 1953）。

1301.01(b)　某特定行为是否构成"服务"

1301.01(b)(i)　竞赛和有奖活动

非常肯定的是，为自己的商品所做的促销活动不是服务。相关判例：*Radio Corp. of America*，205 F.2d 180，98 USPQ 157（C.C.P.A. 1953）（唱片制造商主要为广告和销售唱片而准备的广播节目不属于服务）；*SCM Corp.*，209 USPQ 278（TTAB 1980）（向零售商提供市场拓销和商品陈列不构成独立的服务）；*Wembley*，*Inc.*，111 USPQ 386（Comm'r Pats. 1956）（为向最终购买者销售制造商产品而设计的全国性广告不属于向批发商和零售商提供的服务，因为对于在全国销售的产品通常存在对于全国性产品广告的期待，而且广告的目的是促进广告商品的销售）。

但是，若行为超出了相关行业中通常期待的制造商行为的范围，则可能成为可注册的服务，即使其同时也是为了促销申请者的主要产品或服务。相关判例：*U.S. Tobacco Co.*，1 USPQ2d 1502（TTAB 1986）（烟草公司参与汽车赛被认为构成了一种娱乐服务，因为参与汽车赛并非烟草销售商的通常行为）；*Heavenly Creations*，*Inc.*，168 USPQ 317（TTAB 1971）（申请者的免费发型设计聚会被认为是与其假发

al parties found to be a service separate from the applicant's sale of wigs, because it goes beyond what a seller of wigs would normally do in promoting its goods); *Ex parte Handmacher-Vogel, Inc.*, 98 USPQ 413 (Comm'r Pats. 1953) (clothing manufacturer's conducting women's golf tournaments held to be a service, because it is not an activity normally expected in promoting the sale of women's clothing).

Conducting a contest to promote the sale of one's own goods is usually not considered a service, even though benefits may accrue to the winners of the contest. Such a contest is usually ancillary to the sale of goods or services, and is nothing more than a device to advertise the applicant's products. *In re Dr. Pepper Co.*, 836 F.2d 508, 5 USPQ2d 1207 (Fed. Cir. 1987); *In re Loew's Theatres, Inc.*, 179 USPQ 126 (TTAB 1973); *In re Johnson Publishing Co., Inc.*, 130 USPQ 185 (TTAB 1961). However, a contest that serves to promote the sale of the applicant's goods may be registrable if it operates in a way that confers a benefit unrelated to the sale of the goods, and the benefit is not one that is normally expected of a manufacturer in that field. *In re Congoleum Corp.*, 222 USPQ 452 (TTAB 1984).

A mark identifying a beauty contest is registrable either as a promotional service, rendered by the organizer of the contest to the businesses or groups that sponsor the contest, or as an entertainment service. *In re Miss American Teen-Ager, Inc.*, 137 USPQ 82 (TTAB 1963). *See* TMEP §1402.11.

See TMEP §1301.01(b)(iii) regarding the providing of advertising space in a periodical.

1301.01(b)(ii) Warranty or Guarantee of Repair

While the repair of the goods of others is a recognized service, an applicant's guarantee of repair of its own goods does not normally constitute a separate service because that activity is ancillary to and normally expected in the trade. *In re Orion Research Inc.*, 669 F. 2d 689, 205 USPQ 688 (C.C.P.A. 1980) (guarantee

销售分开的单独的服务，因为这超出了假发销售商通常的商品促销行为）；*Handmacher-Vogel, Inc.*, 98 USPQ 413（Comm'r Pats. 1953）（制衣商举办女子高尔夫巡回赛的行为被认为是服务，因为这在女装推销过程中并非是人们所通常期待的行为）。

举办竞赛促销自己的商品通常不被认为是服务，即使竞赛的优胜者可能获益。这样的竞赛通常是从属于商品或服务的销售，无非是一种为申请者产品做广告的策略。相关判例：*Dr. Pepper Co.*, 836 F.2d 508, 5 USPQ2d 1207（Fed. Cir. 1987）；*Loew's Theatres, Inc.*, 179 USPQ 126（TTAB 1973）；*Johnson Publishing Co., Inc.*, 130 USPQ 185（TTAB 1961）。但是，如果竞赛举办中提供了与商品销售无关的利益，并且在该领域中人们通常是不会期待制造商提供这种利益的，那么竞赛也可以是可注册的服务。相关判例：*Congoleum Corp.*, 222 USPQ 452（TTAB 1984）。

识别选美竞赛的商标可以作为一种竞赛组织者向赞助企业或集团提供的促销服务进行注册，也可以作为一种娱乐服务进行注册。相关判例：*Miss American Teen-Ager, Inc.*, 137 USPQ 82（TTAB 1963）。*参见*：TMEP §1402.11。

参见：TMEP §1301.01(b)(iii)，查阅有关在杂志中提供广告版面的信息。

1301.01(b)(ii)　保修

修理他人的商品被认为是一种服务，但如申请者对自己的商品实施保修，通常不构成一种单独的服务，因为这是一种辅助行为，并且在交易中通常会期待这种行为。相关判例：*Orion Research Inc.*, 669 F.2d 689, 205 USPQ 688（C.C.P.A. 1980）

of repair or replacement of applicant's goods that is not separately offered, promoted or charged for is not a service); *In re Lenox, Inc.*, 228 USPQ 966 (TTAB 1986) (lifetime warranty that is not separately offered, promoted or charged for is not a service). However, a warranty that is offered or charged for separately from the goods, or is sufficiently above and beyond what is normally expected in the industry may constitute a service. *In re Mitsubishi Motor Sales of America, Inc.*, 11 USPQ2d 1312 (TTAB 1989) (comprehensive automobile vehicle preparation, sales and service program held to be a service, where applicant's package included features that were unique and would not normally be expected in the industry); *In re Sun Valley Waterbeds Inc.*, 7 USPQ2d 1825 (TTAB 1988) (retailer's extended warranty for goods manufactured by others held to be a service, where the warranty is considerably more extensive than that offered by others); *In re Otis Engineering Corp.*, 217 USPQ 278 (TTAB 1982) (non-mandatory quality control and quality assurance services held to constitute a registrable service even though the services were limited to applicant's own equipment, where the services were separately charged for, the goods were offered for sale without services, and the services were not merely a time limited manufacturer's guarantee).

1301.01(b)(iii) Publishing One's Own Periodical

The publication of one's own periodical is not a service, because it is done primarily for applicant's own benefit and not for the benefit of others. *In re Billfish International Corp.*, 229 USPQ 152 (TTAB 1986) (activities of collecting, distributing and soliciting information relating to billfishing tournaments for a periodical publication not a separate service, because these are necessary preliminary activities that a publisher must perform prior to publication and sale of goods); *In re Alaska Northwest Publishing Co.*, 212 USPQ 316 (TTAB 1981) (title of magazine section not registrable for magazine publishing services, because the activities and operations associated with designing, producing and promoting applicant's own product are ancillary activities that would be expected by purchasers and readers of any magazine); *In re Landmark Communications, Inc.*, 204 USPQ 692 (TTAB

(并非在申请者商品之外单独提供、促销或收费的包修包换行为不是一种服务);*Lenox, Inc.*, 228 USPQ 966 (TTAB 1986)(并非单独提供、促销和收费的产品终身保修不是一种服务)。但是,在商品之外单独提供或收费的保证,或者超出本行业通常期待的行为,可以构成一项服务。相关判例:*Mitsubishi Motor Sales of America, Inc.*, 11 USPQ2d 1312 (TTAB 1989)(汽车的全面预备、销售和服务计划被认为是一种服务,商标申请者的销售方案中应包含独特的、在该行业中人们通常不会期待的特征);*Sun Valley Waterbeds Inc.*, 7 USPQ2d 1825 (TTAB 1988)(零售商对他人制造的商品提供扩大保证的行为被认为是一种服务,在此,提供的保证应比他人的保证有相当大的扩大);*Otis Engineering Corp.*, 217 USPQ 278 (TTAB 1982)(非强制性质量控制和质量保险服务被认为构成了可注册的服务,即使此类服务仅限于申请者自己的设备,在此服务应为单独收费,商品销售时不含服务,并且服务不仅仅是制造商的限期保证)。

1301.01(b)(iii) 出版自己的期刊

出版自己的期刊的行为不是一项服务,因为这主要是为申请者而非为他人之利益所为。相关判例:*Billfish International Corp.*, 229 USPQ 152 (TTAB 1986)(为出版刊物收集、分发、兜揽长喙鱼垂钓比赛的有关信息的行为不是单独的服务,因为这是出版商在出版和销售产品之前的必要预备行为);*Alaska Northwest Publishing Co.*, 212 USPQ 316 (TTAB 1981)(杂志章节的名称不能作为杂志出版服务进行注册,因为与申请者自己产品的设计、制造和促销有关的行为和运作是杂志购买者和读者对任何杂志期待的辅助行为);*Landmark Communications, Inc.*, 204 USPQ 692

1979) (title of newspaper section not registrable as service mark for educational or entertainment service, because collected articles, stories, reports, comics, advertising and illustrations are indispensable components of newspapers without which newspapers would not be sold); *In re Television Digest, Inc.*, 169 USPQ 505 (TTAB 1971) (calculating advertising rates for a trade publication not a registrable service, because this is an integral part of the production or operation of any publication).

However, providing advertising space in one's own periodical may be a registrable service, if the advertising activities are sufficiently separate from the applicant's publishing activities. *In re Forbes Inc.*, 31 USPQ2d 1315 (TTAB 1994) ("providing advertising space in a periodical" held to be a registrable service, where the advertising services were rendered to a different segment of the public under a different mark than the mark used to identify applicant's magazines); *In re Home Builders Association of Greenville*, 18 USPQ2d 1313 (TTAB 1990) (real estate advertising services rendered by soliciting advertisements and publishing a guide comprising the advertisements of others held to be a registrable service, where advertising was found to be the applicant's primary activity, and the customers who received the publication were not same as those to whom the advertising services were rendered).

1301.01(b)(iv) Soliciting Investors

Offering shares of one's own stock for investment and reinvestment, and publication of reports to one's own shareholders, are not services, because these are routine corporate activities that primarily benefit the applicant. *In re Canadian Pacific Ltd.*, 754 F.2d 992, 224 USPQ 971 (Fed. Cir. 1985). Similarly, soliciting investors in applicant's own partnership is not a registrable service. *In re Integrated Resources, Inc.*, 218 USPQ 829 (TTAB 1983) (syndicating investment partnerships did not constitute a service within the meaning of the Trademark Act, because there was no evidence that the applicant was in the business of syndicating the in-

(TTAB 1979)（报纸栏目的名称不能作为教育或娱乐服务进行注册，因为报纸所收录的文章、故事、报道、连环画、广告及图片是其不可分割的组成部分，若无就难以出售）；*Television Digest*, *Inc*., 169 USPQ 505 (TTAB 1971)（统计商业出版物的广告率不是一项可注册的服务，因为这是任何出版物的生产或运作的组成部分）。

但是，如果广告行为充分独立于申请者的出版行为，那么在自己的期刊上提供广告版面的行为可以成为可注册的服务。相关判例：*Forbes Inc*., 31 USPQ2d 1315 (TTAB 1994)（若使用与申请者的杂志识别商标不同的商标、向不同的大众群体提供的广告服务，则"在期刊上提供广告版面"被认为是可注册的服务）；*Home Builders Association of Greenville*, 18 USPQ2d 1313 (TTAB 1990)（若广告是申请者的主要行为，而且收到出版物的客户与收到广告服务的客户为不同的群体，则通过征求广告并出版含他人广告的指南，提供房产广告服务被认为是一项可注册的服务）。

1301.01(b)(iv)　吸引投资

以吸引投资和再投资为目的提供自己的股份，以及向自己的股东发布报告，不是一种服务，因为它们属于主要使申请者获益的法人的日常行为。相关判例：*Canadian Pacific Ltd*., 754 F.2d 992, 224 USPQ 971 (Fed.Cir.1985)。类似地，在申请者自己的合伙人中吸引投资者也不属于可注册的服务。相关判例：*Integrated Resources*, *Inc*., 218 USPQ 829 (TTAB 1983)（组成辛迪加投资合作伙伴在《商标法》的意义上不能构成服务，因为没有证据表明申请者在从事组成他人辛迪加投资合作

vestment partnerships of others; rather, the applicant partnership was engaged only in syndication of interests in its own organization). On the other hand, investing the funds of others is a registrable service that primarily benefits others. *In re Venture Lending Associates*, 226 USPQ 285 (TTAB 1985) (investment of funds of institutional investors and providing capital for management found to be a registrable service).

In *Canadian Pacific*, 224 USPQ at 974, the court noted that since shareholders are owners of the corporation, an applicant who offers a reinvestment plan to its stockholders is essentially offering the plan to itself and not to a segment of the buying public. The court distinguished *American International Reinsurance Co., Inc. v. Airco, Inc.*, 570 F.2d 941, 197 USPQ 69 (C.C.P.A. 1978), *cert. denied* 439 U.S. 866, 200 USPQ 64 (1978), in which offering an optional retirement plan to applicant's employees was found to be a registrable service that primarily benefits the employees.

1301.01(b)(v) Informational Services Ancillary to the Sale of Goods

Providing general information or instructions as to the purpose and uses of applicant's goods is merely incidental to the sale of goods, not a separate consulting service. *In re Moore Business Forms Inc.*, 24 USPQ2d 1638 (TTAB 1992) (paper manufacturer who rates the recycled content and recyclability of its own products is merely providing information about its goods, not rendering a service to others); *In re Reichhold Chemicals, Inc.*, 167 USPQ 376 (TTAB 1970) ("promoting the sale and use of chemicals" is not a registrable service, where applicant is merely providing "technical bulletins" that contain information about its own products); *Ex parte Armco Steel Corp.*, 102 USPQ 124 (Comm'r Pats. 1954) (analyzing the needs of customers is not registrable as a consulting service, because it is an ordinary activity that is normally expected of a manufacturer selling goods); *Ex parte Elwell-Parker Electric Co.*, 93 USPQ 229 (Comm'r Pats. 1952) (providing incidental instructions on the efficient use of applicant's goods not a service).

伙伴业务；相反，申请者合作伙伴仅仅参与自己组织内的利益辛迪加）。另一方面，以他人的资金进行投资则属于主要受益者为他人的可注册的服务。相关判例：*Venture Lending Associates*，226 USPQ 285（TTAB 1985）（金融机构投资者进行资金投资和提供管理资金被认为是可注册的服务）。

Canadian Pacific（224 USPQ at 974）一案中，法庭认为：由于股东是公司的所有人，因此申请者向自己的股东提出再投资计划实质上是向自己提出计划，而并非向有购买力的部分公众提出。法庭在 *American International Reinsurance Co.，Inc. v. Airco，Inc.*，570 F.2d 941，197 USPQ 69（C.C.P.A. 1978），*cert. denied* 439 U.S.866，200 USPQ 64（1978）一案中对此作了区分，在此案中，向申请者的雇员提出选择性退休金计划被认为是主要为雇员利益的可注册的服务。

1301.01(b)(v)　从属于商品销售的信息服务

为申请者商品的用途及使用提供一般信息或说明仅仅是商品销售的辅助行为，而不是单独的咨询服务。相关判例：*Moore Business Forms Inc.*，24 USPQ2d 1638（TTAB 1992）（造纸商对自己的产品再利用量和可再利用性进行评估只是为自己的商品提供信息，而不是向他人提供服务）；*Reichhold Chemicals，Inc.*，167 USPQ 376（TTAB 1970）（如果申请者仅仅提供包含自己产品信息的“技术公报”，则“促进化学品的销售和使用”就不是可注册的服务）；*Armco Steel Corp.*，102 USPQ 124（Comm'r Pats.1954）（分析客户需求不是一种可注册的咨询服务，因为这是人们通常对销售商品的制造商期待的平常行为）；*Elwell-Parker Electric Co.*，93 USPQ 229（Comm'r Pats.1952）（为申请者商品的有效使用而提供的附带说明书不是服务）。不过，申请者的免费发型设计聚会被认为是一种服务，因为这超出了假发销售商通常

However, an applicant's free hairstyling instructional "parties" were found to be a service, because conducting parties goes beyond what a seller of wigs would normally do in promoting its goods. *In re Heavenly Creations, Inc.*, 168 USPQ 317 (TTAB 1971).

1301.02 What Is a Service Mark

Not every word, combination of words, or other designation used in the sale or advertising of services is registrable as a service mark. To function as a service mark, the asserted mark must be used in a way that identifies and distinguishes the source of the services recited in the application. Even if it is clear that the applicant is rendering a service (*see* TMEP §§1301.01 *et seq.*), the record must show that the asserted mark actually identifies and distinguishes the source of the service recited in the application. *In re Advertising and Marketing Development Inc.*, 821 F.2d 614, 2 USPQ2d 2010 (Fed. Cir. 1987) (stationery specimens showed use of THE NOW GENERATION as a mark for applicant's advertising or promotional services as well as to identify a licensed advertising campaign, where the recited services were specified in a byline appearing immediately beneath the mark).

The fact that the proposed mark appears in an advertisement or brochure in which the services are advertised does not in itself show use as a mark. The record must show that there is a direct association between the mark and the service. *See In re Universal Oil Products Co.*, 476 F.2d 653, 177 USPQ 456 (C.C.P.A. 1973) (term that identifies only a process does not function as a service mark, even where services are advertised in the same specimen brochure in which the name of the process is used); *In re Duratech Industries Inc.*, 13 USPQ2d 2052 (TTAB 1989) (term used on bumper sticker with no reference to the services does not function as a mark); *Peopleware Systems, Inc. v. Peopleware, Inc.*, 226 USPQ 320 (TTAB 1985) (term PEOPLEWARE used within a byline on calling card specimen does not constitute service mark usage of term, even if specimen elsewhere shows that

的商品促销行为。相关判例：*Heavenly Creations*, *Inc*., 168 USPQ 317 (TTAB 1971)。

1301.02 什么是服务商标

并非所有的文字、文字组合或其他在服务销售和广告中使用的商标都可以注册为服务商标。要作为服务商标使用，相关商标必须用于识别和区分申请上所指服务的来源。即使申请者显然是在提供某种服务(*参见* TMEP §§1301.01 以下)，记录材料也必须显示相关商标在实际上识别和区分了相关服务的来源。相关判例：*Advertising and Marketing Development Inc*., 821 F.2d 614, 2 USPQ2d 2010 (Fed. Cir. 1987)(信笺样本显示使用"THE NOW GENERATION"作为申请者广告或宣传服务的商标，该商标还用于识别获得许可的广告活动，而且在紧接商标下方的一行中指明了相关的服务)。

申请的商标出现在广告或宣传服务的宣传手册中，并不表明其作为商标使用。必须有记录显示该商标与服务直接相关。相关判例：*Universal Oil Products Co*., 476 F.2d 653, 177 USPQ 456 (C.C.P.A.1973)(仅仅用于识别一个工序的词语并没有作为服务商标使用，即使在使用这一工序名称的同一个样本宣传手册中对服务进行了广告也是如此)；*Duratech Industries Inc*., 13 USPQ2d 2052 (TTAB 1989)(在保险杆贴纸上使用的词语并未提及服务，因此不作为服务商标使用)；*Peopleware Systems*, *Inc*. *v*. *Peopleware*, *Inc*., 226 USPQ 320 (TTAB 1985)(在名片样本的副线部位使用"PEOPLEWARE"一字，不能认为该字作为服务商标使用，即使

applicant provides the recited services); *In re J. F. Pritchard & Co. and Kobe Steel, Ltd.*, 201 USPQ 951 (TTAB 1979) (proposed mark used only to identify a liquefaction process in brochure advertising the services does not function as a mark, because there is no direct association between mark and offering of services). *See* TMEP §1301.04(b).

The question of whether a designation functions as a mark that identifies and distinguishes the recited services is determined by examining the specimen(s) and any other evidence in the record that shows how the designation is used. *In re Morganroth*, 208 USPQ 284 (TTAB 1980); *In re Republic of Austria Spanische Reitschule*, 197 USPQ 494 (TTAB 1977). It is the perception of the ordinary customer that determines whether the asserted mark functions as a service mark, not the applicant's intent, hope or expectation that it do so. *In re Standard Oil Co.*, 275 F.2d 945, 125 USPQ 227 (C.C.P.A.1960). Factors that the examining attorney should consider in determining whether the asserted mark is used as a service mark include whether wording is physically separate from textual matter, whether a term is displayed in capital letters or enclosed in quotation marks, and the manner in which a term is used in relation to other material on the specimen.

While a service mark does not have to be displayed in any particular size or degree of prominence, it must be used in a way that makes a commercial impression separate and apart from the other elements of the advertising matter or other material upon which it is used, such that the designation will be recognized by prospective purchasers as a source identifier. *In re C. R. Anthony Co.*, 3 USPQ2d 1894 (TTAB 1987); *In re Post Properties, Inc.*, 227 USPQ 334 (TTAB 1985). The proposed mark must not blend so well with other matter on specimens that it is difficult or impossible to discern what the mark is. *In re McDonald's Corp.*, 229 USPQ 555 (TTAB 1985); *In re Royal Viking Line A/S*, 216 USPQ 795 (TTAB 1982); *In re Republic of Austria Spanische Reitschule*, *supra*; *Ex parte National Geographic Society*, 83 USPQ 260 (Comm'r Pats. 1949). On the other hand, the fact that the proposed mark is prominently displayed does not in and of itself make it registrable, if it is not used in a manner that would be perceived by consumers as

在别处的样本也显示申请者提供了所指的服务)；*J. F. Pritchard & Co. and Kobe Steel, Ltd.*, 201 USPQ 951 (TTAB 1979)(所申请的商标仅用于在宣传服务的宣传手册中识别一种液化工艺的，不能作为商标，因为在商标与所提供的服务之间不存在直接的联系)。*参见* TMEP §1301.04(b)。

要确定一种名称是否作为商标来识别并区分相关的服务，应当通过审查样本以及显示该商标使用方式的有记录的任何其他证据来判定。相关判例：*Morganroth*, 208 USPQ 284 (TTAB 1980)；*Republic of Austria Spanische Reitschule*, 197 USPQ 494 (TTAB 1977)。要根据普通消费者的感觉，而非申请者的意图、希望或期待，来判断所申请的商标是否作为服务商标使用。相关判例：*Standard Oil Co.*, 275 F.2d 945, 125 USPQ 227 (C.C.P.A.1960)。在判断所申请的商标是否作为服务商标使用时，审查员应当考虑的因素包括：其用语是否在形式上与文本内容分离，文字是否以大写字母表示或放置于引号内，以及该文字使用时与商标样本的其他部分之间的关系。

尽管服务商标并不一定要以特别大小或显著性来展现，但它在使用时必须给人一种与其他广告内容元素或使用商标的材料分离的商业印象，使潜在的消费者认其为识别服务来源的商标。相关判例：*C. R. Anthony Co.*, 3 USPQ2d 1894 (TTAB 1987)；*Post Properties, Inc.*, 227 USPQ 334 (TTAB 1985)。所申请的商标不能与样本上的其他内容混合在一起，使人难以或无法辨认什么是商标。相关判例：*McDonald's Corp.*, 229 USPQ 555 (TTAB 1985)；*Royal Viking Line A/S*, 216 USPQ 795 (TTAB 1982)；*Republic of Austria Spanische Reitschule*, *supra*；*National Geographic Society*, 83 USPQ 260 (Comm'r Pats. 1949)。另一方面，如果申请商标的使用方式使消费者感觉不出它是一个表明服务来源的符号，那么即使以显著的方

an indicator of source. *In re Wakefern Food Corp.*, 222 USPQ 76 (TTAB 1984). The important question is not how readily a mark will be noticed but whether, when noticed, it will be understood as identifying and indicating the origin of the services. *In re Singer Mfg. Co.*, 255 F.2d 939, 118 USPQ 310 (C.C.P.A.1958).

The presence of the letters "SM" is not dispositive of the issue of whether matter sought to be registered is used as a service mark. *In re British Caledonian Airways Ltd.*, 218 USPQ 737 (TTAB 1983).

See TMEP §1301.02(a) for further information about matter that does not function as a service mark.

See TMEP §§1301.01 *et seq.* regarding what constitutes a service.

See TMEP §§1301.04 *et seq.* regarding service mark specimens.

1301.02(a) Matter That Does Not Function as a Service Mark

To function as a service mark, a designation must be used in a manner that would be perceived by purchasers as identifying and distinguishing the source of the services recited in the application.

Use of a designation or slogan to convey advertising or promotional information, rather than to identify and indicate the source of the services, is not service mark use. *See In re Standard Oil Co.*, 275 F.2d 945, 125 USPQ 227 (C.C.P.A. 1960) (GUARANTEED STARTING found to be ordinary words that convey information about the services, not a service mark for the services of "winterizing" motor vehicles); *In re Melville Corp.*, 228 USPQ 970 (TTAB 1986) (BRAND NAMES FOR LESS found to be informational phrase that does not function as a mark for retail store services); *In re Brock Residence Inns, Inc.*, 222 USPQ 920 (TTAB 1984) (FOR A DAY, A WEEK, A MONTH OR MORE so highly descriptive and informational in nature that purchasers would be unlikely to perceive it as an indicator of the source of hotel services); *In re Wakefern Food Corp.*, 222 USPQ 76

式显示，该商标也不是一个可注册的商标。相关判例：*Wakefern Food Corp.*，222 USPQ 76（TTAB 1984）。问题的重点并不在于商标被注意的难易程度，而在于被注意到之后，商标是否被理解为用来识别和表明服务来源。相关判例：*Singer Mfg. Co.*，255 F.2d 939，118 USPQ 310（C.C.P.A.1958）。

在判断申请注册的内容是否作为服务商标使用这一问题上，字母“SM”是否存在并不是决定性的。相关判例：*British Caledonian Airways Ltd.*，218 USPQ 737（TTAB 1983）。

参见 TMEP §1301.02(a)，查阅有关不作为服务商标使用的内容的更多信息。

参见 TMEP §§1301.01 及以下，查阅什么能够构成服务的信息。

参见 TMEP §§1301.04 及以下，查阅有关服务商标样本的信息。

1301.02(a)　　不作为服务商标使用的内容

一个名称要用作服务商标，其使用方式必须使购买者能够识别和区分所列服务的来源。

如果使用商标或标语的目的是传达广告或促销信息，而非识别和指示服务来源，则不是一种服务商标使用。*参见* 相关判例：*Standard Oil Co.*，275 F.2d 945，125 USPQ 227（C.C.P.A.1960）（“GUARANTEED STARTING”被认为是传达服务信息的普通用语，而非“winterizing”机动车服务的服务商标）；*Melville Corp.*，228 USPQ 970（TTAB 1986）（“BRAND NAMES FOR LESS”被认为是信息短语，不能作为零售服务的商标使用）；*Brock Residence Inns，Inc.*，222 USPQ 920（TTAB 1984）（“FOR A DAY，A WEEK，A MONTH OR MORE”具有高度的描述性和信息性，消费者不可能感觉出这是一个指示宾馆服务来源的符号）；*Wakefern Food Corp.*，

(TTAB 1984) (WHY PAY MORE found to be a common commercial phrase that does not serve to identify grocery store services); *In re Gilbert Eiseman, P.C.*, 220 USPQ 89 (TTAB 1983) (IN ONE DAY not used as source identifier but merely as a component of advertising matter that conveyed a characteristic of applicant's plastic surgery services); *In re European-American Bank & Trust Co.*, 201 USPQ 788 (TTAB 1979) (slogan THINK ABOUT IT found to be an informational or instructional phrase that would not be perceived as a mark for banking services); *In re Restonic Corp.*, 189 USPQ 248 (TTAB 1975) (phrase used merely to advertise goods manufactured and sold by applicant's franchisees does not serve to identify franchising services). *Cf. In re Post Properties, Inc.*, 227 USPQ 334 (TTAB 1985) (the designation QUALITY SHOWS, set off from text of advertising copy in extremely large typeface and reiterated at the conclusion of the narrative portion of the ad, held to be a registrable service mark for applicant's real estate management and leasing services, because it was used in a way that made a commercial impression separate from that of the other elements of advertising material upon which it was used, such that the designation would be recognized by prospective customers as a source identifier). *See also* TMEP §1202.04 regarding informational matter that does not function as a trademark.

A term that is used only to identify a product, device or instrument sold or used in the performance of a service rather than to identify the service itself does not function as a service mark. *See In re Moody's Investors Service Inc.*, 13 USPQ2d 2043 (TTAB 1989) ("Aaa," as used on the specimens, found to identify the applicant's ratings instead of its rating services); *In re Niagara Frontier Services, Inc.*, 221 USPQ 284 (TTAB 1983) (WE MAKE IT, YOU BAKE IT only identifies pizza, and does not function as a service mark to identify grocery store services); *In re British Caledonian Airways Ltd.*, 218 USPQ 737 (TTAB 1983) (term that identifies a seat in the first class section of an airplane does not function as mark for air transportation services); *In re Editel Productions, Inc.*, 189 USPQ 111 (TTAB 1975) (MINI-MOBILE identifies only a vehicle used in rendering services and does not serve to identify the production of television videotapes for others);

222 USPQ76 (TTAB 1984)(“WHY PAY MORE”被认为是一种普通的商业用语，无法用来识别杂货店的服务)；*Gilbert Eiseman，P. C.*，220 USPQ 89 (TTAB 1983)(“IN ONE DAY”只是广告内容的组成部分，传达申请者整形手术服务的特点，而非来源识别符号)；*European-American Bank & Trust Co.*，201 USPQ 788 (TTAB 1979)(标语“THINK ABOUT IT”被认为是一种信息性或指导性的短语，无法被人感觉是银行服务的商标)；*Restonic Corp.*，189 USPQ 248 (TTAB 1975)(仅用于为申请者的特许经营商制造和销售的商品做广告的短语，并非用来识别特许经营的服务)。比较 *Post Properties，Inc.*，227 USPQ 334 (TTAB 1985)(“QUALITY SHOWS”二字以特别巨大的字体使其与广告文本分离，并且在广告旁白的结尾处再次重申，它被认为是可以为申请者的房地产管理和租赁服务注册的服务商标，因为这样的使用方式形成了它与使用它的其他广告材料元素分离的商业印象，能够被潜在的顾客感觉为是识别来源的符号)。*参见* TMEP §1202.04，查阅有关不作为商标使用的信息性内容的信息。

仅用于识别所售产品、装置或仪器或仅在服务实施过程中使用，而非用来识别服务本身的用语不能作为服务商标使用。*参见* 相关判例：*Moody's Investors Service Inc.*，13 USPQ2d 2043 (TTAB 1989)(样本上使用的“Aaa”被认为识别了申请者的等级而非其评定等级的服务)；*Niagara Frontier Services，Inc.*，221 USPQ 284 (TTAB 1983)(“WE MAKE IT，YOU BAKE IT”仅仅识别了比萨饼，并未起识别杂货店服务的商标的功能)；*British Caledonian Airways Ltd.*，218 USPQ 737 (TTAB 1983)(识别飞机头等舱座位的词语不能作为航空客运服务的服务商标)；*Editel Productions，Inc.*，189 USPQ 111 (TTAB 1975)(“MINI-MOBILE”仅仅识别了提供服务时所用的车辆，而未起识别为他人制作电视录像带的服务)；*Oscar Mayer & Co.*

In re Oscar Mayer & Co. Inc., 171 USPQ 571 (TTAB 1971) (WIENERMOBILE does not function as mark for advertising and promoting the sale of wieners, where it is used only to identify a vehicle used in rendering claimed services).

Similarly, a term that only identifies a process, style, method, or system used in rendering the services is not registrable as a service mark unless it is also used to identify and distinguish the service. *See* TMEP §1301.02(e) and cases cited therein.

A term that only identifies a menu item does not function as a mark for restaurant services. *In re El Torito Restaurant Inc.*, 9 USPQ2d 2002 (TTAB 1988).

The name or design of a character or person does not function as a service mark unless it identifies and distinguishes the services in addition to identifying the character or person. *See* TMEP §1301.02(b) and cases cited therein.

A term used only as a trade name is not registrable as a service mark. *See In re Signal Companies, Inc.*, 228 USPQ 956 (TTAB 1986) (journal advertisement submitted as specimen showed use of ONE OF THE SIGNAL COMPANIES merely as an informational slogan, where words appeared only in small, subdued typeface underneath the address and telephone number of applicant's subsidiary). *See* TMEP §1202.01 for additional information about matter used solely as a trade name.

Matter that is merely ornamental in nature does not function as a service mark. *See In re Tad's Wholesale, Inc.*, 132 USPQ 648 (TTAB 1962) (wallpaper design not registrable as a service mark for restaurant services). *See* TMEP §1202.03 *et seq.* for additional information about ornamentation.

See TMEP §1202.02(b)(ii) regarding trade dress.

1301.02(b) Names of Characters or Personal Names as Service Marks

Under 15 U.S.C. §1127, a name or design of a character does not function as a service mark unless it identifies and distinguishes services in addition to identifying-

Inc., 171 USPQ 571 (TTAB 1971)("WIENERMOBILE"香肠汽车并未起香肠广告和促销的商标的作用,而仅仅用于识别提供上述服务时所使用的车辆)。

类似地,仅用于识别提供服务时使用的过程、风格、方法或体系的词语不能作为服务商标注册,除非它也用于识别和区分该服务。*参见* TMEP §1301.02(e)及其引用的判例。

仅用于识别菜单的词语不能作为餐馆服务的商标。相关判例:*El Torito Restaurant Inc.*, 9 USPQ2d 2002 (TTAB 1988)。

人物或人的名字或形象设计不能作为服务商标,除非它在人物或人之外还识别和区分服务。*参见* TMEP §1301.02(b)及其引用的判例。

仅用作商号的词语不能注册为服务商标。*参见* 相关判例:*In Re Signal Companies, Inc.*, 228 USPQ 956 (TTAB 1986)(在作为商标样本提交的刊物广告中使用的"ONE OF THE SIGNAL COMPANIES"仅以小号、淡化字体出现于申请者子公司地址和电话号码下方,因此被认为仅仅是一种信息性标语)。*参见* TMEP §1202.01,查阅仅作为商品名使用的内容的其他信息。

在性质上仅为装饰性的内容不能作为服务商标。*参见* 相关判例:*In re Tad's Wholesale, Inc.*, 132 USPQ 648 (TTAB 1962)(墙纸设计不能作为餐馆服务的服务商标注册)。*参见* TMEP §1202.03 及以下,查阅关于装潢的其他信息。

参见 TMEP §1202.02(b)(ii),查阅关于商品外观的信息。

1301.02(b)　作为服务商标的人物名和人名

根据 15 U.S.C.§1127,人物的名字或形象设计不能作为服务商标,除非在识别

ing the character. If the name or design is used only to identify the character, it is not registrable as a service mark. *In re Hechinger Investment Co. of Delaware Inc.*, 24 USPQ2d 1053 (TTAB 1991) (design of dog appearing in advertisement does not function as mark for retail hardware and housewares services); *In re McDonald's Corp.*, 229 USPQ 555 (TTAB 1985) (APPLE PIE TREE does not function as mark for restaurant services, where the specimens show use of mark only to identify one character in a procession of characters); *In re Whataburger Systems, Inc.*, 209 USPQ 429 (TTAB 1980) (design of zoo animal character distributed to restaurant customers in the form of an iron-on patch not used in a manner that would be perceived as an indicator of source); *In re Burger King Corp.*, 183 USPQ 698 (TTAB 1974) (fanciful design of king does not serve to identify and distinguish restaurant services).

Similarly, personal names (actual names and pseudonyms) of individuals or groups function as marks only if they identify and distinguish the services recited and not merely the individual or group. *In re Mancino*, 219 USPQ 1047 (TTAB 1983) (holding that BOOM BOOM would be viewed by the public solely as applicant's professional boxing nickname and not as an identifier of the service of conducting professional boxing exhibitions); *In re Lee Trevino Enterprises, Inc.*, 182 USPQ 253 (TTAB 1974) (LEE TREVINO used merely to identify a famous professional golfer rather than as a mark to identify and distinguish any services rendered by him); *In re Generation Gap Products, Inc.*, 170 USPQ 423 (TTAB 1971) (GORDON ROSE used only to identify a particular individual and not as a service mark to identify the services of a singing group).

The name of a character or person *is* registrable as a service mark if the record shows that it is used in a manner that would be perceived by purchasers as identifying the services in addition to the character or person. *In re Florida Cypress Gardens Inc.*, 208 USPQ 288 (TTAB 1980) (name CORKY THE CLOWN used on handbills found to function as a mark to identify live performances by a clown, where the mark was used to identify not just the character but also the act or entertainment service performed by the character); *In re Carson*, 197 USPQ 554

角色之外还识别和区分服务。如果名字或设计仅用于识别人物，则不能作为服务商标进行注册。相关判例：*Hechinger Investment Co. of Delaware Inc.*, 24 USPQ2d 1053 (TTAB 1991)(在广告中出现的狗的形象设计不能作为五金和家用器具零售服务的商标)；*McDonald's Corp.*, 229 USPQ 555 (TTAB 1985)(样本显示商标仅用于识别一系列动画人物中的一个，故"APPLE PIE TREE"不能作为餐馆服务的商标)；*Whataburger Systems, Inc.*, 209 USPQ 429 (TTAB 1980)(以烫贴缀片形式向餐馆顾客分发的动画人物设计无法使人感觉是一个识别来源的符号)；*Burger King Corp.*, 183 USPQ 698 (TTAB 1974)(虚拟的国王形象设计不能识别和区分餐馆服务)。

类似地，个人或集体的人名(真名及笔名)只有当其在识别和区分该个人或集体之外，还识别和区分服务时才能作为商标。相关判例：*Mancino*, 219 USPQ 1047 (TTAB 1983)(认为"BOOM BOOM"给大众的感觉只是申请者的职业拳击绰号，而不是识别其职业拳击表演服务的符号)；*Lee Trevino Enterprises, Inc.*, 182 USPQ 253 (TTAB 1974) ("LEE TREVINO"仅被用作识别一位著名的职业高尔夫运动员，而非作为识别和区分任何由他提供的服务的商标使用)；*Generation Gap Products, Inc.*, 170 USPQ 423 (TTAB 1971)("GORDON ROSE"仅被用作识别某一特定个人，而非用来识别某演唱团服务的商标)。

如果记录显示，人物名或人名的使用方式使其在识别人物和人之外，还能使购买者感觉是用来识别服务的，可以注册为服务商标。相关判例：*Florida Cypress Gardens Inc.*, 208 USPQ 288 (TTAB 1980)(在招贴画上出现的"CORKY THE CLOWN"一枚被认为是识别小丑现场表演的商标，因为该商标不仅识别了人物，同时也识别了人物所提供的表演和娱乐服务)；*Carson*, 197 USPQ 554 (TTAB 1977)

(TTAB 1977) (individual's name held to function as mark, where specimens showed use of the name in conjunction with a reference to services and information as to the location and times of performances, costs of tickets, and places where tickets could be purchased); *In re Ames*, 160 USPQ 214 (TTAB 1968) (name of musical group functions as mark, where name was used on advertisements that prominently featured a photograph of the group and gave the name, address and telephone number of the group's booking agent); *In re Folk*, 160 USPQ 213 (TTAB 1968) (THE LOLLIPOP PRINCESS functions as a service mark for entertainment services, namely, telling children's stories by radio broadcasting and personal appearances).

See TMEP §§1202.09 *et seq*. regarding the registrability of the name of an artist or author as a trademark for goods.

1301.02(c) Three-Dimensional Service Marks

The three-dimensional configuration of a building is registrable as a service mark only if it is used in such a way that it is or could be perceived as a mark. Evidence of use might include menus or letterhead that shows promotion of the building's design, or configuration, as a mark. *See In re Lean-To Barbecue, Inc.*, 172 USPQ 151 (TTAB 1971); *In re Master Kleens of America, Inc.*, 171 USPQ 438 (TTAB 1971); *In re Griffs of America, Inc.*, 157 USPQ 592 (TTAB 1968). *Cf. Fotomat Corp. v. Cochran*, 437 F. Supp. 1231, 194 USPQ 128 (D. Kan. 1977); *Fotomat Corp. v. Photo Drive-Thru, Inc.*, 425 F. Supp. 693, 193 USPQ 342 (D. N. J. 1977).

A three-dimensional costume design may function as a mark for entertainment services. *See In re Red Robin Enterprises, Inc.*, 222 USPQ 911 (TTAB 1984).

Generally, a photograph is a proper specimen of use for a three-dimensional mark. However, photographs of a building are not sufficient to show use of the building design as a mark for services performed in the building if they only show

（认为个人名字作为了商标使用，因为样本显示，名字的使用还与服务和有关演出地点、时间、票价、售票地点的信息相关联）；*Ames*，160 USPQ 214 （TTAB 1968）（认为乐团的名称作为了商标使用，因为该名称用在广告上，广告显眼地展现乐团的照片并提供乐团订票代理的名称、地址和电话）；*Folk*，160 USPQ 213 （TTAB 1968）（“THE LOLLIPOP PRINCESS”可以作为娱乐服务的服务商标，亦即通过广播和真人表演讲述童话故事）。

参见 TMEP §§1202.09 及以下，查阅使用艺术家或作者的名字作为商品商标进行注册的信息。

1301.02(c)　立体服务商标

建筑物的立体图形只有被或可以被感觉是商标时，方可作为服务商标进行注册。作为商标使用的证据可以包括：显示推销建筑物的设计或外形的菜单或信笺抬头。参见 相关判例：*Lean-To Barbecue*，*Inc*.，172 USPQ 151 （TTAB 1971）；*Master Kleens of America*，*Inc*.，171 USPQ 438 （TTAB 1971）；*Griffs of America*，*Inc*.，157 USPQ 592 （TTAB 1968）。比较：*Fotomat Corp*. *v*. *Cochran*，437 F. Supp. 1231，194 USPQ 128（D. Kan. 1977）；*Fotomat Corp*. *v*. *Photo Drive-Thru*，*Inc*.，425 F. Supp. 693，193 USPQ 342（D. N. J. 1977）。

立体服装设计可以作为娱乐服务的商标。参见 相关判例：*Red Robin Enterprises*，*Inc*.，222 USPQ 911 （TTAB 1984）。

一般而言，照片是使用立体商标的适当样本。但是，如果建筑物的照片仅仅显示服务是在该建筑物中提供，则无法充分显示把建筑物的形象设计作为在该建筑物中

the building in which the services are performed. The specimen must show that the proposed mark is used in a way that would be perceived as a mark.

See 37 C.F.R. §2.52(a)(2)(iii) and TMEP §807.12 regarding drawings of three-dimensional marks.

When examining a three-dimensional mark, the examining attorney must determine whether the proposed mark is inherently distinctive. *See* TMEP §1202.02(b)(ii).

1301.02(d) Titles of Radio and Television Programs

The title of a continuing series of presentations (*e.g.*, a television or movie "series," a series of live performances, or a continuing radio program), may constitute a mark for either entertainment services or educational services. However, the title of a single creative work, that is, the title of one episode or event presented as one program, does not function as a service mark. *In re Posthuma*, 45 USPQ2d 2011 (TTAB 1998) (term that identifies title of a play not registrable as service mark for entertainment services). *See also In re Cooper*, 254 F.2d 611, 117 USPQ 396 (C.C.P.A. 1958), *cert. denied*, 358 U.S. 840, 119 USPQ 501 (1958); *In re Scholastic Inc.*, 223 USPQ 431 (TTAB 1984), and TMEP §1202.08, in which analogous situations involving book titles are discussed. The record must show that the matter sought to be registered is more than the title of one presentation, performance or recording.

Specimens that show use of a service mark in relation to television programs or a movie series may be in the nature of a photograph of the video or film frame when the mark is used in the program.

Service marks in the nature of titles of entertainment programs may be owned by the producer of the show, by the broadcasting system or station, or by the author or creator of the show, depending upon the circumstances. Normally, an applicant's statement that the applicant owns the mark is sufficient; the examining at-

的服务的商标使用。样本必须显示所申请的商标的使用可以被感觉为是商标。

参见 37 C.F.R.§2.52(a)(2)(iii) 以及 TMEP §807.12,查阅关于立体商标图样的信息。

在检查立体商标时,审查员必须判断所申请的商标是否具有固有的独特性。参见 TMEP §1202.02(b)(ii)。

1301.02(d)　　广播电视节目的名称

连续播放的系列节目(例如,电视或电影“连续剧”,系列现场演出直播,或是连续的广播节目)的名称,可以构成娱乐服务或教育服务的商标。但是,单一的一项创作的名称,亦即:节目中的一个情节或事件的标题不能作为服务商标。相关判例:*Posthuma*, 45 USPQ2d 2011 (TTAB 1998)(识别一个戏剧的名称不能作为娱乐服务的商标进行注册)。另外参见 *Cooper*, 254 F.2d 611, 117 USPQ 396 (C.C.P.A. 1958), *cert. denied*, 358 U.S. 840, 119 USPQ 501 (1958); *Scholastic Inc.*, 223 USPQ 431 (TTAB 1984);以及 TMEP §1202.08,里面讨论了与书名有关的类似情况。记录必须显示,要注册的内容必须不仅仅是一个表演、演出或录音的名称。

显示服务商标与电视节目或电影连续剧结合使用的样本,可以是在节目中使用商标时的电视或电影画面的照片。

娱乐节目名称作为服务商标时,根据具体的情况,其所有者可以是节目制作人、播放机构或者电视台或者作者或创作者。通常,申请者声明自己拥有商标就已足够

torney should not inquire about ownership unless information in the record clearly contradicts the applicant's verified statement that it is the owner of the mark.

1301.02(e) Process, System or Method

A term that only identifies a process, style, method, system, or the like is not registrable as a service mark. A system or process is only a way of doing something, not a service. The name of a system or process does not become a service mark unless it is also used to identify and distinguish the service. *In re Universal Oil Products Co*., 476 F.2d 653, 177 USPQ 456 (C.C.P.A. 1973) (term not registrable as service mark where the specimens show use of the term only as the name of a process, even though applicant is in the business of rendering services generally and the services are advertised in the same specimen brochure in which the name of the process is used); *In re Walker Research, Inc*., 228 USPQ 691 (TTAB 1986) (term that merely identifies computer program used in rendering services does not function as mark to identify market analysis services); *In re Hughes Aircraft Co*., 222 USPQ 263 (TTAB 1984) (term does not function as service mark where it only identifies a photochemical process used in rendering service); *In re Turbine Metal Technology, Inc*., 219 USPQ 1132 (TTAB 1983) (term that merely identifies coating material does not function as mark for repair and reconstruction services); *In re Vsesoyuzny Ordena Trudovogo Krasnogo Znameni Nauchoissledovatelsky Gorno-Metallurgichesky Institut Tsvetnykh Mettalov "Vnitsvetmet"*, 219 USPQ 69 (TTAB 1983) (KIVCET identifies only a process and plant configuration, not engineering services); *In re Information Builders Inc*., 213 USPQ 593 (TTAB 1982) (term identifies only a computer program, not the service of installing and providing access to a computer program); *In re Scientific Methods, Inc*., 201 USPQ 917 (TTAB 1979) (term that merely identifies educational technique does not function as mark to identify educational services); *In re J. F. Pritchard & Co. and Kobe Steel, Ltd*., 201 USPQ 951 (TTAB 1979) (term used only to identify liquefaction process does not function as mark to identify design and engineer ing services); *In re Produits Chimiques Ugine Kuhlmann Societe Anonyme*, 190

了；审查员不应对所有权进行调查，除非记录信息明显有悖于申请者称自己是商标所有人的声明。

1301.02(e) 工序、体系或方法

仅仅识别一个工序、风格、方法、体系或类似的词语，不能作为服务商标进行注册。一个体系或工序只是做事的方式，并非服务。一个体系或工序的名称不能作为服务商标，除非其同时也用于识别和区分服务。相关判例：*Universal Oil Products Co.*，476 F.2d 653，177 USPQ 456（C.C.P.A.1973）（由于样本显示词语只是作为工序名称使用，即便申请者一般从事提供服务的业务，而且在使用工序名的同一个样本宣传册中为服务做了广告宣传，该词语仍不能作为服务商标进行注册）；*Walker Research，Inc.*，228 USPQ 691 （TTAB 1986）（仅用于识别提供服务过程中所使用的电脑程序名不能作为识别市场分析服务的商标）；*Hughes Aircraft Co.*，222 USPQ 263 （TTAB 1984）（仅仅识别提供服务过程中的一种光化学工序名不能作为服务商标）；*Turbine Metal Technology，Inc.*，219 USPQ 1132 （TTAB 1983）（仅仅识别涂料的词语不能作为修理和改建服务的商标）；*Vsesoyuzny Ordena Trudovogo Krasnogo Znameni Nauchoissledovatelsky Gorno-Metallurgichesky Institut Tsvetnykh Metalov "Vnitsvetmet"*，219 USPQ 69 （TTAB 1983）（"KIVCET"所识别的只是一种工艺和工厂配置，并非工程服务）；*Information Builders Inc.*，213 USPQ 593 （TTAB 1982）（此词语仅仅识别一种电脑程序，而非识别提供电脑程序安装和进入电脑程序的服务）；*Scientific Methods，Inc.*，201 USPQ 917 （TTAB 1979）（仅仅识别教育技巧的词语不能作为教育服务的商标）；*J.F. Pritchard & Co. and Kobe Steel，Ltd.*，201 USPQ 951 （TTAB 1979）（仅用于识别液化工艺的词语不能作为识别设计和工程服务的商标）；*Produits Chimiques Ugine Kuhlmann Societe Anonyme*，190 USPQ

USPQ 305 (TTAB 1976) (term that merely identifies a process used in rendering the service does not function as service mark); *In re Lurgi Gesellschaft Fur Mineraloltechnik m. b. H.*, 175 USPQ 736 (TTAB 1972) (term that merely identifies process for recovery of high purity aromatics from hydrocarbon mixtures does not function as service mark for consulting, designing and construction services); *Ex parte Phillips Petroleum Co.*, 100 USPQ 25 (Comm'r Pats. 1953) (although used in advertising of applicant's engineering services, CYCLOVERSION was only used in the advertisements to identify a catalytic treating and conversion process).

If the term is used to identify *both* the process *and* the services rendered by means of the process, the designation may be registrable as a service mark. *See Liqwacon Corp. v. Browning-Ferris Industries, Inc.*, 203 USPQ 305 (TTAB 1979), in which the Board found that the mark LIQWACON identified both a waste treatment and disposal service and a chemical solidification process.

The name of a system or process is registrable only if (1) the applicant is performing a service (*see* TMEP §§1301.01 *et seq.*), and (2) the designation identifies and indicates the source of the service. In determining eligibility for registration, the examining attorney must carefully review the specimens, together with any other information in the record, to see how the applicant uses the proposed mark. The mere advertising of the recited services in a brochure that refers to the process does not establish that a designation functions as a service mark; there must be some association between the offer of services and the matter sought to be registered. *In re Universal Oil Products Co.*, *supra*; *In re J. F. Pritchard & Co.*, *supra*.

1301. 03 Use of Service Mark in Commerce

1301. 03(a) Use of Service Mark in Advertising to Identify Services

In examining an application under 15 U.S.C. §1051(a), an amendment to allege use under 15 U.S.C. §1051(c), or a statement of use under 15 U.S.C. §1051(d), the examining attorney ordinarily should refuse registration if the record shows

305 (TTAB 1976)(仅用于识别提供服务过程中使用的工序的词语不能作为服务商标);*Lurgi Gesellschaft Fur Mineraloltechnik m. b. H.*, 175 USPQ 736 (TTAB 1972)(仅识别一种从烃混合物中提取高纯度芳香剂的工艺的词语不能作为咨询、设计和建筑服务的服务商标);*Phillips Petroleum Co.*, 100 USPQ 25 (Comm'r Pats. 1953)(尽管在申请者工程服务的广告中使用了"CYCLOVERSION"一字,但是它在广告中仅用于识别一种接触反应处理及转化工艺)。

如果某词语不仅用于识别工艺还用于识别通过此工艺提供的服务,则可以作为服务商标进行注册。*参见 Liqwacon Corp. v. Browning-Ferris Industries, Inc.*, 203 USPQ 305 (TTAB 1979),在本案中,委员会认为"LIQWACON"的商标同时识别了一种污水净化处理服务和一种化学固化工艺。

一种体系或工艺的名称可注册的条件是:(1)申请者提供了一种服务(*参见* TMEP §§1301.01 及以下),并且(2)此名称识别并指出服务的来源。在判断是否符合注册条件时,审查员必须仔细审查样本以及记录中的任何其他信息,了解申请者如何使用申请注册的商标。仅仅在宣传手册中引用工艺名称为相关服务做广告宣传不能使该名称成为服务商标;在提供服务和申请注册的内容之间必须存在某种联系。相关判例:*Universal Oil Products Co.*, *同前*;*In re J. F. Pritchard & Co.*, *同前*。

1301.03　在商业中使用服务商标

1301.03(a)　在广告中使用服务商标以识别服务

在审查一项依据 15 U.S.C. §1051(a)规定提出的申请,一项依据 15 U.S.C. §1051(c)规定提交的申报使用修正书或一项依据 15 U.S.C. §1051(d)规定提交的使用声明时,如果记录表明所广告的服务实际上并未实施,则审查员通常应当拒绝给

that the services advertised have not been rendered. For example, the use of a mark in the announcement of a future service does not constitute use as a service mark. *In re Port Authority of New York*, 3 USPQ2d 1453 (TTAB 1987) (advertising and promoting telecommunications services before the services were available insufficient to support registration); *In re Cedar Point, Inc.*, 220 USPQ 533 (TTAB 1983) (advertising of OCEANA marine entertainment park, that was not yet open, held not a valid basis for registration); *In re Nationwide Mutual Ins. Co.*, 124 USPQ 465 (TTAB 1960) (stickers placed on policies, bills and letters announcing prospective name change is mere adoption, not service mark use).

See TMEP 806.03(c) regarding amendment of the basis to intent-to-use under 15 U.S.C. §1051(b) when a §1(a) basis fails; TMEP §1104.10 regarding withdrawal of an amendment to allege use, and TMEP §§1109.16 *et seq*. regarding the time limits for correcting deficiencies in a statement of use under 15 U.S.C. §1051(d).

1301.03(b) Rendering of Service in Commerce Regulable by Congress

In an application under §1(a) or 1(b) of the Trademark Act, 15 U.S.C. §1051(a) or 1051(b), the applicant must use the mark in commerce before a registration may be granted. Section 45 of the Act, 15 U.S.C. §1127, defines "commerce" as "all commerce which may lawfully be regulated by Congress." *See* TMEP §§901.01 and 901.03.

The following are three examples of how a service may be rendered in commerce: (1) the applicant's services are rendered across state lines; (2) customers come across state lines in response to advertising for the services; and (3) the applicant's licensees or franchisees are located in more than one state, and they use the mark. *See* TMEP §901.03 and cases cited therein.

1301.04 Specimens of Use for Service Marks

A service mark specimen must show the mark as actually used in the sale or adver-

予注册。例如，在将来服务的公告中使用商标不能构成服务商标使用。相关判例：*Port Authority of New York*，3 USPQ2d 1453（TTAB 1987）（对于尚未提供的电信服务进行的广告和促销不足以成为支持注册的理由）；*Cedar Point*，*Inc*.，220 USPQ 533（TTAB 1983）（对于尚未开放的"OCEANA"海洋娱乐公园进行广告宣传被认为不是注册的有效基础）；*Nationwide Mutual Ins. Co*.，124 USPQ 465（TTAB 1960）（在保险单、账单及信函上贴上贴纸，宣布即将更名只是一种借用，而非服务商标使用）。

参见 TMEP 806.03(c)，查阅当以 §1(a) 为依据不成立时，根据 15 U.S.C. §1051(b)规定提交意图使用修正书的信息；*参见* TMEP §1104.10 查阅关于撤回使用申报修正的信息，以及参见 TMEP §§1109.16 及以下，查阅对更正依据 15 U.S.C. §1051(d) 作出的使用声明的错误的时间限制的信息。

1301.03(b) 在国会管制的商业中提供服务

依据《商标法》15 U.S.C.§1051(a)或 1051(b)第§1(a)及 1(b) 款的规定提出的申请，申请者必须在获得注册之前将商标用于商业。《商标法》第 45 节 15 U.S.C. §1127 条将"商业"定义为"由国会依法进行管制的一切商业"。*参见* TMEP §§901.01 及 901.03。

以下是如何在商业中提供服务的三个例子：(1)申请者跨州提供服务；(2)随着服务广告的广播，客户跨州而来；以及(3)申请者的受许可人或专卖店跨州分布，且他们使用商标。*参见* TMEP §901.03 及其引用的判例。

1301.04 服务商标使用样本

服务商标样本必须显示在销售或广告申请所指的服务中实际使用了该商标。

tising of the services recited in the application. 37 C. F. R. §2. 56(b)(2). Acceptable specimens may include newspaper and magazine advertisements, brochures, billboards, handbills, direct-mail leaflets, menus (for restaurants), and the like. However, printer's proofs for advertisements, publicity releases to news media, or printed articles resulting from such releases, are not accepted because they do not show use of the mark by the applicant in the sale or advertising of the services. Business documents such as letterhead and invoices may be acceptable service mark specimens if they show the mark and refer to the relevant services. *See* TMEP §1301. 04(b).

See 37 C. F. R. §2. 59 and TMEP §904. 09 regarding substitute specimens.

1301. 04(a) Specimens Must Show Use as a Service Mark

To show service mark usage, the specimens must show use of the mark in a manner that would be perceived by potential purchasers as identifying the applicant's services and indicating their source. *In re Universal Oil Products Co.*, 476 F. 2d 653, 177 USPQ 456 (C. C. P. A. 1973) (term that identified only a process held not registrable as service mark, even though applicant was rendering services and the services were advertised in the same brochure in which the name of the process was used); *In re A La Vieille Russie, Inc.*, 60 USPQ2d 1895 (TTAB 2001) (RUSSIANART perceived as informational matter rather than as service mark for art dealership services, where the term is displayed inconspicuously in specimen brochure amid other informational matter, in the same size and font of type as the rest of the brochure text); *In re Moody's Investors Service Inc.*, 13 USPQ2d 2043 (TTAB 1989) ("Aaa," as used on the specimens, found to identify the applicant's ratings instead of its rating services); *In re McDonald's Corp.*, 229 USPQ 555 (TTAB 1985) (APPLE PIE TREE did not function as mark for restaurant services, where the specimens showed use of mark only to identify one character in a procession of characters, and the proposed mark was no more prominent than anything else on specimens); *In re Signal Companies, Inc.*, 228 USPQ

37 C.F.R.§2.56(b)(2)。可接受的样本包括：报纸和杂志广告、宣传手册、广告牌、招贴画、直邮广告传单、菜单(餐馆用)以及诸如此类。但是，广告印刷校样、向新闻媒体的公开发布以及由此类发布而产生的印刷文章，均为不可接受，因为它们并没有显示申请者在服务的销售或广告活动中使用商标。商业文件，诸如信笺抬头和发票，如果显示了商标并且指出相关的服务，则可以被接受为服务商标的样本。*参见* TMEP §1301.04(b)。

参见 37 C.F.R.§2.59 及 TMEP §904.09，查阅关于替代样本的信息。

1301.04(a)　样本必须显示作为服务商标使用

要显示商标的使用，样本必须显示商标的使用可以被潜在的购买者感觉为识别申请者的服务并指出服务的来源。相关判例：*Universal Oil Products Co*., 476 F.2d 653, 177 USPQ 456 (C.C.P.A.1973)(只是作为工序名称使用的词语不能作为服务商标进行注册，即便申请者提供了服务，并在使用工序名称的同一个样本宣传手册中对服务进行了广告宣传)；*A La Vieille Russie*, *Inc*., 60 USPQ2d 1895 (TTAB 2001)("RUSSIANART"与宣传手册文本的字体大小相同，在样本中不显眼地与其他信息内容混在一起，因而被认为属于信息性内容，而非艺术品经销服务的服务商标)；*Moody's Investors Service Inc*., 13 USPQ2d 2043 (TTAB 1989)(样本所使用的"Aaa"被认为仅识别了申请者的等级而非其评定等级的服务)；*McDonald's Corp*., 229 USPQ 555 (TTAB 1985)(由于样本显示商标仅用于识别一系列动画人物中的一个，并未在样本中表现出显著性，故"APPLE PIE TREE"不能作为餐馆服务的商标)；*Signal Companies*, *Inc*., 228 USPQ 956 (TTAB 1986)(在作为商标样本提交的刊物广告中使用的"ONE OF THE SIGNAL COMPANIES"仅以小号、淡化字体

956 (TTAB 1986) (journal advertisement submitted as specimen showed use of ONE OF THE SIGNAL COMPANIES merely as an informational slogan, where the words appeared only in small, subdued typeface underneath the address and telephone number of applicant's subsidiary); *In re Republic of Austria Spanische Reitschule*, 197 USPQ 494 (TTAB 1977) (use of mark as one of many pictures in applicant's brochure would not be perceived as an indication of the source of the services); *Intermed Communications, Inc. v. Chaney*, 197 USPQ 501 (TTAB 1977) (business progress reports directed to potential investors do not show service mark use for medical services); *In re Restonic Corp.*, 189 USPQ 248 (TTAB 1975) (phrase used merely to advertise goods manufactured and sold by applicant's franchisees does not identify franchising services); *In re Reichhold Chemicals, Inc.*, 167 USPQ 376 (TTAB 1970) (technical bulletins and data sheets on which mark was used merely to advertise chemicals do not show use as a service mark for consulting services).

See TMEP §1301.02(a) regarding matter that does not function as a service mark.

1301.04(b) Association Between Mark and Services

Where the mark is used in advertising the services, the specimen must show an association between the mark and the services for which registration is sought. A specimen that shows only the mark, with no reference to the services, does not show service mark usage. *In re Adair*, 45 USPQ2d 1211 (TTAB 1997) (tags affixed to decorated Christmas tree that bear the mark "TREE ARTS CO. and design" and the applicant's location, but make no reference to services, fail to show use for "design services in the nature of designing handcrafted, permanently decorated Christmas and designer trees"); *In re Johnson Controls, Inc.*, 33 USPQ2d 1318 (TTAB 1994) (labels affixed to packaging of valves do not show use of mark for custom manufacture of valves); *In re Duratech Industries Inc.*, 13 USPQ2d 2052 (TTAB 1989) (bumper stickers showing only the mark do not show use to

出现于申请者子公司地址和电话号码下方,因此被认为仅仅是一种信息性标语);*Republic of Austria Spanische Reitschule*,197 USPQ 494 (TTAB 1977)(商标用作申请者宣传手册诸多图片之一,不能被人感觉为用来指出服务的来源);*Intermed Communications, Inc. v. Chaney*,197 USPQ 501 (TTAB 1977)(向潜在的投资者发送的商业进度报告并未显示作为医疗服务商标使用);*Restonic Corp.*,189 USPQ 248 (TTAB 1975)(仅用于为申请者的特许经营商制造和销售的商品做广告的短语,并非用来识别特许经营的服务);*Reichhold Chemicals, Inc.*,167 USPQ 376 (TTAB 1970)(使用了商标的技术公告和数据表仅仅用来作化学品广告,并不显示作为咨询服务的服务商标)。

参见 TMEP §1301.02(a),查阅有关不作为服务商标的内容的信息。

1301.04(b) 商标与服务之间的联系

如果商标被用于为服务做广告宣传,则样本必须体现商标同申请注册的服务之间的联系。如果样本仅仅显示商标而没有提到服务,则不显示作为服务商标使用。相关判例:*Adair*,45 USPQ2d 1211 (TTAB 1997)(用于装饰圣诞树的饰品标有"TREE ARTS CO. and design"的商标以及申请者的住所,但没有提及服务,则不显示作为"设计手工艺、恒久装饰的圣诞树的设计服务"的商标使用);*Johnson Controls, Inc.*,33 USPQ2d 1318 (TTAB 1994)(粘贴在阀门外包装上的标签并未显示其作为定做阀门服务的商标使用);*Duratech Industries Inc.*,13 USPQ2d 2052 (TTAB 1989)(仅仅显示商标的保险杠贴纸并未显示其作为识别"相关的服务,即推

identify "association services, namely promoting the interests of individuals who censor the practice of drinking and driving"); *In re Riddle*, 225 USPQ 630 (TTAB 1985) (cutouts showing mark with no reference to the services held unacceptable for automotive service center); *In re Whataburger Systems, Inc.*, 209 USPQ 429 (TTAB 1980) (iron-on transfer clothing patches in the form and shape of a cartoon animal mark, distributed as free promotional items to restaurant customers at counters, held insufficient to identify restaurant services). *See also* TMEP §1301.04(c) and cases cited therein.

A specimen that shows the mark as used in the course of performing the services is generally acceptable. Where the record shows that the mark is used in performing (as opposed to advertising) the services, a reference to the services on the specimen itself may not be necessary. *In re Metriplex Inc.*, 23 USPQ2d 1315 (TTAB 1992) (computer printouts showing mark GLOBAL GATEWAY found acceptable to show use of mark to identify data transmission services accessed via computer, because they show use of mark as it appears on computer terminal in the course of rendering the services); *In re Eagle Fence Rentals, Inc.*, 231 USPQ 228 (TTAB 1986) (photograph of rented fence held acceptable for rental of chain link fences, since it shows use of distinctive color scheme in the rendering services); *In re Red Robin Enterprises, Inc.*, 222 USPQ 911 (TTAB 1984) (photograph of costume worn by performer during performance of entertainment services held to be an acceptable specimen). In *Johnson Controls, Inc.*, *supra*, 33 USPQ2d at 1320 (holding that labels attached to the packaging of valves did not show use of the mark for custom manufacturing of valves), the Board distinguished *Metriplex* and *Eagle Fence*, noting that the labels were not used in the rendering of the services, as the custom manufacturing services were complete before purchasers ever see the mark.

In determining whether a specimen is acceptable evidence of service mark use, the examining attorney may consider applicant's explanations as to how the specimen is used, along with any other available evidence in the record that shows how the mark is actually used. *See In re International Environmental Corp.*, 230 USPQ

进审查酒后驾车者的个人的利益”)；*Riddle*，225 USPQ 630 (TTAB 1985)(断流器上显示商标但未提及服务，被认为并未用来识别汽车服务中心的服务)；*Whataburger Systems，Inc.*，209 USPQ 429 (TTAB 1980)(在柜台上作为免费促销品向餐馆顾客分发的卡通动物商标形状的衣服烫贴缀片，被认为不足以识别餐馆服务)。另参见 TMEP §1301.04(c)及其引用的判例。

以在实施服务过程中使用商标的形式显示商标的样本，一般为可接受的样本。如果记录显示在提供服务过程中(相对于广告)使用了商标，那么并不一定要在样本上提及服务。相关判例：*Metriplex Inc.*，23 USPQ2d 1315 (TTAB 1992)(电脑打印输出显示“GLOBAL GATEWAY”商标被认为显示出使用商标来识别通过电脑接入的数据传输服务，因为以在提供服务的过程中商标出现在电脑终端之上的形式，显示了商标的使用)；*Eagle Fence Rentals，Inc.*，231 USPQ 228 (TTAB 1986)(租赁篱笆的照片被认为显示了连锁篱笆的租赁服务，因为它显示了在提供服务过程中使用了独特的色彩设计)；*Red Robin Enterprises，Inc.*，222 USPQ 911 (TTAB 1984)(在娱乐服务表演期间，表演者所穿服装的照片可以被接受为样本)。在 *Johnson Controls，Inc.* *同前*，33 USPQ2d at 1320 一案中(认为粘贴在阀门外包装上的标签并未显示其作为定做阀门服务的商标使用)，委员会区分了 *Metriplex* 案和 *Eagle Fence* 案，指出标签没有在提供服务的过程中使用，因为定制服务在购买者看到商标之前已经完成。

在判断样本是否为可接受的服务商标使用的证据时，审查员应考虑申请者对使用样本的说明，并查看记录，是否有显示商标在实际中如何使用的任何其他证据。参见 相关判例：*International Environmental Corp.*，230 USPQ 688 (TTAB 1986)，在

688 (TTAB 1986), in which a survey distributed to potential customers of applicant's heating and air conditioning distributorship services was held to be an acceptable specimen even though it did not specifically refer to the services, where the applicant stated that the sale of its services involved ascertaining the needs of customers serviced, and the record showed that the surveys were directed to potential customers and were the means by which applicant offered its distributorship services to the public.

1301.04(c) Letterhead

Letterhead stationery, business cards or invoices bearing the mark may be accepted if they create an association between the mark and the services. To create an association between the mark and the services, the specimen does not have to spell out the specific nature or type of services. A general reference to the industry may be acceptable. *In re Ralph Mantia Inc.*, 54 USPQ2d 1284 (TTAB 2000) (letterhead and business cards showing the word "Design" are acceptable evidence of use of mark for commercial art design services); *In re Southwest Petro-Chem, Inc.*, 183 USPQ 371 (TTAB 1974) (use of mark on letterhead next to the name SOUTHWEST PETRO-CHEM, INC. found to be sufficient to show use of the mark for "consulting and advisory services relating to the making and using of lubricating oils and greases," when used for letters in correspondence with customers).

Letterhead or business cards that bear only the mark and a company name and address are not adequate specimens (unless the mark itself has a descriptive portion that refers to the service), because they do not show that the mark is used in the sale or advertising of the particular services recited in the application. *In re Monograms America, Inc.*, 51 USPQ2d 1317 (TTAB 1999) (letterhead specimens showing the mark MONOGRAMS AMERICA and the wording "A Nationwide Network of Embroidery Stores" held insufficient to support registration for consulting services for embroidery stores).

本案中，向申请者的暖通空调经销服务的潜在顾客分发的问卷调查被认为是可接受的样本，尽管在调查中没有特别提到服务，但申请者称其服务的销售包括确定顾客的需求，而且记录也显示该项调查针对的是潜在顾客，并且是申请者将其经销服务向公众推出的手段。

1301.04(c) 信笺抬头

抬头信笺、业务名片或印有商标的发票如果在商标和服务之间建立了某种联系，可以被接受为样本。要在商标和服务之间建立联系，样本并非一定要明确说明服务的具体性质或类型。一般性地提到服务的行业即为可接受。相关判例：*Ralph Mantia Inc.*, 54 USPQ2d 1284 (TTAB 2000)（显示“Design”一字的抬头信笺和业务名片可以作为使用商业艺术设计服务商标的证据）；*Southwest Petro-Chem, Inc.*, 183 USPQ 371 (TTAB 1974)（在与客户的来往信函中，在名称“SOUTHWEST PETRO-CHEM, INC.”旁边的信笺抬头上使用商标，被认为充分显示了使用“有关制造和使用润滑油脂的咨询顾问服务”的商标）。

仅印有商标、公司名称和地址的抬头信笺及业务名片要作为样本还不充分（除非商标本身含有提及服务的描述性部分），因为它们并没有显示商标被用于销售或广告宣传申请上所指的服务。相关判例：*Monograms America, Inc.*, 51 USPQ2d 1317 (TTAB 1999)（显示“MONOGRAMS AMERICA”商标和“A Nationwide Network of Embroidery Stores”词语的抬头信笺样本被认为不足以支持作为刺绣商店的咨询服务进行注册）。

If the letterhead itself does not include a reference to the services, a copy of an actual letter on letterhead stationery bearing the mark is an acceptable specimen of use if the content of the letter indicates the field or service area in which the mark is used. In *Monograms America*, *supra*, the Board indicated that the letterhead specimen might have been accepted if the applicant had submitted a copy of a letter to a store owner describing the services. 51 USPQ2d 1319.

1301.04(d) Specimens for Entertainment Services

For live entertainment services, acceptable specimens include a photograph of the group or individual in performance with the name displayed, *e.g.*, the name printed on the drum of a band. For any entertainment service, advertisements or radio or television listings showing the mark may be submitted, but the specimens must show that the mark is used to identify and distinguish the services recited in the application, not just the performer. *See In re Ames*, 160 USPQ 214 (TTAB 1968) (advertisements for records show use of the mark for entertainment services rendered by a musical group, where the advertisements prominently featured a photograph of musical group and gave the name, address and telephone number of a booking agent).

A designation that identifies only the performer is not registrable as a service mark. *See* TMEP §1301.02(b) regarding the registrability of names of characters or personal names as service marks.

1301.05 Identification and Classification of Services

See TMEP §§1402.11 *et seq*. regarding identification of services, and TMEP §§1401 *et seq*. regarding classification.

1302 Collective Marks Generally

Section 45 of the Trademark Act, 15 U.S.C. §1127, defines "collective mark" as

如果信笺抬头本身并没有提及服务，但如果信件内容说明了商标所使用的领域或服务范围，则以印有商标的抬头信笺写就的实际信函的复印件可以作为样本。相关判例：*Monograms America 同前*，在本案中，委员会认为，如果申请者提交一份向某店主描述服务的信函的复印件，则可以接受抬头信笺为样本。51 USPQ2d 1319。

1301.04(d) 娱乐服务样本

对于现场娱乐服务，可接受的样本包括：显示名称的演出团队或个人的照片，例如，印在鼓上的乐队名称。对于任何娱乐服务，显示商标的广告或广播电视节目表都可以提交，但是样本必须显示出商标被用于识别和区分申请上所指的服务，而不仅仅是表演者。*参见* 相关判例：*Ames*，160 USPQ 214 （TTAB 1968)（广告记录显示乐团使用了娱乐服务商标，因为在广告上显眼地显示了乐团的照片并提供订票代理的名称、地址以及电话号码）。

仅识别表演者的名称不能注册为服务商标。*参见* TMEP §1301.02(b)，查阅关于人物名及人名作为服务商标的可注册性。

1301.05　服务的识别和分类

参见 TMEP §§1402.11 及以下，查阅服务识别的信息，并*参见* TMEP §§1401 及以下，查阅服务分类。

1302　集体商标概述

《商标法》第 45 节，15 U.S.C.§1127 对“集体商标”作了如下定义：

follows:

The term "collective mark" means a trademark or service mark—

(1) used by the members of a cooperative, an association, or other collective group or organization, or

(2) which such cooperative, association, or other collective group or organization has a bona fide intention to use in commerce and applies to register on the principal register established by this Act, and includes marks indicating membership in a union, an association or other organization.

Under the Trademark Act, a collective mark must be *owned by* a collective entity even though the mark is *used by* the members of the collective. There are basically two types of collective marks: (1) collective trademarks or collective service marks; and (2) collective membership marks. The distinction between these types of collective marks is explained in *Aloe Creme Laboratories, Inc. v. American Society for Aesthetic Plastic Surgery, Inc.*, 192 USPQ 170, 173 (TTAB 1976), as follows:

> A *collective trademark or collective service mark* is a mark adopted by a "collective" (*i.e.*, an association, union, cooperative, fraternal organization, or other organized collective group) for use only by its members, who in turn use the mark to identify their goods or services and distinguish them from those of nonmembers. The "collective" itself neither sells goods nor performs services under a collective trademark or collective service mark, but the collective may advertise or otherwise promote the goods or services sold or rendered by its members under the mark. A *collective membership mark* is a mark adopted for the purpose of indicating membership in an organized collective group, such as a union, an association, or other organization. Neither the collective nor its members uses the collective membership mark to identify and distinguish goods or

“集体商标”这个术语是指一种商标或服务商标——

(1) 由合作组织、协会或其他集合团体或组织的成员使用，或者

(2) 此类合作组织、协会或其他集合团体或组织真实地计划将其用于商业活动，并且申请在依据商标法设立的联邦商标登记簿上登记注册，包括表明其为某联盟、协会或其他组织成员的商标。

根据《商标法》，一个集体商标必须由集体实体*拥有*，尽管该商标由集体的成员*使用*。集体商标有两种基本类型：(1)集体商标或集体服务商标；以及(2)集体成员商标。这两种集体商标的区别在 *Aloe Creme Laboratories, Inc. v. American Society for Aesthetic Plastic Surgery, Inc.*, 192 USPQ 170, 173 (TTAB 1976) 一案中有如下解释：

> 一项*集体商标或集体服务商标*是由一个“集体”(即一个协会、联盟、合作组织、共济组织或其他有组织的集合团体)采用的商标，只能由其成员使用，成员使用商标来识别他们的商品或服务，与非成员的商品或服务区分开来。“集体”本身并不通过集体商标或集体服务商标出售商品或提供服务，但是集体可以进行广告宣传或以其他方式促进其成员以该商标销售商品或提供服务。一项*集体成员商标*是一种以表明其为某个有组织的集合团体(如联盟、协会或其他组织)的成员为目的而采用的商标。无论集体还是其成员都不使用集体成员商标来识别和区分商品或服务；相反，这种商标的唯

services; rather, the sole function of such a mark is to indicate that the person displaying the mark is a member of the organized collective group.

See also In re International Institute of Valuers, 223 USPQ 350 (TTAB 1984). *See* TMEP §1303 concerning collective trademarks and service marks; TMEP §1304 concerning collective membership marks; and TMEP §1305, which distinguishes collective trademarks or service marks from trademarks and service marks used by collective organizations.

1302. 01 History of Collective Marks

Section 4 of the Trademark Act of 1946, 15 U.S.C. §1054, provides for registration of both collective marks and certification marks, without distinguishing between them, but §45 of the Act, 15 U.S.C. §1127, defines collective marks and certification marks separately, as distinctly different types of marks. (*See* TMEP §§1306 *et seq*. regarding certification marks.)

A brief history will serve to put these sections in perspective. The earlier statutory provision, out of which §4 and the accompanying definitions in §45 grew, was the June 10, 1938, amendment of the Trademark Act of 1905. Under the Act of 1905, registration could be based only on a person's own use of a mark. The purpose of the 1938 amendment was to provide for registration of a mark by an owner who "exercises legitimate control over the use of a collective mark." "Collective marks," however, were not defined under the Act of 1905, as amended. Section 45 of the Act of 1946 defined the separate types of marks.

See TMEP §1304. 01 for additional history relating to collective membership marks.

1303 Collective Trademarks and Collective Service Marks

Collective trademarks and collective service marks indicate commercial origin of

一功能是表明持有此商标者是某个有组织的集合团体的成员。

另参见 International Institute of Valuers, 223 USPQ 350（TTAB 1984）。*参见* TMEP §1303，查阅关于集体商标和集体服务商标的信息；*参见* TMEP §1304，查阅关于集体成员商标的信息；在 TMEP §1305 中，对集体商标及集体服务商标与集体组织所使用的商标及服务商标区分开来。

1302.01 集体商标的历史

《1946 年商标法》第 4 节 15 U.S.C.§1054，对集体商标和证明商标的注册作了规定，但并未将二者区分开来，但本法 §45，15 U.S.C.§1127 把集体商标和证明商标作为两种不同类型的商标分别作了定义。（*参见* TMEP §§1306 及以下，查阅关于证明商标的信息。）

简要介绍集体商标的历史将有助于理解这些条文规定。早期的法律规定是 1938 年 6 月 10 日颁布的《1905 年商标法》修正案，§4 及 §45 中的相关定义即源自该规定。根据《1905 年商标法》规定，商标只基于某人自己使用商标进行注册。1938 年修正案的目的在于，对注册一个由商标所有者“对某集体商标的使用实施合法控制”的商标作了规定。不过，修订后的《1905 年商标法》也没有对“集体商标”进行定义。《1946 年商标法》第 45 节对各种商标进行了定义。

参见 TMEP §1304.01，查阅有关集体成员商标历史的其他信息。

1303 集体商标和集体服务商标

集体商标和集体服务商标表明了商品及服务的商业来源，但作为*集体商标*它们

goods or services, but as *collective* marks they indicate that the party providing the goods or services is a member of a certain group and meets its standards for admission. The mark is used by all members of the group; therefore, no one member can own the mark, and the collective organization holds the title to the collectively used mark for the benefit of all members of the group. An agricultural cooperative of produce sellers is an example of a collective organization that does not sell its own goods or render services, but promotes the goods and services of its members.

The collective organization itself neither sells goods nor performs services under the mark, but may advertise to publicize the mark and promote the goods or services sold by its members under the mark.

A specimen of use of a collective trademark or service mark must show use of the mark by a member on the member's goods or in the sale or advertising of the member's services. 37 C.F.R. §2.56(b)(3); TMEP 1303.02(b).

1303.01 Use of Collective Trademark and Collective Service Mark Is By Members

Applications for registration of collective trademarks and collective service marks are different in form from applications for registration of other trademarks and service marks because of the difference in ownership and use of collective marks.

Under the definition of "collective mark" in §45 of the Trademark Act, 15 U.S.C. §1127, a collective mark must be owned by a collective entity. The use of a collective trademark or collective service mark is by members of the collective. Therefore, in an application based on use in commerce under 15 U.S.C. §1051 (a), the applicant must assert that the applicant is exercising legitimate control over the use of the mark in commerce by its members.

In an application based on 15 U.S.C. §1051(b) or 15 U.S.C. §1126, the applicant must assert that the applicant has a bona fide intention to exercise legitimate con-

也表明，提供商品及服务的一方是某特定团体的成员，并且符合加入该团体的标准。商标由团体所有成员使用；因此，没有哪一个成员能够拥有该商标，集体组织为团体所有成员的利益而拥有该集体使用的商标。举例来说，一个由农产品销售商组成的农业合作社就是一个集体组织，本身并不销售商品或提供服务，但是促进其成员的商品和服务的销售。

集体组织本身并不以该商标销售商品或提供服务，但是可以通过商标的广告宣传促进其成员以该商标销售商品或服务。

使用集体商标或集体服务商标的样本必须表明某成员在其商品上，或在销售及推销其服务的过程中使用了该商标。*参见* 37 C.F.R.§2.56(b)(3)；TMEP 1303.02(b)。

1303.01 集体商标和集体服务商标由成员使用

由于集体商标在所有权和使用方面同其他商标的差异，因此集体商标和集体服务商标的注册申请在形式上不同于其他商标和服务商标的注册申请。

根据《商标法》§45，15 U.S.C.§1127 对“集体商标”的定义，集体商标必须为某集体实体所拥有。集体商标及集体服务商标由集体成员使用。因此，在以 15 U.S.C.§1051(a)规定的商业使用为依据提出申请时，申请者必须确认其对于其成员在商业中使用商标能够进行合理的控制。

在以 15 U.S.C.§1051(b)或 15 U.S.C.§1126 为依据提出申请时，申请者必须确认其真实地要对其成员在商业中使用商标进行合理的控制。在根据§1(b) 提出申

trol over the use of the mark in commerce by its members. In a §1(b) application, before the mark can register, the applicant must file an amendment to allege use under 15 U.S.C. §1051(c) or a statement of use under 15 U.S.C. §1051(d) alleging that the applicant is exercising legitimate control over the use of the mark in commerce by its members.

In certain situations, notwithstanding the use of a collective trademark or collective service mark by the members of the collective, the collective itself may also use the same mark as a trademark for the goods covered by the collective trademark or service mark registration. *See* TMEP §1305. The "anti-use-by-owner rule" of §4 of the Trademark Act, 15 U.S.C. §1054 does not apply to collective marks. *See Roush Bakery Products Co. v. F. R. Lepage Bakery Inc.*, 4 USPQ2d 1401 (TTAB 1987), *aff'd*, 851 F.2d 351, 7 USPQ2d 1395 (Fed. Cir. 1988), *withdrawn*, *vacated and remanded*, 863 F.2d 43, 9 USPQ2d 1335 (Fed. Cir. 1988), *vacated and modified*, 13 USPQ2d 1045 (TTAB 1989). The Trademark Law Revision Act of 1988, which became effective on November 16, 1989, amended §4 to indicate that the "anti-use-by-owner rule" in that section applies specifically to certification marks.

1303.02 Examination of Collective Trademark and Collective Service Mark Applications

The examination of applications to register collective trademarks and collective service marks is conducted in a manner similar to the examination of applications to register regular trademarks and service marks, using most of the same criteria of registrability. Thus, the same standards generally applicable to trademarks and service marks are used in considering issues such as descriptiveness or disclaimers. However, use and ownership requirements are slightly different due to the nature of collective marks. *See* TMEP §§1303.02(c) *et seq*. *See* TMEP §§1304 *et seq*. regarding examination of applications to register collective membership marks.

请时，商标注册前，申请者必须根据 15 U.S.C.§1051(c)的规定提交使用申报修正书，或根据 15 U.S.C.§1051(d)的规定提交使用声明书，声明申请者对于其成员在商业中使用商标实施合理的控制。

在某些情况下，尽管集体商标或集体服务商标由其成员使用，但集体本身也可以使用同一商标，作为集体商标或集体服务商标注册范围内商品的商标。*参见* TMEP §1305，《商标法》§4，15 U.S.C.§1054 规定的“禁止所有者使用规则”不适用于集体商标。*参见* 相关判例：*Roush Bakery Products Co. v. F. R. Lepage Bakery Inc.*, 4 USPQ2d 1401 (TTAB 1987), *aff'd*, 851 F.2d 351, 7 USPQ2d 1395 (Fed. Cir. 1988), *withdrawn, vacated and remanded*, 863 F.2d 43, 9 USPQ2d 1335 (Fed. Cir. 1988), *vacated and modified*, 13 USPQ2d 1045 (TTAB 1989)。1989 年 11 月 16 日生效的《1988 年商标法修订法》对 §4 作了修正，指出该节中的“禁止所有者使用规则”仅适用于证明商标。

1303.02 集体商标和集体服务商标申请的审查

对申请注册集体商标和集体服务商标的审查，类似于对申请注册普通商标和服务商标的审查，所使用的可注册性判断标准大部分相同。因此，在考虑描述性或放弃权利方面的问题时，应使用一般适用于商标和服务商标的同样的标准。不过，由于集体商标的特性，在使用和所有权方面的要求略微有些不同。*参见* TMEP §§1303.02(c)及以下。*参见* TMEP §§1304 及以下，查阅对申请注册集体成员商标的审查。

1303.02(a) Classification of Goods and Services in Collective Trademark and Collective Service Mark Applications

The goods and services recited in collective trademark and collective service mark applications are assigned to the same classes that are appropriate for those goods and services in general, according to the international and prior United States classification schedules set forth in 37 C.F.R. §§6.1 and 6.2. *See* TMEP §§1401 *et seq*. regarding classification.

1303.02(b) Specimens of Use for Collective Trademark and Collective Service Mark Applications

A specimen of use of a collective trademark or service mark should show use of the mark by a member on the member's goods or in the sale or advertising of the member's services. 37 C.F.R. §2.56(b)(3). The specimen should show use of the mark to indicate that the party providing the goods or services is a member of a certain group and meets its standards for admission.

1303.02(c) Special Elements of Collective Trademark and Collective Service Mark Applications

1303.02(c)(i) Manner of Control

Trademark Rule 2.44(a), 37 C.F.R. §2.44(a), states that, in addition to specifying and containing all elements that are applicable for trademarks, an application for registration of a collective mark under §1(a) of the Act must specify the class of persons entitled to use the mark, indicating their relationship to the applicant and the nature of the applicant's control over the use of the mark.

Trademark Rule 2.44(b), 37 C.F.R. §2.44(b), states that, in addition to specify-

1303.02(a) 对集体商标和集体服务商标申请中的商品和服务进行分类

根据 37 C.F.R.§§6.1 及 6.2 中规定的国际和先前美国分类表的规定，对集体商标和集体服务商标申请中的商品和服务的分类一般与相应商品和服务的分类相同。参见 TMEP §§1401 及以下，查阅有关分类的信息。

1303.02(b) 申请集体商标和集体服务商标所使用的样本

使用集体商标或集体服务商标的样本应当显示某成员在其商品上，或在销售和广告其服务的活动中使用了该商标。37 C.F.R.§2.56(b)(3)。样本应当显示使用商标来表明商品或服务的提供者是某团体的成员并符合加入该团体的标准。

1303.02(c) 集体商标和集体服务商标申请的特别要素

1303.02(c)(i) 控制方式

《商标规则》2.44(a)，37 C.F.R.§2.44(a)规定，除了说明并包含商标适用的所有要素之外，依据本法 §1(a) 提出的集体商标注册申请还必须说明哪一类人有资格使用该商标，指出这一类人与申请者之间的关系，以及申请者对商标使用的控制方式。

《商标规则》2.44(b)，37 C.F.R.§2.44(b)规定，除了说明并包含商标适用的所

ing and containing all elements that are applicable for trademarks, an application for registration of a collective mark under §1(b) or §44 of the Act must specify the class of persons intended to be entitled to use the mark, indicating what their relationship to the applicant will be, and the nature of the control the applicant intends to exercise over the use of the mark.

The following language may be used for the above purpose:

> Applicant controls (or, if the application is being filed under 15 U.S.C. §1051(b) or §1126, applicant intends to control) the use of the mark by the members in the following manner:[specify].

If the applicant's bylaws or other written provisions specify the manner of control, or intended manner of control, it will be sufficient to so state.

1303.02(c)(ii) Use by Members Indicated in Dates-of-Use Clause

When setting out dates of use of a collective mark on goods or in connection with services, in either a §1(a) application or an allegation of use filed in connection with a §1(b) application, the applicant must state that the mark was first used by members (or a member) of the applicant.

1304 Collective Membership Marks

1304.01 History of Membership Marks

Section 4 of the Trademark Act of 1946, 15 U.S.C. §1054, provides that collective marks shall be registrable by persons exercising legitimate control over their use, even though not possessing an industrial or commercial establishment, and the definition of a collective mark in §45, 15 U.S.C. §1127, encompasses marks that indicate membership in a union, association or other organization.

The Trademark Act of 1905 prohibited registration by anyone of symbols of col-

有要素之外，依据本法 §1(b)或§44 提出的集体商标注册申请还必须说明意图让哪一类人享有使用商标的资格、指出将来这些人与申请者之间的关系，以及申请者意欲对商标的使用实施什么样的控制。

下列用语可以用于上述用途：

申请者控制(或者，如果是根据 15 U.S.C.§1051(b)或§1126 提出的申请，申请者将要控制。)其成员对商标的使用，方式如下：[具体说明]。

如果申请者的规章制度或其他书面规定说明了控制(或将要控制)的方式，如此说明就足够了。

1303.02(c)(ii) 在使用日期条款中指出由成员使用

如果规定了服务商标用在商品或相关服务上的日期，不管是根据§1(a) 提出的申请还是根据§1(b)规定提出的申请中提交的使用申报，申请者都必须说明该商标首先由其成员使用。

1304 集体成员商标

1304.01 成员商标的历史

《1946 年商标法》第 4 节 15 U.S.C.§1054 规定了集体商标应当由对商标实施合法控制的人申请注册，即使其并未拥有工商企业；§45，15 U.S.C.§1127 规定的集体商标定义包含了指出商标使用者为联盟、协会或其他组织成员的商标。

《1905年商标法》禁止任何人注册集合团体的标记符号。但是《1946年商标法》

lective groups. The Act of 1946, however, contains no prohibition and thus permits registration by the owners of collective marks, including those used to indicate membership.

Membership marks are not trademarks or service marks in the ordinary sense; they are not used in business or trade, and they do not indicate commercial origin of goods or services. Registration of these marks fills the need of collective organizations who do not use the symbols of their organizations on goods or services but who wish to protect their marks to prevent their use by others. *See Ex parte Supreme Shrine of the Order of the White Shrine of Jerusalem*, 109 USPQ 248 (Comm'r Pats. 1956), regarding the rationale for registration of collective membership marks.

1304.02 Purpose of Membership Mark

The sole purpose of a collective membership mark is to indicate that the user of the mark is a member of a particular organization.

1304.03 Use of Membership Mark Is by Members

Registration of a membership mark is based on actual use of the mark by the members of a collective organization. The owner of the mark exercises control over the use of the mark; however, because the sole purpose of a membership mark is to indicate membership, use of the mark is by members. *See In re Triangle Club of Princeton University*, 138 USPQ 332 (TTAB 1963) (collective membership mark registration denied because specimens did not show use of mark by members). *See also* TMEP §1304.09(c).

Nothing in the Trademark Act prohibits the use of the same mark as a membership mark by members and, also, as a trademark or a service mark by the parent organization (*see* TMEP §1303.01), but the same mark may not be used both as a membership mark and as a certification mark. TMEP §1306.05(a).

并未作出禁止性规定，因此准许集体商标所有者注册商标，包括那些用于指出成员资格的商标。

成员商标不是一般意义上的商标或服务商标；它们并不用于商业或贸易，也并不识别商品或服务的商业来源。注册此类商标满足了不在商品或服务中使用组织符号但希望保护其商标以防止他人使用的集体组织的需要。*参见* 相关判例：*Supreme Shrine of the Order of the White Shrine of Jerusalem*，109 USPQ 248（Comm'r Pats. 1956），查阅注册集体成员商标的基本原理。

1304.02　成员商标的用途

集体成员商标的唯一用途是指出该商标的使用者是某特定组织的成员。

1304.03　成员商标由成员使用

注册成员商标的基础是集体组织成员在实际中使用了该商标。商标所有者控制商标的使用；但是，因为成员商标的唯一用途是指出成员资格，因此是由成员使用商标。*参见* 相关判例：*Triangle Club of Princeton University*，138 USPQ 332（TTAB 1963）（由于样本并未显示由成员使用商标，因此集体成员商标的注册申请被拒）。另*参见* TMEP §1304.09(c)。

《商标法》并未禁止同一商标可以由成员用作成员商标，同时由母组织用作商标或服务商标（*参见* TMEP §1303.01），但是同一商标不得同时用作成员商标和证明商标。TMEP §1306.05(a)。

1304.04 Who May Apply to Register Membership Mark

Application to register a membership mark must be made by the organization that controls or intends to control the use of the mark and, therefore, owns or is entitled to use the mark. Application may not be made by a member. Before a registration may be issued, however, the mark must have been used by appropriate members. *See American Speech-Language-Hearing Association v. National Hearing Aid Society*, 224 USPQ 798 (TTAB 1984); *Constitution Party of Texas v. Constitution Association USA*, 152 USPQ 443 (TTAB 1966).

1304.05 Who May Own Membership Mark

The owner of a collective membership mark is normally the collective organization whose own members use the mark. The organization is usually an association, either incorporated or unincorporated, but is not limited to being an association and may have some other form.

A collective membership mark may be owned by someone other than the collective organization whose members use the mark, and the owner might not itself be a collective organization. An example is a business corporation that forms a club for persons meeting certain qualifications and arranges to retain control of the group and of the mark used by the members of the group. The corporation that has retained control over the use of the mark is the owner of the mark, and is entitled to apply to register the mark. *In re Stencel Aero Engineering Corp.*, 170 USPQ 292 (TTAB 1971).

1304.06 Nature of the Collective Group

Under the definition of "collective mark" in §45 of the Trademark Act, 15 U.S.C. §1127, only a "cooperative, an association or other collective group or organ-

1304.04 谁可以申请注册成员商标

申请注册成员商标必须由控制或将要控制商标从而也拥有或有权使用商标的组织提出。成员不得提出申请。不过，在获准注册之前，商标必须已经为相应的成员所使用。*参见*相关判例：*American Speech-Language-Hearing Association v. National Hearing Aid Society*, 224 USPQ 798 (TTAB 1984); *Constitution Party of Texas v. Constitution Association USA*, 152 USPQ 443 (TTAB 1966)。

1304.05 谁可以拥有成员商标

集体成员商标的所有者通常是其成员使用该商标的集体组织。该组织通常是一个协会，可以是法人组织，也可以不是，但并不限于协会，可以是其他形式的组织。

拥有集体成员商标的人也可以是其成员使用该商标的集体组织以外的其他人，所有者本身并不一定是个集体组织。例如，某商业公司为符合特定条件的人开设一个俱乐部，并对该团体及其成员使用的商标加以控制。这个控制了商标的使用的公司就是该商标的所有者，并有资格申请注册该商标。相关判例：*Stencel Aero Engineering Corp.*, 170 USPQ 292 (TTAB 1971)。

1304.06 集合团体的性质

根据《商标法》§45，15 U.S.C.§1127 对“集体商标”所作的定义，只有“合作组

ization" can become the owner of a collective mark. However, there is great variety in the organizational form of collective groups whose members use membership marks. The terms "group" and "organization" are broad enough to cover all groups of persons who are brought together in an organized manner such as to justify their being called "collective."

In order to apply to register a collective membership mark, the collective organization who owns the mark must be a person capable of suing and being sued in a court of law. *See* 15 U.S.C. §1127. *See* TMEP §§803.01 *et seq*. for further information.

The persons that compose a collective group may be either natural or juristic persons.

1304.07 Character of the Mark

A collective membership mark may be a letter or letters, a word or words, a design alone, a name or nickname, or other matter that identifies the collective organization or indicates its purpose. A membership mark may, but need not, include the term "member" or the equivalent.

In addition to being printed (the most common form), a membership mark may consist of an object, such as a flag, or may be a part of articles of jewelry, such as pins or rings. *See* TMEP §§1304.03 and 1304.09(c) regarding use of membership marks and acceptable specimens.

1304.08 Refusal to Register Membership Mark

An application to register a collective membership mark on the Principal Register must meet all the criteria for registration of other marks on the Principal Register. 15 U.S.C. §1054. *See* 37 C.F.R. §2.46. Likewise, when determining the registrability of a collective membership mark on the Supplemental Register, the same

织、协会或其他集合团体或组织”才能成为集体商标的所有者。不过,其成员使用成员商标的集合团体的组织形式可以多种多样。“团体”和“组织”二词的意义十分广泛,足以包括一切可称为“集体”的有组织的团体。

拥有商标的集体组织必须是能够在法院起诉应诉的人,方可申请注册集体成员商标。*参见* 15 U.S.C.§1127。*参见* TMEP §§803.01 及以下,进一步查询信息。

构成集合团体的人可以是自然人,也可以是法人。

1304.07　　商标的特性

集体成员商标可以是一个或几个字母、一个或几个字、一个单独的图案设计、一个名字或绰号,或者其他可以识别集体组织或指出其目的的内容。成员商标可以包含但并非必须包含“成员”一词或类似的词语。

成员商标除了是印刷之物(最常见的形式)外,还可以由物品构成,比如旗帜或者珠宝首饰的一部分,例如别针或指环。*参见* TMEP §§1304.03 及 1304.09(c),查阅成员商标的使用以及可接受的样本。

1304.08　　拒绝注册成员商标

向联邦商标登记簿申请注册的集体成员商标必须符合联邦登记簿其他商标登记注册的一切标准。15 U.S.C.§1054。*参见* 37 C.F.R.§2.46。同样地,在判断某项集体成员商标是否可以向联邦商标补充登记簿申请注册时,需要适用与其他商标同

standards are used as are applied to other types of marks. *See* 37 C. F. R. §2.47. Thus, the same standards generally applicable to trademarks and service marks are used in considering issues such as descriptiveness or disclaimers. *Racine Industries Inc. v. Bane-Clene Corp.*, 35 USPQ2d 1832, 1837 (TTAB 1994); *In re Association of Energy Engineers, Inc.*, 227 USPQ 76, 77 (TTAB 1985).

1304.08(a) Matter That Does Not Function as a Membership Mark

Whether or not matter functions as a collective membership mark is determined by the specimens and evidence of record. It is the use of the mark to indicate membership rather than the character of the matter composing the mark that determines whether a term or other designation is a collective membership mark. *See Ex parte Grand Chapter of Phi Sigma Kappa*, 118 USPQ 467 (Comm'r Pats. 1958), which held that Greek letter abbreviations are not collective membership marks indicating membership in Greek letter societies simply because some people apply them to athletic jerseys, and *In re Mountain Fuel Supply Co.*, 154 USPQ 384 (TTAB 1967), which held that the design on a jewelry pin indicated longevity rather than membership in an organization. If a proposed mark does not function as a mark indicating membership, the examining attorney should refuse registration under §§1, 2, 4, and 45 of the Trademark Act, 15 U. S. C. §§1051, 1052, 1054, and 1127. *See* TMEP §1304.08(c) as to degrees or titles.

1304.08(b) Likelihood of Confusion

Likelihood of confusion may arise from the contemporaneous use of a collective membership mark on the one hand and a trademark or service mark on the other. The same standards used to determine likelihood of confusion between trademarks and service marks also apply to collective membership marks. *See* 15 U.S.C. §1052 (d); *In re National Novice Hockey League, Inc.*, 222 USPQ 638 (TTAB 1984); *Allstate Life Ins. Co. v. Cuna International, Inc.*, 169 USPQ 313 (TTAB 1971), *aff'd*, 487 F. 2d 1407, 180 USPQ 48 (C.C.P.A. 1973); *Boise Cascade Corp. v.*

样的标准。*参见* 37 C.F.R.§2.47。因此，在考虑描述性或放弃权利方面的问题时，应使用一般适用于商标和服务商标的同样的标准。相关判例：*Racine Industries Inc. v. Bane-Clene Corp.*，35 USPQ2d 1832，1837 (TTAB 1994)；*Association of Energy Engineers, Inc.*，227 USPQ 76，77 (TTAB 1985)。

1304.08(a) 不作为成员商标使用的内容

要确定某个内容是否作为集体成员商标，应通过样本和记录证据来判定。一个词或名称是否为集体成员商标由其是否用来表明成员资格而非由构成商标的内容的特点来判定。*参见* 相关判例：*Grand Chapter of Phi Sigma Kappa*，118 USPQ 467 (Comm'r Pats. 1958)，在本案中认为仅凭有些人将希腊字母缩写用在运动衫上这一点，不能说明该希腊字母缩写是用来表明希腊字母学会成员资格的集体成员商标；另外在 *Mountain Fuel Supply Co.*，154 USPQ 384 (TTAB 1967) 一案中，认为宝石别针上的图案设计表明的是资历深而非组织的成员资格。如果申请的商标不作为识别成员资格的商标使用，那么审查员就应当根据《商标法》§§1，2，4 及 45，15 U.S.C. §§1051，1052，1054 及 1127 的规定拒绝注册。*参见* TMEP §1304.08(c)，查阅有关学位或头衔的信息。

1304.08(b) 混淆的可能性

混淆的可能性可以是由于商标一方面作为集体成员商标使用，另一方面又作为商标或服务商标使用。用于判定商标和服务商标之间混淆可能性的标准同样适用于集体成员商标。*参见* 15 U.S.C. §1052(d)；相关判例：*National Novice Hockey League, Inc.*，222 USPQ 638 (TTAB 1984)；*Allstate Life Ins. Co. v. Cuna International, Inc.*，169 USPQ 313 (TTAB 1971)，*aff'd*，487 F.2d 1407，180 USPQ 48 (C.C.P.A. 1973)；*Boise Cascade Corp. v. Mississippi Pine Manufacturers Assn.*，164 USPQ 364 (TTAB 1969)。

Mississippi Pine Manufacturers Assn., 164 USPQ 364 (TTAB 1969).

The finding of likelihood of confusion between a collective membership mark and a trademark or service mark is not based on confusion as to the source of any goods or services which happen to be provided by the members of the collective organization. Rather, the question is whether relevant persons are likely to believe that the trademark owner's goods or services emanate from, are endorsed by, or are in some way associated with the collective organization. *In re Code Consultants Inc*., 60 USPQ2d 1699, 1701 (TTAB 2001).

1304. 08 (c) Degree or Title Designations Contrasted to Membership Marks

Professional, technical, educational, and similar organizations often adopt letters or similar designations to be used by persons to indicate that the persons have passed certain tests or completed certain courses of instruction that are specified by the organization, or have demonstrated a degree of proficiency to the satisfaction of the organization. When such a symbol is used solely as a personal title or degree for an individual (*i.e*., it is used in a manner that identifies only a title or degree conferred on this individual), then it does not serve to indicate membership in an organization and registration as a membership mark must be refused. *In re International Institute of Valuers*, 223 USPQ 350 (TTAB 1984) (refusal affirmed in collective membership application where use of the mark on specimens indicated award of a degree or title, and not membership in collective entity). *See also In re National Society of Cardiopulmonary Technologists, Inc*., 173 USPQ 511 (TTAB 1972). *Cf. In re Thacker*, 228 USPQ 961 (TTAB 1986); *In re National Association of Purchasing Management*, 228 USPQ 768 (TTAB 1986); *In re Mortgage Bankers Association of America*, 226 USPQ 954 (TTAB 1985).

If the proposed mark functions simply as a degree or title, the examining attorney should refuse registration under §§1,2,4,and 45 of the Trademark Act,15U.S.C. §§1051, 1052, 1054, and 1127, on the ground that the matter does not function

判定集体成员商标与商标或服务商标之间存在混淆的可能性，并不是根据恰巧由集体组织成员提供的任何商品或服务的来源是否混淆。其实，问题在于，相关人员是否可能相信商标所有者的商品或服务是自于集体组织，还是由集体组织提供背书证明或者以某种方式与集体组织相关联。相关判例：*Code Consultants Inc.*, 60 USPQ2d 1699, 1701（TTAB 2001）。

1304.08(c) 与成员商标相对的学位或头衔名称

专业、技术、教育以及类似的组织经常采用证书或者类似的称号，由人们使用以指出其已经通过了该组织指定的某些测试、或完成了组织指定的某些教育课程、或者显示出组织所认可的一种技术熟练程度。如果这类符号只是被用作某个人的个人头衔或学位（即，它只是用来识别授予某个人的头衔或学位），那么它就不能用来识别组织的成员资格，故此必须拒绝将其作为成员商标进行注册。相关判例：*International Institute of Valuers*, 223 USPQ 350（TTAB 1984）（商标使用样本显示这只是授予一种学位或头衔，而非集体实体的成员资格，因此拒绝其作为集体成员商标注册）。*另参见 National Society of Cardiopulmonary Technologists, Inc.*, 173 USPQ 511（TTAB 1972）。比照：*Thacker*, 228 USPQ 961（TTAB 1986）；*National Association of Purchasing Management*, 228 USPQ 768（TTAB 1986）；*Mortgage Bankers Association of America*, 226 USPQ 954（TTAB 1985）。

如果申请的商标只是作为学位或头衔，那么审查员就应当根据《商标法》§§1，2，4 及 45，15 U.S.C. §§1051，1052，1054 及 1127 的规定，以该内容不能作为成员商标为由，拒绝注册。*参见* TMEP §1304.08(a)。

as a membership mark. *See* TMEP §1304.08(a).

1304.09 Examination of Collective Membership Mark Applications

The examination of collective membership mark applications is conducted in the same manner as the examination of applications to register trademarks and service marks, using the same criteria of registrability. Thus, the same standards generally applicable to trademarks and service marks are used in considering issues such as descriptiveness or disclaimers. However, use and ownership requirements are slightly different due to the nature of collective membership marks.

1304.09(a) Classification in Membership Mark Applications

Collective membership marks are classified in Class 200. 37 C.F.R. §6.4.

Class 200 was established as a result of the decision in *Ex parte Supreme Shrine of the Order of the White Shrine of Jerusalem*, 109 USPQ 248 (Comm'r Pats.1956). Before this decision, there was no registration of membership insignia as such on the theory that all collective marks were either collective trademarks or collective service marks. Some marks that were actually membership marks were registered under the Act of 1946 as collective service marks, and a few were registered as collective trademarks. That practice was discontinued upon the clarification of the basis for registration of membership marks and the creation of Class 200.

1304.09(b) Identifications in Membership Mark Applications

An identification of goods or services is not appropriate in connection with a collective membership mark. The purpose of a collective membership mark is to indicate membership in an organization. Appropriate identification language would be, "to indicate membership in an organization (association, club or the like)...," followed by a phrase indicating the nature of the organization or association, *e.g.*,

1304.09　对集体成员商标申请的审查

对于集体成员商标申请的审查，采用同商标和服务商标注册申请同样的审查方式，采用同样的可注册性标准。因此，在考虑描述性或放弃权利方面的问题时，应使用一般适用于商标和服务商标的同样的标准。不过，由于集体成员商标的特性，在使用和所有权方面的要求略微有些不同。

1304.09(a)　成员商标申请中的分类

集体成员商标被分到"200 类"中。37 C.F.R.§6.4。

"200 类"是根据 *Supreme Shrine of the Order of the White Shrine of Jerusalem*, 109 USPQ 248 (Comm'r Pats.1956) 一案的判决结果设立的。在此判决之前，由于在理论上集体商标只存在集体商标和集体服务商标的分类，因此不存在成员商标的注册登记。一些实际上是成员商标的商标，根据《1946 年商标法》注册为集体服务商标，另一些则注册为集体商标。在明确成员商标的注册基础以及设立"200 类"之后，就不再沿用这种做法了。

1304.09(b)　成员商标申请中的识别

商品或服务的识别与集体成员商标之间相关联是不适当的。集体成员商标的用途在于指出是某组织的成员资格。适当的识别用语为："为了指出组织（协会、俱乐部或诸如此类）的成员资格……"后面跟随指出组织或协会性质的语句，例如："为指出

"to indicate membership in an organization of computer professionals."

The nature of an organization can be indicated by specifying the area of activity of its members (*e.g.*, they may sell lumber, or cosmetics, or food, or may deal in chemical products or household goods, or they may provide services as fashion designers or engineers or accountants). If goods or services are not directly involved, the nature of an organization can be indicated by specifying the organization's type or purpose (such as a service or social club, a political society, a trade association, a beneficial fraternal organization, or the like). Detailed descriptions of an organization's objectives or activities are not necessary. It is sufficient if the identification indicates broadly either the field of activity as related to the goods or services, or the general type or purpose of the organization.

1304.09(c) Specimens of Use for Membership Marks

The owner of a collective membership mark exercises control over the use of the mark but does not itself use the mark to indicate membership. A specimen of use of a collective membership mark must show use by members to indicate membership in the collective organization. 37 C.F.R. §2.56(b)(4). *In re International Association for Enterostomal Therapy, Inc.*, 218 USPQ 343 (TTAB 1983); *In re Triangle Club of Princeton University*, 138 USPQ 332 (TTAB 1963). *See also* TMEP §1304.03.

The most common type of specimen is a membership card. Membership certificates are also acceptable. The applicant may submit a blank or voided membership card or certificate.

For trade or professional associations, decals bearing the mark for use by members on doors or windows in their establishments, wall plaques bearing the mark, or decals or plates for use, *e.g.*, on members' vehicles are satisfactory specimens. If the members are in business and place the mark on their business stationery to show their membership, pieces of such stationery are acceptable. Flags, pennants,

电脑专业人员组织的成员资格。”

组织的性质可以通过说明其成员的活动领域来表明(例如,他们可以销售木材,或化妆品,或食品,或者他们可以经营化学品或家庭用品,或者他们可以作为时装设计师、工程师或会计师提供服务)。如果并不直接涉及商品或服务,组织的性质也可以通过说明组织类型或目的来表明(比如服务或社会俱乐部、政治性社团、贸易协会、盈利共济组织,或诸如此类)。无须详细说明组织的目标或活动。识别只要能够广泛地指出与商品或服务有关联的活动领域,或者组织的一般类型或目的即可。

1304.09(c) 成员商标的使用样本

集体成员商标的所有者对商标的使用实施控制,但是本身并不使用商标来表明成员资格。集体成员商标的使用样本必须表明成员使用商标,以表明其为该集体组织的成员。37 C.F.R. §2.56(b)(4)。相关判例:*International Association for Enterostomal Therapy, Inc.*, 218 USPQ 343 (TTAB 1983);*Triangle Club of Princeton University*, 138 USPQ 332 (TTAB 1963)。*另参见* TMEP §1304.03。

最普通的样本类型是会员卡。成员证书也可以。申请者可以提交一份空白或无效的会员卡或证书。

对于行业或专业协会,供成员们在其营业处所的门窗上使用的印有商标的贴纸、印有商标的贴墙砖,或者例如在成员的车辆上使用的贴纸及铭牌等,均为符合要求的样本。如果成员们在业务来往中将商标用于业务信函上以表明成员身份,则此类信函也可作为样本。用于表示政治党派、俱乐部、团体或类似组织的各种旗帜、三角旗

and banners of various types used in connection with political parties, club groups, or the like could be satisfactory specimens.

Many associations, particularly fraternal societies, use jewelry such as pins, rings or charms to indicate membership. *See In re Triangle Club of Princeton University*, *supra*. However, not every ornamental design on jewelry is necessarily an indication of membership. The record must show that the design on a piece of jewelry is actually an indication of membership before the jewelry can be accepted as a specimen of use. *See In re Institute for Certification of Computer Professionals*, 219 USPQ 372 (TTAB 1983) (in view of contradictory evidence in record, lapel pin with nothing more than CCP thereon was not considered evidence of membership); *In re Mountain Fuel Supply Co*., 154 USPQ 384 (TTAB 1967) (design on pin did not indicate membership in organization, but merely showed length of service).

Shoulder, sleeve, pocket, or similar patches, whose design constitutes a membership mark and that are authorized by the parent organization for use by members on garments to indicate membership, are normally acceptable as specimens.

A specimen that shows use of the mark by the collective organization itself, rather than by a member, is not acceptable. Collective organizations often publish various kinds of printed material, such as catalogs, directories, bulletins, newsletters, magazines, programs, and the like. Placing the mark on these items by the collective organization represents use of the mark as a trademark or service mark to indicate that the collective organization is the source of the material. The mark is not placed on these items by the parent organization to indicate membership of a person in the organization.

1304.09(d) Special Elements of Applications for Collective Membership Marks

1304.09(d)(i) Exercise of Control

An application to register a collective membership mark must accurately convey

以及横幅,也是符合要求的样本。

许多协会,尤其是共济会组织,使用诸如别针、指环或小饰物之类的珠宝来识别成员资格。*参见* *Triangle Club of Princeton University*,*同前*。但是,并非珠宝上的每个装饰图案都表明成员资格。在珠宝被接受为使用样本之前,必须有记录表明该珠宝的图案确实用来表明成员资格。*参见* 相关判例:*Institute for Certification of Computer Professionals*, 219 USPQ 372 (TTAB 1983)(由于记录中存在相反的证据,故仅带有"CCP"的衣领夹不被认为是成员资格的证明);*Mountain Fuel Supply Co*., 154 USPQ 384 (TTAB 1967)(别针上的图案并非识别组织的成员身份,而只是显示为组织服务的时间长短)。

经母组织授权由其成员用在服装上,以识别成员资格的肩部、袖子、口袋或类似缀片,如果其图案设计构成成员商标,通常为可接受的样本。

如样本显示使用商标的是集体组织自身而非其成员,则为不可接受的样本。集体组织经常出版各种印刷资料,例如目录册、通讯录、公告、新闻简讯、杂志、计划,以及诸如此类。集体组织将商标用在这类物品上,可以表示将商标作为商标或服务商标使用,以指出集体组织是这些资料的来源。商标并非母组织加在这类物品上用以表明某人为组织成员。

1304.09(d) 集体成员商标申请中的特别要素

1304.09(d)(i) 实施控制

集体成员商标的注册申请,必须通过如下的适当语句,准确地表明对商标的使用

the use or intended use of the mark with appropriate language, as follows.

In an application based on use in commerce under 15 U.S.C.§1051(a), the applicant must assert that the applicant is exercising legitimate control over the use of the mark in commerce by its members.

In an application based on 15 U.S.C.§1051(b) or 15 U.S.C.§1126, the applicant must assert that the applicant has a bona fide intention to exercise legitimate control over the use of the mark in commerce by its members. In a §1(b) application, before the mark can register, the applicant must file an amendment to allege use under 15 U.S.C.§1051(c) or a statement of use under 15 U.S.C.§1051(d) alleging that the applicant is exercising legitimate control over the use of the mark in commerce by its members.

1304.09(d)(ii) Manner of Control

Trademark Rule 2.44(a), 37 C.F.R.§2.44(a), states that, in addition to specifying and containing all elements that are applicable for trademarks, an application for registration of a collective mark under §1(a) of the Act must specify the class of persons entitled to use the mark, indicating their relationship to the applicant and the nature of the applicant's control over the use of the mark.

Trademark Rule 2.44(b), 37 C.F.R.§2.44(b), states that, in addition to specifying and containing all elements that are applicable for trademarks, an application for registration of a collective mark under §1(b) or §44 of the Act must specify the class of persons intended to be entitled to use the mark, indicating what their relationship to the applicant will be, and the nature of the control the applicant intends to exercise over the use of the mark.

The following language may be used for the above purpose:

Applicant controls (or, if the application is being filed under 15 U.S.C.§1051(b) or §1126, applicant intends to control) the use of the mark by the members in the

或意图将要使用。

因此，在根据 15 U.S.C.§1051(a)的规定、基于商业使用而提出的申请中，申请者必须声明其正在对在商业中由其成员使用的商标实施合理的控制。

在根据 15 U.S.C.§1051(b)或 15 U.S.C.§1126 提出的申请中，申请者必须声明其真实意图对由其成员在商业中使用的商标实施合理的控制。在根据§1(b)提出申请时，商标注册前，申请者必须根据 15 U.S.C.§1051(c)的规定提交使用申报修正书，或根据 15 U.S.C.§1051(d)的规定提交使用声明书，声明申请者对于其成员在商业中使用商标实施合理的控制。

1304.09(d)(ii)　控制方式

《商标规则》2.44(a)，37 C.F.R.§2.44(a)规定，除了说明并包含商标适用的所有要素之外，依据本法 §1(a) 提出的集体商标注册申请还必须说明哪一类人有资格使用该商标，指出这一类人与申请者之间的关系，以及申请者对商标使用的控制方式。

《商标规则》2.44(b)，37 C.F.R.§2.44(b)规定，除了说明并包含商标适用的所有要素之外，依据本法 §1(b)或§44 提出的集体商标注册申请还必须说明意图让哪一类人享有使用商标的资格、指出将来这些人与申请者之间的关系，以及申请者意欲对商标的使用实施什么样的控制。

下列用语可以用于上述用途：

申请者控制（或者，如果是根据 15 U.S.C.§1051(b)或§1126 提出的申

following manner:[specify].

If the applicant's by-laws or other written provisions specify the manner of control, or intended manner of control, it will be sufficient to so state.

1304.09(d)(iii) Use by Members Indicated in Dates-of-Use Clause

When setting out dates of use of a collective membership mark, the application or allegation of use must state that the mark was first used by members of the applicant rather than by the applicant, and that the mark was first used on a specified date to indicate membership rather than first used on goods or in connection with services.

1305 Trademarks and Service Marks Used by Collective Organizations

A collective organization may itself use trademarks and service marks to identify its goods and services, as opposed to collective trademarks and service marks or collective membership marks used by the collective's members. *See B. F. Goodrich Company v. National Cooperatives, Inc.*, 114 USPQ 406 (Comm'r Pats. 1957) (mark used to identify tires made for applicant cooperative and sold by its distributors is trademark, not collective mark that identifies goods of applicant's associated organizations; applicant alone provides specifications and other instructions and applicant alone is responsible for faulty tires).

The examination of applications to register trademarks and service marks used or intended to be used by collective organizations is conducted in the same manner as for other trademarks and service marks, using the same criteria of registrability.

The form of the application used by collective organizations is the same as for those used or intended to be used by other applicants. The collective organization should be listed as the applicant, because it uses or intends to use the mark itself.

请，申请者将要控制）其成员对商标的使用，方式如下：[详细说明]。

如果申请者的规章制度或其他书面规定说明了控制（或将要控制）的方式，如此说明就足够了。

1304.09(d)(iii) 在使用日期条款中指出由成员使用

如果规定了服务商标用在商品或相关服务上的日期，申请或使用申报必须说明该商标首先由其成员而非申请者自己使用，而且商标首先在指定的日期使用以表明成员资格，而非首先用在商品或相关服务上。

1305 由集体组织使用的商标和服务商标

与由集体成员使用的集体商标和服务商标或集体成员商标相反，集体组织自身也可以使用商标和服务商标来识别商品和服务。参见 *B. F. Goodrich Company v. National Cooperatives, Inc.*, 114 USPQ 406 (Comm'r Pats. 1957)（为申请者合作者生产并由申请者的经销商销售的轮胎所使用的商标为商标，并非识别申请者相关组织的商品的集体商标；申请者独自提供规范和其他说明，并且独自为有缺陷的轮胎负责）。

审查申请注册由或意图由集体组织使用的商标和服务商标时，采用与审查其他商标和服务商标申请一样的方式，对于可注册性适用同样的标准。

集体组织使用的申请表格同其他申请者使用的申请表格一样。应以集体组织为申请者，因为是它自己使用或意图使用该商标。提交的样本必须是集体组织用于其

The specimen submitted must be material applied by the collective organization to its goods or used in connection with its services.

1306 Certification Marks

1306.01 Definition of Certification Mark

Section 4 of the Trademark Act, 15 U.S.C. §1054, provides for the registration of "certification marks, including indications of regional origin." Section 45 of the Trademark Act, 15 U.S.C. §1127, defines "certification mark" as follows:

> The term "certification mark" means any word, name, symbol, or device, or any combination thereof—
>
> (1) used by a person other than its owner, or
>
> (2) which its owner has a bona fide intention to permit a person other than the owner to use in commerce and files an application to register on the principal register established by this Act,
>
> to certify regional or other origin, material, mode of manufacture, quality, accuracy, or other characteristics of such person's goods or services or that the work or labor on the goods or services was performed by members of a union or other organization.

A certification mark "is a special creature created for a purpose uniquely different from that of an ordinary service mark or trademark ..." *In re Florida Citrus Commission*, 160 USPQ 495, 499 (TTAB 1968).

There are generally three types of certification marks. First, there are certification marks that certify that goods or services originate in a specific geographic region (*e.g.*, ROQUEFORT for cheese). *See Community of Roquefort v. William Faehndrich, Inc.*, 303 F.2d 494, 133 USPQ 633 (2d Cir. 1962); *State of Florida, Department of Citrus v. Real Juices, Inc.*, 330 F.Supp. 428, 171 USPQ 66 (M.D.

商品或相关服务的材料。

1306 证明商标

1306.01 证明商标的定义

《商标法》第 4 节 15 U.S.C.§1054 对“证明商标，包括原产地标记”的注册作了规定。《商标法》第 45 节 15 U.S.C.§1127 对“证明商标”作了如下定义：

> “证明商标”一词是指任何文字、名称、符号或图案，或以上任何组合，并且是——
>
> (1) 由其所有者以外的其他人使用，或
>
> (2) 其所有者真实的意图准许除自己以外的其他人在商业中使用，并提出申请要求在依据本法设立的联邦商标登记簿上注册。
>
> 用以证明该人的商品或服务的原产地或其他来源、材质、生产方式、质量、精确度或其他特性，或者证明该人的商品或服务是由某联盟或其他组织成员来完成。

证明商标“是一种特殊的创造物，有其独特的用途，有别于普通的服务商标或商标……”——*Florida Citrus Commission*，160 USPQ 495，499（TTAB 1968）。

一般有三类证明商标。第一种，证明商标用以证明商品或服务来自特定的地域（例如，干酪证明商标“ROQUEFORT”）。参见 *Community of Roquefort v. William Faehndrich, Inc.*，303 F.2d 494，133 USPQ 633（2d Cir.1962）；*State of Florida, Department of Citrus v. Real Juices, Inc.*，330 F.Supp.428，171 USPQ 66（M.D.

Fla. 1971) (SUNSHINE TREE for citrus from Florida); *Bureau National Interprofessionnel Du Cognac v. International Better Drinks Corp.*, 6 USPQ2d 1610 (TTAB 1988) (COGNAC for distilled brandy from a region in France). *See* TMEP §§1306.02 *et seq*.

Second, there are certification marks that certify that the goods or services meet certain standards in relation to quality, materials, or mode of manufacture (*e.g.*, approval by Underwriters Laboratories). *See Midwest Plastic Fabricators Inc. v. Underwriters Laboratories Inc.*, 906 F.2d 1568, 15 USPQ2d 1359 (Fed. Cir. 1990) (UL certifies, among other things, representative samplings of electrical equipment meeting certain safety standards); *In re Celanese Corporation of America*, 136 USPQ 86 (TTAB 1962) (CELANESE certifies plastic toys meeting certifier's safety standards).

Third, certification marks may certify that the work or labor on the products or services was performed by a member of a union or other organization, or that the performer meets certain standards. *See* TMEP §1306.03 and cases cited therein for further information.

The statutory definition differentiates certification marks from trademarks or service marks by two characteristics. First, a certification mark is not used by its owner and, second, a certification mark does not indicate commercial source nor distinguish the goods or services of one person from those of another person. *See* TMEP §1306.09(a) for a discussion of the distinction between a certification mark and a collective trademark, collective service mark or collective membership mark.

See Holtzman, *Certification Marks: An Overview*, 81 Trademark Rep. 180 (1991).

1306.01(a) Use Is by Person Other than Owner

A certification mark may not be used, in the trademark sense of "used," by the

Fla.1971)(佛罗里达柑橘的证明商标为“SUNSHINE TREE”);*Bureau National Interprofessionnel Du Cognac v. International Better Drinks Corp.*, 6 USPQ2d 1610 (TTAB 1988)(法国某地区蒸馏白兰地的证明商标为“COGNAC”)。*参见* TMEP §§1306.02 及以下。

第二种,证明商标用以证明商品或服务符合有关质量、材质或生产方式的特定标准(例如,UL 实验室的批准)。*参见 Midwest Plastic Fabricators Inc. v. Underwriters Laboratories Inc.*, 906 F.2d 1568, 15 USPQ2d 1359 (Fed. Cir. 1990)(除了证明其他内容外,“UL”这一商标还证明了电器设备的代表性样品符合特定的安全标准);*Celanese Corporation of America*, 136 USPQ 86 (TTAB 1962)(“CELANESE”商标证明塑料玩具符合证明者的安全标准)。

第三种,证明商标可以证明商品或服务是由某工会或其他组织成员来完成,或者证明工作者符合特定的标准。*参见* TMEP §1306.03 及其引用的判例,查阅进一步信息。

法律的定义在两个特性上区分了证明商标与商标或服务商标。首先,证明商标只能由其所有者使用;其次,证明商标并没有指出商品或服务的商业来源,也没有将某人的商品或服务与他人的商品或服务区分开来。*参见* TMEP §1306.09(a),查阅有关证明商标与集体商标、集体服务商标或集体成员商标的区别。

参见 Holtzman, *Certification Marks: An Overview*, 81 Trademark Rep 180 (1991)。

1306.01(a) 使用者为所有者以外的人

如果按商标意义上的“使用”理解,证明商标不能由商标所有者使用;而只能由商

owner of the mark; it may be used only by a person or persons other than the owner of the mark. That is, the owner of a certification mark does not apply the mark to his or her goods or services and, in fact, usually does not attach or apply the mark at all. The mark is generally applied by other persons to their goods or services, with authorization from the owner of the mark.

The owner of a certification mark does not produce the goods or perform the services in connection with which the mark is used, and thus does not control their nature and quality. Therefore, it is not appropriate to inquire about control over the nature and quality of the goods or services. What the owner of the certification mark does control is use of the mark by others on their goods or services. This control consists of taking steps to ensure that the mark is applied only to goods or services that contain the characteristics or meet the requirements that the certifier/owner has established or adopted for the certification. *See* TMEP §1306.06(g)(ii) regarding submission of the standards established by the certifier to determine whether the certification mark may be used in relation to the goods and/or services of others.

1306.01(b) Purpose Is to Certify, Not to Indicate Source

The purpose of a certification mark is to inform purchasers that the goods or services of a person possess certain characteristics or meet certain qualifications or standards established by another person. A certification mark does not indicate origin in a single commercial or proprietary source. In certifying, the same mark is used on the goods or services of many different producers.

The message conveyed by a certification mark is that the goods or services have been examined, tested, inspected, or in some way checked by a person who is not their producer, by methods determined by the certifier/owner. The placing of the mark on goods or its use in connection with services thus constitutes a certification by someone other than the producer that the prescribed characteristics or qualifications of the certifier for those goods or services have been met.

标所有者以外的人(们)使用。也就是说,证明商标的所有者不能将该商标用在其商品或服务上,而且事实上,通常根本不贴或应用该商标。通常,商标经所有者授权,由其他人将其应用在商品或服务上。

证明商标的所有者并不生产或提供使用该商标的商品或服务,因此对于商品或服务的性质和质量也不加控制。因此,询问是否控制商品或服务的性质和质量是不适当的。证明商标的所有者需要控制的是其他人在其商品或服务上使用商标的情况。这种控制包括采取一定的步骤,确保商标只用于含有某些特性或满足要求的商品或服务上,这些特性和要求由证明者/所有者为证明而设立或采用。*参见* TMEP §1306.06(g)(ii),查阅有关提交证明者所设立的、判断证明商标是否可以用在他人的商品和(或)服务的标准。

1306.01(b)　用途是证明,而非指明来源

证明商标的用途在于,告知购买者某人的商品或服务拥有特定的性质或符合特定的资格及标准,而此类要求是由其他人设置的。证明商标并非用来识别一种单一的商业或专有来源。在证明过程中,同一个商标会用于许多不同生产商的商品或服务。

证明商标所传达的信息是,该商品或服务已经经过根据证明人/所有人确定的方式、由生产者以外的人进行的审查、测试、检查或某种形式的查验。将该商标识别于商品或相关服务的使用过程中,构成了由产品生产者以外的人所作的证明,表明该商品或服务已经满足证明人所确定的性质或条件。

1306.02 Certification Marks That Are Indications of Regional Origin

A geographical term may be used, either alone or as a portion of a composite mark, to certify that the goods originate in the particular geographical region identified by the term. As noted in *Community of Roquefort v. William Faehndrich, Inc.*, 303 F.2d 494, 497, 133 USPQ 633, 635 (2d Cir. 1962):

A geographical name does not require a secondary meaning in order to qualify for registration as a certification mark. It is true that section 1054 provides that certification marks are "subject to the provisions relating to the registration of trademarks, so far as they are applicable ..." But section 1052(e)(2), which prohibits registration of names primarily geographically descriptive, specifically excepts "indications of regional origin" registrable under section 1054. Therefore, a geographical name may be registered as a certification mark even though it is primarily geographically descriptive.

When a geographical term is used in a composite certification mark to certify regional origin, the examining attorney should not require a disclaimer or refuse registration of the composite mark on the ground that the mark is primarily geographically descriptive. However, when a geographical term used in a composite certification mark is not used to certify regional origin, the examining attorney should refuse registration or require a disclaimer, as appropriate.

Marks that may be used to certify regional origin are not necessarily limited to terms that comprise precise geographical terminology. A distortion of a geographical term, an abbreviation of a geographical term, or a combination of geographical terms can be used as, or in, a certification mark indicating regional origin. It is also possible for a term that is not technically geographical to have significance as an indication of origin solely in a particular region.

The issue in determining whether a designation is registrable as a regional certifi-

1306.02　表明原产地的证明商标

一个地理名词可以单独或作为混合商标的一部分，证明商品原产于该名称所识别的特定地区。以下摘录于：*Community of Roquefort v. William Faehndrich, Inc.*，303 F.2d 494，497，133 USPO 633，635（2d Cir.1962）：

> 一个地理名称无需第二含义即可作为证明商标注册。尽管在1054节中规定，证明商标"就其可适用性而言，应按与商标注册有关的规定执行……"但在1052(e)(2)节中规定，主要为地理描述性名称的禁止注册，但特别规定"表明原产地"的属于例外情况，可以根据1054节进行注册。因此，即使一个地理名称主要是地理描述性的名称，也可以作为证明商标注册。

当一个地理名词用在复合证明商标中以证明原产地时，审查员不应当以主要为地理描述性名称为由，要求放弃权利或拒绝该复合商标的注册。但是，如果在复合证明商标中使用的地理名词并非用来证明原产地，则审查员应当根据情况拒绝注册或要求放弃权利。

证明原产地的商标可以不必只限于精确的地理名称。地理名词的变体、缩写或几个地理名词的组合，都可以用作或用于指明原产地的证明商标。技术上并非地理性的名称，同样也可以独自在特定的地域内作为原产地商标。

判断某一名称是否可以作为产地证明商标的关键，在于公众是否理解附有该商

cation mark is whether the public understands that goods bearing the mark come only from the region named in the mark, not whether the public is expressly aware of the certification function of the mark per se. If use of the designation in fact is controlled by the certifier and limited to products meeting the certifier's standards of regional origin, and if purchasers understand the designation to refer only to products produced in the particular region and not to products produced elsewhere, then the designation functions as a regional certification mark. *Institut National Des Appellations D'Origine v. Brown-Forman Corp.*, 47 USPQ2d 1875 (TTAB 1998).

A mark that is geographically deceptive may not be registered as a certification mark of regional origin. *See* TMEP §§1210.05 *et seq*. regarding geographically deceptive marks.

1306.02(a) Indicating the Region

The examining attorney should examine the specimens of use and evidence in the record to determine whether the geographical term is being used as a certification mark to indicate the regional origin of the goods upon which it is used. If the record or other evidence available to the examining attorney indicates that a specific term in question has a principal significance as a generic term denoting a type of goods, registration should be refused. *In re Cooperativa Produttori Latte E Fontina Valle D'Acosta*, 230 USPQ 131 (TTAB 1986) (FONTINA held a generic name of a type of cheese rather than a certification mark indicating regional origin, in view of the fact that non-certified producers outside that region use the term to identify non-certified cheeses). The basis for refusal of registration on the Principal Register is 15 U.S.C. §§1052(e)(1), 1054, and 1127, and the basis for refusal of registration on the Supplemental Register is 15 U.S.C. §§1054, 1091 and 1127 (*see* TMEP §1209.02).

When a geographic term is being used as a certification mark to indicate regional origin, the application should define the regional origin that the mark certifies.

标的商品只能来自于商标所指的地区,而不在于公众是否明确意识到该商标本身的证明作用。如果名称的使用事实上受到证明者的控制,并且局限于满足证明者产地证明标准的产品,而且如果购买者理解该名称只能是指某特定产地的产品,而不会是指任何其他地方生产的产品,那么该名称就可以作为原产地证明商标。*Institut National Des Appellations D' Origine v. Brown-Forman Corp.*, 47 USPQ2d 1875 (TTAB 1998)。

具有地理误导性的商标不得作为原产地证明商标进行注册。参见 TMEP §§1210.05 及以下,查阅关于在地理误导性商标的信息。

1306.02(a) 指明地区

审查员应当审查商标使用样本和记录中的证据,判断该地理名词是否被用在商品上作为指出商品原产地的证明商标。如果记录或审查员获得的其他证据表明,申请注册的特定名词是一个主要表示商品种类的一般名称,则应当拒绝其注册。相关判例:*Cooperativa Produttori Latte E Fontina Valle D' Acosta*, 230 USPQ 131 (TTAB 1986)("FONTINA"被认为在更大程度上是某种干酪的一般名称,而非指出原产地的证明商标,因为在该地区以外的非证明生产者同样使用该名词识别非证明的干酪)。拒绝在联邦商标登记簿上注册的依据是 15 U.S.C. §§1052(e)(1), 1054 及 1127;拒绝在联邦商标补充登记簿上注册的依据是 15 U.S.C. §§1054, 1091 及 1127(参见 TMEP §1209.02)。

如果某地理名词被用作指出原产地的证明商标,则申请书应当说明该商标所证明的原产地。

1306.02(b) Authority to Control a Geographical Term

When a certification mark consists solely, or essentially, of a geographical term, the examining attorney should inquire as to the authority of the applicant to control the use of the term, if the authority is not obvious. Normally the entity that has authority to exercise control over the use of a geographical term as a certification mark is a governmental body or a body operating with governmental authorization. The right that a private person can acquire in a geographical term is usually a trademark right, on the basis of exclusive use resulting in the term becoming distinctive of that person's goods. When, however, circumstances make it desirable or necessary for many or all persons in a region to use the name of the region to indicate the origin of their goods, there would be no opportunity for the name to become distinctive for only one person. The term would be used by all persons in the region, not as a trademark indicating commercial origin, but as a certification mark indicating regional origin.

When a geographical term is used as a certification mark, two elements are of basic concern: first, preserving the freedom of all persons in the region to use the term and; second, preventing abuses or illegal uses of the mark that would be detrimental to all those entitled to use the mark. Normally a private individual is not in the best position to fulfill these objectives. The government of a region would be the logical authority to control the use of the name of the region. The government, either directly or through a body to which it has given authority, would have power to preserve the right of all persons and to prevent abuse or illegal use of the mark.

1306.02(c) The Government as Applicant for a Geographical Certification Mark

The applicant may be the government itself (such as the government of the Unit-

1306.02(b)　控制地理术语的权力

当证明商标主要或仅包含某地理名词时，如果控制该词使用的权力不明，审查员就应当对申请者的此种权力进行调查。有权对作为证明商标使用的地理名词行使控制的实体通常是政府机构或者政府授权的机构。对于地理名词，私人能够获得的权利通常是一种商标权，系基于专有使用而导致该名词成为此人商品的特有商标。但是，如果发生某地区的许多或所有人都希望或必须将地名用于识别其商品产地的情况，则该地名不得为某个人专用。该名词将为该地区所有人用作识别原产地的证明商标，而非作为识别商业来源的商标来使用。

如某一地理名词被用作证明商标，则有两个基本要素需要考虑：首先，保留该地区所有人使用该名词的自由；其次，防止商标的滥用或非法使用，造成妨害所有有权使用商标的人使用该商标。通常，私人个体并不是满足这些目标的最佳人选。地区政府是控制地名使用的合理机关。政府直接或通过授权机构，有权为所有人保留权利并防止该商标的滥用和非法使用。

1306.02(c)　政府作为地理证明商标的申请者

申请者可以是政府本身（如美国、某一州或某一市的政府）、政府部门或经政府

ed States, a state or a city), one of the departments of a government, or a body operating with governmental authorization that is not formally a part of the government. There may be an interrelationship between bodies in more than one of these categories and the decision as to which is the appropriate body to apply depends on which body actually conducts the certification program or is most directly associated with it. The determination may be made by the applicant, provided the examining attorney does not find any inconsistency between the selection and the facts indicated in the record.

1306.03 Certification Marks Certifying that Labor Was Performed by Specific Group or Individual

A certification mark may be used to certify that the work or labor on the goods or services was performed by a member of a union or other organization, or by a person who meets certain standards and tests of competency set by the certifier. 15 U.S.C. §1127. The certifier does not certify the quality of the work being performed, but only that the work was performed by a member of the union or group, or by someone who meets certain standards. *In re National Institute for Automotive Service Excellence*, 218 USPQ 744, 747 (TTAB 1983). *See also American Speech-Language-Hearing Association v. National Hearing Aid Society*, 224 USPQ 798 (TTAB 1984). Used in this manner, the mark certifies a characteristic of the goods or services. Whether or not specific matter functions as a certification mark depends on whether the matter is used in connection with the goods or services in such a manner that the purchasing public will recognize it, either consciously or otherwise, as a certification mark.

Occasionally it is not clear whether a term is being used to certify that work or labor relating to the goods or services was performed by someone meeting certain standards or by members of a union or other organization to indicate membership or whether the term is merely being used as a title or a degree of the performer to indicate professional qualifications . Matter that might appear to be simply a title

授权,并非政府正式部门的机构。各机构之间可能在多个类别中相互关联,关于哪个是适合提出申请的机构取决于哪个机构实际执行了证明程序或同其有最直接的联系。只要审查员在所作的选择与记录揭示的事实之间没有发现任何矛盾之处,则决定可以由申请者做出。

1306.03 证明商标证明工作由特定团体或个人完成

证明商标可以用于证明,某项商品或服务的工作或劳务,是由某联盟或其他组织的成员或者由符合证明者设立的特定资格标准和通过资格测试的个人完成或提供的。15 U.S.C.§1127。证明者证明的不是所做工作的质量,而仅仅证明该工作是由联盟或团体的成员或由符合特定标准的个人完成的。相关判例:*National Institute for Automotive Service Excellence*, 218 USPQ 744, 747(TTAB 1983)。另参见 *American Speech-Language-Hearing Association v. National Hearing Aid Society*, 224 USPQ 798(TTAB 1984)。以这种方式使用时,该商标证明了商品或服务的某种特性。某特定内容是否作为证明商标取决于该内容用于商品或服务时的方式是否会使购买公众有意识或无意识地认为其为一种证明商标。

在某些情况下,会分不清某个名词是用作证明相关商品或服务的工作由某联盟或其他组织的成员或由符合特定标准的人员完成,还是仅仅用作一种头衔和学位以表明其专业资格。如果以恰当的方式使用,表面上仅为头衔或学位的内容也可以作

or a degree may function as a certification mark if used in the proper manner. *See In re National Association of Purchasing Management*, 228 USPQ 768 (TTAB 1986) (C. P. M. used merely as title or degree, not as certification mark); *In re National Association of Legal Secretaries (International)*, 221 USPQ 50 (TTAB 1983) (PROFESSIONAL LEGAL SECRETARY not used on the specimens in such a way as to indicate certification significance); *In re National Institute for Automotive Service Excellence*, *supra* (design mark not used simply as a degree or title, but to certify that the performer of the services had met certain standards); *In re Institute of Certified Professional Business Consultants*, 216 USPQ 338 (TTAB 1982) (CPBC not used as a certification mark for business consulting services, but only as a title or degree); *In re Professional Photographers of Ohio, Inc.*, 149 USPQ 857 (TTAB 1966) (CERTIFIED PROFESSIONAL PHOTOGRAPHER used only as the title of a person, not as a certification mark). *Cf. In re University of Mississippi*, 1 USPQ2d 1909 (TTAB 1987) (use of university seal on diplomas did not represent use as a certification mark).

See TMEP §1306.09(a) regarding the difference between a certification mark and a collective mark.

1306.04 Ownership of Certification Marks

The owner of a certification mark is the party responsible for the certification that is conveyed by the mark. The party who affixes the mark, with authorization of the certifier, does not own the mark; nor is the mark owned by someone who merely acts as an agent for the certifier, for example, an inspector hired by the certifier. The certifier, as owner, is the only person who may file an application for registration of a certification mark. *See In re Safe Electrical Cord Committee*, 125 USPQ 310 (TTAB 1960).

Certification is often the sole activity for the owner of a certification mark. However, a person is not necessarily precluded from owning a certification mark because he also engages in other activities, including the sale of goods or the per-

为证明商标。参见相关判例：*National Association of Purchasing Management*，228 USPQ 768（TTAB 1986）（“C. P. M.”只是用作头衔或学位，而非证明商标）；*National Association of Legal Secretaries*（*International*），221 USPQ 50（TTAB 1983）（“PROFESSIONAL LEGAL SECRETARY”样本上显示的使用方式并未表现出有证明意义）；*National Institute for Automotive Service Excellence*，*同前*（设计商标不仅作为学位或头衔使用，也证明了服务的提供者符合特定的标准）；*Institute of Certified Professional Business Consultants*，216 USPQ 338（TTAB 1982）（“CPBC”并非作为咨询服务的证明商标使用，而仅作为头衔或学位使用）；*Professional Photographers of Ohio*，*Inc*.，149 USPQ 857（TTAB 1966）（“CERTIFIED PROFESSIONAL PHOTOGRAPHER”仅作为某人的头衔使用，并不作为证明商标使用）。比照：*University of Mississippi*，1 USPQ2d 1909（TTAB 1987）（在文凭上使用的大学印鉴并不表示作为证明商标使用）。

参见 TMEP §1306.09(a)，查阅证明商标与集体商标之间的区别。

1306.04 证明商标的所有权

证明商标的所有者是对商标所传达的证明内容负有责任的一方。经证明者授权而使用商标的一方并不拥有该商标；证明者的代理人（例如：证明者雇用的检查员）也不拥有该商标。证明者作为所有者，是唯一有权提交申请书申请注册证明商标的人。*参见 Safe Electrical Cord Committee*，125 USPQ 310（TTAB 1960）。

证明通常是证明商标所有者的唯一行为。但是，某人还参与其他活动，包括销售商品或提供服务，并不会使其不能拥有证明商标。不过，在这种情况下，此人在商品

formance of services. In this event, however, the certification mark may not be the same mark that the person uses as a trademark or service mark on goods or services. *See* TMEP §1306.05(a).

Examples of organizations which conduct both types of activities are trade associations and other membership or "club" types of businesses, such as automobile associations. These organizations may perform services for their members, and sell various goods to their members and others, as well as conduct programs in which they certify characteristics or other aspects of goods or services, especially of kinds which relate to the main purpose of the association.

Manufacturing or service companies that do not certify the goods or services of members may nonetheless engage in certification programs under proper circumstances. For example, a manufacturer of chemical wood preservatives might conduct a program certifying certain characteristics of wood or wood products that are treated and sold by others. Among the characteristics or circumstances certified could be the fact that a preservative produced by this manufacturer under a specified trademark was used in the treatment.

As another example, a magazine publisher may conduct a certification program relating to goods or services that are advertised in or have some relevance to the interest area of the magazine.

The certifier/owner determines the requirements for the certification. The standards do not have to be original with the certifier/owner, but may be standards established by another person, such as specifications promulgated by a government agency or standards developed through research of a private research organization. *See* TMEP §1306.06(g)(ii) regarding the standards for certification.

If the name of the organization that developed the standards is part of the mark, an issue could arise as to whether the mark is deceptively misdescriptive under 15 U.S.C. §1052(e)(1) (*see* TMEP §1209.04) or falsely suggests a connection with persons, institutions, beliefs or national symbols under 15 U.S.C. §1052(a) (*see*

或服务中使用的商标或服务商标不能与证明商标相同。*参见* TMEP §1306.05(a)。

参与两类活动的组织的例子有贸易协会和其他成员资格或“俱乐部”类业务，比如汽车协会。此类组织可以向其成员提供服务，并向其成员或他人销售各种商品，同时也可以执行证明商品或服务——尤其是同协会主要目的有关的商品或服务类型——的特性或其他方面的程序。

尽管制造或服务公司不证明成员商品或服务，但在适当的情况下，也可以执行证明程序。例如，某化学木材防腐剂的生产商可以执行证明他人处理和出售的木材或木制品的某些性质的程序。证明的特性或情况可以是，在处理过程中使用了生产商以某特定商标制造的防腐剂。

又例如，某杂志出版商可以对在其杂志上做广告或者与杂志关注领域有某种相关的商品或服务进行证明。

证明者/所有者决定证明的要求。标准不一定要由证明者/所有者原创，也可以是他人所设定的标准，比如政府部门公布的标准或者私人研究组织通过研究建立的标准。*参见* TMEP §1306.06(g)(ii)，查阅有关证明标准的信息。

如果设立标准的组织的名称是商标的一部分，那么可能会产生一个问题，即根据 15 U.S.C.§1052(e)(1)规定，该商标是否存在虚假性误导(*参见* TMEP §1209.04)，或者根据 15 U.S.C.§1052(a)规定，是否虚假地暗示了与某人、机构、信仰或国家象征有关系(*参见* TMEP §1203.03(e))。

TMEP §1203.03(e)).

1306.05 Characteristics of Certification Marks

The Trademark Act does not require that a certification mark be in any specific form or include any specific wording. A certification mark can be wording only, design only, or a combination of wording and design. In other words, there is no particular way that a mark must look in order to be a certification mark.

A certification mark often includes wording such as "approved by," "inspected," "conforming to" or "certified," or similar wording, which is natural since certification (or approval) is practically the only significance the mark is to have when it is used on goods or in connection with services. However, this wording is not required, and a mark that entirely lacks this wording can perform the function of certification.

The examining attorney must look to the facts disclosed in the record to determine whether the mark is used in certification activity and is in fact a certification mark.

It is not necessary to show that the mark is instantly recognizable as a certification mark, or that the mark has already become well known to the public as a certification mark. However, it should be clear from the record in the file that the circumstances surrounding the use or promotion of the mark will give certification significance to the mark in the marketplace. *See Ex parte Van Winkle*, 117 USPQ 450 (Comm'r Pats. 1958).

1306.05(a) Same Mark Not Registrable as Certification Mark and as Any Other Type of Mark

Trade or service marks and certification marks are different and distinct types of marks designed to serve different purposes. A trademark or service mark is used

1306.05　证明商标的特点

《商标法》并未要求证明商标必须具有特定的形式或包含特定的措辞。证明商标可以是词语、图案或者词语和图案的组合。换言之，即没有对证明商标的外观有特别的要求。

证明商标经常包括诸如“经……批准”、“经审查”、“符合……”、“经证明”或类似的词语，这是很自然的，因为在商标用于商品或相关服务时，证明（或批准）实际上是其唯一的意义。不过，此类词语并不是必需的，完全不带有此类词语的商标也可以作为证明使用。

审查员必须审查记录所揭示的事实，以判定商标是否用于证明活动并且实际上是一个证明商标。

作为证明商标的商标并不要求必须立即就能被认为是证明商标，也不要求其已经为公众所熟知。但是，档案记录应当清楚地表明，商标的使用或推广使商标在市场中被赋予证明的意义。参见 *Van Winkle*, 117 USPQ 450 (Comm'r Pats.1958)。

1306.05(a)　同一商标不能同时注册为证明商标和任何其他类型的商标

商标或服务商标与证明商标是截然不同的类型，为不同的目的服务。商标或服

by one person on his or her goods or services alone, whereas a certification mark is used by persons other than the owner of the mark. A certification mark does not distinguish between producers, but represents a certification regarding some characteristic that is common to the goods or services of many persons. Using the same mark for two contradictory purposes would result in confusion and uncertainty about the meaning of the mark and would invalidate the mark for either purpose.

Section 4 of the Trademark Act, 15 U.S.C. §1054, prohibits the registration of a certification mark "when used so as to represent falsely that the owner or a user thereof makes or sells the goods or performs the services on or in connection with which such mark is used," and §14(5)(B) of the Act, 15 U.S.C. §1064(5)(B), provides for the cancellation of a registered certification mark where the registrant engages in the production or marketing of any goods or services to which the certification mark is applied. *See* TMEP §1306.07 regarding §14(5) of the Act. Thus, if a party has a registration as a trademark or service mark for any goods or services, he or she may not register the same mark as a certification mark for those goods or services. Conversely, a registration as a certification mark precludes registration of the same mark by its owner as a trademark or service mark for any goods or services to which the certification mark applies. *See In re Florida Citrus Commission*, 160 USPQ 495 (TTAB 1968).

The prohibition against registration both as a trademark or service mark and as a certification mark applies to marks that are identical or so similar as to constitute essentially the same mark. Variations in wording or design, even though small, can, if meaningful, create different marks; on the other hand, inconsequential differences, such as the style of lettering or the addition of wording of little importance, normally would not prevent marks from being regarded as the same. *See In re 88 Open Consortium Ltd.*, 28 USPQ2d 1314 (TTAB 1993), in which the mark 88OPEN COMPATIBILITY CERTIFIED and design was found registrable as a certification mark even though applicant owned six registrations for the marks 88OPEN in typed and stylized form as trademarks, service marks and collective membership marks. The Board noted that the words COMPATIBILITY

务商标由一人单独用于其商品或服务上，而证明商标则是由所有者以外的其他人使用。证明商标并不识别生产者，而是代表一种证明，即有关许多人的商品或服务所共有的特性的证明。如果将同一个商标用于背道而驰的两种目的，就会使商标的含义产生混淆和不确定，从而使两方面的目的都无法实现。

《商标法》第 4 节 15 U.S.C.§1054 规定，如果某证明商标"在使用中会产生误导，使人误解商标的所有者或使用者制造或销售使用商标的商品或提供使用商标的服务"，则禁止注册；而且《商标法》§14(5)(B)，15 U.S.C.§1064(5)(B)规定，如果商标注册人参与应用商标的商品或服务的生产或销售，应取消已注册的证明商标。参见 TMEP §1306.07，查阅有关《商标法》§14(5)的规定。因此，如果某人已经为任何商品或服务注册了某商标或服务商标，他（她）就不能再将同样的商标注册为那些商品或服务的证明商标。反过来，已经注册的证明商标就不能注册为应用该商标的商品或服务的商标或服务商标。参见 *Florida Citrus Commission*，160 USPQ 495 (TTAB 1968)。

禁止同时注册为商标或服务商标和证明商标这一规定，适用于相同或者极其相似从而在本质上构成相同商标的两个商标。在用词或图案上的差异，即使很小，但如果是有意义的，即构成不同的商标；另一方面，无关紧要的差异，比如字体风格或增加一些无关紧要的字，通常会被认为是相同的商标。参见 *88 Open Consortium Ltd.*，28 USPQ2d 1314 (TTAB 1993)，在本案中，"88OPEN COMPATIBILITY CERTIFIED"及图案被认为可以作为证明商标注册，尽管申请者同时还拥有六个获得注册的手写体及印刷体"88OPEN"商标、服务商标和集体成员商标。委员会认为，"COM-

CERTIFIED served to inform those seeing the mark that it is functioning as a certification mark, and that the certification mark included a design feature not found in the previously registered marks). *See also* TMEP §§1306.04, 1306.06(d) and 1306.09.

1306.05(b) Cancellation of Applicant's Prior Registration Required by Change from Certification Mark Use to Trademark or Service Mark Use, or Vice Versa

The nature of the activity in which the mark is used or intended to be used may change from use to certify characteristics of goods or services to use on the party's own goods or services, or on goods or services produced for the party by related companies. The change might also be the other way around, from trade or service mark use to certification mark use.

If there is already a registration as one type of mark and the registrant files an application for registration of the mark as the other type, the applicant must surrender the previous registration under §7(e) of the Trademark Act, 15 U.S.C. §1057(e), before the examining attorney approves the new application for publication of the mark or for issuance of a registration on the Supplemental Register. *See* 37 C.F.R. §2.172 and TMEP §1608 regarding surrender. The registration certificate for the new application should not issue until the prior registration actually has been cancelled.

In examining the new application, the examining attorney must carefully review the application to ensure that the facts of record support the new application.

1306.06 Examination of Certification Mark Applications

1306.06(a) Refusal to Register Certification Mark

The same standards are used to determine the registrability of certification marks

PATIBILITY CERTIFIED"二字用于告知看见商标的人这是一个证明商标，而且该证明商标还包含了与已注册商标不同的图案特征。另参见 TMEP §§1306.04，1306.06(d)及1306.09。

1306.05(b)　要从证明商标用途变更为商标或服务商标，申请者先前的注册要注销，反之亦然

使用或意图使用商标的行为性质可以从用于证明商品或服务的特性转变为用于当事人自己的商品或服务上，或用于相关公司为当事人生产的商品或服务。也可以反过来，从商标或服务商标的用途变更为证明商标的用途。

如果已经注册为一种商标类型，然后提出申请注册为另一种商标类型，审查员在批准要求发行商标的新申请或者在联邦商标补充登记簿注册之前，根据《商标法》§7(e)，15 U.S.C.§1057(e)规定，申请者必须放弃原有的注册。参见 37 C.F.R.§2.172 及 TMEP §1608，查阅关于放弃的信息。新申请的注册证书必须在原注册实际注销之后方可签发。

在审查新申请的过程中，审查员必须仔细审查申请书，确保记录资料中的事实支持新申请。

1306.06　证明商标申请的审查

1306.06(a)　拒绝注册证明商标

判断证明商标可注册性的标准同其他类型的商标相同。因此，在考虑描述性、放

that are used for other types of marks. Thus, the standards generally applicable to trademarks and service marks are used in considering issues such as descriptiveness, disclaimers, and likelihood of confusion. (*But see* TMEP §§1306.02 *et seq*. regarding certification marks indicating regional origin only.)

Regarding the application of §2(e) of the Trademark Act, 15 U.S.C. §1052(e), to certification marks, *see Community of Roquefort v. Santo*, 443 F.2d 1196, 170 USPQ 205 (C.C.P.A. 1971); *In re National Association of Legal Secretaries (International)*, 221 USPQ 50 (TTAB 1983). Regarding the application of §2(d), 15 U.S.C. §1052(d), to certification marks, *see Procter & Gamble Co. v. Cohen*, 375 F.2d 494, 153 USPQ 188 (C.C.P.A. 1967); *Stabilisierrungsfonds fur Wein v. Peter Meyer Winery GmbH*, 9 USPQ2d 1073 (TTAB 1988). *See also E. I. duPont de Nemours & Co. v. Yoshida International, Inc.*, 393 F. Supp. 502, 185 USPQ 597 (E.D.N.Y. 1975).

A refusal to register because the subject matter does not function as a certification mark is predicated on §§1, 2, 4, and 45 of the Trademark Act, 15 U.S.C. §§1051, 1052, 1054, and 1127. Educational or other degrees or titles awarded to individuals, and used only as personal titles or degrees, are not certification marks. So used, titles and degrees indicate qualifications or attainments of the person; they do not pertain to or certify services that have been performed by the person. *See* TMEP §1306.03.

1306.06(b) The Mark on the Drawing

The drawing in the application must include the entire certification mark, but it should not include anything that is not part of the mark. The examining attorney must refer to the specimens to determine what constitutes the mark. *See In re National Institute for Automotive Service Excellence*, 218 USPQ 744 (TTAB 1983). In evaluating the drawing, the same standards used in relation to trademark and service mark drawings apply to certification marks (*see* TMEP §§807 *et seq.*).

弃权利以及混淆的可能性方面的问题时，应使用一般适用于商标和服务商标的同样的标准。（但是请*参见* TMEP §§1306.02 及以下，查阅关于仅识别原产地的证明商标的信息）。

关于《商标法》§2(e) 15 U.S.C. §1052(e) 适用证明商标的信息，*参见 Community of Roquefort v. Santo*, 443 F.2d 1196, 170 USPQ 205 (C.C.P.A.1971)；*National Association of Legal Secretaries (International)*, 221 USPQ 50 (TTAB 1983)。关于 §2(d), 15 U.S.C. §1052(d) 适用证明商标的信息，*参见 Procter & Gamble Co. v. Cohen*, 375 F.2d 494, 153 USPQ 188 (C.C.P.A.1967)；*Stabilisierrungsfonds fur Wein v. Peter Meyer Winery GmbH*, 9 USPQ2d 1073 (TTAB 1988)。*另参见 E.I.duPont de Nemours & Co. v. Yoshida International, Inc.*, 393 F.Supp.502, 185 USPQ 597 (E.D.N.Y.1975)。

由于相关内容不能作为证明商标而拒绝注册，在《商标法》§§1、2、4 及 45 的 15 U.S.C. §§1051、1052、1054 及 1127 中有详细的规定。授予个人的教育或其他学位或头衔，并且仅用于表示个人头衔或学位的，不是证明商标。若如此使用，则头衔和学位用来表明该人的资格或成就；并不适用或证明该人提供的服务。*参见* TMEP §1306.03。

1306.06(b)　　商标图样

申请书中的图样必须包含整个证明商标，但是不应包含任何不属于商标的部分。审查员必须参考样本以判断什么构成了该商标。*参见* 相关判例：*National Institute for Automotive Service Excellence*, 218 USPQ 744, 747 (TTAB 1983)。在评估图样的过程中，适用于商标和服务商标图样的判断标准同样适用于证明商标（*参见* TMEP §§807 及以下）。

1306.06(c) Specimens of Use for Certification Marks

Certification mark specimens must show use to certify. Although a certification mark performs a different function from a trademark or a service mark, it is used in a manner analogous to that of a trademark or a service mark (*i.e.*, on a label, tag, or container for the goods, a display associated with the goods, or in the sale or advertising of services rendered).

A certification mark specimen must show how a person other than the owner uses the mark to certify regional or other origin, quality, or other characteristics of that person's goods or services; or that members of a union or other organization performed the work or labor on the goods or services. 37 C.F.R. §2.56(b)(5).

Materials that bear the mark and are actually attached or applied to the goods or used in relation to the services by the persons authorized to use the mark constitute proper specimens.

The same standards used to evaluate trademark and service mark specimens also apply to certification marks. *See* TMEP §§904 *et seq*.

Sometimes the owner/certifier prepares tags or labels that bear the certification mark that are supplied to the authorized users to attach to their goods or for use in relation to their services. *See Ex parte Porcelain Enamel Institute, Inc.*, 110 USPQ 258 (Comm'r Pats. 1956). These tags or labels are acceptable specimens.

1306.06(d) Relation Between Certification Mark and Trademark or Service Mark on Specimens

It is customary for trademarks or service marks to be placed on goods or used with services in conjunction with certification marks. However, it is also possible for a certification mark to be the only mark used on goods or with services. Some producers market their goods or services without using a trademark or service mark,

1306.06(c) 证明商标的使用样本

证明商标样本必须显示证明的用途。尽管证明商标与商标或服务商标的功能不同,但其使用方式类似于商标或服务商标(即用在标签、标牌、商品的容器或展品上,或者用在相关服务的销售或广告中)。

证明商标样本必须显示所有者以外的人如何将商标用于证明产地或其他来源、质量或其商品或服务的其他特性;或者证明商品或服务是由某联盟或其他组织的成员提供劳务。37 C.F.R.§2.56(b)(5)。

材料若带有商标,并事实上附挂在或应用在获准使用该商标的人的商品或相关服务中,即可构成适当的样本。

评价商标或服务商标样本的标准同样适用于证明商标。*参见* TMEP §§904 及以下。

有时候,由所有者(证明者)制作带有证明商标的标签或标牌,并向授权使用者提供,用于使用者的商品或相关服务上。*参见* 相关判例:*Porcelain Enamel Institute, Inc.*, 110 USPQ 258 (Comm'r Pats.1956)。这些标牌或标签是可接受的样本。

1306.06(d) 证明商标和商标或服务商标在样本方面的关系

习惯上,商标或服务商标常与证明商标一起用在商品或服务上。不过,也有证明商标单独用在商品或服务上的情况。有些生产商在销售商品或服务中并不使用商标

yet these producers may be authorized to use a certification mark and, as a result, the certification mark would be the only mark on the goods or services. In these situations, the significance of the mark might not be readily apparent and the examining attorney should request an explanation of the circumstances to ascertain whether the mark is a certification mark rather than a trademark or service mark. *See also* TMEP §1306.09.

When a trademark or a service mark appears on the specimens in addition to a certification mark, the certification mark can be on a separate label, or can be included on a single label along with the user's own trademark or service mark.

A composite certification mark may include a trademark or service mark, provided the composite mark functions to certify, with the trade or service mark serving only to inform, or to suggest the certification program, rather than to indicate origin of the goods or services with which the mark is used. These situations usually are created when a company that produces goods or performs services wants to develop a program and a mark to certify characteristics of the goods or services of others that are related to the producer's own goods or services. *See* the examples in TMEP §1306.04.

The trademark or service mark must be owned by the same person who owns the certification mark. A party may not include the trademark or service mark of another in a certification mark, even with a disclaimer. If the examining attorney believes that a trademark or service mark included in a certification mark is owned by another, the examining attorney should refuse registration of the certification mark.

1306.06(e) Classification of Goods and Services in Certification Mark Applications

In applications to register certification marks, all goods are classified in Class A and all services are classified in Class B. 37 C.F.R. §6.3.

或服务商标，但他们经授权可以使用某个证明商标，这样，证明商标就成为该商品或服务的唯一商标了。在这种情况下，商标的意义可能不很明显，审查员应当要求对相关情况作出解释，以确定该商标是否为证明商标而非商标或服务商标。另*参见* TMEP §1306.09。

如果在样本上，除了证明商标之外还有商标或服务商标，证明商标可以是单独标签，也可以与使用者自己的商标或服务商标放在同一标签上。

一个复合证明商标可以包括商标或服务商标，但要求复合商标的功能是证明，而商标或服务商标仅仅用于告知或提示证明程序，而非用于表明商品或服务的来源。出现这种情况通常是，一家生产某商品或提供某服务的公司想创建一个程序和商标，用以证明与自己商品或服务相关的他人商品或服务的特性。*参见* TMEP §1306.04 中所举的例子。

商标或服务商标与证明商标的所有者必须为同一人。在证明商标中不得包含他人的商标或服务商标，即使已经放弃权利者。如果审查员相信，在证明商标中包含了其他人的商标或服务商标，则应当拒绝证明商标的注册。

1306.06(e)　证明商标申请中对于商品和服务的分类

在证明商标的注册申请中，一切商品都归入 A 类，而一切服务都归入 B 类。37 C.F.R.§6.3。

Classes A and B (but not any other classes) may be included in one application. *See* TMEP §§1403 *et seq*. regarding multiple class applications.

NOTE: When the Trademark Act of 1946 went into effect, the goods and services for which certification marks were registered were classified in the regular classes for goods and services. It was later concluded that this was not reasonable, because a certification mark is commonly used on a great variety of goods and services, and the specialized purpose of these marks makes it unrealistic to divide the goods and services into the competitive groups that the regular classes represent. The change to classification in Classes A and B for certification marks was made by amendment of the Trademark Rules on August 15, 1955.

1306.06(f) Identification of Goods and Services in Certification Mark Applications

In a certification mark application, the goods or services that are certified may be identified less specifically than in an application for a trademark or service mark.

Ordinarily it is only necessary to indicate general kinds of goods and services, such as food, agricultural commodities, electrical products, textile materials, printed material, or insurance agency services, machinery repair, restaurant services. However, if the certification program itself is limited to specific goods or services, for example, wine, wood doors, bakery machinery, then the identification in the application should be more specific.

1306.06(g) Special Elements of Certification Mark Applications

1306.06(g)(i) Statement of What the Mark Certifies

The application must contain a statement of the characteristic, standard, or other feature that is certified or intended to be certified by the mark. The statement may begin with the wording, "The certification mark, as used (or intended to be

一项申请中可以包含 A 类或 B 类(但不包括其他任何类别)。参见 TMEP §§1403 及以下,关于涉及多种类别的申请。

注:当《1946 年商标法》生效时,注册证明商标的商品和服务按普通的商品和服务分类法进行分类。后来认为这种做法不合理,因为证明商标通常用于各种各样的商品和服务,由于证明商标的专门用途,将这类商品和服务按普通分类法划分为互为竞争的类别是不切实际的。1955 年 8 月 15 日颁布的《商标规则》对此作了更改,将证明商标分为 A 类和 B 类。

1306.06(f)　证明商标申请中的商品和服务的识别

与申请注册商标或服务商标相比,在申请证明商标时,对被证明的商品或服务的识别不是那么具体明确。

通常只需要指明商品和服务的一般类别,比如食品、农产品、电器产品、纺织品、印刷品,或是保险代理服务、机械修理、餐饮服务。但是,如果证明程序本身限定为某具体商品或服务,例如酒、木门、面包机,那么应在申请中予以更具体的识别。

1306.06(g)　证明商标申请的特殊要素

1306.06(g)(i)　对于商标证明对象的陈述

在申请时,必须对商标所证明或意图证明的特性、标准及其他特性作一项声明。声明可以如下开头:“此证明商标由(意图由)被授权者使用,证明(或意图证明)……”。

used) by authorized persons, certifies (or is intended to certify) ... ." *See* 37 C.F.R. §2.45.

All of the characteristics or features that the mark certifies should be included. A mark does not have to be limited to certifying a single characteristic or feature.

The characteristics or features that the mark certifies should be explained in reasonable detail, so that they are clear. The broad suggestive terms of the statute, such as quality, material, mode of manufacture, are generally not satisfactory by themselves because they do not accurately reveal the nature of the certification. How specific the statement should be depends in part on the narrowness or breadth of the certification. For example, "quality" would not inform the public of the meaning of the certification where the characteristic being certified is limited, for example, to the strength of material, or the purity of a strain of seed.

The statement of certification in the application is printed on the registration certificate. For that reason it should be reasonably specific but does not have to include the details of the specifications of the characteristic being certified. If practicable, however, more detailed specifications should be made of record in the application file.

Although the information as to what the mark certifies may appear in the same statement as the identification of goods and/or services, it is preferable that these elements be recited separately in the application.

1306.06(g)(ii) Standards

The applicant (certifier) must submit a copy of the standards established to determine whether others may use the certification mark on their goods and/or in connection with their services. 37 C. F. R. §2.45. For an intent-to-use application, under §1(b) of the Act, 15 U.S.C. §1051(b), the standards are submitted with the amendment to allege use or the statement of use. 37 C.F.R. §2.45(b).

参见37 C.F.R.§2.45。

商标所证明的所有特性或特征都应包含在内。一个商标并不限于只证明一个特性或特征。

应当对商标所证明的特性或特征进行合理详细的解释,使之明确。法令使用的泛指语,比如质量、材质、制造方式,一般不能满足这项要求,因为它们并没有准确揭示证明的性质。声明的具体程度应部分取决于证明范围的宽窄。例如,如果证明的性质限定为比如材料的强度,或种子的纯度,则"质量"一词就不足以向公众传达证明的含义。

申请书中对证明内容的声明将印刷在注册证书上。因此,声明应当合理地具体,但不必包含所证明特性的规格的详细信息。不过,如果可能,应当在申请文件备案资料中包含更详细的规格说明。

尽管关于商标证明内容的信息可以与识别商品和(或)服务的信息置于同一声明中,但是申请时,最好还是分开叙述。

1306.06(g)(ii) 标准

申请者(证明者)必须提交一份用于判断他人是否可以在其商品和服务中使用证明商标的标准。C.F.R.§2.45。对于根据《商标法》§1(b),15 U.S.C.§1051(b)规定提出的意图使用申请,判断标准应与使用申报修正书或使用声明书一起提交。37 C.F.R.§2.45(b)。

The standards do not have to be original with the applicant. They may be standards established by another party, such as specifications promulgated by a government agency or standards developed through research of a private research organization.

1306.06(g)(iii) Exercise of Control

In an application based on use in commerce under 15 U.S.C. §1051(a), the applicant must assert that the applicant is exercising legitimate control over the use of the certification mark in commerce. 37 C.F.R. §2.45(a).

In an application based on 15 U.S.C. §1051(b) or 15 U.S.C. §1126, the applicant must assert that the applicant has a bona fide intention to exercise legitimate control over the use of the certification mark in commerce. 37 C.F.R. §2.45(b). In a §1(b) application, before the mark can register, the applicant must file an amendment to allege use under 15 U.S.C. §1051(c) or a statement of use under 15 U.S.C. §1051(d) alleging that the applicant is exercising legitimate control over the use of the certification mark in commerce.

If there is doubt as to the existence or nature of such control by the applicant, the examining attorney should require an explanation and sufficient disclosure of facts or the filing of appropriate documents to support the applicant's statement regarding the exercise of control over the use of the mark.

1306.06(g)(iv) Use by Others Indicated in Dates-of-Use Clause

When specifying the dates of first use, the applicant must indicate that the certification mark was first used under the authority of the applicant, or by persons authorized by the applicant, because a certification mark is not used by the applicant itself.

1306.06(g)(v) Statement That Mark is Not Used by Applicant

The application must contain a statement that the applicant is not engaged in (or,

这种标准无须为申请者原创。可以是他人设立的标准，比如政府机构公布的规范，或是私人研究组织通过研究开发的标准。

1306.06(g)(iii) 实施控制

因此，申请者根据 15 U.S.C.§1051(a)规定，提出申请商业使用的证明商标时，必须声明其正在对在商业中使用的证明商标实施合理的控制。37 C.F.R.§2.45(a)。

在根据 15 U.S.C.§1051(b)或 15 U.S.C.§1126 提出申请时，申请者必须声明其真实地意图对在商业中使用的证明商标实施合理的控制。37 C.F.R.§2.45(b)。申请者根据§1(b) 提出申请时，必须提交一份 15 U.S.C.§1051(c)规定的使用申报修正书，或一份 15 U.S.C.§1051(d)规定的使用声明书，声明申请者对在商业中使用的证明商标实施合理的控制。

如果对于申请者是否有此控制或控制的性质有疑问，审查员应当要求解释和充分揭示事实，或者提交相应的文件，支持申请者关于对商标实施控制的声明。

1306.06(g)(iv) 在使用日期条款中指明由他人使用

在说明首次使用的日期时，申请者必须表明证明商标是在申请者的授权下得到首次使用，或者由获得申请者授权的人使用，因为证明商标不能由申请者自己使用。

1306.06(g)(v) 关于商标并非由申请者使用的声明

申请资料中必须包含一份声明，表明申请者并未参与（或者，如果是根据《商

if the application is filed under §1(b) of the Act, 15 U.S.C. §1051(b), will not engage in) the production or marketing of the goods or services to which the mark is applied. *See* 37 C.F.R. §2.45. This statement does not have to be verified, and can therefore be entered by examiner's amendment.

1306.06(g)(vi) Amendment to Different Type of Mark

If an application is filed to register a mark as a certification mark and the mark is actually another type of mark, or if an application is filed to register a mark as another type when it is actually a certification mark, the application may be amended (without additional fee) to request registration as the proper type of mark. It is preferred that the applicant completely rewrite the application to provide a clean copy, rather than amend the original papers. Also, the application should be re-executed because some essential allegations differ for the different types of marks.

1306.07 Relationship of §14 (Cancellation) to Examination of Certification Mark Applications

Extract from 15 U.S.C. §1064. Cancellation. A petition to cancel a registration of a mark, stating the grounds relied upon, may, upon payment of the prescribed fee, be filed as follows by any person who believes that he is or will be damaged, including as a result of dilution under section 43(c), by the registration of a mark on the principal register established by this Act, or under the Act of March 3, 1881, or the Act of February 20, 1905 ...

...

(5) *At any time in the case of a certification mark on the ground that the registrant (A) does not control, or is not able legitimately to exercise control over, the use of such mark, or (B) engages in the production or marketing of any goods or services to which the certification mark is applied, or (C) permits the use of*

标法》§1(b),15 U.S.C.§1051(b)提出申请,将不会参与。)应用该商标的商品或服务的生产或销售。*参见* 37 C.F.R.§2.45。此项声明不必认证,因此可以通过审查员的修正书的方式进行输入。

1306.06(g)(vi) 对于不同类型商标的修正

如果申请注册的是证明商标,而它实际上是另一类型的商标,或者如果申请注册的是其他类型的商标,而它实际上却是证明商标,那么可以将申请修正为(无需另外缴费)要求注册正确商标类型的申请。但申请者最好还是重写一份申请,提供一份整洁的申请,而不要在原申请上作修正。当然,申请应当重新处理,因为不同类型的商标具有一些本质上不同的要求。

1306.07 §14(撤销)与证明商标申请审查之间的关系

摘自 15 U.S.C.§1064"撤销"一节。任何人如果认为某商标在依本法设立的联邦商标登记簿上注册会或将会使他(她)遭受损失,包括导致产生 43(c)所规定的商标淡化、或者产生 1881 年 3 月 3 日法案、或 1905 年 2 月 20 日法案所规定的结果时,可以在交纳规定的收费之后,采用以下方式要求撤销该商标的注册,并说明要求撤销的理由……

……

(5)对于证明商标,可以在任何时候,以申请者(A)没有或无法对商标进行合理的控制,或(B)参与应用证明商标的商品或服务的生产或销售,或(C)准许证明商标

the certification mark for purposes other than to certify, or (D) discriminately refuses to certify or to continue to certify the goods or services of any person who maintains the standards or conditions which such mark certifies ...

...

Nothing in paragraph (5) shall be deemed to prohibit the registrant from using its certification mark in advertising or promoting recognition of the certification program or of the goods or services meeting the certification standards of the registrant. Such uses of the certification mark shall not be grounds for cancellation under paragraph (5), so long as the registrant does not itself produce, manufacture, or sell any of the certified goods or services to which its identical certification mark is applied.

Section 14 of the Trademark Act, 15 U.S.C. §1064, provides for petitions to cancel registrations. Subsection (5) lists specific circumstances when petitions to cancel certification marks may be filed. The concepts implicit in §14(5) are reflected in examination as follows:

Subsection A: In an application, the applicant states under oath or declaration that the applicant is exercising, or has a bona fide intention to exercise, legitimate control over the use of the certification mark. TMEP §1306.06(g)(iii). Such statement is accepted unless the examining attorney has knowledge of facts which indicate that it should not be accepted.

Subsection B: The applicant is required to state, as appropriate, that he or she is not engaged in, or will not engage in, the production or marketing of any goods or services to which the certification mark is applied. TMEP §1306.06(g)(v). Such statement is accepted unless the examining attorney has knowledge of facts indicating the contrary.

Subsection C: This subsection concerns whether a party permits use of the certification mark for purposes other than to certify. No statements are required in the application specifically on this point. The existence of un-

用于证明以外的其他用途，或(D)歧视性地拒绝给符合证明商标标准或条件的商品或服务证明或继续证明为由……

……

第(5)段落的规定，不得视为禁止证明商标的注册人将商标用于广告或推广证明程序或符合证明标准的商品或服务。证明商标的此类使用不能成为第(5)段落规定的撤销商标的理由，只要注册人本身并不生产、制造或销售任何应用相同证明商标的商品或服务。

《商标法》第14节15 U.S.C.§1064对撤销注册请求作了规定。第(5)段落列举了可以提出撤销证明商标请求的具体情况。§14(5)规定的隐含概念反映在审查中为：

小节A：申请时，申请者以宣誓或声明的形式表示：申请者正在或有真实意图，对证明商标的使用进行合理的控制。TMEP §1306.06(g)(iii)。此类声明可以被接受，除非审查员了解的事实显示不应接受该声明。

小节B：相应地，申请者必须声明：他或她没有参与或将要参与应用证明商标的商品或服务的生产或销售。TMEP §1306.06(g)(v)。此类声明可以被接受，除非审查员了解到与之相反的事实。

小节C：本小节是关于当事人是否准许证明商标用于证明以外的用途。关于这一点，在申请时并没有要求作任何声明。他人未经申请者授权擅自

authorized or illegal uses by others without the applicant's authorization is not within the examining attorney's province and cannot be used as a basis for refusal to register, provided that use authorized by the applicant, as supported by the record, is proper certification use.

Subsection D: This subsection relates to the obligation of the owner not to discriminately refuse to certify. This subject is not mentioned in §§4 or 45, 15 U.S.C. §1054 or §1127. The Office has never undertaken to evaluate, in *ex parte* examination, whether the standards or characteristics which the mark certifies, as set out by the applicant, are discriminatory per se; nor is it in the province of *ex parte* procedure to investigate or police how the certification is practiced.

1306.08 Registration of Certification Mark on Basis of Foreign Registration

A certification mark may be registered in the United States under §44 of the Trademark Act, 15 U.S.C. §1126, on the basis of a foreign registration. However, whether a particular foreign registration is acceptable as the basis for a United States registration depends on the scope of the foreign registration.

A person may not obtain a registration in the United States that is broader in scope than the foreign registration on which the United States application is based. *See In re Löwenbräu München*, 175 USPQ 178 (TTAB 1972); TMEP §1402.01(b). Therefore, a registration as a certification mark in the United States may not be based on a foreign registration that is actually a trademark registration, *i.e.*, a registration that is based on the registrant's placement of the mark on his or her own goods as a trademark. The scope of the registration, *i.e.*, the nature of the registration right, would not be the same.

The scope and nature of the registration right is not always immediately apparent from a foreign registration certificate. Foreign registration certificates are not al-

或非法使用商标不在审查员的审查范围之内，不能作为拒绝注册的理由，只要记录资料表明经申请者授权的使用是适当的证明使用即可。

小节 D：本小节是关于所有者负有不得歧视性地拒绝证明的义务。在 §§4 及 45，15 U.S.C. §1054 及 §1127 中并没有提到这个问题。办公室从未在单方面审查中评价申请者确定的商标所证明的标准或特性是否在本质上具有歧视性；也未建立单方面的程序，以调查或管制证明的实际使用。

1306.08 国外注册的证明商标在国内注册

一项在国外注册的证明商标，可以根据《商标法》§44，15 U.S.C. §1126 的规定在美国注册。不过，一项外国注册是否可以作为在美国注册的基础，取决于该外国注册的适用范围。

如果外国注册的适用范围小于在美国注册的适用范围，则不可注册。*参见*相关判例：*Löwenbräu München*，175 USPQ 178（TTAB 1972）；以及 TMEP §1402.01(b)。因此，如果在外国注册为商标，即注册人将商标作为商标用在自己的商品上，则不能在美国以证明商标进行注册。因为注册的范围，即注册权利的性质，有所不同。

注册权利的范围和性质并非总是能够立即从外国注册证书上显现出来。外国注

ways labeled as pertaining to a trademark, service mark, collective mark or certification mark and, when they are labeled, the significance of the term is not always clear. For example, the designation "collective" represents a different concept in some foreign countries than it does in the United States. Moreover, while a certificate printed on a standardized form may be headed with the designation "trademark," the body of the certificate might contain language to the contrary.

Since certification is an exception in the larger world of trademarks, an indication of certification in the registration certificate would normally represent a conscious decision that a certification situation exists. Therefore, if a foreign registration certificate has a heading that designates the mark as a certification mark or if the body of the foreign certificate contains language indicating that the registration is for certification, the foreign registration normally may be accepted to support registration in the United States as a certification mark.

Whenever there is ambiguity about the scope or nature of the foreign registration or whenever the examining attorney believes that the foreign certificate may not reflect the actual registration right, the examining attorney should inquire regarding the basis of the foreign registration.

1306.09 Uncertainty Regarding Type of Mark

When the facts in the application are insufficient to provide an adequate basis for determining whether the mark is functioning as a trademark or service mark or as a certification mark, the examining attorney should ask for further explanation as to the activities in which the mark is used and should require a sufficient disclosure of the facts to enable a proper examination to be made. The manner in which the activities associated with a mark are conducted is the main factor that determines the type of mark. The conduct of parties involved with the mark evidences the relationship between the parties, and the responsibilities of each to the goods or services and to the mark.

册证书并非总是标明为商标、服务商标、集体商标或证明商标，即使标明，其用语的意义也未必清楚。例如，“集体”一词在某些外国代表了与美国不同的概念。此外，在标准格式上印制的证书可能以“商标”为标题，但证书的主体可能包含相反的内容。

由于证明是范围更广阔的商标中的一个例外情况，在注册证书中表明证明通常代表了有意识地判定存在证明的情况。因此，如果外国注册证书的标题指出商标为证明商标，或者证书主体包含了表明注册为证明商标的用语，则一般可以以该外国注册为基础，在美国注册为证明商标。

如果外国注册的范围或性质含糊不清，或者审查员认为该外国注册未能反映真实的注册权利，则审查员应当对该外国注册的基础进行调查。

1306.09 商标的类型不确定

如果申请书中的事实不足以判断该商标是商标、服务商标还是证明商标，则审查员应当要求申请者对使用商标的活动作进一步的解释说明，并且应当要求申请者充分披露事实以进行适当的审查。确定商标类型的主要因素是商标与活动如何相关。商标有关各方的行为证明了各方之间的关系，以及各方对商品或服务以及商标的责任。

1306.09(a) Distinction Between Certification Mark and Collective Mark

A collective trademark or collective service mark indicates origin of goods or services in the members of a group. A collective membership mark indicates membership in an organization. A certification mark certifies characteristics or features of goods or services. *See American Speech-Language-Hearing Association v. National Hearing Aid Society*, 224 USPQ 798, 806-808 (TTAB 1984), for a discussion of the distinction between collective marks and certification marks.

Both collective marks and certification marks are used by more than one person, but only the users of collective marks are related to each other through membership in a collective group. The collective mark is used by all members and the collective organization holds the title to the collective mark for the benefit of all members.

A certification mark may be used to certify that the work or labor on the goods or services was performed by a member of a union or other organization. *See* TMEP §1306.03. Used in this manner, the certification mark certifies not that the user is a member of an organization but that the labor on the user's goods or services was performed by a member of an organization.

An application to register a mark that is used or intended to be used by members of a collective group must be scrutinized carefully to determine the function of the mark. If the mark is used or intended to be used by the members as a trademark on goods they produce or as a service mark for services they perform, then the mark is a collective trademark or collective service mark. If the mark is used or intended to be used by members to indicate membership in an organization, then the mark is a collective membership mark. However, if use of the mark is or will be authorized only under circumstances designated by the organization to certify characteristics or features of the goods or services, the mark is a certification mark.

1306.09(a)　证明商标与集体商标的区别

集体商标或集体服务商标表明商品或服务来自于某团体的成员。集体成员商标表明某组织的成员资格。证明商标证明商品或服务的特性或特征。*参见 American Speech-Language-Hearing Association v. National Hearing Aid Society*, 224 USPQ 798, 806－808（TTAB 1984）,查阅有关集体商标与证明商标之间区别的讨论。

集体商标和证明商标都为多人所用,但只有集体商标的使用者才可以通过集合团体的成员资格而彼此相关。集体商标由所有成员使用,并且集体组织为所有成员的利益拥有集体商标。

证明商标可以用于证明商品或服务的劳务是由某联盟或其他组织的成员提供的。*参见* TMEP §1306.03。证明商标以这种方式使用时,所证明的并非商标使用者是某组织的成员,而是商标使用者的商品或服务是由某组织的成员提供劳务。

对于一项要求注册集合团体成员使用或意图使用的商标的申请,必须仔细审查以确定商标的功能。如果商标是作为商标用于或意图用于成员生产的商品或提供的服务上,则商标为集体商标或集体服务商标。如果商标是由成员用于或意图用于表明其为某组织的成员资格,则商标为集体成员商标。但是,如果商标只有在组织指定的条件下经授权或将要授权才可使用,以证明商品或服务的特性或特征,则商标为证明商标。

1306.09(b) Distinguishing Certification Mark Use from Related-Company Use of Trademark or Service Mark

Sometimes an application requests registration of a certification mark, but there is a contractual relationship in the nature of a franchise or license between the applicant and the user of the mark, whereby the applicant, as the franchisor or licensor, specifies the nature or quality of the goods produced (or of the services performed) under the contract. These situations require care in examination because they usually indicate trademark or service mark use (through related companies) rather than certification mark use, because the applicant, as franchisor or licensor, controls the nature of the goods or services and has the responsibility for their quality.

The key distinction between use of subject matter as a certification mark and use as a trademark or service mark through a related company is the purpose and function of the mark in the market place, and the significance that it would have to the relevant purchasing public. A trademark or service mark serves to indicate the origin of goods or services, whereas a certification mark serves to guarantee certain qualities or characteristics. *See In re Monsanto Co.*, 201 USPQ 864, 870 (TTAB 1978); *In re Celanese Corp. of America*, 136 USPQ 86 (TTAB 1962).

Furthermore, the owner of a certification mark must permit use of the mark if the goods or services meet the certifier's standard, whereas a trademark owner may, but is not obligated to, license use of its mark to third parties. *Monsanto*, 201 USPQ at 870.

1306.09(c) Patent Licenses

Sometimes the owner of a patent asserts ownership of the mark that is applied to goods that are manufactured under license from the patent owner, in accordance with the terms and specifications of the patent. In most cases, these marks have

1306.09(b) 区分证明商标的使用与相关公司对商标或服务商标的使用

有时，一项申请要求注册证明商标，但是从特许或许可的性质上看，申请者与商标的使用者之间存在合同关系，其中申请者作为特许人或许可人，对根据合同生产的商品（或提供的服务）的性质或质量进行规定。对于这种情况需要仔细审查，因为它们通常显示的是商标或服务商标用途（通过相关公司），而非证明商标用途，因为申请者作为特许人或许可人，控制商品或服务的性质并且对商品或服务的质量负责。

对于商标是作为证明商标使用，还是通过相关公司作为商标或服务商标，主要区别在于该商标在市场中的用途和功能，以及商标对相关购买公众的意义。商标或服务商标用于识别商品或服务的来源，而证明商标用于保证某种品质或特性。*参见*相关判例：*Monsanto Co.*，201 USPQ 864，870（TTAB 1978）；*Celanese Corp. of America*，136 USPQ 86（TTAB 1962）。

此外，作为证明商标的所有者，只要商品或服务符合证明者的标准，就必须准许使用商标，而商标的所有者则可以，但没有义务，许可第三人使用其商标。*Monsanto*，201 USPQ at 870。

1306.09(c) 专利许可

有时，专利所有者认为自己拥有在其专利许可下生产的、符合专利要求和规范的商品上使用的商标。在大多数情况下，这种商标是以相关公司使用为基础注册为商标。

been registered as trademarks, on the basis of related-company use. Generally, the patent owner's purpose, in arranging for the application of a mark to the goods manufactured under his or her license, would be to identify and distinguish those goods whose nature and quality the patent owner controls through the terms and specifications of the patent. Therefore, registration as a trademark (on the basis of related-company use) rather than registration as a certification mark would be appropriate.

1307 Registration as Correct Type of Mark

The examining attorney should take care to ascertain the correct type of mark during examination, and to require amendment if necessary. If a registration is issued for the wrong type of mark, it may be subject to cancellation. *See National Trailways Bus System v. Trailway Van Lines, Inc.*, 269 F. Supp. 352, 155 USPQ 507 (E.D.N.Y. 1965); *American Speech-Language-Hearing Association v. National Hearing Aid Society*, 224 USPQ 798 (TTAB 1984).

一般而言，专利所有者安排在其许可下生产的商品上应用商标，目的是识别和区分那些由其通过专利要求和规范控制性质和质量的商品。因此，（根据相关公司的使用）将商标注册为商标比注册为证明商标更为恰当。

1307　以正确的类型注册商标

在审查过程中，审查员应当注意确定正确的商标类型，必要时可要求修正。如果已签发类型错误的商标注册，可予以撤销。*参见 National Trailways Bus System v. Trailway Van Lines, Inc.*, 269 F. Supp. 352，155 USPQ 507（E. D. N. Y. 1965）；*American Speech-Language-Hearing Association v. National Hearing Aid Society*, 224 USPQ 798（TTAB 1984）。